PROSPECTIVE MEMORY

PROSPECTIVE MEMORY

Cognitive, Neuroscience, Developmental, and Applied Perspectives

Edited by

Matthias Kliegel • Mark A. McDaniel • Gilles O. Einstein

LEA Lawrence Erlbaum Associates
Taylor & Francis Group

New York   London

Lawrence Erlbaum Associates
Taylor & Francis Group
270 Madison Avenue
New York, NY 10016

Lawrence Erlbaum Associates
Taylor & Francis Group
2 Park Square
Milton Park, Abingdon
Oxon OX14 4RN

Library of Congress Cataloging-in-Publication Data

Prospective memory : cognitive, neuroscience, developmental, and applied
    perspectives / [edited by] Matthias Kliegel, Mark A. McDaniel, Gilles O. Einstein.
        p. cm.
    Includes bibliographical references and index.
    ISBN 978-0-8058-5858-7 (alk. paper) -- ISBN 978-1-4106-1843-6 (alk. paper)
    1. Prospective memory. I. Kliegel, Matthias. II. McDaniel, Mark A. III. Einstein,
Gilles O., 1950-

BF378.P76P76 2007
153.1'3--dc22   2007006642

Visit the Taylor & Francis Web site at
http://www.taylorandfrancis.com

and the LEA and Routledge Web site at
http://www.routledge.com

Contents

Preface

[T]here are no cases of principles emerging that would cause us ... to believe that prospective tasks fundamentally differ from retrospective tasks.

—Roediger (1996, p. 151)

*M*ore than 10 years ago, this conclusion was drawn in a commentary on chapters discussing fundamental processes of prospective memory in the first edition book on prospective memory (Brandimonte, Einstein, & McDaniel, 1996). Since then, a lot has happened!

Over the last decade, the topic of prospective memory (i.e., the encoding, storage, and delayed retrieval of intended actions) has attracted much interest, and this is reflected in a rapidly growing body of literature. The first edition provided a foundation for furthering prospective memory research by capturing the main developments in the field of prospective memory. However, because research was progressing at a relatively slow rate at that time (with only 45 papers published during the previous 20 years), it was primarily designed to identify important avenues for future prospective memory research.

Research in the area of prospective memory has exploded during the last decade. Approximately 350 scientific articles have been published on this topic since the appearance of the first edition book in 1996. In addition, in 2000, the First International Conference on Prospective Memory was organized in Hatfield, UK, and the Second International Conference on Prospective Memory was held in Zurich in 2005. The field is developing rapidly in the quality, quantity, and diversity of approaches to examining prospective remembering. Accordingly, we felt it was time to gather contributions of active prospective memory researchers for a second book that would provide an accessible, integrated source to the expanded literature in prospective memory.

Whereas many of the authors in this volume contributed to the 1996 book and can be regarded as the founders of current prospective memory research, other contributions come from authors who are relatively new to the field and who are examining broader aspects of prospective memory and, as a result, extending our understanding of it. We asked authors to focus their contributions on their work, but also more generally to review the expanded literature in their area of expertise in prospective memory research. Furthermore, the authors have been encouraged to consider future directions for research and to raise questions that they believe all researchers in this area will need to address.

The book is divided into four parts that together provide a broad and deep introduction to the cognitive, neuroscience, developmental, and applied aspects of prospective memory. Conceptually following up on Roediger's (1996) challenging comment, the 16 chapters and four commentaries can be taken as offering a fine-grained analysis of both the similarities and differences between prospective and retrospective memory. Part I is aimed at summarizing recent theoretical advances in the understanding of prospective memory. To achieve this, important current theoretical models are introduced, models that emphasize the complexity and mul-tifaceted nature of prospective remembering and attempt to reveal its underlying cognitive processes. Part II reflects the continued and still growing interest in the developmental trajectories of prospective memory. When the 1996 book appeared, research on this topic was largely limited to the upper age ranges and investigated prospective memory within a relatively narrow set of paradigms. Since then, con-siderable advances in the investigation of prospective memory development have occurred. For instance, the chapters in this volume provide an examination of pro-spective memory development across the entire life span, from preschool children to the oldest of the old. Part III is dedicated to the neuroscience of prospective memory and thus reflects the trend in contemporary psychology research of inves-tigating the neuropsychological and neurophysiological underpinnings of human cognitive processes. Topics range from the investigation of the neural correlates of prospective memory using neuroimaging techniques and event-related brain potentials to the clinical neuropsychology of prospective memory. Part IV expands the discussion to a broad range of real-world applications such as the assessment and treatment of prospective memory deficits, the social importance of prospec-tive memory, the usefulness of strategies for improving prospective memory, and the role of prospective remembering in general health behavior (e.g., medical adherence).

Following the model of the first prospective memory volume, prominent mem-ory researchers evaluate the chapters in each part and comment more generally on the state of prospective memory research in the four major areas targeted.

ACKNOWLEDGMENTS

We thank the authors for their exciting contributions. We are deeply grateful to Lori Handelman, Stephen Rutter, and Tony Messina at Lawrence Erlbaum Associ-ates for their encouragement, advice, and support during all stages of the book's development. Finally, we express gratitude to the organizations that supported our efforts during the editorial process: Matthias Kliegel to the Swiss National Science Foundation (SNF), Mark McDaniel to the National Institute on Aging (NIA), and Mark McDaniel and Gil Einstein to NASA.

REFERENCES

Brandimonte, M.A., Einstein, G.O. & McDaniel, M.A. (Eds.) (1996). *Prospective memory: Theory and applications.* Mahwah, NJ: Erlbaum.

Roediger III, H.L. (1996). Commentary: Prospective memory and episodic memory. In M. Brandimonte, G.O. Einstein & M.A. McDaniel (Eds.), *Prospective memory: Theory and applications* (pp. 149–155). Mahwah, NJ: Erlbaum.

Editors

Gilles O. Einstein received his PhD from the University of Colorado in experimental psychology in 1977. He has taught at Furman University since 1977 and chaired the department from 1994 until 2006. Dr. Einstein won Furman University's Meritorious Teaching Award in 1985 and was the first recipient of Furman University's Excellence in Teaching Award in 2006. He is past president of the Southeastern Workers in Memory, and he has served on the editorial boards of the *Journal of Experimental Psychology: Learning, Memory, and Cognition* and *Memory & Cognition*. He is a Fellow of Divisions 2, 3 and 20 of the American Psychological Association, and he is a member of the Association of Psychological Science and the Psychonomic Society. His research focuses on the processes involved in prospective remembering, how these processes break down in important real-world situations, and how they are affected by aging. He has published more than 75 articles, chapters, and books, and his research has been supported by the National Institute on Aging, the National Institute of Mental Health, and NASA. He and Mark McDaniel are coauthors of recent books titled *Memory Fitness: A Guide for Successful Aging* and *Prospective Memory: An Overview and Synthesis of an Emerging Field*.

Matthias Kliegel received his PhD in psychology from the University of Heidelberg, Germany. Afterward he worked as a research associate at the German Centre for Research on Aging. In 2002, he was appointed assistant professor of psychology at the Department of Psychology at the University of Zurich, Switzerland. Here, he teaches lifespan developmental psychology and leads a research group on the development of intentional behavior across the lifespan. He is an International Affiliate of Division 20 of the American Psychological Association, and he is a member of the Gerontological Society of America as well as of the German and Swiss Psychological Associations. His research focuses on cognitive development across the lifespan with a major interest in the development of intentional behavior, especially prospective remembering. He has published more than 70 articles in peer-reviewed journals as well as a German textbook on adult developmental psychology. His research has been supported by the Swiss National Science Foundation as well as the German Research Foundation. In 2003, he received the Vontobel Award for Research on Aging. Starting October 2007, Matthias Kliegel will become full professor of psychology and chair of the Developmental Psychology Unit at the Department of Psychology at the Dresden University of Technology, Germany.

Mark McDaniel is a professor of psychology at Washington University in St. Louis. He received his Ph.D. from University of Colorado in 1980, has research interests in the general area of human learning and memory, and has served as associate editor of the *Journal of Experimental Psychology: Learning, Memory, and Cognition* (1995-2000) and as president of the Rocky Mountain Psychological Association. He and Gilles Einstein are coauthors of two recent books: *Memory Fitness: A Guide for Successful Aging* and *Prospective Memory: A Synthesis of an Emerging Field*.

Contributors

Marcike Altgassen
Department of Psychology
University of Zurich
Zurich, Switzerland

Maria A. Brandimonte
Suor Orsola Benincasa Università
Naples, Italy

Paul W. Burgess
Institute of Cognitive Neuroscience
    and Psychology Department
University College London
London, United Kingdom

Anna-Lisa Cohen
Department of Psychology
New York University
New York, New York

Gabriel I. Cook
Department of Psychology
Claremont McKenna College
Claremont, California

R. Key Dismukes
NASA Ames Research Center
Moffett, California

Iroise Dumontheil
Institute of Cognitive Neuroscience
    and Psychology Department
University College London
London, United Kingdom and
    Laboratoire de Physiologie de la
    Perception et de l'Action
Collège de France
Paris, France

Gilles O. Einstein
Department of Psychology
Furman University
Greenville, South Carolina

Judi A. Ellis
School of Psychology
University of Reading
Reading, United Kingdom

Donatella Ferrante
Suor Orsola Benincasa University
Naples, Italy
    and University of Trieste
Trieste, Italy

J. E. Freeman
School of Psychology
University of Reading, United Kingdom

Sam J. Gilbert
Institute of Cognitive Neuroscience
    and Psychology Department
University College London
London, United Kingdom

Peter M. Gollwitzer
Department of Psychology
New York University
New York, New York
    and University of Konstanz
Konstanz, Germany

Melissa Guynn
Department of Psychology
New Mexico State University
Las Cruces, New Mexico

Julie D. Henry
School of Psychology
University of New South Wales
New South Wales, Australia

Christopher Hertzog
School of Psychology
Georgia Institute of Technology
Atlanta, Georgia

Jason L. Hicks
Department of Psychology
Louisiana State University
Baton Rouge, Louisiana

Theodor Jäger
Department of Psychology
Saarland University
Saarbrücken, Germany

Lia Kvavilashvili
School of Psychology
University of Hertfordshire
Hertfordshire, United Kingdom

Matthias Kliegel
Gerontopsychology Department
University of Zurich
Zurich, Switzerland

Fiona E. Kyle
Deafness, Cognition, and Language
   Research
University of Cambridge
Cambridge, United Kingdom

Rachael Mackinlay
Department of Psychology
University of Zürich
Zurich, Switzerland

Richard L. Marsh
Department of Psychology
University of Georgia
Athens, Georgia

Mike Martin
Department of Psychology
University of Zurich
Zurich, Switzerland

Elizabeth A. Maylor
Department of Psychology
University of Warwick
Coventry, United Kingdom

Mark A. McDaniel
Department of Psychology
Washington University
St. Louis, Missouri

David J. Messer
Centre for Child Development
Faculty of Education and Language
   Studies
Open University
United Kingdom

Morris Moscovitch
Department of Psychology
University of Toronto
Toronto, Ontario, Canada

Jiro Okuda
Institute of Cognitive Neuroscience
   and Psychology Department
University College London
   and Tamagawa University
   Research Institute
Tokyo, Japan

Denise Park
The Beckman Institute
The University of Illinois
   at Urbana-Champaign
Urbana, Illinois

Louise H. Phillips
School of Psychology
University of Aberdeen
Aberdeen, Scotland, United Kingdom

Peter G. Rendell
Department of Psychology
Australian Catholic University
Melbourne, Australia

Marieke L. Schölvinck
Institute of Cognitive Neuroscience
    and Psychology Department
University College London
London, United Kingdom

David Shum
School of Psychology
Griffith University
Brisbane, Australia

Jon S. Simons
Brain Mapping Unit
Addenbrooke's Hospital,
University of Cambridge
Cambridge, United Kingdom

Rebekah E. Smith
Department of Psychology
The University of Texas at San Antonio
San Antonio, Texas

Angelika T. Thöne-Otto
Outpatient Clinic of Cognitive Neurology
University of Leipzig
Leipzig, Germany

Katrin Walther
Outpatient Clinic of Cognitive
    Neurology
University of Leipzig
Leipzig, Germany

Robert West
Department of Psychology
Iowa State University
Ames, Iowa

Elizabeth A. H. Wilson
The Beckman Institute
The University of Illinois
    at Urbana-Champaign
Urbana, Illinois

1

Ten Years On
Realizing Delayed Intentions

JUDI A. ELLIS and J. E. FREEMAN

School of Psychology
University of Reading, UK

O ur capacity to shape and direct our future behavior is of fundamental importance in the development, pursuit, and maintenance of an independent and autonomous lifestyle from early childhood to late adulthood. It is dependent, to a large extent, on our ability to enact intended actions at an appropriate moment in the future, in the absence of direct reminders to do so, and without the support of highly practiced action sequences triggered by specific environmental cues. Actions such as brushing our teeth at bedtime, for example, are supported not only by environmental or physiological cues (e.g., being in the bathroom, feeling sleepy, late evening) but also numerous instances of prior performance of this action in the same or very similar contexts. By contrast, the performance of other intended actions, such as relaying a message to a family member later in the day, cannot inherently rely on these sources of support. The term *prospective memory* is commonly used to describe the means by which we succeed or fail in carrying out the latter types of activities and thereby identifies a key set of processes that support the pursuit of an independent and fulfilling life.

In many ways, prospective memory is an umbrella term, used to describe both a type of task and the processes underlying the performance of these tasks. Moreover, the particular processes that individual researchers seek to investigate and explain tend to focus either on the unaided (with respect to the absence of a direct reminder or well-rehearsed activity sequence) retrieval of an intended action or on its progression from inception to the record of its success or recovery from failure. Although prospective memory is a useful and commonly accepted descriptor, it is an unfortunate one insofar as it implies that memory processes are the key (and to some the only) factor in determining performance on the task, despite the observation that many variables influence outcome, including planning, attention,

1

action control, and so on (see, e.g., Ellis, 1996; Kliegel, Eschen, & Thöne-Otto, 2004; Kliegel, McDaniel, & Einstein, 2000; Martin, Kliegel, & McDaniel, 2003). Thus, this description can (often unwittingly) constrain research activity and lead to ambiguity at best and incompleteness at worst with respect to the theoretical proposals and models that emerge from one's research activity. In this context, it is interesting to note occasions (and their frequency) on which researchers in this area find the term restrictive and revert to arguably more precise alternatives such as intentions, intended actions, and so on, in the course of their development of a theoretical point or explanation of empirical findings.

In this chapter, as in an earlier one (Ellis, 1996), we explicitly adopt a broad definition of prospective memory—both task and processes—that begins with the decision to act in a particular way in the future and ends with the evaluation of the outcome of that intention. In the light of subsequent chapters in this volume we focus primarily on the earlier (formation and encoding) and later (execution and evaluation) aspects of these intended actions, and on the processes underpinning them, as expressed in the performance of young adults. In so doing, we examine similarities and differences in the way in which they are investigated in social as well as in cognitive psychology, focusing in particular on theoretical and empirical work on goal and implementation intentions. As our earlier example of a prospective memory task illustrated, many if not all such tasks occur in a social context or carry implications for social relationships (cf. Winograd, 1988). This chapter illustrates the considerable progress that has been achieved in the past ten years in our knowledge and understanding of the nature of prospective memory tasks and the processes underpinning performance on these tasks.

It is commonly accepted that prospective remembering proceeds through the following phases: encoding, retention, retrieval, execution, and evaluation (Ellis, 1996; see also Brandimonte, 1991; Einstein & McDaniel, 1996). These are summarized briefly here and described in more detail in Ellis (1996). In the first phase, three components and the associations among them are encoded: the when (retrieval criterion), what (action to be performed), and that (intent or decision to act) components. This is followed by a period of delay, which can vary from minutes to weeks, during which the intention representation must be retained until a performance interval or opportunity to fulfill one's intention occurs. If this situation maps onto the encoded retrieval criteria, success on the task requires the timely retrieval of the intention followed by its enactment. Finally, evaluation of the outcome of the preceding activities allows one to record a successful outcome or replan or reevaluate the intention in the event of failure. For clarity, we focus primarily on event-based intentions, that is, intentions for which the retrieval cues are events rather than times or activities (Kvavilashvili & Ellis, 1996; Einstein & McDaniel, 1996).

ENCODING

Behavioral Studies

Twelve years ago only one modern study had been conducted on the formation, encoding, and representation of delayed intentions. In the intervening period a reasonable body of research has replicated and extended the findings reported in this seminal paper by Goschke and Kuhl (1993) that identified an intention superiority effect (ISE). This effect describes the enhanced activation or increased accessibility (Marsh, Hicks, & Bink, 1998) of materials associated with intended actions, relative to other types of information in memory, reflected in reduced response latencies for these materials in a recognition test. The ISE has been investigated using a postponed-intention paradigm in which recognition latencies for nouns and verbs from a simple action script intended for subsequent enactment are contrasted with those for comparable items not intended for enactment. Using this design, Goschke and Kuhl (1993) observed shorter latencies for items intended for enactment relative to neutral items: the ISE. Subsequent research by Marsh, Hicks, and colleagues, using a lexical decision task as a potentially more direct measure of activation and accessibility, has replicated the ISE. Moreover, it has revealed that this effect is maintained when these actions are interrupted and removed when they are cancelled or completed. Indeed, cancellation and completion appear to lead to the inhibition of intention-related information relative to other, neutral materials—an intention completion effect (Marsh et al., 1998; Marsh, Hicks, & Bryan, 1999). The ISE has also been observed with young adults under more naturalistic conditions in the laboratory in which participants are required to self-initiate an intention that has personal relevance (Dockree & Ellis, 2001).

Reliable (and equivalent) ISEs have been observed in older as well as younger adults, using a laboratory paradigm similar to that employed by Goschke and Kuhl (1993) and Marsh and colleagues (Freeman & Ellis, 2003a). In contrast, age-related differences have been observed when naturally occurring intentions are employed. Indeed, Maylor, Darby, and Della Sala (2000) observed an intention inferiority effect, insofar as older adults' completed intentions appeared to be more accessible than their to-be-completed ones. Their study, however, not only used naturally occurring intentions, but also investigated the ISE by comparing the accessibility of intentions to be performed in the next few days with the accessibility of those completed in the past few days. Unlike laboratory paradigms, this contrast between retrospective (completed) and prospective (to-be-completed) fluency does not include a comparable set of non-intention-related information. Thus it is unclear whether older adults' performance is a consequence of an age-related decline in the accessibility of to-be-completed intentions or impaired inhibition of completed intentions.

Freeman and Ellis (2003b) modified Maylor et al.'s (2000) design by asking young and (healthy) older adults to attend two sessions 1 week apart. In the first session they named the intentions they planned to carry out in the following week and in the second, 1 week later, they named the intentions that they had completed during the previous week. This allowed us to explore possible age differences in the proportion of intentions that were accessible prior to but not after completion, and vice versa. We obtained a reliable ISE for young adults in the absence of any evidence of intention superiority in older adults; moreover, there was no indication of an intention inferiority effect in these older adults. Furthermore, the findings suggest that the absence of a reliable ISE in healthy older adults reflects age-related differences in the accessibility of to-be-completed intentions, rather than the heightened accessibility (reduced inhibition) of completed ones. This finding is not consistent with Goschke and Kuhl's (1993) assertion that the ISE is a nonstrategic phenomenon. Instead, it indicates that the ISE may depend on attentionally demanding encoding or rehearsal operations that establish the intentional status of information in memory (see also Altmann & Trafton, 2002), perhaps through a commitment marker. This would be compatible with neuropsychological evidence that successful intentional tagging may be dependent on the integrity of executive functions supported by the frontal cortex (e.g., Shallice & Burgess, 1991). We return to this issue and the related one concerning the apparent discrepancy between naturally occurring and experimental intentions on the occurrence of an ISE in older adults.

Neurophysiological Studies

Lebiere and Lee (2001) simulated the findings reported by Marsh et al. (1998) and Marsh et al. (1999) in an adaptation of J.R. Anderson's (1990) ACT-R model. In this model the ongoing task (a lexical decision task) is a goal in longer term memory and the to-be-completed intended action is a context associated with that goal, when it is either uncompleted or partially completed. In these circumstances a context primes items related to that intention and inhibits unrelated ones (ISE). Once completed, however, the intention is removed from the current goal. The model includes an assumption that when an intention has been performed the context changes to the next expected intention. This change raises the activation of items relevant to that intention and lowers the activation of unrelated items, thereby producing an inhibitory effect on items relevant to the previously completed intention (intention completion effect) that enables a new context (intention) to be primed.

Subsequent research, reported by Watanabe and Kawaguchi (2005), indicates that Lebiere and Lee's (2001) model might need to be extended to take account of temporally ordered yet unrelated prospective memory tasks. Watanabe and Kawaguchi's (2005) findings suggest that processing of a current intention activates first the immediately preceding intention, followed by the subsequent intention in the current temporal sequence. Interestingly, however, these effects occurred only when the intended actions were associated with contextualized temporal information (e.g., times in a single day or days in a particular month) and with some degree of personal relevance (see also Watanabe, 2003; Watanabe & Kawaguchi, 1999). These authors suggested that their findings reflect a process in which one checks that a prior action has been completed before engaging in a new one. Their findings also indicate the potential relevance of personal importance or involvement and contextual cues, if the ISE (or the intention completion effect) is to accommodate the complexity of intentions in everyday activity, including multiple intentions (se also Leynes, Marsh, Hicks, Allen, & Mayhorn, 2003). In this context it is interesting to note that Dockree and Ellis (2001) obtained an ISE in young adults using a laboratory task that required people to self-initiate an intention that had personal relevance.

Neuroimaging studies have recently shed light on the processes activated when an intention is formed or encoded. Using electrophysiological response potentials (ERPs), Leynes, Allen, and Marsh (1998), for example, examined neural activity associated with preparatory processes for motoric and semantic tasks. They used contingency negative variations that appear to have two main components that reflect the processes operating between a warning signal and a stimulus. Early contingency negative variation is primarily observed over the frontal lobes and is thought to reflect processing of a warning signal. Late contingency negative variation, by contrast, is associated with central-parietal activity and believed to reflect preparatory activities. Leynes et al. observed topographical differences in preparatory activities for motor (central/late contingency negative variation) and cognitive and semantic (frontal/early contingency negative variation) tasks. Motor preparation, moreover, was accompanied by cortical activity in motor regions, and cognitive task preparation was associated with reduced activity in these areas, along with excitation in the frontal regions. Leynes et al. argued that this pattern of activity is consistent with cortical activity localization when these tasks are actually executed (e.g., Penfield & Boldrey, 1937; Shallice et al., 1994). Thus this study suggests that motor regions may be activated when an intention to perform a motor action is encoded, thereby indicating a possible role for motoric information in the ISE.

ISE and Motoric Processing

Goschke and Kuhl (1993, 1996) attributed the ISE to the intrinsic tendency of material with an intentional status and refer to the "special dynamic status of intention" (Goschke & Kuhl, 1993, p. 1224). We investigated this assertion in a series of experiments designed to explore an alternate (action superiority) account that draws parallels between the ISE and the subject-performed task effect (Freeman & Ellis, 2003c). On this account, the relatively high activation or increased accessibility observed for intention-related information is thought to reflect an advantage for the motor or sensorimotor information that is present in an intention that specifies a motor response (see also Brandimonte & Passolunghi, 1994; Koriat, Ben-Zur, & Nussbaum, 1990). Thus we proposed that there is a functional similarity between the benefits observed on memory for material enacted at encoding—the subject-performed-task effect—and the heightened accessibility of to-be-enacted material—the ISE. This account conceptualizes the advantage for to-be-enacted intentions as a prospective analog of the subject-performed-task encoding effect, arguing that the heightened accessibility of both performed and to-be-performed information reflects the availability of motor information. This sensorimotor information serves to make the item more distinctive, benefiting memory for that material as seen in the subject-performed-task effect, and thus more readily accessible, as seen in the ISE, from longer term memory.

The findings from a series of five experiments were consistent with the action superiority account (Freeman & Ellis, 2003c). Following verbal encoding, we observed an advantage for to-be-enacted material in two different paradigms (postponed intention and subject-performed task), in the absence of any evidence for heightened accessibility of to-be-performed information following enactment at encoding (Experiments 1–4). Moreover, the advantage for to-be-performed information (ISE) after verbal encoding was eliminated when motor processing was prevented using a selective motor interference task that had minimal attentional demands: "drawing" circles in the air (Experiment 5). Thus our findings suggest that there is an overlap between overt and intended enactment and indicate that motor information may be activated when to-be-performed intentions are verbally encoded.

Freeman and Ellis's (2003a) findings are consistent with those reported by Leynes et al. (1998) and in a recent functional MRI (fMRI) study by Eschen et al. (in press). They may also shed light on the discrepancy, discussed earlier, between naturally occurring and experimental intentions such that older adults show a reliable ISE for the latter but not the former type of task (Freeman & Ellis, 2003a, 2003b). We have argued that this discrepancy reflects a fundamental difference in the nature of the activities involved in the two paradigms (Freeman & Ellis, 2003b). Specifically, we argue that the exact motoric requirements of many everyday intentions (e.g., buy a birthday present) may be insufficiently well specified at encoding to benefit from the preparatory processing that we suggest supports the representation of more well-defined laboratory tasks. Of course, it is also the case that many naturally occurring intentions that describe activities could be described as more verbal (e.g., pass on a message) or cognitive (choose holiday destination). However, our findings indicate the absence of an ISE, in younger adults, for actions that are designated for verbal report (Freeman & Ellis, 2003c).

Freeman and Ellis's (2003c) findings question Goschke and Kuhl's (1993) assertion that intentions have some special status in memory by virtue of their intentional quality and instead propose that their enhanced accessibility is a function of the availability of motor information, in the preceding paradigms at least. This is perhaps unsurprising given that all reported studies focus on investigating the accessibility of either verbs or nouns and verbs from a short activity script or a set of single verbs, and thus could reasonably be described as investigating the accessibility of information related only to the action component of an intention. As noted earlier, intentions are comprised of (at least) three components: the action, a retrieval criterion or cue, and an intent or decision to act. Moreover, the realization of an intention requires the timely retrieval of an intended action, that is, retrieval of an action when the associated retrieval cue is present. Thus, although the heightened activation of action information may assist in the recovery of that action, if the accessibility of intention-relevant information does indeed influence the probability of successful retrieval, it could be argued that the ease with which a retrieval cue is recognized and recalled as such should be more influential in this context. We have conducted a preliminary study that partially addresses this question in which we inserted a recognition test between the encoding of a prospective memory task and the start of an ongoing task (Freeman & Ellis, under review). This allowed us to examine young adults' recognition latencies for a series of retrieval cue target words (nouns) following the encoding of prospective memory task instructions (to respond to these words by making a simple key press whenever they saw them in a later ongoing task, a sentence judgment task). These cue words were recognized more quickly ($M = 766$ ms, $SD = 204$ ms) than matched neutral words ($M = 810$ ms, $SD = 128$ ms) designated for verbal recall only, $t(71) = -3.70$, $p < .001$. However, it remains to be established whether the accessibility of this (or action-related) information affords any benefit for intention performance, a point to which we return in our discussion of retrieval processes.

The design of our experiment to examine the accessibility of retrieval cue information is similar to one employed by Einstein et al. (2005, Experiment 5). In contrast to our observation of shorter latencies, however, they observed slowed responses to target words when these words were presented in an interpolated task that occurred prior to the ongoing task in which the prospective memory task was embedded. As in our study, Einstein et al. examined latencies to their cue words after instructing people to suspend their intention temporarily. However, in our study the interpolated task was a recognition test in which people were explicitly asked to recognize the prospective memory target items as well as other nontarget words they had learned at encoding and thus respond appropriately to these items. In contrast, Einstein et al. used a lexical decision test that clearly does not examine memory for target items. It is perhaps understandable then that recall of the intentional status of these target items leads to slower lexical decisions, whereas a recognition test elicits faster responses (relative to responses to nontarget items).

Prospective Memory Tasks and Implementation Intentions

A further important but often neglected aspect of delayed intentions—in cognitive psychology at least—is the third component: the intent or decision or readiness to act. Following Kuhl (1985), one of us suggested that this may vary from a *wish* or *want* to a *must, ought,* or *will* and proposed that this "strength" of an intention may reflect not only that intention's personal importance[1] but also the perceived benefits of a successful outcome as well as the potential consequences of failure (Ellis, 1996). Moreover, it is an aspect that is likely to be influenced further by the nature of the originator (self, other) and the primary beneficiary (self, other) as well as the relative importance of any relevant other person. Therefore, the strength of a delayed intention should be influenced by the relationship between it and other concurrent or longer term goals, aims, or intentions. Information on this facet of an intention comes primarily from studies of goal and implementation intentions in social psychology.

Gollwitzer (1999; Gollwitzer & Brandstätter, 1997; Gollwitzer & Schaal, 1998) postulated the concept of an implementation intention as a means of specifying more precisely the conditions under which a longer term or more encompassing goal intention (e.g., to eat more healthily) can be realized through a specific action. Thus, whereas a goal intention defines what one intends to achieve, an implementation intention describes a particular means of resolving the discrepancy between one's current and desired behavior by specifying when, where, and how a goal can be instantiated (e.g., eat an extra portion of fruit at your coffee break tomorrow). A substantial body of research, with experimental as well as naturally occurring

---

[1] Recent research suggests that the importance of an intention may have its greatest effect on performance during the retrieval phase. Thus we discuss the role of this variable later in this chapter.

intentions, of varying degrees of personal importance, significance, and implications for failure, has demonstrated that the encoding of an implementation intention improves performance relative to that of a goal intention. Thus, for example, difficult goal intentions (participants' ratings) were completed three times more often when they were associated with implementation intention instructions (Gollwitzer & Brandstätter, 1997, Experiment 1).

In abstract terms, a goal intention takes the form "I intend to achieve X," whereas an implementation intention is expressed in the form "When situation X occurs (e.g., coffee break), then I will perform response Y (eat fruit)" (Gollwitzer, 1999, p. 494). From this description it is difficult to discern any notable difference between an implementation intention and a delayed intention or prospective memory task, for example, a decision (intent) to do X (action) when Y (retrieval cue) occurs (Ellis, 1996). Moreover, all experimental prospective memory tasks include a definition of the retrieval cue (e.g., perform this action when a particular word or words occur). Thus all such tasks are comparable to implementation intentions. Clearly, greater variability is possible in naturally occurring intentions, which can range from "Ask Paul to feed the cat tomorrow" to "Ask Paul to feed the cat tomorrow, when I see him at work during our coffee break." Both of these intentions, however, are more specific—in terms of both the action and the retrieval cue— than a corresponding goal intention such as "Ask someone to feed the cat at some time." It is unlikely that prospective memory researchers would classify the latter as a prospective memory task; the specification of a retrieval cue is an inherent property of a prospective memory task (e.g., "Ask Jack to feed the cat before I go on vacation next week").

Interestingly, in many studies the encoding of an implementation intention frequently includes a third element: repetition of the task instruction. This element invokes a degree of commitment because people are asked either to say aloud or subvocally or to write down the instruction "When I encounter (situation) Y then I will perform (action) X." In contrast to most prospective memory experiments, therefore, the volitional link—the intent or decision to act—between a cue (Y) and an action (X) is explicitly encoded. Clearly it is of interest to investigate whether this explicit volitional link has a particular effect on performance that is separate from the benefits of increased specificity. To examine this question we need to include a control condition in which the same cue and action are provided in the absence of explicit volitional encoding. Unfortunately, such a control condition has been employed infrequently and the findings are equivocal. Cohen and Gollwitzer (chap. 17, this volume), for example, used a conventional prospective memory design in which participants were asked to learn three unrelated word pairs and instructed to say the second member of each pair if they saw the first during a lexical decision task. Participants in the implementation intention condition were asked to form an explicit volitional link between one of the pairs by writing down the relevant phrase three times (e.g., "If I see the word *window* at any point in the task, then I will say *wrapper* as fast as possible!"). Although this manipulation led to better performance, the difference was marginal and performance in both the conventional prospective memory and the implementation intention conditions was close to ceiling.

Another study, conducted by Stellar (1992; reported in Gollwitzer, 1999), used the Embedded Figures Test (Witkin, 1950) in which a small geometric figure is hidden in a larger one. Stellar's participants were told that they would be asked to use one of these smaller figures to create a traffic sign later in the experiment (goal intention). A second group was asked to plan how they would do this (implementation intention) and a third was given the additional instruction to say to themselves "I will do this in exactly this way" (implementation intention + explicit commitment). Similar to the ISE studies described earlier, Stellar examined the accessibility of these intentions by looking at response latencies to detect smaller figures, including the target figure, in a series of new larger ones. In comparison to the goal condition, she observed reliably shorter latencies for the implementation + commitment group; however, there was no reliable difference between the implementation intention condition and either the goal or the implementation + commitment conditions. Thus an explicit commitment did not appear to increase the accessibility of a specific intention, in terms of its action component (the implementation intention condition).

A comprehensive review of similarities and differences between implementation intention and prospective memory tasks is neither possible nor appropriate here. However, it is important to consider at least three other experiments that have attempted to link the two research programs by examining the benefits of forming an implementation intention for a prospective memory task. All three illustrate potential confusion with respect to the specific features of an implementation intention that might serve to differentiate it from a prospective memory task, a confusion that is perhaps understandable given the variability in experimental instructions used to describe or define an implementation intention in the social and health psychology literature. Thus, Chasteen, Park, and Schwartz (2001) asked participants to write the day of the week on the right side of sheets of paper used in an experiment. The implementation intention group was given the additional instructions to not only say aloud "I will," and so on, but also to visualize themselves carrying out this action. These extra instructions enhanced performance in their older participants. Similarly, Einstein, McDaniel, Williford, Pagan, and Dismukes (2003) asked their participants to press a certain key on a computer keyboard whenever the computer screen had a red background and their task had changed. Their implementation intention group was given the additional instruction to visualize this situation and to imagine themselves carrying out the required key press. Although the extra instructions did not improve performance, it should be noted that—unusually—they did not include an explicit commitment to carry out the intention. Finally, Liu and Park (2004) investigated the possibility of improving performance in monitoring blood sugar levels in older adults without a history of diabetes or related disorders. Following practice in completing the procedure, participants were asked to take these tests at four specified times a day for 3 weeks. The implementation group was asked to decide not only when and where they would do this, but also to imagine and describe (in writing) this situation, including the events leading up to the situation. The behavioral control group was asked to recite the instructions (take test at 12:00, 1:30, etc.) and the deliberative control group was asked to consider the pros and cons of success and failure.

Participants in the implementation group were more successful than those in each of the two control groups.

To summarize, it is clear from research on implementation intentions that a number of manipulations, singly or in combination, could be employed at encoding to enhance the probability that a delayed intention will be realized. These manipulations, moreover, may be particularly effective for older adults. However, most can be subsumed under the description of planning processes concerned with planning how, when, and where (cf. Ellis, 1996). Others are elaboration strategies that have a long history of improving performance on a variety of cognitive tasks (e.g., imagery). Nevertheless, it is important to identify the conditions under which these additional instructions at encoding enhance prospective remembering, given the considerable variability that is possible in the components of a prospective memory task (e.g., number of target events or target–action pairings). Perhaps the most interesting question is whether and when an explicit commitment to enact an intention (without further embellishment) improves performance. Examination of the preceding findings suggests that it is possible that this will be effective when either the prospective memory and ongoing tasks are more challenging (e.g., multiple and separate target–action pairs) or the participant population is compromised with respect to its attentional demands at retrieval (see Cohen & Gollwitzer, chap. 17, this volume, for a related suggestion). We are currently engaged in a systematic program of work that is investigating these possibilities. For the moment, we would argue that the increasingly common description in the prospective memory literature—investigating the potential enhancement of a prospective memory task by the "addition of an implementation intention" (operationalized in different ways in different experiments)—is a misleading one. It would be more accurate to describe such a manipulation as examining the potential benefits for prospective memory performance when encoding of the prospective memory task includes an explicit commitment, imagery, and so on.

Retention Interval

In retrospective memory, performance declines with increasing delays between study and test. Over a century ago Ebbinghaus (1887–1964) observed that this forgetting took the form of a logarithmic function, initially rapid (in the first minutes or hours after encoding) with a slower decline as the delay extended to several weeks. This phenomenon, moreover, has been observed in a number of subsequent experiments using a variety of materials (e.g., Bahrick & Phelps, 1987). In contrast, research on the effects of delay on prospective remembering has yielded apparently equivocal findings. Loftus (1971), for example, observed poorer performance after a longer (answering 15 questions) rather than after a shorter (5 questions) delay. Similarly, Meacham and Leiman (1982) observed a greater decline in performance after a 5- to 8-day delay than after a 1- to 4-day delay, in the absence of an external memory aid. In contrast, however, Wilkins (1986) failed to observe any decline in performance across a 1- to 36-day delay period, and similar findings were reported using far shorter intervals of 15 versus 30 minutes (Einstein, Holland, McDaniel, & Guynn, 1992) and 4 versus 20 minutes (Guynn, McDaniel, & Einstein, 1998).

One explanation of these apparently contradictory findings, initially proposed by Brandimonte and Passolunghi (1994), is that forgetting in a prospective memory task occurs primarily within the first 3 minutes after encoding. Forgetting over a very short interval—less than 1 minute—has also been observed by Harris and Wilkins (1984) and Einstein, McDaniel, Manz, Cochran, and Baker (2001). Surprisingly, Brandimonte and Passolunghi's (1994) experiments are the only reported investigations on the effects of different delay periods on prospective remembering that include a no-delay condition and are thus directly comparable to tests of immediate recall or recognition in retrospective memory. Potentially, the inclusion of a no-delay condition could provide a more sensitive measure of prospective memory forgetting, particularly if this is combined with progressively longer filled or unfilled retention intervals such as 30 seconds, 1 minute, 1.5 minutes, and so on. At the least, replication of their findings would be a useful addition to the literature on this question.

In everyday life as well as the laboratory, retention intervals are typically filled by one or more activities. The character of these activities may also influence prospective memory performance. Sellen, Louie, Harris, and Wilkins (1997), for example, suggested that we might evaluate unfulfilled intentions during natural breaks in activity. One of us observed a similar phenomenon in unpublished data collected during a study of the factors associated with the recollection of naturally occurring intentions (Ellis & Nimmo-Smith, 1993); these occasions were associated with small or large breaks in action (e.g., finish washing dishes and prepare to dry them). These observations have been corroborated in a comparable study, using experimenter-provided intentions designated for completion in everyday life, where thoughts about one's intentions in general frequently coincided with a break or change in activity (Kvavilashvili, 2005).

Hicks, Marsh, and Russell (2000) reported findings from a systematic investigation of this hypothesis, in a series of experiments in which both the nature (single or multiple activities) and extent (2.5–15 minutes) of a retention period were varied. The findings from these experiments revealed that providing breaks in activity led to improved performance, after both shorter and longer intervals (2.5, 5, and 15 minutes). Moreover, Hicks et al. observed that longer intervals per se led to higher performance than shorter ones, perhaps because natural fluctuations in attention across longer periods provide opportunities to review one's current goals. It would be interesting to extend these experiments further, by not only exploring the effects of one's activity during very short retention intervals (30–180 seconds), but also investigating the influence of variations in the characteristics of the intention (cf. Kvavilashvili, 2005) and the attentional demands and nature of one's activity on performance. One question that comes to mind is the effect on prospective memory performance of one's expectations of whether or not a cue will appear during a retention interval. Typically, participants in laboratory experiments are explicitly led to believe that a retrieval cue for their intention will not occur during this period; they are usually informed that it will occur in a subsequent ongoing task that they have practiced beforehand. If these instructions are not provided and the nature of the interpolated task is such that a retrieval cue or target event could conceivably occur during the retention interval, the frequency of intention recollections may decrease over time (e.g., repeated nonappearance of a target event may lower expectations that it will occur in the future). At the least, this possibility highlights the potential importance of the exact instructions that a participant receives, a point raised earlier in the discussion of implementation intentions and prospective memory tasks and one to which we return later.

RETRIEVAL

Logically, if an intention has been successfully encoded and retained, then successful performance relies on processing a target event in the ongoing task, recognizing that it constitutes a retrieval cue for an intention, retrieving the action associated with that intention, and performing that action. Failures could be due to errors in any of these processes. Moreover, failure to perform an intention does not necessarily imply failure to recall that intention when the target event appeared. People may, for example, recall their intention when the target occurs but be recaptured by the demands of the ongoing task before the appropriate action is executed (see also Einstein, McDaniel, Smith, & Shaw, 1998). Performance measures based on a simple binary measure (did or did not perform action), therefore, are likely to include both successful and unsuccessful intention retrieval, as indicated by some studies that have examined response latencies to target events (e.g., West & Craik, 1999). Theoretical expositions, however, do not always acknowledge this possibility and thus do not consider the potentially separate impact of experimental manipulations on retrieval and on the implementation of the retrieved intention (for an exception see Cohen, West, & Craik, 2001).

Attentional Requirements of Intention Retrieval and Performance

Several subsequent chapters focus on the different processes operating during this period. Therefore, we limit this section to a few comments on the key question of the attentional requirements of intention retrieval (and performance), a subject on which others will elaborate in more depth, from different perspectives. Einstein and McDaniel (1996) provided a succinct and useful summary of the two different positions on this question: the automatic activation (automatic retrieval) and notice + search (strategic retrieval) models. Thus, they presented two contrasting positions in which the performance of all prospective memory tasks was either achieved automatically or required strategic processing. Both models underwent a number of developments, in the light of subsequent research findings, culminating in the proposition of a multiprocess framework (McDaniel & Einstein, 2000; see also Ellis, Milne, & McGann, 1997). According to this framework, the attentional or strategic demands of retrieval vary as a function of the characteristics of all of the components and phases of the prospective memory task (including the retention interval and ongoing task) and of the individual undertaking that task.

Many different methods have thus far been used to investigate the parameters that reduce or increase reliance on strategic processes, including contrasts between the performance of young and healthy (and impaired) older adults (healthy older adults are presumed to have reduced or attenuated attentional capacity) and young adults under full and divided attention (using divided attention tasks that make lower or higher demands on strategic resources). We have recently begun a program of research that looks at age effects at the other end of the life span, based on research that has demonstrated age-related increases in attentional capacity and the development of strategic skills. Thus, if retrieval of a particular prospective memory task can be completed without strategic resources, then there should be little or no change as a function of increasing age. Similarly, if a task is shown to rely on attentional resources, as evidenced by age effects in children, we can examine the influence of factors thought to mitigate reliance on attentional demands. In one pair of experiments, we looked at the effects of target distinctiveness or salience on performance of an event-based prospective memory task in 4-, 5-, and 6-year-old children (McGann, Defeyter, Ellis, & Read, 2005). Following the predictions of the multiprocess model, we reasoned that distinctive or salient target events are more likely to capture attention and induce an automatic switch of attention from the ongoing task to that target event, thereby facilitating intention retrieval. Our findings were consistent with the predictions of the multiprocess model: Reliable age effects between all three age groups were observed in the nonsalient target conditions only (means in the nonsalient conditions were 0.14, 0.43, and 0.73 for the 4-, 5-, and 6-year-olds, respectively). In the salient conditions there was a reliable difference between the 4- and 6-year-olds only ($M = 0.41, 0.61, 0.71$, respectively). In a complementary series of studies we looked at age-related changes in the specificity effect, the finding that young adults show higher prospective memory performance when the target event is encoded as specific exemplars of a category (e.g., apple, pear, plum) than when the category label is encoded (e.g., a type of fruit; Einstein, McDaniel, Richardson, Cunfer & Guynn, 1995; Ellis & Milne, 1996). The provision of (typical) specific exemplars at encoding should facilitate noticing and recognizing when these targets appear in the ongoing task. We reasoned, therefore, that age-related effects were more likely to occur in the general than in the specific cue condition. In a study of 6- and 8-year-olds' prospective memory performance, we observed a reliable effect of age in the general ($M = 0.64$ and 0.92, respectively) but not the specific cue ($M = 0.89$, 0.95) conditions (Zhang & Ellis, 2005).

A contrasting theory of intention retrieval, the preparatory attentional and memory processes (PAM) model, assumes that resource-demanding preparatory attentional processes are obligatory for successful performance (Smith, 2003; Smith & Bayen, 2004). An important aspect of Smith's research is the introduction of a new method of investigating the attentional demands of intention retrieval and performance: examination of the costs of prospective remembering on ongoing task performance by contrasting accuracy and response latency on nontarget ongoing task trials when an intention is present or absent (see also Ellis & Milne, 1995). Smith and others refer to these costs as *monitoring costs*. As Marsh, Hicks, and Cook (2005) observed, however, this is a potentially misleading description as it implies that when such costs are observed participants are necessarily engaging in an "active, strategic process of searching for intention-related cues" (p. 69). In common with Marsh et al., we do not find that this is an experience that participants typically report.

As will become clear, the exact nature of the control (non-prospective-memory) condition varies across even the relatively limited number of experiments conducted thus far using this method. Smith (2003), for example, contrasted ongoing task performance with a prospective memory task with that when the prospective memory task was absent or when it was postponed until after execution of the ongoing task. In one respect the latter is a more stringent test of prospective memory task costs as it takes account of the memory component of having an intention to complete at some later point. If costs are observed, one can be confident that these are likely to be due to processes underpinning the attentional component. More commonly, the simple control condition of completing the ongoing task alone (using either a within- or between-participants design) is employed. Because this contrast does not take account of the memory component of an intention (i.e., its content), if reliable costs are not observed, one can be fairly confident that these are minimal at best. However, if costs are observed using this contrast, then the origin of these costs is unclear.

Smith's (2003) initial studies reported costs (with and without the memory component in the control condition) of performing a prospective memory task when six target events were embedded in a lexical decision task. Subsequent research has demonstrated that when a lexical decision ongoing task is employed, these costs occur only when two or more target events are prescribed (Cohen, Jaudas & Gollwitzer, 2005). Einstein and McDaniel (2005), however, reported reliable costs with a single target, but in this case the prospective memory task was embedded in a sentence completion ongoing task, one that arguably required greater attentional resources to complete in comparison to a lexical decision task. (Both studies employed the simple control condition of ongoing task only.) Thus, it is possible that the costs of undertaking a prospective memory task are mediated by both the number of prospective memory targets and the nature of the ongoing task, an observation that is more consistent with a multiprocess model than with PAM.

Recent findings reported by Marsh et al. (2005) apparently challenge predictions of both the multiprocess framework and the PAM model. They explored the effects of variable effort on the ongoing task, a match or mismatch between the processing required to recognize a target event and to perform the ongoing task on prospective memory performance, and the costs of that performance. They reasoned that high effort should decrease target event detection. However, they also proposed that this relationship would hold only when target detection and ongoing performance competed for the same or similar processing resources, that is, in the matched condition (e.g., semantic ongoing task and target event defined by its semantic features). Following the rationale of a task appropriate processing approach (Maylor, Darby, Logie, Della Sala, & Smith, 2002), they expected to observe higher performance in the matched than in the mismatched (e.g., semantic processing ongoing task and target event defined by its perceptual features) conditions.

When the ongoing task was a lexical decision task (semantic processing) and the prospective memory task was to detect either an animal word (matched processing) or a palindrome (mismatched condition; e.g., *civic*), Marsh et al. (2005, Experiment 1) observed costs in both prospective memory conditions (relative to a simple control) and better prospective memory performance in the matched conditions under low effort but no difference between the matched and mismatched conditions under high effort, due to a reliable drop in performance in the matched condition. Thus, high effort appears to deplete resources needed to support prospective memory performance in (matched) conditions where performance of both the ongoing and prospective memory tasks rely on similar processes. In a second experiment, a perceptually based ongoing task was employed and the mirror image of the preceding findings was observed. Here the prospective memory task of detecting palindromes formed the matched condition and Marsh et al. found that performance here was better than in the mismatched (animal word) condition under low effort with no reliable difference under high effort, due to a reliable reduction in performance in the matched condition. Moreover, in both experiments, there was a cost associated with prospective memory task performance in both the matched and mismatched conditions, relative to performance on the ongoing task only (simple control).

Marsh et al. (2005) argued that the multiprocess framework predicts higher performance in matched conditions occurs because the ongoing task requirements focus attention on relevant features of the cue and thus facilitates automatic cue detection. In contrast, their findings indicate that high performance in this condition is capacity consuming. Similarly, Smith's (2003; Smith & Bayen, 2004) PAM model has difficulty accommodating Marsh et al.'s (2005) findings, as it would predict that higher costs (on the ongoing task) lead to higher prospective memory performance. However, it should be noted that Marsh et al.'s predictions with respect to the multiprocess model are based on an assumption that matched and mismatched processing describes a distinction that maps onto the one employed by McDaniel and Einstein (2000) between focal and nonfocal processing. As the latter point out in this volume, this need not necessarily be a valid assumption. Thus, as M'Daniel and Einstein point out in this volume, although making a lexical decision about a word (ongoing task) and identifying that word as a member of a particular category (prospective memory target) both require semantic processing, they would argue that the lexical decision does not require processing the semantic features necessary to make a semantic decision.

Marsh et al. (2005) argued that their findings indicate that we need a more sophisticated model of resource demands that differentiates between the attentional demands of performing the whole task (ongoing and prospective memory)—generic processing resources—and the more specific processing resources called on by a particular prospective memory task, that is, those required to detect critical target features. This is an important observation that is consistent with recent findings in research on executive processes that identify a number of different components (e.g., Miyake et al., 2000). Thus, Marsh et al. (2005) suggested that divided attention reduces the attentional resources available for the whole task, whereas variations in the importance or effort directed to an ongoing task potentially impact on specific processing that may be required to identify a prospective memory target event.

Interestingly, Marsh et al.'s (2005) findings appear to conflict with those that we have reported (McGann, Ellis, & Milne, 2002). We observed detrimental effects of divided attention when there was a conceptual match between the ongoing and prospective memory tasks in the absence of such an effect with a perceptual match.

(We should note that our findings also conflict with the predictions of the multi-process model as advanced by McDaniel & Einstein, 2000. Interestingly, however, the processing requirements for both the ongoing task and target identification in our matched conditions do satisfy the definition of focal processing described by McDaniel & Einstein & Rendell, Chap. XX, this volume.) Marsh et al.'s (2005) explanation suggests that the demands of the whole task are greater when the match is conceptual than when it is perceptual. We are currently engaged in a series of studies examining the costs of matched and mismatched processing that should inform this debate.

Performance Interval

Ellis (1996) drew a distinction between the activities that we engage in after encoding a prospective memory task and the identification of a situation that might afford an opportunity for realizing a delayed intention—a performance interval. The relevance of this distinction has been highlighted by the findings from recent studies. Nowinski and Dismukes (2005), for example, observed better prospective memory performance when the ongoing task in which the prospective memory target events should occur was explicitly named during encoding. Moreover, their findings suggest that the locus of this effect lies in the incorporation of this information into the representation of the intention at encoding, that is, the further specification of retrieval cue information. A complementary study, looking at time-based intentions, was reported recently by Cook, Marsh, and Hicks (2005). They observed better performance when the time cue (6–7 minutes into the study) occurred during the expected ongoing task than when no context was specified at study.

When a context (ongoing task) is not provided, from the participant's perspective, the performance interval for an event-based intention encompasses all the different tasks to be undertaken during the study in which the retrieval cue might conceivably occur, including the filler task employed during a retention interval. In contrast, naming a particular task at encoding provides information about when the retrieval cue is likely to appear; this information is in addition to the identification (e.g., a specific word) of that cue. This is a situation that is common for naturally occurring intentions, when one knows not only the cue (e.g., give a message to *Mary*) but also the potential situations when that cue might be expected to appear (e.g., at a meeting, in the cinema) and is therefore able to engage in when-realization planning (Ellis, 1996). In most laboratory tasks, by contrast, planning is not possible due to lack of knowledge about the nature, structure, or duration of an ongoing task.

The preceding findings suggest that we should take particular care with the instructions that people are given about when a retrieval cue is likely to occur and that we should give sufficient information about these instructions in our reports of the studies that we conduct. In general, as far as it is possible to tell, most reported studies have provided some information about the ongoing task in which a cue might appear, if only by virtue of the common practice of allowing people to undertake a practice version of that ongoing task before encoding an intention to perform an extra (prospective memory) action when the main version is presented later in the study. In some respects, this request for more detail in task instructions parallels our request for clarity in the definition of an implementation intention and in the exact instructions that are provided in implementation intention studies.

Importance and Retrieval

It has been suggested that the relative importance of an intention may contribute to one's decision or readiness to act (the intent component), along with the perceived benefits of a successful outcome or consequences of failure, and the nature of the originator and beneficiary of that intention (Ellis, 1996). Thus it was proposed that importance would exert an influence on the encoding of an intention. Recent research, however, suggests that the major impact of intention importance on performance may occur during a retrieval phase. In a series of studies, Kliegel and colleagues reported findings that indicate importance improves performance when the characteristics of the intention make it more likely that retrieval will require the employment of strategic processes (Kliegel, Martin, McDaniel, & Einstein, 2001, 2004). Thus importance improved performance on a time-based but not an event-based task (Kleigel et al., 2001). However, they have demonstrated that importance can impact the performance of some event-based tasks, specifically those in which there is a mismatch between the processing focus required to complete the ongoing task and that required to identify the retrieval cue; in this instance the cue was defined by its perceptual features (specific letters in a word) and the ongoing task elicited conceptual processing (rating the pleasantness, concreteness, familiarity, or seriousness of a set of words; Kliegel et al., 2004).

ISE and Retrieval

We noted earlier the paucity of experimental research on the possible link between the heightened accessibility of a delayed intention (observed in the ISE) and success or failure in the retrieval or execution of that intention. An exception to the resounding silence on this important question comes from a study by Marsh, Hicks, and Watson (2002), who examined response latencies to target items in an ongoing task. They suggested the shorter latencies observed on failed PM trials reflect the operation of the ISE, whereas the longer ones for successful trials reflect additional processes such as noticing the target event, retrieving the intention, and coordinating execution, including task switching, of the ongoing and prospective memory tasks. As Marsh et al. noted, these additional processes may mask any benefits afforded by the ISE. It is clearly important to conduct further research on this relationship between accessibility and performance and to devise experimental paradigms that enable separation of the impact of the ISE to noticing and retrieval in particular. However, the time course sensitivity of electrophysiological measures (ERPs) may prove to be the most effective and informative of the currently available techniques for answering this question (see West, chap. 12, this volume).

Implementation Intentions

One of the hypothesized benefits of forming an implementation intention, in contrast to a goal intention, is that they "delegate the control of goal-directed responses to anticipated situational cues, which (when actually encountered) elicit these responses automatically" (Gollwitzer, 1999, p. 493). This claim for the automatic retrieval of implementation intentions has been qualified recently as referring to those "features of automaticity as identified by Bargh (1992, 1994)" (Gollwitzer & Sheerhan, 2005, p. 24). These features are immediacy (e.g., speed of response), efficiency (e.g., independent of cognitive load such as a secondary task), and lack of awareness (e.g., evidence in favor of nonconscious priming effects). It is not possible to present a detailed review of these claims here. Certainly, although many studies appear to support these assertions, for the most part this support occurs when performance on an implementation intention is contrasted with that for a goal intention, on a particular measure such as speed of response or accessibility. In prospective memory terms, this could be seen as similar to the contrast between intentions with a general (category) cue with those in which specific exemplars of that category are named at encoding (the specificity effect referred to earlier). As such, the claim for the relative automaticity of implementation intentions is not at odds with the multiprocess model proposed by McDaniel and Einstein (2000), which predicts that the characteristics of a retrieval cue will influence the attentional demands of retrieval and therefore prospective memory performance. However, it would be interesting to see an approach to the study of attentional demands in the implementation intention literature that examines not only variations in the retrieval cue (or situational cues) but also different measures of cost, that is, one that mirrors the methodological approach to this question in prospective memory research. Thus implementation intentions, like prospective memory tasks, may vary with respect to the demands they place on the attentional or strategic resources; the claim that all use relatively few attentional resources is a potentially oversimplistic one that does not take account of variations between implementation intentions.

Cohen and Gollwitzer (chap. 17, this volume) draw a different comparison between non-cue-specific (e.g., I intend to write a letter) and cue-specific intentions (e.g., If and when I finish my meeting, then I will write the recommendation letter) in prospective memory. They argue that a cue-specific intention (prospective memory task) is similar to an implementation intention. Certainly this distinction between cue-specific and non-cue-specific intentions exists for naturally occurring intentions and could be seen as comparable to a contrast drawn by one of us between general and specific cues (Ellis, 1996). However, in the latter some notion of when an intention should be realized is provided, for example, in the morning (general) versus at coffee time (specific). As noted earlier, the inclusion of a when component or retrieval cue is an inherent property of the delayed intentions that we study under the description of prospective memory. Moreover, all laboratory tasks of prospective memory describe such a component; indeed, it is difficult to envisage how one would describe a laboratory task without such a component. Finally, as noted earlier, implementation intentions (in everyday as well as laboratory instantiations) not only specify when an action should be executed, but also provide additional instructions at encoding such as overt or covert commitment, imagery, explicit planning, and so on. The research program in which we are engaged examines the effects of these additional manipulations on the requirement of strategic processing resources for retrieval and performance.

Output Monitoring

Whether or not an intention has been retrieved and performed successfully, it is important to be able to recall the outcome of one's endeavors to adjust future action accordingly. The term *output monitoring* was employed by Koriat and Ben-Zur (1988) to describe processes concerned with recording whether or not an intended action has been completed. Two errors are possible here: omissions that are due to the incorrect belief that one has completed an uncompleted intention, and repetitions due to the incorrect belief that one has not completed an executed intention (Marsh, Hicks, Hancock, & Munsayac, 2002).

Marsh, Hicks, Hancock, et al. (2002) developed a laboratory paradigm that can distinguish between these errors by asking people to make a different response (e.g., /key on a computer keyboard) when they encountered a target word on the first occasion and a different response (e.g., = key) if it appeared for a second occasion and they remembered responding earlier to the first appearance of that word. Thus one can examine performance on the second appearance of target words after correct as well as incorrect (no action) responses to the first appearance of these words. Their findings, from a series of five experiments with young adults, are consistent with the assumption that one's beliefs about one's past performance can lead to prospective memory failures. Thus, some omission errors occurred because people erroneously believed that they had previously fulfilled an intention, and some repetition errors were due not to failure to recall seeing a target word previously, but to the erroneous belief that an action had not been made in response to that word.

Einstein et al. (1998), using a different paradigm, asked people to engage in eleven 3-minute activities and to make a specific response (prospective memory task) at some point after 30 seconds had elapsed in that task. After each activity they asked participants whether they had successfully performed the most recent prospective memory task. Their findings suggest that both young and older adults can become confused about whether or not they have carried out their intentions. Clearly this could lead to repetitions, omissions, or both types of errors.

We have conducted a series of experiments that address possible differences in the numbers and types of errors that older and younger adults commit and explore the possible causes of these errors, using the Marsh, Hicks, Hancock, et al. (2002) paradigm (Harvey & Ellis, 2005). For these, we used a condition that they described as distinctive in which the prospective memory task is to respond to any word that names an animal. The participants' task was to press the key corresponding to the first letter of a target word on the first presentation and to press the = key if it appeared for a second time and he or she remembered making the correct action on the first occurrence (Marsh, Hicks, Hancock, et al., 2002, Experiment 5).

In one experiment we compared the performance of young and older adults on this task. Our findings indicate that if they had failed to make a response to the first appearance of a target word, then both young and older adults were equally likely to make a correct response (press first letter key) as an incorrect one (press = key); that is, there was no reliable difference in young and older adults' propensity to make omission errors. In contrast, when a correct response (first letter key) had been made to the first appearance of a target word, young adults made more correct responses (= key) and fewer incorrect responses (first letter key) than older adults. Thus older adults appear to be vulnerable to repetition errors (cf. Koriat & Ben-Zur, 1988).

In a second experiment we contrasted the performance of young adults under full or divided attention (Craik's odd digit task; Craik, 1987), using the distinctive condition described by Marsh, Hicks, Hancock, et al. (2002). Following failure to respond to the first target appearance, the data were similar to those reported earlier in that there were no reliable differences between the two groups in the number of correct and incorrect responses (propensity to make omission errors). Similarly, following a correct response to the first target appearance, young adults in the divided attention condition were more likely than those under full attention to make an incorrect response; that is, divided attention increases one's vulnerability to repetition errors. This suggests that older adults' propensity to commit repetition errors may be due, in large part, to reduced attentional capacity. Koriat and Ben-Zur's (1988) distinction between online and retrospective output monitoring processes may be relevant to this observation. Online processes occur when an act has been completed and result in either the deletion of an intention representation or the addition of a marker to indicate that it has been performed. In contrast, retrospective processes occur when an occasion (retrieval cue) reappears. They suggested that errors in these retrospective processes may occur as a consequence of errors in online ones (e.g., inappropriate deletion of an uncompleted intention or failure to mark a successfully completed one). Thus reductions in the attentional capacity of older adults may impact online output monitoring processes in recording successful performance. An alternate hypothesis is that older adults' recall of past performance may be operating relatively successfully and their repetition errors may be a consequence of underconfidence in their recall of this event. We are currently exploring these different explanations.

Although researchers of implementation intentions have not conducted experimental investigations of output monitoring, theories in this area place more emphasis on this aspect of a delayed intention. Gollwitzer, in particular, has described in detail the processes that are likely to operate in this evaluation phase (see, e.g., Gollwitzer, 1990). These include a comparison between the goals that have been achieved and the desired goal. If one has fallen below expectations (e.g., poorer than anticipated performance), then one may reexamine that goal by reducing expected standards or reconsidering alternate goals (considered at encoding when a decision to follow a particular goal is made). They also include an evaluation of whether the outcome that has been achieved satisfies the goal intention from which the implementation intention was derived. Thus social psychologists pay greater attention and regard to the function that a particular intention plays in our current and future goal hierarchy than most prospective memory researchers, paralleling the greater attention that they give to the operation and influence of these variables during the formation of an intention.

CONCLUSIONS AND FUTURE DIRECTIONS

The different contributions contained in this volume illustrate the increased attention and interest that research in this area has received in the last 10 years from cognitive psychologists, social psychologists, and neuropsychologists. They also bear testimony to the considerable progress that has been made in exploring the various aspects and phases of different prospective memory tasks and the processing that underpins these. The knowledge that we have gained and the progress that has been made in developing theoretical explanations of prospective memory processes—from encoding to output monitoring—has been remarkable. For example, 10 years ago research on the encoding and representation of delayed intentions consisted of the single seminal paper by Goschke and Kuhl (1993), models of retrieval processes failed to capture the complexity of a prospective memory task, and our knowledge of output monitoring processes came from a single study by Koriat and Ben-Zur (1988).

Although the review presented here is necessarily incomplete, it has illustrated a growing and welcome trend toward acknowledging and addressing variations in the characteristics of not only delayed intentions, but also the context in which these intentions are encoded, retained, realized, and evaluated. It also reveals the ingenuity of researchers in the area in employing different techniques and devising new methodologies to clarify, for example, when and why attentional resources are required to enhance the probability of a successful outcome. One challenge for the future is to directly compare the findings that are obtained from these different techniques and methods. For example, we need to compare the effects of age (in children as well as young and older adults), divided attention, and ongoing task costs on a particular instantiation of a prospective memory task and then systematically vary that task, on the basis of previous findings, to explore in more detail the nature of and extent to which attentional resources are required to support performance in different prospective memory tasks (cf. Marsh et al.'s [2005] distinction between generic and specific resources).

We believe that it is also important to acknowledge, more often than is currently the case, that a performance failure does not necessarily imply a failure of retrieval. It is also important to develop methods of distinguishing more clearly between these two events to identify where the depletion of attentional resources has an impact. This is true also for studies of the influence of one's activities during a retention interval on later retrieval and performance and on output monitoring. Activities during a retention interval vary not only in their nature, number, and duration, but also in their attentional demands and processing focus. Similarly, do older adults' repetition errors arise because attentional resources are insufficient to fully encode the original action or because this impacts on their ability to retrieve that information? Are these generic or specific processing resources? On a more mundane but potentially important level, supplying more detail in the exact instructions that are provided to participants might illuminate the underlying reasons we might observe different patterns of performance using superficially similar designs. Did one group of researchers specify which task in a series the targets would appear in while another retained some ambiguity and thus uncertainty for a participant?

Another important development that would benefit research on delayed intentions is to integrate theoretical proposals, methods, and findings from prospective memory and implementation research. These should at least be regarded as complementary lines of study of similar phenomena in which differences of emphasis can be used constructively to plug the gaps of understanding in each tradition. Social psychologists, for example, have traditionally paid greater regard to the origin of intentions, asking questions such as why we decide on one course of action rather than another in the pursuit of an overarching goal. Cognitive psychologists, by and large, have neglected this, potentially to the detriment of fully appreciating the myriad of influences on the encoding of an intention and the motivational forces that might impact the outcome of that intention. Thus far, cognitive psychologists have focused primarily on the action component of an intention, with some work on the cue component but scant regard to the intent (strength of decision to act, including will or commitment) and thus the relationship among all three components at encoding and the potential impact of this on retrieval.

Complementarily, cognitive psychologists have a long history of exploring the attentional or strategic requirements of different processes and tasks, expending an increasing amount of effort on exploring the impact of variations between designs and the exact nature of the strategic processes that might be employed (inhibition, task switching, etc.). These could usefully be applied to explore variations between implementation intentions. (The earlier request for precise instructions also applies to reports of research on the latter.) Ideally, greater collaboration between social and cognitive psychologists (and neuroscientists), working in intradisciplinary research groups, would allow us to develop a greater understanding of this vitally important research area: how we develop, maintain, and sustain our ability to determine and enact intentions at appropriate future moments.

REFERENCES

Altmann, E. M., & Trafton, J. G. (2002). Memory for goals: An activation-based model. *Cognitive Science, 26,* 39–83.

Anderson, J. R. (1990). *The adaptive character of thought.* Hillsdale, NJ: Erlbaum.

Bahrick, H. P., & Phelps, E. (1987). Retention of Spanish vocabulary over 8 years. *Journal of Experimental Psychology: Learning, Memory and Cognition, 13,* 344–349.

Bargh, J. A. (1992). The ecology of automaticity: Towards establishing the conditions needed to produce automatic processing effects. *American Journal of Psychology, 105,* 181–199.

Bargh, J. A. (1994). The four horsemen of automaticity: Awareness, efficiency, intention and control in social interaction. In R. S. Wyer, Jr. & T. K. Srull (Eds.), *Handbook of social cognition* (2nd ed., pp. 1–40). Hillsdale, NJ: Lawrence Erlbaum Associates, Inc.

Brandimonte, M. A. (1991). Ricordare il futuro Remembering the future. *Giornale Italiano di Psicologia, 3,* 351–374.

Brandimonte, M. A., & Passolunghi, M. C. (1994). The effect of cue-familiarity, cue-distinctiveness and retention interval on prospective remembering. *The Quarterly Journal of Experimental Psychology, 47A,* 565–587.

Chasteen, A. L., Park, D. C., & Schwartz, N. (2001). Implementation intentions and facilitation of prospective memory. *Psychological Science, 12,* 457–461.

Cohen, A.-L., Jaudas, A., & Gollwitzer, P. M. (2005, July). *Working memory load and self-regulatory strategies modulate the cost of remembering to remember.* Paper presented at the 2nd International Conference on Prospective Memory, Zurich.

Cohen, A.-L., West, R., & Craik, F. I. M. (2001). Modulation of the prospective and retrospective components of memory for intentions in younger and older adults. *Aging, Neuropsychology and Cognition, 8,* 1–13.

Cook, G. I., Marsh, R. L., & Hicks, J. L. (2005). Associating a time-based prospective memory task with an expected context can improve or impair intention completion. *Applied Cognitive Psychology, 19,* 345–360.

Craik, F. I. M. (1987). A functional account of age differences inmemory. In F. Klix & H. Hagendorf (Eds.), *Human memory and cognitive capabilities: Mechanisms and performances* (pp. 409–422). Amsterdam: Elsevier.

Dockree, P. M., & Ellis, J. A. (2001). Forming and canceling everyday intentions: Implications for prospective remembering. *Memory and Cognition, 29,* 1139–1145.

Ebbinghaus, H. (1964). Memory: A contribution to experimental psychology. In K. W. Spence & J. T. Spence (Eds.), *The psychology of learning and motivation* (Vol. 1, pp. 229–325). New York: Academic. (Original work published 1887.)

Einstein, G. O., Holland, L. J., McDaniel, M. A., & Guynn, M. J. (1992). Age-related deficits in prospective memory: The influence of task complexity. *Psychology and Aging, 7,* 471–478.

Einstein, G. O., & McDaniel, M. A. (1996). Retrieval processes in prospective memory: Theoretical approaches and some new empirical findings. In M. Brandimonte, G. O. Einstein, & M. A. McDaniel (Eds.), *Prospective memory: Theory and applications* (pp. 115–141). Mahwah, NJ: Lawrence Erlbaum Associates, Inc.

Einstein, G. O., & McDaniel, M. A. (2005, July). *Evidence for spontaneous retrieval processes in prospective memory.* Paper presented at the 2nd International Conference on Prospective Memory, Zurich.

Einstein, G. O., McDaniel, M. A., Richardson, S. L., Cunfer, A. R., & Guynn, M. J. (1995). Aging and prospective memory: Examining the influence of self-initiated retrieval processes. *Journal of Experimental Psychology: Learning, Memory, and Cognition, 21,* 996–1007.

Einstein, G. O., McDaniel, M. A., Smith, R. E., & Shaw, P. (1998). Habitual prospective memory and aging: Remembering intentions and forgetting actions. *Psychological Science, 9,* 284–288.

Einstein, G.O., McDaniel, M.A., Manzi, M., Cochran, B., & Baker, M. (2000). Prospective memory and aging: Forgetting intentions over short delays. *Psychology and Aging, 15,* 671–683.

Einstein, G. O., McDaniel, M. A., Thomas, R., Mayfield, S., Shank, H., Morrisette, N., et al. (2005). Multiple processes in prospective memory retrieval: Factors determining monitoring versus spontaneous retrieval. *Journal of Experimental Psychology: Learning, Memory, and Cognition, 134,* 327–342.

Einstein, G. O., McDaniel, M. A., Williford, C. L., Pagan, J. L., & Dismukes, R. K. (2003). Forgetting of intentions in demanding situations is rapid. *Journal of Experimental Psychology: Applied, 9,* 147–162.

Ellis, J. A. (1996). Prospective memory or the realization of delayed intentions: A conceptual framework for research. In M. Brandimonte, G. O. Einstein, & M. A. McDaniel (Eds.), *Prospective memory: Theory and applications* (pp. 1–22). Mahwah, NJ: Lawrence Erlbaum Associates, Inc.

Ellis, J. A., & Milne, A. (1995, November). *Realizing intentions in a multiple task environment.* Poster presented at the 36th Annual Meeting of the Psychonomic Society, Los Angeles.

Ellis, J. A., & Milne, A. (1996). Retrieval cue specificity and the realization of delayed intentions. *Quarterly Journal of Experimental Psychology, 49A,* 862–887.

Ellis, J. A., Milne, A., & McGann, D. (1997). *Prospective remembering in a multiple-task environment.* Poster presented at the 37th Annual Conference of the Psychonomic Society, Los Angeles.

Ellis, J. A., Milne, A., & McGann, D. (March, 1997). *Conceptual and perceptual processes in prospective remembering.* Paper presented at the International Workshop on Prospective Memory, Leuven, Belgium.

Ellis, J. A., & Nimmo-Smith, I. (1993). Recollecting naturally-occurring intentions: A study of cognitive and affective factors. *Memory, 1,* 107–126.

Eschen, A., Freeman, J. E., Dietrich, T., Martin, M., Ellis, J. A., Martin-Fiori, E. et al. (in press). Motor brain regions involved in the encoding of delayed intentions: An fMRI study. *International Journal of Psychophysiology.*

Freeman, J. E., & Ellis, J. A. (2003a). Aging and the accessibility of performed and to-be-performed activities. *Aging, Neuropsychology and Cognition, 10,* 298–309.

Freeman, J. E., & Ellis, J. A. (2003b). The intention-superiority effect for naturally-occurring intentions: The role of intention accessibility in everyday prospective remembering in young and older adults. *International Journal of Psychology, 38,* 215–228.

Freeman, J. E., & Ellis, J. A. (2003c). The representation of delayed intentions: A prospective subject-performed task? *Journal of Experimental Psychology: Learning, Memory, and Cognition, 29,* 976–992.

Freeman J. E & Ellis J. A. (2007). Retrieval cue activation in prospective memory tasks: Effects of age and intention completion. Unpublished manuscript.

Gollwitzer, P. M. (1990). Action phases and mindsets. In E. T. Higgins & R. M. Sorrentino (Eds.), *The handbook of motivation and cognition* (Vol. 2, pp. 53–92). New York: Guilford.

Gollwitzer, P. M. (1999). Implementation intentions: Strong effects of simple plans. *American Psychologist, 54,* 493–503.

Gollwitzer, P. M., & Brandstätter, V. (1997). Implementation intentions and effective goal pursuit. *Journal of Personality and Social Psychology, 73,* 186–199.

Gollwitzer, P. M., & Schaal, B. (1998). Metacognition in action: The importance of implementation intentions. *Personality and Social Psychology Review, 2,* 124–136.

Goschke, T., & Kuhl, J. (1993). Representation of intentions: Persisting activation in memory. *Journal of Experimental Psychology: Learning, Memory, and Cognition, 19,* 1211–1226.

Goschke, T. & Kuhl, J. (1996). Remembering what to do: Explicit and implicit memory for intentions. In M. Brandimonte, G.O. Einstein & M.A. McDaniel (Eds.). *Prospective memory: Theory and applications.* Mahwah, NJ: Lawrence Erlbaum Associates.

Guynn, M. J., McDaniel, M. A., & Einstein, G. O. (1998). Prospective memory: When reminders fail. *Memory and Cognition, 26,* 287–298.

Harvey, D. A., & Ellis, J. A. (2005, July). *Prospective memory and output monitoring in older adults: Deficits in attention or reduced confidence?* Poster presented at the 2nd International Conference on Prospective Memory, Zurich.

Hicks, J. L., Marsh, R. L., & Russell, E. J. (2000). The properties of retention intervals and their affect on retaining prospective memories. *Journal of Experimental Psychology: Learning, Memory, and Cognition, 26,* 1160–1169.

Kliegel, M., Eschen, A., & Thöne-Otto, A. I. T. (2004). Planning and realization of complex intentions in traumatic brain injury and normal aging. *Brain and Cognition, 56,* 43–54.

Kliegel, M., Martin, M., McDaniel, M. A., & Einstein, G. O. (2001). Varying the importance of a prospective memory task: Differential effects across time- and event-based prospective memory. *Memory, 9,* 1–11.

Kliegel, M., Martin, M., McDaniel, M. A., & Einstein, G. O. (2004). Importance effects on performance in event-based prospective memory tasks. *Memory, 12,* 553–561.

Kliegel, M., McDaniel, M. A., & Einstein, G. O. (2000). Plan formation, retention, and execution in prospective memory: A new approach and age-related effects. *Memory and Cognition, 28,* 1041–1049.

Koriat, A., & Ben-Zur, H. (1988). Remembering that I did it: Processes and deficits in output monitoring. In M. M. Gruneberg, P. E. Morris, & R. N. Sykes (Eds.), *Practical aspects of memory: Current research and issues* (Vol. 1, pp. 203–208). Chichester, UK: Wiley.

Koriat, A., Ben-Zur, H., & Nussbaum, A. (1990). Encoding information for future enactment: Memory for to-be-performed versus memory for to-be-recalled tasks. *Memory and Cognition, 18,* 568–578.

Kuhl, J. (1985). Volitional mediators of cognitive-behavior consistency: Self-regulatory processes and actions versus state orientation. In J. Kuhl & J. Beckmann (Eds.), *Action control: From cognition to behavior* (pp. 101–128). New York: Springer.

Kvavilashvili, L. (2005, July). *Automatic or controlled? Rehearsal and retrieval processes in everyday time- and event-based prospective memory tasks.* Paper presented at the 2nd International Conference on Prospective Memory, Zurich.

Kvavilashvili, L., & Ellis, J. A. (1996). Varieties of intention: Some distinctions and classification. In M. Brandimonte, G. O. Einstein, & M. A. McDaniel (Eds.), *Prospective memory: Theory and applications* (pp. 23–51). Mahwah, NJ: Lawrence Erlbaum Associates, Inc.

Lebiere, C., & Lee, F. J. (2001). Intention superiority effect: A context-sensitivity account. In *Proceedings of the Fourth International Conference on Cognitive Modelling* (pp. 139–144). Mahwah, NJ: Lawrence Erlbaum Associates, Inc.

Leynes, P. A., Allan, J. D., & Marsh, R. L. (1998). Topographic differences in CNV amplitude reflect different preparatory processes. *International Journal of Psychophysiology, 31,* 33–44.

Leynes, P. A., Marsh, R. L., Hicks, J. L., Allen, J. D., & Mayhorn, C. B. (2003). Investigating the encoding and retrieval of intentions with event-related potentials. *Consciousness and Cognition, 12,* 1–18.

Liu, L. L., & Park, D. C. (2004). Aging and medical adherence: The use of automatic processes to achieve effortful things. *Psychology and Aging, 19,* 318–325.

Loftus, E. F. (1971). Memory for intentions: The effect of presence of a cue and interpolated activity. *Psychonomic Science, 23,* 315–316.

Marsh, R. L., Hicks, J. E., & Bink, M. L. (1998). The activation of completed, uncompleted and partially completed intentions. *Journal of Experimental Psychology: Learning, Memory, and Cognition, 24,* 350–361.

Marsh, R. L., Hicks, J. L., & Bryan, E. S. (1999). The activation of unrelated and canceled intentions. *Memory and Cognition, 27,* 320–327.

Marsh, R. L., Hicks, J. L., & Cook, G. I. (2005). On the relationship between effort toward an ongoing task and cue detection in event-based prospective memory. *Journal of Experimental Psychology: Learning, Memory, and Cognition, 31,* 68–75.

Marsh, R. L., Hicks, J. L., Hancock, T. W., & Munsayac, K. (2002). Investigating the output monitoring component of event-based prospective memory performance. *Memory and Cognition, 30,* 302–311.

Marsh, R. L., Hicks, J. L., & Watson, V. (2002). The dynamics of intention retrieval and coordination of action in event-based prospective memory. *Journal of Experimental Psychology: Learning, Memory, and Cognition, 28*, 652–659.

Martin, M., Kliegel, M., & McDaniel, M. A. (2003). The involvement of executive functions in prospective memory performance of adults. *International Journal of Psychology, 38*, 195–206.

Maylor, E. A., Darby, R. J., & Della Sala, S. (2000). Retrieval of performed versus to-be-performed tasks: A natutralistic study of the intention-superiority effect in normal aging and dementia. *Applied Cognitive Psychology, 14*, 83–98.

Maylor, E. A., Darby, R. J., Logie, R., Della Sala, S., & Smith, G. (2002). Prospective memory across the lifespan. In P. Graf & N. Ohta (Eds.), *Lifespan development of human memory* (pp. 235–256). Cambridge, MA: MIT Press.

McDaniel, M. A., & Einstein, G. O. (2000). Strategic and automatic processes in prospective memory retrieval: A multiprocess framework. *Applied Cognitive Psychology, 14*, S127–S144.

McGann, D., Defeyter, M. A., Reid, C., & Ellis, J. A. (2005, July). *Prospective memory in children: The effects of age and target salience.* Paper presented at the 2nd International Conference on Prospective Memory, Zurich.

McGann, D., Ellis, J. A., & Milne, A. (2002). Conceptual and perceptual processes in prospective remembering: Differential influence of attentional resources. *Memory and Cognition, 30*, 1021–1032.

McGann, D., Defeyter, M.A., Ellis, J.A. & Reid, C. (2005). Prospective memory in children: The effects of age and target salience. Paper presented at the 2nd International Conference on Prospective Memory, Zurich.

Meacham, J. A., & Leiman, B. (1982). Remembering to perform future actions. In U. Neisser (Ed.), *Memory observed: Remembering in natural contexts* (pp. 327–336). San Francisco: Freeman.

Miyake, A., Friedman, N. P., Emerson, M. J., Witzki, A. H., Howerter, A., & Wager, T. D. (2000). The unity and diversity of executive functions and their contributions to complex "frontal lobe" tasks: A latent variable analysis. *Cognitive Psychology, 41*, 49–100.

Nowinski, J. L., & Dismukes, R. K. (2005). Effects of ongoing task context and target typicality on prospective memory performance: The importance of associative cueing. *Memory, 13*, 649–657.

Penfield, W., & Boldrey, E. (1937). Somatic motor and sensory representation in the cerebral cortex as studied by electrical stimulation. *Brain, 60*, 389–443.

Sellen, A. J., Louie, G., Harris, J. E., & Wilkins, A. J. (1997). What brings intentions to mind? An in situ study of prospective memory. *Memory, 5*, 483–507.

Shallice, T., & Burgess, P. (1991). Deficits in strategy application following frontal lobe damage in man. *Brain, 114*, 727–741.

Shallice, T., Fletcher, P., Frith, C. D., Grasby, P., Frackowiak, R. S. J., & Dolan, R. J. (1994). Brain regions associated with acquisition and retrieval of verbal episodic memory. *Nature, 368*, 633–635.

Smith, R. E. (2003). The cost of remembering to remember in event-based prospective memory: Investigating the capacity demands of delayed intention performance. *Journal of Experimental Psychology: Learning, Memory, and Cognition, 29*, 347–361.

Smith, R. E., & Bayen, U. J. (2004). A multinomial model of event-based prospective memory. *Journal of Experimental Psychology: Learning, Memory, and Cognition, 30*, 756–777.

Watanabe, H. (2003). Effects of encoding style, expectation of retrieval mode, and retrieval style on memory for action phrases. *Perceptual and Motor Skills, 96*, 707–727.

Watanabe, H., & Kawaguchi, J. (1999). Temporal aspects of everyday activities and events. *Studies in Informatics and Science (Nagoya University), 10*, 159–178.

Watanabe, H., & Kawaguchi, J. (2005). Representation of plans: Activation in memory. *Memory, 13,* 174–188.

West, R., & Craik, F. I. M. (1999). Age-related decline in prospective memory: The roles of cue accessibility and cue sensitivity. *Psychology and Aging, 14,* 264–272.

Wilkins, A.J. (1986). Remembering to do things in the laboratory and everyday life. *Acta Neurologica Scandinavica, 74* (Spple. 109), 109–112.

Winograd, E. (1988). Some observations on prospective remembering. In M. M. Gruneberg, P. E. Morris, & R. N. Sykes (Eds.), *Practical aspects of memory: Current research and issues* (Vol. 1, pp. 348–353). Chichester, UK: Wiley.

Witkin, H. A. (1950). Individual differences in ease of perception of embedded figures. *Journal of Personality, 19,* 1–15.

Zhang, X., & Ellis, J. A. (2006). *The development of prospective remembering: Effects of cue specificity.* Unpublished manuscript.

Zhang, X. & Ellis, J.A. (2007). The development of prospective memory: Influence of target specificity. Unpublished manuscript.

2

Connecting the Past and the Future
Attention, Memory, and Delayed Intentions

REBEKAH E. SMITH

Department of Psychology
The University of Texas at San Antonio

An agent who is contemplating what to do at a given time sees the future of the world from that time on branching out into many alternatives, and he also sees that those alternatives can be tied to the past just by his making certain instantiations true. Those selected instantiations become special just by their being selected: they are the junctions at which the agent's causality can connect the future containing the truth of the complex proposition to the given past.

—Hector-Neri Castañeda (1975, p. 280)

This quote from Castañeda's discussion of intentions refers to the fundamental relationship between intentions and memory. When an individual has an intent, he or she has selected a particular path of action, and when that intent has a particular relationship to the past it has a special status: It is an intention. This current discussion of the relationship between memory and delayed intentions begins by defining intentions, drawing heavily on action theory to do so. The definition process includes the clarification of such terms as immediate and delayed intentions, as well as distinguishing intentions from intents.

I begin this chapter by defining precisely what is meant by delayed intentions for two reasons. First, as pointed out by McDaniel and Einstein (2000), one challenge for prospective memory researchers "has been to define the characteristics that distinguish prospective memory tasks" (p. S127) from retrospective tasks. Rather than just listing potential characteristics of these tasks, I describe a fundamental definition of what constitutes a delayed intention. The second reason for starting with precise definitions is that clarification of what exactly is meant by the term delayed intentions has implications for theoretical explanations of how delayed intentions are accomplished. Therefore it is important not just to provide an operational definition for what constitutes a delayed intention in a given task context, but to consider the basic aspects of a delayed intention. Following the discussion of terminology, this chapter focuses on one particular theoretical position, the preparatory attentional and memory processes (PAM) theory.

PRELIMINARY CLARIFICATIONS

Delayed Intentions

In addition to pointing out the connection between memory and intent, the introductory quote draws attention to the importance of a decision in any discussion of action. An individual has alternative pathways to follow at any given moment, and it is the act of choosing one particular alternative at a given point in time that determines what action an individual will take. *Volition* is the act of making such a decision. Although intentions and volition are related, the terms are not synonymous. Volition as just defined is more closely related to the term *intent*. Not everyone discriminates between volition and intent (Castañeda, 1975); however, I see the distinction, although subtle, in the following way. Recall that volition was defined as the act of choosing a course of action. An intent is the decision. That is, volition could be thought of as encompassing intent: The act of deciding is volition and the result of this act, which is really embedded within and inseparable from the act, is the decision. This particular aspect of volition is intent. For example, I might make the decision to make a phone call, which results in the intent to pick up and dial the phone that is the immediate cause of this action. The volition leads to the intent, but does not itself immediately cause the action. Beyond stating that an intent is the result of the act of deciding on a course of action, a more detailed definition of intent is required. The distinction between volitions and intents, as well as the following definitions, is depicted in Figure 2.1.

Defining Intent   As a starting point, consider an intent to be a mental event that is the proximate cause of action (Brand, 1984). Of course, rather than illuminating the issue, this simply begs the question of what sort of mental event can cause action (Brand, 1980). An intent is the full endorsing of a practitional copula at a time at which it can be endorsed (Brand, 1984; Castañeda, 1975). The term *copula* simply refers to the joining of the agent and the action in such a way that the action describes the agent's state. This connection between the agent and action takes a special form. The connection is practitional (i.e., the connection exists), as opposed to propositional, which refers to a connection that could be or could not be. In other words, a proposition has a truth value, whereas a practitioner does not (Castañeda, 1980). For example, suppose that I decide, "I will read this book"; it is possible that this statement could be made false in that I might not read

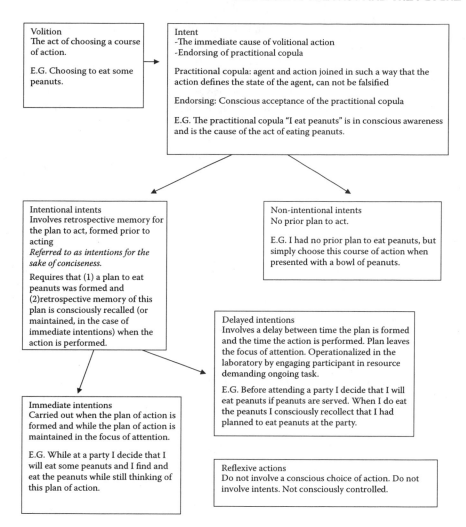

FIGURE 2.1 A summary presentation of the definitions involved in specifying what constitutes a delayed intention and how delayed intentions differ from immediate intentions, reflexes, and nonintentional intents.

the book. In contrast, if I decide "I read this book," the statement is neither true nor false; it describes my current state. The decision makes up the endorsing part of the definition. This means that I completely accept the statement "I read this book." In other words, the state represented by the practitional copula comes into existence. An intent is the mental event that causes action through the complete acceptance of a particular relationship between an agent and an action at such time that the action can occur. It is a choice of a particular action α: It is not an "I will α" choice, it is a choice of "I α."

Defining Intentions   How do intentions differ from other forms of intent? It is a reference to the past that distinguishes intentions from intents. Intents can be broken into two groups: intentional and nonintentional intents. Intentional actions involve reference to a "prior representation of a complex action" (Brand, 1984, p. 47). An intentional action is one that is in some way part of a plan that was formed before the action occurred. An example might help to clarify the distinction. Suppose that the phone rings unexpectedly and I pick up the receiver. At that moment my intent was to pick up the receiver, but I did not plan to do so before the action occurred. This is a nonintentional intent. In contrast, suppose I plan to make a phone call. This time my intent to pick up the receiver is intentional because it was planned before the action occurred. Although the plan of action is formed prior to the action occurring, the full endorsing of the associated practitional copula is concurrent with the action and is undertaken by the agent that is the intender (Beardsley, 1980). It is these planned actions that are the focus of this discussion, and rather than using the cumbersome terminology of an intentional intent, I will use the term *intention*.[1]

The intentional aspect of intentions, which requires the formation of a plan prior to the execution of action, thus requires that all intentions are prospective. An immediate intention still requires that a plan of action be formulated prior to acting, but in this case the transition from a plan to an action occurs without the intention ever leaving the focus of attention. The agent decides to perform a particular action and does so while the plan to act remains as the focus of conscious awareness. Generally this would be a fairly immediate performance of the action, but could involve a period of time in which the person maintains the plan continuously as the focus of attention. For example, I decide that I should go to the other room to take my medicine, and I maintain this plan in the focus of attention while I go get the medicine to avoid the situation of arriving in the room and not being able to remember what I went in the room for.

In this chapter, the term *delayed intention* refers to what is generally considered to be a prospective memory task. A delayed intention is one in which the prior representation of an action leaves the focus of attention for some amount of time prior to the eventual execution of the action. That is, in the case of delayed intentions, the plan of action, once formed, does not remain as the focus of conscious awareness. The requirement that the action plan not be maintained as the focus of attention for an intention to be a delayed intention is a strict definition of an idealized case and presents a complication that likely contributed to the relative paucity of prospective memory studies prior to the publication of Einstein and McDaniel's (1990) groundbreaking study.

---

[1] *Intention*, as I use the word, is not the same as intentionality. *Intentionality*, in philosophical terms, is the "property of mental states and events by which they are directed at or about or of objects and states of affairs in the world" (Searle, 1983, p. 1). This meaning of intentionality refers to a larger class of events that includes intentions, beliefs, and desires; however, intentions are different from beliefs and desires (Brand, 1984; Castañeda, 1975; Searle, 1983).

Intentional should be distinguished from intensional. *Intensional* refers to the "*of*-ness property" that is characteristic of intentions and thus if something is intentional, it is also intensional (Rey, 1983).

One of the complications for studying prospective memory in a controlled setting is how to provide an appropriate analog task, within a controlled setting and relatively short time frame, to real-world prospective memory tasks in which an intention may be formed far in advance of the time at which the action can be performed. A solution was provided by Einstein and McDaniel (1990) when they developed what has now become the standard type of prospective memory task used in controlled laboratory studies. The "essential characteristic" of the Einstein and McDaniel paradigm "was to have subjects busily working on one task, while at the same time requiring them to perform an activity at future specified times" (p. 718). The argument was that the engagement in the ongoing task would prevent continual maintenance of the action plan as the focus of attention. Furthermore, many studies involve a filled delay between the prospective memory instructions and the ongoing task with which the prospective memory task is associated. Although we cannot be perfectly sure that the action plan has left the focus of attention following the prospective memory instructions in each and every case, these techniques mimic real-world demands and provide what has been accepted by the research community as an appropriate analogy to real-world delayed intention tasks.

Intentions and Consciousness

What exactly does the term *endorsing* in the definition of intents mean? The practitional copula exists only as an aspect of consciousness. When an otherwise propositional copula becomes practitional (i.e., the relationship between the agent and the action achieves the state of neither potential truth nor potential falsity, but existence) this copula is now an "item before consciousness" (Castañeda, 1975, p. 284). Therefore, an intent, when it is causing an action, is conscious. Thus, at the time of performance a delayed intention has at its base a conscious intent. Consciousness in this case refers to something that is in the focus of attention and to which some of our limited cognitive resources are directed. By stating that intents are conscious, I have ruled out certain behaviors that one might attempt, under other circumstances, to group together with intentions. The necessity of consciousness eliminates such things as reflexes from the category of intents. Behaviors that cannot be consciously controlled would not by this view be considered intents.

Retrospective Memory and Delayed Intentions

Defining intentions as the sanctioning of a choice at the point in time when the resulting action is possible seems to leave no room for retrospective memory to play a role. The intention "is" regardless of what happened in the past. However, although the endorsement of the practitional copula "is," prior to this particular choice there were alternatives. The selection of an alternative can be influenced by the past. When the past influences an intent such that the agent is conscious of the influence, the intent is called an intentional action. An action is intentional when it includes the feature of having been part of a representational plan of a complex activity. Intentional action is action that involves reference to the past; in other words, action that involves conscious recollection of the intended action. In the absence of memory (i.e., in the absence of the previous existence of a plan), we cannot have intentional action, and thus in the absence of retrospective memory, we would have only nonintentional immediate intents. Thus, given our definition of intentions as intentional intents, retrospective memory is a fundamental aspect of intentions.

Before beginning a discussion of how memory influences intentions, two distinctions must be made. By defining intentions as intents that reference the past, I mean that the intent was part of a plan. The intent that drives the corresponding action is not the same as that which drives a recollection of the plan. Memory for an intention—remembering that you planned to do α—is not the same as the performance of action α. This distinction and the distinction to be made in the next paragraph are not random declarations; rather, they are based on a careful consideration of the selected definition of intentions. Although the past is a defining element in intentions, memory in this case serves as a tool, rather than as an object (see Kelley & Jacoby, 1990, for further discussion of this distinction). The intent is part of a previously made plan, and thus the past experience influences current mental processes; however, the past is not the focus of the mental processes, the intent is. This is different from memory as the focus of mental processes. Therefore, the performance of a delayed intention is not the same as retrieving the plan of that action for inspection.

The second distinction to be made is that memory that I intend is not the same as the intention. In other words, remembering that I meant to do something in the absence of memory for what the something was is a different mental event from remembering to α. Recall that an intent (the base of an intention) is the acceptance of a statement connecting the agent and the action. Thus, if the action is absented from the copula in question, then the copula is not the same. If an individual recalls he or she was to do something without recalling what he or she was to do, the action is undefined and, therefore, it is not possible to have the same intent. The copula that specifies the relationship between the agent and action α is not the same as the copula that connects the agent and action $\alpha_?$. The agent and the action cannot be separated.

These distinctions are consistent with Crowder's (1996) argument that memory for the intention cannot fully explain performance of the intention and that performance of intentions is not an accurate reflection of memory for those intentions. As noted by Crowder, memory for an intention and performance of the intention at the appropriate time are often not correlated (e.g., Dobbs & Rule, 1987; Kliegel, McDaniel, & Einstein, 2000; Kvavilashvili, 1987; Mäntylä, 1994). This finding indicates that the performance of delayed intentions depends on more than just retrospective memory for the intentions. Although I agree with Crowder's conclusion that performance does not accurately reflect memory for an intention, I do not agree with his argument in support of this position. Crowder provided the example of an impossible intention (e.g., determining the exact value of π) that can be remembered but never performed. This argument is invalid given the definition of intentions. An intention has at its heart an intent, and given that intents are the cause of action, there cannot be an impossible intent: The copula of I α_π can never be endorsed and thus cannot be an intent. The corresponding intention cannot exist. You could have the intention of *trying* to determine the exact value of π, but not of actually determining the exact value of π.

Time-Based and Event-Based Prospective Memory Tasks

Prospective memory tasks can be classified in a variety of different ways (e.g., Kvavilashvili & Ellis, 1996). A common distinction involves differentiating time-based and event-based prospective memory tasks. Time-based prospective memory tasks are tasks that involve an action that is to be carried out at a certain clock time or after a set amount of time has elapsed. Remembering to place a phone call at 2:30 or remembering to turn off the oven after 15 minutes are both examples of time-based prospective memory tasks. Event-based tasks are tasks that must be performed when a specific target event occurs in the environment, such as remembering to give your colleague a message when you see him or her. The focus of this chapter is on event-based prospective memory.

Because prospective memory tasks often involve interruption of some other activity (Einstein & McDaniel, 1996), as discussed earlier, laboratory versions of event-based prospective memory tasks generally involve embedding the prospective memory task in an ongoing activity (Einstein & McDaniel, 1990). For instance, in Einstein, Smith, McDaniel, and Shaw (1997), participants engaged in a word rating task as the ongoing activity. In addition to the word rating task, participants were asked to try to remember to press a special key if a target word appeared during the word rating task. This additional task was the prospective memory task.

THE PREPARATORY ATTENTIONAL AND MEMORY PROCESSES THEORY

The definitions and distinctions already outlined provided an important starting point for the PAM theory (Smith, 2003; Smith & Bayen, 2004, 2005, 2006; Smith, McVay & McConnell, Hunt, 2007). These definitions lead to an important role for consciousness in the performance of delayed intentions. An individual must be conscious of the plan to perform an action (in other words, the plan is in the focus of attention) at both encoding, when the plan is formed, and at retrieval, when the action is performed. The endorsement of the practitional copula is a conscious activity. Furthermore, this endorsement occurs along with a conscious recollection of the prior plan of action.

In addition, intents are volitional and volition is a decision. Thus, an intention is a decision about action that consciously references a prior plan. The importance of the decision making rests in a key aspect of prospective memory tasks: The agent must often remember to perform the action when other activity is underway (Einstein & McDaniel, 1996). Refer again to the characteristic that distinguishes delayed intentions and immediate intentions. Immediate intentions are performed as the intention is formed. In contrast, delayed intentions, by definition, require that the plan of action leaves the focus of attention for some amount of time between the decision to perform the action and the time at which the action is to be performed. In this interim, ongoing activity will occupy the focus of attention.

How is it that the intent is returned to focal attention? One might argue that the return to focal attention of the intent could be achieved through automatic processes (e.g., Guynn, McDaniel, & Einstein, 2001; McDaniel & Einstein, 2000). These automatic processes could take several different forms. For instance, the "associative linkage between target and intended action" could lead to "activation of the intended action upon encounter of the target event, with such activation presumably being reflexive and nonstrategic" (McDaniel & Einstein, 2000, p. S130). McDaniel and Einstein also argued that an environmental event can lead to "spontaneous and relatively resource-free retrieval of the action" (McDaniel & Einstein, 2000, p. S131). In both the automatic associative activation case and the spontaneous and resource-free retrieval of the action case the prospective memory task is performed automatically and a decision process would not be required. Careful application of the definitions outlined earlier would exclude these two cases of automatic performance as reflexive action that is not subject to conscious control and is therefore not an intention. Alternatively, one would require different but equally precise definitions of intentions to include these cases.

McDaniel and Einstein (2000) also suggested that there are cases in which an environmental event spontaneously captures attention (e.g., because the target is salient) due to a noticing process, perhaps because of a differential ease of processing for the target event. The attention capture is followed by a "controlled search for memory" (p. S131), as would be the noticing of a target. In these cases the initial orienting to the target event may be automatic, but this is followed by a controlled decision process about how to respond to the stimulus. In this alternative situation an individual must devote capacity to active decision making (McDaniel & Einstein, 2000). Similarly, in this sort of situation PAM would predict that the attention capture is followed by preparatory attentional processing, with the preparatory attentional processing likely in the focus of attention.

When prospective memory tasks involve targets that are not going to spontaneously capture attention, which thereby force active decision making, there must be other means for preparing to respond to a target. To perceive the target as such, the individual must be prepared in some way for the potential occurrence of the target (Smith, 2003). The PAM theory argues that some of our limited cognitive resources must be devoted to evaluating the environment and responses to the environment for an event to be recognized as a target event. This particular point arises from the basic assumption of transfer appropriate processing (Morris, Bransford, & Franks, 1977). The intended action plan will return to the focus of attention through reinstatement of the processes that occurred at encoding. For the same processes to be reinstated, the retrieval context must sufficiently match the encoding context.

With respect to the external context, or environment, there will always be a difference in time and often in other factors. For example, if you plan in the morning at home to stop and pick up dry cleaning after work, the location at encoding and at retrieval will be different. What might match are the internal context of retrieval and the internal context that was part of the plan. The same external information can be viewed in very different ways depending on an individual's own information and experience. This is perhaps one reason that laboratory prospective memory tasks do not always suffer from ceiling effects, despite very good physical matches between encoding and retrieval contexts. The internal context has been changed sufficiently by the ongoing task to reduce the chances of reinstating the processing necessary for completion of the prospective memory task.

Reinstatement of the processing that will lead to the performance of a delayed intention depends on the match between the external or internal context at retrieval and the internal context at encoding. This requires that the agent's internal context be ready for the reinstatement to occur. If the agent is devoting all available resource capacity to some ongoing activity, the external environment will only match the context that existed at encoding if the ongoing activity sets the same context. Given that the intent of the background task is by definition not the same as the delayed intention, the match will always be less than ideal. This problem can be overcome by devoting some amount of capacity to evaluating the environment and the appropriateness of your responses to events in the environment. (The importance of the relationship between the external context at retrieval and the internal expectations about that context are highlighted nicely in a recent study by Marsh, Hicks, & Cook, 2006; see also Cook, Marsh, & Hicks, 2005; Nowinski & Dismukes, 2005.)

As alluded to earlier, there are cases in which preparatory attentional processes need be engaged for only a short time prior to performing the delayed intention. For instance, if one sets a loud alarm as a reminder, the alarm, if sufficiently obnoxious, may intrude into one's focus of attention and demand consideration. This would lead to an evaluation of how one is to respond to the stimulus or what the meaning of the stimulus is; that is, preparatory attentional processes are engaged. It is still the case that the task involves resource-demanding preparatory processes; however, in this case they would be initiated in response to an attention-capturing event in the environment.

Figure 2.2 presents a depiction of how a delayed intention is performed according to the PAM theory. First an individual decides to perform an action. This is the formation of an intention,[2] shown in Figure 2.2 as the point at which the individual decides to perform a particular action, "I will α_1." The action could occur immediately, "I α_1" (an immediate intention, arrow 1), or it could be delayed, in other words, "I engage in some other action, α_2." In the case of a delayed intention in which we engage in some ongoing activity after forming the intent to perform α_1, we would have a different intent, "I α_2," and the planned action α_1 leaves the focus of attention (arrow 2).

---

[2] It should be noted that until an action is carried out, there is no intention in a strict sense. An intention is a kind of intent and intents do not exist in the absence of action because they are the cause of action. Thus, until an intention is acted out we cannot know for sure that it is an intention. However, I use the term intention with the understanding that at encoding this represents something that could be an intention.

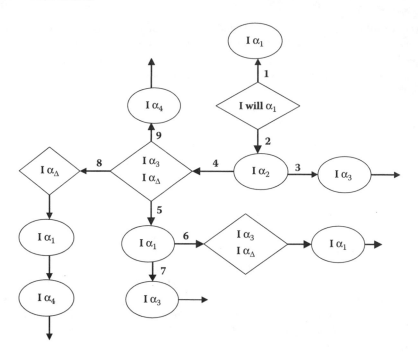

FIGURE 2.2 Diagram of the possible stages in the performance, or failed performance, of an intention. The process begins with the formation of an intention to perform action α_1. Following arrow 1 illustrates the case of an immediate intention. The action is carried out with the plan leaving consciousness. Following arrow 2 illustrates the case of a delayed intention. The intention leaves consciousness and capacity is devoted to the ongoing task α_2. If insufficient capacity is devoted to preparatory attentional processing (arrow 3), or if retrospective recognition of the targets or retrospective recall of the action fails (arrow 9), then the individual will move on to some other action α_4. Selecting either arrow 5 or 8 will lead to performance of the delayed intention. Following arrow 5, once the delayed intention is performed, the individual could continue with action α_3 if the ongoing task is incomplete (arrow 7). If there are multiple target events to which the individual needs to respond with action α_1, the individual could continue with preparatory attentional processing (arrow 6). Following arrow 8, the individual stops performing the ongoing task and devotes capacity only to deciding what to do.

For the intention to be executed, I must devote some amount of my limited cognitive resources to making decisions about how to respond to my environment, at the point at which the intended action can be carried out. In other words, I must be prepared for the possibility that I will make a decision to change from an ongoing action to some other action. This does not mean that considering the change to a specific action is the focus of attention. Rather, this simply means that I am prepared for the possibility in a general sense represented by α_Δ. The processes involved in considering the possibility of a change in a general sense, α_Δ, are referred to as preparatory attentional processes. Although these preparatory attentional processes need not be the constant focus of attention, they do require resources and they prepare the individual for the return of the intended action to the focus of attention.

The PAM theory proposes that preparatory attentional processes are required during the performance interval, but does not require constant engagement of these processes prior to the performance interval. That is, if we must remember to stop at the store on the way home, we must engage in preparatory processing during the interval when the opportunity to stop at the store is possible, but we need not engage in preparatory attentional processing throughout the entire day.

What might lead to the initiation of preparatory processing? It is possible that through developmental processes we learn to reevaluate our behavior and potential responses to the environment at various points during our daily lives. For instance, when finishing one task, but before starting the next, we might consider whether we can focus only on that task or must also accomplish something else, with the latter leading to the engagement of preparatory attentional processes. Event-based prospective memory tasks that can be accomplished at such switch points, called combination time- and activity-based prospective memory tasks by Kvavilashvili and Ellis (1996), may have an advantage. These tasks must be performed at natural points for initiation of preparatory attentional processes, and these processes can be engaged without also devoting resources to an ongoing task. Kvavilashvili and Ellis suggested that the fact that these combination time- and activity-based prospective memory tasks can be performed without interrupting an ongoing activity may contribute to an advantage in performance success rates for these sorts of tasks.

Referring again to Figure 2.2, assume that the performance interval or opportunity for α_1 is associated with an ongoing activity α_3. The individual must engage preparatory attentional processes during the performance interval to have successful prospective memory performance. The individual need not engage in preparatory attentional processing outside of the performance interval, in this case, during the performance of α_2. This would be similar to saying to participants that they should remember to press the Enter key if they see the word *dog* during a lexical decision task, but then having them perform a filler task of math problems between the time they get the instructions and the time they perform the lexical decision task. Participants may or may not also engage in preparatory attentional processing during the math problem task. PAM theory proposes that they must be engaging in preparatory attentional processing when the target occurs during the lexical decision task to be successful at this task.

It is possible that the individual does not engage in preparatory processing during the performance interval and fails to perform the delayed intention (arrow 3). Alternatively, as suggested earlier, participants may routinely evaluate potential changes in activity or the need to be prepared for such changes when switch points occur in the environment. This would lead to the initiating of preparatory attentional processing while engaging in the action α_3 associated with the performance opportunity for the intended action α_1 (arrow 4). If the target occurs and is correctly identified and the action correctly recalled, then the individual can perform the delayed intention (arrow 5). Execution of the delayed intention could be followed by additional preparatory processing, in the case where participants anticipate opportunities to perform the task again (arrow 6), or participants may stop engaging in preparatory attentional processing and continue with the ongoing task only (arrow 7).

Another way to achieve success is to engage only in preparatory attentional processing, which would be accompanied by complete neglect of the ongoing task (arrow 8). This could lead to successful prospective memory performance assuming accurate target recognition and action recall, but this would be at the expense of the other activity.

Even if participants engage in preparatory attentional processing, they may fail to recognize the target event as a performance opportunity or may fail to recall the intended action. Both of these cases would lead to a failure to perform the intended action. In this case the performance of α_3 would be completed and followed by the next action α_4 (pathway 9).

What is the relationship between the preparatory attentional processes and the processing needed for the ongoing task? The PAM theory proposes that we switch back and forth between actions α_3 and α_A. This is thought to be similar to situations in which secondary tasks are imposed during encoding. The switching between the perception and comprehension processes involved in encoding information and the processes required for the secondary task, according to Craik, Govoni, Naveh-Benjamin, and Anderson (1996), is controlled and must therefore require capacity. The allocation of capacity to α_A, the preparatory attentional processes, is necessary for stimuli to be interpreted; if the situation for action is correctly interpreted, this will lead to the case of "I α_1." Thus, capacity is involved in the initiation of a delayed intention, not just in the execution of the action.

The likelihood of initiating a delayed intention to a particular target will be determined in part by the amount of capacity devoted to preparatory attentional processes. The capacity available for preparatory attentional processes is a function of the capacity devoted to ongoing activities, motivation, and overall available capacity. Furthermore, even though some minimal amount of capacity might be devoted to preparatory attentional processes, as mentioned earlier, these processes need not be the focus of attention; that is, participants need not be explicitly checking for performance opportunities. In fact it is more likely the case that preparatory attentional processes will operate outside of the focus of attention and instead on the periphery of awareness. The distinction between focal attention and peripheral awareness idea is analogous to Wundt's (1912/1973) distinction between apprehension and apperception. This distinction was drawn to explain the relationship between the contents of focal attention and the contents of consciousness. Consciousness is limited, but focal attention is even more restricted. When the contents of attention reach full-blown awareness, they are apperceived. In contrast, contents that are above the threshold of consciousness, but of which we are only minimally aware or perhaps unaware, are apprehended. Although outside the focus of attention, apprehended contents occupy some of our limited cognitive capacity. Analogous to Wundt's ideas, the preparatory attentional processes can be the focus of attention but also can operate outside of focal attention, and are therefore called preparatory attentional processes.

Importantly, neither the target nor the action is occupying capacity; rather, it is the processes of evaluating how to respond to our environment that occupy capacity.

Although resource-demanding preparatory attentional processes are required, they are not sufficient to guarantee correct performance. In addition to being prepared to change responses to the environment, one must also correctly recognize when to change the response to the environment. Performing the intention correctly depends on recognizing the target as a target. The probability of correctly recognizing a target event is likely to depend on a number of factors, such as how well the target is processed at the time the intention is formed or the number of different target events to be remembered. Accurate recall of the intended action is also required for successful prospective memory performance. The processes involved in the recognition of target events and recall of the action are thought to be similar to the processes involved in retrospective recognition and recall tasks. It is the requirement for preparatory attentional processes that distinguishes prospective memory tasks from retrospective memory tasks.

The PAM theory is similar in some respects to the multiprocess framework (McDaniel & Einstein, 2000), which proposes that sometimes retrieval of an intention will require resource-demanding strategic processes, and in these cases the predictions made by the multiprocess framework and the PAM theory will generally parallel each other. However, the two explanations differ when it comes to some types of prospective memory tasks. As explained earlier, the PAM theory proposes that prospective memory tasks will always require resource-demanding preparatory processes for successful performance. In contrast, the multiprocess framework proposes that there are some cases in which the intention is retrieved automatically. Specifically, the multiprocess framework proposes that if the action is simple, the target is salient, there is a strong association between the target and the action, and the focal processes involved in the ongoing task include processing of the target, then the intention will be retrieved automatically on presentation of the target. In these select cases, the PAM theory and the multiprocess framework will make different predictions regarding the automaticity of the prospective memory task.

Summary of PAM Theory

A delayed intention is performed, according to the PAM theory, in the following way. An individual—call him or her the agent—consciously forms a plan concerning a future action. A delay ensues during which the agent cannot maintain that plan as the focus of attention. By definition, the agent must consciously recollect the plan to act for the action to be an intention. An important distinguishing characteristic of the PAM theory concerns how this recollection occurs. An individual must make decisions about what action to take at a given moment. Engaging in these decision-making processes, which are argued to involve cognitive capacity, allows one to be prepared to change how one responds to stimuli in the environment; thus, the theory refers to these as preparatory attentional processes. If the preparatory attentional processes lead to the conscious recollection of a prior plan for the action, then we have acted intentionally. When action is thrust upon us, as in a reflexive movement, this action does not involve the endorsing of a practitional copula and is not an intent.

According to the PAM theory, capacity must be devoted to evaluating the environment and our responses to the environment. The probability that an intention is completed is influenced by the amount of capacity available and how much capacity is devoted to ongoing activities. In addition to the capacity-absorbing preparatory attentional processes, successful prospective memory involves recognizing a target event as a target event and correctly recalling the intended action.

EMPIRICAL SUPPORT FOR THE PAM THEORY

Much of the supporting evidence for the PAM theory comes from examining performance on the ongoing activity. A second line of support comes from the application of multinomial modeling techniques. With respect to the former, consider that the PAM theory proposes that successful prospective memory performance requires resource-demanding preparatory attentional processes. If we assume that an individual has a limited pool of conscious capacity, and if the individual assigns some of these resources to engaging in preparatory, attentional processes, this leaves fewer resources for the ongoing task. If the ongoing task is sufficiently resource demanding, it should be affected negatively by the addition of the prospective memory task. We can evaluate this specific prediction by comparing performance on the ongoing task when the ongoing task is performed alone with performance on the ongoing task when the prospective memory task is embedded in the ongoing task. The preparatory attentional processes must be engaged prior to the retrospective recognition processes, so the preparatory attentional processes will be engaged on nontarget trials as well as target trials. Thus, evidence for preparatory attentional processes should be found on nontarget trials.

A number of studies have demonstrated a cost to ongoing activities. Smith (2003) found that participants who had to perform a prospective memory task that was embedded in an ongoing lexical decision task were 200 to 300 ms slower on non-prospective-memory-target trials than were participants in a control condition who performed the lexical decision task alone. A cost to ongoing activities has been shown in a number of different laboratories using different ongoing tasks, different target events, and different age groups (Einstein et al., 2005; Loft & Yeo, in press; Marsh et al., 2005, 2006; Marsh, Hicks, Cook, Hansen, & Pallos, 2003; Smith, 2003; Smith & Bayen, 2004, 2006; Smith et al., 2007, under review; West, Krompinger, & Bowry, 2005). West et al. (2005) demonstrated that the cost was found on trials that preceded successful prospective memory hits, but not prospective memory misses, indicating that the cost associated with the prospective memory task is caused by functionally important processes.

Although many of these demonstrations do not distinguish between the multiprocess framework and the PAM theory, recent work by Smith et al., 2007; see also Smith, 2001) does provide a direct comparison of these two explanations. As mentioned earlier, the multiprocess view proposes that when prospective memory tasks involve salient target events, a strong association between the target and the action, a target that is processed in the course of completing the ongoing task, and a simple action, the intention will be retrieved automatically. Smith et al. found evidence of a cost to ongoing activities when using a task that meets these criteria. For instance, when participants are asked to respond to their own name (a very salient target), their performance on an ongoing lexical decision task was poorer in comparison to participants in a control condition who performed only the lexical decision task. In a different experiment conducted by Smith et al., participants performed an ongoing color-matching task (Smith & Bayen, 2004, 2006). All of the participants performed two blocks of 62 trials of a color-matching task that involved seeing four colored rectangles followed by a string of Xs. Their task was to decide if the color in which the Xs were displayed matched one of the four colored rectangles presented on that trial. The colors used were red, green, blue, yellow, and white rectangles and X strings on a black background. Half of the participants, those in the control condition, performed the color-matching task only, and the other half performed a prospective memory task in the second block of trials. The prospective memory task was to press the P key if they saw a pink string during the color-matching task. The occurrence of the pink string was salient: The color change was spontaneously detected by participants in the control condition, despite not having been told about the appearance of an unusual color. This task simultaneously meets all of the criteria outlined by the multiprocess framework for a prospective memory task to be considered automatic: The action is simple (press a key), the action and target are well associated (press the P key for a pink string), the target is salient, and the dimension along which the target was defined (color) was processed as part of the focal processing engaged by the ongoing task. Thus, the multiprocess view would not predict a cost to ongoing task performance in this case. In contrast, the PAM theory would predict a cost to the ongoing task.

Performance on the ongoing task was evaluated for the five trials preceding each trial (the six prospective memory target trials and the four trials following each target were excluded from the analysis). There was no difference in baseline (block 1 before the prospective memory instructions were given) reaction time or accuracy on the color-matching task between the two conditions. Each individual's baseline reaction time was subtracted from his or her reaction time in block 2. This difference score was evaluated to determine whether the addition of the prospective memory task affected the ongoing task. The control condition showed a significant practice effect; on average this group was over 100 ms faster in the second block than in the first block. In contrast, the prospective memory group failed to show a practice effect and importantly, the difference scores for the prospective memory group were significantly related to performance on the prospective memory task, with larger difference scores (i.e., a greater cost) associated with better performance. In other words, resource-demanding processes were being engaged even on non-prospective-memory-target trials, and these processes are functionally related to success on the prospective memory task.

Why did we find a cost in a task that simultaneously met all of the criteria for automaticity, whereas in some cases others have not found a significant cost using single targets? Marsh et al. (2003) failed to find a significant cost in one condition, but the difference was in the direction of a cost. Einstein et al. (2005) did demonstrate a significant cost in all experiments in which a control condition was compared with a prospective memory condition, but they failed to find a significant cost in three out of nine comparisons of control and prospective memory conditions. In two of these three nonsignificant cases, the direction was consistent with a cost. It is possible that a lack of power contributed to the nonsignificant findings. As demonstrated in the Smith, et al. (2007) study, the cost appeared as a lack of a practice effect for the prospective memory condition, whereas a practice effect was demonstrated in the control condition. This is a cost nonetheless, but clearly indicates that the resource demands of preparatory attentional processing can be very subtle. In the Einstein et al. (2005) study, the power to detect small effects was less than .13 in all cases, and never better than .6 for detecting even medium-sized effects. Highlighting power as a potential factor, a comparison in Experiment 3 of Einstein et al. that failed to reach significance with 32 participants was significant in Experiment 4 using the identical procedures, but including 104 participants.

Importantly, the control and prospective memory conditions in Einstein et al. (2005) were always manipulated within subjects in a counterbalanced design. The choice to use a within-subjects control condition in a counterbalanced design, as opposed to using both a within-subjects baseline block that always preceded the prospective memory block combined with a true control condition as used in Smith, et al. (2007), could have contributed to the different outcomes. When using the within-subjects counterbalanced control condition, for half of the participants the control block comes after the prospective memory condition. This could interfere with their performance on the control block, despite the fact that they are told that they do not have to perform the prospective memory task during the control block. Guynn (2005) demonstrated just such a side effect: Participants who were given prospective memory instructions prior to the control block were slower on the control trials than participants who received the prospective memory instructions after the control block, even though the participants knew that they did not need to perform the prospective memory task during the control block. Thus, the particular procedures used could have contributed to the lack of a significant cost in Einstein et al. (2005).

Although there have been four failures to find a significant cost (one case in Marsh et al., 2003; three cases in Einstein et al., 2005), on the whole, the results of the effect of a prospective memory task on ongoing task performance support the proposal made by the PAM theory that resource-demanding preparatory attentional processes are involved in successful prospective memory performance. In particular, when avoiding potential problems associated with a counterbalanced design for control blocks and while using a task that meets all of the multiprocess framework's criteria for automaticity, performance on a prospective memory task is associated with a cost to ongoing task performance (Smith, et al., 2007).

Evidence regarding a cost to the ongoing task is encouraging but limited in a number of different ways. First, the cost measures provide only an indirect indicator that participants are engaging in preparatory attentional processes. Cost to ongoing tasks could be caused in part by factors such as rehearsal in addition to the basic preparatory attentional processes. Second, given that the cost is most often found on reaction time measures (often with relatively few observations per participant), issues such as noise, baseline differences, and insufficient power can complicate interpretations of these findings, particularly in the case of small differences. Fortunately, many prospective memory tasks lend themselves to multinomial modeling, which provides converging evidence for evaluating the PAM theory.

Smith and Bayen (2004, 2005, 2006) introduced a multinomial model of prospective memory. The model provides estimates of the contributions of underlying cognitive processes, specifically preparatory attentional processes and retrospective recognition processes, to observable prospective memory performance. The model has been shown to be identifiable and has been validated (Smith & Bayen, 2004). With respect to what sorts of variables would be expected to influence the estimates of the underlying cognitive processes, the retrospective recognition processes should be influenced by variables that influence recognition, such as the discriminability of targets and nontargets and the amount of time allowed for target encoding (Smith & Bayen, 2004). Other variables that influence recognition performance would also be expected to influence the parameter estimates of retrospective memory in many cases. However, the small number of target events generally used in prospective memory makes predictions based on findings in the typical retrospective recognition tasks, employing many more target events, complicated.

Factors that influence the availability of cognitive resources or the allocation of resources would also be expected to influence the likelihood of engaging in preparatory attentional processes. Motivation, task importance, expectations about when preparatory attentional processes should be engaged or how difficult a task will be, and reminders could all potentially affect preparatory attentional processes. Task importance and task context have both been shown to affect estimates of preparatory attentional processes (Smith & Bayen, 2004). Using the model, Smith and Bayen (2005) showed that preparatory attentional processing is sensitive to differences in working memory capacity and working memory load, as would be expected if preparatory attentional processes are resource demanding. In addition, Smith and Bayen (2006) found that adult age differences in prospective memory performance were driven by age differences in preparatory attentional processes, also as would be expected if preparatory attentional processes are resource demanding, given evidence of reduced resources for older adults (Zacks, Hasher, & Li, 2000). As a brief aside, one might wonder about the demonstration of age differences in the resource-demanding preparatory attentional processes in light of demonstrations of no adult age differences on naturalistic tasks. It could well be that in noncontrolled settings, the older adults are devoting a larger component of their cognitive resources to engaging in preparatory attentional processing and thereby performing as well as the younger adults. We do not know exactly how it is that the tasks are being accomplished, nor how this might affect other ongoing activities, in these naturalistic tasks. The fact that we find age differences in preparatory processes in a relatively demanding laboratory task does not rule out the possibilities that under the right circumstances older adults could choose or be encouraged to redirect sufficient resources to the preparatory attentional processes to increase their performance to a level matching that seen with younger adults. The results of the Smith and Bayen (2006) study are consistent with other work showing no age differences in recall of the action and failure to maintain intentions (Cohen, Dixon, Lindsay, & Masson, 2003; Cohen, West, & Craik, 2001; West & Craik, 1999; West, Murphy, Armilio, Craik, & Stuss, 2002; see Smith & Bayen, 2006, for discussion). The results of Smith and Bayen also converge with Kliegel et al. (2000), in which no age differences were found in plan retention, albeit Kliegel et al. employed a much more complicated task context.

ADDITIONAL ISSUES AND FUTURE DIRECTIONS

The Nature of Real-World Prospective Memory Tasks

Although the debate over whether prospective memory tasks are accomplished automatically has motivated a fair amount of prospective memory research, and while this work is important, it might be time to shift our focus somewhat. As mentioned earlier, the PAM theory and the multiprocess framework make similar predictions regarding when a cost would be demonstrated in many prospective memory tasks. Only cases involving a salient target, simple action, well-associated target, and action and focal processing of the target meet the criteria for automaticity according to the multiprocess framework, and only these cases will produce diverging predictions. It seems that prospective memory tasks that simultaneously meet these criteria are likely to make up a very small proportion of prospective memory tasks in the real world. Of course this speculation regarding the preponderant nature of real-world tasks is just that: speculation. However, there is no inherent reason to dismiss this view, nor any inherent reason to embrace the opposite position proposed by the multiprocess framework that most tasks in the real world are automatic, implying that the tasks simultaneously meet all the criteria for automaticity.

Self-Reports and Subjective Experience   One of the motivating issues for the multiprocess framework's proposal that tasks can be accomplished automatically is that participants reported that intentions "popped" into mind (Einstein & McDaniel, 2005, p. 287). Interestingly, one of the original motivations that lead to the development of the PAM theory also came from participants' posttest self-reports. While collecting data during my first involvement in prospective memory research (Einstein, McDaniel, Smith, & Shaw, 1998; Einstein et al., 1997), I found that during posttest questioning, older adults would often say such things as, "I completely forgot about that [the prospective memory] task," or "I did not think about it [the prospective memory task] at all." I began to wonder then how an automatic retrieval explanation would deal with this. If retrieval of the task is automatic, it should not matter if the participant thinks about the task: The presence of the cue in the environment should have triggered the response or at least thoughts about the task. Of course, perhaps the target did lead to spontaneous retrieval of the target in these cases, but the participant did not have sufficient resources to carry out the prospective memory task in the current task context and also failed to encode or retrieve the fact that the prospective memory task had come to mind.

It might also be the case that when people have the subjective experience of something popping into mind, they had in fact been engaging in subtle but necessary processes that facilitated the retrieval of the intention and that it only seemed that the intention popped into mind of its own accord. The point is that self-reports and subjective experiences can be misleading with respect to what processes are really contributing to performance on any given task (Nisbett & Wilson, 1977; Toth & Hunt, 1990). However, self-reports and subjective experience can provide an instigation for deeper consideration of issues. In my case, the sorts of reports just mentioned eventually lead me to question existing explanations and to in turn build a new theory based on very specific definitions of the behavior of interest.

The prevailing nature of prospective memory tasks in the real world is an issue that remains to be evaluated empirically. However, based on my own self-reports and experiences, it is certainly the case that many of the actions I have to remember to perform in the real world are not as simple as pressing a key, and often the association between targets and actions is not highly associated. In cases in which the target and action have become overly associated, these tasks very likely have become more procedural or reflexive rather than truly intentional (thus the need for clear and precise definitions of what sorts of tasks we are talking about). In this case the highly learned tasks might in fact have become habits that will be carried out unless counteracted through the use of delayed intentions.

Importance of Prospective Memory in Daily Life   In a related vein, a commonly touted argument in support of the idea that prospective memory tasks can be automatic is that because prospective memory tasks are such an important part of daily functioning, it would be inefficient for these tasks not to be accomplished in an automatic fashion. For example, regarding the cost associated with prospective memory tasks as demonstrated by Smith (1999, 2000), McDaniel and Einstein (2000) proposed that, "Given these kinds of costs and given the prevalence of prospective memory demands in our lives, it seems that it would be adaptive in many situations to rely on automatic processes" (p. S142). The presumption may be true enough, but it is also true that the way things seem is not always the way they are.

The fact that a task is important for our survival does not necessitate that the task be automatic, nor does the perception that a task has become automated mean that the task does not require resources. For many adults, at least in many cities in the United States, driving is an essential aspect of daily life, in some cases required for earning a living. Whether this is a good situation or not is a different issue, but driving is a task that plays an important "survival" role for many people. At the same time, driving for most adults has the subjective experience of being automatic. Yet, when resources are devoted to something else, driving suffers (e.g., Strayer, Drews, & Johnston, 2003), indicating that this important task requires resources. The prevalence of a task in our lives does determine its automaticity.

No Role for Automatic Processes?

One common misinterpretation of the PAM theory concerns the role of automatic processing in prospective memory. For instance, Einstein and McDaniel (2005) suggested that what is "at issue is whether monitoring is the sole process in PM [prospective memory] retrieval or whether spontaneous processes can also accomplish PM retrieval]" (p. 287). This is a mischaracterization of the issue under debate. The debate is whether resource-demanding processes are required *in addition to* automatic processes or whether the task can be accomplished through automatic processes only. The PAM theory says that resource-demanding processes are required for successful prospective memory. This does not rule out a contribution from automatic processes: Automatic processes almost certainly will play a role. Just as other memory tasks can involve a combination of automatic and nonautomatic processes, prospective memory involves both kinds of processes according to the PAM theory. What distinguishes the PAM theory is the proposal that while automatic processes contribute to performance, they never act alone in determining performance; in other words, prospective memory tasks are never entirely automatic.

The point here is not whether automatic processes play a role in real-world task—they surely do. It is that these tasks are not *entirely* automatic. This point is deduced from the definitions on which the PAM theory is based. However, even in the view of the multiprocess framework, it is unclear that real-world prospective memory tasks simultaneously meet the criteria for automaticity. Thus, focusing on cases that meet the multiprocess framework's criteria for automaticity in the laboratory might limit the generality of various findings. A more fruitful approach might lie in developing and applying new methods for measuring the underlying processes that contribute to prospective memory. The development and validation of a multinomial model provides an important first step in this direction.

Alternative Data-Analytic Approaches

Formal models have considerable potential for providing a clearer understanding of how underlying cognitive processes contribute to prospective memory and how different manipulations influence those processes. The development and application of formal models require specificity and precision regarding various processes and how those processes are related to one another. It is fine to propose that different kinds of processes are involved in prospective memory, but it is much more useful to delineate exactly when those particular processes come into play and how they interact with other types of processes. Smith and Bayen (2004) provided the first introduction of these sorts of methods to prospective memory, and it would be advantageous to see expanded use of these and other new measurement and analytic techniques in the field. Smith and Bayen (2004, 2005, 2006) evaluated a submodel in which the preparatory attentional processes do not contribute to performance. This model does not fit the data, which point to the importance of preparatory attentional processing. However, rather than evaluating the automatic retrieval case through a submodel, the best case would be to have alternative theory-based formal models to evaluate the different views.

There has been only one meta-analysis of existing prospective memory research (Henry, MacLeod, Phillips, & Crawford, 2004). The body of published research is rapidly growing and additional meta-analyses will be able to add clarification and cohesiveness to the literature. Likewise, there has been only one study employing factor-analytic techniques to evaluate the validity of prospective memory as a distinct construct (Salthouse, Berish, & Siedlecki, 2004). The field will benefit greatly from more extensive development and application of alternative methods of data analysis.

The continued development and application of techniques for determining how underlying processes are affected by various manipulations has the potential to advance another aspect of research in this area. A very important applied question concerns how we might improve prospective memory for individuals who are having difficulty with these kinds of tasks. The pursuit of an answer to this question will be greatly facilitated by an improved understanding of exactly which of the underlying processes are contributing to prospective memory failures for a given group of individuals. Once we know which processes are diminished we can better develop ways to address these changes.

On the flip side to knowing which underlying processes are diminished in a certain situation, it is equally useful to have clear measures of how techniques for improving prospective memory affect the various underlying processes. For instance, one technique for improving prospective memory in older adults is to use implementation intention instructions (Chasteen, Park, & Schwarz, 2001; Gollwitzer, 1999; Liu & Park, 2004). Implementation intention instructions request that participants imagine themselves performing the task. Implementation intention instructions are argued to improve goal achievement by increasing automatic retrieval of the goal when certain conditions are met (Gollwitzer, 1999). In contrast to this hypothesis, Smith, McConnell, and Little (2005) demonstrated one case in which implementation intention instructions did improve prospective memory performance, but did so through increased preparatory attentional processes, which suggests that implementation intention instructions may work through different nonautomatic mechanisms when applied to prospective memory tasks.

In summary, the future of prospective memory research will be improved through the use of an expanded repertoire of methods and analytic techniques. In particular, the application of formal models, which encourage increased specificity in the description of underlying processes and provide a means of measuring those underlying processes, hold considerable promise for advancing research in this area.

REFERENCES

Beardsley, M. (1980). Motives and intentions. In M. Bradie & M. Brand (Eds.), *Action and responsibility* (pp. 71–79). Bowling Green, OH: Bowling Green State University, Applied Philosophy Program.

Brand, M. (1980). A brief reply to Kim. In M. Bradie & M. Brand (Eds.), *Action and responsibility* (pp. 27–29). Bowling Green, OH: Bowling Green State University, Applied Philosophy Program.

Brand, M. (1984). *Intending and acting.* Cambridge, MA: MIT Press.

Castañeda, H.-N. (1975). *Thinking and doing.* Boston: D. Reidel.

Castañeda, H.-N. (1980). The doing of thinking: Intending and willing. In M. Bradie & M. Brand (Eds.), *Action and responsibility* (pp. 80–92). Bowling Green, OH: Bowling Green State University, Applied Philosophy Program.

Chasteen, A. L., Park, D. C., & Schwarz, N. (2001). Implementation intentions and facilitation of prospective memory. *Psychological Science, 12,* 457–461.

Cohen, A.-L., Dixon, R. A., Lindsay, D. S., & Masson, M. E. J. (2003). The effects of perceptual distinctiveness on the prospective and retrospective components of prospective memory in young and old adults. *Canadian Journal of Experimental Psychology, 57,* 274–289.

Cohen, A.-L., West, R., & Craik, F. I. M. (2001). Modulation of the prospective and retrospective components of memory for intentions in younger and older adults. *Aging, Neuropsychology, and Cognition, 8,* 1–13.

Cook, G. I., Marsh, R. L., & Hicks J. L. (2005). Associating time-based prospective memory with an expected context can improve intention completion. *Applied Cognitive Psychology, 19,* 345–366.

Craik, F. I. M., Govoni, R., Naveh-Benjamin, M., & Anderson, N. D. (1996). The effects of divided attention on encoding and retrieval processes in human memory. *Journal of Experimental Psychology: General, 125,* 159–180.

Crowder, R. G. (1996). The trouble with prospective memory: A provocation. In M. Brandimonte, G. O. Einstein, & M. A. McDaniel (Eds.), *Prospective memory: Theory and applications* (pp. 143–148). Mahwah, NJ: Lawrence Erlbaum Associates, Inc.

Dobbs, A. R., & Rule, B. G. (1987). Prospective memory and self-reports of memory abilities in older adults. *Canadian Journal of Psychology, 41,* 209–222.

Einstein, G. O., & McDaniel, M. A. (1990). Normal aging and prospective memory. *Journal of Experimental Psychology: Learning, Memory, and Cognition, 16,* 717–726.

Einstein, G. O., & McDaniel, M. A. (1996). Retrieval processes in prospective memory: Theoretical approaches and some new empirical findings. In M. Brandimonte, G. O. Einstein, & M. A. McDaniel (Eds.), *Prospective memory: Theory and applications* (pp. 115–142). Mahwah, NJ: Lawrence Erlbaum Associates, Inc.

Einstein, G. O., & McDaniel, M. A. (2005). Prospective memory: Multiple retrieval processes. *Current Directions in Psychological Science, 14,* 286–290.

Einstein, G. O., McDaniel, M. A., Smith, R. E., & Shaw, P. (1998). Habitual prospective memory and aging: Remembering intentions and forgetting actions. *Psychological Science, 9,* 284–288.

Einstein, G. O., McDaniel, M. A., Thomas, R. A., Mayfield, S., Shank, H., Morrisette, N. et al. (2005). Multiple processes in prospective memory retrieval: Factors determining monitoring versus spontaneous retrieval. *Journal of Experimental Psychology: General, 134,* 327–342.

Einstein, G. O., Smith, R. E., McDaniel, M. A., & Shaw, P. (1997). Aging and prospective memory: The influence of increased task demands at encoding and retrieval. *Psychology and Aging, 12,* 479–488.

Gollwitzer, P. M. (1999). Implementation intentions: Strong effects of simple plans. *American Psychologist, 54,* 493–503.

Guynn, M. J. (2005, November). *Monitoring in event-based prospective memory: Retrieval mode instantiation plus target event checks.* Poster presented at the annual meeting of the Psychonomic Society, Toronto.

Guynn, M. J., McDaniel, M. A., & Einstein, G. O. (2001). Remembering to perform actions: A different type of memory? In H. D. Zimmer, R. L. Cohen, M. J. Guynn, J. Engelkamp, R. Kormi-Nouri, & M. A. Foley (Eds.), *Memory for action: A distinct form of episodic memory?* (pp. 25–48). New York: Oxford University Press.

Henry, J. D., MacLeod, M. S., Phillips, L. H., & Crawford, J. R. (2004). A meta-analytic review of prospective memory and aging. *Psychology & Aging, 19,* 27–39.

Kelley, C. M., & Jacoby, L. L. (1990). The construction of subjective experience: Memory attributions. *Mind and Language, 5,* 49–68.

Kliegel, M., McDaniel, M. A., & Einstein, G. O. (2000). Plan formation, retention, and execution in prospective memory: A new approach and age-related effects. *Memory & Cognition, 28,* 1041–1049.

Kvavilashvili, L. (1987). Remembering intention as a distinct form of memory. *British Journal of Psychology, 78,* 507–518.

Kvavilashvili, L., & Ellis, J. (1996). Varieties of intention: Some distinctions and classifications. In M. Brandimonte, G. O. Einstein, & M. A. McDaniel (Eds.), *Prospective memory: Theory and applications* (pp. 115–142). Mahwah, NJ: Lawrence Erlbaum Associates, Inc.

Liu, L. L., & Park, D. C. (2004). Aging and medical adherence: The use of automatic processes to achieve effortful things. *Psychology and Aging, 19,* 318–325.

Loft, S., & Yeo, G. (in press). An investigation into the resource requirements of event-based prospective memory. *Memory & Cognition.*

Mäntylä, T. (1994). Remembering to remember: Adult age differences in prospective memory. *Journals of Gerontology, 49,* 276–282.

Marsh, R. L., Hicks, J. L., & Cook, G. I. (2005). On the relationship between effort toward an ongoing task and cue detection in event-based prospective memory. *Journal of Experimental Psychology: Learning, Memory, and Cognition, 31,* 68–75.

Marsh, R. L., Hicks, J. L., & Cook, G. I. (2006). Task interference from prospective memories covaries with contextual associations of fulfilling them. *Memory & Cognition.*

Marsh, R. L., Hicks, J. L., Cook, G. I., Hansen, J. S., & Pallos, A. (2003). Interference to ongoing activities covaries with the characteristics of an event-based intention. *Journal of Experimental Psychology: Learning, Memory, and Cognition, 29,* 861–870.

McDaniel, M. A., & Einstein, G. O. (2000). Strategic and automatic processes in prospective memory retrieval: A multiprocess framework. *Applied Cognitive Psychology, 14,* S127–S144.

Morris, C. D., Bransford, J. D., & Franks, J. J. (1977). Levels of processing versus test-appropriate strategies. *Journal of Verbal Learning and Verbal Behavior, 16,* 519–533.

Nisbett, R. E., & Wilson, T. D. (1977). Telling more than we can know: Verbal reports on mental processes. *Psychological Review, 84,* 231–259.

Nowinski, J. L., & Dismukes, R. K. (2005). Effects of ongoing task context and target typicality on prospective memory performance: The importance of associative cuing. *Memory, 13,* 649–657.

Rey, G. (1983). A reason for doubting the existence of cosnciousness. In R. J. Davidson, G. E. Schwartz, & D. Shapiro (Eds.), *Consicousness and self-regulation: Advances in research and theory* (Vol. 3, pp. 1–39). New York: Plenum.

Salthouse, T. A., Berish, D. E., & Siedlecki, K. L. (2004). Construct validity and age sensitivity of prospective memory. *Memory & Cognition, 32,* 1133–1148.

Searle, J. R. (1983). *Intentionality: An essay on the philosophy of mind.* New York: Cambridge University Press.

Smith, R. E. (1999). A new conceptualization of delayed intention performance: Initiation requires capacity (Doctoral dissertation, University of North Carolina at Greensboro, 1999). *Dissertation Abstracts International, 60B,* 2977.

Smith, R. E. (2000, July). *Successful initiation of delayed intentions requires capacity.* Paper presented at the First International Conference on Prospective Memory, Hatfield, UK.

Smith, R. E. (2001, November). *Intentions, capacity, and salient target events.* Poster presented at the 42nd Annual Meeting of the Psychonomics Society, Orlando, FL.

Smith, R. E. (2003). The cost of remembering to remember in event-based prospective memory: Investigating the capacity demands of delayed intention performance. *Journal of Experimental Psychology: Learning, Memory, and Cognition, 29,* 347–361.

Smith, R. E., & Bayen, U. J. (2004). A multinomial model of event-based prospective memory. *Journal of Experimental Psychology: Learning, Memory, and Cognition, 30,* 756–777.

Smith, R. E., & Bayen, U. J. (2005). The effects of working memory resource availability on prospective memory: A formal modeling approach. *Experimental Psychology, 52,* 243–256.

Smith, R. E., & Bayen, U. J. (2006). The source of age differences in event-based prospective memory: A multinomial modeling approach. *Journal of Experimental Psychology: Learning, Memory, and Cognition, 32,* 623–635.

Smith, R. E., Hunt, R. R., McVay, J. C., & McConnell, M. D. (2007). *The cost of event-based prospective memory: Salient target events. Journal of Experimental Psychology: Learning, Memory, 2nd Cognition.*

Smith, R. E., McConnell, M. D., & Little, J. C. (2005, November). *Implementation intentions and prospective memory.* Poster presented at the annual meeting of the Psychonomics Society, Toronto.

Strayer, D. L., Drews, F. A., & Johnston, W. A. (2003). Cell phone-induced failure of visual attention during simulated driving. *Journal of Experimental Psychology: Applied, 9,* 23–32.

Toth, J. P., & Hunt, R. R. (1990). Effect of generation on a word-identification task. *Journal of Experimental Psychology: Learning, Memory, and Cognition, 16,* 993–1003.

West, R., & Craik, F. I. M. (1999). Age-related decline in prospective memory: The roles of cue accessibility and cue sensitivity. *Psychology and Aging, 14,* 264–272.

West, R., Krompinger, J., & Bowry, R. (2005). Disruptions of preparatory attention contribute to failures of prospective memory. *Psychonomic Bulletin & Review, 12,* 502–507.

West, R., Murphy, K. J., Armilio, M. L., Craik, F. I. M., & Stuss, D. T. (2002). Lapses of intention and performance variability reveal age-related increases in fluctuations of executive control. *Brain and Cognition, 49,* 402–419.

Wundt, W. (1973). *An introduction to psychology.* New York: Arno. (Original work published 1912.)

Zacks, R. T., Hasher, L., & Li, K. Z. H. (2000). Human memory. In F. I. M. Craik & T. A. Salthouse (Eds.), *The handbook of aging and cognition* (pp. 293–358). Mahwah, NJ: Lawrence Erlbaum Associates, Inc.

3

Theory of Monitoring in Prospective Memory
Instantiating a Retrieval Mode and Periodic Target Checking

MELISSA J. GUYNN

Department of Psychology
New Mexico State University

S ince the publication of the first edited book (Brandimonte, Einstein, & McDaniel, 1996) devoted entirely to prospective memory, or memory to execute an intended action at an appropriate point in the absence of an explicit request to remember, attention has increasingly been paid to the processes that mediate prospective memory. This has been made possible at least in part by clever new methods and alternate dependent measures that have permitted more sophisticated study of these processes. Traditionally, the primary dependent measure in prospective memory experiments has been a measure of prospective memory accuracy, such as whether a correct prospective memory response is made or the proportion of correct prospective memory responses that are made (e.g., Einstein & McDaniel, 1990). More recently, attention has turned to include alternate dependent measures. These include neural correlates of prospective memory (e.g., Burgess, Quayle, & Frith, 2001; West, Herndon, & Crewdson, 2001; West & Ross-Munroe, 2002), accuracies and latencies on the ongoing activity in which the prospective memory task is embedded (e.g., Guynn, 2003; Kliegel, Martin, McDaniel, & Einstein, 2001, 2004; Smith, 2003), and reaction times to prospective memory target stimuli in a context other than a prospective memory task (e.g., Einstein et al., 2005; Goschke & Kuhl, 1993; Marsh, Hicks, & Bink, 1998). These alternate dependent measures have enabled more analytic study of the processes underlying prospective memory. One of these processes, the evidence for which is provided by performance on the ongoing activity in which the prospective memory task is embedded, is monitoring for the prospective memory target stimuli. These targets indicate when it is appropriate to execute the intended action (i.e., perform the prospective memory task), and monitoring for these targets is the focus of this chapter.

Monitoring actually has an older history in the field than the preceding discussion might imply, as monitoring has been a central feature of explanations of time-based prospective memory since the beginning of research on the topic. Time-based tasks are those in which either a particular time or a particular amount of elapsed time indicates when it is appropriate to execute the intended action. The early focus on monitoring (i.e., time monitoring or clock monitoring) in time-based tasks no doubt reflects at least in part the fact that there has been a fairly obvious way to measure this process. The thing that is monitored (i.e., the time or a clock) is separate from the prospective memory task and the ongoing activity in which it is embedded. Thus, monitoring can be measured by an overt behavior such as a head turn to inspect a clock in the room (e.g., Ceci, Baker, & Bronfenbrenner, 1988; Ceci & Bronfenbrenner, 1985; Harris & Wilkins, 1982) or a key press to reveal a clock on a computer display (e.g., Einstein, McDaniel, Richardson, Guynn, & Cunfer, 1995). In contrast, monitoring has only more recently become a focus in event-based tasks, where an external target event indicates when it is appropriate to execute the intended action. This more recent focus no doubt reflects at least in part the fact that there has not been as obvious a way to measure monitoring in event-based tasks, until recently.

In particular, the technique for measuring event monitoring derives from the fact that in event-based tasks, the target events are embedded in an ongoing activity (i.e., a cover task). This is to simulate the real-world necessity of interrupting an ongoing activity at an appropriate point (i.e., when a designated target occurs) to execute an intended action. To measure monitoring, performance on the ongoing activity in which the prospective memory targets are embedded (i.e., the experimental trials of the ongoing activity) is compared to performance on the ongoing activity when no prospective memory task is assigned (i.e., the control trials of the ongoing activity). Impaired performance (i.e., lower accuracies, higher latencies, or both) on the experimental trials (and, specifically, on the nontarget experimental trials, to measure monitoring uncontaminated by a retrieval or a response) relative to the control trials provides the evidence of monitoring. A number of researchers have used this type of measure and have obtained evidence for monitoring in event-based prospective memory (e.g., Brandimonte, Ferrante, Feresin, & Delbello, 2001; Guynn, 2001, 2003, 2005; Hicks, Marsh, & Cook, 2005; Kliegel et al., 2001, 2004; Kvavilashvili, 1987; Marsh, Hicks, & Cook, 2005; Marsh, Hicks, Cook, Hansen, & Pallos, 2003; Smith, 2003).

THEORIES OF PROSPECTIVE MEMORY

Perhaps not coincidentally, monitoring is featured in existing theoretical perspectives on event-based prospective memory. The earliest approach, a model of the attentional control of behavior (Norman & Shallice, 1986; see also Burgess &

Shallice, 1997; Shallice & Burgess, 1991), accounts for prospective memory retrieval in the context of other ongoing behaviors. The first component in the model, contention scheduling, is used to control behaviors that are routine. With contention scheduling, a thought schema or an action schema is selected automatically when it is sufficiently activated and its trigger conditions are met. However, contention scheduling is not always sufficient to guarantee an intended outcome, such as when an intended action is not routine and thus not normally associated with its trigger conditions (e.g., when there is a prospective memory task to perform). Under these conditions, the second component in the model, the executive or supervisory attentional system (SAS), is used to control behavior. The SAS operates by biasing contention scheduling, specifically by increasing the activation of intended schemas and decreasing the activation of unintended schemas. Another function of the SAS is monitoring the environment for the markers or target events (the trigger conditions) that indicate when it is appropriate to execute the intended action.

A more recent approach, a multiprocess model (Einstein et al., 2005; McDaniel & Einstein, 2000; McDaniel, Guynn, Einstein, & Breneiser, 2004), proposes that prospective memory retrieval is mediated by relatively automatic processes under some conditions and by more strategic processes under other conditions. One of the strategic processes is monitoring for the targets that indicate when it is appropriate to execute the intended action. This monitoring is more likely to play a role under some conditions than others. These conditions include when the prospective memory task is more important, when the prospective memory target events are not particularly salient, when there is no preexisting association between a target event and an intended action, when the ongoing activity does not elicit focal processing of the target events, and for certain types of individuals.

Another recent approach, a preparatory attentional and memory processes model (Smith, 2003; Smith & Bayen, 2004), proposes that prospective memory retrieval is always mediated by nonautomatic preparatory attentional and retrospective memory processes. This is the case for all types of individuals, even when the prospective memory task is not important, the target events are salient, there is an association between a target event and its intended action, and the ongoing activity elicits focal processing of the target events. The preparatory attentional processes are engaged throughout the ongoing activity in which the prospective memory task is embedded, and the retrospective memory processes are engaged when a prospective memory target is detected via the preparatory attentional processes. One of the possible preparatory attentional processes is monitoring for the targets that indicate when it is appropriate to execute the intended action.

Although all of these accounts allow that prospective memory retrieval can be mediated by monitoring for the targets or markers that indicate when to perform the prospective memory task, none specifies what monitoring actually entails. Accordingly, work in my laboratory has been directed toward developing and evaluating a theory of monitoring. In this chapter, I outline the theory as developed to this point and describe the results that have been interpreted as providing support for the theory (i.e., evidence for the two component processes of monitoring). I also suggest a possible mechanism underlying one of the component processes, extend the theory to time-based prospective memory, highlight the relationship between monitoring and vigilance, and outline possible directions for future research.

THEORY OF MONITORING

Before describing the theory, two points deserve mention. First, the theory is not inherently incompatible with any theoretical perspective that allows that monitoring can mediate prospective memory (e.g., the three models already described). Thus, the present theory of monitoring may complement the existing theories of prospective memory. Some ideas along these lines are offered in the last section of the chapter. Second, the focus of the experiments described here was monitoring rather than prospective memory per se. Thus, the experiments were designed to create situations in which participants would be likely to monitor for the prospective memory targets. Some might complain that these procedures would have obscured any automatic process that mediates prospective memory. There certainly may be occasions where prospective memory is automatic and thus not mediated by monitoring, but this theory does not apply to those situations, and thus these experiments were not designed to illuminate those processes.

According to the theory, monitoring comprises two processes that demand resources, namely, instantiating a prospective memory retrieval mode and making periodic checks of the environment for an appropriate occasion (i.e., a target) to execute the intended action. For convenience, the theory will be abbreviated as the retrieval mode + target checking (RM + TC) theory of monitoring.

The concept of a retrieval mode is borrowed from the retrospective memory literature, where a retrieval mode is conceptualized as a mental *set* that is a prerequisite for the attempt to retrieve information and independent of the success or failure of that attempt (e.g., Tulving, 1983, 1998, 2002). Lepage, Ghaffar, Nyberg, and Tulving (2000) provided a useful definition in terms of a "neurocognitive set, or state, in which one mentally holds in the background of focal attention a segment of one's personal past, treats incoming and on-line information as 'retrieval cues' for particular events in the past, refrains from task-irrelevant processing, and becomes consciously aware of the product of successful ecphory, should it occur, as a remembered event" (p. 506).

Evidence for a retrieval mode has been found mainly in neuropsychological studies, and, specifically, a "brain region can be regarded as a neuroanatomical correlate" of a retrieval mode if it "becomes differentially active during attempted retrieval of past events" and "does so independently of the level of ecphory" (Lepage et al., 2000, p. 506). Evidence for this differential activation that is independent of the level of ecphory is provided by a variety of approaches; positron emission tomography (PET), event-related potential (ERP), and functional magnetic resonance imaging (fMRI) studies have all revealed a particular pattern of right frontal activation when individuals try to remember information, regardless of whether they do remember the information (e.g., Buckner et al., 1998; Kapur et al., 1995; McIntosh, Nyberg, Bookstein, & Tulving, 1997; Morcom & Rugg, 2002; Nyberg et al., 1995; Rugg, Fletcher, Frith, Frackowiak, & Dolan, 1997; Schacter,

Alpert, Savage, Rauch, & Albert, 1996; Wagner, Desmond, Glover, & Gabrieli, 1998). A behavioral analog of this dissociation is that across levels of attention, there is no systematic relationship between the number of items that are retrieved and the cost on a concurrent task in which the retrieval attempts are embedded (e.g., Craik, Govoni, Naveh-Benjamin, & Anderson, 1996). The idea is that differences in the numbers of items that are retrieved reflect differences in ecphory, whereas differences in the costs on concurrent tasks reflect differences in the demands of instantiating a retrieval mode.

In the domain of prospective memory, a retrieval mode is also conceptualized as a task set to treat stimuli as cues to retrieve stored intentions, a prerequisite for prospective memory when prospective memory is mediated by monitoring, and may be independent of the extent of target checking. Moreover, the literature on task switching might be useful in understanding the prospective memory retrieval mode. This is because switching between different tasks produces a cost to task performance, which is interpreted as reflecting the reconfiguration of a task set (Rogers & Monsell, 1995). Because a prospective memory retrieval mode is also conceptualized as a task set, costs would be expected when individuals instantiate a retrieval mode or switch between retrieval modes. Thus, the literature on task-switching costs may help to understand the costs that accompany the retrieval mode.

The retrieval mode is a more or less continuous or constant process that operates after a prospective memory task has been assigned and until it has been completed or canceled (cf. Marsh et al., 1998; Marsh, Hicks, & Bryan, 1999). In contrast, checking the environment for the targets is a more periodic or intermittent process. This is perhaps the more intuitive process, and it seems likely that this is the process that researchers had in mind when they suggested that monitoring is not continuous (Dobbs & Reeves, 1996; Harris & Wilkins, 1982). In fact, this is in part the reason for proposing the retrieval mode. Specifically, it does not seem reasonable to require target checking on every occasion where monitoring mediates prospective memory, because the appearance of the targets in the environment is also periodic or intermittent. Such a requirement would mean that a target check would have to be made at the exact moment that a target is present, and it seems unlikely that this would occur to any beneficial extent; moreover, the costs of continuous checking are prohibitive (Harris & Wilkins, 1982). Thus, when a target is present and a target check is made, the combination of the retrieval mode and target checking can support monitoring, but when a target is present and a target check is not made, then just the retrieval mode can support monitoring.

To conclude, the retrieval mode is a necessary component of monitoring that might be sufficient on some occasions. Target checking is not sufficient for monitoring and is not always even necessary (e.g., when a target and a target check do not occur at the same moment). Thus, when prospective memory retrieval is mediated by monitoring, either both the retrieval mode and target checking may be involved, or just the retrieval mode may be involved. Of course, prospective memory retrieval may be mediated by automatic processes on some occasions (Einstein et al., 2005), in which case neither the retrieval mode nor target checking would be involved. The efforts to gather evidence for the theory of monitoring have been directed toward gathering evidence for each component process.

EVIDENCE FOR THE COMPONENT PROCESSES

In all of the experiments described here, a prospective memory task was embedded in an ongoing short-term memory task and a concurrent four-choice reaction time task. For the short-term memory task, five words appeared in a row in the center of the computer screen for a short period of time, and participants recalled the words when they disappeared. Performance was scored as the number of words that were recalled correctly on each trial. In all cases these trials were arranged into six-trial sets and each set was followed by a 10-second rest break. For the reaction time task, asterisks appeared in one of four horizontal positions on the computer screen, and participants pressed one of four keys that corresponded to the asterisk location. The task was continuous and concurrent with the short-term memory task. Whenever a participant pressed a key, asterisks immediately appeared in another location, and this continued while the words were studied and recalled. Performance was scored as the number of keys that were pressed correctly on each trial and the reaction time to press the keys correctly. Thus, better performance could be evidenced as either increased accuracy on the short-term memory task or increased accuracy or decreased latency on the reaction time task. Finding better performance (on any of these dependent measures) on the control trials (when just the short-term memory and reaction time tasks were assigned) than on the experimental trials (when a prospective memory task was also assigned) provided evidence for monitoring. Specific manipulations were implemented in each experiment to address the component processes of instantiating a retrieval mode and checking for targets.

The RM + TC theory was actually motivated by the mixed results of one such experiment (Guynn, 2001) using the general method described above. In this experiment, participants performed separate blocks of experimental and control trials. On control trials, participants were assigned just the short-term memory and reaction time tasks, without an embedded prospective memory task. On experimental trials, participants were assigned a prospective memory task (i.e., press the Enter key if you encounter a fruit word) in the context of the ongoing short-term memory and reaction time tasks. During these experimental trials, one group was instructed to check for the fruits (i.e., the prospective memory targets) constantly, on each of the six trials in a set, and one group was instructed to check for the fruits occasionally, on half of the six trials in a set. (Participants were allowed to decide which trials to check; most reported that they tended to check the first three trials.) Participants were later asked to estimate on a scale from 1 to 6 the number of trials per set on which they checked for fruits. For participants in both the constant and occasional checking groups, a retrieval mode (if operating) would be maintained throughout the experimental trials. Both groups would engage in periodic target checking (if operating), with relatively more target checks in the constant checking group than in the occasional checking group.

The predictions for performance on the ongoing tasks (on any of the dependent measures) are illustrated in Table 3.1. Note that more + signs in the tables indicate worse predicted performance. This is because in all but one of the experiments reported here, the cost of monitoring was reflected in just the reaction time task

TABLE 3.1   Target Checking and Retrieval Mode
Predictions for Performance in the Ongoing
Tasks

	Control Trials	Experimental Trials
Target Checking Prediction		
Occasional checking instruction	+	+ +
Constant checking instruction	+	+ + +
Retrieval Mode Prediction		
Occasional checking instruction	+	+ +
Constant checking instruction	+	+ +

Note.   More + signs indicate worse performance (i.e., more impairment, lower accuracy, or higher latency) in any ongoing task-
dependent measure.

latencies (where longer latencies reflect worse or slower performance). Thus, using
more + signs to indicate worse predicted performance should increase the transfer
between understanding the predictions in the tables and understanding the results
in the figures.

If target checking is the only process operating, then performance in experimental trials should be worse than in control trials, and this difference should
occur to a greater extent in the constant checking group than in the occasional
checking group. Further, self-reports should indicate greater checking in the constant group than in the occasional group. In contrast, if a retrieval mode is the only
process operating, then performance in experimental trials should still be worse
than in control trials, but this difference should occur to an equal extent in the
constant and occasional groups. Further, self-reports should indicate equivalent
checking in the constant and occasional groups.

The actual results did not exactly conform to either pattern (see Figure 3.1),
in such a way that they motivated the conclusion that both processes were operating. The self-report results (i.e., number of trials out of six for which participants
reported checking for the targets) indicated a difference between the groups, with
greater checking by the constant group (an average of 5.86 checks per set) than by
the occasional group (an average of 2.92 checks per set). Further, although there
was a significant difference between the experimental and control trials in the
reaction time task latencies, the interaction between group and trial type was not
significant, suggesting a similarity between the groups in another process.

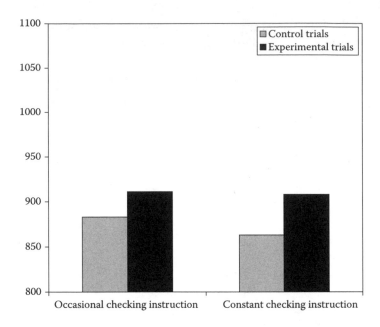

FIGURE 3.1   Latency on the reaction time task.

The most parsimonious interpretation of these results is that although the constant and occasional checking groups differed in target checking, they did not differ in the retrieval mode.

This mixed pattern of results also resembled a pattern from the retrospective memory literature that had been interpreted as providing evidence for a retrieval mode that was separate from the ecphory or actual retrieval of stored episodes (i.e., a lack of a systematic relationship between the cost of the reaction time task and the number of items that were retrieved; Craik et al., 1996). Thus, this pattern of results from the prospective memory experiment was similarly interpreted as providing evidence for two processes. There was no systematic relationship between the cost on the reaction time task and the extent of checking for the targets because the groups differed in target checking but not in the extent to which they instantiated a retrieval mode. This post hoc interpretation is entirely consistent with the particular groups in question, in that participants in the constant and occasional checking groups should have differed in the extent of target checking, but there is no reason to expect that they should have differed in the extent to which they instantiated a retrieval mode. Several other experiments, described below, were directed toward testing this post hoc interpretation.

In an experiment designed to evaluate the involvement of both processes (Guynn, 2003), experimental and control trials either alternated trial by trial or they were blocked. For the alternating trials, there were 48 alternating control and experimental trials (arranged in sets of six), counterbalanced across participants in terms of which trial type appeared first. For the blocked trials, there were 24 consecutive control trials (arranged in sets of six) and 24 consecutive experimental trials (arranged in sets of six), counterbalanced across participants in terms of which trial type appeared first. Participants were cued before each new type of trial as to whether they should perform just the short-term memory and reaction time tasks (control trials) or both tasks plus the prospective memory task (experimental trials).

Predictions for this experiment were based on two assumptions. First, if a retrieval mode were operating, then it would be operating on both types of experimental trials (those that were blocked and those that alternated with control trials) and on control trials that alternated with experimental trials. A retrieval mode of course would be expected to operate on experimental trials, but it would also be expected to operate on control trials that alternated with experimental trials, as it would not be efficient, or perhaps even possible, to switch in and out of a retrieval mode between the alternating trial types. Second, if target checking were operating, then it would be operating on both types of experimental trials, and on neither type of control trial. This is because target checking is a more flexible process than switching in and out of a retrieval mode, and so it would be possible (and not inefficient) to check for the targets on the experimental trials, even when they alternated with control trials, and not to check on the control trials, even when they alternated with experimental trials. The predictions in Table 3.2 regarding performance on the ongoing activity were based on these assumptions.

If target checking is the only process operating, then performance should be better on control trials than on experimental trials, and this difference should not vary as a function of whether the trial types are alternating or blocked. If instantiating a retrieval mode is the only process operating, then performance should be better

TABLE 3.2   Target Checking and Retrieval Mode Predictions for Performance in the Ongoing Tasks

	Control Trials	Experimental Trials
Target Checking Prediction		
Blocked trial types	+	+ +
Alternating trial types	+	+ +
Retrieval Mode Prediction		
Blocked trial types	+	+ +
Alternating trial types	+ +	+ +
Target Checking + Retrieval Mode Prediction		
Blocked trial types	+	+ + +
Alternating trial types	+ +	+ + +

Note. More + signs indicate worse performance (i.e., more impairment, lower accuracy, or higher latency) in any ongoing task-dependent measure.

on blocked control trials than on alternating control trials and on both types of experimental trials, and this difference should not vary across these latter three trial types. Finally, if target checking and instantiating a retrieval mode both are operating, then performance should be best on blocked control trials, intermediate on alternating control trials, and worse on both types of experimental trials. The results are illustrated in Figure 3.2. The reaction time task accuracy results appear in the top panel and the latency results appear in the bottom panel. In both cases, there was a larger difference in performance between the experimental and control trials when the trial types were blocked than when they alternated, and this was because performance on the control trials, but not on the experimental trials, varied as a function of whether the trial types alternated or were blocked. The results thus conformed to the third prediction and were interpreted as providing evidence for both component processes of monitoring.

Two alternate interpretations, although implausible, could not be ruled out by these results, however. That is, one possibility is that target checking was the only process operating, and thus the differential costs reflected target checking occurring to the greatest extent on both types of experimental trials, to the least extent on the blocked control trials, and to an intermediate extent on the alternating control trials. The other possibility is that a retrieval mode was the only process operating, and thus the differential costs reflected the differential resource demands of instantiating a retrieval mode (i.e., the greatest demand on both types of experimental trials, the least demand on the blocked control trials, and an intermediate demand on the alternating control trials). The difficulty in ruling out these alternate interpretations may reflect in part the fact that a single manipulation (alternating vs. blocked trial types) was used to provide evidence for both component processes of monitoring.

Accordingly, in a subsequent experiment, different manipulations were used to explore each component process (Guynn, 2005). To investigate target checking, participants performed one block of 24 control trials and two blocks of 24 experimental trials (the order of the three blocks was counterbalanced across participants). The critical manipulation was that participants were given information about the possible locations of the prospective memory targets (i.e., the fruits). On one block of experimental trials, participants were informed that the fruits could appear as any one of the five words in a short-term memory trial, and on one block of experimental trials participants were informed that the fruits could appear as just the first word in a short-term memory trial.

The retrieval mode should be equivalent regardless of the number of locations to be checked, but target checking should be affected by this manipulation. Thus, if monitoring is affected by the information about possible target location, then the implication would be that target checking is what is affected; if this manipulation does not affect monitoring, then target checking would not be implicated (see Table 3.3). Again, a retrieval mode should be equivalent across the two blocks of experimental trials, and thus this manipulation would not provide information on the operation (or lack thereof) of a retrieval mode. The reaction time task latencies revealed that participants performed worse on the experimental trials when informed that targets could appear as any of the five words than as just the first

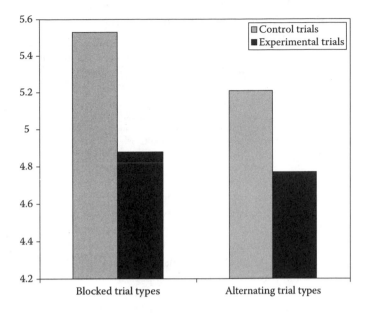

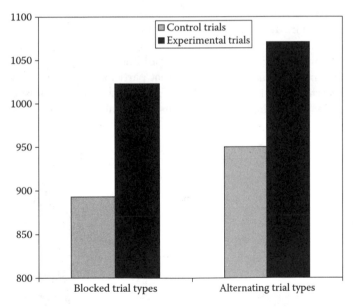

FIGURE 3.2 Accuracy (top panel) and latency (bottom panel) on the reaction time task.

word in a short-term memory trial (see Figure 3.3), consistent with the interpretation that participants were checking for the targets on the experimental trials.

To investigate instantiating a retrieval mode, participants also performed one block of 24 control trials and two blocks of 24 experimental trials. The control block was

TABLE 3.3   Target Checking Predictions
for Performance on the Ongoing Tasks

	Control Trials	Experimental First Trial	Experimental All 5 Trials
Target checking	+	+ +	+ + +
No target checking	+	+ +	+ +

Note.   More + signs indicate worse performance (i.e., more impairment, lower accuracy, or higher latency) on any ongoing task-dependent measure.

performed first and the order of the two experimental blocks was counterbalanced across participants. The critical manipulation was that participants performed the control trials either before or after the instructions about the prospective memory task. On the control trials, participants did not perform (nor were expected to perform) the prospective memory task. If a retrieval mode is instantiated upon the prospective memory instructions, then the retrieval mode would be operating on the control trials that follow the prospective memory instructions, but not on the control trials that precede the prospective memory instructions. Target checking should be nonexistent on both types of control trials. Thus, if monitoring is affected by whether the control trials are preceded or followed by the prospective memory instructions, the implication would be that instantiating a retrieval mode is what is affected; if this manipulation does not affect monitoring, then a retrieval mode would not be implicated (see Table 3.4). The reaction time task latencies revealed that participants performed worse on the control trials when they had already been instructed about the prospective memory task than when they had not yet been instructed about the prospective memory

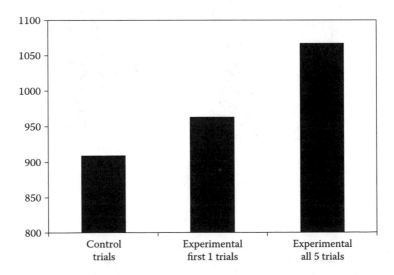

FIGURE 3.3   Latency on the reaction time task.

TABLE 3.4   Retrieval Mode Predictions for
Performance on the Ongoing Tasks (Control Trials)

	PM Instructions, Then Control Trials	Control Trials, Then PM Instructions
Retrieval mode	+ +	+
No retrieval mode	+	+

Note. More + signs indicate worse performance (i.e., more impairment, lower accuracy, and/or higher latency) on any ongoing task dependent measure. PM = prospective memory.

task (see Figure 3.4), consistent with the interpretation that participants were instantiating a retrieval mode on the control trials after having been instructed about the prospective memory task (and, by extension, on the experimental trials).

A final experiment was conducted to rule out the possibility that this latter cost actually reflected target checking (i.e., participants checking for the targets during the control trials after having been instructed about the prospective memory task). In this experiment, all participants were instructed about the prospective memory task before they performed the control trials; the number and the order of the control and experimental trials were the same as in the prior experiment. However, one group was informed that the fruits in the later experimental trials could appear as any one of the five words, and one group was informed that the fruits could appear as just the first word, in a short-term memory trial (see Table 3.5 for predictions).

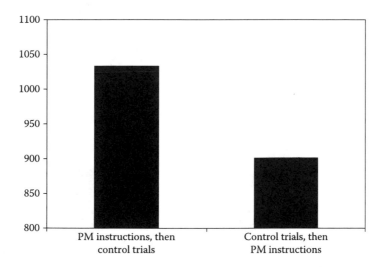

FIGURE 3.4   Latency on the reaction time task (control trials).

TABLE 3.5   Target Checking Versus Retrieval Mode
Predictions for Performance on the Ongoing Tasks
(Control Trials)

	Experimental First PM Instructions, Then Control Trials	Experimental All 5 PM Instructions, Then Control Trials
Retrieval mode	+	+
Target checking	+	+ +

Note.   More + signs indicate worse performance (i.e., more impairment, lower accuracy, and/or higher latency) on any ongoing task dependent measure. PM = prospective memory.

If participants just instantiated a retrieval mode on the control trials in the prior experiment, then performance on the control trials should not be affected by this manipulation in this experiment. If participants checked for the targets on the control trials in the prior experiment, however, then performance on the control trials should be affected by this manipulation in this experiment (i.e., better performance in the one-word condition than in the five-word condition). The reaction time task latencies indicated that performance on the control trials was not affected by this manipulation (see Figure 3.5), consistent with the interpretation that the cost in the prior experiment occurred because participants instantiated a retrieval mode but did not check for the targets during the control trials after having been instructed about the prospective memory task.

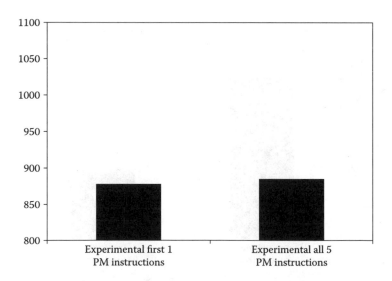

FIGURE 3.5   Latency on the reaction time task (control trials).

Although the results just described were interpreted as providing evidence for the involvement of both component processes in monitoring, it has been difficult to obtain evidence that uniquely implies the separate processes (e.g., a double dissociation) of a retrieval mode and target checking. In fact, it could be that an alternate approach (e.g., a neuropsychological approach) might be most useful in providing evidence for the component processes of monitoring. This would be similar to the neuropsychological evidence for the retrospective memory retrieval mode (vs. ecphory) that was reported earlier. Similarly, West and colleagues (West et al., 2001; West & Ross-Munroe, 2002) have used ERP results to separate the noticing and search components of prospective memory retrieval, and Burgess et al. (2001) have used PET results to separate the maintenance of an intention and the realization of an intention. Such an approach could also be useful for separating the retrieval mode and target checking components of monitoring. Another approach could be to apply a quantitative technique for providing separate estimates of the two components; one such possibility is raised in the last section of this chapter.

ACTIVATION AND RETRIEVAL MODE

Researchers have proposed that prospective memory may be supported by stronger and longer lasting levels of activation of the intention representation compared to other (e.g., retrospective memory) representations (Goschke & Kuhl, 1993). The evidence for these stronger and longer lasting levels of activation comes from a finding known as the *intention superiority effect* (Goschke & Kuhl, 1993; Marsh et al., 1998). In this effect, participants are faster to make a decision (e.g., a recognition decision or a lexical decision) about words that are part of a prospective script (a script to be executed) than a neutral script. In contrast, they are not faster to respond to words that are part of a retrospective script (a script to be observed and verified for accuracy) than a neutral script. Goschke and Kuhl (1993) interpreted this effect in terms of the ACT* model of cognition (Anderson, 1983). In this model, goals in working memory are represented as source nodes that maintain increased levels of activation without rehearsal. In interpreting the intention superiority effect, the proposal was that goals in long-term memory (i.e., intentions or prospective memory representations) are also source nodes that maintain increased levels of activation without rehearsal.

This interpretation of the intention superiority effect is included here because this increased level of activation may be related to the retrieval mode component of monitoring (Guynn, 2003). In particular, the increased level of activation may provide the mechanism for the retrieval mode (i.e., in effect, they may be the same process). (Alternative possibilities are that the increased level of activation increases the likelihood of target checking or that target checking increases the level of activation of the intention representation.) Several lines of work are consistent with there being a relationship between the increased level of activation and the retrieval mode component of monitoring. Specifically, there may be a similarity in both their resource demands and their time parameters; the concept of activation also plays a role in explaining the costs that are incurred when participants switch between different tasks (i.e., task switching costs).

Regarding the resource demands, researchers have developed a computational account of the intention superiority effect using the ACT-R (a successor of ACT*; Anderson & Lebiere, 1998) cognitive architecture (Lebiere & Lee, 2001; see also Lovett, Reder, & Lebiere, 1999). In this model, the current context or task to be accomplished (e.g., the prospective memory task) is a source of activation in the current goal. This activation occurs when the task is expected to be performed in the near future and persists until the task is performed. The most important implication of this computational model for the retrieval mode is that "maintaining a context in the goal exacts some costs, including the additional splitting of the total attentional level" (Lebiere & Lee, 2001, p. 142). Thus, maintaining the increased level of activation places demands on the cognitive system, much as instantiating the retrieval mode is proposed to do.

Further, work on neuroanatomical correlates indicates that in the domain of retrospective memory, a retrieval mode is effortful to adopt, maintain, and switch in and out of; depends on the frontal cortex; and persists until the desired material is retrieved or the retrieval goal changes (Duzel, 2000; McIntosh et al., 1997; Morcom & Rugg, 2002; Nyberg, 1999; Nyberg et al., 1995; Tulving, 1983, 1998). Similar conclusions have been drawn about the increased level of activation that produces the intention superiority effect (Goschke & Kuhl, 1993; Marsh et al., 1998; Marsh et al., 1999), suggesting another parallel between the increased level of activation and the proposed characteristics of the retrieval mode.

Finally, the task switching literature suggests a relationship between a task set (or a retrieval mode) and the concept of level of activation. The task switching literature was mentioned earlier as possibly relevant to the retrieval mode, because the cost of task switching can be viewed as caused by a switch from one task set to another. Related to the concept of activation playing a role in a retrieval mode, Allport, Styles, and Hsieh (1994) proposed that task set inertia also contributes to the cost of task switching. The task set inertia occurs because the prior task set remains partially activated on subsequent trials. A different perspective on the role of activation is Rubinstein, Meyer, and Evans's (2001) model of executive control in task switching. In this model, rule activation is one of the two stages of executive control (the other is goal shifting), in which the rules for selecting the next task's response are activated and the rules for selecting the prior task's response are deactivated.

TIME MONITORING

Although the RM + TC theory was developed in the context of event-based prospective memory, the theory may also apply to time-based prospective memory. As mentioned earlier, monitoring for the appropriate occasion to execute an intended action has been proposed to mediate time-based prospective memory since the beginning of research on the topic (Ceci et al., 1988; Ceci & Bronfenbrenner,

1985; Einstein et al., 1995; Harris & Wilkins, 1982). This is perhaps not coinciden-
tal because there has been a fairly obvious way to measure time monitoring, with
either an observable head turn to inspect a clock in the room or a measurable key
press to bring up a clock on a computer display. It has been less obvious how to
measure event monitoring. An analog to the time-based scenario would be to present target events in a different spatial location than the ongoing activity stimuli.
Monitoring could then be indexed by an observable head turn to the location of
the potential target event or a measurable key press to bring up the potential target event. This method would restrict one to a type of checking model of event
monitoring, however, in that it is difficult to imagine this overt process of monitoring as corresponding to a psychological process other than that of checking. This
analog to the time-based scenario suggests that the method for studying time-
based prospective memory has actually restricted one to a checking model of time
monitoring. In fact, a model of monitoring in time-based prospective memory, the
Test-Wait-Test-Exit (TWTE) model (Harris & Wilkins, 1982), can be thought of as
a checking model, with the tests corresponding to checks of the environment for
an appropriate occasion to execute the intended action.

In contrast, the method for measuring event monitoring that has actually been
used (i.e., impairment on nontarget experimental trials relative to control trials,
with the target event appearing as a stimulus embedded in the ongoing activity)
does not restrict one to a checking model of event monitoring. This method could
thus be extended to time-based prospective memory, such that the RM + TC theory could be evaluated for its applicability to time monitoring. Checking would
still be revealed by a head turn or a key press, and the retrieval mode would be
revealed by impairment on nontarget experimental trials relative to control trials,
after the time-check trials are omitted. Any resulting monitoring cost uncontaminated by checking would then be interpreted as reflecting the instantiation of a
retrieval mode. Harris and Wilkins (1982) might have even anticipated that there
was a process of interest other than checking the time or a clock (e.g., the retrieval
mode that is proposed here) when they suggested that "the most interesting questions" are "those that deal with the cognitive events intervening between observations of the clock" (pp. 134–135). Of course, any absence of a monitoring cost after
the time-check trials are omitted would imply that a retrieval mode does not play
a role in time-based prospective memory.

MONITORING AND VIGILANCE

The recent interest in monitoring has helped to bring to the fore an inconsistency
in the prospective memory literature. On the one hand, researchers suggest that
vigilance can be used to accomplish prospective memory tasks (Baddeley & Wilkins,
1984; Brandimonte et al., 2001; Craik & Kerr, 1996; Maylor, 1996; Meacham &
Leiman, 1982; Meier & Graf, 2000; cf. Dobbs & Reeves, 1996). On the other hand,
researchers prescribe conditions to reduce or eliminate the possibility that
vigilance processes will be operative in prospective memory experiments
(Einstein & McDaniel, 1990; Ellis & Kvavilashvili, 2000; Kvavilashvili, 1992;

McDaniel & Einstein, 1993). The basic idea behind these prescribed conditions is that participants must not be aware that prospective memory is the main purpose of the experiment, and instead, they must view the prospective memory task as an "extra" part of the experiment. The most common guideline is to interpolate a delay between the prospective memory instructions and the ongoing activity in which the prospective memory task is embedded (e.g., Einstein & McDaniel, 1990; McDaniel & Einstein, 1993).

This inconsistency is troubling in light of the theoretical and empirical work already described that suggests that monitoring plays a role in prospective memory (e.g., Guynn, 2003; McDaniel & Einstein, 2000; Norman & Shallice, 1986). Rarely is anything explicit said about the relationship between vigilance and monitoring, but one exception (which is the preferred interpretation here) is that vigilance and monitoring refer to the same basic process that differs only in its likelihood of occurrence (Brandimonte et al., 2001). On this interpretation, monitoring refers to situations where it occurs to a relatively lesser extent and vigilance refers to situations where it occurs to a relatively greater extent.

A difference in likelihood is entirely plausible given the two different types of target detection experiments. In prospective memory experiments, an ongoing activity must be interrupted to respond to embedded targets. Cognitive resources must be used to perform the ongoing activity, leaving fewer resources available to monitor for the targets. In vigilance experiments, more often the target detection task is the only task to be performed. Cognitive resources do not have to be shared between tasks and thus can be used exclusively to monitor for the targets. Also, vigilance tasks, but not prospective memory tasks, are referred to as monitoring tasks, perhaps reflecting an assumption about the relative likelihood of monitoring in the two types of target detection tasks (i.e., it is possible for monitoring *not* to play a role in prospective memory tasks, but not in vigilance tasks).

To the extent that the primary (or only) difference between monitoring and vigilance is the likelihood of the same basic process, it seems misguided to demand that all prospective memory experiments be conducted so as to reduce or eliminate vigilance. Such a demand would be tantamount to demanding that all prospective memory experiments be conducted so as to reduce or eliminate monitoring. This extreme position seems unwarranted given the role of monitoring in the leading theoretical perspectives on prospective memory and the empirical evidence for monitoring in prospective memory. Further, researchers do not even necessarily follow the guidelines to reduce or eliminate vigilance in prospective memory experiments (i.e., interpolate a delay) when doing so would likely mask the primary process of interest in the experiment. For example, when the purpose of the experiment is to investigate the increased level of activation of the prospective memory representation (Goschke & Kuhl, 1993; Marsh et al., 1998; Marsh et al., 1999), the neural correlates of prospective memory (West & Covell, 2001; West, Herndon, & Covell, 2003; West et al., 2001; West & Ross-Munroe, 2002), holding a retrieved intention in mind before performing the prospective memory task (Einstein, McDaniel, Manzi, Cochran, & Baker, 2000; Einstein, McDaniel, Williford, Pagan, & Dismukes, 2003), monitoring in time-based prospective memory (Ceci et al., 1988; Ceci & Bronfenbrenner, 1985; Einstein et al., 1995; Harris & Wilkins, 1982), and even monitoring in event-based prospective memory (Guynn, 2003; Kliegel et al., 2001, 2004; Smith, 2003), a delay has not been interpolated between the prospective memory instructions and the activity in which the primary dependent variable is measured. This is presumably because introducing such a delay could result in the process of primary interest not being detectable.

Of course, the position at the other extreme, that all prospective memory experiments should be conducted to allow or enhance monitoring or vigilance, also seems misguided, as such conditions could interfere with the detection of any automatic process mediating prospective memory. Rather, the most productive course of action would be to identify the process(es) of interest in any given research endeavor and to conduct the studies that allow the process(es) to come to the fore.

FUTURE DIRECTIONS

As a theory of monitoring, the RM + TC theory may complement theories of prospective memory that do not specify what monitoring actually entails. Future work may profitably focus on integrating this theory with theories of prospective memory. For example, in the Norman and Shallice (1986) model, the executive or supervisory attentional system is responsible for monitoring for the targets or markers. One challenge for integrating this model with the RM + TC theory is to explain how this attentional system could accomplish the separate processes of instantiating a retrieval mode and periodic target checking. This explanation could possibly be in terms of how the executive attentional system would bias contention scheduling to accomplish both component processes. According to the multiprocess model (McDaniel & Einstein, 2000), there are conditions under which monitoring is more likely to play a role, including when the prospective memory task is more important, when the prospective memory target events are not particularly salient, when there is no preexisting association between a target event and an intended action, when the ongoing activity does not elicit focal processing of the target events, and for certain types of individuals. Thus, future work to integrate this model with the RM + TC theory could focus on the effects of these factors on the separate processes of instantiating a retrieval mode and periodic target checking. A unique feature of the preparatory attentional and memory processes model (Smith & Bayen, 2004) is that it is a multinomial model that yields numerical estimates of its two parameters. Thus, future work to integrate this model with the RM + TC theory could focus on the relationship between these parameters and the component processes of monitoring. A reasonable first hypothesis is that the preparatory attentional processes, one of which is monitoring, subsume both instantiating a retrieval mode and periodic target checking. Future work to integrate these views could focus on modeling the preparatory attentional processes, including the retrieval mode and target checking components of monitoring.

Much work also remains to be done with regard to the RM + TC theory itself, independent of work to integrate it with the existing theories of prospective memory. For example, the assumptions about the component processes as described earlier remain to be evaluated. These include the assumptions that the retrieval mode is a prerequisite for target checking, that the retrieval mode is necessary for monitoring, and that the retrieval mode may be sufficient for monitoring. The mechanism of the retrieval mode and the relationship between the retrieval mode and the increased level of activation of the prospective memory representation also remain to be evaluated. The functionality of the relationship between each component process and prospective memory also has not yet been investigated. For example, one possibility is that only the extent of target checking is functionally related to prospective memory. In other words, perhaps more target checking benefits prospective memory, but there is more of an all-or-none relationship between the retrieval mode and prospective memory, such that a retrieval mode is necessary (when prospective memory is mediated by monitoring), but incurring further costs on the ongoing activity as a result of the retrieval mode does not further benefit prospective memory. Neuropsychological approaches may help to provide separate estimates of the two component processes and thereby resolve some of these issues. Another approach that may be useful in this regard is to apply distributional analysis techniques to the reaction time distributions from the ongoing task (e.g., Dawson, 1988; Hockley, 1984; Ratcliff, 1979; Wenger & Townsend, 2000). Work on the retrospective memory retrieval mode, task sets and task switching, and vigilance may also prove useful in the efforts to understand monitoring and its component processes, and the retrieval mode in particular. Needless to say, despite any progress reported herein, most of the work obviously remains yet to be done on this topic. The ultimate goal of this chapter is to stimulate further interest in and research on these issues.

ACKNOWLEDGMENTS

Portions of this research were presented at the 2nd International Conference on Prospective Memory, July 2005, Zurich, Switzerland.

Appreciation is expressed to Gilles Einstein and Mark McDaniel for feedback on earlier versions of this chapter.

REFERENCES

Allport, D. A., Styles, E. A., & Hsieh, S. (1994). Shifting intentional set: Exploring the dynamic control of tasks. In C. Umilta & M. Moscovitch (Eds.), *Attention and performance XV: Conscious and nonconscious information processing*, (pp. 421–452). Cambridge, MA: MIT Press.

Anderson, J. R. (1983). *The architecture of cognition*. Cambridge, MA: Harvard University Press.

Anderson, J. R., & Lebiere, C. (1998). *The atomic components of thought*. Mahwah, NJ: Lawrence Erlbaum Associates, Inc.

Baddeley, A. D., & Wilkins, A. (1984). Taking memory out of the laboratory. In J. E. Harris & P. E. Morris (Eds.), *Everyday memory: Actions and absent-mindedness* (pp. 1–17). London: Academic.

Brandimonte, M., Einstein, G. O., & McDaniel, M. A. (Eds.). (1996). *Prospective memory: Theory and applications*. Mahwah, NJ: Lawrence Erlbaum Associates, Inc.

Brandimonte, M. A., Ferrante, D., Feresin, C., & Delbello, R. (2001). Dissociating prospective memory from vigilance processes. *Psicologica, 22*, 97–113.

Buckner, R. L., Koutstaal, W., Schacter, D. L., Dale, A. M., Rotte, M., & Rosen, B. R. (1998). Functional-anatomic study of episodic retrieval: II. Selective averaging of event-related fMRI trials to test the retrieval success hypothesis. *NeuroImage, 7,* 163–175.

Burgess, P. W., Quayle, A., & Frith, C. D. (2001). Brain regions involved in prospective memory as determined by positron emission tomography. *Neuropsychologia, 39,* 545–555.

Burgess, P. W., & Shallice, T. (1997). The relationship between prospective and retrospective memory: Neuropsychological evidence. In M. A. Conway (Ed.), *Cognitive models of memory* (pp. 247–272). Cambridge, MA: MIT Press.

Ceci, S. J., Baker, J. G., & Bronfenbrenner, U. (1988). Prospective remembering, temporal calibration, and context. In M. M. Gruneberg, P. E. Morris, & R. N. Sykes (Eds.), *Practical aspects of memory: Current research and issues* (Vol. 1, pp. 360–365). Chichester, UK: Wiley.

Ceci, S. J., & Bronfenbrenner, U. (1985). "Don't forget to take the cupcakes out of the oven": Prospective memory, strategic time-monitoring, and context. *Child Development, 56,* 152–164.

Craik, F. I. M., Govoni, R., Naveh-Benjamin, M., & Anderson, N. D. (1996). The effects of divided attention on encoding and retrieval processes in human memory. *Journal of Experimental Psychology: General, 125,* 159–180.

Craik, F. I. M., & Kerr, S. A. (1996). Commentary: Prospective memory, aging, and lapses of intention. In M. Brandimonte, G. O. Einstein, & M. A. McDaniel (Eds.), *Prospective memory: Theory and applications* (pp. 227–237). Mahwah, NJ: Lawrence Erlbaum Associates, Inc.

Dawson, M. R. W. (1988). Fitting the ex-Gaussian equation to reaction time distributions. *Behavior Research Methods, Instruments, & Computers, 20,* 54–57.

Dobbs, A. R., & Reeves, M. B. (1996). Prospective memory: More than memory. In M. Brandimonte, G. O. Einstein, & M. A. McDaniel (Eds.), *Prospective memory: Theory and applications* (pp. 199–225). Mahwah, NJ: Lawrence Erlbaum Associates, Inc.

Duzel, E. (2000). When, where, what: The electromagnetic contribution to the WWW of brain activity during recognition. *Acta Psychologica, 105,* 195–210.

Einstein, G. O., & McDaniel, M. A. (1990). Normal aging and prospective memory. *Journal of Experimental Psychology: Learning, Memory, and Cognition, 16,* 717–726.

Einstein, G. O., McDaniel, M. A., Manzi, M., Cochran, B., & Baker, M. (2000). Prospective memory and aging: Forgetting intentions over short delays. *Psychology and Aging, 15,* 671–683.

Einstein, G. O., McDaniel, M. A., Richardson, S. L., Guynn, M. J., & Cunfer, A. R. (1995). Aging and prospective memory: Examining the influences of self-initiated retrieval processes. *Journal of Experimental Psychology: Learning, Memory, and Cognition, 21,* 996–1007.

Einstein, G. O., McDaniel, M. A., Thomas, R., Mayfield, S., Shank, H., Morrisette, N., et al. (2005). Multiple processes in prospective memory retrieval: Factors determining monitoring versus spontaneous retrieval. *Journal of Experimental Psychology: General, 134,* 327–342.

Einstein, G. O., McDaniel, M. A., Williford, C. L., Pagan, J. L., & Dismukes, R. K. (2003). Forgetting of intentions in demanding situations is rapid. *Journal of Experimental Psychology: Applied, 9,* 147–162.

Ellis, J., & Kvavilashvili, L. (2000). Prospective memory in 2000: Past, present, and future directions. *Applied Cognitive Psychology, 14,* S1–S9.

Goschke, T., & Kuhl, J. (1993). Representation of intentions: Persisting activation in memory. *Journal of Experimental Psychology: Learning, Memory, and Cognition, 19,* 1211–1226.

Guynn, M. J. (2001). Footprints of monitoring in event-based prospective memory (Doctoral dissertation, University of New Mexico, 2001). *Dissertation Abstracts International: Section B: The Sciences and Engineering, 62,* 1108.

Guynn, M. J. (2003). A two-process model of monitoring in event-based prospective memory: Activation/retrieval mode and checking. *International Journal of Psychology, 38,* 245–256.

Guynn, M. J. (2005). *Monitoring in event-based prospective memory: Adopting a retrieval mode and checking for target events.* Unpublished manuscript.

Harris, J. E., & Wilkins, A. J. (1982). Remembering to do things: A theoretical framework and an illustrative experiment. *Human Learning, 1,* 123–136.

Hicks, J. L., Marsh, R. L., & Cook, G. I. (2005). Task interference in time-based, event-based, and dual intention prospective memory conditions. *Journal of Memory and Language, 53,* 430–444.

Hockley, W. E. (1984). Analysis of response time distributions in the study of cognitive processes. *Journal of Experimental Psychology: Learning, Memory, and Cognition, 10,* 598–615.

Kapur, S., Craik, F. I. M., Jones, C., Brown, G. M., Houle, S., & Tulving, E. (1995). Functional role of the prefrontal cortex in retrieval of memories: A PET study. *NeuroReport, 6,* 1880–1884.

Kliegel, M., Martin, M., McDaniel, M. A., & Einstein, G. O. (2001). Varying the importance of a prospective memory task: Differential effects across time- and event-based prospective memory. *Memory, 9,* 1–11.

Kliegel, M., Martin, M., McDaniel, M. A., & Einstein, G. O. (2004). Importance effects on performance in event-based prospective memory tasks. *Memory, 12,* 553–561.

Kvavilashvili, L. (1987). Remembering intention as a distinct form of memory. *British Journal of Psychology, 78,* 507–518.

Kvavilashvili, L. (1992). Remembering intentions: A critical review of existing experimental paradigms. *Applied Cognitive Psychology, 6,* 507–524.

Lebiere, C., & Lee, F. J. (2001). Intention superiority effect: A context-sensitivity account. In E. M. Altmann, A. Cleeremans, C. D. Schunn, & W. D. Gray (Eds.), *Proceedings of the 2001 Fourth International Conference on Cognitive Modeling* (pp. 139–144). Mahwah, NJ: Lawrence Erlbaum Associates, Inc.

Lepage, M., Ghaffar, O., Nyberg, L., & Tulving, E. (2000). Prefrontal cortex and episodic memory retrieval mode. *Proceedings of the National Academy of Sciences, 97,* 506–511.

Lovett, M. C., Reder, L. M., & Lebiere, C. (1999). Modeling working memory in a unified architecture: An ACT-R perspective. In A. Miyake & P. Shah (Eds.), *Models of working memory: Mechanisms of active maintenance and executive control* (pp. 135–182). Cambridge, UK: Cambridge University Press.

Marsh, R. L., Hicks, J. L., & Bink, M. L. (1998). Activation of completed, uncompleted, and partially completed intentions. *Journal of Experimental Psychology: Learning, Memory, and Cognition, 24,* 350–361.

Marsh, R. L., Hicks, J. L., & Bryan, E. S. (1999). The activation of unrelated and canceled intentions. *Memory & Cognition, 27,* 320–327.

Marsh, R. L., Hicks, J. L., & Cook, G. I. (2005). On the relationship between effort toward an ongoing task and cue detection in event-based prospective memory. *Journal of Experimental Psychology: Learning, Memory, and Cognition, 31,* 68–75.

Marsh, R. L., Hicks, J. L., Cook, G. I., Hansen, J. S., & Pallos, A. L. (2003). Interference to ongoing activities covaries with the characteristics of an event-based intention. *Journal of Experimental Psychology: Learning, Memory, and Cognition, 29,* 861–870.

Maylor, E. A. (1996). Does prospective memory decline with age? In M. Brandimonte, G. O. Einstein, & M. A. McDaniel (Eds.), *Prospective memory: Theory and applications* (pp. 173–197). Mahwah, NJ: Lawrence Erlbaum Associates, Inc.

McDaniel, M. A., & Einstein, G. O. (1993). The importance of cue familiarity and cue distinctiveness in prospective memory. *Memory, 1,* 23–41.

McDaniel, M. A., & Einstein, G. O. (2000). Strategic and automatic processes in prospective memory retrieval: A multiprocess framework. *Applied Cognitive Psychology, 14,* S127–S144.

McDaniel, M. A., Guynn, M. J., Einstein, G. O., & Breneiser, J. (2004). Cue-focused and reflexive-associative processes in prospective memory retrieval. *Journal of Experimental Psychology: Learning, Memory, and Cognition, 30,* 605–614.

McIntosh, A. R., Nyberg, L., Bookstein, F. L., & Tulving, E. (1997). Differential functional connectivity of prefrontal and medial temporal cortices during episodic memory retrieval. *Human Brain Mapping, 5,* 323–327.

Meacham, J. A., & Leiman, B. (1982). Remembering to perform future actions. In U. Neisser (Ed.), *Memory observed: Remembering in natural contexts* (pp. 327–336). San Francisco: Freeman.

Meier, B., & Graf, P. (2000). Transfer appropriate processing for prospective memory tests. *Applied Cognitive Psychology, 14,* S11–S27.

Morcom, A. M., & Rugg, M. D. (2002). Getting ready to remember: The neural correlates of task set during recognition memory. *NeuroReport, 13,* 149–152.

Norman, D. A., & Shallice, T. (1986). Attention to action: Willed and automatic control of behavior. In R. J. Davidson, G. E. Schwartz, & D. Shapiro (Eds.), *Consciousness and self-regulation: Advances in research and theory* (Vol. 4 pp. 1–18). New York: Plenum.

Nyberg, L. (1999). Functional neuroanatomy of component processes of episodic memory retrieval. In L.-G. Nilsson & H. J. Markowitsch (Eds.), *Cognitive neuroscience of memory* (pp. 43–54). Kirkland, WA: Hogrefe & Huber.

Nyberg, L., Tulving, E., Habib, R., Nilsson, L.-G., Kapur, S., Houle, S., et al. (1995). Functional brain maps of retrieval mode and recovery of episodic information. *NeuroReport, 7,* 249–252.

Ratcliff, R. (1979). Group reaction time distributions and an analysis of distribution statistics. *Psychological Bulletin, 86,* 446–461.

Rogers, R. D., & Monsell, S. (1995). Costs of a predictable switch between simple cognitive tasks. *Journal of Experimental Psychology: General, 124,* 207–231.

Rubinstein, J. S., Meyer, D. E., & Evans, J. E. (2001). Executive control of cognitive processes in task switching. *Journal of Experimental Psychology: Human Perception and Performance, 27,* 763–797.

Rugg, M. D., Fletcher, P. C., Frith, C. D., Frackowiak, R. S. J., & Dolan, R. J. (1997). Brain regions supporting intentional and incidental memory: A PET study. *NeuroReport, 8,* 1283–1287.

Schacter, D. L., Alpert, N. M., Savage, C. R., Rauch, S. L., & Albert, M. S. (1996). Conscious recollection and the human hippocampal formation: Evidence from positron emission tomography. *Proceedings of the National Academy of Sciences, 93,* 321–325.

Shallice, T., & Burgess, P. W. (1991). Deficits in strategy application following frontal lobe damage in man. *Brain, 114,* 727–741.

Smith, R. E. (2003). The cost of remembering to remember in event-based prospective memory: Investigating the capacity demands of delayed intention performance. *Journal of Experimental Psychology: Learning, Memory, and Cognition, 29,* 347–361.

Smith, R. E., & Bayen, U. J. (2004). A multinomial model of event-based prospective memory. *Journal of Experimental Psychology: Learning, Memory, and Cognition, 30,* 756–777.

Tulving, E. (1983). *Elements of episodic memory*. New York: Oxford University Press.

Tulving, E. (1998). Brain/mind correlates of human memory. In M. Sabourin, F. Craik, & M. Robert (Eds.), *Advances in psychological science: Vol. 2. Biological and cognitive aspects* (pp. 441–460). Hove, UK: Psychology Press.

Tulving, E. (2002). Episodic memory: From mind to brain. *Annual Review of Psychology, 53*, 1–25.

Wagner, A. D., Desmond, J. E., Glover, G. H., & Gabrieli, J. D. E. (1998). Prefrontal cortex and recognition memory: Functional-MRI evidence for context-dependent retrieval processes. *Brain, 121*, 1985–2002.

Wenger, M. J., & Townsend, J. T. (2000). Basic response time tools for studying general processing capacity in attention, perception, and cognition. *Journal of General Psychology, 127*, 67–99.

West, R., & Covell, E. (2001). Effects of aging on event-related neural activity related to prospective memory. *NeuroReport, 12*, 2855–2858.

West, R., Herndon, R. W., & Covell, E. (2003). Neural correlates of age-related declines in the formation and realization of delayed intentions. *Psychology and Aging, 18*, 461–473.

West, R., Herndon, R. W., & Crewdson, S. J. (2001). Neural activity associated with the realization of a delayed intention. *Cognitive Brain Research, 12*, 1–9.

West, R., & Ross-Munroe, K. (2002). Neural correlates of the formation and realization of delayed intentions. *Cognitive, Affective, & Behavioral Neuroscience, 2*, 162–173.

4

On Beginning to Understand the Role of Context in Prospective Memory

RICHARD L. MARSH

Department of Psychology
University of Georgia

JASON L. HICKS

Department of Psychology
Louisiana State University

GABRIEL I. COOK

Department of Psychology
Claremont McKenna College

A t least since the days of William James's functionalism, context information has been regarded as paramount in importance to human cognitive processing (e.g., Carr, 1925). More specifically, we have known for quite some time that retrospective memory is sensitive to the explicit manipulation of context (e.g., Feingold, 1914), as would be the case when students perform somewhat more poorly on examinations when tested in a room different from the one where the original instruction took place (e.g., Abernathy, 1940). Our contribution to this volume examines the role of context information in prospective memory because it has received so little explicit attention to date. Recently, we made the claim that the field of prospective memory could benefit greatly if it attempted to tie its findings back more directly to the theories and principles of retrospective memory from whence it originally sprung (Marsh, Cook, & Hicks, 2006a). Our chapter represents a slightly larger scale attempt at doing so than we would expect of the average scholar examining data in his or her laboratory for a given line of research. Nevertheless, we hope that our contribution will provide a good example of how prospective memory data can be tied back to important principles and canons of retrospective memory. We begin with a very brief summary of the kinds of context effects that are typically found in research on retrospective memory. We then selectively revisit published prospective memory work that has profitably capitalized on contextual manipulations to affect intention completion. Finally, we define two contextual associations that may be important in fulfilling intentions. We also provide the reader with examples of our most recent work demonstrating that context effects occur robustly in prospective memory, and moreover, that they probably deserve more attention than they have heretofore received.

THE ROLE OF CONTEXT IN RETROSPECTIVE MEMORY

Context has been defined in sundry ways, but all manner of classifications basically arrive at a similar distinction. For example, Wickens (1987) distinguished between what he called context alpha and context beta. *Context alpha* effects refer to manipulations of context that are external to the stimulus or event itself. Such effects are generally labeled environmental context effects (see S. M. Smith & Vela, 2001). The citation classic in this regard is Godden and Baddeley's (1975) extreme manipulation of having university diving club members learn a list of words on land or 20 feet under water. When crossed with whether the test took place on land or under water, there were two conditions each where the environment at learning and test matched or mismatched. Recall was better when they matched. Of course, this basic finding on retrospective memory has been replicated a number of different times in a myriad of ways with variables as diverse as sound, odor, and posture. By contrast, *context beta* is defined as when the stimulus or event combines with another stimulus or event that somehow changes its semantic or contextual meaning. The citation classic in this case is Light and Carter-Sobell's (1970) demonstration that homographs (*grade*) learned under one sense (steep *grade*) will not be remembered as well if tested under another sense (good *grade*). Unfortunately, both kinds of effects are labeled context-dependent memory effects although their operative underlying principles are actually very different.

Similar retrospective memory effects are found with *state-dependent* manipulations. For example, manipulating inebriation (or not) at study and test will lead to the same sort of interactions as described for manipulations of context alpha (e.g., Eich, 1989). Other drugs such as nicotine, caffeine, and marijuana produce the same result, as do ambient temperatures, body position, odors, music, and states of pain. Another variant on state-dependency context effects is *mood-dependent* effects, which are not exactly the same thing as *mood-congruency* effects. In the former, placing people in slightly positive or negative mood states at both study and test produces the same crossover interactions (i.e., memory is better in the match conditions than in the mismatch conditions). By contrast, in the latter, mood congruency is when a person's current mood cues him or her either to learn or to remember information that is consistent with that mood (e.g., Hertel, 1992). For example, if after learning a list of positive, negative, and neutral words, people are placed in a slightly positive mood, they will recall more positive than negative words (and the opposite occurs if placed in a sad mood; Teasdale & Russell, 1983). As another example, Bower (1981) placed participants in either a happy or sad mood and had them learn a story about two characters, one of whom was happy and the other of whom was sad. People learned more about the protagonist that was related to their current learning state. Not all theorists agree on the underlying mechanisms involved with mood-dependent and mood-congruency retrieval. Nevertheless, to our mind, mood-dependent retrieval is caused by the current mood state adding unique retrieval cues that otherwise would not have been present if one was in a different mood. Therefore, mood-dependent retrieval, in our mind, is a time-of-retrieval effect. By contrast, mood-congruency effects are better described as a time-of-encoding effect. Material that better matches one's concurrent mood is related to one's current state of mind and one's self, and thus, the context interacts with the material to produce superior learning. As the reader will see later, we take a page from this difference in theoretical explanations and later argue that contextual effects on prospective memory can arise either from context information at intention formation or intention retrieval.

Another sort of consistent context effect on retrospective memory is *transfer-appropriate processing*. The idea here is that the cognitive processing that was used at encoding will yield better memory if it is recapitulated at test. The classic citation for this effect has participants learning words under what could be construed as a levels of processing judgment (Morris, Bransford, & Franks, 1977). Participants generated some words to fit into a sentence frame, and others as a rhyme to particular words. Two types of tests were administered, a standard recognition test and a rhyme recognition test. The latter test had participants mark items that rhymed with the studied words. Consistent with the preceding summary, items studied in the rhyme context were better recognized on the rhyme test than the standard test (and the reverse was also true). In other words, cognitive processing on an item that is recapitulated at test will lead to better memory than if the item receives a different sort of processing at test. With these issues now refreshed in the reader's mind, we would like to argue that event-based and time-based prospective memory should be sensitive to the same sort of context effects that are found in retrospective memory. We begin by revisiting published prospective memory work that demonstrates that some of these same principles affect intention completion.

PUBLISHED WORK REVISITED

Capitalizing on Context

In this section we describe five separate lines of work that have used explicit manipulations of context to affect the rate at which intentions are completed. In the first, McDaniel, Robinson-Riegler, and Einstein (1998) examined the degree to which event-based prospective memory is conceptually versus perceptually driven. In Experiment 2 of that report, they manipulated the room (context alpha) in which an intention was learned versus where the ongoing task was actually conducted. One room was spacious and had stark white walls, whereas the other was small and decorated with colorful posters. As we describe later, they also manipulated the format of the cues as pictures versus words. For the present purposes, the pictures resulted in ceiling performance, but the word cues displayed a standard environmental context effect such that event-based prospective memory was best when the intention was learned and the ongoing task was performed in the same room. In Experiment 1 of that report, participants learned homographs as event-based cues. For example, the cue was delivered in a sentence converging on the meaning of *bat* as in baseball or as in animal (a context beta manipulation). Event-based performance was better when the meaning was reinstated (81%) as compared with when it was not (48%). From this evidence McDaniel et al. concluded that event-based prospective memory was largely conceptually driven.

That conclusion, however, would only stand for a few short years before McGann and her colleagues demonstrated analogous benefits for perceptual as well as conceptual study-test changes. In a generalized replication of McDaniel et al.'s (1998) results, McGann, Ellis, and Milne (2003) used homographs (bank) and manipulated the semantic sense of the target at study (e.g., money) and test (e.g., river). McGann et al. replicated the advantage in event-based prospective memory when the homograph's meaning was reinstated during the ongoing task. Moreover, McGann, Ellis, and Milne (2002), as well as McGann et al. (2003), demonstrated that the advantage also extends to the font of the cue. When cues are studied in a particular font, and the font varies during the ongoing task, reinstating the font that was used during intention formation leads to better event-based prospective memory than if the cues were printed in a different font. One important feature of the work of McGann and her colleagues was that their conceptual results (i.e., with homographs) were obtained with a sentence verification task, whereas their font results were obtained with a readability judgment task. What remains unclear is whether the same results would have been obtained had the two ongoing tasks been switched. We believe that it may be the case that font changes only event-based performance because the ongoing task is focusing participants on font judgments, and furthermore, the sentence verification task is a semantic task that is focusing participants on the semantic meaning of the homographs. If the ongoing processing tasks were switched, perhaps the differences in event-based performance would evaporate.

In our own work, we have tried to capitalize on changes in context to affect the output-monitoring component of event-based performance (Marsh, Hicks, Cook, & Mayhorn, 2007; Marsh, Hicks, Hancock, & Munsayac, 2002). In this work, we repeated event-based cues later in the ongoing activity and asked participants to press a different, repeat key if they could remember successfully making a response to the cue on the earlier occasion when it appeared. The goal was to devise a paradigm that would capture real-world commission and omission errors that reflect repeating or omitting an event-based intention. We were generally successful in this regard as we discovered that younger adults tend to believe that they responded earlier when in fact they missed the cue entirely. We believe this occurred because they remembered encountering the cue on the previous occasion and inferred that they responded earlier when they did not. Thus, they are likely to omit completing more intentions than they are to repeat them. By contrast, older adults did not commit this error as often, perhaps because they have worse retrospective memory for encountering the cue previously. The younger adults can avoid making the equivalent of omission errors if their initial response to cues is more elaborated and distinctive. However, as it relates to the focus of this chapter, if one changes the processing context (i.e., ongoing task) from pleasantness ratings to imageability ratings (or vice versa) between the first and second encounters with the cue, younger adults forget that they successfully responded earlier and start committing the equivalent of repetition errors (i.e., believing they did not respond earlier when in fact they did). In this case, the context of making one judgment versus another on an item changes the processing of that cue in much the same way as it does for the transfer-appropriate processing effects discussed earlier.

Another means of capitalizing on context is very much related to transfer-appropriate processing, and unfortunately it is named *task-appropriate* processing, which can be somewhat confusing. Nonetheless, the basic effect occurs when there is a match (semantic or orthographic) between the processing task (i.e., ongoing task) and the type of intention (semantic or orthographic) that is given (Maylor, Darby, Logie, Della Salla, & Smith, 2002). For example, Marsh, Hicks, and Hancock (2000) gave participants the intention to respond either to animal words or to palindromes (words spelled the same forward and backward: *civic*). We classified the animal intention as essentially semantic and the palindrome intention as orthographic. One ongoing activity was to rate the pleasantness of words (which we classified as semantic) and another ongoing activity was to determine if words had double letters (which we classified as orthographic). When the ongoing activity focused participants on the relevant aspects of the cues, performance was higher (about 70% cue detection) as compared with when the processing task was incongruent with the intention (about 55% cue detection). In addition, Meier and Graf (2000) showed virtually the same thing. The task-appropriate processing effect has become one prong in the multiprocess view's argument for the automatic detection of event-based cues. The problem with this argument is that Marsh, Hicks, and Cook (2005) recently demonstrated that task-appropriate processing actually requires resources, which is inconsistent with a more automatic view of cue detection. Of course, we used a categorical intention, which might be more resource demanding than, say, using specific prospective memory cues.

Ceci and Bronfenbrenner (1985) conducted a time-based study in which children were asked to monitor the passage of time needed to bake cupcakes or to charge a motorcycle battery. Both tasks lasted 30 minutes. The important result for the present purposes was that strategic monitoring of a clock depended on whether the children were tested in the laboratory or in their home context. In the home context, children were less anxious and were able to check the clock less frequently. By contrast, in the unfamiliar context, clock checking was more frequent. Ceci and Bronfenbrenner attributed the difference in clock checking to a difference in the level of anxiety that the children had about the task. Twenty years later, we may reinterpret this finding as having been a consequence of the perceived importance of the task that depended on the context in which the ongoing task was performed (Kliegel, Martin, McDaniel, & Einstein, 2001, 2004). After all, 21 children (out of 96) were late at performing the task, and only one of these late responders was observed in the laboratory. Nevertheless, the results clearly show that the environment in which one performs the identical prospective memory task can affect performance.

Multiprocess View

Because the multiprocess view is described elsewhere (see McDaniel, Einstein, & Rendell, chap. 7, this volume; Smith, chap. 2, this volume), we mention only briefly our interpretation of McDaniel, Guynn, Einstein, and Breneiser's (2004) article. In that article, a discrepancy plus search mechanism is posited to replace the older familiarity plus search mechanism described originally by Einstein and McDaniel (1996). At the very heart of this discussion is how cues come to be noticed as different from the background constellation of information being processed. Barring for the moment any discussion of automatic detection, highly unusual cues, those that are distinctive from the background, and those of low frequency in their class of items generally increase event-based prospective memory because they ensure that a cue is noticed and a search of memory for their meaning ensues (cf. McDaniel & Einstein, 1993). Take for example their manipulation of *monad* and *yolif* versus *movie* and *rake* as event-based cues. The former, low-frequency words went undetected in the context of a short-term memory task consisting of low-frequency words, whereas the latter, more common words stuck out. The results were the opposite for the same two cues being processed against a background context of high-frequency words. Consequently, the effectiveness of a particular cue is not absolute but, rather, has a relative effectiveness depending on the prevailing context; and that context is only partially defined by the type of information being processed, but also by the cue itself.

Our point is that cue detection as described in the multiprocess view (i.e., discrepancy plus search) must appeal in part to the importance of context. What makes an item salient or not depends in part on the information surrounding it, or the context in which it occurs. West, Wymbs, Jakubek, and Herndon (2003, Experiment 2) recently used this principle effectively. Participants were asked to form the intention that when a pair of words appeared on a trial in the same color, they should press a special key. West et al. compared a condition in which all of the words were colored to a control condition where the majority of the background trials were in the same color. When many colors were presented, the cue trials became less distinct against their background, which decreased event-based performance from 93% to 80%. So in summary, cue detection in the multiprocess view is a process of discrepancy assessment that will depend on the surrounding context information.

Lures

There are several different ways to create near-cues that do not fulfill the criteria for making an event-based response. These are essentially lures, and they have not received much attention outside of the work conducted by West and his colleagues. West and Craik (1999, 2001) asked participants to respond to green uppercase words and defined lures as either gray uppercase words or green lower-case words. Although younger adults did not false alarm to them, older adults did. However, everybody exhibited some slowing in reacting to those lures, which is evidence in support of a verification component to the microstructure of an event-based response (Marsh, Hicks, Cook, Hansen, & Pallos, 2003; Marsh, Hicks, & Watson, 2002). West and Craik (2001) extended the same basic findings to semantic lures as well. Lures defined in this way essentially have compound conditions about the cues that make them mismatch one of the preconditions for responding (e.g., green and uppercase). Taylor, Marsh, Hicks, and Hancock (2004) used a similar manipulation when we asked participants to respond to animal words beginning with the letter *L*. In that work, we interpreted mismatches (animal lures not beginning with *L*) as something akin to reminders. The more animals we placed in the ongoing task prior to a valid cue, the higher the event-based prospective memory performance. The same was not true of explicit reminders (i.e., no concomitant increase in performance with more reminders), which we interpreted as the lures providing practice at retrieving the intention. Admittedly, that interpretation remains open to speculation and reinterpretation.

Returning to the theme of this chapter, another way to define lures is to have items appear in the wrong environmental context. Einstein et al. (2005, Experiment 5) gave participants an intention about a specific word that would appear in an imagery rating task. Other times, the word was not associated with a prospective memory but, rather, a retrospective memory task. After associating the word with a prospective versus retrospective task, they administered a brief lexical decision task prior to the imagery-rating task. The intention to respond should have been suspended during the lexical decision task, but instead they found about a 40-ms slowing. They interpreted this finding as a *spontaneous retrieval* of the intention in the wrong context even when no resources should have been devoted to the prospective memory task. Our own belief is that this slowing is probably associated with the verification stage of the microstructure of an event-based response, which of course would only happen after the cue had been detected. However, the overarching point is that a cue can be defined by the specific context in which it occurs, and when it occurs outside of that context it can engage some of the microstructure processes involved with event-based responding. We return to this idea later when describing some of our more recent work.

TWO CONTEXTS: INTENTION FORMATION AND INTENTION RETRIEVAL

In this section, we offer the idea that contextual information is important both at intention formation and retrieval. We first define what we mean by encoding and retrieval. We then describe some new ongoing work in our laboratory that is currently at various states of completion. The work on context at intention formation is further subdivided into whether the contextual information is made explicit or is left implicit. We then conclude this section with a brief rejoinder to the question about what role attention plays in prospective memory.

Formation Versus Retrieval

Everyone has had the experience of walking into a room, pausing, and then wondering just what intention brought them into that particular room in the first place. The trip back to the room where we formed the intention is usually a period of bewilderment broken by the intention coming to mind when we arrive back in the room where the intention had been formed originally. Anecdotes such as these highlight that contextual associations, even to the physical or mental context of when and where an intention is formed, are important to prospective memory. In this example, the reinstatement of the context at retrieval served to bring the intention to mind more effectively. As such, this is an everyday example of the environmental context effects described earlier. Therefore, the context that one is in when one forms the intention and when one retrieves the intention both can have consequential effects on prospective memory. Good examples of these have been described in the work of McDaniel et al. (1998) and McGann et al. (2002, 2003).

Another type of contextual association that is often made at intention formation is encoding the future context that one expects to be in at intention completion. For example, if you have a question to ask a friend and you form the intention to ask him over lunch at the end of the week, what is the fate of that intention if you run into him at a store before the lunch date? Very little is known about the expectations that people have about the future context they will be in when they could potentially complete the intention. On the one hand, elaboration of the intention in this way may transform it into an implementation intention and increase the probability of actually completing it (see Cohen & Gollwitzer, chap. 17, this volume). On the other hand, if the opportunity arises to fulfill the intention earlier, or a different opportunity arises after a missed opportunity, the potential exists that linking an intention to a specific context may actually reduce performance. The way we have just been talking about a future performance context applies to those intentions where the future context is made quite explicit, either by one's self or another. However, with some intentions the future context may only be implied or assumed, and thus the relationship to the future context is more implicit. Because very little is known about how such associations affect performance, we have directed some of our research efforts to better understand these contextual associations. In the next section we consider the implications of contextual associations made at intention formation.

Expectations of Context at Intention Formation

When people expect to be in a particular future context, part of their intention may include information about that future context. If so, then either being in that expected context or a different one may affect intention completion. In one pioneering study, Nowinski and Dismukes (2005) implicitly associated an event-based task with one ongoing task context versus another. More specifically, they gave their participants (in Experiment 1) the intention to press the A key when a fruit word occurred during the experiment. The instructions were clear and unambiguous that the fruit word could appear in either of the two ongoing tasks.

However, in a clever manipulation, they linked the intention to one of the two ongoing tasks by use of an example. Their two ongoing tasks were a matching and an anagram task. So, if the intention was linked to the anagram task, the instructions were, "If you see the name of a fruit word as one of the words in the anagram task, or any other task, press the A key." Participants were then led into a block of the anagram ongoing task before even receiving instructions about how to perform the matching task. In this way, the prospective memory task was much more highly associated with the anagram than the matching task. They found that this significantly affected performance insofar as cue detection was better when the cues occurred in the associated task (.50) as compared with the other task (.38).

The implications of this outcome are that, with event-based performance anyway, associating an intention to a future context can benefit performance. Nowinski and Dismukes's (2005) article tests the effect of having versus not having an association. Or perhaps that would be better stated as having an association versus having a weaker association. What their paradigm does not address is what effect there is of having an intention, but the cues occur in the wrong context. So, one could imagine a between-subject manipulation where the instructions are made clear that the software was written to present fruit words in the anagram (or matching) task and then they actually appear in the anagram versus matching task. Of course a control condition that is told nothing about when the prospective cues should occur would be necessary to assess the relative benefit versus decrement of holding either the correct or incorrect association.

In unpublished work from our laboratory we have also tested the effect of implying that cues would appear in a specific context (Marsh, Hicks, & Cook, 2002). In this case, we had three different conditions that were each given four specific animal exemplars to study at intention formation. In one case it was four specific words, in another condition it was four pictures, and in the third it was four animal words along with their corresponding pictures (i.e., both). We asked participants to form an intention to say the name of each out loud any time they encountered those four specific cues. The ongoing activity was to rate the frequency of occurrence in the past 2 weeks of a series of pictures and words intermixed with one another. Like Nowinski and Dismukes (2005), our instructions were clear and unambiguous that participants should respond regardless of the format (picture or word), but the page we handed them with the four cues implied that cues would occur in one or the other of the two contexts (except in the third and final condition). A portion of the data from this experiment is displayed in Figure 4.1. Each pair of bars represents cue detection from a given condition of implying that cues would be experienced as words, pictures, or in either format. There were two each of the pictures and word cues embedded in the ongoing activity, two of which they had seen in that exact format and two they had not. The darker bars depict performance for the picture cues and the lighter bars for words.

The first four bars show a nice crossover interaction in which the implied context resulted in higher event-based performance for that class of cues than the one that was not implied. In explaining why mismatched detection is lower, performance for the word cues at study is presumably driven by the fact that seeing the word, say *horse*, cannot activate a mental image of the specific horse seen as a

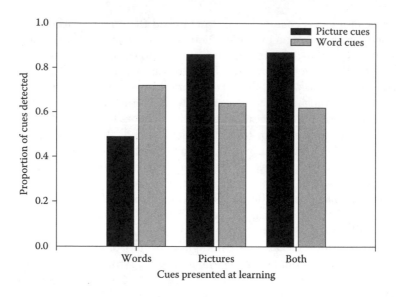

FIGURE 4.1   Pairs of bars denote the formats of the cues at learning and darker versus lighter bars denote the formats of the cues as actually experienced in the ongoing task.

picture at test. Likewise, performance for the picture cues at study is driven by the fact that seeing a picture of a horse does not activate the written form of the word *horse*. When both pictures and words are studied, pictures at test received better cue detection than the words, thereby mirroring performance for the picture condition. That effect replicates McDaniel et al.'s (1998) finding that pictures are more effective retrieval cues, *ceteris paribus*. However, by comparison to the studied word condition, pictures are not always the most effective cue if the implied context is that the cue will be delivered as a word.

To our knowledge, the Nowinski and Dismukes (2005) and our unpublished experiments are the only ones that have tested an implied context about the format of or when event-based cues will be encountered. By contrast, we have done quite a bit more work in which our instructions have been explicit about the context in which an intention should be carried out. In a recently published study, we gave participants the time-based intention to respond in the window of 6 to 7 minutes after the experiment began (Cook, Marsh, & Hicks, 2005). We told two groups of participants that this window would occur during the third phase of the experiment when they were doing a syllable counting task and after the Phase 1 pleasantness rating and the Phase 2 demographic questionnaire had been completed. The two groups differed in only the fact that for one group this information was correct—the window opened in the syllable counting task—and for the other the window actually opened and closed during the first phase. All participants could check a clock as frequently as they wanted throughout the experiment. Compared to control conditions that had no context information associated with their intention (.52 accuracy), the condition with the correct context information performed much better than the control (.71) and the condition with the wrong context association did the worst (.28). In subsequent experiments in this package, we tried very hard to identify factors (e.g., reminders) that might ameliorate having an incorrect association but found that such an association, once formed, is very hard to overcome.

In another study, we examined the effect on *task interference* of associating an intention to a future context (Marsh, Hicks, & Cook, 2006). Task interference is the slowing of reaction times to an ongoing activity when holding an intention as compared with not having an intention (R. E. Smith, 2003; R. E. Smith & Bayen, 2004). We used a variant of our three-stage paradigm in which participants were making lexical decision judgments in Phases 1 and 3, but the two phases were separated by a short demographic questionnaire. In one condition, no event-based intention was given. In this case, reaction times hovered in the 650-ms range for both Phases 1 and 3. In another condition, we told participants to respond to animal words in the third and final phase in which we embedded four animal cues. Event-based performance in this condition was 93%, but the interesting aspect of the data was that no task interference occurred over Phase 1 (i.e., reaction times were approximately 650 ms, as in the no-intention control condition). However, marked interference occurred when participants holding an intention embarked on Phase 3 (approximately 700 ms). Therefore, linking an intention to a future context suspended task interference over the intervening contexts until the context arrived to which the intention was linked. These data are entirely consistent with Einstein, McDaniel, Williford, Pagan, and Dismukes's (2003) claim that the cumulative effect would be prohibitively costly over the course of a normal day if all intentions produced a task interference effect all of the time. Our data suggest that linking intentions to specific contexts is one way to avoid such task interference effects. In a second experiment in that paper, we showed that essentially the same thing occurs with a time-based intention to respond in Phase 3. The major difference was that we also found some evidence for the dissipation of the task interference effect after the time window had expired.

One important question (to us anyway) that stems from the sorts of contextual manipulations described thus far is what happens when an item related to an intention is encountered in the wrong context? As described earlier, this essentially makes the item a lure because it should not receive a response. In the sorts of manipulations just described where we linked an intention to a future context (i.e., Phase 3 of the experiment), encountering a related item or a perfect cue might or might not cause the intention to be retrieved in a context preceding the performance context. According to Marsh et al.'s (2003) analysis of the microstructure of event-based prospective memory, recognition, verification, retrieval, and coordination processes take place on a successful trial where the cue is detected. When a lure is encountered, only recognition and verification need to take place to reject the lure as occurring in the wrong context. However, those two processes alone may be sufficient to produce what Einstein et al. (2005) called *spontaneous retrieval* in their report of embedding the cue word in the wrong context (i.e., in the lexical decision task preceding the imagery rating task). To investigate this

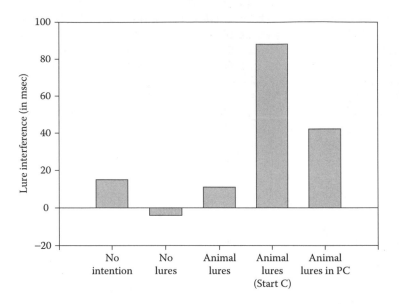

FIGURE 4.2 Lure interference as a function of the type of lures experienced in the first phase of the experiment.

process in a bit more detail, we conducted an unpublished study in which we asked participants to respond to animal words that began with the letter C, but only during Phase 3 of the experiment (cf. Taylor et al., 2004). Both Phases 1 and 3 were lexical decision tasks interrupted by a short demographic questionnaire.

Based on the earlier results, we expected no task interference in Phase 1 and significant task interference in Phase 3, which is indeed what we found. The main manipulation, however, was the type of lure that we placed in Phase 1 of the experiment. The results can best be understood by referring to Figure 4.2. The dependent variable for this graph is the average reaction time on the four lure trials subtracting the average latency to word trials during Phase 1 in which the lures occurred. In other words, that variable gives us a metric of how much more slowly lures were processed than other word items in Phase 1. Focusing for the moment on the first four bars of that graph, the first represents lure interference when there was no intention. These items were control-matched words to the animal items on the relevant dimensions, but were not words denoting animals. These same items were placed in the second condition to observe performance with an intention to respond to animals starting with the letter C in Phase 3. As the reader can see, both of these conditions produced negligible amounts of interference on lure items that do not statistically differ from zero. Of some interest, however, animal lures that matched the intention with the exception of starting with a different letter (e.g., horse) also produced negligible interference (see the middle bar in Figure 4.2). Therefore, even semantically related lures encountered outside of the performance context of Phase 3 received no special recognition as evidenced by these reaction time data.

By contrast, when there was a direct match to a cue (i.e., an animal that did start with the letter *C*) outside the performance context, a very large lure interference effect was observed. Based on the results from the third and fourth conditions, we concluded that linking an intention to a future context protects the rememberer from both task and lure interferences unless the cue is an exact copy of what is to be responded to later during the performance context (cf. Einstein et al., 2005). We believe the large interference effect is a consequence of recognizing the cue word and having to engage in verification that the context is incorrect and concluding that no response should be issued (no participant false alarmed). We found it very interesting that animal words attracted no attention when they were encountered in the wrong context (middle bar). Consequently, we conducted a fifth and final condition in which people were told to respond to animals starting with the letter *C* in both Phases 1 and 3. Note that this fifth condition is identical to the third condition and differs only in that the third condition has a contextual association to the third phase, whereas the fifth condition does not. Now, animals encountered in the first phase actually received some attention and an interference effect of about half the magnitude of the fourth condition was obtained. Therefore, a direct comparison of the third and fifth conditions affords the opportunity to observe performance on lures when they occur outside versus inside the performance context, respectively. Once again, linking an intention to a future context appears to be protecting people from lure interference.

One question that often arises when we describe these effects to our colleagues concerns the degree to which the change in attentional allocation policies is more strategic or automatic when a new context cues the intention. In our experiments, as in everyday life, we assume that linking an intention to a future context requires that an association be formed between that distal context and the intention itself. On arriving into the correct context, we assume memory-based cuing processes cause the intention to receive activation if not an overt retrieval. The realization that an intention is related to this context then causes more conscious attentional allocation policies to be set about how one is going to approach the entire task set (i.e., the new ongoing activity and the prospective memory task). In other words, we do not necessarily believe that detection of the new context is just like detection of an event-based cue, although a parsimonious theory of prospective memory might argue so. Another memory-based explanation about how a distal context can cue an intention when that context arrives is through explicit retrieval strategies. By this we mean explicitly reminding ourselves, say, about the instructions for the new task and what was expected about performance. This type of retrieval strategy is bound to cause recollection of the intention. Such thoughts about future plans and activities have been shown to occur in between activities and transition points in the workday (Sellen, Louie, Harris, & Wilkins, 1997). Therefore, our feeling is that the association between the context and the intention may cause the intention to come to mind, or there may be an explicit retrieval or search strategy that is evoked by transition points in activities and day schemas. Which of these operates in our experiments, we do not know. Moreover, we do not know which of these explanations dominates for real-world intentions, or if it is some combination of both. Thus, this is one question that is ripe for future empirical work.

The contexts we have discussed thus far have tended to be coarse periods of time, similar to what would be encountered in the macrostructure of one's daily life. We were interested in whether the reduction in task interference could be found with even finer grained manipulations more akin to the specific material being processed. In one experiment, we asked whether the task interference effect on pictures versus words would covary with whether one had an intention about pictures versus words (Marsh, Cook, & Hicks, 2006b, Experiment 1b). We predicted that if we gave participants an intention about words, task interference on word trials would be greater than on picture trials (and the same would be true for pictures with an intention about pictures). In this experiment, participants named pictures and words that triggered a voice key to obtain naming latencies. The first 90 trials were a baseline measure, and the second 90 trials were performed with either an intention to respond to pictures of furniture items or words denoting the same. We operationalized task interference as the slowing in the second block of trials relative to the first baseline block of trials. One key feature of this experiment was that pictures and words were experienced in small blocks of 10 items each, and this feature was explained to participants at the outset. This manipulation should have allowed participants to predict what material would be processed on the vast majority of the upcoming trials, and therefore allowed them to adjust their attentional allocation policies accordingly. The data are displayed in Figure 4.3 and support this analysis. The darker bars denote performance for people given an intention about detecting furniture words. Notice that task interference was greater during the word blocks and was almost entirely eliminated for picture

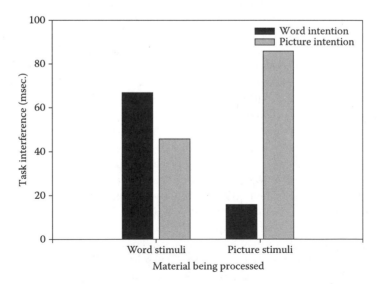

FIGURE 4.3 Task interference as a function of the material being processed in the ongoing task and the type of intention being held.

blocks. The lighter bars show virtually the same relative effect except that there was no total elimination of the task interference effect on words when participants held a picture intention.

The effect just described is not obtained when the pictures and words are intermixed unpredictably (Marsh et al., 2006b, Experiment 1a). However, when a cue word appears as the fixation point and that word denotes whether a picture or a word will have to be named on that trial, the effect depicted in Figure 4.3 reappears. The same is also true when people are asked to respond to animals printed in a red or a green font; namely, task interference is smaller for the items printed in the opposite font color from the intention (in this experiment, the color of the asterisk fixation point was perfectly correlated with the color of the font used on that trial). More generally, we believe that people are able to change dynamically their attentional allocation policies between the ongoing and prospective memory task at a very fined grained level. Thus, preparatory attention (R. E. Smith, 2003, chap. 2, this volume) must be a fairly complicated set of attentional mechanisms that is tuned to both more general as well as specific, local contexts. The fact that participants needed some warning to alleviate task interference suggests that post-stimulus checking may not be the best way to depict task interference. Guynn (2003) argued that task interference comes from being in a retrieval mode and also from poststimulus checking (see also Guynn, chap. 3, this volume). If a component of task interference was poststimulus checking, then we should have obtained the effects in Figure 4.3 with a totally random sequence, and we did not.

The preceding discussion summarizes our empirical data and theoretical thinking about how linking an intention to a future context can dramatically affect prospective memory processes. More specifically, doing so affects general attentional allocation policies as well as more local ones, and it affects the microstructure of an event-based response as we have demonstrated with lures. As mentioned earlier, West and his colleagues have done quite a bit of work that includes lure trials, but they were, to our knowledge, always presented in the performance context. In the next section of our chapter, we argue that the context in which an intention is retrieved, or the immediately preceding context, can also affect prospective memory.

Expectations of Context at Intention Retrieval

In a *delay-execute* prospective task, participants receive a salient event-based cue but must delay their response for anywhere from 5 to 30 seconds until some other part of the ongoing task is reached (e.g., Einstein, McDaniel, Manzi, Cochran, & Baker, 2000; Einstein et al., 2003). The general goal of this research is to simulate those times in everyday life when an intention cannot be completed immediately, such as remembering that medication needs to be taken but the trip to the kitchen to retrieve it takes time. As compared with younger adults who generally perform quite well at this task, older adults forget the intention quite rapidly (in a matter of seconds), even when they are asked to rehearse what it is they have to do over the intervening filled retention interval (McDaniel, Einstein, Stout, & Morgan, 2003). The same is true if a salient cue occurs in the ongoing activity and the participant is interrupted with a different task that draws his or her attention away from the computer monitor before returning to the ongoing task at hand (Einstein et al., 2003; McDaniel, Einstein, Graham, & Rall, 2004). Generally, the interruption has a very deleterious effect on intention completion, and that disruption is not a function of the duration of the interruption.

In the work that Einstein and McDaniel have done on the task interruption effect, they always presented the cue in the ongoing activity that preceded the interruption, and they always returned to the same ongoing activity in which the cue had occurred originally. In their experiments, they asked participants to respond when the task changed (e.g., from pleasantness ratings to picking synonyms). In his dissertation work, Cook examined this task interruption effect in some detail. Cook compared performance when the cue occurred before the interrupting task to when the cue occurred during the interrupting task itself. Despite it being temporally closer to the task change, when the cue occurred in the interrupting task, performance was much worse (proportion responding was .39) than when it occurred before the interrupting task (.69). There are several ways to think about that effect. Because the interrupting task had to be inhibited, perhaps the intention to respond becomes associated with the interrupting task and it too becomes inhibited. By contrast, when the cue occurs before the interruption, the intention may become associated with the particular ongoing task, which is then reinstated before the task change requiring a prospective response. To examine this latter interpretation, Cook manipulated whether the ongoing task was reinstated after the interruption or if participants proceeded directly from the interrupting task to the task change, requiring a prospective response.

The results are displayed in Figure 4.4. The left two bars reflect a replication of the previously described results. That is, when the ongoing task in which the cue occurred is reinstated for several trials just before the task change, performance is much better than when the cue occurs during the interrupting task. By contrast, the right two bars show what happened when the ongoing activity is not reinstated after the interrupting task. Basically, if the cue occurs before the interruption, not reinstating that task prior to a task change reduces performance dramatically. We believe that these effects demonstrate the importance of the context at retrieval. Reinstating the ongoing task must have served either as a reminder or acted more implicitly to reactivate the intention to respond at the task change. Either way, these results demonstrate that intentions become linked to the contexts in which they are formed, and later the context during or just directly preceding it is functionally involved in these sorts of delay-execute prospective memory tasks. These results clearly mirror the context effects in retrospective memory described earlier.

The Role of Attention

Thus far, we have avoided discussing in any detail our position on the debate of whether event-based prospective memory requires cue-focused effort and resources or whether there are circumstances in which cues can be detected automatically. Our position long ago was that it required resources (Marsh & Hicks, 1998), but we admit that all it would take is a single demonstration of automatic detection outside of the performance context (e.g., Einstein et al., 2005) to prove that a continuum

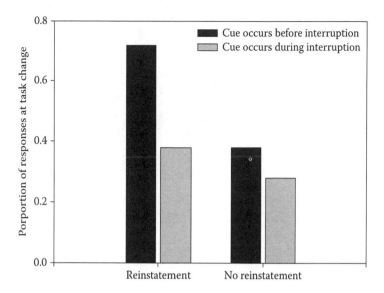

FIGURE 4.4 Proportion of delayed-execute responses as a function of whether the ongoing task was reinstated after the interruption (pairs of bars) and whether the cue occurred before or during the interrupting task (shading of bars).

of resources that depends on task conditions is probably the best depiction of the actual state of affairs. Nevertheless, we have been interested in what it means to be inside versus outside the performance context, as many of the previous sections in this chapter should make abundantly clear. We believe that in many cases being in the performance context changes people's attentional allocation policies away from the ongoing task and toward the prospective memory task, even if that latter task still remains only on the periphery of attention. So, we believe that attention is important and have not changed our opinion that event-based prospective memory lies squarely at the crossroads of memory and attention.

To show this in a novel way using a dependent measure other than reaction times, we gave different groups of participants various event-based intentions to be performed while studying a list of words to be learned for a later, unspecified memory test. Besides a no-intention control condition, we gave one group a categorical intention, a different group an intention about one specific cue, and a final group an intention about six specific cues. After learning, we tested their performance with a free recall test for the 40 studied items. These three groups of participants were compared to a condition that had no intention. Although a reader might quibble with our definition, we believe that based on the other results from our laboratory, this no-intention control group is essentially comparable to operating outside the performance context. At the outset, we had two alternative predictions for free recall performance. On the one hand, possessing an intention may increase the degree or quality of evaluating the words being studied and thereby improve free recall. On the other hand, the major interpretation lent to the preparatory attention and memory model by

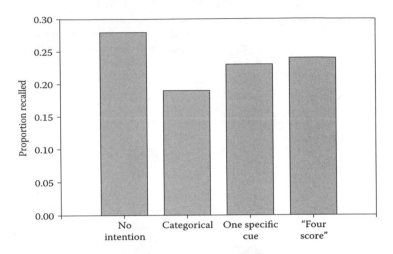

FIGURE 4.5 Free recall performance as a function of the intention being held during learning of the list.

R. E. Smith (2003) and others is that having an event-based intention interferes with other cognitive processes. By this account, free recall may be lower for the groups given an intention because it negatively impacts their learning strategies.

The results are summarized in Figure 4.5. In none of the conditions where an intention was given did participants actually find an event-based cue because none was placed in the study list, so that aspect of performance was constant. The first bar denotes free recall when no intention was given, or what we are essentially equating with being outside the performance interval (or context). The second bar represents performance for a group of 30 participants given the intention to respond to furniture words. (Incidentally, all of the conditions had a 4-minute distractor task intervene in between the prospective memory instruction and the commencement of the study phase and another distractor task after studying the words.) As the reader can see, free recall was lower by about 9% when participants held a categorical intention. Although not a dramatic effect, the decrement was statistically significant. A similar effect is seen with the specific intention to respond to the single, specific cue *desk*. Moreover, the same effect is found when participants were asked to respond to six specific cues coming from the first sentence of President Lincoln's Gettysburg Address (i.e., the words *four, score, seven, years, ago, today*). Statistically, all three conditions with intentions differ from the first, and the same is true by direct statistical contrast of the first control condition to the remaining three conditions.

Therefore, a variety of intentions disrupted the learning of the list. These results seem to stand in stark contrast to any claims that very sensitive measures such as response latencies are needed to find a task interference effect. Our interpretation of this outcome is that participants given the intentions altered their attentional allocation strategies, probably at intention formation, and decided to devote some resources to detecting the event-based cues. Because the 40 words were presented at a rate of one every 5 seconds, the entire list of words took only

3.33 minutes to present. We doubt that this is long enough to allow participants to adjust their attentional allocation strategies as they might in longer performance contexts (e.g., Einstein et al., 2005) where task interference grows smaller as the performance context lengthens. Consequently, if we had used longer lists, perhaps the free recall decrement would have been somewhat smaller.

Technically, the decrement in free recall from holding an intention about a single cue is inconsistent with Marsh et al.'s (2003) finding of no task interference to latencies from holding an intention to respond to the cue *dog* in a lexical decision task. One way to reconcile the inconsistency is to assume that latencies are not necessarily the most sensitive dependent measure for finding task interference from holding an intention. Speed in an ongoing task is determined by many factors, such as the nature of the items being processed. We used high-frequency words in our free recall task to observe a robust level of free recall that benefits from the formation of interitem associations during learning. We assume that the intention has disrupted the ability to form some of these interitem associations and consequently weakened overall learning of the 40-item list. Holding the same intention obviously did not affect lexical decision latency, but it does not necessarily have to if one assumes that latency is not necessarily the sine qua non in task interference research.

Because we have adopted a fairly liberal definition of the term *context* in this chapter (e.g., material-specific slowing with pictures and words), we mention one last experiment concerning the roles of attention and context that may have eluded some readers to date (Hicks, Cook, & Marsh, 2005). In that study, we manipulated the size of a perceptual cue that was either inside or outside the focus of attention for performing the ongoing task. More specifically, we gave participants a lexical decision task and on each trial a letter string appeared with a rectangular border around it. For the present purposes, the border was irrelevant to making the lexical decision and it represented a piece of background context information. One group of participants was given the intention to respond to red words and another group was given the intention to respond to a red border. The color red appeared only eight times and it was always on the prospective memory cue trial, whereas five other colors were used approximately equally often for the letter string and border. Participants given an intention about the border responded more often when the border was large (i.e., fat lines: 83%) than when the border was small (i.e., thin lines: 67%). Thus, manipulating the size of a cue in the periphery increased performance. By contrast, manipulating the size of the word, which is already in the focus of attention, had no consequent effect (all conditions in the neighborhood of 72%).

Therefore, if one defines context as what is in the focus of attention for successfully performing the ongoing task versus irrelevant to that task, then manipulations designed to attract attention in the periphery change performances but similar manipulations are unimportant for material already receiving focal processing. The important point of our free recall study, and the one just described, is that the role of attention in prospective memory tasks is not limited to simply measuring reaction time costs to an ongoing task. Admittedly, that was an outstanding place to start, but the field should neither be limited by that measure nor should it treat it as some kind of gold standard against which to evaluate direct attentional manipulations or other types of consequences of holding an intention on subsequent task performance.

We do not know how any of our results would have changed if we would have explicitly manipulated the relative importance of the prospective memory versus ongoing activity as others have done (Kliegel et al., 2001, 2004; R. E. Smith & Bayen, 2004). Much would hang in the balance of the type of intention given to participants. For example, specific cues that are in the focus of attention do not benefit from making the intention more important, whereas nonfocal cues (e.g., letters or syllables within words as the prospective memory cues) do tend to benefit from increasing the importance of the prospective task. We would assume that increasing the importance of intentions linked to specific contexts would increase the probability that these intentions influence both the frequency with which they come to mind when the correct context is encountered, as well as the attentional allocation policy in place when the new ongoing task is encountered. Whether an importance instruction would have exacerbated the free recall deficit is an empirical question that has yet to be determined. However, if an importance manipulation affects the attentional allocation policies as we suspect that it does, then making the study phase more important than cue detection should result in no recall deficit, and making the prospective task more important should result in a greater deficit than already observed (both compared to no explicit instruction at all).

MAJOR ISSUES AND FUTURE DIRECTIONS

The role that context information plays in retrospective memory has been acknowledged for the better part of a century. Consequently, we doubt that readers will be extraordinarily surprised that context information plays an important role in whether or not intentions are fulfilled. However, what we are surprised about is that the number of investigations directly related to the interaction of prospective memory with contextual information can be counted with less than the number of fingers on two hands. For those of us who study prospective memory because it is relevant to tangible, real-world phenomena in our everyday lives, we understand that our lives transpire in an ever-changing multitude of different contextual situations. The characteristics of the contexts surrounding intention formation, future contexts to which intentions may be associated, and the retrieval context itself are the three key variables that have not received enough attention to date. Therefore, studying these three characteristics, and their interactions, should be fruitful paths for researchers interested in studying prospective memory.

Consider the context of intention formation. We form intentions in a variety of places such as in our homes, in our offices, in our automobiles, and on the way through the front door of a grocery store (to name a few). Does the context at intention formation matter? We believe that it does, and we believe that McDaniel et al.'s (1998) room change experiment proves that it does. However, besides a match or a mismatch, everyday life brings with it more complicated situations. For example, suppose one forms the intention to ask one's secretary to perform a particular task. One could do that at home, in one's office, or in the presence of the cue itself, but the person is currently occupied, necessitating that the intention be formed. We do not know how these different contexts that differ in psychological distance to the cue would affect performance. Experiments are needed along these lines to ascertain whether our anecdote about returning to the room where one formed an intention indeed increases the probability of recollection. Further experiments are needed that go beyond the environmental context at encoding. There are a variety of internal contexts that, whether reinstated or not during a performance interval, may affect intention completion. One's mood or prevailing emotional state has not been investigated in any detail (but see Harris & Menzies, 1999). In unpublished work, we have tested obsessive-compulsive individuals and discovered that with an intention about neutral material they are disadvantaged in cue detection, but with an intention related to bodily fluids (e.g., *mucus* and *urine*) they are not. The idea there is that individuals with obsessive-compulsive disorder behave as cognitively distracted for material other than that related to their compulsion. Work along these lines with populations such as depressed and euphoric individuals may also fit a broader definition of what it means to form an intention in a variety of contexts.

The retrieval context has been studied in prospective memory, but in many cases the studies have been concerned with task load or difficulty of the ongoing task, and then that work is devoid of any appeal to the fact that the retrieval context is being manipulated. Perhaps those authors (including ourselves) thought that it was implicit, but our point is that making an explicit appeal to it as a context manipulation may help others see exciting new ways to pursue work in this area. For example, let us take a page out of the transfer-appropriate processing book. If one generates versus reads event-based cues during learning, will those cues be better detected if the generation versus reading processing is recapitulated at test? Granted this example manipulates both encoding and retrieval contexts, but our point is that there are many principles of retrospective memory in which context plays a role that have gone unstudied in prospective memory. Often memory for the retrieval context will be important later as our studies on the output monitoring component of event-based prospective memory demonstrate.

Some intentions are linked to specific contexts, whereas others are more decontextualized. We have already stated that we know of very little work comparing those sorts of intentions. Are intentions to return books to the library, this week, this afternoon, or right after lunch completed with different frequencies? Would a participant's intention to tell the experimenter his or her date of birth sometime during the experiment (but not right now) versus during debriefing (or a break) affect performance? When an intention is associated with a future context, do similar contexts also cause the intention to be retrieved? Are the task interference effects in which reaction time is slowed when holding an intention graded such that being in a similar context, but not the correct one, yields an intermediate degree of slowing? Or are the context effects on task interference all or none? We do not have answers to these questions, but we do believe that retrieval contexts will interact with how the intention was formed originally.

We understand that there may be finicky readers who do not appreciate our open-ended and quite liberal definition and usage of the term *context*. For this we make no apologies because we believe the abuse of the term will lead to more interesting articles on prospective memory that will bring those experiments external validity and improve our theoretical understandings of this important topic. To the finicky reader we say that we appreciate the definition of context as all things incidental to what is currently in the focus of attention. Our broader usage is necessarily imprecise because it must cover a multitude of heretofore unstudied variables. As we see it, there have been two major developments in the arena of event-based prospective memory recently, namely the multiprocess view (McDaniel et al., 2004) and the preparatory attention and memory model (R. E. Smith, 2003). All other contributions, including our own, should be considered fine pieces of incremental science. This section of each chapter in this volume was intended to provide the interested research scientist with some directions for future research. By construing context more broadly, we believe that a researcher new to this area can find some effect of interest in the retrospective memory literature and ask if the same or a similar effect applies to prospective memory. We have made a similar assertion in a different chapter that also contains many possible ideas for future research (Marsh et al., 2006a). Although we may have been unabashedly guilty for our liberal definition when writing about context effects in prospective memory, we do not feel that we can be faulted for our suggestion for how to perform good incremental science and we look forward to reading the work of any new investigators who we have managed to attract to this interesting and exciting field of inquiry.

REFERENCES

Abernathy, E. M. (1940). The effect of changed environmental conditions upon the results of college examinations. *Journal of Psychology, 10,* 293–301.

Bower, G. H. (1981). Mood and memory. *American Psychologist, 36,* 129–148.

Carr, H. A. (1925). *Psychology: A study of mental activity.* New York: Longmans, Green.

Ceci, S. J., & Bronfenbrenner, U. (1985). "Don't forget to take the cupcakes out of the oven": Prospective memory, strategic time-monitoring, and context. *Child Development, 56,* 152–164.

Cook, G.I., Marsh, R.L., Clark-Foos, A., & Meeks, J.T. (2007). Learning is impaired by activated intentions. *Psychonomic Bulletin & Review, 14,* 101–106.

Cook, G. I., Marsh, R. L., & Hicks, J. L. (2005). Associating a time-based prospective memory task with an expected context can improve or impair intention completion. *Applied Cognitive Psychology, 19,* 345–360.

Eich, E. (1989). Theoretical issues in state dependent memory. In H. L. Roediger & F. I. M. Craik (Eds.), *Varieties of memory and consciousness: Essays in honor of Endel Tulving* (pp. 331–354). Hillsdale, NJ: Lawrence Erlbaum Associates, Inc.

Einstein, G. O., & McDaniel, M. A. (1996). Retrieval processes in prospective memory: Theoretical approaches and some new empirical findings. In M. Brandimonte, G. O. Einstein, & M. A. McDaniel (Eds.), *Prospective memory: Theory and applications* (pp. 115–142). Hillsdale, NJ: Lawrence Erlbaum Associates, Inc.

Einstein, G. O., McDaniel, M. A., Manzi, M., Cochran, B., & Baker, M. (2000). Prospective memory and aging: Forgetting intentions over short delays. *Psychology & Aging, 12,* 671–683.

Einstein, G. O., & McDaniel, M. A., Thomas, R., Mayfield, S., Shank, H., Morrisette, N. et al. (2005). Multiple processes in prospective memory retrieval: Factors determining monitoring versus spontaneous retrieval. *Journal of Experimental Psychology: General, 134,* 327–342.

Einstein, G. O., McDaniel, M. A., Williford, C. L., Pagan, J. L., & Dismukes, R. K. (2003). Forgetting of intentions in demanding situations is rapid. *Journal of Experimental Psychology: Applied, 9,* 147–162.

Feingold, C. A. (1914). The influence of environment on identification for persons and things. *Journal of Criminal Law and Police Science, 5*, 39–51.

Godden, D. R., & Baddeley, A. D. (1975). Context dependent memory in two natural environments: On land and underwater. *British Journal of Psychology, 66*, 325–331.

Guynn, M. J. (2003). A two-process model of strategic monitoring in event-based prospective memory: Activation/retrieval mode and checking. *International Journal of Psychology, 38*, 245–256.

Harris, L. M., & Menzies, R. G. (1999). Mood and prospective memory. *Memory, 7*, 117–127.

Hertel, P. T. (1992). Emotion, mood and memory. In L. Squire (Ed.), *Encyclopedia of learning and memory* (pp. 157–161). New York: Macmillan.

Hicks, J. L., Cook, G. I., & Marsh, R. L. (2005). Detecting event-based prospective memory occurring within and outside the focus of attention. *American Journal of Psychology, 118*, 1–11.

Kliegel, M., Martin, M., McDaniel, M. A., & Einstein, G. O. (2001). Varying the importance of a prospective memory task: Differential effects across time- and event-based prospective memory. *Memory, 9*, 1–11.

Kliegel, M., Martin, M., McDaniel, M. A., & Einstein, G. O. (2004). Importance effects on performance in event-based prospective memory tasks. *Memory, 12*, 553–561.

Light, L. L., & Carter-Sobell, L. (1970). Effects of changed semantic context on recognition memory. *Journal of Verbal Learning and Verbal Behavior, 9*, 1–11.

Marsh, R. L., Cook, G. I., & Hicks, J. L. (2006a). An analysis of prospective memory. In B. H. Ross (Ed.), *Psychology of learning and motivation* (pp. 115–153). San Diego, CA: Elsevier Academic.

Marsh, R. L., Cook, G. I., & Hicks, J. L. (2006b). Task interference from event-based intentions can be material specific. *Memory & Cognition*.

Marsh, R. L., & Hicks, J. L. (1998). Event-based prospective memory and executive control of working memory. *Journal of Experimental Psychology: Learning, Memory, and Cognition, 24*, 336–349.

Marsh, R. L., Hicks, J. L., & Cook, G. I. (2005). On the relationship between effort toward an ongoing task and cue detection in event-based prospective memory. *Journal of Experimental Psychology: Learning, Memory, and Cognition, 31*, 68–75.

Marsh, R. L., Hicks, J. L., & Cook, G. I. (2006). Task interference from prospective memories covaries with contextual associations of fulfilling them. *Memory & Cognition, 34*, 1037–1045.

Marsh, R. L., Hicks, J. L., & Cook, G. I. (unpublished). *On the interaction between intention specificity and the format of retrieval cues in event-based prospective memory.* Unpublished manuscript.

Marsh, R. L., Hicks, J. L., Cook, G. I., Hansen, J. S., & Pallos, A. L. (2003). Interference to ongoing activities covaries with the characteristics of an event-based intention. *Journal of Experimental Psychology: Learning, Memory, and Cognition, 29*, 861–870.

Marsh, R. L., Hicks, J. L., Cook, G. I., & Mayhorn, C. B. (2007). Comparing older and younger adults in an event-based prospective memory paradigm containing an output monitoring component. *Aging, Neuropsychology, & Cognition, 14*, 168–188.

Marsh, R. L., Hicks, J. L., & Hancock, T. W. (2000). On the interaction of ongoing cognitive activity and the nature of an event-based intention. *Applied Cognitive Psychology, 14*, S29–S42.

Marsh, R. L., Hicks, J. L., Hancock, T. W., & Munsayac, K. (2002). Investigating the output monitoring component of event-based prospective memory performance. *Memory & Cognition, 30*, 302–311.

Marsh, R. L., Hicks, J. L., & Watson, V. (2002). The dynamics of intention retrieval and coordination of action in event-based prospective memory. *Journal of Experimental Psychology: Learning, Memory, and Cognition, 28*, 652–659.

Maylor, E. A., Darby, R. J., Logie, R. H., Della Sala, S., & Smith, G. (2002). Prospective memory across the lifespan. In P. Graf & N. Ohta (Eds.), *Lifespan development of human memory* (pp. 235–256). Cambridge, MA: MIT Press.

McDaniel, M. A., & Einstein, G. O. (1993). The importance of cue familiarity and cue distinctiveness in prospective memory. *Memory, 1,* 23–41.

McDaniel, M. A., Einstein, G. O., Graham, T., & Rall, E. (2004). Delaying execution of intentions: Overcoming the costs of interruptions. *Applied Cognitive Psychology, 18,* 553–561.

McDaniel, M. A., Einstein, G. O., Stout, A. C., & Morgan, Z. (2003). Aging and maintaining intentions over delays: Do it or lose it. *Psychology & Aging, 18,* 823–835.

McDaniel, M. A., Guynn, M. J., Einstein, G. O., & Breneiser, J. (2004). Cue-focused and reflexive-associative processes in prospective memory retrieval. *Journal of Experimental Psychology: Learning, Memory, and Cognition, 30,* 605–614.

McDaniel, M. A., Robinson-Riegler, B., & Einstein, G. O. (1998). Prospective remembering: Perceptually driven or conceptually driven processes? *Memory & Cognition, 26,* 121–134.

McGann, D., Ellis, J. A., & Milne, A. (2002). Conceptual and perceptual processes in prospective remembering. *European Journal of Cognitive Psychology, 15,* 19–41.

McGann, D., Ellis, J. A., & Milne, A. (2003). Conceptual and perceptual processes in prospective remembering: Differential influence of attentional resources. *Memory & Cognition, 30,* 1021–1032.

Meier, B., & Graf, P. (2000). Transfer appropriate processing for prospective memory tests. *Applied Cognitive Psychology, 14,* S11–S27.

Morris, C. D., Bransford, J. D., & Franks, J. J. (1977). Levels of processing versus transfer appropriate processing. *Journal of Verbal Learning and Verbal Behavior, 16,* 519–533.

Nowinski, J. L., & Dismukes, R. K. (2005). Effects of ongoing task context and target typicality on prospective memory: The importance of associative cuing. *Memory, 13,* 649–657.

Sellen, A. J., Louie, G., Harris, J. E., & Wilkins, A. J. (1997). What brings intentions to mind? An *in situ* study of prospective memory. *Memory, 5,* 483–507.

Smith, R. E. (2003). The cost of remembering to remember in event-based prospective memory: Investigating the capacity demands of delayed intention performance. *Journal of Experimental Psychology: Learning, Memory, and Cognition, 29,* 347–361.

Smith, R. E., & Bayen, U. (2004). A multinomial model of prospective memory. *Journal of Experimental Psychology: Learning, Memory, and Cognition, 30,* 756–777.

Smith, S. M., & Vela, E. (2001). Environmental context-dependent memory: A review and meta-analysis. *Psychonomic Bulletin & Review, 8,* 203–220.

Taylor, R. S., Marsh, R. L., Hicks, J. L., & Hancock, T. W. (2004). The influence of partial-match cues on event-based prospective memory. *Memory, 12,* 203–213.

Teasdale, J. D., & Russell, M. L. (1983). Differential effects of induced mood on the recall of positive, negative and neutral words. *British Journal of Clinical Psychology, 22,* 163–171.

West, R., & Craik, F. I. M. (1999). Age-related decline in prospective memory: The roles of cue accessibility and cue sensitivity. *Psychology & Aging, 14,* 264–272.

West, R., & Craik, F. I. M. (2001). Influences on the efficiency of prospective memory in younger and older adults. *Psychology & Aging, 16,* 682–696.

West, R., Wymbs, N., Jakubek, K., & Herndon, R. W. (2003). Effects of intention load and background context on prospective remembering: An event-related brain potential study. *Psychophysiology, 40,* 260–276.

Wickens, D. D. (1987). The dual meanings of context: Implications for research, theory, and applications. In D. S. Gorfein & R. R. Hoffman (Eds.), *Memory and learning: The Ebbinghaus centennial conference.* (pp. 135–152). Hillsdale, NJ: Lawrence Erlbaum Associates, Inc.

5

Commentary
Theories of Prospective Memory

CHRISTOPHER HERTZOG

School of Psychology
Georgia Institute of Technology

*I*t is a privilege and a pleasure to be able to comment on the excellent set of chapters regarding theoretical perspectives on prospective memory for this volume. I have organized the commentary as follows. First, I share an anecdote about a prospective memory failure I recently experienced as I was working on this commentary. Then, I provide specific comments in chapters 1, 2, 3, and 4. Finally, I return to several general themes raised by the comments on each chapter, and raise some issues and possible directions for the future of prospective memory theory and research.

THE ANECDOTE

I was driving into work recently, preparing to run two errands on my way. First, I planned on stopping at the post office to mail a package and to buy some stamps. The post office is fairly close to my house, less than a mile away. Second, I planned on stopping at the cleaners and picking up some dry cleaning. The dry cleaner I use is about half a mile off my usual route to work, and roughly two thirds of the way to the office from my home in Atlanta. To complete that errand I needed to turn off my usual route to work, go to the cleaners, and then double back to the route to work.

I completed the errand at the post office, got in the car, and pulled the red dry cleaning receipt out of the glove compartment and placed it on the passenger seat in the car. I assumed the act of doing this would aid me in remembering to go to the dry cleaners. I am aware of the research on implementation intentions and prospective memory (e.g., Chasteen, Park, & Schwarz, 2001) and had read Ellis and Freeman's chapter discussing such effects just a few days before. My belief was that if I clearly thought about the need to turn to go to the dry cleaners, I would do so, and that the act of pulling out the receipt would both reinforce the intention and provide a cue. (Perhaps I should have pasted it to the window!) I thought about the route I would need to take: Turn off of North Avenue onto Monroe Boulevard. This was the implementation intention. Make the turn onto Monroe and proceed to the dry cleaners. I then set off down the road. The route would take me about 10 minutes to reach my right turn. While on North Avenue, I was engaged in thinking about this commentary. I was late in submitting it, partly because of chronic overcommitment and a hectic life of late and partly because I was struggling with how to frame the commentary. As I drove along, thinking about the chapter by Melissa Guynn I had just read and what I would want to say about it, I drove through the Monroe intersection, the turn I needed to make to go to the dry cleaner. Two intersections later, I realized that I had indeed missed the turn. This realization came over me suddenly, without any apparent prompting by an environmental cue, although it could have been prompted by seeing the traffic light and recognizing it as one already past Monroe. (Regarding the dry cleaning receipt, I had not looked down at the passenger seat at any point.) After about one more block of hearty laughter at myself, I changed my plans. Instead of retracing my steps, more or less, and spending an extra several minutes en route, I resolved to pick up the dry cleaning on the way home, even though this would require me to leave work earlier than I had wanted to so I could get there before they closed. I would rearrange one appointment and plan on working more at home that evening. At the end of my day, I did exactly that, and picked up the dry cleaning.

This kind of experience is one we have all had, and in fact, these are far from rare events. Some of us absent-minded professors experience it more than others. Some might claim that this kind of prospective forgetting increases as we get older, and would attribute this failure to my advancing age. Indeed, research I have done suggests that people of all ages believe that prospective memory declines as we get older (Lineweaver & Hertzog, 1998). Actually, like most of us, I suspect, I have had such incidents of forgetting throughout my adult life, and I have not experienced these kinds of events as being more frequent in recent years. However, I cannot rule out that explanation. For one thing, I do not systematically record my memory failures (for an interesting report of such errors, including prospective memory errors, see Herrmann, Gruneberg, Fiore, Schooler, & Torres, 2006). Moreover, I often use external aids and specific strategies to try to avoid such errors, and this behavior has certainly increased as I have gotten older (e.g., Intons-Peterson & Fournier, 1986). Perhaps these strivings represent a kind of age-related compensatory behavior for perceived memory problems (e.g., de Frias, Dixon, & Bäckman, 2003) that keeps the rates of forgetting steady despite age-related increases in the risk of unaided prospective forgetting. The more important question is this: What is the process by which such forgetting occurs, in general, and in this specific instance? As I reflected on it, it occurred to me that this specific act of forgetting was relevant to some of the theoretical arguments I comment on, if only as a vehicle for me to frame my thinking about them. I return to this anecdote as I discuss each of the chapters, asking how their theoretical perspectives would account for the event.

INTRODUCTORY COMMENTS

One feature that all of these chapters share is a focus on experimental approaches to understanding prospective memory. Prospective memory research started out, more or less, being grounded in the observational literature reported by practical memory researchers (e.g., Morris, 1992). The kind of anecdote I just recounted might be a datum in early prospective memory studies that used diary methods to study prospective remembering and forgetting. Other studies used techniques like asking individuals to call the laboratory at specific days and times, and observing whether they did so. Research on prospective memory changed radically when Einstein and McDaniel (1990) published their experiments that simulated prospective memory in a laboratory task. Now, more than 15 years later, the field is dominated by experiments studying prospective memory using a variety of experimental tasks, manipulating conditions that may lower or elevate the probability of prospective memory errors. The first four chapters review different aspects of that literature and make claims about the origins of prospective memory errors. Usually, the experimental task environment is a dual-task condition in which the primary task, or the ongoing task, requires discriminations that place demands on attention and memory. The prospective task is the secondary task, which differs from prototypical secondary tasks in that prospective cues are relatively infrequent events. I return to this point later. The more important point is that the field has moved into modified dual-task paradigms as ways of experimentally evaluating the mechanisms that govern prospective remembering.

By definition, in essence, prospective memory is remembering to perform an intended act at an appropriate time and place when enactment must be delayed. The different chapters in this section all accept, in principle, that there are multiple stages of processing required in situations demanding prospective remembering, including the creation of an intention to act, along with conditions for enactment, maintenance of that intention over some delay period, retrieval of the intention at a time and place appropriate for action, and then action. All the authors are essentially in agreement that the "plan of action," as Smith calls it, is not actively held in working memory during the delay interval between the formation of the intention to act and the opportunity for enactment. Instead, typically, attention is occupied with other events and planned actions during the delay. The chapters differ in some important respects about the mechanisms underlying processing at different stages, however, both in terms of key variables in their theoretical accounts and in the role different mechanisms play in prospective memory. In particular, the issue of how the plan of action is reactivated in the appropriate context, enabling successful remembering and fulfillment of intent through action, is a point of diverging emphases, if not conflicting views.

ELLIS AND FREEMAN'S CHAPTER

Ellis and Freeman (chap. 1, this volume) provide an admirable review of recent developments in prospective memory, highlighting in part their own work on the intention superiority effect, motivation (task importance), and individual differences that may influence prospective remembering. Ellis and Freeman do an excellent job in framing prospective memory in terms of the types of executive control mechanisms that may be critical for successful intention representation and retrieval in the context of an ongoing task. I particularly appreciate their arguments that the intention superiority effect does not necessarily imply a lack of strategic processing, and that output monitoring is an important mechanism mediating the intention completion effect. Output monitoring can be considered a type of metacognition. It could be highly beneficial if perspectives from metacognition for retrospective memory (where issues of monitoring with and without awareness have been widely considered; see Reder, 1996) were brought into the arena of prospective memory (see, as modest examples, Kidder, Park, Hertzog, & Morrell, 1997; Reese & Cherry, 2002). Ellis and colleagues' work on action superiority, both in terms of intention superiority and in terms of creating a mismatch between encoded intentions and the act embodied in the intention, is both clever and important.

Ellis and Freeman provide an excellent and critical discussion of the literature on implementation intentions and successful prospective remembering. As they point out, a number of manipulations can be employed at encoding to increase the probability that a delayed intention will be realized (e.g., visualized enactment). From this point of view, my prospective memory failure may have occurred because, although I did create an implementation intention at the post office, it was represented in abstract propositional form (turn right on Monroe to go the cleaners) rather than visualized as an action (see the intersection and what it looks like, imagine turning to proceed to the cleaners). Planning did indeed occur, but perhaps not in a form that would maximize the likelihood of intention retrieval at the propitious moment (see also Maylor, 1996).

Finally, Ellis and Freeman's wonderful review of the controversy between the preparatory attention view and the multiprocess view bears reading and rereading (see my further commentary on this topic in the next section). The apparent contradiction between results from Marsh, Hicks, and Cook (2005) and McGann, Ellis, and Milne (2002) is also a wonderful example of how puzzling through apparent inconsistencies can lead to new insights, new experiments, and progress in the field.

SMITH'S CHAPTER

Smith's chapter (chap. 2, this volume) builds off of her recent line of work, principally with Bayen, indicating that there is a cost of a prospective memory instruction embedded in an ongoing task. In Smith (2003), the ongoing task was a lexical decision task, but the phenomena that she and her colleagues have replicated was with other ongoing tasks. Smith and colleagues have shown that being under prospective memory instructions slows performance on the ongoing task (e.g., slower correct lexical decision times). Smith argues that this effect implicates allocation of attentional resources to words to determine whether they are indeed prospective cues. In essence, being in prospective performance mode has costs due to the need to monitor words for event-based cues.

Smith argues that prospective memory requires preparatory attentional processing, and that this preparation stage is "likely in the focus of attention." She further argues that this requires allocation of limited cognitive resources to evaluating the environmental events to determine whether they satisfy the requirements for action embodied in the intent. She argues that reinstatement of processes that occurred at encoding, as in the transfer-appropriate-processing hypothesis, must lead to the retrieval context matching the encoding context, leading to retrieval of the intention. Preparatory processing is not required continuously during the delay, but must occur prior to encountering an environmental cue for a prospective action so that the intent and plan of action may be retrieved and acted on.

Certainly, the available evidence suggests that being in a prospective memory task has costs, in terms of performance of the primary or ongoing task. However, Smith's theory requires not merely that there are costs, but that these costs reflect the operation of preparatory attentional processes, without which one would fail to act. Smith cites her multinomial modeling work with Bayen as indicating that variables such as working memory capacity influence prospective memory and measures of preparatory attentional processing (ongoing task costs).

Obviously, Smith's explanation of my prospective memory failure, described earlier, would simply be that I did not prepare to recognize the intersection I needed to turn at prior to arriving at it. Because of this, I did not recognize the street sign, the buildings, and other cues that would have shown me I had arrived at Monroe and a right turn was required.

Smith is currently engaged in a debate with Einstein and McDaniel regarding whether prospective memory requires allocation of attentional resources to prepare for event-cue processing (e.g., McDaniel, Einstein, & Rendell, chap. 7, this volume). Those authors have offered a multiprocess model of prospective memory (McDaniel & Einstein, 2000) emphasizing that cue detection can proceed by relatively automatic (and resource-free) recognition of event cues. The multiprocess view would state that my failure to go the dry cleaners could be attributed to one or more of several processes. Let's focus on the spontaneous cuing mechanism. There were several available prospective cues in my environment (the receipt, the traffic sign at Monroe), all of which could have cued me without being in a preparatory monitoring mode, had I only looked at them. Or, as I was thinking about the Guynn chapter, successful retrieval of the action intention could have been triggered simply by spreading activation from the topic of event-based prospective memory to the intention I had stored in memory.

The possibility of spontaneous cuing of intention retrieval is anathema to Smith's obligatory preparatory attentional account. To counter claims of spontaneous cuing without attention allocation, Smith cites new research conducted with Hunt. They created prospective cues that were highly salient and distinctive, satisfying conditions she claims should lead to automatic cue detection, if it can actually occur. They detected costs of prospective memory instructions on the ongoing task in this condition as well, leading Smith to argue against automatic cue detection. She also cites a number of potential issues with studies showing no costs (and hence indirectly claiming spontaneous retrieval), including (a) low statistical power to detect costs, and (b) use of within-subjects manipulations that do not include a between-subject control, thereby underestimating processing costs.

Certainly, I am sympathetic to this argument, because my own work with Park and colleagues (Kidder et al., 1997; Park, Hertzog, Kidder, Morrell, & Mayhorn, 1997) showed exactly the pattern of ongoing task costs that Smith is describing: A between-subject control showed substantial practice benefits on the ongoing task, meaning that the no-prospective memory control group was needed to gain an accurate estimate of costs on the ongoing task. And we found such costs. We also produced evidence that the costs increased with the number of different prospective events individuals were monitoring (Kidder et al., 1997). Smith would probably explain this effect as evidence of a graded attentional resource demand. Power and precision are certainly known to be issues in event-based prospective memory tasks. If one increases the frequency of events in the direction of a more traditional secondary task context, then the intention could be argued to be in constant production mode, with attention continuously allocated to it. However, studying infrequent events can produce misleading results due to a lack of precision in the dependent variable.

I have no appetite for trying to referee this debate, but I comment on it briefly. In fact, I have little to say about the specifics of the arguments that Ellis and Freeman have not said in their chapter's incisive treatment of the controversy. I merely add a couple of general points. First, such arguments are healthy and a very good sign for the field of prospective memory. Most of the time when such debates occur, the opposing viewpoints are both correct in certain critical aspects, and resolution (if it is ever found), usually involves an integration of the two perspectives. In this case Einstein and McDaniel are arguing that both preparatory attention and automatic cue detection mechanisms operate (among others), whereas Smith contends successful prospective memory inevitably requires allocation of resources to event cue detection. Einstein and McDaniel have already opted for integration, and Smith demurs. It is useful to have a strong theoretical position like Smith's in play, and to have a full discussion of the results that are pertinent to each viewpoint. It will inevitably lead to better experiments and more critical thinking.

Having said that, it is important to recognize that such arguments are rarely, if ever, resolved by critical experiments in the muddy scientific waters that are experimental cognitive psychology. On the one hand, the structure of the arguments does not necessarily afford critical experimental tests. Smith argues, for example, that preparatory attention is not always evoked (but must be for successful prospective remembering), and that it is not necessarily accessible to awareness, even when it is operating. So awareness cannot be, by this argument, a criterion for attention allocation. On the other hand, interpretation of empirical results depends on a number of auxiliary assumptions in both cases, and these assumptions are difficult to disentangle from the tests themselves. It is difficult to prove that automatic cue detection has not occurred, because the costs Smith bases her study on are at best indirect measures of resource allocation. Costs could occur, even when they are not central to event cue detection per se. Likewise, it will be difficult to prove that there has been no preparatory allocation of attention, because there is no direct behavioral measure of that mechanism. Here, use of ancillary measures, such as evoked potentials, as in work by West and colleagues, might be helpful in showing preparatory attention (e.g., West, Krompinger, & Bowry, 2005). Even then, however, showing evidence of controlled attention allocation during a given prospective memory task context does not imply it occurs in all task settings.

In fact, what we might be observing here is the inevitable consequence of designing prospective memory tasks as dual-task paradigms that can be carried out in a single lab session. It could be the dark side of a move to controlled experiments as a way of assessing event-based prospective memory. As Smith points out, "One of the complications for studying prospective memory in a controlled setting is how to provide an appropriate analog task, within a controlled setting and relatively short time frame, to real-world prospective memory tasks in which an intention may be formed far in advance of the time at which an action can be performed" (p. 6). It is not clear to me that the types of event-based tasks discussed at length in these chapters have external validity to a variety of contexts in which successful prospective memory must occur (e.g., my failure to pick up the laundry). Smith's demonstration of ongoing task costs with highly salient cues that could afford automatic cue detection may simply imply that participants in laboratory dual task contexts maintain an activated preparatory response set over long periods of time, especially when they remain in the laboratory testing context. It might not signify that it is a necessary condition for event cue detection.

GUYNN'S CHAPTER

Guynn (chap. 3, this volume) builds a case for the existence of a retrieval mode for prospective memory, in which one must be, in effect, prepared to retrieve intentions to act at the appropriate time and place. Certainly, the idea that individuals must have an activated prospective response set makes sense. Furthermore, Guynn's arguments about the potential importance of models of the central executive (she cites in particular Shallice and Burgess's [1991] supervisory attentional system model) and the possible relevance of the task-switching literature resonate with my perspective. As Guynn notes, there is good evidence of global switch costs (the overhead created by the need to monitor the environment for signals to switch processing algorithms) and the local cost of actually making a shift. The relevance of this literature to both Guynn's arguments about a retrieval mode and Smith's claim of preparatory attention is obvious. What is not obvious is whether the retrieval mode Guynn cites is actually distinct from preparatory attention. Guynn claims the mechanisms are complementary, that controlled attention is not required to be in a retrieval mode, and that could well be true. However, research directly addressing this issue is needed. I do not attempt to methodologically deconstruct Guynn's experimental evidence; she does a reasonable job herself in identifying several of the potential issues involved. I would simply say that more evidence for the retrieval mode as a Tulving-style retrieval mode in prospective memory is still needed.

Guynn's perspective might explain my prospective lapse in terms of the degree of absorption in the ongoing task, combined with the secondary load of automated driving. It is well known that individuals can drive and think about something else at the same time, often without apparent costs for normal driving, but with potential costs for recruitment of attention in emergency situations (Strayer, Drews, & Johnston, 2003). However, when one is thinking and driving, both the central executive and ancillary processing modules relevant to intention retrieval may be fully engaged, preventing establishment of a retrieval mode. Under these circumstances, event-based prospective cues may be noticed as such, but their processing does not elicit retrieval of the intention to turn on to the appropriate street. Notice that this account may have something in common with the perspective of Jacoby and his colleagues regarding mechanisms of habit versus recollection in creating retrospective memory errors (e.g., Jacoby, 1999). Given that I was engaged in the habitual behavior of driving to work, recollection of the intention to turn could have been triggered by recognizing the appropriate intersection. However, perhaps a retrieval mode must be activated for that triggering to occur. Absent that, one remains in a relatively automated state, recognizing familiar streets and scenes as they pass by, but without a high probability of detecting the event cue when it occurs.

MARSH, HICKS, AND COOK'S CHAPTER

Marsh, Hicks, and Cook (chap. 4, this volume) are far too modest when they imply, at the end of their wonderful chapter, that they are merely doing incremental science after the contributions of Einstein and McDaniel, on the one hand, and Smith on the other. Their research beautifully illustrates the importance of continued development and elaboration of theoretical accounts of how event-based cues are processed, in their situational context. We need a theory of cue processing that explains the differential probability of intention retrieval, and Marsh et al. take major steps in the right direction.

First, their work on phases of task context clearly shows that individuals do use instruction-based expectations about probabilities of events to turn on and off preparatory attention and cue monitoring mechanisms. Second, their work also demonstrates nicely that it is how cues are interpreted in context that determines whether they are noticed and lead to the intended action. These interpretations can be created at the time of intention formation, in terms of expectancies for when appropriate cues will appear and how they will be manifested. Marsh et al. invoke the concept of transfer-appropriate processing (see also Smith's chapter on this point); namely, that effective cue detection requires a match between processing at the time of encoding (intention formation) and at the time of event occurrence for intention retrieval to be successful. The notion that cues may be noticed and processed but not trigger intention retrieval, because they occur at unexpected times or because their processing does not focus on the critical aspects that defined the expected manifestation of the cue, is a critical insight.

Marsh et al.'s perspective suggests that my prospective failure might not have occurred because I failed to notice that I was approaching Monroe, but rather, because I was processing that information in the context of driving toward and through intersections rather than processing the features of the intersection that would have cued me to the fact that this was, indeed, the street where I needed to turn. Indeed, even if I had taped the laundry receipt to the window, I might have been so engaged in looking around it at the traffic through my windshield that I would not have processed it as an event cue (or anything other than an obstacle to vision that must be ignored) during the critical time of approaching the intersection.

Note that Marsh et al.'s account suggests that cue detection is not merely a by-product of where one's attention is focused. McDaniel, Guynn, Einstein, and Breneiser (2004) showed that cue recognition and intention retrieval are more likely when the cue is processed in focal attention, as opposed to when the task requires a shift of attention to other information. This finding makes perfect sense, because detecting a stimulus as an event cue has a higher probability when one is attending to it than when one is not, and is even more likely when the dimension of information being extracted from the cue is relevant to the intention–cue association as originally encoded. Apparently, however, the focus of attention itself cannot fully account for prospective cue effectiveness. Marsh et al. demonstrate that there is a gradient of probability that focally processed cues will trigger intention retrieval (see also Mäntylä, 1994, and Penningroth, 2005, who showed that the typicality of a focally processed category cue influences whether it will trigger a prospective response). What is critically important about Marsh et al.'s approach is that they begin to lay out for us the wealth of variables that can influence how cues are effectively and ineffectively processed to achieve prospective remembering.

GENERAL REMARKS AND CONCLUSION

This excellent set of chapters does an admirable job of sketching the current state of prospective memory theory, pointing to opportunities for further advancement. What is truly remarkable about them, as a set, is that the authors have clearly read and considered each other's work and perspectives. The result is a great deal of commonality in treatment, yet important differences in perspective.

In the remaining space I have, I would like to raise two sets of issues for future consideration. First, although I agree with Marsh et al. regarding the value of grounding prospective memory research in theory and method derived from memory research in general, I would claim that new advances in experimental approaches toward prospective memory research also require more careful explication of theoretical concepts like limited central resources, attentional resources, and the central executive. The chapters by Guynn and Ellis and Freeman do this to an extent, but more work is probably required (see also Burgess et al., chap. 11, this volume). The central executive, its constituent processes and mechanisms, and the degree to which operations of the central executive require awareness and controlled attention are a focus of current research in areas such as working memory and attention (e.g., Engle & Kane, 2004; Miyake et al., 2000). New neurologically grounded models of cognitive control mechanisms are emerging (e.g., Braver & Barch, 2002; Buckner, 2003; O'Reilly & Frank, 2006) that are relevant to ways one should conceptualize issues such as preparatory attention sets in the larger context of the multiple pathways by which we achieve cognitive control, including over memory and memory retrieval. These theoretical models have great promise for assisting prospective memory researchers to conceptualize how attentional and response sets may operate, both within and outside phenomenal awareness. Ultimately, they may be critical for further leverage on the debate between proponents of automatic detection of event-based cues versus proponents of resource-demanding preparation for cue detection.

From a methodological point of view, the existing literature on attention allocation in dual-task paradigms may have something important to offer prospective memory researchers. Attention research in the 1970s and 1980s put a great deal of emphasis on the problems of scaling dual-task performance in terms of relative emphasis on primary and secondary tasks, using so-called performance operating characteristics (POCs; e.g., Navon & Gopher, 1979; Norman & Bobrow, 1975). Progress in prospective memory research may require a more explicit way of evaluating and controlling for the degree to which participants in event-based experimental tasks emphasize the monitoring and attentional preparation for prospective events, on the one hand, relative to optimal performance on the ongoing (primary) task, on the other hand. Studies that explicitly manipulate relative emphasis through the use of incentives, instructions, and other independent variables may be needed to address critical questions, including whether event-based cues can be detected without preparatory attention. The work by Kliegel and colleagues (e.g., Kliegel, Martin, McDaniel, & Einstein, 2004) on the importance of the task is a laudable effort in this direction (see also Ellis & Freeman, chap. 1, this volume). There are formidable measurement issues here, and these issues probably contributed to attention researchers moving away from POC estimation to other research questions without fully resolving the attending problems. Nevertheless, more explicit effort to conceptualize how people set criteria for emphasis of the ongoing task and the prospective memory task is needed.

Such an approach might also be necessary to evaluate individual differences, including age differences, in prospective memory performance. When Park et al. (1997) found age differences in event-based prospective memory, Einstein and colleagues (e.g., Einstein, Smith, McDaniel, & Shaw, 1997) argued that the difficult ongoing task strained the attentional resources of older adults, producing an apparent age deficit in prospective memory. Instead, the argument went, the observed difference was due to age differences in available cognitive resources, which constrained older adults' ability to monitor event-based cues. In other words, the observed age differences in prospective memory were an artifact of the resource demands on older adults (at the time, Einstein and McDaniel were conceptually committed to the claim that there were no age differences in event-based prospective memory, a position that has softened over the years). Adjusting the ongoing task difficulty to make the ongoing task more difficult can eliminate age differences in event-based prospective memory, even in the type of nonfocal cuing task used by Park et al. (1997; see Bastin & Meulemans, (2002). Logie, Maylor, Della Salla, and Smith (2004) reported that age differences in prospective memory were found only in a high working-memory demanding condition; such findings indicate that attentional load or working memory constraints may influence age differences, but the jury is out on how to find the right point of between-groups comparison when there are age differences in attention and working memory resources.

However, the earlier literature on POCs in dual tasks suggests another, more fundamental problem in a dual-task environment. Attempts to equate on the difficulty of the primary task are problematic if one does not conjointly manipulate relative emphasis on both elements of the dual task (in our case, the ongoing task and the prospective task). Data we collected (Kidder et al., 1997) suggested older adults were putting more emphasis on the prospective task than younger adults. Moreover, one can argue that if the differential resource demand hypothesis is to be properly tested, any adjustments of task difficulty cannot merely be made at the group level, but should be calibrated at the level of individual participants. Otherwise, individual differences in available resources will cause some persons within an age group to be severely taxed, whereas others might not be taxed. Variance due to individual differences is almost always much greater than variance due to systematic age differences. Given that consensus is emerging on the importance of attentional mechanisms for event-based prospective memory, more heroic attention to task demands and relative task emphases may be required for an optimal test of age differences in event-based prospective memory.

The second major point that needs to be made is that it is important that prospective memory researchers take lessons learned from laboratory tasks and test their importance in accounting for prospective remembering and forgetting in the natural ecology. The types of experimental task paradigms used to study time-based and event-based prospective memory might do a poor job of simulating actual prospective memory performance. In everyday life a whole new set of variables operate that can lead to excellent everyday prospective memory even when the underlying mechanisms of prospective memory, as measured by laboratory tasks, would predict otherwise. For example, Park and colleagues (Park et al., 1999) studied individual differences in remembering to take medications, a prototypic prospective memory task. We measured actual medication adherence in the ecology through the use of pill bottles with electronic caps that could record when the bottles were opened. Our sample was a group of rheumatoid arthritis patients, varying from young adulthood through old age. Our original expectation was that we would see large age differences in prospective memory performance, given cognitive declines that accompany normal aging. It is well known, for example, that older adults are impaired in a variety of dual-task situations (see Salthouse, 1991). We did find age differences, but with older adults actually doing somewhat better in their medication adherence. When we adjusted for performance on a set of abilities, including working memory and reasoning, the positive age differences increased. This finding suggested that the older arthritis patients were using strategies for remembering to take medication that, in effect, took the cognition out of prospective memory. We also found that other personal characteristics of individuals, such as self-reported level of daily life demands and the use of routines to structure everyday life, predicted future medication adherence, controlling on cognitive ability.

Findings that older adults perform well on everyday prospective memory tasks are not new (e.g., West, 1988). What was important here was that they performed well in actual medication adherence in everyday life. Moreover, their reports of past difficulty or success in remembering to take the medications, elicited in an intake interview, successfully predicted later levels of medication adherence (Hertzog, Park, Morrell, & Martin, 2000). When individuals had difficulty remembering to take medications they were apparently aware of that fact, and these difficulties were consistent over time. Other work by Park and colleagues does suggest adherence problems in other populations of older adults (e.g., hypertensives; Morrell, Park, Kidder, & Martin, 1997) who are taking medications that may be easier to forget than medication to protect against rheumatoid inflammation, which punishes the patient with pain when a medication is forgotten. Nevertheless, the point remains that individuals often show better performance in the actual ecology than would be expected based on laboratory task performance. Laboratory research on prospective memory tasks might tell us much about underlying mechanisms for unsupported prospective memory, but it might not tell us much at all about the mechanisms that matter for successful prospective remembering in everyday life, including the kinds of compensatory behaviors I alluded to earlier in this chapter. An exciting prospect is that the types of mechanisms discussed in these chapters operate in both the laboratory and real life, but are conditional on the characteristics of particular person–context conjunctions—when individuals face prospective memory challenges in certain situations while behaving in specific ways (see Rendell & Craik, 2000, for a step in this direction). Such issues remain a topic for further research, and it would indeed be exciting to see this kind of thinking emerge more fully in empirical prospective memory research in the upcoming years.

REFERENCES

Bastin, C., & Meulemans, T. (2002). Are time-based and event-based prospective memory affected by normal aging in the same way? *Current Psychology Letters: Behaviour, Brain, and Cognition, 7,* 105–121.

Braver, T. S., & Barch, D. M. (2002). A theory of cognitive control, aging cognition, and neuromodulation. *Neuroscience and Biobehavioral Reviews, 26,* 809–817.

Buckner, R. L. (2003). Functional-anatomic correlates of control processes in memory. *Journal of Neuroscience, 23,* 3999–4004.

Chasteen, A. L., Park, D. C., & Schwarz, N. (2001). Implementation intentions and facilitation of prospective memory. *Psychological Science, 12,* 457–461.

de Frias, C. M., Dixon, R. A., & Bäckman, L. (2003). Use of memory compensation strategies is related to psychosocial and health indicators. *Journal of Gerontology: Psychological Sciences, 58B,* P12–P22.

Einstein, G. O., & McDaniel, M. A. (1990). Normal aging and prospective memory. *Journal of Experimental Psychology: Learning, Memory, and Cognition, 16,* 717–726.

Einstein, G. O., Smith, R. E., McDaniel, M. A., & Shaw, P. (1997). Aging and prospective memory: The influence of increased task demands at encoding and retrieval. *Psychology and Aging, 12,* 479–488.

Engle, R. W., & Kane, M. J. (2004). Executive attention, working memory, and a two-factor theory of cognitive control. In B. H. Ross (Ed.), *The psychology of learning and motivation: Advances in research and theory* (Vol. 44, pp. 145–199). San Diego, CA: Elsevier Academic Press.

Herrmann, D., Gruneberg, M. M., Fiore, S., Schooler, J. W., & Torres, R. (2006). Memory failures and their causes in everyday life. In L.-G. Nilsson & N. Ohta (Eds.), *Memory and society: Psychological perspectives* (pp. 255–272). New York, NY: Psychology Press.

Hertzog, C., Park, D. C., Morrell, R. W., & Martin, M. (2000). Ask and ye shall receive: Behavioral specificity in the accuracy of subjective memory complaints. *Applied Cognitive Psychology, 14,* 257–275.

Intons-Peterson, M. J., & Fournier, J. (1986). External and internal memory aids: When and how often do we use them? *Journal of Experimental Psychology: General, 115,* 267–280.

Jacoby, L. L. (1999). Ironic effects of repetition: Measuring age-related differences in memory. *Journal of Experimental Psychology: Learning, Memory, and Cognition, 25,* 3–22.

Kidder, D. P., Park, D. C., Hertzog, C., & Morrell, R. W. (1997). Prospective memory and aging: The effects of working memory and prospective memory task load. *Aging, Neuropsychology, and Cognition, 4,* 93–112.

Kliegel, M., Martin, M., McDaniel, M. A., & Einstein, G. O. (2004). Importance effects on performance in event-based prospective memory tasks. *Memory, 12,* 553–561.

Lineweaver, T. T., & Hertzog, C. (1998). Adults' efficacy and control beliefs regarding memory and aging: Separating general from personal beliefs. *Aging, Neuropsychology, and Cognition, 5,* 264–296.

Logie, R. H., Maylor, E. A., Della Salla, S., & Smith, G. (2004). Working memory in event-based and time-based tasks: Effects of secondary demand and age. *European Journal of Cognitive Psychology, 16,* 441–456.

Mäntylä, T. (1994). Remembering to remember: Adult age differences in prospective memory. *Journal of Gerontology: Psychological Sciences, 49B,* P276–P282.

Marsh, R. L., Hicks, J. L., & Cook, G. I. (2005). On the relationship between effort toward and ongoing task and cue detection in event-based prospective memory performance. *Memory & Cognition, 30,* 302–311.

Maylor, E. A. (1996). Does prospective memory decline with age? In M. Brandimonte, G. O. Einstein, & M. A. McDaniel (Eds.), *Prospective memory: Theory and applications* (pp. 173–197). Mahwah, NJ: Lawrence Erlbaum Associates, Inc.

McDaniel, M. A., & Einstein, G. O. (2000). Strategic and automatic processes in prospective memory retrieval: A multiprocess framework. *Applied Cognitive Psychology, 14,* S127–S144.

McDaniel, M. A., Guynn, M. J., Einstein, G. O., & Breneiser, J. (2004). Cue-focused and reflexive-associative processes in prospective memory retrieval. *Journal of Experimental Psychology: Learning, Memory, and Cognition, 30,* 605–614.

McGann, D., Ellis, J. A., & Milne, A. (2002). Conceptual and perceptual processes in prospective remembering: Differential influence of attentional resources. *Memory & Cognition, 30,* 1021–1032.

Miyake, A., Friedman, N. P., Emerson, M. J., Witzki, A. H., Howerter, A., & Wager, T. D. (2000). The unity and diversity of executive functions and their contributions to complex "frontal lobe" tasks: A latent variable analysis. *Cognitive Psychology, 41,* 49–100.

Morrell, R. W., Park, D. C., Kidder, D. P., & Martin, M. (1997). Adherence to antihypertensive medications across the life span. *Gerontologist, 37,* 609–619.

Morris, P. E. (1992). Prospective memory: Remembering to do things. In M. M. Gruneberg & P. E. Morris (Eds.), *Aspects of memory: The practical aspects* (Vol. 1, pp. 196–222). London: Routledge.

Navon, D., & Gopher, D. (1979). On the economy of the human-processing system. *Psychological Review, 86,* 214–255.

Norman, D. A., & Bobrow, D. J. (1975). On data-limited and resource-limited processes. *Cognitive Psychology, 7,* 44–64.

O'Reilly, R. C., & Frank, M. J. (2006). Making working memory work: A computational model of learning in the prefrontal cortex and basal ganglia. *Neural Computation, 18,* 283–328.

Park, D. C., Hertzog, C., Kidder, D. P., Morrell, R. W., & Mayhorn, C. B. (1997). The effect of age on event-based and time-based prospective memory. *Psychology and Aging, 12,* 314–327.

Park, D. C., Hertzog, C., Leventhal, H., Morrell, R. W., Leventhal, E., Birchmore, D. et al. (1999). Medication adherence in rheumatoid arthritis patients: Older is wiser. *Journal of the American Geriatric Society, 47,* 172–183.

Penningroth, S. L. (2005). Effects of attentional demand, cue typicality, and priming on an event-based prospective memory task. *Applied Cognitive Psychology, 19,* 885–897.

Reder, L. M. (Ed.). (1996). *Implicit memory and metacognition.* Mahwah, NJ: Lawrence Erlbaum Associates, Inc.

Reese, C. M., & Cherry, K. E. (2002). The effects of age, ability, and memory monitoring on prospective memory task performance. *Aging, Neuropsychology, and Cognition, 9,* 98–113.

Rendell, P. G., & Craik, F. I. M. (2000). Virtual week and actual week: Age-related differences in prospective memory. *Applied Cognitive Psychology, 14,* S43–S62.

Salthouse, T. A. (1991). *Theoretical perspectives on cognitive aging.* Hillsdale, NJ: Lawrence Erlbaum Associates, Inc.

Shallice, T., & Burgess, P. W. (1991). Deficits in strategy application following frontal lobe damage in man. *Brain, 114,* 727–741.

Smith, R. E. (2003). The cost of remembering to remember in event-based prospective memory: Investigating the capacity demands of delayed intention performance. *Journal of Experimental Psychology: Learning, Memory, and Cognition, 30,* 756–777.

Strayer, D. L., Drews, F. A., & Johnston, W. A. (2003). Cell phone-induced failure of visual attention during simulated driving. *Journal of Experimental Psychology: Applied, 9,* 23–32.

West, R. L. (1988). Prospective memory and aging. In M. M. Gruneberg, P. E. Morris, & R. N. Sykes (Eds.), *Practical aspects of memory: Current research and issues: Volume 2. Clinical and educational implications* (pp. 119–125). Chichester, UK: Wiley.

West, R., Krompinger, J., & Bowry, R. (2005). Disruptions of preparatory attention contribute to failures of prospective memory. *Psychonomic Bulletin & Review, 12,* 502–507.

6

The Development of Prospective Memory in Children

Methodological Issues, Empirical Findings, and Future Directions

LIA KVAVILASHVILI

School of Psychology
University of Hertfordshire, UK

FIONA E. KYLE

Deafness, Cognition, and Language Research Centre
University College London, UK

DAVID J. MESSER

Centre for Child Development and Learning, Faculty of Education
and Language Studies, The Open University, UK

Research on prospective memory has now reached the point at which it is no longer necessary to start a chapter with a definition of prospective memory or a discussion about its defining features and how it differs from retrospective memory. This has been done repeatedly elsewhere (e.g., see Einstein & McDaniel, 1996; Ellis, 1996; Graf & Uttl, 2001; Guajardo & Best, 2000; Kvavilashvili, 1992; Kvavilashvili & Ellis, 1996). Instead, we start the chapter by examining briefly some statistics on prospective memory research in the past 30 years, and possible reasons for the almost complete lack of research on the development of prospective memory. We then discuss methodological issues that arise in this research, review some experimental data, and outline future directions in this unduly neglected area of prospective memory.

Recently, researchers have started to express their concerns about the scarcity of developmental studies. For example, Ellis and Kvavilashvili (2000), in their editorial for a special issue on prospective memory, were hoping that "the increasing body of research on executive functions—which develop gradually throughout childhood and adolescence—may provide the spur for further research on prospective memory development" (p. S8), and cited a study by Kerns (2000) as a promising example of such research. However, in the following 5 years (from 2001 to 2005), out of more than 150 published studies on prospective memory, only 4% of studies were developmental (Kerns & Price, 2001; Kliegel, Ropeter, & Mackinlay, 2006; Kvavilashvili, Messer, & Ebdon, 2001; Martin & Kliegel, 2003; Maylor, Darby, Logie, Della Sala, & Smith, 2002; McCauley & Levin, 2004; Nigro, Senese, Natullo, & Sergi, 2002).

It is interesting that this was not the case in the first 15 years of prospective memory research. From 1971 to 1985, out of 10 (published) experimental studies, 4 were developmental, thus constituting 40% of the total output (Ceci & Bronfenbrenner, 1985; Meacham & Colombo, 1980; Meacham & Dumitru, 1976; Somerville, Wellman, & Cultice, 1983). This trend, however, was not preserved in the next 15 years of research. Although the number of published studies increased dramatically from 1986 to 2000 (to approximately 180), the percentage of developmental studies dropped equally dramatically from 40% to 3%, with only six developmental studies published in that period (Beal, 1988; Ceci, Baker, & Bronfenbrenner, 1988; Guajardo & Best, 2000; Kerns, 2000; Kurtz-Costes, Schneider, & Rupp, 1995; Passolunghi, Brandimonte, & Cornoldi, 1995). Moreover, as pointed out earlier, this pattern did not change in the last 5 years of prospective memory research (since 2001; see Table 6.1 for a list of developmental studies published since 1976).

TABLE 6.1   Developmental Studies of Prospective Memory as a Function of Type of Reported Study (Questionnaire, Theoretical/Review and Experimental). The Studies in the Boxes Refer to Papers in which Prospective Memory in Children was not a Primary Focus of Investigation/Review.

Developmental studies on prospective memory		
Questionnaire studies	Theoretical and review papers	Experimental studies
Kreutzer et al., 1975 (4 to 11 years) Cavanaugh & Borkowski, 1980 (4 to 11 years) Kurtz & Borkowski, 1984 (4 to 11 years) Beal, 1985 (5, 6, 8 years & young adults) Farrant et al., 1999 (8 to 16 years)	Meacham, 1982 Harris, 1984 Winograd, 1988	Meacham & Dumitru, 1976 (5, 7 years) Meacham & Colombo, 1980 (5, 7 years) Somerville et al., 1983 (2, 3, 4 years) Ceci & Bronfenbrenner, 1985 (10, 14 years) Ceci et al., 1988 (10-years) Passolunghi et al., 1995 (7, 10 years) Guajardo & Best, 2000 (3, 5 years) Kerns, 2000 (7 to 12 years) Kerns & Price, 2001 (8 to 13 years) Kvavilashvili et al., 2001 (4, 5, 7 years) Nigro et al., 2002 (7 to 11 years) Martin & Kliegel, 2003 (6 to 11 years) McCauly & Levin, 2004 (10 to 19 years) Kliegel et al., in press (8 to 9 years) Beal, 1988 (4 to 9 years) Kurtz-Costes et al., 1995 (5, 7, 9 years) Maylor et al., 2002 (6- to 11years)

The lack of interest in the development of prospective memory in children is surprising given that "remembering to do things in the future is a common everyday memory task that even young children are expected to perform" (Beal, 1985, p. 631). For preschool children, typical prospective memory tasks involve remembering "to dress properly to go outside, to bring appropriate objects to games, to deliver messages, to carry out chores on a regular basis" (Meacham, 1982, p. 129). The list of prospective memory tasks increases even further with school-age children who may also have to remember to take routine medications, complete errands, show up for appointments in- and outside of school, bring home special permission slips, call their friends or parents at work, return books to the library, bring completed homework to school, and so on (McCauley & Levin, 2004). Meacham (1982) stressed the social aspect of these tasks and that they were markedly different from the social context of retrospective memory tasks such as remembering what one did yesterday. Similarly, according to Winograd (1988), "if one remembers to perform an activity, one is rewarded. This is not the case with retrospective remembering by and large, until schooling begins with its demands on memorisation of arbitrary information" (p. 351). Therefore, both Meacham (1982) and Winograd (1988) believed that the early development of prospective memory skills was necessary for children to successfully cope with the everyday situations previously described. Meacham and Colombo (1980) even argued that "children's attempts at prospective remembering may be an important precursor to the development of strategies for retrospective remembering" (p. 299).

These were novel and theoretically challenging ideas. Moreover, they even received some empirical support in several early studies of prospective memory (e.g., Ceci & Bronfenbrenner, 1985; Kreutzer, Leonard, & Flavell, 1975; Meacham & Colombo, 1980; Somerville et al., 1983). Unfortunately, this initial and promising line of research was not pursued any further. In the 1990s, developmental psychologists shifted their attention to other practically relevant issues such as autobiographical memory, eyewitness suggestibility, false beliefs, and so on. On the other hand, prospective memory researchers concentrated on studying prospective memory at the other end of the developmental spectrum (i.e., in old age). This was mainly due to the publication of Einstein and McDaniel's (1990) highly influential and seminal paper on aging and prospective memory, in which they developed a simple and successful paradigm for studying and measuring prospective memory in the laboratory.

However, there are at least two other possible explanations for this lack of interest and the motivation to study prospective memory development in children. First, there may be an implicit assumption that research on children cannot produce any new insights into the mechanisms of prospective memory and that it is simply an extension of research on adults. If this is the case, then it is understandable why the developmental research might be less attractive to prospective memory researchers. Second, research on children is methodologically more difficult than research on adults (Schneider & Pressley, 1997, p. 136). In addition, there is a lack of well-established methods and tasks suitable for studying prospective memory in children of wide age range.

The first explanation is not that convincing. Even with a small number of developmental studies there are plenty of examples of novel findings that are theoretically important for the general field of research on prospective memory in adults. For example, a study by Ceci and Bronfenbrenner (1985) on children's clock monitoring patterns as a function of context (home vs. lab) has been frequently cited and has had lasting influence on theorizing about time-based prospective remembering. Furthermore, research on adults has demonstrated that the remembering of event-based tasks is not affected or even improved with increased delay intervals (e.g., Hicks, Marsh, & Russell, 2000). However, in the study of Nigro et al. (2002), manipulating the delay interval from 5 to 10 minutes did not affect children's performance on event-based tasks, replicating previous findings with adults, but did impair their performance on the time-based tasks. This is a novel finding that is worth pursuing in adult studies that have not yet systematically examined the effects of delays on time-based tasks.

Further examples of novel results include a study by Kvavilashvili et al. (2001) that demonstrated the effects of task interruption on children's performance in an event-based task, and a study by Guajardo and Best (2000) that obtained positive correlations between prospective and retrospective memory tasks in 3- but not in 5-year-old children. Findings with 5-year-olds are more in line with several other adult studies that have also failed to establish the reliable correlations between the two forms of memory (e.g., Brandimonte & Passolunghi, 1994; Einstein & McDaniel, 1990; Kvavilashvili, 1987; McDaniel, Robinson-Riegler, & Einstein, 1998). Findings with 3-year-olds, however, emphasize the possible difficulties that very young children may have with the retrospective component of the prospective memory tasks (i.e., what needs to be done and when), and show that prospective and retrospective memory scores can be correlated when the retrospective component of the prospective memory tasks is too difficult for the individual. This finding also demonstrates some inherent difficulties of studying prospective memory in children especially when studying the developmental trajectory across the wide age range.

METHODOLOGICAL ISSUES OF STUDYING PROSPECTIVE MEMORY IN CHILDREN

With the exception of the diary method, research on children has used similar methods to those used in adult studies: an interview and questionnaire method and the experiments conducted in- and outside the laboratory. Because the laboratory method has become predominant in both adult and developmental research, we concentrate on the laboratory method. Consequently, important questions that need to be addressed are whether children's prospective memory can be studied with laboratory methods used with adults and what the possible difficulties with these methods are.

A Laboratory Paradigm of Studying Prospective Memory

Figure 6.1(a) shows the basic components of a standard laboratory method of studying prospective memory in adults originally developed by Einstein and McDaniel (1990). In this paradigm, participants are initially introduced to a task (mostly run on computer) that they will be performing at a later point during the experiment. This task may consist of short-term memory trials, answering general knowledge questions, rating silly sentences as true–false, rating words for pleasantness, and so on.

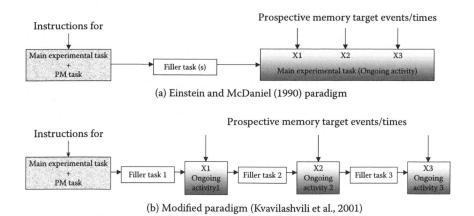

(a) Einstein and McDaniel (1990) paradigm

(b) Modified paradigm (Kvavilashvili et al., 2001)

FIGURE 6.1 A schematic representation of laboratory paradigms of prospective memory.

After some practice with this main experimental task, participants receive instructions for a prospective memory task that usually consists of remembering to press a key in response to a target word that will occur several times in the course of the main experimental task. This corresponds to the first stage of the prospective memory task (i.e., the formation of intention to act in the future; see Ellis, 1996; Brandimonte & Passolunghi, 1994). It is followed by a delay interval that is filled with performing some unrelated (filler) tasks. This ensures that participants switch their attention from the prospective memory task to elsewhere and mimics everyday situations where, after forming an intention to make a phone call later on, one switches to other ongoing tasks and concerns. When participants finish the filler tasks, they are asked to carry out the main experimental task they practiced earlier, without any mention of the prospective memory instructions. In the course of the ongoing experimental task, participants encounter the target word several times, and they have to remember to press the key without any explicit prompt from the experimenter. Prospective memory is measured as a number or proportion of cases in which participants remembered to press the key. To ensure that targets occur relatively infrequently in the course of the main experimental task, the latter usually consists of dozens or hundreds of trials that last on average between 15 and 30 minutes.

A Modified Version of the Paradigm

When we started our research on children at the end of 1990s, it was obvious to us that certain components of this basic paradigm needed modification for it to work with young children between 3 and 7 years old. With respect to an initial encoding stage, we reckoned that it would be difficult to introduce young children to the main experimental and prospective memory tasks in the manner usually done with adults (e.g., "We are additionally interested in your ability to remember to do things in the future"). Unlike adult volunteers, children might not have proper understanding of the value of doing experimental tasks for scientific research. Also, unlike psychology undergraduates who receive course credits for their participation, it is not always possible to compensate the participation of children with rewards. To keep children engaged and motivated in the procedure, both tasks have to be introduced as a form of a game. For that reason, in every experiment we have conducted we used (various versions of) a toy mole, "Morris," who children are told cannot see very well and needs their help in various tasks (e.g., naming pictures, drawing pictures, etc.). Prospective memory tasks consist of telling children that Morris is scared of animals, and if they happen to see a picture of any animal during the future tasks, they have to hide that picture in the box situated behind them (see Kvavilashvili et al., 2001).

We had more serious concerns about the final retrieval phase of the procedure, when participants have to perform the main ongoing experimental task with occasional prospective memory targets embedded in it. Initial piloting showed that it would not be possible to have preschool children performing the same task for dozens or hundreds of trials without them becoming bored and disinterested in the task. For this reason we slightly modified the basic paradigm so that each prospective memory target was embedded into a relatively short block of trials (e.g., naming 20 line drawings of familiar objects) that were alternated by brief 2-minute-long and engaging filler tasks such as drawing a picture for a mole. This modified paradigm for children is depicted in Figure 6.1(b) and was successfully used in our study on the effects of age and task interruption on young children's prospective memory (Kvavilashvili et al., 2001).

It is important to point out that the basic characteristics of the standard Einstein and McDaniel (1990) paradigm and the modified paradigm are similar. The difference between the two lies only in the ongoing activity, which, in the case of the modified paradigm, consists of two different types of alternating tasks with a relatively small number of trials (or duration). This ensures that young children do not lose their concentration and interest in the ongoing activity. Moreover, several developmental studies have used the standard paradigm (e.g., Guajardo & Best, 2000; Passolunghi et al., 1995) and some adult studies have used ongoing tasks similar to those in the modified paradigm (e.g., see Cook, Marsh & Hicks, 2005).

Eliminating Possible Ceiling Effects in the Modified Paradigm

Using the modified paradigm, Kvavilashvili et al. (2001) showed that children enjoyed "helping out Morris" and were engaged in the ongoing task of naming four separate stacks of cards of line drawings. Most important, prospective memory performance was not at ceiling even in the oldest age group. However, it later turned out that the absence of ceiling effects was due to prospective memory instructions asking children to do something in response to a general target (i.e., a category of animals) without the children knowing in advance which specific exemplars of this category would occur in the ongoing task. Several studies of adults have shown reduced performance levels with such general targets (i.e., animals) compared to specific targets like, for example, tiger, leopard, and lion (Cherry et al., 2001; Einstein, McDaniel, Richardson, Guynn, & Cunfer, 1995; Ellis & Milne, 1996).

Indeed, when in subsequent projects we wanted to test 3-, 5-, and 7-year-old children with a specific prospective memory target (e.g., a picture of a dog) we had serious troubles avoiding ceiling effects even in the youngest age group. For example, in the initial pilot study children had to give a toy dog a toy bone every time they named a different picture of a dog in each of the three stacks of cards. It was apparent that this task was intrinsically too motivating. It almost seemed as if the children could not wait for a moment when they could actually carry out this exciting task of "feeding the dog."

Therefore we had to make the prospective memory task less "exciting" by asking the children to perform a more arbitrary activity of placing a small dog figure into a small box (that was behind the child) every time they named a picture of a dog. However, even with this modification, performance levels were still unacceptably high. To reduce performance further we had to make the ongoing picture-naming task more difficult. This was achieved by asking children to look at the very first picture in the booklet and tick it off with a felt pen every time it occurred in the booklet. Thus, in addition to naming the pictures, the children also had to detect the (nonprospective) target picture that was different across all three picture books. Only after making these adjustments to the prospective memory task itself and the ongoing task did we manage to eliminate the ceiling effects in a prospective memory task with specific targets.

Additional Problems with Both Paradigms

Apart from ceiling effects, there are at least two additional problems facing the developmental researchers of prospective memory. The first problem involves the possibility that some younger children may forget to perform the prospective memory task because of a retrospective memory failure to remember that they had been given the prospective memory instructions in the first place. Therefore, children's retrospective memory for prospective memory instructions should be assessed at the end of the experimental session via a series of successive probes increasing in specificity. It is especially important to do so for children who forget to perform the prospective memory task on all occasions. For example, in Kvavilashvili et al. (2001), the postexperimental probing procedure consisted of asking the children if, in addition to naming the pictures, they were also supposed to do something else. If the children could not answer this question, the next more specific prompt involved asking them whether they were supposed to do something when they saw certain pictures in the picture naming task. If the children were unable to answer this question as well, the final most specific prompt involved asking them what they were supposed to do when they saw a picture of an animal. All those children who were unable to answer this final question were excluded from the analyses, as they clearly demonstrated having no memory of receiving prospective memory instructions at the beginning of the experimental session. It should be noted, however, that in all the studies that we have conducted so far, the number of such children was usually very small (but see Guajardo & Best, 2000). It is therefore unlikely that the exclusion of these children from the sample will result in the overestimation of prospective memory ability in young children.[1]

The second and more serious problem faced by developmental researchers of prospective memory concerns the necessity to adjust the difficulty and duration of the ongoing task for children in cross-sectional (and longitudinal) studies. It is obvious that naming 20 pictures will be a more difficult and resource-demanding task for 4-year-olds than it will be for 7- or 9-year-olds. For example, in a study by Kvavilashvili et al. (2001) there was a significant age effect in the time taken to name each of the four stacks of cards, with 4-year-olds being the slowest and 7-year-olds the fastest. Given that ongoing task difficulty has been shown to adversely affect prospective memory performance in adults, it is possible that age effects obtained in a particular developmental study are due to deficits in processing resources for carrying out an ongoing task rather than deficits in prospective memory per se. One way to overcome this difficulty is to adjust the task duration by giving younger children fewer pictures to name than the older children. For example, in two subsequent studies Kvavilashvili, Kornbrot, and Messer (2002) and Kvavilashvili, Messer, and Kyle (2002) had 3-, 5-, 7-, and 9-year-old children process 10, 15, 20, and 25 pictures, respectively. However, even when the task duration is controlled there is still a possibility that the task is still more demanding for younger children. As shown later, if the task difficulty is not adjusted or controlled, this could significantly influence the outcomes of the study.

Another possible and perhaps more naturalistic way of equating the levels of interest in and the task difficulty of ongoing activity is to ask children to watch cartoons or play video games as part of their main ongoing activity. Playing video games is a particularly interesting possibility given that children start playing such games at a very young age and these games have become part of their everyday life.

Other Possible Methods and Tasks

Video games were initially used by Ceci and Bronfennbrenner (1985) in their famous study where children had to remember to take cupcakes out of the oven or recharge the batteries in 30 minutes and were allowed to play the video game during the delay interval. More recently, Kerns (2000) developed a simple and elegant method in which a prospective memory task is embedded in the computer game itself (see also Kerns & Price, 2001). Thus, children are introduced to a short, 5-minute video game consisting of driving a car along the road. The goal is to drive as fast and as accurately as possible without hitting other vehicles on the road. For this main ongoing task children gain scores that are prominently displayed on the screen all the time. The prospective memory task consists of refueling the gas tank every time it is less than one quarter full by pressing a button on a joystick. The fuel tank can be monitored by pressing another button that brings the image of the fuel tank on the screen for 3 seconds. If the children forget to refuel the tank at an appropriate time and run out of gas, they lose all their scores accumulated at that point. Prospective memory is scored as the number of times (out of five) children run out of gas.

One remarkable aspect of this new method is that it studies time-based prospective memory in children without requiring them to have any clock-reading skills. Kerns (2000) tested children across the wide age range of 7 to 12 years. The J-shaped pattern of monitoring the fuel tank, demonstrated even by 7-year-olds, clearly indicates that the task measures time-based prospective memory (cf. Harris & Wilkins, 1982). It is obvious that this method can be used with even preschool children. Furthermore, the method can also be easily adapted to study event-based prospective memory by asking children to press the button every time they encounter a certain type of vehicle (e.g., ambulance) on their way (e.g., Wilde, 1998, cited in Kerns & Price, 2001). Clearly, this simple method opens several interesting avenues for intensive research on children's prospective memory. Another interesting and promising method developed by Martin and Kliegel (2003) involves studying children's performance in complex prospective memory tasks requiring planning, initiation, and the execution of a set of related tasks. This method is described in more detail in Chapter 9 of this volume.

Having discussed methodological issues of studying prospective memory development in children, we can now move on to the main findings that have emerged from published studies as well as some unpublished and current research from our laboratory.

REVIEW OF DEVELOPMENTAL RESEARCH ON PROSPECTIVE MEMORY

Research on children's prospective memory has primarily concentrated on two related and equally important questions: First, what are the effects of age on prospective memory, both in terms of the earliest age at which prospective memory skills and the development of these skills in preschool and school-age children? Second, do children possess metamemory knowledge about the best strategies for various everyday prospective memory tasks, and, if yes, how effectively can they use this knowledge in their day-to-day life? We review research addressing each of these questions in turn below.

Effects of Age on Prospective Memory in Children

So far, only two studies have examined prospective memory in very young (preschool) children (Guajardo & Best, 2000; Somerville et al., 1983). All other published studies have concentrated on the development of prospective memory primarily in school-age children covering relatively short developmental age spans of 2 to 3 years and using a cross-sectional methodology. Some studies have compared prospective memory performance in either preschool to school-age children from 4 to 7 years (Kvavilashvili et al., 2001) or early school-age children from 5 to 7 years (Meacham & Colombo, 1980; Meacham & Dumitru, 1976). Other studies have used older school children comparing prospective memory performance in 7- and 10-year-olds (Passolunghi et al., 1995) or in 10- and 14-year-olds (Ceci et al., 1988; Ceci & Bronfenbrenner, 1985). Finally, only a few published papers have studied the development of prospective memory across wider age ranges of 4 to 5 years. For example, Nigro et al. (2002) studied children between 7 and 11 years, and Kerns (2000) studied children between 7 and 12 years old (see also Maylor et al., 2002). All these studies have reported variable results. We briefly review these findings before we discuss possible reasons for obtaining discrepant results across the studies.

Prospective Memory in 2- to 5-Year-Old Children

The question about the earliest age at which prospective memory skills can be observed has so far been addressed only in a naturalistic study of Somerville et al. (1983). In this study, 2-, 3-, and 4-year-old children were assigned to eight different reminding tasks by their usual caregivers (mothers) over a period of 2 weeks. These tasks varied in the level of motivation, like "Remind me to buy candy at the store tomorrow morning" (high interest) or "Remind me to bring in the wash after the nap" (low interest), and in the length of delay between receiving these instructions and the opportunity to carry them out (5–10 minutes vs. several hours).

The results that were obtained about the motivation and delay manipulation were highly interesting and novel at the time, and were later replicated in several adult studies on prospective memory. There was a highly significant effect of motivation explaining up to 25% of variance in children's prospective memory performance (cf. Kliegel, Martin, McDaniel, & Einstein, 2001, 2004; Kvavilashvili, 1987). There was also a significant effect of delay in that performance was better with short delays of several minutes than long delays of several hours. However, this effect was much smaller and explained only 5% of the variance in performance. This finding is in line with adult studies showing only a small or no reliable effects of delays on prospective memory performance (e.g., Einstein, Holland, McDaniel, & Guynn, 1992; Harris & Wilkins, 1982; Nigro & Cicogna, 2000). However, the most important results that emerged from this study concern the absence of any age effects on children's prospective memory. Thus, 2-year-olds were as good as 4-year-olds, with 80% success in remembering tasks with high interest and short delays (the success rate was still 50% with high interest and long delay intervals of several hours).

It was this remarkable finding that prompted researchers like Meacham (1982) and Winograd (1988) to suggest that prospective memory skills may develop particularly early for a child to cope successfully in everyday social contexts. Unfortunately, no attempt has been made to replicate this finding using similar age groups. The only other published study that has compared preschool children belongs to Guajardo and Best (2000), who studied 3- and 5-year-old children's prospective memory with a laboratory task using the Einstein and McDaniel (1990) paradigm depicted in Figure 6.1(a). The ongoing task was introduced to the children as a computer game in which they received six blocks of 10 pictures of familiar objects (5 seconds per picture) and at the end of the block they had to recall as many pictures as possible. The prospective memory task consisted of pressing a key on the keyboard every time they saw a picture of a house (or a duck) as part of this "computer game."

Unlike Somerville et al. (1983), Guajardo and Best (2000) obtained a significant effect of age: 5-year-olds were reliably better at remembering to press the key than the 3-year-olds. However, postexperimental probing of the children showed that 52% of the 3-year-olds had difficulty remembering prospective memory instructions, as they were unable to answer the question about what it was that they were asked to do when they saw the picture of a house or duck. In addition, the ongoing free recall task was undoubtedly more difficult to the 3-year-olds, who recalled significantly fewer pictures than the 5-year-olds. Given these problems with methodology, it is difficult to draw firm conclusions about the nature of prospective memory development between the ages of 3 and 5 years. However, what is remarkable in this study is that 5-year-old children performed near ceiling in this computerized prospective memory task, with 50% of the children remembering on all six occasions and mean prospective scores ranging between 5.05 and 5.58 across different conditions.

Prospective Memory in 5- to 7-Year-Old Children   Discrepant findings have been obtained in studies covering late preschool and early school years. For example, in Meacham and Dumitru (1976), 7-year-old children were reliably better at remembering to post their drawing at the end of the session than 5-year-olds. However, no age effects were obtained in a study by Meacham and Colombo (1980) in which children had to remind the experimenter, at the end of the session, to open the surprise box. One possible explanation for the discrepant findings across these two studies could be that the task of opening the surprise box was more interesting or motivating than posting the drawing and that this high level of motivation eliminated age effects.

Somewhat discrepant results for 5- and 7-year-olds were also obtained by Kvavilashvili et al. (2001), who used a modified paradigm presented in Figure 6.1(b), and described earlier. Whereas 7-year-olds performed reliably better than 5-year-olds in Experiments 1 and 2, no age effect was obtained in Experiment 3 between these age groups even though broadly similar tasks and materials were used in all three studies. Interestingly, in this study no age effects were obtained between 4- and 5-year-old children but, in both experiments, 7-year-olds were reliably better than 4-year-olds.

Prospective Memory in 7- to 14-Year-Old Children   Two other studies that investigated prospective memory in older school children both found reliable age effects that, however, were qualified by interactions with some other independent variables manipulated by the researchers. For example, in Passolunghi et al. (1995), 7- and 10-year-old children were tested with a standard Einstein and McDaniel (1990) paradigm where the ongoing task consisted of 40 trials of five two-syllable words presented simultaneously on the screen for 6 seconds, which children had to read as quickly and as accurately as they could. The prospective memory tasks consisted of pressing a key on the computer keyboard whenever the word *boat* appeared on the screen as part of the ongoing word reading task. The encoding modality of prospective memory instructions was manipulated by showing children either a picture of the boat (pictorial encoding), the written word *boat* (verbal encoding), or asking them to enact the prospective memory task by actually pressing the designated key on the keyboard (motoric encoding). The results showed that age effects were present only in motoric encoding conditions, but not in pictorial and verbal encoding conditions. If anything, 7-year-olds had reliably higher scores than 10-year-olds in pictorial encoding conditions in Experiment 1, and the difference between the means in Experiment 2 was in the same direction.

Furthermore, in a study by Ceci and Bronfenbrenner (1985) on 10- and 14-year-old children, the prospective memory task was remembering to take cupcakes out of the oven (or recharge the batteries) in exactly 30 minutes while being busily engaged in an ongoing task of playing a computer game in two different contexts (laboratory vs. home). Although the primary emphasis of this study was on children's time-monitoring strategies (discussed in the next section), the results concerning prospective memory performance are equally important even though they are less well known and almost never discussed in the literature. In the laboratory, prospective memory performance was at ceiling as all but one child remembered to remove the cupcakes or recharge the batteries on time (i.e., within the first 60 seconds of the critical time). An age effect was only present when children were tested in their own homes, with 10-year-olds being more likely to be late than 14-year-olds (58% vs. 25%). One possible explanation of this age by context interaction could be differences in motivation across the two contexts in younger children. Thus, it is possible that 10-year-olds took the prospective memory task less seriously in their own homes than in the anxiety-provoking laboratory situation.

Finally, as pointed out earlier, there are very few published studies that have examined the development of prospective memory across larger age ranges of 4 to 5 years, and these studies have also produced mixed results. For example, in Nigro et al. (2002), children whose ages ranged from 7 to 11 years were busily engaged in an ongoing activity of solving problems (mathematical additions and puzzles) for 15 minutes and, in addition, had to remember to remind the experimenter to do something either at a particular time (time-based task) or when seeing another experimenter (event-based condition). Although children were more likely to remind the experimenter in the event-based than in the time-based condition, there was no effect of age ($F < 1$). On the other hand, Kerns (2000), who tested 7- to 12-year-old children using her novel computerized Cyber Cruiser task for studying time-based prospective memory (described earlier), did report a reliable age effect in a form of negative correlation between the chronological age and prospective memory performance assessed by the number of times children ran out of gas ($r = -.29$; see also Martin & Kliegel, 2003; Maylor et al., 2002).

Possible Reasons for Discrepant Findings and Conclusions What can be concluded from this brief review of findings concerning the development of prospective memory in children? At first sight this diverse set of data may seem confusing and contradictory. We would argue that there are at least two major points that need to be taken into account when trying to interpret the variable pattern of findings. The first point is methodological, and concerns the importance of equating the difficulty of ongoing tasks across the age groups in the laboratory experiments. The second point concerns the size of age effects that have been reported. These issues are now discussed in more detail.

With two exceptions (Martin & Kliegel, 2003; Nigro et al., 2002), none of the published studies have made an attempt to equate the difficulty of ongoing tasks across the age groups used. It is obvious, for example, that in Passolunghi et al. (1995), reading sets of five words in 6 seconds would have been a much more difficult task for 7-year-olds than for 10-year-olds. Similarly, in Guajardo and Best

(2000), studying lists of 10 pictures was a substantially more demanding task for 3-year-olds than for 5-year-olds. Furthermore, Kvavilashvili et al. (2001) also reported that 4- and 5-year-old children took significantly longer to name 20 pictures in each of the four stacks of cards than 7-year-olds.

In most studies, however, age effects in the performance of ongoing tasks are not even reported. On the other hand, Kerns (2000) stressed that the ongoing task of playing Cyber Cruiser was equally engaging to children of various ages who took part in her study. Even if the game was equally interesting to children aged 7 to 12 years, this still does not eliminate the possibility that the game was more difficult to 7-year-olds than to 12-year-old children. Unfortunately, Kerns did not analyze children's performance on the Cyber Cruiser to see if there were any age effects on this ongoing computer task. It is interesting that Nigro et al. (2002), who covered a similar age range (7–11 years), but at the same time adjusted the level of difficulty of problems and puzzles that children were solving as part of their ongoing activity, did not report any age effects in event-based or time-based prospective memory. Moreover, when we reanalyzed the data of Kvavilashvili et al. (2001) and entered the time spent on naming the pictures as a covariate, the effects of age reported in this paper disappeared.

This issue is obviously less important for naturalistic studies as participants would be engaged in their habitual everyday (and mostly age-appropriate) tasks. For example, naturalistic studies on aging and prospective memory have consistently failed to obtain any significant age effects between young and old (Moscovitch, 1982; Rendell & Thompson, 1999; West, 1988, Study 1). Similarly, in the only existing naturalistic study conducted by Somerville et al. (1983) on 2- to 4-year-old children, no age effect was obtained. Taken together, the evidence seems to support the idea that in many cases significant age effects may be attenuated or even disappear when children of various ages are engaged in ongoing activities that are matched in their difficulty across the age groups.

On the other hand, it would be incorrect to conclude that prospective memory is largely age invariant and that adjusting task difficulty in the developmental studies of prospective memory will always eliminate the age effects. For example, in two unpublished studies we modified the method developed by Kvavilashvili et al. (2001) so that younger children had to process a smaller number of pictures during an ongoing activity than older children (with 3-, 5-, and 7-year-olds processing 10, 15, and 20 pictures, respectively). Nevertheless, in a study by Kvavilashvili, Kornbrot, and Messer (2002, Experiment 2) a significant age effect was found in children's prospective memory so that 7-year-olds were significantly better than 5- and 3-year-olds, who did not differ from each other. In another study using an identical ongoing activity, but a different prospective memory task (i.e., instead of putting a dog figure into a box, children had to remember to say something to the toy mole when seeing a particular picture), Kvavilashvili, Messer, and Kyle (2002) also found a significant age effect. Thus, 3-year-olds were significantly worse than 5-year-olds, who did not differ from 7-year-olds, who, in turn, did not differ from 9-year-olds.

Given that age effects can be obtained even when the length and the difficulty of ongoing activities have been controlled for, an important issue that needs to be examined is the size of these age effects. Unfortunately, very few studies have reported effect sizes and often insufficient information is provided to calculate the effect sizes in these studies. However, the examination of existing studies and available data shows that effect sizes are relatively modest, especially in comparison to often dramatic developmental changes in a variety of retrospective memory tasks covering the same age range (e.g., Gathercole, 1998; Schneider & Pressley, 1997).

For example, in two experiments reported by Kvavilashvili et al. (2001), age explained a relatively small percentage of variance in 4-, 5-, and 7-year-old children's prospective memory performance (with $\eta^2 = .08$ and .07, respectively). Moreover, in Experiment 3, the effect size was twice as large for a free recall task ($\eta^2 = .15$) than for the prospective memory task ($\eta^2 = .07$). Similarly, in the published study that has used the largest age range (7–12 years), Kerns (2000) reported a relatively small negative correlation between chronological age and the performance on the prospective memory task embedded in the Cyber Cruiser game ($r = -.29$), indicating that age explained only 8% of the variance in children's prospective memory performance.

Interestingly, when the length or the difficulty of ongoing tasks is controlled, the effect sizes can become even smaller. For example, although Kvavilashvili, Kornbrot, and Messer (2002) did find an age effect in 3-, 5-, and 7-year-old children, as described earlier, this effect explained only 3% of variance in children's prospective memory of remembering to put a dog figure in the box. In contrast, very large age effects were obtained in the same study on children's performance on standard retrospective memory tasks such as digit span ($\eta^2 = .45$), picture recognition ($\eta^2 = .44$), and immediate and delayed free recall ($\eta^2 = .20$ and $\eta^2 = .16$, respectively; for the latter two tasks only the data of 5- and 7-year-olds were available).

Similar results were also obtained by Kvavilashvili, Messer, and Kyle (2002) in a study conducted on 3-, 5-, 7-, and 9-year-old children in which the difficulty of an ongoing task was controlled and the prospective memory task involved a verbal response instead of an overt action of putting a dog figure in the box. Initial analyses showed a large effect size ($\eta^2 = .16$). However, this turned out to be entirely due to 3-year-olds' difficulty in remembering this verbal prospective memory task (saying something to the mole when seeing a particular picture). Indeed, when 3-year-olds were excluded from the analyses the effect of age explained only 3% of the variance in 5-, 7-, and 9-year-olds' prospective memory performance. Incidentally, the data of 3-year-olds in these two experiments seem to provide some support for the idea that "prospective memory may be superior for intentions requiring motor response than for those requiring verbal ... response" (Freeman & Ellis, 2003, p. 990). This is clearly an issue that merits further investigation in adults and especially in young children.

One final example of dramatic changes that may occur in effect sizes due to experimental manipulations was recently reported by McGann, Defeyter, Ellis, and Reid (2005). They conducted two experiments on 4-, 5-, and 7-year-old children using a modified paradigm presented in Figure 6.1(b). In Experiment 1, children had to name each of the four blocks of 20 pictures presented on the computer screen (the ongoing task), with each block being preceded by drawing a picture for Rosie the rag doll. The prospective memory task involved remembering to press a key on the computer keyboard every time they saw a food picture that Rosie "could collect for her picnic." In Experiment 2, children had to name and manually sort the four stacks of 20 cards into categories. Moreover, the length of the ongoing task was controlled by allowing each child to engage in this task for only 1 minute. Finally, the prospective memory task consisted of taking a picture with a food item and putting it into Rosie's lunch box. Significant age effects were obtained in both experiments. However, whereas age explained 20% of the variance in Experiment 1, it explained only 7% of the variance in Experiment 2, in which children were engaged in a more meaningful prospective memory task and in which the length and possibly the difficulty of the ongoing card naming and sorting task were controlled. In addition, in Experiment 2, there was an interesting age by target salience interaction so that the effect of age was present only when prospective memory targets were the same size as the nontarget pictures. When prospective memory targets were slightly larger in size than most of the nontarget pictures, there were no age effects in 4-, 5- and 7-year-old children.

Taken together, the existing evidence appears to suggest that although prospective memory does develop with age, the developmental changes are modest at best and can be reduced even further by testing children with meaningful and interesting prospective memory tasks (e.g., McGann et al., 2005) or by adjusting the difficulty of ongoing activities (Kvavilashvili, Kornbrot, & Messer, 2002). Is this relatively good ability of remembering to carry out prospective memory tasks accompanied by equally good metamemory for processes and strategies involved in successful prospective remembering?

Effects of Age on Metamemory for Prospective Memory Tasks in Children

As pointed out earlier, this question consists of two related issues. The first concerns children's knowledge of processes and strategies that can enhance performance in everyday prospective memory tasks. This issue has been examined by Kreutzer et al. (1975) and Beal (1985) by using an interview and questionnaire method. The second issue concerns children's actual ability to utilize these strategies in prospective memory tasks that they have to carry out in everyday life. This question has so far been addressed in a study by Ceci and Bronfenbrenner (1985; see also Ceci et al., 1985) and Kerns (2000), who studied children's monitoring behavior in time-based tasks.

Children's Knowledge of Strategies for Prospective Memory Tasks   Kreutzer et al. (1975) conducted the first and seminal study on children's strategic knowledge of several everyday (primarily retrospective) memory tasks such as remembering where one could have left one's jacket at school, remembering Christmas when a particular present was given, or how to memorize a categorical set of nine pictures (three pictures from three different categories). The most famous and often cited question concerned children's strategic knowledge of a typical prospective memory task. Specifically, children were asked to list every possible strategy they could think of to ensure that they would remember to take their skates to school the next morning. Four age groups were tested: kindergarten (4–5 years), first grade (6–7 years), third grade (8–9 years), and fifth grade (10–11 years) children. Children's answers to the skates question fell into four categories, three of which referred to external strategies and one to an internal strategy (i.e., periodic rehearsal of the task in one's mind). The external strategies involved the physical manipulation of skates (e.g., putting them near the door), the use of external reminder cues other than the skates (e.g., writing a note), or soliciting help from others (e.g., asking a parent to provide a reminder).

The results showed that there were no marked age effects in the tendency to list one versus another of these four strategies. Even the kindergarteners were able to come up with at least one strategy each. There was also a clear preference for external strategies, as only 16% of the children suggested using the internal rehearsal strategy. It is interesting that in a naturalistic study, when college undergraduates had to remember to send postcards to the experimenter on prearranged dates, a similar small percentage of students (i.e., 20%) reported having actually used the internal strategy of rehearsing the task in their mind (Meacham & Singer, 1977). Overall, however, older children (the third and fifth graders) listed more strategies than younger children (kindergarteners and first graders) and the strategies that they described were more explicitly planful and means-ends-oriented than those reported by younger children. Similar results were obtained for another prospective item from the Kreutzer et al. (1975) questionnaire that asked children what they needed to do to ensure that they would not forget an upcoming event (e.g., a friend's birthday). Here again, even the youngest children could come up with a strategy or two, with more and increasingly planful strategies reported by older children.

In contrast, marked age effects were obtained in the same study with several retrospective items, such as how to remember an event from a previous Christmas or how to memorize a categorical list of nine pictures. For example, in relation to the Christmas question, 5-year-olds could hardly understand the task, whereas 7- and 9-year-olds said they would solicit help from adults. Only 11-year-olds produced more varied strategies, but even with this age group there was plenty of scope for further improvement. This contrasting pattern of findings concerning prospective and retrospective items was subsequently replicated in several other studies using similar questions (e.g., Cavanaugh & Borkowski, 1980; Kurtz & Borkowski, 1984; see also Farrant, Boucher, & Blades, 1999, for using the prospective questions in children with autism).

Another well-known study on children's metamemory of prospective memory tasks, using a similar interview method, was conducted by Beal (1985, Study 1). Unlike Kreutzer et al. (1975), Beal tested children's knowledge of the effectiveness of different types of cues in everyday prospective memory tasks. Moreover, in addition to children, she also tested a group of college undergraduates. Children (5-, 6-, and 8-year-olds) and young adults were given the descriptions of six different prospective memory task scenarios together with two alternative reminder cues that the protagonist could use to help him or her successfully remember the task (e.g., remembering to take out trash or calling a friend after school). Participants had to choose the effective reminder out of two and provide justification for their choice. The three scenarios concerned the cue informativeness (e.g., that the cue should be nonambiguous or sufficiently detailed to act as an effective reminder), and the other three, the cue placement (e.g., that the cue should be easily noticeable or that it should be encountered at the right time).

The results showed that there were no statistically reliable differences in the number of correct responses in 5-, 6-, and 8-year-old children. However, whereas 5- and 6-year-olds were significantly less accurate than adults, 8-year-olds were as good as adults in four out of six target scenarios. It is also important to note that, in comparison to adults and 8-year-olds, young children were somewhat disadvantaged by having to provide verbal justification for their choices. In addition, both 8-year-olds and especially adults performed at ceiling in several of the six target scenarios. Despite these difficulties in interpreting the results, on the whole, the results seem to be in line with the findings of Kreutzer et al. (1975) and indicate that young children, and especially 8-year-olds, may have a fairly good understanding of the basic nature and functions of reminders in prospective memory tasks.

One problem that these studies share is that they assess children's metamemory knowledge of memory situations (i.e., declarative metamemory) rather than their actual strategic behavior in everyday prospective memory tasks (i.e., procedural metamemory). There is evidence in the literature showing that although children may have an adequate knowledge of a strategy suitable for a particular retrospective memory task, they might not use it in an actual memory test situation (e.g., Fabricius & Wellman, 1983; Schneider & Pressley, 1997). None of the developmental studies have examined children's spontaneous use of external strategies in prospective memory tasks such as remembering to take skates to school. This is an interesting topic that awaits future investigation. There are, however, three published studies that have examined children's strategic monitoring behavior in time-based prospective memory tasks.

Children's Use of Strategies in Prospective Memory Tasks

In their cupcake and battery recharging study, Ceci and Bronfenbrenner (1985) were primarily interested in 10- and 14-year-old children's strategic clock-monitoring behavior during the 30-minute delay interval filled with playing a computer game. An earlier study by Harris and Wilkins (1982) had shown that when young adults had to remember to carry out a time-based task at 3- or 9-minute intervals while watching a film, their clock checking prior to each critical time resembled the J-shaped pattern: Participants checked the clock initially a few times, then the clock checking dropped for some time until it dramatically increased in the period immediately preceding the critical time. Ceci and Bronfenbrenner wanted to see if 10- and 14-year-olds would also engage in this strategic clock monitoring displayed by adults and whether this behavior would vary as a function of context. Thus, an interesting aspect of this study was that half of the children were tested in the laboratory by a trained psychology undergraduate who was unknown to them and the other half were tested at home by their older siblings (also psychology undergraduates).

The results showed entirely different clock-monitoring patterns in these two contexts. In the more anxiety-provoking environment of the psychology laboratory, in which the prospective memory task was probably perceived as quite important, the number of clock checks linearly increased, with the highest number being made in the last 5 minutes of the delay interval. Although this strategy was not most parsimonious, given the large number of clock checks that children had to make, it paid off in that all but one child remembered to take out the cupcakes (or recharge the batteries) on time. In contrast, in the more relaxing and familiar environment (i.e., at home), those children who remembered to take out the cupcakes on time demonstrated strategic monitoring that resembled the U-shaped pattern. Thus, children checked the clock quite frequently in the first 10 minutes of the delay interval as if trying to synchronize or calibrate their internal clock with the elapsed time shown by the external clock. After this, the number of clock checks dropped markedly for some time until it again sharply increased in the last 5 minutes of the delay period. Interestingly, there were no marked age effects in clock monitoring. Although overall younger children made more clock checks than older children, the pattern of clock checks was similar across age groups in both contexts.

These findings are remarkable for two reasons. First, they show that children can use different clock monitoring strategies as a function of context. In the laboratory, where the consequences of forgetting the prospective memory task were probably perceived as less acceptable, children chose to use the less parsimonious but safer strategy of linearly increasing monitoring. At home, however, where children were more relaxed and probably deemed the forgetting of the prospective memory task as more acceptable, they chose to use a completely different U-shaped pattern of monitoring. Second, this U-shaped pattern of monitoring indicates that 10- and 14-year-old children, if necessary, can engage in fairly complex strategic behavior that involves temporal calibration of internal clocks at the beginning of the delay interval. As a result of this calibration, the overall number of clock checks is substantially reduced, allowing children to deploy their attentional resources elsewhere (in this case on playing the computer game).

To study this temporal calibration strategy in more detail, Ceci et al. (1988) conducted a follow-up study in which 10-year-old children had to carry out the same prospective memory task at home as before, but the speed of clocks was manipulated (accelerated or decelerated by 10%, 33%, or 50%). The results showed that 10-year-olds managed to successfully use the temporal calibration strategy (reflected in the U-shaped pattern of monitoring) in conditions in which the time on the external clocks was accelerated or decelerated by 10% and 33%. However, when the time was accelerated or decelerated by as much as 50%, children chose a linearly increasing pattern of monitoring instead, as if realizing that they could no longer trust their internal estimation of time that did not seem to match the one shown by the external clock.

The findings of Ceci and his colleagues were recently replicated by Kerns (2000) in 7- to 12-year-old children who, in the course of the computer game Cyber Cruiser, had to periodically check the levels of a gas tank and refuel it whenever it reached a certain critical level. The gas tank ran out of the fuel five times in the course of this computer game (approximately once every 60 seconds). The findings showed that there was no age effect in the pattern of strategic monitoring. All children, irrespective of age, displayed the J-shaped pattern of monitoring originally reported by Harris and Wilkins (1982) on young adult participants. Mäntylä and Carelli (2005) also reported the J-shaped pattern when they studied time monitoring and time estimation across the life span in children (8- to 12-year-olds), young adults, and older adults. Moreover, children were as good as young adults at a time estimation task in which they had to reproduce short time intervals of 4 to 32 seconds.[2]

Conclusions   Taken together, the results of Ceci and colleagues and Kerns (2000) show that young children can use fairly complex monitoring strategies in time-based prospective memory tasks. However, an intriguing aspect of these findings is that children may be using these strategies fairly automatically without much conscious knowledge of what they are doing. For example, when Ceci and Bronfenbrenner (1985) probed their participants at the end of the session, children seemed to be unaware or unable to verbally formulate the temporal calibration strategy that they were exhibiting in their behavior (i.e., they seemed to be unaware of the fact that they checked the clock more frequently at the beginning than in the middle of the delay period). Ceci and Bronfenbrenner (1985) argued that if the temporal calibration strategy is indeed deployed automatically, then "this would help explain why young children appear to be adept at its use, as automatic processing has been shown to be age-invariant" (p. 162).[3]

CONCLUSIONS AND FUTURE DIRECTIONS

The research on prospective memory development in children is surprisingly small and still in an embryonic stage, even after almost three decades of prospective memory research. Moreover, the few studies conducted in this area have varied considerably in their choice of age range, research questions, manipulated variables, and the research methodology. This diversity is also reflected in the highly variable and often inconsistent patterns of results obtained in these studies. However, despite these problems, an overriding theme that is starting to emerge from the studies reviewed in this chapter is that the age effects are often weak and highly dependent on experimental manipulations (e.g., target event salience, modality, etc.) and changes in methodology (e.g., equating the difficulty or the length of the ongoing activity, task interest, etc.).

Thus, even 2- to 4-year-old children seem to be able to remember high-interest tasks over short delays 80% of the time (Somerville et al., 1983), and in the past, in our own work, we have experienced difficulties eliminating ceiling effects in the performance of preschool children with such meaningful (and interesting) tasks as remembering to feed a toy dog with a bone (see also Guajardo & Best, 2000, for near-ceiling performance obtained in 5-year-olds). Moreover, in those studies that do obtain reliable age effects, the effects are relatively small (e.g., Kerns, 2000; Kvavilashvili et al., 2001), and they can disappear altogether when the difficulty of the ongoing activity is adjusted across the age groups (e.g., Nigro et al., 2002). In addition, the age effects seem to be highly sensitive to different experimental manipulations reflected by interactions of age with several different independent variables such as experimental context (Ceci & Bronfenbrenner, 1985), target salience (McGann et al., 2005, Experiment 2), and target modality (Passolunghi et al., 1995).

Taken together, these initial findings and observations seem to suggest that prospective memory may be relatively well developed in preschoolers as originally proposed by Meacham (1982) and Winograd (1988). Moreover, the developmental trajectory from preschool to early and later school years might not be as sharp as in the case of some retrospective memory tasks (but see Maylor et al., 2002). Additional support for this idea comes from the studies on metamemory and strategy use in children showing that even children as young as 7 years old can use a fairly complex temporal calibration strategy in time-based prospective memory tasks (e.g., Kerns, 2000; see also Ceci et al., 1988; Ceci & Bronfenbrenner, 1985). Somewhat surprisingly, Ceci and Bronfenbrenner (1985) found that 10- and 14-year-old children were unable to verbalize the key aspects of the temporal calibration strategy, suggesting that it was probably used automatically without much effort or conscious awareness on their part.

There is currently much debate and research about the underlying mechanisms of prospective memory. Several contrasting theoretical models have been developed and tested, with some models suggesting that prospective remembering entirely relies on automatic retrieval processes (Guynn, McDaniel, & Einstein, 2001; McDaniel et al., 1998) and others that it is due to self-initiated rehearsal and strategic monitoring (Shallice & Burgess, 1991; Smith, 2003). However, McDaniel and Einstein (2000) proposed that the retrieval of prospective memory tasks can be mediated by either of these processes. According to their multiprocess account, although prospective remembering relies predominantly on automatic processes, under particular conditions (e.g., when the target event is not salient) it is necessary to adopt a more strategic mode of operation like periodic rehearsal of an intention or monitoring the time or environment. Direct empirical evidence in support of this new framework comes from several recent experiments conducted by McDaniel and Einstein and their colleagues (e.g., Einstein et al., 2005; McDaniel & Einstein, 2000).

Interestingly, the pattern of findings emerging from developmental research appears to provide additional support for this model. Thus, the findings that young children display fairly good prospective memory performance under some conditions (e.g., high motivation, salient target event), and that they can employ a temporal calibration strategy without being consciously aware of it, indicate that prospective remembering is indeed (at least partly) mediated by automatic processes. On the other hand, the significant age effects obtained in several studies indicate that prospective memory can also be mediated by more conscious strategic processes. Thus, the future developmental research on prospective memory may turn out to be a particularly useful testing ground for the multiprocess framework. Of particular importance would be to investigate the interactions of age with several variables such as motivation, target salience, and cue action association to find the conditions that are more conducive for automatic or strategic processing.

There are at least two other lines of research that can further inform and contribute to the debate about the nature of underlying mechanisms of prospective memory. The first line would be to study prospective memory performance in very young children. Currently there is only one published study on

2- to 4-year-olds (Somerville et al., 1983) with encouraging results, and it will be necessary to replicate and extend these initial findings. Second, it will be necessary to conduct studies in which children's prospective memory performance will be compared to adults' performance. Making the ongoing activities and experimental situation comparable across such a wide age range is quite challenging method-ologically but not entirely impossible, as shown by the results of a recent study conducted in our laboratory (Kvavilashvili & Taylor, 2004).

In this study, 5-year-olds and young undergraduates with a mean age of 21 years ($SD = 6.76$) had to remember to say something when they encountered a pic-ture of a horse (specific instruction) or a picture of an animal (general instruction) in a later picture naming task containing either 10 or 30 line drawings, depending on the age group (children and adults, respectively). The participants had to also make a prediction of whether they thought they would remember to carry out this task or not. After a short 10- to 15-minute delay interval filled with listen-ing to a story from a picture book (children) or a taped story by Edgar Allan Poe (adults), participants had to name the line drawings presented either on the com-puter screen (adults) or manually on picture cards (children). The target picture of a horse occurred only once in the 7th or 21st position for children and adults, respectively.

The results showed that 5-year-olds were much more accurate in predicting their prospective memory performance than adults. In addition, although there were no differences across age groups in the general instruction condition, 5-year-olds were significantly better than adults in the specific instruction condition. Although these results are both interesting and encouraging, they need to be interpreted with caution as experimental tasks and instructions were not identical in the two age groups. For example, children were introduced to the toy mole Morris, who was absent in the adult group, and children and adults were exposed to different storybooks in the delay period. Most important, due to experimenter error, the children's storybook contained several animals (but no prospective memory target, the horse), which could have served as inadvertent reminders and enhanced the children's performance (see, e.g., Taylor, Marsh, Hicks, & Hancock, 2004). We are currently conducting a follow-up experiment in which the tasks and instructions are more comparable across the two age groups.

Another very useful avenue for future research is studying the developmental trajectories of prospective memory tasks and comparing them to those of retro-spective memory tasks (e.g., Kvavilashvili, Kornbrot, & Messer 2002; Kvavilashvili et al., 2001, Experiment 3; Maylor et al., 2002). The question about the relation-ship between prospective and retrospective memory is an important one and has been examined since the beginning of prospective memory research in the 1970s. However, the results of correlational studies have proved to be disappointing due to the difficulty of obtaining significant correlations between the two tasks. An alternative way of addressing this issue, suggested by McDaniel (1995), is to exam-ine the effects of important variables, such as age, motivation, delay interval, and so on, on both prospective and retrospective memory tasks to see if different pat-terns emerge under these two conditions. The best example of such study is the one conducted by Hicks et al. (2000) in which the contrasting effects of delay intervals

(2.5 minutes vs. 5 minutes vs. 15 minutes) were obtained for an event-based prospective memory task and the retrospective memory tasks of free and cued recall that were closely matched with the event-based task on several task dimensions. It is obvious that directly comparing the age effects on a variety of closely matched prospective and retrospective memory tasks in future developmental studies can provide invaluable insights into the question about the similarities and differences that may exist between these two types of tasks.

One additional and fruitful avenue for research on this question would be to compare children's (as well as adults') metamemory predictions in simple prospective and retrospective tasks. For example, in Kvavilashvili and Taylor (2004), described earlier, 5-year-old children were quite good at predicting their performance on a prospective memory task but grossly overestimated their performance on a simple retrospective memory task (i.e., recalling 10 line drawings). Findings concerning retrospective prediction accuracy are in line with the results of several early metamemory studies on retrospective remembering (e.g., Levine, Yussen, DeRose, & Pressley, 1977; Yussen & Berman, 1981). Interestingly, young adults seemed to perform at chance level for both prospective and retrospective memory tasks.

In conclusion, we believe that the developmental studies have a lot to offer to the general research on prospective memory as shown by this discussion and the review of the relevant literature. Moreover, there are already promising signs of renewed interest into this unduly neglected area, with several papers presented at the 2nd International Conference on Prospective Memory in July 2005 being developmental. If this trend continues, we may witness particularly important and rapid developments in the research on children's prospective memory in the future.

REFERENCES

Beal, C. R. (1985). Development of knowledge about the use of cues to aid prospective retrieval. *Child Development, 56,* 631–642.

Beal, C. R. (1988). The development of prospective memory skills. In M. M. Gruneberg, P. E. Morris, & R. N. Sykes (Eds.), *Practical aspects of memory: Current research and issues* (Vol. 1, pp. 366–370). Chichester, UK: Wiley.

Brandimonte, M. A., & Passolunghi, M. C. (1994). The effect of cue familiarity, cue-distinctiveness, and retention interval on prospective remembering. *Quarterly Journal of Experimental Psychology, 47A,* 565–588.

Cavanaugh, J. C., & Borkowski, J. G. (1980). Searching for metamemory–memory connections: A developmental study. *Developmental Psychology, 16,* 441–453.

Ceci, S. J., Baker, J. G., & Bronfenbrenner, U. (1988). Prospective remembering and temporal calibration. In M. M. Gruneberg, P. E. Morris, & R. N. Sykes (Eds.), *Practical aspects of memory: Current research and issues* (Vol. 1, pp. 360–365). Chichester, UK: Wiley.

Ceci, S. J., & Bronfenbrenner, U. (1985). "Don't forget to take the cupcakes out of the oven": Prospective memory, strategic time-monitoring, and context. *Child Development, 56,* 152–164.

Cherry, K. E., Martin, R. C., Simmons-D'Gerolamo, S. S., Pinkston, J. B., Griffing, A., & Gouvier, W. D. (2001). Prospective remembering in younger and older adults: Role of prospective cue. *Memory, 9,* 177–193.

Cook, G. I., Marsh, R. L., & Hicks, J. L. (2005). Associating a time-based prospective memory task with an expected context can improve or impair intention completion. *Applied Cognitive Psychology, 19*, 345–360.

Einstein, G. O., Holland, L. J., McDaniel, M. A., & Guynn, M. J. (1992). Age related deficits in prospective memory: The influence of task complexity. *Psychology and Aging, 7*, 471–478.

Einstein, G. O., & McDaniel, M. A. (1990). Normal aging and prospective memory. *Journal of Experimental Psychology: Learning, Memory and Cognition, 16*, 717–726.

Einstein, G. O., & McDaniel, M. A. (1996). Retrieval processes in prospective memory: Theoretical approaches and some new empirical findings. In M. Brandimonte, G. O. Einstein, & M. A. McDaniel (Eds.), *Prospective memory: Theory and applications* (pp. 115–141). Mahwah, NJ: Lawrence Erlbaum Associates, Inc.

Einstein, G. O., McDaniel, M. A., Richardson, S. L., Guynn, M. J., & Cunfer, A. R. (1995). Aging and prospective memory: Examining the influences of self-initiated retrieval. *Journal of Experimental Psychology: Learning, Memory and Cognition, 21*, 996–1007.

Einstein, G. O., McDaniel, M. A., Thomas, R., Mayfield, S., Shank, H., Morrisette, N., et al. (2005). Multiple processes in prospective memory retrieval: Factors determining monitoring and spontaneous retrieval. *Journal of Experimental Psychology: General, 134*, 327–342.

Ellis, J. A. (1996). Prospective memory or the realization of delayed intentions: A conceptual framework for research. In M. Brandimonte, G. O. Einstein, & M. A. McDaniel (Eds.), *Prospective memory: Theory and applications* (pp. 1–22). Mahwah, NJ: Lawrence Erlbaum Associates, Inc.

Ellis, J. A., & Kvavilashvili, L. (2000). Prospective memory in 2000: Past, present and future directions. *Applied Cognitive Psychology, 14*, S1–S9.

Ellis, J. A., & Milne, A. (1996). Retrieval cue specificity and the realization of delayed intentions. *Quarterly Journal of Experimental Psychology, 49A*, 862–887.

Fabricius, W. V., & Wellman, H. M. (1983). Memory development. *Journal of Children in Contemporary Society, 16*, 171–187.

Farrant, A., Boucher, J., & Blades, M. (1999). Metamemory in children with autism. *Child Development, 70*, 107–131.

Freeman, J. E., & Ellis, J. A. (2003). The representation of delayed intentions: A prospective subject-performed task? *Journal of Experimental Psychology: Learning, Memory, and Cognition, 29*, 976–992.

Gathercole, S. E. (1998). The development of memory. *The Journal of Child Psychology and Psychiatry, 39*, 3–27.

Graf, P., & Uttl, B. (2001). Prospective memory: A new focus of research. *Consciousness and Cognition, 10*, 437–450.

Guajardo, N. R., & Best, D. L. (2000). Do preschoolers remember what to do? Incentive and external cues in prospective memory. *Cognitive Development, 15*, 75–97.

Guynn, M. J., McDaniel, M. A., & Einstein, G. O. (2001). Remembering to perform actions: A different type of memory? In H. D. Zimmer, R. L. Cohen, M. J. Guynn, J. Engelkamp, R. Kormi-Nouri, & M. A. Foley (Eds.), *Memory for action: A distinct form of memory?* (pp. 25–48). Oxford, UK: Oxford University Press.

Harris, J. E., & Wilkins, A. J. (1982). Remembering to do things: A theoretical framework and an illustrative experiment. *Human Learning, 1*, 123–136.

Hicks, J. L., Marsh, R. L., & Russell, E. J. (2000). The properties of retention intervals and their affect on retaining prospective memories. *Journal of Experimental Psychology: Learning, Memory, and Cognition, 26*, 1160–1169.

Kerns, K. (2000). The CyberCruiser: An investigation of development of prospective memory in children. *Journal of the International Neuropsychological Society, 6*, 62–70.

Kerns, K. A., & Price, K. J. (2001). An investigation of prospective memory in children with ADHD. *Child Neuropsychology, 7,* 162–171.

Kliegel, M., Martin, M., McDaniel, M. A., & Einstein, G. O. (2001). Varying the importance of a prospective memory task: Differential effects across time- and event-based prospective memory. *Memory, 9,* 1–11.

Kliegel, M., Martin, M., McDaniel, M. A., & Einstein, G. O. (2004). Importance effects on performance in event-based prospective memory tasks. *Memory, 12,* 553–561.

Kliegel, M., Ropeter, A., & Mackinlay, R. J. (2006). Complex prospective memory in children with ADHD. *Child Neuropsychology.*

Kreutzer, M. A., Leonard, C., & Flavell, J. H. (1975). An interview study of children's knowledge about memory. *Monographs of the Society for Research in Child Development, 40*(Serial No. 159).

Kurtz, B. E., & Borkowski, J. G. (1984). Children's metacognition: Exploring relations among knowledge, process and motivational variables. *Journal of Experimental Child Psychology, 37,* 335–354.

Kurtz-Costes, B., Schneider, W., & Rupp, S. (1995). Is there evidence for intraindividual consistency in performance across memory tasks? New evidence on an old question. In F. E. Weinert & W. Schneider (Eds.), *Memory performance and competencies: Issues in growth and development* (pp. 245–262). Mahwah, NJ: Lawrence Erlbaum Associates, Inc.

Kvavilashvili, L. (1987). Remembering intention as a distinct form of memory. *British Journal of Psychology, 78,* 507–518.

Kvavilashvili, L. (1992). Remembering intentions: A critical review of existing experimental paradigms. *Applied Cognitive Psychology, 6,* 507–524.

Kvavilashvili, L., & Ellis, J. A. (1996). Varieties of intention: Some distinctions and classifications. In M. Brandimonte, G. O. Einstein, & M. A. McDaniel (Eds.), *Prospective memory: Theory and applications* (pp. 23–51). Mahwah, NJ: Lawrence Erlbaum Associates, Inc.

Kvavilashvili, L., Kornbrot, D. E., & Messer, D. J. (2002, November). *Effects of age on prospective and retrospective memory in young children and old adults.* Poster presented at the 43rd Psychonomic Society Meeting, Kansas City, MO.

Kvavilashvili, L., Messer, D., & Ebdon, P. (2001). Prospective memory in children: The effects of age and task interruption. *Developmental Psychology, 37,* 418–430.

Kvavilashvili, L., Messer, D. J., & Kyle, F. E. (2002, April). *Event-based prospective memory in 3- to 9-year old children: The effects of age, explanation and type of action.* Paper presented at the Experimental Psychology Society Conference, Leuven, Belgium.

Kvavilashvili, L., & Taylor, K. (2004, August). *Metamemory for prospective and retrospective memory tasks.* Paper presented at the 28th International Congress of Psychology, Beijing, China.

Levine, J. R., Yussen, S. R., DeRose, T. M., & Pressley, M. (1977). Developmental changes in assessing recall and recognition memory capacity. *Developmental Psychology, 13,* 608–615.

Mäntylä, T., & Carelli, M. G. (2005, July). *Time monitoring and executive functions in children and adults.* Paper presented at the 2nd International Conference on Prospective Memory, University of Zurich, Zurich, Switzerland.

Martin, M., & Kliegel, M. (2003). Die Entwicklung komplexer prospektiver Gedachtnisleistung im Kindesalter [The development of complex prospective memory performance in children]. *Zeitschrift-fur-Entwicklungspsychologie-und-Padagogische-Psychologie, 35,* 75–82.

Maylor, E. A., Darby, R. J., Logie, R. H., Della Sala, S., & Smith, G. (2002). Prospective memory across the life span. In P. Graf & N. Ohta (Eds.), *Lifespan development of human memory* (pp. 235–256). Cambridge, MA: MIT Press.

McCauley, S. R., & Levin, H. S. (2004). Prospective memory in pediatric traumatic brain injury: A preliminary study. *Developmental Neuropsychology, 25,* 5–20.

McDaniel, M. A. (1995). Prospective memory: Progress and processes. In D. L. Medin (Ed.), *The psychology of learning and motivation* (Vol. 33, pp. 191–221). San Diego, CA: Academic.

McDaniel, M. A., & Einstein, G. O. (2000). Strategic and automatic processes in prospective memory retrieval: A multiprocess framework. *Applied Cognitive Psychology, 14,* S127–S144.

McDaniel, M. A., Robinson-Riegler, B., & Einstein, G. O. (1998). Prospective remembering: Perceptually driven or conceptually driven processes? *Memory & Cognition, 26,* 121–134.

McGann, D., Defeyter, M. A., Ellis, J. A., & Reid, C. (2005, July). *Prospective memory in children: The effects of age and target salience.* Paper presented at the 2nd International Conference on Prospective Memory, University of Zurich, Zurich, Switzerland.

Meacham, J. A. (1982). A note on remembering to execute planned actions. *Journal of Applied Developmental Psychology, 3,* 121–133.

Meacham, J. A., & Colombo, J. A. (1980). External retrieval cues facilitate prospective remembering in children. *Journal of Educational Research, 73,* 299–301.

Meacham, J. A., & Dumitru, J. (1976). Prospective remembering and external retrieval cues. *Catalog of Selected Documents in Psychology, 6*(No. 65), Ms. No. 1284.

Meacham, J. A., & Singer, J. (1977). Incentive effects in prospective remembering. *Journal of Psychology, 97,* 191–197.

Moscovitch, M. (1982). A neuropsychological approach to memory and perception in normal and pathological aging. In F. I. M. Craik & Trehub (Eds.), *Aging and cognitive processes* (pp. 55–78). New York: Plenum.

Nigro, G., & Cicogna, P. C. (2000). Does delay affect prospective memory performance? *European Psychologist, 5,* 228–233.

Nigro, G., Senese, V. P., Natullo, O., & Sergi, I. (2002). Preliminary remarks on type of task and delay in children's prospective memory. *Perceptual and Motor Skills, 95,* 515–519.

Passolunghi, M. C., Brandimonte, M., & Cornoldi, C. (1995). Encoding modality and prospective memory in children. *International Journal of Behavioral Development, 18,* 631–648.

Rendell, P. G., & Thompson, D. M. (1999). Aging and prospective memory: Differences between naturalistic and laboratory tests. *Journal of Gerontology: Psychological Sciences, 54B,* 256–269.

Schneider, W., & Pressley, M. (1997). *Memory development between two and twenty* (2nd ed.). Mahwah, NJ: Lawrence Erlbaum Associates, Inc.

Shallice, T., & Burgess, P. (1991). Deficits in strategy application following frontal lobe damage in man. *Brain, 114,* 727–741.

Smith, R. E. (2003). The cost of remembering to remember in event-based prospective memory: Investigating the capacity demands of delayed intention performance. *Journal of Experimental Psychology: Learning, Memory, and Cognition, 29,* 347–361.

Somerville, S. C., Wellman, H. M., & Cultice, J. C. (1983). Young children's deliberate reminding. *Journal of Genetic Psychology, 143,* 87–96.

Taylor, R. S., Marsh, R. L., Hicks, J. L., & Hancock, T. W. (2004). The influence of partial-match cues on event-based prospective memory. *Memory, 12,* 203–213.

West, R. L. (1988). Prospective memory and aging. In M. M. Gruneberg, P. E. Morris, & R. N. Sykes (Eds.), *Practical aspects of memory: Current research and issues* (Vol. 2, pp. 119–125). Chichester, UK: Wiley.

Winograd, E. (1988). Some observations on prospective remembering. In M. M. Gruneberg, P. E. Morris, & R. N. Sykes (Eds.), *Practical aspects of memory: Current research and issues* (Vol. 1, pp. 348–353). Chichester, UK: Wiley.

Yussen, S. R., & Berman, L. (1981). Memory predictions for recall and recognition in first-, third-, and fifth-grade children. *Developmental Psychology, 17,* 224–229.

ENDNOTES

[1] We are grateful to Matthias Kliegel for pointing out this possibility to us.

[2] You may have noticed some discrepancy in the findings of Ceci and Bronfenbrenner (1985), who found the U-shaped curve, and all the other studies reviewed in this chapter that reported the J-shaped curve. According to Kerns (2000), this slight discrepancy could be entirely due to the repeated nature of the prospective memory task in her (and the other) studies. Thus, with each consecutive delay interval, the calibration of the internal clock would be less and less necessary resulting in the J-shaped rather than the U-shaped pattern when averaged over several delay intervals.

[3] However, if children use temporal calibration strategy automatically, as suggested by Ceci and Bronfenbrenner (1985), this raises an issue about the definition of strategy. Is an automatically deployed strategy a strategy in its traditional sense used in the developmental research? We are grateful to Matthias Kliegel for pointing this out to us. However, the discussion of this important question is outside the scope of this chapter.

7

The Puzzle of Inconsistent Age-Related Declines in Prospective Memory
A Multiprocess Explanation

MARK A. MCDANIEL

Department of Psychology
Washington University in St. Louis

GILLES O. EINSTEIN

Department of Psychology
Furman University

PETER G. RENDELL

School of Psychology
Australian Catholic University

*P*rospective memory serves an important function for older adults. Some prospective memory tasks help foster and maintain social relations, such as remembering to send a grandchild or a friend a birthday card. Other prospective memory tasks are necessary for normal maintenance, such as remembering to stop at the store for bread, remembering to pay utility bills when they are due, and remembering to turn off the oven. Many other tasks are central to the health needs of older adults, such as remembering to take medication (see McDaniel & Einstein, 2007) and remembering to monitor indexes of physical function (e.g., blood sugar levels; Liu & Park, 2004). Accordingly, in the past 15 years, researchers have begun to focus on age-related changes in prospective memory.

In this chapter, we examine aging and event-based prospective memory. Event-based tasks involve remembering to perform an intended action when a specific event occurs. Examples include remembering to give a friend a message when you see her and remembering to buy bread when you pass the grocery store.

In a seminal analysis, Craik (1986) suggested that prospective memory involves more self-initiated retrieval than retrospective memory and thus should be especially difficult for older adults. Consistent with this analysis, many studies using laboratory event-based paradigms have reported robust age-related decrements in prospective memory (e.g., d'Ydewalle, Luwel, & Brunfaut, 1999; Mäntylä & Nilsson, 1997; Maylor, 1993, 1996; Park, Hertzog, Kidder, Morrell, & Mayhorn, 1997; Vogels, Dekker, Brouwer, & de Jong, 2002), and a recent meta-analytic review of prospective memory and aging (laboratory-based) experiments reinforces the view that prospective memory generally declines with age (Henry, MacLeod, Phillips, & Crawford, 2004).

However, some event-based laboratory prospective memory studies have found small or no age differences (e.g., Cherry & LeCompte, 1999; Einstein & McDaniel, 1990; Einstein, McDaniel, Richardson, Guynn, & Cunfer, 1995; Reese & Cherry, 2002). Given the ubiquity of prospective memory tasks in everyday life and the demographics of an increasingly aging society, it is important to understand the conditions under which older adults do and do not perform comparably to younger adults on prospective memory tasks. In this chapter, we focus on several theories that identify various factors in the prospective memory task as central to age-related changes in prospective remembering. In addition, we present new experiments conducted in our laboratories that directly measure and manipulate the theoretical factors highlighted next.

THE MULTIPROCESS THEORY

The specific event signaling the appropriateness of executing an intended action can be considered a prospective memory cue or target (McDaniel & Einstein, 1993). The multiprocess framework of McDaniel and Einstein (2000) makes a distinction between prospective memory cues that overlap with the information constellation relevant to performing the ongoing task[1] (we label these *focal* cues) versus those cues that are present in the environment but not part of the information being considered by the person (labeled *nonfocal* cues). An everyday example of a focal cue would be encountering and pausing to converse with the friend to whom you intended to give a message. An example of a nonfocal cue would be a grocery store (for stopping to buy bread) located a bit off the road when you are traveling in rush hour traffic (and thus attending closely to the other cars). Table 7.1 provides descriptions of how various laboratory-based tasks could be implemented with either focal or nonfocal cues.

It is important to clarify several aspects of our distinction between focal and nonfocal cues. First, a nonfocal cue might still be in the visual field; the key is that

---

[1] Other terms for the activity in which the prospective memory task is embedded have been used in the literature, including *background, foreground,* and *cover task/activity. Ongoing task* was the term agreed on by a meeting of the participants at the First International Conference on Prospective Memory, Hatfield, UK, July 2000.

TABLE 7.1   Representative Examples of Task Conditions That We
Assume Are Low and High in Focal Processing (Some Used
in Published Research)

Processing	Ongoing Task	Prospective Memory
Nonfocal	Words are presented in the center of a computer monitor and participants are told to learn them for recall tests that occur at unpredictable times.	Respond when you see a particular background pattern (background pattern changes every 3 seconds).
Focal	Keep track of the number of occurrences of each background screen pattern.	Respond when you see a particular background pattern (background pattern is changed every 3 seconds).
Nonfocal	Lexical decision task.	Respond to items from the "animal" category.
Focal	Lexical decision task.	Respond to the word cat.
Nonfocal	Pairs of words are presented and participants decide whether the word on the left is a member of the category on the right.	Respond to the syllable tor.
Focal	Pairs of words are presented and participants decide whether the word on the left is a member of the category on the right.	Respond to the word tortoise.
Nonfocal	Pictures of famous faces are presented, and the task is to name the face.	Respond when you see a face in which a person is wearing eyeglasses.
Focal	Pictures of famous faces are presented, and the task is to name the face.	Respond when you see a face with the first name of John.

Note. Adapted from Einstein and McDaniel (2005).

the prospective memory cue is not a feature directly relevant to the ongoing task. For instance, in a laboratory prospective memory task used by Maylor (1996), the ongoing activity was to name pictures of famous faces. The prospective memory cue was the presence of eyeglasses on the face. Certainly when looking at the face (the picture), eyeglasses are in the visual field. However, the features processed to name the face did not depend on considering whether the face has eyeglasses.

Second, some theorists have noted that task-appropriate processing is an important determinant of prospective memory performance in general (Marsh, Hicks, & Cook, 2005) and of age-related effects in particular (Maylor, Darby, Logie, Della Sala, & Smith, 2002). The notion here is that prospective memory will be improved to the extent that the level of processing of the target cue and the ongoing task are congruent. For example, a task-appropriate prospective memory task would be one in which both the target cue and the ongoing task require nonsemantic processing or semantic processing. Theoretical work has sometimes equated the task-appropriate processing notion with the multiprocess distinction of focal and nonfocal cues (e.g., Marsh et al., 2005). The two ideas are not the same, however. Task-appropriate prospective memory tasks can reflect focal processing as described earlier, but need not do so. Instantiations of task-appropriate processing in the literature as often as not produce nonfocal cue conditions. For instance, performing lexical decisions as an ongoing task and executing the prospective memory intention when a member of the animal category is presented are both semantic tasks. However, making a decision about whether a letter string is a word (lexical decision) does not require processing the semantic features necessary to make a category determination. Although this is a task-appropriate prospective memory task, it is not a task with a focal cue. Consequently, performance aspects of the task would not be expected to show predicted behaviors for a focal cue, as some have suggested (cf. Marsh et al., 2005).

Pertinent to the issue of aging and prospective memory, the multiprocess view further suggests that focal cues can stimulate a relatively automatic spontaneous retrieval of the intended action, whereas nonfocal cues require more strategic attentional resources to monitor for the cue signaling the appropriateness of performing the intended action (see Einstein et al., 2005, for empirical support). Based on this idea, McDaniel and Einstein (2000) reasoned that older adults should show relatively intact remembering (relative to young adults) when the prospective memory task involves a focal event-based cue because focal cues do not require self-initiated retrieval and because spontaneous retrieval processes are thought to be preserved in older adults (e.g., Craik, 1986). In contrast, older adults will be disproportionately challenged by nonfocal cues because these cues place more demands on attentional resources (e.g., for monitoring for the cue), resources that presumably decline with age (e.g., Craik & Byrd, 1982). Because of these resource challenges, McDaniel and Einstein suggested that age-related declines in prospective memory would be more robust for nonfocal cues.

The foregoing analysis is consistent with the literature. Studies that have found no significant age differences in prospective memory have used focal cues. For instance, in Cherry and LeCompte's (1999) and Einstein and McDaniel's (1990) research, the target cue was the appearance of a particular word and the ongoing task was remembering a set of presented words (see also Einstein et al., 1995, Experiments 2 & 3).[2] By comparison, studies that have found robust age differences have used nonfocal target cues. In Maylor's (1993, 1996) research, the target cue was the presence of eyeglasses or a pipe (depending on the experiment) in the picture of a famous face, and the ongoing task was to name the famous face (eyeglasses do not have to be processed to name a face). In Park et al. (1997) the ongoing task involved remembering items, and the target cue was a particular background pattern on which the to-be-remembered items for the ongoing task were displayed. More directly, in an experiment contrasting focal and nonfocal cues across younger and older adults, age-related declines were significantly larger for nonfocal than for focal cues (Maylor et al., 2002).

Our focus in this chapter is in understanding how focal and nonfocal cues influence retrieval processes in prospective memory as it relates to age differences. It is important to note, however, that the multiprocess theory also assumes that other variables, such as the length of the delay between intention formation

---

[2] One puzzling exception is the finding of age-related decrements in prospective memory when a focal cue is related to the initiation of a complex task (the six-elements task), which itself contains prospective memory demands (Kliegel, McDaniel, & Einstein, 2000). Although entirely speculative, perhaps the embeddings of several prospective tasks present additional complexities that disadvantage older adults.

and the anticipated opportunity for execution, the importance of the prospective memory task, and the number of different target cues can affect whether people rely on spontaneous retrieval versus monitoring processes in a prospective memory situation (Einstein et al., 2005; McDaniel & Einstein, 2000).

MONITORING AND RESOURCE ALLOCATION

Another theoretical view is advocated by Smith (2003; see also Smith, chap. 2, this volume). She argues that capacity-demanding attentional processes are always necessary for successfully interpreting an environmental event as a prospective memory target event. In this view, a capacity-consuming monitoring process is needed for successful prospective memory, regardless of whether the target cue is focal or nonfocal. This view explicitly places prospective memory in a dual-task framework, in which the ongoing task and the prospective memory task are essentially competing for limited resources, and as such prospective memory (as well as ongoing task) performance will depend on one's resource allocation policies. Such resource allocation policies can theoretically produce a continuum of combinations of trade-offs in performance between task x (e.g., ongoing task) and task y (prospective memory; Navon & Gopher, 1979).

Applying these ideas to aging and prospective memory (e.g., Smith & Bayen, 2006), the expectation is that age-related declines in prospective memory will generally be observed because older adults presumably will try to hold ongoing task performance at a reasonable level, and thus prospective memory will decline (given age-related decrements in attentional resources; Salthouse, 1991b). Note, however, that this approach can possibly account for the results reviewed showing no age-related decline with focal cues. The idea is that in these studies older adults' resource allocation policies were selected to maintain relatively high levels of prospective memory, but did so at a disproportionate cost to the ongoing task. That is, older adults in some cases may be willing to sacrifice ongoing task performance to maintain respectable levels of prospective memory performance. To date, however, this idea is virtually untested because with the exception of Rendell, McDaniel, Forbes, and Einstein (2007, Experiment 1) published studies on prospective memory and aging have not been designed to evaluate the costs of prospective memory performances on ongoing task performance.

In the next sections we review the Rendell et al. (2007) experiment and then report two new experiments, all of which manipulated the nature of the target cues (focal vs. nonfocal) and evaluated younger and older adults' performance on both (a) levels of prospective memory remembering and (b) costs of the prospective memory task. These designs thus involved control conditions in which the ongoing task was performed in the absence of the prospective memory task, and costs of the prospective memory task were assessed by comparing ongoing performance in the control and prospective memory conditions. According to the multiprocess framework, a focal target should produce minimal age differences, and critically, older (and younger) adults' performance on the ongoing task should not be compromised by the prospective memory task. With a nonfocal cue, however, both older and younger adults should show costs for the ongoing activity. Further, older adults should either show declines in prospective memory (relative to younger adults and relative to the focal cue condition), or older adults might maintain prospective memory performance but at the expense of disproportionate costs (relative to younger adults) to the ongoing activity.

Alternatively, given a common view that age differences in prospective memory are generally found in laboratory prospective memory tasks (Craik, 2003), negative effects of age should emerge on the prospective memory task. Further, the Smith and Bayen (2006) view anticipates some indication of decrements on the ongoing task (costs) when a prospective memory task is present and especially so for older adults. According to this view, it is possible that no age differences will occur, but such an effect should be accompanied by robust costs for older adults relative to younger adults to the ongoing activity for both focal and nonfocal cue conditions. The idea here is that resources ordinarily directed at performing the ongoing task in the control condition will be significantly diminished for older adults because of the demand for their limited attentional resources to monitor for the prospective memory target event.

RENDELL, MCDANIEL, FORBES, AND EINSTEIN EXPERIMENT

The ongoing task in Rendell et al. (2007, Experiment 1) closely followed Maylor's (1993, 1996, 1998) famous faces task as participants were shown 120 pictures of famous faces one at a time and asked to name the faces. The nonfocal prospective memory condition was similar to the Maylor (1996) version as participants were asked to make a response whenever they saw a famous face wearing eyeglasses. In the focal prospective memory condition, participants were asked to make a response whenever they saw a face with the first name of John. The pacing of the ongoing task was identical for the 78 younger adults ($M = 19.6$ years) and the 60 older adults ($M = 75.4$ years). Twenty-six younger adults and 20 older adults were assigned to each of two prospective memory conditions (focal, nonfocal) and to a control condition in which participants performed only the ongoing task.

The central finding was a significant interaction between age and target cue for the proportion of correct prospective memory responses. The age deficit was significantly larger in the nonfocal condition (younger adults: $M = .87$; older adults: $M = .55$; effect size in terms of $\eta^2 = .23$) than in the focal condition (younger adults: $M = .90$; older adults: $M = .78$; $\eta^2 = .07$). Another way to view this interaction is that the prospective memory of older adults was significantly higher in the focal condition than in the nonfocal condition, but this was not the case for younger adults, who showed similar levels of performance regardless of the type of target. Ongoing task performance in the three conditions (focal, nonfocal, control), which in this experiment was measured by the proportion of faces correctly named, did not interact with age, and this performance was not significantly affected by performing the prospective memory task. These results directly demonstrate the reduction of age differences with a focal relative to a nonfocal cue, and importantly show that this reduction cannot be attributed to older adults sacrificing ongoing task performance.

These results are consistent with the multiprocess framework (McDaniel & Einstein, 2000). Although the cues of eyeglasses and John were both within the visual field of the participants, the cues differed in their relevance to the features processed to name the face. John is directly relevant to the ongoing task, whereas the presence of eyeglasses is not directly relevant. This opportunity for related processing with the focal rather than nonfocal cue reduced age deficits and therefore indicates that prospective memory retrieval with focal cues could be relatively automatic.

The pattern reported here neatly matches the previous studies that have reported substantial age deficits on the prospective memory tasks with nonfocal cues (Maylor, 1993, 1996; Park et al., 1997) and no significant age differences with focal cues (Cherry & LeCompte, 1999; Einstein & McDaniel, 1990; Einstein et al., 1995, Experiments 1 & 2). The match is not perfect, though, because the age differences were reduced but not eliminated in the focal cue condition. Rendell et al. (2007) proposed this could reflect older adults' relative difficulty with the time limitations on the ongoing task, difficulty due to age-related cognitive slowing (Salthouse, 1991a). Specifically, the presentation times for the faces were identical for younger and older partcipants, and, given cognitive slowing that occurs with age, the ongoing task could have been functionally more demanding for older adults (see Kvavilashvili, Kyle, & Messer, chap. 6, this volume, for further specification of this point).

NEW EXPERIMENTS

Experiment 1

This experiment was a variation of Rendell et al. (2007, Experiment 1), but rather than asking participants to write down the names of the faces, we asked them to write down the occupations of the faces. The focal target cue was a particular occupation (politician), whereas the nonfocal cue was the presence of eyeglasses on the face. As in Rendell et al., to examine possible trade-offs between the prospective and ongoing tasks, we compared participants' performance on the ongoing task in the prospective memory groups with performance on the ongoing task in control groups that performed only the ongoing task.

Fourteen younger and 14 older adults were assigned to each of the prospective memory conditions (focal vs. nonfocal cues). In addition, 18 younger and 18 older adults were assigned to the control condition in which participants performed only the ongoing task. The younger adults (undergraduates from the University of New Mexico) ranged in age from 18 to 46 years ($M = 21.5$). The older adults (from the greater Albuquerque, New Mexico, area) ranged in age from 63 to 86 years ($M = 73.5$).

The proportions of successful prospective memory responses (out of eight trials) are displayed in Figure 7.1 as a function of age group and type of prospective memory cue (focal, nonfocal). As can be seen, the focal cue produced substantially higher performance than the nonfocal cue ($Ms = .86$ vs. $.42$), but prospective memory levels did not significantly differ as a function of age ($Ms = .66$ and $.62$ for younger and older adults, respectively). This finding was not modulated by the type of cue, as the absence of age differences was observed for both the focal and nonfocal cues.

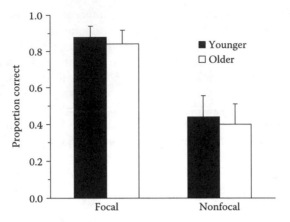

FIGURE 7.1   Mean proportion of correct responses on the prospective memory task (out of a possible eight) in Experiment 1. Error bars represent standard errors of the mean.

To shed light on the possible explanations outlined earlier for the absence of age deficits in prospective memory, we examined performance on the ongoing activity. Control group performance on the ongoing activity was used as a baseline against which to gauge the degree to which the ongoing activity performance declined in the presence of the prospective memory task. We scored the proportion of correct responses for the occupation identification task, and Figure 7.2 gives the mean proportions for the experimental and control groups. In general, performance was worse for older adults than for younger adults. Inspection of Figure 7.2 indicates

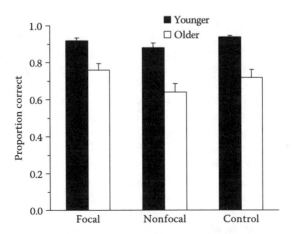

FIGURE 7.2   Mean proportion of the correct occupations identified (out of a possible 120) in Experiment 1, according to prospective memory condition (Control = no prospective memory task). Error bars represent standard errors of the mean.

that the decline for older adults occurred in both the prospective memory and the control conditions. Thus, even without prospective memory demands, this occupation identification task was harder for older adults. Whether the age decrement was knowledge based (i.e., older adults knew fewer of the occupations for the famous faces) or whether it was based on retrieval difficulties (e.g., retrieval demands of the task disfavored older adults), or both, is not certain.

The critical issue for purposes here, however, concerns how performance on the occupation identification task fared for each age group in the presence of focal cue and nonfocal cue prospective memory demands relative to performance when prospective memory was not required (the control group). Statistical analyses revealed that for younger adults performance on the occupation task did not significantly decline with the addition of either type of prospective memory task. Likewise, for older adults with a focal prospective memory cue, performance on the ongoing activity ($M = .75$) did not decline relative to performance in the no-prospective memory control ($M = .73$). By contrast, with a nonfocal cue, older adults showed a significant drop in performance on the occupation identification task ($M = .64$) relative to the no-prospective memory control.

These results are again consistent with the multiprocess framework (McDaniel & Einstein, 2000; see also Maylor et al.'s, 2002, task-appropriate processing view). When the prospective memory task was signaled by a cue that is focal to the processing of the ongoing activity, there were no significant age differences in prospective memory performance. More critically, we found no costs to the occupation identification activity for older (and younger) adults when the prospective cue was focal. The pattern thus converges on the theoretical position that with focal cues, prospective memory retrieval can be relatively automatic (McDaniel & Einstein, 2000) and therefore exhibits minimal or no age-related decline.

Another new finding was that older adults maintained prospective memory performance at levels displayed by younger adults even when the prospective memory task used nonfocal cues. This result can be understood by the observation that older but not younger adults incurred significant expense to the ongoing activities in the presence of the nonfocal cue prospective memory task. In the next experiment we investigated whether a different set of older adults with different prospective memory and ongoing tasks would also operate with this particular trade-off (i.e., maintain prospective memory with nonfocal cues at the expense of the ongoing activity). We also used an ongoing activity that provided reaction times (a more telling index of cost; Smith, 2003) and relied on within-subjects comparisons to test for converging support for these patterns just reported.

Experiment 2

The ongoing activity was a category judgment task patterned after that used by Einstein et al. (2005, Experiment 2), who demonstrated that response latencies were sensitive to costs produced in conditions in which participants were explicitly encouraged to adopt monitoring strategies for the prospective memory task. The category judgment activity involved presenting a word and a category label, and participants were required to decide as quickly as possible whether the word was a category coordinate. In the focal cue condition, the target cue was a particular word (e.g., *dormitory*), whereas in the nonfocal cue condition the target cue was a syllable (e.g., *tor*). We measured each participant's attention allocated toward the prospective memory task by comparing the participant's accuracy and speed of performance on the ongoing task with and without the prospective memory task.

Two issues were of central interest. First, we wanted to see if older adults would again maintain levels of prospective memory performance at levels evidenced by younger adults even with demanding nonfocal cues. Second, we were interested in the age-related pattern of costs on the category judgment task produced in the focal cue and the nonfocal cue conditions. By most if not all views of prospective memory, in the nonfocal cue condition older adults should show poorer prospective memory performance or disproportionately more costs than younger adults, or both. Predictions start to diverge for the focal condition. The multiprocess framework (McDaniel & Einstein, 2000) anticipates no costs for either younger or older adults. By contrast, views assuming that capacity-demanding attentional processes are necessary for prospective remembering (e.g., Smith, 2003) predict significant costs to the ongoing activity for both younger and older adults in the focal cue condition accompanied by age-related decrements in prospective memory, disproportionate costs for older adults (given age-related declines in attentional resources; Salthouse, 1991b), or both.

There were 24 participants from each age group assigned to each condition (focal vs. nonfocal target). The younger adults were students at Furman University, ranging in age from 18 to 23 years ($M = 20.29$). The older adults lived in the Greenville, South Carolina, area and ranged in age from 68.6 to 82 years ($M = 0$). The younger and older participants were included from the outset of the experiment (i.e., tested during the same time period and by the same experimenters), however, the data from the younger participants have been reported for other purposes in Einstein et al. (2005). They are described here as baselines for evaluating age-related changes in prospective memory.

Table 7.2 provides the proportion of successful prospective memory responses as a function of target condition (focal, nonfocal), prospective memory trial (Trials 1–4), and age (younger, older). The results were entirely in line with Experiment 1. There was no significant difference between the prospective memory performance of younger adults and older adults ($Ms = .77$ and $.72$). Prospective memory performance was significantly better with the word (focal) target ($M = .92$) than with the syllable (nonfocal) target ($M = .57$), and this effect did not interact with age. In addition, prospective memory significantly declined by Trial 4 relative to the initial trials.[3] Importantly, this decline over trials significantly interacted with the type of target. As can be seen in Table 7.2, prospective memory declined across trials for the syllable condition but not for the word condition.

Participants' accuracy on the category decision task was generally high ($M = .97$) and varied only slightly across conditions (see Table 7.3 for means). To

---

[3] With trial as a variable, the prospective memory data are dichotomous (0, 1) for each cell. When degrees of freedom are not low (e.g., less than 20), as in this analysis, analysis of variance gives accurate results with such data (Rosenthal & Rosnow, 1991, p. 521).

TABLE 7.2   Mean Proportion Correct on the Prospective Memory Task in Experiment 2

Age Group	Quadrant	Target Condition	
		Focal (Word)	Nonfocal (Syllables)
Younger	1	.92	.71
	2	.96	.71
	3	.96	.63
	4	.88	.42
Older	1	.83	.63
	2	1.00	.54
	3	.92	.58
	4	.88	.38

determine whether performing a prospective memory task exacted costs on the reaction times in the ongoing task, we tabulated the reaction times of those trials that the participants answered correctly in both the prospective memory section and the nonprospective memory section of the experiment. The results from the trimmed and untrimmed data did not differ, so we report only the trimmed data here (given in Table 7.4).

TABLE 7.3   Mean Proportion Correct on the Ongoing Activity (Category Judgment) in Experiment 2

Age Group	Quadrant	Target Condition					
		Focal (Word)			Nonfocal (Syllable)		
		Control	PM	Cost	Control	PM	Cost
Younger	1	.97	.96	.01	.95	.96	−.01
	2	.95	.96	−.01	.96	.96	.00
	3	.97	.94	.03	.96	.96	.00
	4	.96	.95	.01	.96	.97	−.01
	Overall			.01			.00
Older	1	.98	.96	.02	.98	.97	.01
	2	.98	.98	.00	.97	.97	.00
	3	.97	.98	−.01	.97	.97	.00
	4	.97	.98	−.01	.98	.96	.02
	Overall			.00			.01

Note. PM = prospective memory

TABLE 7.4   Mean Response Times (in ms) to the Ongoing Activity (Category Judgment) in Experiment 2

Age Group	Quadrant	Focal (Word)			Nonfocal (Syllable)		
		Control	PM	Cost	Control	PM	Cost
Younger	1	1,108.76	1,160.54	51.78	969.02	1,240.36	271.34
	2	1,122.50	1,096.72	−25.78	971.36	1,190.24	218.88
	3	1,096.18	1,175.57	79.39	957.19	1,122.55	165.36
	4	1,108.99	1,120.33	11.34	952.68	1,090.58	137.90
	Overall			29.18			198.37
Older	1	1,419.56	1,521.07	101.51	1,445.00	2,239.12	794.12
	2	1,397.02	1,446.76	49.74	1,404.60	2,073.24	668.64
	3	1,376.36	1,447.83	71.47	1,440.87	1,888.63	447.76
	4	1,351.35	1,398.86	47.51	1,437.62	1,828.79	391.17
	Overall			67.56			575.42

Note. PM = prospective memory

Importantly, the cost incurred by the prospective memory task was significantly greater when the target was nonfocal (the syllable condition) than when the target was focal (the word condition). Further, there was a significant cost of the prospective memory task with the nonfocal cue ($M = 386.89$, for the cost), but not with the focal cue ($M = 48.38$). As can be seen in Table 7.4, both young and older adults showed the same pattern (no significant cost with focal cues for either age group). However, older adults showed more pronounced costs with the nonfocal cue than did younger adults. That is, with the nonfocal cue, older adults showed significantly greater increases in response times in the presence of the prospective memory task (relative to when it was not present; i.e., greater cost) than did younger adults.

Another interesting finding was that the costs of the prospective memory task generally declined throughout the experiment. This pattern of costs signals true reduction in costs: Response times in the prospective memory condition became faster as the experiment progressed, whereas the control response times were virtually unchanged from quadrant to quadrant. Also of note, the decline in costs across quadrants was significantly modulated by the type of target. As can be seen in Table 7.4, the cost to the ongoing activity incurred by the prospective memory task decreased prominently over the four blocks of trials with the nonfocal (syllable) targets, but less so for the focal (word) targets.

These results reinforce and extend the important findings from Experiment 1. Once again, older adults performed as well as younger adults in prospective memory across both focal and nonfocal cue conditions. Critically, this is the first experiment that has directly demonstrated that the absence of age differences with focal cues is not accompanied by significant costs to the ongoing activity for the older adults, when costs are assessed with sensitive reaction time measures (cf. Smith, 2003). Indeed, the small and nonsignificant costs (due to the presence of a prospective memory demand) in response times for the ongoing task observed for older adults did not differ from the small and nonsignificant costs observed for the younger adults. Importantly, the nonsignificance of the costs did not reflect inadequate power to detect an effect. The overall power to detect an effect for possible costs of the focal cue was .92 for a medium size effect and 1.00 for a large size effect, with the usual reaction time costs falling between medium and large effect sizes (Smith, 2003, Experiments 1 & 2). By contrast, the absence of age differences with nonfocal cues was accompanied by significant costs in response times to the ongoing activity, costs that were especially pronounced for the older adults. As outlined in previous sections, this entire pattern is consistent with a framework that assumes that focal cues support relatively spontaneous prospective memory retrieval, whereas nonfocal cues require more resource-demanding monitoring processes (Einstein et al., 2005; McDaniel & Einstein, 2000).

This pattern is inconsistent with general views proposing that prospective memory necessarily requires high levels of self-initiated retrieval processes (e.g., Craik, 1986) or requires resource-demanding preparatory attentional processes (Smith, 2003; Smith & Bayen, 2006). These views generally anticipate age-related declines in prospective memory. In the absence of such declines, however, these views must assume that older adults are trading off performance on the ongoing activity to maintain reasonable levels of prospective memory performance. Clearly, for focal prospective memory cues, such trade-offs did not occur in this experiment. Older adults were as accurate and as fast on the category decision task in the presence of the prospective memory task (relative to its absence) and still achieved levels of prospective memory performance comparable to younger adults.

Another telling finding was that monitoring declines across the course of the experiment (as indicated by costs to the ongoing activity) were associated with reduced prospective memory in the nonfocal condition but not the focal condition. This pattern converges on the idea that prospective memory with focal cues is not overly dependent on monitoring (or other attention-demanding processes). Finally, the decline in monitoring (costs) as the experiment progressed indicates that capacity-consuming monitoring processes are difficult to maintain. This dovetails with the claim of the multiprocess framework that it would be maladaptive to rely exclusively on monitoring processes because doing so quickly taxes limited attention resources (Einstein et al., 2005). Monitoring appears to be difficult to sustain over relatively short intervals, making it implausible that monitoring would be prominently engaged across the substantial intervals present in everyday prospective memory tasks (cf. Smith, chap. 2, this volume).

DIRECT EVIDENCE FOR PRESERVED SPONTANEOUS RETRIEVAL IN OLDER ADULTS

Our assumption throughout has been that spontaneous retrieval processes are relatively unaffected by aging (e.g., Craik, 1986; Dywan & Jacoby, 1990). In recent years, we have developed an experimental paradigm for directly measuring spontaneous retrieval processes as they occur in prospective memory contexts (Einstein et al., 2005, Experiment 5; Einstein & McDaniel, 2005). The general rationale underlying this paradigm is to give participants a prospective memory intention (e.g., press a key whenever they see a target item) in the context of a particular ongoing task and then to ask participants to suspend this prospective memory intention while performing a different "speed" task in which their only demand is to perform the task as accurately and quickly as possible. Critically, we present the prospective memory target during this speed task, and our interest is in the accuracy and speed of responding. Because participants were specifically instructed to suspend the prospective memory intention during the speed task, there should be no monitoring. Given, however, that a characteristic of a spontaneous retrieval process is that it should occur without intention, any slowing in responding to the prospective memory target relative to a matched control item (which also had been exposed earlier) should reflect spontaneous retrieval processes. Using this paradigm, we (Einstein et al., 2005, Experiment 5) found that younger adults were about 55 ms slower to respond to the prospective memory targets. Our interpretation of this slowing was that presenting a prospective memory target in the context of this other task caused participants to spontaneously retrieve components of the prospective memory intention, and this slowed down responding to the speed task.

In a recent study in our laboratory conducted by Arnold, Bishop, Roberts, and Scullin, we found preliminary evidence for preserved spontaneous retrieval processes in older adults. In the initial phase of the experiment, we gave groups of 32 younger and 32 older participants instructions and practice on an image-rating ongoing task. In the next phase, we gave participants instructions and practice for the prospective memory task. Specifically, participants were asked to press the 8 key on the computer keyboard whenever they saw either of two target words (e.g., *corn* and *dancer*) in the context of the image-rating task. In the next phase, participants were told that we would return to these tasks later and that we first wanted them to perform a lexical decision task. We defined this as a speed task, told participants to suspend all previous task demands, and told them to focus exclusively on responding as quickly and accurately as possible on this task. Despite these instructions, we presented each prospective memory target (and matched control items) five times during this task. Consistent with the previously described results, there was significant slowing to prospective memory targets relative to control items; importantly, this slowing was at least as large in older adults (720 ms for control items and 764 ms for target items, a slowing of 44 ms) as for younger adults (536 ms for control items and 553 ms for target items, a slowing of 17 ms). Although the slowing was nominally larger with older adults, the interaction between type of item and age condition was not significant. Because older adults were slower in general to perform lexical decisions, it is interesting to note that the percentage slowing was at least nominally larger in older adults ($M = 6.0\%$) than in younger adults ($M = 3.2\%$).

In general, then, these initial results with older adults suggest that the presentation of specific prospective memory target events, even in a context in which they are not anticipated, leads to the reflexive retrieval of intention-related information. These items are in some sense "loaded," and their presentation produces an additional response in the system. This response appears to be at least as large in older adults as in younger adults.

DISCUSSION AND CONCLUSIONS

A common generalization in the aging literature is that age differences are found in prospective memory (e.g., see Craik, 2003; West & Craik, 1999). Although this generalization has received support from laboratory examinations of prospective memory (see Henry et al.'s, 2004, meta-analysis), there are a number of studies that report no age differences (see the introduction to this chapter). Moreover, the idea that age produces decrements in prospective memory has not received support in naturalistic studies (Rendell & Thomson, 1993, 1999). In naturalistic paradigms, age differences rarely occur, and when they do it is older adults who outperform younger adults (Henry et al., 2004; Phillips, Henry & Martin, Chapter 6, this volume). The set of experiments presented in this chapter provides a basis for understanding this mixed pattern and perhaps especially for reconciling the contrary patterns reported between laboratory and naturalistic prospective memory tasks.

To recapitulate, we (Rendell et al., 2007) demonstrated an interaction between the extent of age-related differences in prospective memory and the nature of the target cue: With focal target cues, the age difference was significantly attenuated. Second, in two new experiments, the results were even more pronounced. We found that older adults performed as well as younger adults on prospective memory tasks across very different paradigms and contexts. The paradigms incorporated different ongoing activities, different prospective memory target events, different experimenters (postgraduate students in Experiment 1 and undergraduate students in Experiment 2), participants from different geographical locations of the country, and participants with different experiential backgrounds and characteristics (in Experiment 1, older participants were from a long-term aging study and younger participants were from a state university with modest admission criteria, whereas in Experiment 2 older participants were recruited for the single experimental session and younger participants were enrolled in a highly selective private university). The consistent age invariance in prospective memory was obtained in the context of these divergent laboratory conditions, thereby promoting confidence that the patterns are not limited to rather narrow boundary conditions.

One might question the power of these experiments to detect age differences in prospective memory. In a meta-analysis of event-based laboratory experiments, the overall age-related deficit was reported to be of medium size (Henry et al., 2004). The power to detect a medium size age effect in prospective memory performance was modest in the new Experiment 1 (.44) and more respectable in Experiment 2 (.67). To augment the statistical power, we collapsed the prospective memory data from both experiments into one analysis of variance, with age and the type of cue (focal, nonfocal) as between-subject variables. The results were identical to those reported in each experiment, with substantial power (.86) to detect both an age difference and an interaction between age and cue type. This pattern compels the conclusion that there were no age differences in prospective memory performance.

There are three novel and critical aspects of these patterns that merit emphasis. First, the absence (or attenuation) of age differences in prospective memory when a (single) target cue was focal to the ongoing task occurred without significant costs to the ongoing task for the older adults. Even when costs were measured in terms of speed of performing the ongoing task (new Experiment 2), a measure advocated by theorists for assessing prospective-memory related costs to the ongoing activity (Smith, 2003), there was no indication that older adults maintained high levels of prospective memory at the expense of performing the cover activity (nor did younger adults show costs to the ongoing activity in the presence of the prospective memory task). These data, therefore, provide the strongest support to date for the idea that when the prospective memory cue is focal to the ongoing task, for older adults prospective memory retrieval can be accomplished with few resources. That is, focal cues seem to promote spontaneous prospective memory retrieval (see McDaniel & Einstein, 2000, for details with young adults). The second critical finding is the direct evidence that this spontaneous retrieval is spared in older adults (the experiment with Arnold, Bishop, Roberts, & Scullin), a claim that is consistent with theoretical accounts of aging and memory (Craik, 1986; Hasher & Zacks, 1979). Accordingly, for prospective memory tasks with focal cues, age-related decline in prospective memory is not especially likely.

Consequently, in naturalistic prospective memory situations in which the target event is focal to one's ongoing activity (e.g., encountering a neighbor to whom one intends to give a message, or encountering a garbage can on trash pick-up day), age-related deficits would not be expected, nor are they found. Further, in naturalistic settings, the delays between forming an intention and the opportunity to execute it are often substantial. Based on our finding (in the new Experiment 2) that attention-demanding self-initiated processes (e.g., monitoring) are taxing and decline over relatively short delays, we believe that both younger and older adults most often tend to rely on spontaneous retrieval processes. Given the theoretical assumption that spontaneous retrieval processes are preserved with age and our additional new finding that supports this assumption, the failure to obtain age decrements in naturalistic tasks can be understood (see also Kvavilashvili & Fisher, 2005, Study 2).

The third critical finding concerns the absence of age differences when the ongoing task did not encourage focal processing of the target event (i.e., the target event of a face with glasses during the ongoing task of naming the occupations of the people pictured; the target event of a particular syllable during the ongoing task of deciding whether the word was a category coordinate). With such nonfocal targets, we (McDaniel & Einstein, 2000) have argued that successful prospective memory retrieval is more dependent on strategic processes that monitor environmental events for the target (see also Guynn, 2003; Smith, 2003). This strategic monitoring is thought to invoke attentional or working memory resources, and given that the ongoing task requires attentional resources as well, then performance theoretically will be characterized by the person's resource allocation policy to the two demanding activities (Navon & Gopher, 1979). From previous work (Einstein et al., 2005; Guynn, 2001; Smith, 2003), we expected that younger adults would support prospective memory at the expense of the ongoing activity. We were uncertain what older adults' resource allocation poli-cies would be. It seemed possible that older adults might be able to support relatively high levels of prospective memory performance, if they were willing to allow reductions in performance on the ongoing activity. Previous studies, however, had typically reported age-related declines in prospective memory for nonfocal targets (Maylor, 1993, 1996; Park et al., 1997; Rendell et al., 2007). According to some views that posit that prospective memory exerts substantial attentional demands, and an accompanying reduction in these resources with age (Salthouse, 1991b; Verhaeghen, Marcoen, & Goossens, 1993; Zacks & Hasher, 1988), older adults might be unable even through appropriate resource allocation to maintain prospective memory levels evidenced by younger adults (e.g., Craik, 1986; Smith & Bayen, 2004).

In the two new experiments reported here, at least, older adults' resource allo-cation policies with nonfocal target events clearly supported prospective memory at levels comparable to those of younger adults. Performing at levels equivalent to the younger adults in the nonfocal condition came at a price, however. In Experi-ments 1 and 2, older adults had exaggerated costs (relative to younger adults) on the ongoing activity in the presence of the nonfocal prospective memory task. One important methodological implication is that it seems important when examining age differences in prospective memory to include measures that enable you to examine resource allocation policies (cf. Park et al., 1997; Smith, 2003).

More important, these findings illuminate another possible reason for why age differences in prospective memory are not found in naturalistic settings. Older adults can maintain prospective memory performance equivalent to that of younger adults, but doing so might involve some sacrifice in the speed or accuracy of the ongoing activity. In many naturalistic situations, such a cost, especially in terms of speed, may not be especially penalizing and accordingly quite acceptable to older adults. Further, naturalistic prospective memory tasks may seem more important to older adults than to younger adults (see, e.g., Kvavilashvili & Fisher, 2007), thereby stimulating resource allocations for older adults that favor prospec-tive memory performance. From this perspective, the absence of age differences in naturalistic prospective memory studies (Henry et al., 2004) is understandable. Indeed, in naturalistic settings, older adults may often be able to slow the pace of ongoing activity for the purpose of supporting prospective memory (Rendell & Craik, 2000). This conjecture is in line with a recent finding reported by Rendell et al. (2007, Experiment 2). When the ongoing task (the famous faces task as implemented by Maylor, 1993, in which participants are required to name the face) was presented at a slow pace, older adults performed as well as younger adults with a nonfocal target (face wearing glasses).

In conclusion, we urge prospective memory researchers to appreciate the variability in age differences in prospective memory that has been observed across studies. There is now ample evidence that age differences are exagger-ated under some conditions and greatly attenuated and sometimes even elim-inated under others. We suspect that important modulating variables beyond the focal–nonfocal distinction highlighted in this chapter include the extent to which demands of the ongoing task are functionally equivalent for young and older adults (see Einstein, Smith, McDaniel, & Shaw, 1997), the importance of the prospective memory task (cf. Kliegel, Martin, McDaniel, & Einstein, 2004), the complexity of the prospective memory task (Einstein, Holland, McDaniel, & Guynn, 1992; Kliegel et al., 2000), time of day (Leirer, Tanke, & Morrow, 1994), and possibly genetic factors (Driscoll, McDaniel, & Guynn, 2005). We believe that further research examining the variables that moderate age differences will improve our understanding of both the underlying processes involved in different kinds of prospective memory situations and the nature of the effects of aging on cognitive processes.

ACKNOWLEDGMENTS

The National Aeronautics and Space Administration Grant NCC-2-1085 to Gilles Einstein and Mark McDaniel supported the completion of the new Experiment 1. These experiments were reported in part at the 2005 and 2006 Meetings of the Psychonomic Society, Toronto, Canada and Houston, Texas, respectively. We thank Nova Morrisette and Tom Graham for assistance in testing participants in the new Experiment 1 and Meredith Edwards and Mary Neil Hagood for assistance in testing participants in the new Experiment 2.

REFERENCES

Cherry, K. E., & LeCompte, D. C. (1999). Age and individual differences influence prospective memory. *Psychology and Aging, 14,* 60–76.

Craik, F. I. M. (1986). A functional account of age differences in memory. In F. Klix & H. Hagendorf (Eds.), *Human memory and cognitive capabilities: Mechanisms and performances* (pp. 409–422). Amsterdam: Elsevier Science.

Craik, F. I. M. (2003). Aging and memory in humans. In J. H. Byrne (Ed.), *Learning and memory* (2nd ed., pp. 10–14). New York: Macmillan.

Craik, F. I. M., & Byrd, M. (1982). Aging and cognitive deficits: The role of attentional resources. In F. I. M. Craik & S. Trehub (Eds.), *Advances in the study of communication and affect: Vol. 8. Aging and cognitive processes* (pp. 191–211). New York: Plenum.

Driscoll, I., McDaniel, M. A., & Guynn, M. J. (2005). Apolipoprotein E and prospective memory in normally aging adults. *Neuropsychology, 19,* 28–34.

d'Ydewalle, G., Luwel, K., & Brunfaut, E. (1999). The importance of on-going concurrent activities as a function of age in time- and event-based prospective memory. *European Journal of Cognitive Psychology, 11,* 219–237.

Dywan, J., & Jacoby, L. (1990). Effects of aging on source monitoring: Differences in susceptibility to false fame. *Psychology and Aging, 5,* 379–387.

Einstein, G. O., Holland, L. J., McDaniel, M. A., & Guynn, M. J. (1992). Age-related deficits in prospective memory: The influence of task complexity. *Psychology and Aging, 7,* 471–478.

Einstein, G. O., & McDaniel, M. A. (1990). Normal aging and prospective memory. *Journal of Experimental Psychology: Learning, Memory, and Cognition, 16,* 717–726.

Einstein, G. O., & McDaniel, M. A. (2005). Prospective memory: Multiple retrieval processes. *Current Directions in Psychological Science, 14,* 286–290.

Einstein, G. O., McDaniel, M. A., Richardson, S. L., Guynn, M. J., & Cunfer, A. R. (1995). Aging and prospective memory: Examining the influences of self-initiated retrieval processes. *Journal of Experimental Psychology: Learning, Memory, and Cognition, 21,* 996–1007.

Einstein, G. O., McDaniel, M. A., Thomas, R., Mayfield, S., Shank, H., Morrisette, N. et al. (2005). Multiple processes in prospective memory retrieval: Factors determining monitoring versus spontaneous retrieval. *Journal of Experimental Psychology: General, 134,* 327–342.

Einstein, G. O., Smith, R. E., McDaniel, M. A., & Shaw, P. (1997). Aging and prospective memory: The influence of increased task demands at encoding and retrieval. *Psychology and Aging, 12,* 479–488.

Guynn, M. J. (2001). *Footprints of monitoring in event-based prospective memory.* Unpublished doctoral dissertation, University of New Mexico, Albuquerque, NM.

Guynn, M. J. (2003). A two-process model of strategic monitoring in event-based prospective memory: Activation/retrieval mode and checking. *International Journal of Psychology, 38,* 245–256.

Hasher, L., & Zacks, R. T. (1979). Automatic and effortful processes in memory. *Journal of Experimental Psychology: General, 108,* 356–388.

Henry, J. D., MacLeod, M. S., Phillips, L. H., & Crawford, J. R. (2004). A meta-analytic review of prospective memory and aging. *Psychology and Aging, 19,* 27–39.

Kliegel, M., Martin, M., McDaniel, M. A., & Einstein, G. O. (2004). Importance effects in event-based prospective memory tasks. *Memory, 12,* 553–561.

Kliegel, M., McDaniel, M. A., & Einstein, G. O. (2000). Plan formation, retention, and execution in prospective memory: A new approach and age-related effects. *Memory & Cognition, 28,* 1041–1049.

Kvavilashvili, L, & Fisher, L. (2007). Is time-based prospective remembering mediated by self-initiated rehearsals? Role of incidental cues, ongoing activity, age and motivation. *Journal of Experimental Psychology: General, 136,* 112–132.

Leirer, V. O., Tanke, E. D., & Morrow, D. G. (1994). Time of day and naturalistic prospective memory. *Experimental Aging Research, 20,* 127–134.

Liu, L. L., & Park, D. C. (2004). Aging and medical adherence: The use of automatic processes to achieve effortful things. *Psychology and Aging, 19,* 318–325.

Mäntylä, T., & Nilsson, L. G. (1997). Remembering to remember in adulthood: A population-based study on aging and prospective memory. *Aging, Neuropsychology, and Cognition, 4,* 81–92.

Marsh, R. L., Hicks, J. L., & Cook, G. I. (2005). On the relationship between effort toward an ongoing task and cue detection in event-based prospective memory. *Journal of Experimental Psychology: Learning, Memory, and Cognition, 31,* 68–75.

Maylor, E. A. (1993). Aging and forgetting in prospective and retrospective memory tasks. *Psychology and Aging, 8,* 420–428.

Maylor, E. A. (1996). Age-related impairment in an event-based prospective memory task. *Psychology and Aging, 11,* 74–78.

Maylor, E. A. (1998). Changes in event-based prospective memory across adulthood. *Aging, Neuropsychology and Cognition, 5,* 107–128.

Maylor, E. A., Darby, R. J., Logie, R., Della Sala, S., & Smith, G. (2002). Prospective memory across the lifespan. In P. Graf & N. Ohta (Eds.), *Lifespan development of human memory* (pp. 235–256). Cambridge, MA: MIT Press.

McDaniel, M. A., & Einstein, G. O. (1993). The importance of cue familiarity and distinctiveness in prospective memory. *Memory, 1,* 23–41.

McDaniel, M. A., & Einstein, G. O. (2000). Strategic and automatic processes in prospective memory retrieval: A multiprocess framework. *Applied Cognitive Psychology, 14,* S127–S144.

McDaniel, M. A., & Einstein, G. O. (in press). Components of prospective memory most at risk for older adults and implications for medical adherence. In D. C. Park & L. Liu (Eds.), *Social and cognitive perspectives on medical adherence.* Washington, DC: American Psychological Association.

Navon, D., & Gopher, D. (1979). On the economy of the human-processing system. *Psychological Review, 86,* 214–255.

Park, D. C., Hertzog, C., Kidder, D. P., Morrell, R. W., & Mayhorn, C. B. (1997). Effect of age on event-based and time-based prospective memory. *Psychology and Aging, 12,* 314–327.

Reese, C. M., & Cherry, K. E. (2002). The effects of age, ability, and memory monitoring on prospective memory task performance. *Aging, Neuropsychology and Cognition, 9,* 98–113.

Rendell, P. G., & Craik, F. I. M. (2000). Virtual and actual week: Age-related differences in prospective memory. *Applied Cognitive Psychology, 14,* S43–S62.

Rendell, P. G., McDaniel, M. A., Forbes, R. D., & Einstein, G. O. (2007). Age-related effects in prospective memory are modulated by ongoing task complexity and relation to target cue. *Aging, Neuropsychology, and Cognition, 14,* 236–256.

Rendell, P. G., & Thomson, D. M. (1993). The effect of ageing on remembering to remember: An investigation of simulated medication regimens. *Australian Journal of Ageing, 12,* 11–18.

Rendell, P. G., & Thomson, D. M. (1999). Aging and prospective memory: Differences between naturalistic and laboratory tasks. *Journal of Gerontology: Psychological Sciences, 54B,* P256–P269.

Rosenthal, R., & Rosnow, R. L. (1991). *Essentials of behavioral research: Methods and data analysis* (2nd ed.). New York: McGraw-Hill.

Salthouse, T. A. (1991a). Mediation of adult age differences in cognition by reductions in working memory and speed of processing. *Psychological Science, 2,* 179–183.

Salthouse, T. A. (1991b). *Theoretical perspectives on cognitive aging.* Hillsdale, NJ: Lawrence Erlbaum.

Smith, R. E. (2003). The cost of remembering to remember in event-based prospective memory: Investigating the capacity demands of delayed intention performance. *Journal of Experimental Psychology: Learning, Memory, and Cognition, 29,* 347–361.

Smith, R. E., & Bayen, U. J. (2006). The source of adult age differences in event-based prospective memory: A multinomial modeling approach. *Journal of Experimental Psychology: Learning, Memory, and Cognition, 32,* 623–635.

Verhaeghen, P., Marcoen, A., & Goossens, L. (1993). Facts and fiction about memory aging: A quantitative integration of research findings. *Journal of Gerontology, 48,* 157–171.

Vogels, W. W. A., Dekker, M. R., Brouwer, W. H., & de Jong, R. (2002). Age-related changes in event-related prospective memory performance: A comparison of four prospective memory tasks. *Brain and Cognition, 49,* 341–362.

West, R., & Craik, F. I. M. (1999). Age-related decline in prospective memory: The roles of cue accessibility and cue sensitivity. *Psychology and Aging, 14,* 264–272.

Zacks, R. T., & Hasher, L. (1988). Capacity theory and the processing of inferences. In L. L. Light & D. M. Burke (Eds.), *Language, memory, and aging* (pp. 154–170). New York: Cambridge University Press.

8

Adult Aging and Prospective Memory
The Importance of Ecological Validity

LOUISE H. PHILLIPS

School of Psychology
University of Aberdeen, United Kingdom

JULIE D. HENRY

School of Psychology
University of New South Wales, Australia

MIKE MARTIN

Institute of Psychology
University of Zurich, Switzerland

A n important focus in the literature on prospective memory (PM) concerns the impact of adult aging on this important memory skill. In Brandimonte, Einstein, and McDaniel's (1996) previous book on PM, Maylor (1996) reviewed the available literature on the effects of aging on a range of PM tasks and concluded that, for PM tasks in a naturalistic setting, "Older adults are at least as good as younger adults (and sometimes better)" (p. 182). In contrast, on laboratory-based PM tasks, "there is not a single laboratory study in the literature in which the elderly significantly outperformed the young, although there are some studies in which older and younger subjects did not differ. In contrast, there are several reports of age-related impairments" (p. 184).

This pattern of age-related impairment on lab-based PM tasks, along with age improvements in naturalistic PM tasks has since been replicated in a single

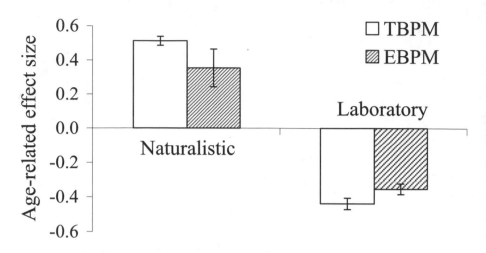

FIGURE 8.1   Direction and magnitude of age-related effect sizes on naturalistic and laboratory-based prospective memory tasks. TBPM = time-based prospective memory task; EBPM = event-based prospective memory task. Meta-analytic data from Henry et al. (2004).

sample (Rendell & Thomson, 1999). Further, a recent meta-analytic review confirmed that across the many published studies of age and PM, age-related deficits in lab-based PM tasks are equivalent in magnitude to the age-related benefits observed in naturalistic PM tasks (Henry, MacLeod, Phillips, & Crawford, 2004; see Figure 8.1). Note that corresponding with most other literature in this area (and the classification of tasks used in the Henry et al. meta-analysis), in this chapter we begin by classifying tasks based on the setting in which they are carried out. In other words, lab-based tasks are those carried out in a laboratory setting, whereas naturalistic tasks are those carried out in the everyday environment of the participant, however artificial the PM demands might be. Of course the ecological validity of a task depends on more than just the environment in which it is carried out, and the roles of both the nature of the PM task and the variants in the setting in which it is carried out are discussed in the latter part of this chapter. The finding of different directions of age effects on PM tasks carried out in different settings has been referred to as the *age prospective memory paradox* (Rendell & Craik, 2000). This apparent paradox is the key focus of this chapter.

Specific methodological and theoretical issues arise when considering the effects of aging on lab-based tasks, and different issues are relevant to the study of naturalistic tasks. In this chapter we therefore begin by providing an overview of the issues associated with age effects on lab-based PM tasks, then consider naturalistic PM tasks, before considering how the total picture of age differences in both types of PM can best be explained.

AGE EFFECTS ON LABORATORY-BASED PROSPECTIVE MEMORY TASKS

It is beyond the scope of this review to provide detailed descriptions of the many laboratory-based studies of PM that include aging as a factor. Other chapters in this volume (e.g., Kliegel, Mackinlay & Jäger, chap. 9, this volume; McDaniel, Einstein & Rendell, chap. 7, this volume) cover aging effects on such PM tasks in more detail (see also West, Jakubek, & Wymbs, 2002). Instead, we focus on the issues that have absorbed much of the debate in the literature: Are the lab-based deficits associated with aging specific to PM, or do they reflect more general changes in memory and other cognitive resources? Further, what task-related factors systematically influence the magnitude of age-related differences in lab-based PM tasks?

Are Age Changes in Lab-Based PM Specific or General?

There is some disagreement in the literature about whether age differences in lab-based PM reflect age declines in episodic memory and other cognitive components such as processing speed or inhibition, or instead reflect at least a partially unique deficit. Whereas Dobbs and Reeves (1996) argued that PM is more than memory, Craik and Kerr (1996) posited that prospective and retrospective memory depend largely on the same set of cognitive processes, with PM-specific components including the planning of an intention and the setting up of retrieval cues.

Relative to retrospective memory, PM has been argued to be more dependent on self-initiated processes (Craik, 1986). This is because, according to Craik's (1986) theoretical model, recollection is dependent on reconstructing events in memory. It is suggested that this process must be guided either by external cues, or, in their absence, self-initiated cues. In retrospective memory tasks, explicit prompts to recall are provided, whereas in PM tasks the cue is not an explicit request for action, but instead requires either interpretation of an external event or an internal impetus. It has often been argued that this requirement for self-initiated remembering means that PM tasks should be more susceptible to the effects of adult aging than retrospective memory tasks (e.g., Craik, 1986; Maylor, 1995; McDaniel & Einstein, 2000).

PM tasks must inevitably involve a retrospective mnemonic component (Cohen, West, & Craik, 2001; McDaniel & Einstein, 1992). Successfully performing a PM task requires not only remembering that something has to be done, but also retrieval of the contents of the intention. Cherry et al. (2001) reported that two measures of retrospective memory accounted for 68% of the age-related variance in PM performance. Further, it has been noted that age differences in PM tasks increase with the retrospective memory load of the PM task, for example, where the number of cues to be remembered is incremented (Einstein, Holland, McDaniel, & Guynn, 1992). The influence of retrospective memory may be different on the varying components of complex prospective memory tasks (Kliegel, McDaniel, & Einstein, 2000). Because there is considerable evidence of age-related decline in retrospective memory, age deficits in this aspect of cognition are likely to impact

PM performance in older adults. The issue therefore is whether the deficit in retrospective memory is the major or only cause of age-related declines in PM.

Age variance in PM partially overlaps with other cognitive measures, but
there is evidence of an additional age-related variance in detecting PM cues. For
example, Salthouse, Berish, and Siedlecki (2004) reported age differences in four
lab-based PM tasks in a large sample of adults. There was some statistical overlap
in the age variance in PM and other pertinent cognitive measures (executive functioning, episodic memory, processing speed). Further, age differences in PM performance were reduced when retrospective memory for the PM task instructions
was taken into account. Despite this overlap there was also evidence of unique age-
related influences on PM, separate from other cognitive operations, particularly
for the age range from 50 and older. In this study, Salthouse et al. reported rare
data on life-span effects in the four lab-based PM tasks studied, indicating that
performance remains stable until age 50 or 60 and declines thereafter. This clearly
contrasts with some measures of executive function and processing speed that tend
to show substantial declines much earlier in the age range (e.g., MacPherson,
Phillips, & Della Sala, 2002).

Age and the Nature of Lab-Based PM Tasks   It is clear from reading
the Brandimonte et al. (1996) book on PM that there was considerable excitement
about the possibility that time- and event-based PM might be differentially influenced by variables such as age, and therefore might be reliant on different cognitive processes. Time-based PM tasks require the participant to perform a specified
behavior after the passage of a given amount of time, whereas for event-based PM
tasks the required behavior is prompted by an external cue (Einstein & McDaniel,
1990; Einstein, McDaniel, Richardson, Guynn, & Cunfer, 1995). Time-based PM
tasks have therefore been argued to be the most reliant on internal control
mechanisms because, assuming no external mnemonic aid is used, the use of time
cues is more dependent on self-initiated mental activities, such as active time monitoring (d'Ydewalle, Bouckaert, & Brunfaut, 2001). Thus, of the two types of PM, it
has been argued that time-based PM should be especially sensitive to age-related
decline (Einstein & McDaniel, 1996; Einstein et al., 1995; Maylor, 1995, 1996).

Initial experiments bore out this prediction. In comparison to event-based
tasks, studies of time-based tasks have more consistently revealed age-related deficits (d'Ydewalle et al., 2001; Einstein et al., 1995; Park, Hertzog, & Kidder, 1997).
It has been reported that during the performance of time-based PM tasks, older
adults tend to monitor the clock less often than their younger counterparts
(Einstein et al., 1995; Park et al., 1997), and this may be attributable to deficits in attentional resources or poorer estimation of time intervals (Einstein et al.,
1995). Where both time- and event-based tasks have been examined in the same
participants, age-related deficits are more consistently associated with the time-
based PM tasks (Einstein & McDaniel, 1996; Einstein et al., 1995) or conditions
(McDaniel & Einstein, 1992; Park et al., 1997).

However, in some studies older adults have been found to perform better on
time-based relative to event-based PM tasks (d'Ydewalle, Luwel, & Brunfaut,
1999). Moreover, in our meta-analysis of age effects on PM (Henry et al., 2004)

there was not a significant difference between the size of the age effect on time-based laboratory PM tasks (age effect size = −.39) and event-based laboratory PM tasks (age effect size = −.34; see Figure 8.1). This collapses across a large number of different PM paradigms, using different tasks and stimuli, and leads to the conclusion that there is no differential effect of aging on time-based as compared to event-based PM performance.

Instead, evidence increasingly suggests that a more useful way of determining the size of age effects on a lab-based PM task is to consider levels of complexity, memory load, and the amount of strategic monitoring required. Age differences in PM tasks are often larger when the task involves greater complexity (Einstein et al., 1992; Mantyla, 1994). McDaniel and Einstein (2000) proposed a multiprocess framework of event-based PM tasks in which it is argued that prospective remembering can be supported by either strategically monitoring the environment for the presence of the prospective cue, or by relying on the prospective cue to automatically prompt the target action. Because aging is presumed to be associated with deficits in attentional capacities, this framework therefore predicts that the magnitude of age effects on event-based tasks will be determined by the extent to which the task depends on automatic processing versus controlled resource-demanding processing. McDaniel and Einstein (2000) suggested that the following factors may increase the strategic, controlled demands of PM paradigms, and thus may increase any age deficits: (a) nondistinctive PM cues, (b) a weak association between the cue and the intended action, (c) processing of the PM cue being peripheral to the processing carried out in the ongoing task, or (d) a highly attention-demanding or engaging ongoing task.

A number of studies have shown that these factors are important in determining the magnitude of age differences in PM. For example, the nature of the ongoing task in which the PM task is embedded is important in determining the size of age differences in lab-based tasks (d'Ydewalle, 1995; d'Ydewalle et al., 1999; Einstein, Smith, McDaniel, & Shaw, 1997; Martin & Schumann-Hengsteler, 2001), with age effects typically reduced if the cognitive demands of the ongoing task are relatively low (see Maylor, 1995). Varying the typicality of cues to action influences age effects (Cherry et al., 2001; Mantyla, 1993, 1994). The most complex PM tasks require more executive resources and result in the largest age-related deficits (Martin, Kliegel, & McDaniel, 2003).

Henry et al. (2004) directly tested the predictions of the multiprocess framework in a meta-analytic review and found that age effects were indeed significantly higher when event-based PM tasks involved higher strategic demands. Moreover, although the magnitude of the age deficit associated with time-based PM tasks did not differ from age effects on high-strategic-demand event-based tasks, it was substantially in excess of the deficit for low-strategic-demand event-based PM tasks. Thus, the moderating effect of level of strategic demand may account for apparent discrepancies in the relative magnitude of age effects on event- and time-based tasks. For more details on the multiprocess framework in relation to age differences in PM see McDaniel et al. (chap. 7, this volume).

To conclude this short section on the effects of lab-based tasks, there is a clear pattern of age-related deficits on many lab-based PM tasks, and although this is partly related to other aspects of cognitive decline such as poorer retrospective memory and slower processing, there also seems to be a unique age impairment associated with PM tasks. Initial evidence pointed toward the importance of the type of PM cue, whether based on time intervals or event cues. However, more important in estimating the size of age deficits in PM tasks appears to be the extent to which the task demands strategic, effortful monitoring.

AGE EFFECTS ON PM TASKS SET IN EVERYDAY LIFE

As noted previously, older adults tend to perform as well or better than their younger counterparts in PM tasks that are carried out in naturalistic rather than laboratory settings. These tasks include measures artificially introduced by the experimenter to the naturalistic setting, such as when the participant is required to telephone the experimenter at a specific time over 4 weeks (Devolder, Brigham, & Pressley, 1990), 2 weeks (Moscovitch, 1982), and 5 days (Maylor, 1990); mail postcards to the experimenter (Patton & Meit, 1993); or periodically log the time on an electronic organizer (Rendell & Thomson, 1993, 1999). Older adults have also been reported to show better PM for naturalistic behavior in realistic settings, such as attending appointments (Martin, 1986) and following intended medication regimes (Hertzog, Park, & Morrell, 2000; Park et al., 1999; Park & Kidder, 1996). More detail on the nature of age-related changes in all of these tasks is provided in the sections that follow.

Maylor (1996) argued that because older adults have had more experience with real-world PM tasks across their life span, they will have gained feedback on the frequency and nature of any lapses in intention realization. This may result in the development of compensatory strategies that improve PM performance in naturalistic settings. The superior performance of older adults in naturalistic conditions may reflect more experience with time management, knowledge of their memory's fallibility, fewer distractions, greater opportunity to plan how they will remember to execute the tasks, or more efficient use of PM reminder cues. These explanations are considered in detail later in the section on factors that might explain the age–PM paradox.

FACTORS THAT MIGHT EXPLAIN THE AGE-RELATED BENEFITS IN NATURALISTIC PM

Motivation

It has long been argued that younger and older adults may differ in their motivation to successfully complete PM tasks outside of the laboratory (Moscovitch, 1982; Patton & Meit, 1993; Rendell & Craik, 2000). Thus, the level of motivation of younger participants to complete PM tasks among the other demands of everyday life may be relatively low, and this is particularly likely to be the case for undergraduate students completing studies for course credits, who represent the majority of younger participants in such studies (Maylor, 1993). Noncompliance with instructions among younger participants is therefore regarded as a serious issue in PM tasks with real-world settings (Dobbs & Reeves, 1996) as it raises the possibility that naturalistic task data among younger participants may not be meaningful (Craik & Kerr, 1996). A number of specific factors relating to age differences in motivation to complete naturalistic PM tasks have been raised. These include generational differences in attitudes to punctuality, age differences in personality dimensions such as conscientiousness, and age differences in lifestyle factors.

Generational differences in attitudes to politeness and ideas about social norms have been argued to be a potential confounding factor in evaluating naturalistic PM tasks (Maylor, 1993). Dobbs and Reeves (1996) argued that young and old might have different evaluations of when it is appropriate to send a letter, for example, because older participants might think early completion of the task is more acceptable than younger participants. Cuttler and Graf (2005) presented evidence that age-related increases in the personality dimension of conscientiousness might explain age improvements in a prospective memory task in a real-world setting (making a phone call). Further information about the interaction among motivation, personality, and PM is clearly needed.

It has been suggested that, relative to older adults, younger people lead lives that are less structured and predictable, and busier and more engaging (e.g., Henry et al., 2004; Maylor, 1996; Rabbitt, 1996). It may be important to separate out these two issues that might be critical to the role of lifestyle in naturalistic PM tasks: the structuredness of life and the busyness of life. It has been suggested that older people follow more structured and predictable daily routines compared to younger adults (Rendell & Thomson, 1999). In contrast, Rendell and Craik (2000) argued that age improvements in naturalistic PM are not due to age differences in structure of lifestyle, but acknowledge the need for further empirical research on this topic. For instance, it was suggested that one manner of investigating the role of structure as a potential moderator of any age effects would be to test groups of younger and older adults who have similar occupations, and thus have similar daily activities.

In terms of busyness of lifestyle, a number of studies have attempted to address this issue empirically. Of course, the majority of older adults participating in studies are retired, whereas the majority of younger participants are in education. Retirement might lead to more available time to devote to setting up strategies and carrying out PM tasks in everyday settings. Rendell and Thomson (1999) reported age-related improvements in logging times on a personal organizer and specifically investigated the effect of retirement status on PM performance of those aged 60 to 69. There was no difference between participants who were working, retired, or carrying out home duties in terms of accuracy of PM responding. However, when Rendell and Thompson (1999) looked at posttask reports in their whole sample, younger adults (aged 18–28) had more difficulty in keeping the organizer with them than older adults (60–69 and 80–92), which might suggest that the relative busyness of younger participants influenced their ability to perform the task. Park et al. (1999) investigated the adherence of middle-aged and older adults with rheumatoid arthritis to a medication regimen, where errors were quantified as failures to take the correct amount of medication on a particular day. Older adults were more accurate at remembering to take medication and also reported less busy lifestyles. Martin and Park (2003) described a new method of assessing lifestyle busyness, the Martin and Park Environmental Demands Questionnaire, which correlates with medication adherence and may prove useful in future research in this field.

Another key aspect that links to potential age differences in motivation is the nature of the PM task and materials used in the artificial laboratory compared to real-life settings. Most lab-based PM tasks consist of highly abstract material and tasks with no context or emotional salience, and this may be important in explaining age differences (Ellis & Kvavilashvili, 2000; Rendell & Thomson, 1999). Lack of salience may lower the perceived importance of the PM task, resulting in more PM failures (McDaniel & Einstein, 2000). For older adults, the social salience of activities such as making a phone call may boost performance on natu-ralistic PM tasks, and the abstract nature of most lab-based PM tasks is unlikely to provide such motivation. There is evidence from other cognitive domains that increasing the emotional salience of task material reduces age deficits in prob-lem solving (Blanchard-Fields, Jahnke, & Camp, 1995) and recognition memory (Charles, Mather, & Carstensen, 2003). This may be particularly important for PM tasks, where older adults are impaired at noticing cues. Further, in a skill highly related to PM, cognitive planning, increasing the extent to which lab-based tasks resemble familiar situations reduces age-related impairments (Garden, Phillips, & MacPherson, 2001; Kliegel, Martin, McDaniel, & Phillips, in press; Phillips, Kliegel, & Martin, 2006). Despite recognition of the potential importance of moti-vational factors such as the emotional significance of task materials in PM per-formance (e.g., Kvavilashvili & Ellis, 1996), we are not aware of any published aging studies to date that have experimentally manipulated the emotionality, social importance, or contextual salience of PM tasks in either lab-based or more realistic settings. This means we have very little knowledge about the role of these aspects of motivation in relation to the age–PM paradox.

Recent evidence on lab-based PM performance suggests that the motivational factor of perceived task importance may be important where PM tasks impose sub-stantial demands on monitoring resources (Kliegel, Martin, McDaniel, & Einstein, 2004). Lab-based dual-task PM situations are likely to result in higher levels of strategic demand for older compared to younger adults, and indeed Maylor (1998) reported that older adults think less about the PM aspects of a lab-based task during its execution. In a recent study Kliegel, Phillips, and Jäger (in preparation) found that older adults were particularly susceptible to importance manipulations in a lab-based PM task. All lab-based PM tasks depend on a dual-task situation where an ongoing task must be interrupted to respond to the PM cue, and the results of Kliegel et al. (in prep.) suggest that for older adults to do well in such a situation, they must be instructed to prioritize the PM task over the performance of the ongoing task. It would therefore be useful in future lab-based and naturalis-tic studies to look in more detail at the relative motivation for the PM and ongoing tasks in younger and older adults.

To summarize, despite frequent reference to the issue of motivation to explain the age benefit in naturalistic PM, there is relatively little empirical evidence that directly addresses the role of developmental or cohort differences in social mores and the busyness and structure of everyday life in PM performance. Similarly, few studies have directly measured or manipulated motivation in relation to age differences in PM tasks.

Use of Reminders

An obvious potential explanation for the pattern of age improvements in naturalistic PM is that older adults are more likely to use memory aids, an opportunity that is only available outside of the watchful eye of the experimenter in the lab. It has often been suggested that older adults are aware of the fallible nature of their memory and therefore are more likely to equip themselves with external cues to prospective intentions (e.g., Craik & Kerr, 1996; Dobbs & Reeves, 1996; Glisky, 1996; Hertzog et al., 2000; Kvavilashvili & Ellis, 2004; Logie, Maylor, Della Sala, & Smith, 2004; Maylor, 1990; Moscovitch, 1982; Patton & Meit, 1993); this is only possible in naturalistic tasks. This view is so widespread in the aging literature that it could be classed as the prevailing wisdom, and it seems to have resulted in otherwise careful authors misinterpreting empirical evidence. As detailed later, studies that clearly do not provide evidence to support the idea that the use of memory cues explains the age benefit in naturalistic tasks (Maylor, 1990; Rendell & Craik, 2000) have often been interpreted as providing just such supporting evidence (e.g., Henry et al., 2004; Logie et al., 2004; see more examples later). This widespread misciting of available evidence makes it particularly important to go back to the original sources.

The idea that age benefits in naturalistic PM are due to increased use of reminder cues is sometimes phrased to suggest that the use of PM tasks in real-life settings is of no scientific interest (Dobbs & Reeves, 1996; Glisky, 1996; Kvavilashvili & Ellis, 2004; Logie et al., 2004). Craik and Kerr (1996) argued that age benefits on naturalistic PM tasks are attributable to "the greater attention paid to compensatory strategies by older participants, rather than to the maturation of cognitive abilities" (p. 227). However, if older adults show enough metacognitive prescience to spontaneously generate and use effective mnemonic cues in the face of many other deficits in metacognition, this suggests effective development of some aspects of cognitive skill. For an aging researcher this should therefore be an interesting and potentially rich source of evidence, rather than being seen as a confound. Also, in opposition to the prevailing wisdom on this topic, other authors have explicitly argued that age benefits in implementing intentions in naturalistic settings are not caused by the use of external aids (d'Ydewalle & Brunfaut, 1996; Patton & Meit, 1993; Rendell & Thomson, 1999).

Three types of reminder cues are usually considered important in researching prospective memory: internal, external, and conjunction cues (Maylor, 1990). First, internal cues may be used as reminders; that is, the intention to carry out an activity reaches a critical level of conscious awareness and "pops into mind." Most laboratory-based PM tasks rely to some extent on setting up and activating effective internal cues. Internal cues are also frequently used in everyday PM tasks. External cues to carry out an intention might include explicit reminders to carry out an activity such as a note in a diary or organizer. Many people spontaneously use such external cues in everyday settings, and it has often been argued that older people are more likely to use these types of reminders during naturalistic PM tasks. Conjunction cues occur where the intention to act is associated with a specific ongoing event, so that when an event (e.g., preparing breakfast) occurs, an intention (e.g., taking medication) should be implemented. There is evidence that conjunction cues are a particularly efficient way to remember intentions (Maylor, 1990).

The actual evidence as to whether older adults make more use of external or conjunction cues in PM tasks is mixed (Maylor, 1996). In some naturalistic PM studies, older adults have been reported to make greater use of external cues (Jackson, Bogers, & Kerstholt, 1990; Lovelace & Twohig, 1990), whereas in other studies younger adults report greater use of external cues (Dobbs & Rule, 1987; Rendell & Thomson, 1993; West, 1988). However, Maylor (1993) noted that evidence from most of these studies is inconclusive because of the very small samples involved. Park et al. (1999) reported that age improvements in medication adherence were not due to older adults being more reliant on external cues to memory. Also, Rendell and Craik (2000) instructed participants not to use memory cues in a naturalistic PM task, and at a posttask debriefing interview young and old participants reported low use of reminder strategies: There was still an age benefit in PM performance. It is likely that the nature of the PM task may influence age differences in the likelihood of using external cues (Maylor, 1996). Gould, McDonald, and King (1997) reported that a group of older adults reported widespread use of external memory strategies for a range of different situations, apart from when remembering to take medication, when they mostly reported the use of internal strategies. The most commonly used category of internal strategies was concentrating on understanding and remembering medication instructions. Gould et al. (1997) reported that the most commonly used external reminder strategy was leaving the pills in a prominent place; the use of more effective external reminders such as lists of medication times or records of medication taking was rare in the population sampled. Some conjunction cues relating taking pills to everyday activities were relatively common.

In an influential study of aging and naturalistic PM, Maylor (1990) asked participants between 52 and 95 years old to make five phone calls at specified times, and further asked for information on what cues were used to aid memory. The most common type of cue was the use of external reminders, particularly the prominent positioning of the task instructions or the use of a calendar or diary. Those who used external reminders were more likely to remember to phone than those relying on internal cues. Within this sample of older adults, there was no age effect on PM performance. However, Maylor noted that among those who used external memory cues, age was positively related to accurate PM performance, whereas in the minority of participants who relied on internal cues, age was negatively correlated with PM (for further analysis of these data, see Maylor, 1996). It is interesting to note that this result has often been interpreted to support an external reminder explanation for age benefits in naturalistic PM (e.g., Freeman & Ellis, 2003; Gould, 1999; Henry et al., 2004; Johansson, Andersson, & Ronnberg, 2000; Maylor, 1998). However, as Maylor (1990) concluded, "In the past, the superior performance by the elderly in the latter [i.e., naturalistic PM] studies has been attributed to their greater use of external aids compared to the young. The present results suggest that this is an oversimplification, as *within* a middle-aged and elderly population age did not influence the choice of cue, and for those using the *same* conjunction and external cues, the older subjects were still superior" (p. 490). In other words, the results from Maylor (1990) do not provide direct evidence that older adults do well on naturalistic PM tasks because of greater use of reminders, contrary to the predominant interpretation of this article in the literature. Instead, the results indicate that older adults are more efficient in their use of external cues than young adults, which raises interesting issues about the types of cues used and the roles of skills and experience in cue use.

Kvavilashvili (2005) asked participants to call the experimenter at a set time and record a diary of all occasions when the intention came to mind on the day of the task, particularly noting whether the intention just popped into mind without obvious reason, was triggered by external cues in the environment, or was internally cued by self-initiated retrieval. No differences between a young and old group in the frequency of intention retrieval or performance on the telephone task were found, but older adults made more uncued rehearsals and fewer self-initiated retrievals compared to the young. This suggests that older adults are relying more on automatic retrieval of intentions than the young.

In an initial experiment, Rendell and Thomson (1999) looked at the interaction between age group and the type of time-based cues that might be used in a PM task involving logging prespecified times in a personal organizer. In particular, they varied the regularity of the time cues for making a PM response: Either four responses were required at regular intervals for a week (e.g., 8:00 a.m., 12:30 p.m., 5:00 p.m., 9:30 p.m.) as compared to irregular time intervals that varied each day. They argued that the irregular time interval condition would be less susceptible to the use of conjunction cues because the intervals could not be so easily tied into everyday events such as meals. Also, when they asked participants to report, posttask, whether they had developed a strategy for carrying out the time-logging task, younger adults were more likely to say they had developed such a strategy. These results were interpreted as evidence against a reminder explanation of age improvements in naturalistic PM. A second experiment had two different task conditions that increased the availability of (a) external cues to carry out a PM intention, through the use of an alarm reminder; and (b) conjunction cues, where participants were told that they could choose times to best connect with events in their everyday routine. There was no age group interaction with type of reminder, suggesting that lack of using external or conjunction cues was not the cause of poorer PM performance among younger participants. However, it is possible that it was more difficult for younger participants to identify four regular events that occurred at the same time every day to use as conjunction cues.

Despite the widespread view that age benefits in naturalistic PM tasks may be attributable to increased use of external reminders, there is remarkably little evidence that supports this idea, and indeed evidence that contradicts this interpretation (Patton & Meit, 1993; Rendell & Thomson, 1999). The most widely cited paper to support the idea that age improvements in naturalistic PM are caused by increased use of reminder cues (Maylor, 1990) actually found no age effect on PM performance, and no age difference between those relying on internal and external reminders. Maylor (1996) argued that there may be age differences in the efficiency with which external cues can be used, reflecting life experience. Further, older adults might use more effective types of external cues. These issues remain to be explored in the empirical literature.

AGE, PROSPECTIVE MEMORY, AND ECOLOGICAL VALIDITY

It remains unclear which properties of naturalistic and lab-based tasks are critical in determining the direction of age effects. Some factors that have been considered to be potentially important in PM cannot explain the pattern of results. The differential aging effects on PM tasks cannot simply be attributed to the greater complexity of laboratory tasks: Age deficits are found even on very simple laboratory tasks (e.g., Huppert, Johnson, & Nickson, 2000), whereas age benefits are retained in complex naturalistic tasks (Rendell & Craik, 2000). Although increasing the complexity and memory load of lab-based PM tasks exacerbates age deficits (e.g., Einstein & McDaniel, 1996), manipulations of complexity and memory load do not influence the magnitude of age effects on naturalistic PM tasks (Rendell & Thomson, 1993, 1999). Although the majority of naturalistic tasks require a PM response at a specific time, whereas most lab-based tasks require a PM response to a specific event, this time–event distinction also cannot explain the paradoxical results (Henry et al., 2004; Park et al., 1997; Rendell & Craik, 2000). In the next section, we consider which properties of lab-based and naturalistic tasks might explain the pattern of aging effects found. First, though, we briefly consider the pattern of age differences in performance in relation to manipulations of ecological validity in other domains of cognition.

Age and Ecological Validity in Other Domains of Cognition

It would be useful to compare the pattern of reversed age effects on PM in naturalistic compared to lab settings with the effects of ecological validity in other cognitive skills. It is not the case that increasing the ecological validity of cognitive tasks inevitably reverses the direction of age effects on cognitive tasks. For example, in tasks of *retrospective memory*, age-related declines in performance are found even when more naturalistic materials, tasks, and settings have been used (see, e.g., Hess & Pullen, 1996; Light, 1991). There are reductions in the size of age-related memory deficits when task materials are more contextualized (e.g., Wingfield, Lahar, & Stine, 1989), the relationship between different task elements complies with expectations (e.g., Hess & Pullen, 1994), and when the task materials are more age relevant (e.g., Bäckman, 1991). However, age-related declines in retrospective memory still tend to occur even when ecological validity is increased.

One of the skills that is particularly important in PM is planning. Planning consists of both mental formulation of a method to carry out a task, and accurate execution of the formulated plan. There are age-related declines in the ability to formulate and execute plans in novel tasks (e.g., Gilhooly, Phillips, Wynn, Logie, & Della Sala, 1999). Where a planning task is set in a more familiar environment, no age differences are found (Garden et al., 2001; Lachman & Burack, 1993; Phillips et al., 2006). In relation to problem solving, many authors have argued against the use of traditional psychometric problem-solving tasks such as IQ tests to study aging. However, there are many measurement problems associated with assessing more ecologically valid problem solving, such as how to score such tasks (Berg & Klaczynski, 1996), and this has fuelled contradictory results. Influential work in this field (e.g., Denney, 1989) concludes that (a) older people perform better on more everyday problem-solving tasks compared to artificial tasks, but (b) there are consistent age-related declines in most naturalistic problem-solving tasks, which occur later in the aging process than is evident for artificial problem-solving tasks. A recent meta-analytic review (Thornton & Dumke, 2005) concluded that there was a significant age-related decrement in everyday problem solving, but that this was smaller for interpersonal compared to instrumental problem-solving tasks.

The evidence from literature on retrospective memory and problem solving therefore suggests that significant age-related impairments remain, even when more naturalistic tasks are used. This can be contrasted to the results from planning and PM studies, which indicate the elimination or reversal of age effects in more naturalistic tasks. However, most manipulations of ecological validity in relation to retrospective memory and problem solving involve using more realistic or contextualized materials, but remaining within the confines of the laboratory. In contrast, the role of ecological validity in relation to PM and aging has mostly been examined through contrasting performance in laboratory and real-world settings and there have been very few direct manipulations of, for example, how realistic a PM task is within a lab-based setting. This raises some important questions about how ecological validity should be conceptualized.

WHAT IS ECOLOGICAL VALIDITY?

The age–PM paradox arises from clear evidence of age-related improvements in implementing intentions in an everyday setting, along with age declines in PM performance in the laboratory. A critical factor therefore seems to be the ecological validity of the task. But what do we mean by ecological validity, and is it possible to identify which aspects of ecological validity are most important in this pattern of aging results? There is no agreement on the definition of ecological validity (Kvavilashvili & Ellis, 2004), but here we focus on the extent to which a PM task resembles the demands of everyday life, as opposed to the more artificial constraints imposed by an experimenter.

Table 8.1 shows a continuum representing relatively strong versus weak versions of ecological validity. The strongest type of ecological validity (Type 1 in the

TABLE 8.1   Types of Ecological Validity in Prospective Memory Tasks (Ecological Validity Decreases Down the Table)

Type of Ecological Validity	Setting	Task: Naturally Occurring or Artificial[a]	Familiarity of Task[b]	Example(s) from PM Literature	Pattern of Age Effects
		High Ecological Validity			
Type 1. Part of everyday life	Everyday life	Natural	Familiar	Taking medication	Mixed
Type 2. Experimental task embedded in an everyday setting	Everyday life	Artificial	Familiar Novel	Making phone calls Logging times in organizer	Improvement Improvement
Type 3. Set in a complex environment (but outside everyday experience)	Complex real or virtual environment	Artificial	Familiar Novel	Shopping errand task Signal presence of particular item	No evidence No evidence
Type 4. Lab setting but realistic task	Laboratory	Artificial	Familiar	Remind experimenter to carry out action	Decline
Type 5. Lab setting, artificial task	Laboratory	Artificial	Novel	Signal presence of particular item	Decline
		Low Ecological Validity			

[a] Naturally occurring tasks are those that would occur anyway in everyday life without the interference of the experimenter, and artificial tasks are those put in place by the experimenter.

[b] The familiarity of a task is the extent to which the content and task demands are familiar and likely to have been encountered in everyday life, as opposed to more novel tasks, which tend to be abstract and involve carrying out tasks not previously encountered in everyday life. Clearly this dimension is a continuum rather than a dichotomy.

table) occurs where the task under investigation is part of everyday life. Here, both the setting of the task and the actual intentions to be carried out must be part of the routine of the participant, with only observation of behavior rather than experimental intervention. Relatively few PM studies achieve this level of ecological validity, and most use medication adherence as the critical task, although clearly this task depends on many other social, physical, and cognitive factors, too. From studies of medication compliance in the medical literature, it is not straightforward to evaluate age effects. As Cramer & Rosenheck (1998) noted, "Although many physicians assume that elderly patients are more likely to be poorly compliant than younger patients, because of the high number of medications and complexity of regimens, this relationship has not been proven" (p. 8). Thus, whereas some studies report that patient compliance is higher in older relative to younger adults (Park et al., 1999; Schulz, O'Donnell, McDonough, Sasane, & Meyer, 2005), other studies report a negative effect of ageing (Roe, Motheral, Teitelbaum, & Rich, 2000), or no age effect (Lorenc & Branthwaite, 1993). Discrepancies between studies have been attributed to differences in the ages of participants, number of medications, medical conditions, periods of dosing, dosing frequencies, and the measurement and definition of compliance (see Greenberg, 1984; Park & Kidder, 1996). In some studies, adherence is measured by looking at participants' errors in taking medication they had explicitly *stated* they intended to take. Different from this approach, most compliance studies record errors when participants do not take the mediations prescribed by their physicians. Whereas physician-compliance studies often report error rates of around 50%, intention-adherence errors are below 10% across age groups matched for education, severity and duration of illness, and number of medications (Park et al., 1999). The findings in this area may therefore be related to the error criterion; that is, people may not comply with the prescription of their physicians, but adhere to their own intended regimen well.

It would be of interest to know more about everyday PM (Type 1) in more varied types of tasks in older and younger adults. For example, Rendell and Thomson (1999) argued that some types of everyday PM tasks are likely to suffer age-related decline, particularly where the need to remember an intention crops up unexpectedly and does not fit well into everyday routines, or the task demands memory for specific content. It would be very useful to see more information on the nature of age effects on these different aspects of everyday PM.

Most naturalistic PM tasks reported in the literature involve the experimenter setting specific tasks to be carried out during everyday routines, such as making phone calls at specified times. The PM tasks set are usually artificial in the sense that there is no meaning of the tasks to the participant, but the types of tasks are usually relatively familiar and straightforward. This corresponds to Type 2 ecological validity in Table 8.1. There is evidence of age-related improvements in performing this type of task (e.g., Rendell & Thomson, 1999), irrespective of whether the task itself is relatively familiar such as making phone calls, or relatively novel such as logging times on a personal organizer. This strongly suggests that the task itself need not be inherently part of an everyday routine to show age improvements.

The next level of ecological validity (Type 3 in Table 8.1) is where tasks are set in a real (or complex virtual) environment, but not in the everyday routine of the participant. Here the experimenter could have more control over the experimental setting than when relying on everyday life, and could observe all aspects of the participant's behavior, rather than relying on self-reported use of memory cues. For example, in the Multiple Errands task (Shallice & Burgess, 1991) participants are observed carrying out an experimentally determined set of tasks in a real shopping center. Tasks of work-based generation and implementation of plans have also been investigated in real and virtual environments (Funke & Krüger, 1993; McGeorge et al., 2001). However, as far as we are aware, no previous studies have investigated age differences in the efficiency of PM under such circumstances. It would be extremely interesting to observe age differences in PM in complex real environments such as a workplace or shopping center, or in artificial environments set up to resemble real life (e.g., inbox tasks), or in virtual environments that parallel real-world settings but allow better experimental control and recording of performance. Using a range of environments and task manipulations in such settings would improve understanding of the factors that improve or impair PM in older adults.

Another aspect of ecological validity (Type 4 in Table 8.1) occurs when tasks are set in the laboratory but provide some context or familiarity that encourages participants to engage with the task and apply learned skills and strategies. Although this issue had been extensively investigated in relation to age effects in other cognitive domains, relatively few studies have looked at age differences in PM tasks that are laboratory based but contextualized. Nearly all lab-based PM tasks in aging studies have been entirely abstract and novel. One recent exception is a study by McDermott and Knight (2004) that used more naturalistic stimuli of video clips of a visit to a shopping center to investigate age differences in PM. However, the tasks that participants were asked to do in this study were not familiar: The ongoing task was to count the number of objects such as bicycles, and the PM task consisted of remembering and implementing 27 different intentions associated with different cues. The retrospective memory load of these task instructions was extremely high, particularly because PM was tested by participants writing down the cue–action associations in response to seeing the cue, rather than actually implementing an intention. Older adults' performance was much worse than that of young adults, and this was interpreted as suggesting that "the decline in PR [prospective remembering] in numerous laboratory-based tests ... has parallels in the real-life performance of older adults" (p. 357). However, the PM task in this study was highly artificial and placed very substantial demands on episodic memory, so it is not clear how this conclusion could be justified. There were no age differences in the ongoing counting task, suggesting that older participants may have prioritized this over the daunting PM task.

Finally, Type 5 ecological validity is represented by the traditional lab-based PM tasks on which age-related deficits are often found, where the setting, task materials, and PM task instructions tend to be both novel and abstract.

Some studies have looked at an incidental but meaningful task during a lab-based testing session to investigate PM. For example, Dobbs and Rule (1987) found that older adults were particularly poor at remembering to ask for a red pen when completing a drawing task. Also, Mantyla and Nilsson (1997) found age declines in a PM task that they described as relatively realistic, in which older participants had to remind the experimenter to sign a paper during an experiment. These results suggest that the use of more familiar stimuli or tasks may not reduce age deficits in PM in laboratory settings, but more precise manipulations are needed to better understand the role of naturalistic materials and task demands in relation to age effects on PM tasks set in the lab.

In sum, age benefits in PM performance are most readily seen when tasks are set in the day-to-day environment of the participant. Age deficits in PM have been reported when a task is set in a laboratory but has some more familiar or incidental context. This suggests that the most critical factor in determining the direction of age effects in PM is the task setting, rather than providing more familiar contexts within the lab, but this has not been directly tested by manipulating task setting or familiarity while keeping other aspects constant. The lack of direct observational information about performance of older adults carrying out PM tasks in naturalistic or more constrained but realistic settings limits current understanding of the age benefits in naturalistic PM.

What Does the Age–Prospective Memory Paradox Mean?

For an experimental psychologist, the key message from this chapter may be the finding that older adults perform poorly in PM tasks in the lab, because it is only in the laboratory that participants' performance can be experimentally controlled and monitored. So, for example, Dobbs and Reeves (1996) argued that outside the lab situation, participants will alter the PM task to suit their needs, and we can no longer draw any theoretical conclusions about the nature of any PM changes with age. However, for a gerontologist, the key message may be that older adults are extremely capable of remembering to carry out intentions in their everyday lives, contrary to common stereotypes of memory loss with age. Given the pattern of results reported in this chapter, experimental psychologists have a responsibility to take great care in extending the findings from the controlled but sterile environment of the lab to draw assumptions about the effects of aging in the richer context of everyday life. All of those interested in aging and cognition might want to consider the following scenario, which highlights this tension between empirically rigorous lab-based findings and less controlled real-life performance.

> As a cognitive psychologist you have been asked to advise a government department on issues concerned with aging and employment. One of the questions they ask is, "Are older people worse than younger people at scheduling and carrying out tasks and appointments at the appropriate time?" What would your answer be? Should we be guided by the lab-based theoretical results, or are the studies set in everyday life a better guide to this issue?

Thinking about this scenario also helps to focus attention on what some of the debates around the paradoxical age effects on PM tasks might mean. For example, the poorer performance of younger adults on naturalistic PM tasks might depend on factors such as motivation, personality factors, adherence to social rules, or life structure, and the effects of these factors on automatization and monitoring of performance on PM tasks. These factors have often been dismissed as *artefactual*—explaining away age differences—because they may reflect social norms or cohort differences rather than developmental age-related changes in basic cognitive functions. However, these motivational and organizational factors may impact on important aspects of PM that go beyond the simple skills involved in making phone calls to more general use of memory resources in everyday life, for example to organize health behaviors, work schedules, and family life. It is striking that we have so little knowledge of age differences in everyday PM performance in complex settings. Kvavilashvili and Ellis (2004) argued that PM tasks in naturalistic settings may have low ecological validity in the sense that there are confounding variables (e.g., motivation or reminder use) that impair the generalizability and hence external validity of such tasks. However, we do not know (and it is an interesting empirical question) whether lab-based or naturalistic PM tasks best predict everyday PM performance in the workplace and social lives of older adults.

MAJOR ISSUES AND FUTURE DIRECTIONS

Ecological validity is a key issue in investigating prospective memory. Both laboratory and naturalistic settings have provided valuable information about the nature of age differences in PM. Any theory of PM that considers only lab-based or real-world results would be inadequate. However, we still do not understand the reasons for the paradox indicated by strong age benefits in naturalistic settings along with age deficits in lab-based settings. This pattern is not generally seen in other aspects of cognitive function (with the possible exception of the related construct of planning; see Phillips, McLeod & Kliegel, 2005, for a review), however this might be because age differences in few other domains of cognition have been investigated outside of the laboratory. One problem in interpreting this paradox is that the natures of samples and tasks used in lab-based and naturalistic PM settings are often very different, making it more difficult to compare across studies. It is essential that more studies are carried out looking at a range of lab-based and naturalistic PM tasks within the same sample; to our knowledge, the only published study to do this so far is Rendell and Thomson (1999). This may be particularly important because published PM studies vary considerably in the range of ages in young and old groups, including a number that study middle-aged participants as the younger comparison group, and a number of PM tasks may show nonmonotonic relationships with age (e.g., Mantyla & Nilsson, 1997; Maylor, 1998). Also, there is substantial variation in both the presence and magnitude of age effects in PM tasks within each setting.

The nature of published lab-based and naturalistic PM tasks differs dramatically. To develop a better understanding of the mechanisms underlying age differences in both types of tasks, manipulations that alter tasks in both settings but along the same dimensions are needed. There are many possible manipulations that would help us to understand the nature of age differences in PM better, and the following are just a few suggestions.

Measuring and Manipulating Reminder Strategies

It would be extremely useful to develop PM task analogs in both lab and everyday settings that can be manipulated in terms of retrospective memory load, and the reminder strategies used by participants. It would be of particular interest to introduce different types of reminder strategies (internal, external, conjunction) and to monitor the occurrence of rehearsal of intentions. Another factor of importance here would be to investigate participants' awareness of their own memory fallibility, a factor that has often been theoretically linked to assumed increases in the use of reminder strategies among older adults. Kvavilashvili (2005) reported that older adults made more uncued rehearsals of PM intentions than young adults in a naturalistic task. This suggests that in everyday tasks, older adults are more likely to review their pending intentions, and thus more likely to encounter the correct time to start monitoring for the appropriate time or event for the prospective action. If that is the case, then triggering rehearsal of intentions in everyday environments should improve performance for younger adults, too. An interesting question is whether methods of encouraging rehearsal and review of intentions could improve older adults' performance on lab-based tasks, where the cognitive load of managing a dual task situation might make extraneous cognitive load too problematic.

Manipulating Motivation

Developing PM tasks in both settings that can be varied in the motivational quality of the task to the individual participant would add to our understanding of this component of PM. A number of motivational issues have been suggested to explain the age–PM paradox, and it would be useful to see more careful measurement of task attitudes and perceived importance of both ongoing task activities and the embedded PM task. Of particular interest would be controlled manipulation, in both lab and realistic settings of the various aspects of motivation that have been argued to explain the paradox: social goals, the realism of the PM task, emotional involvement in the task, busyness and demands of everyday life or the ongoing task, and so on.

Participant Control

A further issue that may be important in considering the pattern of age effects on PM may be the level of control participants have over the task. In most naturalistic tasks, the participant has freedom to choose the best way to recall and implement intentions, whereas in laboratory tasks the experimenter exerts much more control over the nature of implementation cues. To date, this issue of choice of memory strategies has not been directly addressed through instruction manipulations in PM tasks. Cockburn (1996) observed that even when PM cues are built into an interview, older people are unlikely to make spontaneous use of reminder cues because they perceive the task as under the control of the interviewer, and this suggests that further exploration of participant and experimenter control in PM tasks could be fruitful.

Experience and Practice

Practice on a task may be important, and have different implications for age differences in lab-based and naturalistic tasks. With experience, people may seek to reduce the retrospective component of everyday PM tasks; for example, always making sure to put pills in the same place every day to make the PM task of taking medication become as routine and noneffortful as possible. If participants receive a large amount of practice with appropriate feedback on a lab-based task, they may eventually recognize environmental contingencies in the experimental paradigm and thus rely more and more on precursory trials to trigger their monitoring (Zöllig, 2005): This should reduce age differences in lab-based PM tasks. The age advantage on naturalistic tasks may disappear with extended practice in the task environment for the younger adults. Examining in detail the time course of extended PM performance in terms of monitoring, cue–action associations, intention rehearsal, and errors would be useful. This offers the possibility of making more use of repeated measures designs in PM performance, and creating lab-based tasks that model the demands of everyday tasks more closely.

Direct Manipulation of Task Setting and Materials

As discussed earlier, we still do not fully understand which aspects of ecological validity underpin the paradoxical results obtained, and it would be extremely useful to have some studies that manipulate the specific aspects of task setting and nature of task in a more methodological manner, within the same or matched samples. For example, use of the same PM task in an artificial but complex setting, a complex virtual environment, and in participants' everyday life would allow better understanding of the role of task setting in age differences in PM. Further, manipulating the familiarity and realism of the materials used in a PM task while keeping the task complexity and task setting the same would elucidate age differences in the importance of task realism.

CONCLUSION

The age–PM paradox is the repeated finding of a substantial age-related decline in performing many lab-based PM tasks, along with a substantial age-related improvement in PM tasks carried out in naturalistic settings. The limited empirical evidence available to date does not support the widespread assumption in the literature that this pattern reflects artefacts in the use of naturalistic methods. Current understanding of the role of memory aids, motivation, practice, and lifestyle in both types of PM tasks is poor, and this needs to be addressed through the use of controlled manipulations in large-scale studies. Exploration of this puzzling paradox will enhance theoretical models of PM and shed light on the importance of PM in everyday behavior. Understanding why older people show better performance in naturalistic PM tasks may provide clues as to how to improve other aspects of everyday cognition in old age.

REFERENCES

Bäckman, L. (1991). Recognition memory across the lifespan: The role of prior knowledge. *Memory and Cognition, 19,* 63–71.

Berg, C. A., & Klaczynski, P. A. (1996). Practical intelligence and problem solving: Searching for perspectives. In F. Blanchard-Fields & T. M. Hess (Eds.), *Perspectives on cognitive change in adulthood and aging* (pp. 323–357). New York: McGraw-Hill.

Blanchard-Fields, F., Jahnke, H. C., & Camp, C. (1995). Age differences in problem-solving style: The role of emotional salience. *Psychology and Aging, 10,* 173–180.

Brandimonte, M., Einstein, G. O., & McDaniel, M.A. (1996). *Prospective memory: Theory and applications.* Mahwah, NJ: Lawrence Erlbaum Associates, Inc.

Charles, S. T., Mather, M., & Carstensen, L. L. (2003). Aging and emotional memory: The forgettable nature of negative images for older adults. *Journal of Experimental Psychology: General, 132,* 310–324.

Cherry, K. E., Martin, R. C., Simmons-D'Gerolamo, S. S., Pinkston, J. B., Griffing, A., & Gouvier, W. D. (2001). Prospective remembering in younger and older adults: Role of the prospective cue. *Memory, 9,* 177–193.

Cockburn, J. (1996). Assessment and treatment of prospective memory deficits. *In M.* Brandimonte, G. O. Einstein, & M. A. McDaniel (Eds.), *Prospective memory: Theory and applications* (pp. 327–350). Mahwah, NJ: Lawrence Erlbaum Associates, Inc.

Cohen, A. L., West, R., & Craik, F. I. M. (2001). Modulation of the prospective and retrospective components of memory for intentions in younger and older adults. *Aging Neuropsychology and Cognition, 8,* 1–13.

Craik, F. I. M. (1986). A functional account of age differences in memory. In F. Klix & H. Hagendorf (Eds.), *Human memory and cognitive capabilities: Mechanisms and performances* (pp. 409–422). Amsterdam: Elsevier-North-Holland.

Craik, F. I. M., & Kerr, S. A. (1996). Commentary: Prospective memory, aging, and lapses of intention. *In M.* Brandimonte, G. O. Einstein, & M. A. McDaniel (Eds.), *Prospective memory: Theory and applications* (pp. 227–237). Mahwah, NJ: Lawrence Erlbaum Associates, Inc.

Cramer, J. A., & Rosenheck, R. (1998). Compliance with medication regimens for mental and physical disorders. *Psychiatric Services, 49,* 196–201.

Cuttler, C., & Graf, P. (2005, July). *Personality and cognitive ability underlie age-related differences in prospective memory.* Poster presented at the Second International Conference on Prospective Memory, Zurich, Switzerland.

Denney, N. W. (1989). Everyday problem-solving: Methodological issues, research findings, and a model. In L. W. Poon, D. C. Rubin, & B. A. Wilson (Eds.), *Everyday cognition in adulthood and late life* (pp. 330–351). Cambridge, UK: Cambridge University Press.

Devolder, P. A., Brigham, M. C., & Pressley, M. (1990). Memory performance awareness in younger and older adults. *Psychology and Aging, 5,* 291–303.

Dobbs, A. R., & Reeves, M. B. (1996). Prospective memory: More than memory. In M. A. Brandimonte, G. O. Einstein, & M. A. McDaniel (Eds.), *Prospective memory: Theory and applications* (pp. 199–226). Mahwah, NJ: Lawrence Erlbaum Associates, Inc.

Dobbs, A. R., & Rule, B. G. (1987). Prospective memory and self-reports of memory abilities in older adults. *Canadian Journal of Psychology, 41,* 209–222.

d'Ydewalle, G. (1995). Age-related interference of intervening activities in a prospective memory task. *Psychologica Belgica, 35,* 189–203.

d'Ydewalle, G., Bouckaert, D., & Brunfaut, E. (2001). Age-related differences and complexity of ongoing activities in time- and event-based prospective memory. *American Journal of Psychology, 114,* 411–423.

d'Ydewalle, G., & Brunfaut, E. (1996). Are older subjects necessarily worse in prospective memory tasks? In M. Georgas, E. Manthouli, E. Besevegis, & A. Kokkevi (Eds.), *Contemporary psychology in Europe: Theory, research and applications* (pp. 161–172). Göttingen, Germany: Hogrefe & Huber.

d'Ydewalle, G., Luwel, K., & Brunfaut, E. (1999). The importance of on-going concurrent activities as a function of age in time- and event-based prospective memory. *European Journal of Cognitive Psychology, 11,* 219–237.

Einstein, G. O., Holland, L. J., McDaniel, M. A., & Guynn, M. J. (1992). Age-related deficits in prospective memory: The influence of task complexity. *Psychology and Aging, 7,* 471–478.

Einstein, G. O., & McDaniel, M. A. (1990). Normal aging and prospective memory. *Journal of Experimental Psychology: Learning, Memory, and Cognition, 16,* 717–726.

Einstein, G. O., & McDaniel, M. A. (1996). Retrieval processes in prospective memory: Theoretical approaches and some new empirical findings. In M. Brandimonte, G. O. Einstein, & M. A. McDaniel (Eds.), *Prospective memory: Theory and applications* (pp. 115–141). Mahwah, NJ: Lawrence Erlbaum Associates, Inc.

Einstein, G. O., McDaniel, M. A., Richardson, S. L., Guynn, M. J., & Cunfer, A. R. (1995). Aging and prospective memory: Examining the influences of self-initiated retrieval processes. *Journal of Experimental Psychology: Learning, Memory and Cognition, 21,* 996–1007.

Einstein, G. O., Smith, R. E., McDaniel, M. A., & Shaw, P. (1997). Aging and prospective memory: The influence of increased task demands at encoding and retrieval. *Psychology and Aging, 12,* 479–488.

Ellis, J., & Kvavilashvili, L. (2000). Prospective memory in 2000: Past, present and future directions. *Applied Cognitive Psychology, 14,* S1–S9.

Freeman, J. E., & Ellis, J. A. (2003). The intention-superiority effect for naturally occurring activities: The role of intention accessibility in everyday prospective remembering in young and older adults. *International Journal of Psychology, 38,* 215–228.

Funke, J., & Krüger, T. (1993). *"Plan-A-Day" (PAD).* Bonn, Germany: Psychologisches Institut der Universität Bonn.

Garden, S., Phillips, L. H., & MacPherson, S. E. (2001). Mid-life aging, open-ended planning and laboratory measures of executive function. *Neuropsychology, 15,* 472–482.

Gilhooly, K. J., Phillips, L. H., Wynn, V. E., Logie, R. H., & Della Sala, S. (1999). Planning processes and age in the 5 disc Tower of London task. *Thinking and Reasoning, 5,* 339–361.

Glisky, E. L. (1996). Prospective memory and the frontal lobes. In M. A. Brandimonte, G. O. Einstein, & M. A. McDaniel (Eds.), *Prospective memory: Theory and applications* (pp. 249–266). Mahwah, NJ: Lawrence Erlbaum Associates, Inc.

Gould, O. N. (1999). Cognition and affect in medication adherence. In D. C. Park, R. W. Morrell, & K. Shifren (Eds.), *Processing of medical information in aging patients: Cognitive and human factors perspectives* (pp. 167–183). Mahwah, NJ: Lawrence Erlbaum Associates, Inc.

Gould, O. N., McDonald-Miszczak, L., & King, B. (1997). Metacognition and medication adherence: How do older adults remember? *Experimental Aging Research, 23,* 315–342.

Greenberg, R. N. (1984). Overview of patient compliance with medication dosing: A literature review. *Clinical Therapeutics, 6,* 592–599.

Henry, J. D., MacLeod, M., Phillips, L. H., & Crawford, J. R. (2004). Meta-analytic review of prospective memory and aging. *Psychology and Aging, 19,* 27–39.

Hertzog, C., Park, D. C., & Morrell, R. W. (2000). Ask and ye shall receive: Behavioural specificity in the accuracy of subjective memory complaints. *Applied Cognitive Psychology, 14,* 257–275.

Hess, T. M., & Pullen, S. M. (1994). Adult age differences in impression change processes. *Psychology and Aging, 6,* 237–250.

Hess, T. M., & Pullen, S. M. (1996). Memory in context. In F. Blanchard-Fields & T. M. Hess (Eds.), *Perspectives on cognitive change in adulthood and aging* (pp. 387–427). New York: McGraw-Hill.

Huppert, F. A., Johnson, T., & Nickson, J. (2000). High prevalence of prospective memory impairment in the elderly and in early-stage dementia: Findings from a population-based study. *Applied Cognitive Psychology, 14,* S63–S81.

Jackson, J. L., Bogers, H., & Kerstholt, J. (1988). Do memory aids aid the elderly in their day-to-day remembering? In M. M. Gruneberg, P. E. Morris, & R. N. Sykes (Eds.), *Practical aspects of memory: Current research and issues: Volume 2. Clinical and educational implications* (pp. 137–142). Chichester, UK: Wiley.

Johansson, O., Andersson, J., & Ronnberg, J. (2000). Do elderly couples have a better prospective memory than other elderly people when they collaborate? *Applied Cognitive Psychology, 14,* 121–133.

Kliegel, M., Martin, M., McDaniel, M. A., & Einstein, G. O. (2004). Importance effects on performance in event-based prospective memory tasks. *Memory, 12,* 553–561.

Kliegel, M., Martin, M., McDaniel, M.A., & Phillips, L.H. (2007). Adult age differences in errand planning: The role of task familiarity and cognitive resources. *Experimental Aging Research, 33,* 145–161.

Kliegel, M., McDaniel, M. A., & Einstein, G. O. (2000). Plan formation, retention, and execution in prospective memory: A new approach and age-related effects. *Memory and Cognition, 28,* 1041–1049.

Kliegel, M., Phillips, L. H., & Jäger, T. (in preparation). *Importance effects on age differences in performance in event-based prospective memory.*

Kvavilashvili, L. (2005, July). *Automatic or controlled? Rehearsal and retrieval processes in everyday time- and event-based prospective memory tasks.* Paper presented at the Second International Conference on Prospective Memory, Zurich, Switzerland.

Kvavilashvili, L., & Ellis, J. (1996). Varieties of intention: Some distinctions and classifications. In M. A. Brandimonte, G. O. Einstein, & M. A. McDaniel (Eds.), *Prospective memory: Theory and applications* (pp. 23–51). Mahwah, NJ: Lawrence Erlbaum Associates, Inc.

Kvavilashvili, L., & Ellis, J. (2004). Ecological validity and the real-life/laboratory controversy in memory research: A critical (and historical) review. *History and Philosophy of Psychology, 6,* 59–80.

Lachman, M. E., & Burack, O. R. (1993). Planning and control processes across the life span: An overview. *International Journal of Behavioral Development, 16,* 131–143.

Light, L. L. (1991). Memory and aging: Four hypotheses in search of data. *Annual Review of Psychology, 43,* 333–376.

Lorenc, L., & Branthwaite, A. (1993). Are older adults less compliant with prescribed medication than younger adults? *British Journal of Clinical Psychology, 32,* 485–492.

Lovelace, E. A., & Twohig, P. T. (1990) Healthy older adults' perceptions of their memory functioning and use of mnemonics. *Bulletin of the Psychonomic Society, 28,* 115–118.

MacPherson, S., Phillips, L. H., & Della Sala, S. (2002). Age, executive function and social decision-making: A dorsolateral prefrontal theory of cognitive aging. *Psychology and Aging, 17,* 598–609.

Martin, M. (1986). Aging and patterns of change in everyday memory and cognition. *Human Learning, 5,* 63–74.

Martin, M., Kliegel, M., & McDaniel, M. (2003). The involvement of executive functions in prospective memory performance of adults. *International Journal of Psychology, 38,* 195–206.

Martin, M., & Park, D. C. (2003). The Martin and Park Environmental Demands Questionnaire (MPED): Psychometric properties of a newly developed questionnaire to measure environmental demands. *Aging: Clinical and Experimental Research, 15,* 77–82.

Martin, M., & Schumann-Hengsteler, R. (2001). How task demands influence time-based prospective memory performance in young and older adults. *International Journal of Behavioral Development, 25,* 386–391.

Mantyla, T. (1993). Priming effects in prospective memory. *Memory, 1,* 203–208.

Mantyla, T. (1994). Remembering to remember: Adult age-differences in prospective memory. *Journals of Gerontology, 49,* 276–282.

Mantyla, T., & Nilsson, L. (1997). Remembering to remember in adulthood: A population-based study on aging and prospective memory. *Aging, Neuropsychology and Cognition, 4,* 81–92.

Maylor, E. A. (1990). Age and prospective memory. *Quarterly Journal of Experimental Psychology, 42A,* 471–493.

Maylor, E. A. (1993). Minimized prospective memory loss in old age. In J. Cerella, J. Rybash, W. Hoyer, & M. L. Commons (Eds.), *Adult information processing: Limits on loss* (pp. 529–551). San Diego, CA: Academic.

Maylor, E. A. (1995). Prospective memory in normal ageing and dementia. *Neurocase, 1,* 285–289.

Maylor, E. A. (1996). Does prospective memory decline with age? In M. Brandimonte, G. O. Einstein, & M. A. McDaniel (Eds.), *Prospective memory: Theory and applications* (pp. 173–197). Mahwah, NJ: Lawrence Erlbaum Associates, Inc.

Maylor, E. A. (1998). Changes in event-based prospective memory across adulthood. *Aging, Neuropsychology and Cognition, 5,* 107–128.

McDaniel, M. A., & Einstein, G. O. (1992). Aging and prospective memory: Basic findings and practical applications. *Advances in Learning and Behavioral Disabilities, 7,* 87–105.

McDaniel, M. A., & Einstein, G. O. (2000). Strategic and automatic processes in prospective memory retrieval: A multiprocess framework. *Applied Cognitive Psychology, 14,* S127–S144.

McDermott, K., & Knight, R. G. (2004). The effects of aging on a measure of prospective remembering using naturalistic stimuli. *Applied Cognitive Psychology, 18,* 349–362.

McGeorge, P., Phillips, L. H., Crawford, J. R., Garden, S. E., Della Sala, S., Milne, A. B. et al. (2001). Using virtual environments in the assessment of executive dysfunction. *Presence: Teleoperators and Virtual Environments, 10,* 375–383.

Morris, L. S., & Schulz, R. M. (1992). Patient compliance: An overview. *Journal of Clinical Pharmacology Therapeutics, 17,* 283–295.

Moscovitch, M. (1982). A neuropsychological approach to memory and perception in normal and pathological aging. In F. I. M. Craik & S. Trehub (Eds.), *Aging and cognitive processes* (pp. 55–78). New York: Plenum.

Park, D. C., Hertzog, C., & Kidder, D. P. (1997). Effect of age on event-based and time-based prospective memory. *Psychology & Aging, 12,* 314–327.

Park, D. C., Hertzog, C., Leventhal, H., Morrell, R. W., Leventhal E., Birchmore, D. et al. (1999). Medication adherence in rheumatoid arthritis patients: Older is wiser. *Journal of the American Geriatric Society, 47,* 172–183.

Park, D. C., & Kidder, D. P. (1996). Prospective memory and medication adherence. In M. Brandimonte, G. O. Einstein, & M. A. McDaniel (Eds.), *Prospective memory: Theory and applications* (pp. 369–390). Mahwah, NJ: Lawrence Erlbaum Associates, Inc.

Patton, G. W., & Meit, M. (1993). Effect of aging on prospective and incidental memory. *Experimental Aging Research, 19,* 165–176.

Phillips, L. H., Kliegel, M., & Martin, M. (2006). Age and planning tasks: The influence of ecological validity. *International Journal of Aging and Human Development, 62,* 175–184.

Phillips, L. H., MacLeod, M., & Kliegel, M. (2005). Adult aging and cognitive planning. In G. Ward & R. Morris (Eds.), *The cognitive psychology of planning* (pp. 111–134). Hove, UK: Psychology Press.

Rabbitt, P. M. A. (1996). Commentary: Why are studies of "prospective memory" planless? *In* M. Brandimonte, G. O. Einstein, & M. A. McDaniel (Eds.), *Prospective memory: Theory and applications* (pp. 239–248). Mahwah, NJ: Lawrence Erlbaum Associates, Inc.

Rendell, P. G., & Craik, F. I. M. (2000). Virtual week and actual week: Age-related differences in prospective memory. *Applied Cognitive Psychology, 14,* S43–S62.

Rendell, P. G., & Thomson, D. M. (1993). The effect of ageing on remembering to remember: An investigation of simulated medication regimens. *Australian Journal of Ageing, 12,* 11–18.

Rendell, P. G., & Thomson, D. M. (1999). Aging and prospective memory: Differences between naturalistic and laboratory tasks. *Journals of Gerontology Series B: Psychological Sciences and Social Sciences, 54,* 256–269.

Roe, C. M., Motheral, B. R., Teitelbaum, F., & Rich, M. W. (2000). Compliance with and dosing of angiotensin-converting-enzyme inhibitors before and after hospitalization. *American Journal of Health Systems Pharmacy, 57,* 139–145.

Salthouse, T. A., Berish, D. E., & Siedlecki, K. L. (2004). Construct validity and age sensitivity of prospective memory. *Memory and Cognition, 32,* 1133–1148.

Schultz, J. S., O'Donnell, J. C., McDonough, K. L., Sasane, R., & Meyer, J. (2005). Determinants of compliance with statin therapy and low-density lipoprotein cholesteral goal attainment in a managed care population. *American Journal of Managed Care, 11,* 306–312.

Shallice, T., & Burgess, P. (1991). Deficits in strategy application following frontal lobe damage in man. *Brain, 114,* 727–741.

Thornton, W. J. L., & Dumke, H. A. (2005). Age differences in everyday problem-solving and decision-making effectiveness: A meta-analytic review. *Psychology and Aging, 20,* 85–99.

West, R., Jakubek, K., & Wymbs, N. (2002). Age-related declines in prospective memory: Behavioral and electrophysiological evidence. *Neuroscience & Biobehavioral Reviews, 26,* 827–833.

Wingfield, A., Lahar, C. J., & Stine, E. A. L. (1989). Age and decision strategies in running memory for speech: Effects of speech rate, linguistic structure and processing time. *Journal of Gerontology: Psychological Sciences, 44,* 106–113.

Zöllig, J. (2005, July). What do we know about neural and behavioral correlates of prospective memory in children? Paper presented at the Second International Conference on Prospective Memory, Zurich, Switzerland.

9

A Life Span Approach to the Development of Complex Prospective Memory

MATTHIAS KLIEGEL and RACHAEL MACKINLAY

Department of Psychology
University of Zürich, Switzerland

THEODOR JÄGER

Department of Psychology
Saarland University, Saarbrücken, Germany

OPTING FOR A LIFE SPAN PERSPECTIVE

Extreme Age Group Comparisons versus Life Span Development

Prospective memory concerns activities such as having to remember to do homework after returning home from school or to switch off the stove after cooking. As such, prospective remembering is an important and pervasive aspect of real-life memory processes and can be regarded as a major factor supporting the attainment and preservation of autonomy in everyday life across the life span (e.g., Cockburn & Smith, 1988; Kliegel & Martin, 2003; Mills et al., 1997).

Reviewing the literature on prospective memory development, however, reveals that the major focus of research so far has been on age differences between distinct and more or less extreme age groups in the adult age range (for a meta-analytic overview, see Henry, MacLeod, Phillips, & Crawford, 2004; see also Phillips, Henry, & Martin, chap. 8, this volume; McDaniel, Einstein, & Rendell, chap. 7, this volume, for discussions of this literature in detail). Although there has been some work on prospective memory at the other end of the life span, in children this issue has received considerably less attention (but see Kvavilashvili, Kyle, & Messer, chap. 6, this volume, for a comprehensive overview and some indications that this area is growing again). Investigations of children's prospective memory development have also been limited to comparing prospective memory performance between distinct age groups, ranging from preschool to early adolescence. Surprisingly few contributions have focused on a life span developmental perspective of prospective memory; thus, a comprehensive theoretical approach and empirical data sets comprising both ends of the human life span are largely absent from the published literature (for a notable exception see Maylor, Darby, Logie, Della Sala, & Smith, 2002).

We strongly believe that a life span perspective on prospective memory development is necessary to give focus to this ubiquitous phenomenon of human cognition. This is because the delayed realization of intended actions is a frequent (e.g., Crovitz & Daniel, 1984; Kliegel & Martin, 2003; Terry, 1988) and important autonomy-related (Elvevåg, Maylor, & Gilbert, 2003; Meacham, 1982; Meacham & Colombo, 1980; Shum, Leung, Ungvari, & Tang, 2001; Winograd, 1988) developmental task that is not limited to a specific age period. Furthermore, cross-sectional investigations of prospective memory at different stages of the life span suggest significant changes in this ability across the entire life span.

Thus, in this chapter we argue in favor of describing prospective memory development and elaborating on mechanisms of this development within a life span developmental framework. In doing so, we will apply four core principles of life span developmental psychology that have been outlined by Baltes and colleagues (e.g., Baltes & Baltes, 1990; Baltes, Lindenberger & Staudinger, 1998; Baltes, Reese & Nesselroade, 1977). First, we outline how these principles might be applicable to prospective memory development, describing findings we have obtained in our lab over the past several years. Here, besides summarizing and delineating results from a number of studies that (mostly but not exclusively) follow the traditional approach of extreme group comparisons within a certain age segment, we also—by pooling data from previous studies—provide for the first time life span trajectories of performance in distinct prospective memory phases. Moreover, we extend this descriptive level of analyses by offering a rough outline of a model that aims to explain developmental processes in prospective memory, and discuss initial evidence for the proposed mechanisms.

Four Principles of Life Span Developmental Psychology

One central idea of life span developmental psychology is that development concerns not only the biologically determined differentiation and growth of psychological factors in children. Development is rather seen as taking place from the very beginning until the end of human life, with any phase having its own specific importance for the entire course of development (e.g., Baltes & Baltes, 1990). For the life span development of prospective memory, this means that we need to describe and explain developmental differences and changes from childhood into old age and aim to identify mechanisms that drive these developmental processes.

Importantly, this includes both mechanisms that may be similar across the entire life span and mechanisms that may be specific to particular developmental phases.

A second principle is the multidimensionality of development. *Multidimensionality* describes the observation that development—even within one developmental domain—does not follow a parallel or unitary path but is different for many subdomains; for instance, free recall and recognition memory follow different developmental trajectories despite both being aspects of memory (e.g., Craik & McDowd, 1987). One other prominent example is the differentiation of fluid and crystallized intelligence in the developmental psychology of intelligence (e.g., Schaie, 2005). In consequence, when describing the development of cognitive functions, distinct developmental trends have to be specified for distinct subdomains. For the life span development of prospective memory, this means that we will need to decompose the process of prospective memory to accurately describe the various dimensions of prospective memory development across the life span.

In fact, within domains and subdomains there may even be opposite developmental trajectories involving growth, decline, and stability (Baltes et al., 1998). This concerns the third principle of life span developmental psychology and has been labeled *multidirectionality*. Importantly, it has been argued that growth, decline, and stability are present and possible at each phase of the human life span, with only the relative importance of these three processes changing over time (from growth being dominant in early phases and decline becoming dominant in late life). For the life span development of prospective memory this means that, in relation to the identified dimensions, we need to target all three potential developmental trends in those dimensions; in other words, where do we find growth, where decline, and where stability?

Finally, resting on the idea of growth being possible even very late in life, the fourth principle is the *plasticity* of developmental domains. Acknowledging that plasticity is a very broad concept comprising the possibility of change in neural structures as well as behavioral domains, we use the term plasticity to argue that one's cognitive (e.g., prospective memory) capacity is not entirely predetermined at any stage of the life span. Many skills can be trained or improved, even in very early or late life, although there are of course limits to the degree of potential improvement (e.g., Kliegl, Smith, & Baltes, 1989). For the life span development of prospective memory this means that we will particularly need to search for the processes where plasticity does happen; that is, where we can find ways of improving prospective memory performance across the life span.

MULTIDIMENSIONALITY: DECOMPOSING THE PROCESS OF PROSPECTIVE MEMORY

The first principle, that development is a process that takes place right across the life span, is the motivation for and somewhat inherent to the entire chapter. Thus, we begin our outline of life span prospective memory development by decomposing the developmental object of interest, the process of prospective memory.

The Four Phases of Prospective Remembering: A Process Model

From a theoretical point of view, it has been argued that the term *prospective memory* is an umbrella term representing several distinct phases and cognitive processes involved in the realization of delayed intentions (McDaniel & Einstein, 2000). Kliegel, Martin, McDaniel, and Einstein (2002; see also Ellis, 1996) thus proposed a process model that disentangles the process of prospective remembering into four phases: (a) *intention formation*—the point at which the intention is formed, which often involves forming a plan; (b) *intention retention*—a period during which the intention is retained, which is typically filled with an "ongoing" activity (Ellis & Kvavilashvili, 2000) that precludes continuous rehearsal of the intended task; (c) *intention initiation*—the point in time at which execution of the intention is (or should be) initiated; and (d) *intention execution*—where the intended action (or actions) is executed (normally) in accordance with the previously formed plan (see Figure 9.1). To give a concrete example, this process model may be used to describe an everyday prospective memory task of (a) forming the intention to take medication after the meal, (b) keeping the intention in mind during the meal without continuous mental rehearsal, (c) recollecting and initiating the intention on one's own initiative after the meal, and (d) actually executing the intention according to the previously formed plan by getting the medication from the chest of drawers and taking it with a glass of water.

In consideration together with the principle of multidimensionality, we propose to utilize this descriptive process model to study potential multiple facets within prospective memory development. How can we do this empirically?

The Four Phases of Prospective Remembering: An Empirical Paradigm

Most studies on time- or event-based prospective memory have employed prospective memory tasks that consist of a single, isolated act that has to be remembered and performed at appropriate points in the experiment, for example, to press a designated key on the computer keyboard whenever a prospective memory cue appears or at a specific time (e.g., Einstein & McDaniel, 1990; Einstein, McDaniel, Richardson, Guynn, & Cunfer, 1995; Einstein, Smith, McDaniel, & Shaw, 1997; Marsh & Hicks, 1998; Maylor, 1996; Park, Hertzog, Kidder, Morrell, & Mayhorn, 1997; West & Craik, 1999). Because these paradigms comprise of a simple (although often repeated) intended action, they might not completely capture the phases of prospective remembering already described as they potentially obviate the need

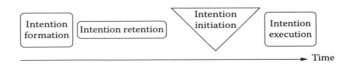

FIGURE 9.1   Decomposing the process of prospective remembering (after Kliegel et al., 2002).

to explicitly plan delayed actions and minimize the retrospective memory load of intention content during the delay phase. Thus, most of the paradigms applied in the literature focus on prospective memory initiation only (Ellis & Kvavilashvili, 2000).

To be able to study all four phases of prospective memory and their interplay, as well as their development, we have proposed a prospective memory paradigm that provides empirical scores for performance in all four phases by applying a modified version of the six-elements task (SET; see Kliegel, Eschen, & Thöne-Otto, 2004; Kliegel, Martin, & Moor, 2003; Kliegel, McDaniel, & Einstein, 2000; see also Kliegel et al., 2002; Kliegel, Phillips, Lemke, & Kopp, 2005). The SET was initially proposed by Shallice and Burgess (1991) to assess multitasking performance in neurological patients. To perform the SET, participants have to remember to self-initiate six different, open-ended tasks in a limited time period. Therefore, they have to schedule the tasks efficiently and keep track of time (see also Burgess, Veitch, Costello, & Shallice, 2000; Groot, Wilson, Evans, & Watson, 2002).

Materials   We kept the basic format of the original SET. In our modified SET, participants must remember to perform six tasks that are subdivided into two parallel versions of three types of tasks: words, arithmetic, and pictures. In all tasks, stimuli are presented on a sheet of paper and participants can move down the sheet from one item to the next to continue working on the task. In the word finding tasks (Parts A and B), participants must score out a word from a list of several possibilities (e.g., nonword distracters: *haz–haif–house–hool*). In the arithmetic tasks (Parts A and B), participants write down the answers to sets of arithmetic problems of varying difficulty. In the picture tasks (Parts A and B), participants must write down the names of line drawings of everyday objects. Total performance time is limited to 6 minutes. Two rules govern performance: (a) All tasks must be attempted, and (b) participants cannot attempt both parallel versions of the same task type sequentially, hence restricting the order in which tasks can be attempted.

Procedure   We extended the original SET instructions to require participants to both explicitly state a verbal performance plan that they intend to follow when working on this multitask set and to delay the self-initiated execution of this plan (Kliegel et al., 2000). A score is generated for each component of the modified SET so that performance at each phase of prospective remembering can be evaluated (Kliegel et al., 2000).

1. *Intention formation component.* First participants plan their later performance. This verbal plan is recorded on a cassette tape and transcripts are scored according to how elaborate the plan is.[1]
2. *Intention retention component.* Second, participants have to retain their plan over a delay period. This delay is filled by heavily engaging activities

---

[1] This plan is scored as follows: It is noted whether the participant makes an explicit plan or not. If a plan is made, does the participant include the intention to attempt all tasks? Furthermore, does the participant plan to adhere to the rule that constrains the order in which tasks can be performed? Finally, the number of executable substeps is analyzed.

(e.g., IQ subtests) that prevent participants from continuously rehearsing the prospective memory task in working memory. Moreover, intention retention itself is examined, as participants are required to recall their plan during this delay period. When compared to their original plan, this gives a measure of how accurately participants are able to retrospectively recall their intention content.[2]

3. *Intention initiation component.* At the end of this delay period, the paradigm requires that participants self-initiate performance of the multitask set on presentation of an appropriate cue.[3]

4. *Intention execution component.* When the multitask set is finally performed, participants' performance and adherence to task rules are scored.[4]

Importantly for the present purposes, these modifications allow us to disentangle the intention formation or planning phase of a prospective memory task from the execution phase, because intention formation itself is explicitly assessed and evaluated in the form of a verbal plan. Similarly, the intention initiation phase can be scored independently of the intention execution phase during which the multitask set is performed. As an additional point of interest, *plan fidelity*, the extent to which participants execute their original plan, can also be measured.

This modified SET was initially applied as a paper-and-pencil test to investigate complex prospective memory development throughout adulthood (Kliegel et al., 2002; Kliegel, Martin, & Moor, 2003; Kliegel et al., 2000; Martin, Kliegel, & McDaniel, 2003) and in clinical populations (Kliegel et al., 2004, Kliegel et al., 2005). It has also been implemented as a computerized version, the *Heidelberger Exekutivfunktionsdiagnostikum* (HEXE; Kliegel & Martin, 2002), which has so far been used to examine the development of complex prospective memory in typically (Martin & Kliegel, 2003) and atypically (Kliegel, Ropeter, & Mackinlay, 2006) developing children. In the next section, we review the results obtained in these cross-sectional studies and examine all four stages of prospective memory at distinct phases of the human life span.

At this point we should comment that our complex prospective memory task enables explicit differentiation of the four phases of prospective remembering at the cost of being a fairly resource-demanding task. In their multiprocess framework, McDaniel and Einstein (2000; see also Einstein et al., 2005) argued that

---

[2] This recalled plan is scored using the same elements as the initial plan generated in the intention formation phase. The two plans are then compared and points are awarded for correct recall of the original plan (i.e., matching elements).

[3] The cue to begin the multitask set is when participants are asked to write their date of birth at the top of a questionnaire given to them by the experimenter. If participants fail to act on presentation of this cue, the experimenter reminds participants to begin performing the multitask set and a failure of self-initiation is recorded.

[4] Multitask performance is scored according to the following elements. The number of tasks attempted within the given time limit and whether the task order rule is adhered to or broken. Additional scores of interest include whether participants adopt an optimal performance sequence by beginning with a single item from each task and the accuracy of their responses to items in each task.

the need for planning in prospective memory tasks increases the probability of strategic processing as the underlying mechanism of prospective retrieval. Moreover, in the execution phase of our task, participants have to keep track of time and schedule six different tasks, which according to the multiprocess view will result in conscious monitoring. Thus, we acknowledge that the task applied in the research and theoretical reasoning presented in this chapter represents only one—albeit fairly common—prospective memory scenario.[5] Other, more automatically triggered prospective memory tasks are likely to show distinct developmental patterns (see McDaniel et al., chap. 7, this volume).

The Four Phases of Prospective Remembering: Age Differences and Age Invariance across the Life Span

Overview and Predictions   The theoretical rationale for expecting differential age effects on the four phases of prospective memory comes from the proposition of differential involvement of specific cognitive resources in each phase. Specifically, in proposing an explanatory model (see Figure 9.2 for a revised version of a previously presented model schema) we argue that the task requirements in intention formation, intention initiation, and intention execution components can be assumed to require (specific) executive processes, whereas the requirements of the intention retention component may demand mainly retrospective storage capacity (Kliegel et al., 2002).

Although the model assumes that, in principle, there may be task- and individual-dependent variations in the extent to which a specific mechanism will be involved at each phase; it generally assumes that age affects each prospective memory phase through the task- and individual-specific interplay of (at least) four distinct major variables: planning, storage, monitoring, and inhibition.

Planning is assumed to be the most influential function at the intention formation phase. We have previously reported (Kliegel et al., 2002; Martin et al., 2003) that performance at this stage of the model correlates with performance on tests of planning including the Tower of London (Shallice, 1982) and the "Plan-a-Day" test (Funke & Krüger, 1993). Intention initiation may rely on somewhat different executive functions; in particular it correlates with performance on tests of monitoring and cognitive flexibility. Similarly, strong predictors of intention execution are tests that require inhibition (e.g., the Wisconsin Card Sort Test; Heaton, Chelune, Talley, Kay, & Curtis, 1993) and a nonverbal fluency measure (5-points test; Lee, Strauss, Loring, & McLoskey, 1997), reflecting the importance of cognitive flexibility to the execution of a complex set of intentions.

---

[5] An example is the daily requirement of planning and executing a set of multiple intentions when starting a busy workday during which one has to call a colleague before he or she leaves for a vacation, mark a research paper before the student author arrives, ask the student to read a specific book chapter but not before explaining a specific flaw in the student's paper, and so on. Similar multiple intention problems are likely to occur in many work settings (e.g., health care, aviation) but also in everyday nonprofessional environments where multiple intentions have to be scheduled and their execution has to be delayed.

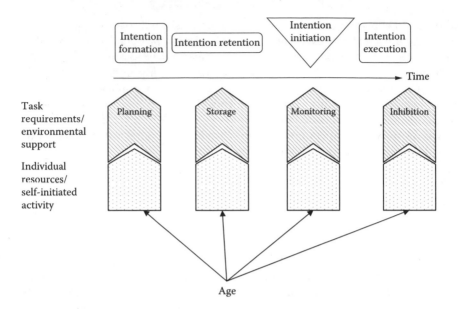

FIGURE 9.2 A requirement-resource-interaction model of prospective memory development.

We anticipate that the strongest age effects will be evident in those phases of the model most reliant on executive resources. This assumption rests on results supporting a strong relationship between prospective remembering and executive functions, as it has been shown in studies examining frontal lobe patients (e.g., Burgess, 2000; Burgess et al., 2000; Cockburn, 1995; Fortin, Godbout, & Braun, 2003; Groot et al., 2002), neuroimaging studies (Burgess, Quayle, & Frith, 2001; Okuda et al., 1998), and other mainly correlation-based findings in healthy adults (e.g., McDaniel, Glisky, Rubin, Guynn, & Routhieaux, 1999). Indeed, an executive functioning hypothesis of prospective memory development has been proposed in which the deterioration of prospective memory with increasing age, as well as improvements in the prospective memory performance of children, might be associated with the age-related decay and growth of the efficiency of executive functioning (see Dempster, 1992; Glisky, 1996; Hasher, Stoltzfus, Zacks & Rypma, 1991; Kliegel & Jäger, 2006; Kliegel et al., 2006; West, 1996). Specifically, it is predicted that the higher the degree to which executive functioning is involved in a particular prospective memory task, the higher the probability that age differences will emerge. Note that this hypothesis has initially been offered for prospective memory in general. In light of the multiprocess framework, however, the role of executive functions is likely to be much stronger in tasks that require monitoring processes than in tasks that rely on spontaneous retrieval. As this hypothesis awaits empirical testing, the complex prospective memory paradigm is more likely to be conceived of as a task relying on strategic executive resources in terms of the multiprocess framework.

Age-related predictions regarding the intention-retention component of the model are somewhat less clear. The specific retrospective memory processes that underlie intention retention are not well defined. It is likely that different prospective memory tasks place different demands on retrospective memory. Some prospective memory tasks, for example, in which the required response is a simple key press, are likely to place lower demands on retrospective storage capacity than tasks that require the retention of complex plans over a longer delay period. Because there is evidence that long-term retrospective storage capacity may alter to a similar degree as executive functioning (e.g., Park et al., 2002) one might expect intention retention in adulthood and old age to be affected by the aging process. In contrast, several previous studies have shown that age-related prospective memory performance is not mainly due to age-related decline in retrospective storage of the intended actions (e.g.,Kliegel & Jäger, 2006; Kliegel, Ramuschkat, & Martin, 2003). In children, there is well-documented evidence that retrospective memory storage capacity develops significantly throughout childhood (for a review see Schneider, 2002), providing the possibility for a somewhat more straightforward expectation of the importance of intention-retention abilities for prospective memory performance at the beginning of the life span. Particularly, performance on tests of long-term retention show consistent improvements from preschool to adolescence (Howe & Brainerd, 1989). In sum, age-related predictions for intention retention in older adulthood are not fixed, and it is possible that intention retention plays a more significant role in complex prospective memory in childhood.

Intention Formation   Using the paper-and-pencil version of the modified SET, Kliegel and colleagues (2000) showed that the plans formed by 31 older adults (M = 71.3 years) were less elaborate and complex than those of 31 younger adults (M = 26.5 years). Older adults tended to make simple plans involving the intention to first perform version A of all tasks followed by version B of all tasks, thus avoiding breaking the task order rule. Younger adults typically made more elaborate plans that involved planning task performance according to their own preferences and generating cues that signaled when to switch to another task. This result was replicated in two other studies employing the paper-and-pencil version of the modified SET: Kliegel, Martin, and Moor (2003) found a similar lack of elaborate planning in 48 older adults (M = 69.7 years) compared to 51 younger adults (M = 25 years), as did Kliegel and colleagues (2004) working with 21 older (M = 70.81 years) and 19 younger adults (M = 24.26 years).

Intention Retention   In contrast to robust age-related differences in planning, no significant age-group differences in plan retention were reported in two of these studies (Kliegel et al., 2004; Kliegel et al., 2000). Older adults were able to retain the details of their plan as well as younger adults, and the overall level of plan retention was consistently high. However, Kliegel, Martin, and Moor (2003) observed a small but significant age-related difference, with older adults retaining their plans less well than younger adults, rendering age differences in plan retention less clear.

Intention Initiation   In all three studies younger adults were significantly better at self-initiating performance of the modified SET on presentation of the appropriate cue (Kliegel et al., 2004; Kliegel, Martin, & Moor, 2003; Kliegel et al., 2000).

Intention Execution   A similarly robust age effect was observed for the execution of the complex intention (remembering to attempt each of the six tasks); SET performance was significantly better in younger than older adults (Kliegel et al., 2004; Kliegel, Martin, & Moor, 2003; Kliegel et al., 2000; see also Rendell & Craik, 2000). Younger adults switched between tasks more fluently and frequently and thus attempted more tasks than older adults. It is difficult to attribute this effect to a lack of salience of the requirement to attempt all tasks; robust age group differences remained even when the need to switch between tasks was highlighted by awarding bonus points for each task switch (Kliegel, Martin, & Moor, 2003). A second point of interest is that, in general, the plans initially formulated by participants did not overlap substantially with the manner in which the complex intentions were subsequently executed (plan fidelity). There is some suggestion that the fidelity with which a plan is executed may be higher in younger adults relative to older adults, although this finding awaits replication (Kliegel et al., 2004).

To sum up the main findings, healthy older adults have been shown to demonstrate deficits in the formation, planning, and self-initiation of a complex intention. Furthermore, strong age effects have repeatedly been found in the phase during which the complex intention has to be executed. Age effects regarding plan retention have been somewhat mixed, indicating no or only a slight advantage for younger adults.

In addition to these initial studies of younger and older adults, we have recently started to extend the use of the modified SET to the study of prospective memory earlier in the course of development, investigating typically (Martin & Kliegel, 2003) and atypically developing children (Kliegel et al., 2006). For this purpose, we developed a computer version of the SET called the HEXE that keeps all important features and phases of the original version but transfers the setting to a computer game (see Figure 9.3 for a screenshot of the computer program).

Like our paper-and-pencil modification of the SET, the HEXE involves six tasks, subdivided into three types of tasks: words, arithmetic, and pictures. In all tasks stimuli are represented on the computer screen in stacks of cards and participants can select which stack to work on by pressing a key. Once selected, the items in a stack continue to appear until the participant selects a different task. In all HEXE tasks participants make yes–no judgments in response to stimuli. In the word tasks participants judge whether a word presented on the screen is real or not. In the picture tasks participants judge whether the line drawing presented on the screen is an item from their local area (i.e., middle Europe) or not (e.g., a pyramid or a cuckoo clock). In the arithmetic tasks participants judge whether the solution presented for a problem (e.g., $2 + 2 = 5$) is correct or not. The difficulty level of HEXE task items is adjusted according to the age of the participants.

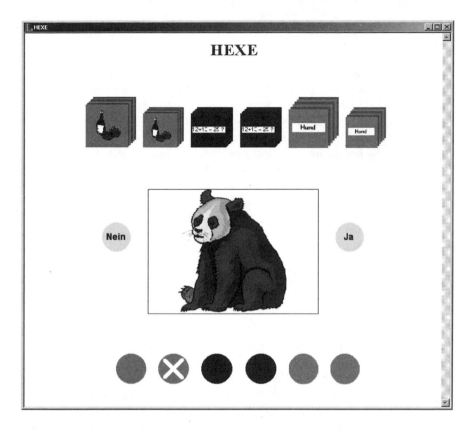

FIGURE 9.3 Schematic overview of the Heidelberger Exekutivdiagnostikum (HEXE – Six-Task Version).

The HEXE is administered in the same stages as the modified SET. Following an instruction and practice phase in which the different "games" (tasks) are introduced, participants are asked to generate a plan of what they intend to do (intention formation). They are subsequently asked to recall their plan after a delay phase (intention retention). Finally, after another delay, they have to self-initiate (intention initiation) and execute (intention execution) the HEXE task procedure on their own in response to an initiation cue and corresponding to their plan, working in a time limit of 2 (or 6) minutes. Participants who fail to self-initiate the HEXE task are reminded to do so by the experimenter.

Martin and Kliegel (2003) administered the HEXE to 115 typically developing children from five distinct age groups (*M* ages = 6.5, 7.0, 8.0, 9.0, and 10.0 years, respectively). This version of the HEXE included only four tasks rather than six (two picture tasks and two arithmetic tasks), and the tasks were adapted for difficulty into three levels (preschool, first and second grade, and third and fourth grade) to allow for developmental differences in arithmetic and verbal ability and to control for ongoing task difficulty.

Intention Formation   In contrast to the adult studies involving the modified SET, only half the children (47%) formed a plan of how to perform the HEXE task when asked to do so, whereas initial findings show that only a very low percentage of adults failed to form an explicit plan (e.g., Kliegel et al., 2004). In terms of complexity, the plans provided by children resembled those of older adults with very few plans including personal reasons for the chosen order or containing any specifications for intended task switching at a certain point. Although there was no overall age effect in plan formation, the two youngest age groups were less likely to provide an explicit plan when directly compared to the oldest age group studied. Regarding the low number of children who stated an explicit plan, it could be argued that the 53% of children who did not provide an explicit plan had planned but simply did not explicate their plan; however, results showed that children who had provided an explicit plan performed significantly better in the intention execution phase than children who had not, which goes against this interpretation.

Intention Retention   Similar to adults, older children who had provided a plan were able to remember the plan they had made. This initial finding seems to suggest that retrospective memory for intentions may not show significant developments in either childhood or adulthood, which would be in contrast to well-documented age differences in performance on more traditional retrospective memory tasks (Gathercole, 1998; Schneider, 2002). Perhaps memory for self-generated intentions, as required in the modified SET, is less problematic for young and older age groups; this hypothesis awaits direct empirical testing.

The preschoolers in our study, however, did show substantial retrospective forgetting of intended plans. This result is congruent with other studies of prospective memory in children which suggest that the retrospective component of prospective memory may be more critical in children than in adults (Guajardo & Best, 2000; Martin & Kliegel, 2003; Zöllig, Schwank, Lemke, & Kliegel, 2005). Unfortunately, the high number of nonplanners in our study prevents a sufficiently powerful test of either hypothesis and further work clearly needs to be done.

Intention Initiation   Self-initiation of the modified SET was only poorer in preschoolers when compared to the oldest age group. However, the data for intention execution showed that children attempted more tasks with increasing age and thus showed a more pronounced improvement in complex prospective memory execution across childhood.

In a recent study, 20 typically developing boys (aged 8–9 years) and 20 boys with a diagnosis of Attention Deficit Hyperactivity Disorder (ADHD; aged 8–9 years) performed the HEXE task (Kliegel et al., 2006). Because ADHD is a developmental disorder with a strong profile of executive dysfunction, we anticipated group differences in intention formation, initiation, and execution. A four-task version of the HEXE was used (two picture tasks and two arithmetic tasks) and task administration was identical to that described in the earlier study (Martin & Kliegel, 2003).

Intention Formation   Similar to the results of the previous study, not all children generated an explicit plan of how to perform the HEXE task. It is interesting to note that only 40% of typically developing control children provided a plan (47% in the previous study), whereas 100% of children with ADHD did so. However, participants with ADHD produced less elaborate and complex plans than their typically developing counterparts, a result that mirrors differences in planning observed between younger and older adults (Kliegel et al., 2004; Kliegel et al., 2000).

Intention Retention   The group difference observed in plan formation may have impacted plan retention, as participants with ADHD who had formed poor plans remembered them less well than participants who had formed better plans. In line with results of the previous study, control children remembered their plans well.

Intention Initiation   Although there was a tendency for typically developing children to self-initiate performance on the HEXE more than children with ADHD, we had predicted a stronger group difference on this measure than we observed. It is possible that the cue we used to indicate self-initiation was too distinctive (placing a red triangle on the table in front of the child) and therefore facilitated performance.

Intention Execution   Children in both groups attempted a similar number of tasks, but children with ADHD did so at the cost of performance accuracy, giving more incorrect answers to mathematics and picture naming questions than controls. It is likely that some sort of speed–accuracy trade-off was present in the performance of this group.

In sum, the performance of typically developing children of different ages and children with developmental disorders on the HEXE complex prospective memory task highlights a performance pattern that is fairly consistent with that of older adults. At the intention formation phase, children are less likely to form an explicit plan than adults, indicating that intention formation may be more challenging for children, much as it appears to be for older adults. It remains to be seen whether developmental differences in plan formation are also apparent between different age groups of typically developing children. Like adults of all ages, the majority of typically developing children retained their intentions well, although again it is difficult to draw firm conclusions because so many children failed to provide an initial plan to test for retention. In contrast, intention retention may be problematic for preschool children and does appear to be impaired in atypical development. In primary school-aged children, intention initiation develops gradually in typical development and seems to be only somewhat affected in atypical development. This pattern may not be as pronounced as intention initiation deficits observed in older adults. However, developmental differences in the intention execution of both typically and atypically developing children are highly consistent with performance difficulties observed in older adults.

Just as in the aging literature, an executive function account can be used to explain this pattern of results. With regard to intention formation, planning skills are known to develop significantly throughout childhood and adolescence (e.g., Anderson, Anderson, & Lajoie, 1996; Levin et al., 1991). Other executive functions such as cognitive flexibility and inhibitory control also develop progressively during childhood (Anderson, 2002; Christ, White, Mandernach, & Keys, 2001; Welsh, Pennington, & Groisser, 1991) and this could underlie the (rather slight) differences in intention initiation and the marked differences in execution in both typical and atypical development. In conclusion, in accordance with evidence from the adult literature supporting a relationship between executive functioning and prospective memory development, this seems to also be true for children (see also Glisky, 1996; Guajardo & Best, 2000; Kliegel, Ramuschkat, & Martin, 2003; West, 1996).[6] With regard to the multidimensionality of prospective memory development, our cross-sectional extreme group comparison data suggest that the influence of executive functioning on age-related prospective memory performance might be especially present for the phases of prospective remembering that require high degrees of executive control (i.e., intention formation, intention initiation, and intention execution), but in contrast have little or lesser impact on the intention retention phase.

MULTIDIRECTIONALITY: DEVELOPMENTAL TRAJECTORIES OF INTENTION FORMATION, INTENTION RETENTION, INTENTION INITIATION, AND INTENTION EXECUTION

To date, four reports on prospective memory development across a wider adult age range have been published (Huppert, Johnson, & Nickson, 2000: 65–90 + years; Kliegel & Jäger, 2006: 22–31/60–91 years; Mäntylä & Nilsson, 1997: 35–80 years; Uttl, Graf, Miller, & Tuokko, 2001: 65–95 years). Although these studies differ with respect to the age trajectories reported (e.g., Huppert and colleagues [2000] reported a linear decline in prospective memory performance in a subtest of the Rivermead Behavioral Memory Test, whereas Kliegel and Jäger [in press]reported an accelerated decline within older adults using the delayed-execute paradigm of Einstein, McDaniel, Manzi, Cochran, and Baker [2000]), they are also limited in two other ways. First, all studies use (different) prospective memory tasks that only focus on prospective initiation. Second, none of the studies included children in their analyses. Thus, no report has been published that describes age trajectories that truly capture the life span. Later, we extend the extreme group comparisons

---

[6] We note that this relationship might be particularly present in complex prospective memory paradigms given their high degree of executive control demands. Indeed, although age-related deficits in younger children have been observed in our complex prospective memory task, this does not hold for all studies using rather simple prospective memory tasks that do not involve such a high degree of executive control (e.g., Meacham & Colombo, 1980; Somerville, Wellman, & Cultice, 1983; Wang, Kliegel, Liu, & Yang, in press).

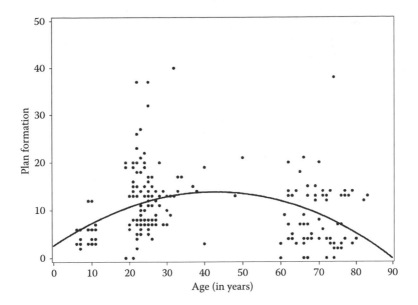

FIGURE 9.4   Life span trajectory in intention formation.

we featured in the previous section and report analyses that search for growth, loss, and stability in the life span development of prospective memory.

To apply the multidirectionality principle to prospective memory development we have pooled some of the data from the studies already described with some unpublished data sets that use the paper-and-pencil modified SET or the computerized HEXE version of our complex prospective memory task; all data we include used the six-task version.[7] By doing so we have compiled a data sample comprising indicators of all four prospective memory phases in 555 participants, ranging in age from 6 to 84 years ($M = 39.4$, $Mdn = 27$, $SD = 25.1$; 58% female), in particular adding to the children's database. Because few of the data sets combined for the present analyses included middle adulthood, the age distribution is bimodal with two peaks at 20.3 years and 69.0 years, respectively. Consequently, we report overall age trajectories as well as trajectories for predefined lower and upper sections of the human life span separately to address the following research question: Can we find evidence for a typical developmental inverted U-shaped function and where do we find growth, where stability, and where decline?

Figure 9.4 depicts the pooled data for the first phase of prospective memory, intention formation (note that most data points represent more than one observation).

---

[7] It is important to note that we only used the six-task versions and only included participants who were able to recall all task rules. Moreover, procedural delays were largely comparable across all studies, and by adjusting for subtask item and distracter task difficulty, overall task difficulty can also be assumed to be comparable across age groups and across studies. Finally, we examined the impact of study type (computer vs. paper-and-pencil) on the results, but the results did not change systematically with the type of administration.

First, using the whole sample, we analyzed age trajectories by testing several potential regression equations to fit the observed data set. A linear function did not describe the data adequately ($F < 1$), but a quadratic function received the best fit ($R^2 = .13$). As illustrated in Figure 9.4, this function describes an increase in performance from childhood to young adulthood and a decline within older adulthood, with age explaining 13% of the variance. As noted, due to the small number of participants in the middle adulthood age range, we additionally computed those analyses separately for the younger and the older sections of the sample. These analyses revealed that from childhood into young adulthood (age < 30) there is an accelerated growth that levels off at about 20 years of age (quadratic regression, $R^2 = .23$). Looking at age trends across the adult age range (age 20+), a linear but only slight decline was observed ($R^2 = .07$). Focusing only on the group of older adults (age 60+) revealed stability in performance as no age-related regression function reached the significance criterion. This pattern of results suggests that at the intention formation phase of prospective remembering, growth mostly happens in childhood and levels off by around 20 years of age, which is congruent with evidence supporting the development of planning skills in childhood (e.g., Friedman & Scholnick, 1997).[8] Across adulthood there appears to be a slight decline, a pattern that fits data from experimental studies in which extreme groups of younger and older adults are compared (see Phillips, MacLeod, & Kliegel, 2005, for an overview). What should be particularly noted is a period of relative stability of intention formation within older adulthood, something that is often missed in extreme group comparison studies but demonstrates the importance of looking at performance levels across the life span.

The data regarding intention retention are depicted in Figure 9.5. In contrast to the majority of the experimental analyses reported earlier in which no age effects were reported, when all the data are pooled, a small but significant age effect emerges. This is represented by a quadratic inverted U-shaped function that explains 4% of the variance.

An examination of this effect in separate analyses for different age groups revealed that this overall age trend was mostly due to an accelerated increase in performance across childhood, again leveling off at about 20 years ($R^2 = .09$) and a marginally significant linear decline within the older adults ($R^2 = .03$). Across the entire adult age range, however, no significant age effect emerged. How do

---

[8] One criticism that could be leveled at these comments is that our instructions force planning. It is, of course, true that we explicitly ask participants to form a plan because we need to generate a reliable score for the intention formation phase. As an alternative, we could have asked participants about their plans retrospectively, but this method comes with its own criticisms attached. In defense of our method, we believe that prospective memory always involves some degree of planning in terms of anticipating what is to be done. However the need to explicitly activate this planning resource varies, depending on the complexity of the task and the situation. In a less complex prospective memory task we might not expect to find the same U-shaped pattern of development of intention formation. We imagine that adult participants at least would have planned anyway, even if we had not asked them to. Future studies could be designed with prevented and enhanced planning groups to examine the effects of planning on performance.

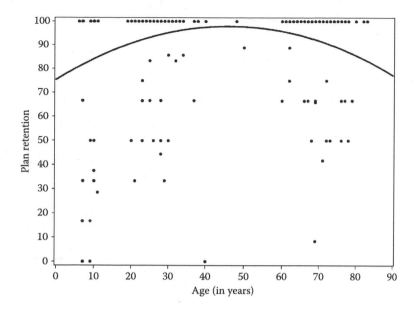

FIGURE 9.5 Life span trajectory in intention retention.

we explain these age-related effects where previously we found none? It is likely that the power afforded by our pooled data set enables detection of a small but nonetheless significant influence of age on intention retention. In smaller sample experimental studies, these effects were almost always in the right direction, but there was a lack of power to detect them. In previous sections, we highlighted the ambiguity surrounding age-related predictions in intention retention. The analyses reported here lend support to the hypothesis that the retrospective component of prospective memory is not age invariant and may therefore rely on long-term retrospective memory processes. Of particular interest is the fact that the growth slope is steepest in children, the effect being three times larger than that in older adults. This heightened importance of intention retention early in the life span fits well with data from other studies (e.g., Guajardo & Best, 2000) and with experimental observations from our lab (Zöllig et al., 2005).

Analyzing intention initiation, logistic regression analyses were utilized to explore the age trends. Overall, a quadratic age function had the best model fit ($R^2 = .23$). Follow-up analyses showed that there was a strong accelerated growth from early childhood into young adulthood that leveled off only at age 25 ($R^2 = .29$) and an accelerated decline across adulthood ($R^2 = .22$) that turned into a linear decline within old age ($R^2 = .09$). Finally, regarding intention execution, Figure 9.6 demonstrates that the overall developmental trend obtained was again a quadratic function ($R^2 = .21$), which could be decomposed into an accelerated increase across childhood into young adulthood, leveling off at about 20 years ($R^2 = .12$), and an accelerated decline across adulthood ($R^2 = .25$) that remained accelerated even within old age ($R^2 = .11$).

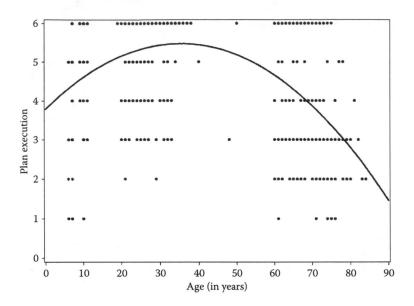

FIGURE 9.6   Life span trajectory in intention execution.

Intention initiation and intention execution phases show broadly similar patterns of development and fit most closely to an inverted U-shaped developmental function. Intention initiation, the most typically prospective element of our model of prospective memory, appears to develop well into young adulthood. A possible mechanism underlying this is the protracted development of the frontal lobes, in particular frontopolar Brodmann area 10 (see Burgess et al., chap. 11, this volume; West, chap. 12, this volume, for an elaboration of this theory). Both intention initiation and intention execution evidence an accelerated decline in older adulthood, a pattern that contrasts with the stability of intention retention. Here, development still happens within older adulthood, a fact we might miss by comparing only extreme age groups (see Kliegel & Jäger, 2006).

In sum, these analyses support an inverted U-shaped age-related function in all four prospective memory dimensions across the entire life span. Although, due to the age distribution of our pooled sample, we cannot conclude precise estimates of the actual performance peaks, our data demonstrate for the first time that prospective memory development appears to follow the typical pattern of growth in childhood, relative stability in young to middle adulthood, and gradual or accelerated decline in older adulthood. Additionally, and perhaps more importantly, the analyses revealed that depending on the prospective memory dimension studied, the overall age effect is (a) of differential size, and (b) more or less accelerated. Moreover, the slope of this function was found to be differentially pronounced when examining the different phases of prospective memory.

Having identified age trends in prospective memory, the next step is to explore potential mechanisms that may explain them. Can we find evidence for the mechanisms underlying age-related changes in prospective memory? More important, can we use this knowledge to show potential for improvement, for plasticity in prospective remembering, even in older adults? In the following section, we discuss two studies conducted in our lab that have addressed precisely these questions. They represent an important first step toward a deeper understanding of the mechanisms underlying prospective memory development and give an early indication of methods by which prospective memory may be rehabilitated.

PLASTICITY: HOW TO IMPROVE COMPLEX PROSPECTIVE MEMORY PERFORMANCE

Planning

One potential mechanism underlying age-related changes in prospective memory is planning. In a recent study we sought to provide direct support for the model-based prediction (see Figure 9.2) that appropriate planning improves the delayed realization of complex intentions (Kliegel, Martin, McDaniel, Einstein, & Moor, in press). To investigate this hypothesis, we applied the paper-and-pencil version of the modified SET to samples of 90 younger ($M = 25$ years) and 90 older ($M = 68$ years) adults, who were comparable in health and educational status. Conceptually, this study was linked to previous studies that have provided indirect evidence (via correlations) that planning may exert an influence on delayed intention realization (e.g., Kliegel et al., 2004; Kliegel et al., 2005). However, these studies did not substantiate this relationship experimentally, nor did they answer the question of whether poor planning plays a causal role in performance impairments. Therefore, to directly examine the impact of planning on complex prospective memory performance, we experimentally manipulated the degree to which participants engaged in detailed and elaborate planning during the intention formation phase.

For this purpose, we introduced two conditions. In the planning aid condition, participants were instructed to consider planning aids that might help them to successfully realize the delayed complex intention (to self-initiate and successfully perform the SET). One planning aid targeted the intention initiation component: Participants were asked to elaborate on initiation-related elements of their plan and to explicitly mention the specific cue that determined when they had to start working on the SET. Another planning aid targeted the intention execution component and was aimed at increasing the specificity of the intention to switch between multiple subtasks. When planning, participants were told to consider switching among SET subtasks after working on no more than two items of each subtask. According to model-based predictions, we anticipated that the two planning aids should improve performance in the intention formation phase and thereby also in the intention initiation and the intention execution phases. By contrast, participants assigned to a no planning aid condition were asked to develop a plan on their own without any guidance and thus we predicted no performance enhancements in this group.

The second goal of this study relates to the plasticity question of potential improvements. By investigating groups of younger and older adults, we were able to ask whether effective planning could reduce or even eliminate age differences in prospective memory performance. Our reason for expecting that this might be possible stems from the findings discussed earlier, which indicate that performance deficits observed in older adults during the intention initiation and the intention execution phases may result from the older adults developing less elaborate plans than younger adults in the intention formation phase. To summarize, first we predicted that our planning manipulations would improve performance at the intention initiation and intention execution phases in general. Second, we predicted that older adults in our planning aid condition would perform as well as, or almost as well as, younger adults. The main results of the study were as follows.

Intention Formation   A marginally significant main effect of age group and a significant main effect of planning aid were revealed, indicating that older adults developed less elaborate plans than younger adults and that providing planning aids generally improved the elaborateness of the plans. More important, a significant age group by planning aid interaction revealed that the planning aid increased the elaborateness of the plans only for the older adults to a level comparable to the younger adults.

Intention Retention   No main effects or interactions were observed. No age group differences in the accuracy of plan retention emerged, and the provision of planning aids did not influence plan retention.

Intention Initiation   Significant main effects of both age group and planning aid, but no interaction effect, were found. This indicates that younger adults initiated the SET tasks by themselves more frequently than older adults and that providing a planning aid targeting initiation improved the self-initiation of SET tasks in both groups of participants.

Intention Execution   A significant main effect of age group emerged, showing that the younger adults made more switches between the SET tasks than the older adults. Although there was no main effect of planning aid, there was a significant age group by planning aid interaction indicating that only the older adults' self-initiated switching benefited from the planning aids. However, as a note of caution, the performance of young adults in the no planning aid condition was almost at ceiling, thus allowing little chance to detect an improvement in young adults. It is interesting to note, however, that the performance of older adults in the planning aid condition was still substantially lower than that of younger adults, indicating that the planning aid did not enable older adults to perform at a similar level to (aided or unaided) younger adults.

To summarize, it is clear that providing planning aids enabled participants to produce better plans and participants were able to make use of the aids provided. This study provides evidence that enhancing intention planning directly affects performance on a complex prospective memory task: A main effect of planning aid was observed at the intention initiation phase for both age groups and using a planning aid facilitated intention execution in older adults. Second, with regard to plasticity (or, more specifically, the possibility of behavioral improvement), the performance of both younger and older participants was enhanced by the planning aids, indicating a degree of plasticity in both groups. As predicted, older adults benefited most from the planning aids, but this was still not enough to raise their performance to the level of young adults. Does this imply that age-related improvement is limited with respect to prospective memory? It is highly likely that plasticity in prospective memory, as in other areas of cognitive functioning, has limits. What is interesting to note is that in our prospective memory study, older adults not only improved their performance after our training manipulation, they also appeared to narrow the gap between their performance and that of younger adults. This finding contrasts with studies investigating retrospective memory, in which training techniques also benefit all participants but the gap between young and older adults does not narrow and even increases (e.g., Kliegl et al., 1989; although note that this study differs from ours because participants were trained on a general processing strategy, the Method of Loci, whereas our intervention was specifically linked to the paradigm and the material supplied). If supported, however, this difference in plasticity would have implications for prospective memory rehabilitation techniques, although at present we interpret it cautiously because of ceiling effects in the younger adults. Replication of this finding avoiding ceiling effects and an examination of possible transfer effects of planning aids to other stimuli sets is desirable.

Inhibition

A second potential mechanism proposed in the component model (see Figure 9.2) is the influence of inhibition on the execution phase of complex prospective memory. The hypothesis is that to successfully remember to switch between multiple intentions, one has to inhibit attention to the current, ongoing activity to switch to one of the remaining (intended) tasks. The executive resource assumed to be involved in this process is inhibition of the prepotent response to continue with the ongoing task. Importantly, for the life span perspective of this chapter, inhibitory resources are a key construct involved in cognitive development in children (Welsh et al., 1991) as well as in older adults (Hasher & Zacks, 1988). Thus, in a recently conducted study (Kliegel, Mackinlay, & Jäger, in press), we directly targeted the role of inhibiting ongoing task performance in a life span sample.

In a cross-sectional design we investigated four different age groups across the life span: 51 first-grade children (M age = 7), 52 fourth-grade children (M age = 10), 79 younger adults (M age = 26), and 79 older adults (M age = 67). All participants were healthy, the children had normal IQs, and the two adult age groups did not evidence any differences in education or verbal ability. Participants performed the computerized HEXE, six-task version.

Based on the suggestion that inhibitory control should be involved in the intention execution phase, we predicted that the degree to which age differences emerge in the ability to execute a complex intention depends on the extent to which those inhibitory resources are required. An experimental manipulation was introduced to test this hypothesis. In the interruption condition, participants performed the six open-ended HEXE tasks in which the next item of any chosen task appeared on the computer screen immediately after a response to the previous item was made. Hence, to be able to successfully execute the intention to attempt each of the six HEXE tasks, the participants had to actively inhibit responding to the next appearing item of a given task to change to another task. By contrast, in the no interruption condition, the next item of a given task did not appear on the computer screen unless it was requested by a button press. Thus, the next item of any task appeared only after the participants opted to continue, which reduced the inhibitory requirements necessary to change among the six tasks. Participants of each age group were randomly assigned to the two conditions. The results are reported next. For the first three phases of the model (intention formation, retention, and initiation) the experimental procedure was identical in both experimental condition groups, thus when discussing these results we group participants by age, but not by age and condition.

Intention Formation   Not all children generated an explicit plan of how to perform the HEXE, in contrast to adults, who invariably generated plans of action. Significant developmental differences in plan generation were observed. Seven-year-old children were less likely to formulate a plan of how to perform the HEXE than either 10-year-olds or adults. Similarly, 10-year-olds were less likely to generate an explicit plan of performance than either young or old adults. No differences in the likelihood of forming a plan were observed between younger and older adults; however, in line with previous findings, significant differences in the complexity of plans made were observed, with older adults producing less complex plans than younger adults.

Intention Retention   The majority of participants who had formed a plan were able to correctly recall it during the intention retention phase and no significant age group differences were observed.

Intention Initiation   The proportions of participants who initiated the HEXE task by themselves at the appropriate cue were 10%, 38%, 71%, and 38% among the 7-year-olds, 10-year-olds, younger adults, and older adults, respectively.[9] Significant age group differences were observed: 7-year-olds were different from all other groups, and the proportion of 10-year-olds' and older adults' self-initiating performance was significantly different from younger adults.

Intention Execution   Most central to this study was the intention execution phase, as in this phase we manipulated the amount of inhibitory control that was required to execute the complex intention. An Age × Condition analysis of variance

---

[9] In this study we changed the initiation cue into a less salient event, which is probably responsible for the lower levels of performance, particularly in older adults, when compared to the HEXE studies reported earlier.

(ANOVA) yielded significant main effects of age group and experimental condition and a significant interaction, indicating that the size of the age differences was modulated by inhibitory requirements. Separate ANOVAs for each condition (interruption vs. no interruption) revealed a significant main effect of age group in the no interruption condition ($\eta^2 = .18$), but in the interruption condition this effect was substantially stronger ($\eta^2 = .35$), confirming that the age differences were more exaggerated when the demands for inhibitory control were greater (see Figure 9.7). In the no interruption condition, post hoc tests showed that 7-year-old children were significantly impaired compared to all other age groups and no other age group differences were significant. By contrast, in the interruption condition there were additional significant differences between the 10-year-olds and the younger adults and between the younger adults and the older adults.

To sum up the main findings, the results are consistent with the expectation that the extent to which a prospective memory task requires executive (i.e., inhibitory) control in the intention execution phase influences the degree to which younger children and older adults are impaired relative to older children or younger adults in their ability to execute a complex intention. Age differences were strongest under conditions in which greater inhibitory control was necessary to successfully perform the complex intention. This is in line with the specific prediction of the model and a demonstration of plasticity that is a result of a task-related modification.

In conclusion, although research on underlying processes, developmental mechanisms, and plasticity in prospective memory across the life span is still in its infancy, the studies presented here have identified two mechanisms that at least partially account for developmental trajectories in the ability to execute complex intentions. The strength of these studies lies in their exploration of model-based hypotheses and (in the case of the second study) the use of life span developmental samples. A further examination of the model presented in Figure 9.2 shows that

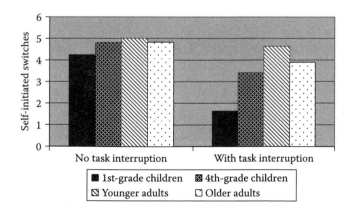

FIGURE 9.7   Effects of age and task interruption on intention execution across the life span.

other hypotheses can be generated and tested within the context of the complex prospective memory paradigm; for example, a manipulation of the retrospective memory requirements of the task might be expected to induce age effects in intention retention. Manipulations that affect age-related performance in the initiation component through the degree of required monitoring (vs. spontaneous retrieval) have been discussed somewhat more extensively in the context of the multiprocess framework (see McDaniel et al., chap. 7, this volume).

SUMMARY OF MAJOR ISSUES AND FUTURE DIRECTIONS

Although this chapter aims at highlighting important aspects of a life span developmental view on prospective memory, it can only serve as an initial impulse that leaves open many more questions than it answers. The major issues for future research in the context of life span development in prospective memory can be organized along the four key principles discussed.

We have shown that pooling cross-sectional data adds to our current understanding of the life span development of prospective memory. However, for a true life span developmental perspective, the collection of longitudinal data needs to be addressed. So far, every single developmental study on prospective memory in children and adults (our own included) has relied on cross-sectional age differences to estimate developmental changes. As several studies in the field of intelligence and retrospective memory development have indicated (e.g., Hofer & Sliwinski, 2006; Schaie, 2005), only longitudinal data will allow us to adequately test core hypotheses such as the causal role of maturing executive resources for the development of prospective memory. In addition, adult aging studies that rest on cross-sectional age differences are particularly prone to the influence of cohort effects: Longitudinal studies will show if controlling for cohort differences in early education, lifelong intellectual activities, professional involvement in more complex occupations, or lifestyle will change the pattern of results obtained so far.

We have argued that our process model of prospective memory provides a good starting point for investigating the multidimensionality of prospective remembering; that is, investigating four phases rather than focusing exclusively on intention initiation. Most current process models of prospective memory identify four or five dimensions that are quite similar to those applied in this chapter (see, e.g., Ellis, 1996; Kvavilashvili & Ellis, 1996). However, it is likely that in time this level of analysis will prove to not be sufficiently fine-grained. In the future it will be important to further decompose these processes of prospective remembering to detect with increasing precision those process components that are most crucial for developmental changes. For example, one phase that has been largely neglected in most research paradigms, but that may be especially important in childhood, is the intention retention phase. Because there are indications that the retrospective storage component of the intention may be a more relevant aspect in the first part of the human life span, it will be necessary to more clearly delineate the nature of this phase. Is it only a relatively passive storage phase or are periodically occurring or initiated recollections of the intention supporting the maintenance of the intention? Are there age differences in the frequency or controllability of the occurrence of such intention refreshments? Are self-generated intentions remembered more easily than other-generated intentions? These and other questions will help us to further understand which task requirements and which individual resources are involved at a given stage in the process and where to target more precise investigations of developmental changes in those process components.

In addition, the model presents stages at which age may affect prospective memory phases through the interplay of task demands and individual resources. Most models of cognitive functioning rest on the assumption that we have task characteristics and cognitive resources, and that if these fit, a satisfactory level of performance will be achieved. However, in real life the interaction between these elements is likely to be more dynamic. It is likely that task demands can be (more or less optimally) changed by the individual, and that individual resources that a person may have developed, maintained, or partially lost can still be more or less efficiently mobilized and applied. For example, research on (retrospective) metamemory strategies in children has shown that strategy knowledge does not necessarily predict strategy application (e.g., Schneider & Lockl, 2002). A similar explanation could be applied to the finding that older adults are sometimes more successful at performing naturalistic prospective memory tasks than younger adults (Rendell & Craik, 2000); perhaps older adults compensate better and redefine naturalistic tasks to suit their own strengths. Thus, to comprehend life span prospective memory development we will have to further understand how the individual learns to actively engage (maturing) resources to a (given but potentially modifiable) task and how this multiple interaction of task, resources, and active resource employment develops across the life span. Importantly, future research will have to show if those mechanisms are similar or distinct across the life span.

With regard to the *multidirectionality* of prospective memory, the analyses presented here suggest differences in the pattern of developmental trends across the life span identified for the different phases of our model (evidenced by differential slopes, fits of both linear and quadratic functions to patterns of growth, stability, and decline). This indicates that development truly occurs across the whole life span and that to only measure prospective memory by the end result misses much of this rich detail. One proposal that we would like to make for the future is to opt for more research into stability across the life span. Although most research targets growth and decline, studying stability, especially in old age, will help to identify areas of age invariance for which interventions may not be necessary but which may be used as strengths to build on when targeting areas of decline. Moreover, studying stability will also be relevant for detecting mechanisms of compensation, as stability is likely to partly occur due to effective counterbalancing of declines. In addition, there may also be areas of age benefit, even in old age, as the line of research on laboratory versus naturalistic prospective memory performance has shown (Rendell & Craik, 2000). To understand how stability can be maintained or how growth can be perpetuated into old age will serve as a basis for effective interventions in this part of the human life span.

In terms of plasticity, we have described two studies that demonstrate how prospective memory performance can be impaired (by high inhibitory requirements) or improved (by use of planning aids), even in old age. These are only two of the variables suggested in our model; their influence needs to be further established and the influence of other variables (e.g., monitoring) should be systematically evaluated in the context of the present paradigm (see also Guynn, chap. 3, this volume; Smith, chap. 2, this volume; Smith & Bayen, 2004). We also raised the possibility that the plasticity of prospective memory in older adulthood is likely to be limited. Given that there have been very few systematic training studies in prospective memory (e.g., Schmidt, Berg, & Deelman, 2001; Villa & Abeles, 2000), it remains an open question as to what extent prospective memory can be improved and whether these interventions have a lasting effect. It will be particularly important to determine if one needs to train specific components (e.g., the planning aid training presented here), cognitive resources, or strategies, and if there are age differences in the ways prospective memory is optimally trained across the life span. One final question of interest is whether plasticity comes at a cost. Is mustering the cognitive resources necessary to improve performance so effortful that it results in fatigue, or even worse leads to impairments in other areas of functioning (potentially related to ongoing task performance)? These questions, derived by adopting a life span approach to prospective memory development, provide the basis for many future investigations.

REFERENCES

Anderson, P. (2002). Assessment and development of executive function during childhood. *Child Neuropsychology, 8*, 71–82.

Anderson, P., Anderson, V., & Lajoie, G. (1996). The Tower of London test: Validation and standardization for pediatric populations. *The Clinical Neuropsychologist, 10*, 54–65.

Baltes, P. B., & Baltes, M. M. (1990). Psychological perspectives on successful aging: The model of selective optimization with compensation. In P. B. Baltes & M. M. Baltes (Eds.), *Successful aging: Perspectives from the behavioral sciences* (pp. 1–34). New York: Cambridge University Press.

Baltes, P. B., Lindenberger, U., & Staudinger, U. M. (1998). Life span theory in developmental psychology. In W. Damon & R. M. Lerner (Eds.), *Handbook of child psychology: Vol. 1. Theoretical models of human development* (pp. 321–356). New York: Wiley.

Baltes, P. B., Reese, H. W., & Nesselroade, J. R. (1977). *Life span developmental psychology: Introduction to research methods.* Monterey, CA: Brooks-Cole.

Burgess, P. W. (2000). Strategy application disorder: The role of the frontal lobes in human multitasking. *Psychological Research, 63*, 279–288.

Burgess, P. W., Quayle, A., & Frith, C. D. (2001). Brain regions involved in prospective memory as determined by positron emission tomography. *Neuropsychologia, 39*, 545–555.

Burgess, P. W., Veitch, E., Costello, A., & Shallice, T. (2000). The cognitive and neuroanatomical correlates of multitasking. *Neuropsychologia, 38*, 848–863.

Christ, S. E., White, D. A., Mandernach, T., & Keys, B. A. (2001). Inhibitory control across the life span. *Developmental Neuropsychology, 20*, 653–669.

Cockburn, J. (1995). Task interruption in prospective memory: A frontal lobe function. *Cortex, 31*, 87–97.

Cockburn, J., & Smith, P. T. (1988). Effects of age and intelligence on everyday memory tasks. In M. M. Gruneberg, P. E. Morris, & R. N. Sykes (Eds.), *Practical aspects of memory: Current research and issues: Vol. 2. Clinical and educational implications* (pp. 132–136). Chichester, UK: Wiley.

Craik, F. I. M., & McDowd, J. M. (1987). Age differences in recall and recognition. *Journal of Experimental Psychology: Learning, Memory, and Cognition, 13,* 474–479.

Crovitz, H. F., & Daniel, W. F. (1984). Measurements of everyday memory: Toward the prevention of forgetting. *Bulletin of the Psychonomic Society, 22,* 413–414.

Dempster, F. N. (1992). The rise and fall of the inhibitory mechanism: Toward a unified theory of cognitive development and aging. *Developmental Review, 12,* 45–75.

Einstein, G. O., & McDaniel, M. A. (1990). Normal aging and prospective memory. *Journal of Experimental Psychology: Learning, Memory, and Cognition, 16,* 717–726.

Einstein, G. O., McDaniel, M. A., Manzi, M., Cochran, B., & Baker, M. (2000). Prospective memory and aging: Forgetting intentions over short delays. *Psychology and Aging, 15,* 671–683.

Einstein, G. O., McDaniel, M. A., Richardson, S. L., Guynn, M. J., & Cunfer, A. R. (1995). Aging and prospective memory: Examining the influences of self-initiated retrieval processes. *Journal of Experimental Psychology: Learning, Memory, and Cognition, 21,* 996–1007.

Einstein, G. O., McDaniel, M. A., Thomas, R., Mayfield, S., Shank, H., Morrisette, N., et al. (2005). Multiple processes in prospective memory retrieval: Factors determining monitoring versus spontaneous retrieval. *Journal of Experimental Psychology: General, 134,* 327–342.

Einstein, G. O., Smith, R. E., McDaniel, M. A., & Shaw, P. (1997). Aging and prospective memory: The influence of increased task demands at encoding and retrieval. *Psychology and Aging, 12,* 479–488.

Ellis, J. (1996). Prospective memory or the realization of delayed intentions: A conceptual framework for research. In M. Brandimonte, G. O. Einstein, & M. A. McDaniel (Eds.), *Prospective memory: Theory and applications* (pp. 1–22). Mahwah, NJ: Lawrence Erlbaum Associates, Inc.

Ellis, J., & Kvavilashvili, L. (2000). Prospective memory in 2000: Past, present, and future directions. *Applied Cognitive Psychology, 14,* 1–9.

Elvevåg, B., Maylor, E. A., & Gilbert, A. L. (2003). Habitual prospective memory in schizophrenia. *BMC Psychiatry, 3,* 1–7.

Fortin, S., Godbout, L., & Braun, C. M. J. (2003). Cognitive structure of executive deficits in frontally lesioned head trauma patients performing activities of daily living. *Cortex, 39,* 273–291.

Friedman, S. L., & Scholnick, E. K. (Eds.). (1997). *The developmental psychology of planning.* Mahwah, NJ: Lawrence Erlbaum Associates, Inc.

Funke, J., & Krüger, T. (1993). *Plan-A-Day (PAD).* Bonn, Germany: Psychologisches Institut der Universität Bonn.

Gathercole, S. E. (1998). The development of memory. *Journal of Child Psychology and Psychiatry, 39,* 3–27.

Glisky, E. L. (1996). Prospective memory and the frontal lobes. In M. Brandimonte, G. O. Einstein, & M. A. McDaniel (Eds.), *Prospective memory: Theory and applications* (pp. 249–266). Mahwah, NJ: Lawrence Erlbaum Associates, Inc.

Groot, Y. C. T., Wilson, B. A., Evans, J., & Watson, P. (2002). Prospective memory functioning in people with and without brain injury. *Journal of the International Neuropsychological Society, 8,* 645–654.

Guajardo, N. R., & Best, D. L. (2000). Do preschoolers remember what to do? Incentive and external cues in prospective memory. *Cognitive Development, 15,* 75–97.

Hasher, L., Stoltzfus, E. R., Zacks, R. T., & Rypma, B. (1991). Age and inhibition. *Journal of Experimental Psychology: Learning, Memory, and Cognition, 17,* 163–169.

Hasher, L., & Zacks, R. T. (1988). Working memory, comprehension, and aging: A review and a new view. In G. H. Bower (Ed.), *The psychology of learning and motivation* (Vol. 22, pp. 193–225). New York: Academic.

Heaton, R. K., Chelune, G. J., Talley, J. L., Kay, G. G., & Curtis, G. (1993). *Wisconsin Card Sorting Test manual: Revised and expanded.* Odessa, FL: Psychological Assessment Resources.

Henry, J. D., MacLeod, M. S., Phillips, L. H., & Crawford, J. R. (2004). A meta-analytic review of prospective memory and aging. *Psychology and Aging, 19,* 27–39.

Hofer, S. M., & Sliwinski, M. J. (2006). Design and analysis of longitudinal studies on aging. In J. E. Birren & K. W. Schaie (Eds.), *Handbook of the psychology of aging* (pp. 15–37). Amsterdam: Elsevier.

Howe, M. L., & Brainerd, C. J. (1989). Development of children's long-term retention. *Developmental Review, 9,* 301–340.

Huppert, F. A., Johnson, T., & Nickson, J. (2000). High prevalence of prospective memory impairment in the elderly and in early-stage dementia: Findings from a population-based study. *Applied Cognitive Psychology, 14,* S63–S81.

Kliegel, M., Eschen, A., & Thöne-Otto, A. I. T. (2004). Planning and realization of complex intentions in traumatic brain injury and normal aging. *Brain and Cognition, 56,* 43–54.

Kliegel, M., & Jäger, T. (2006). Delayed-execute prospective memory performance: The effects of age and working memory. *Developmental Neuropsychology, 30,* 819–843.

Kliegel, M., Mackinlay, R., & Jäger, T. (in press). Complex prospective memory: Development across the lifespan and the role of task interruption. *Developmental Psychology.*

Kliegel, M., Mackinlay, R., & Jäger, T. (in preparation). *The role of inhibitory efficiency in complex prospective memory: A lifespan approach.*

Kliegel, M., & Martin, M. (2002). *Heidelberger Exekutivfunktionsdiagnostikum (HEXE 3.01).* Taunustein, Germany: Scolaware.

Kliegel, M., & Martin, M. (2003). Prospective memory research: Why is it relevant? *International Journal of Psychology, 38,* 193–194.

Kliegel, M., Martin, M., McDaniel, M. A., & Einstein, G. O. (2002). Complex prospective memory and executive control of working memory: A process model. *Psychologische Beiträge, 44,* 303–318.

Kliegel, M., Martin, M., McDaniel, M. A., Einstein, G. O., & Moor, C. (in press). *Realizing complex delayed intentions in younger and older adults: The role of planning aids.*

Kliegel, M., Martin, M., & Moor, C. (2003). Prospective memory and ageing: Is task importance relevant? *International Journal of Psychology, 38,* 207–214.

Kliegel, M., McDaniel, M. A., & Einstein, G. O. (2000). Plan formation, retention, and execution in prospective memory: A new approach and age-related effects. *Memory and Cognition, 28,* 1041–1049.

Kliegel, M., Phillips, L. H., Lemke, U., & Kopp, U. A. (2005). Planning and realization of complex intentions in patients with Parkinson's disease. *Journal of Neurology, Neurosurgery, and Psychiatry, 76,* 1501–1505.

Kliegel, M., Ramuschkat, G., & Martin, M. (2003). Executive functions and prospective memory performance in old age: An analysis of event-based and time-based prospective memory. *Zeitschrift für Gerontologie und Geriatrie, 36,* 35–41.

Kliegel, M., Ropeter, A., & Mackinlay, R. J. (2006). Complex prospective memory in children with ADHD. *Child Neuropsychology, 12,* 407–419.

Kliegl, R., Smith J., & Baltes P. B. (1989). Testing-the-limits and the study of age differences in cognitive plasticity of a mnemonic skill. *Developmental Psychology, 25,* 247–256.

Kvavilashvili, L., & Ellis, J. (1996). Varieties of intentions: Some distinctions and classifications. In M. Brandimonte, G. O. Einstein, & M. A. McDaniel (Eds.), *Prospective memory: Theory and applications* (pp. 23–51). Mahwah, NJ: Lawrence Erlbaum Associates, Inc.

Lee, G. P., Strauss, E., Loring, D. W., McCloskey, L., & Haworth, J. M. (1997). Sensitivity of figural fluency on the Five-Point Test to focal neurological dysfunction. *Clinical Neuropsychologist, 11,* 59–68.

Levin, H., Culhane, K., Hartmann, H., Evankovich, K., Mattson, A. J., Harward, H., et al. (1991). Developmental changes in performance on tests of purported frontal lobe functioning. *Developmental Neuropsychology, 7,* 377–395.

Mäntylä, T., & Nilsson, L.-G. (1997). Remembering to remember in adulthood: A population-based study on aging and prospective memory. *Aging, Neuropsychology, and Cognition, 4,* 81–92.

Marsh, R. L., & Hicks, J. L. (1998). Event-based prospective memory and executive control of working memory. *Journal of Experimental Psychology: Learning, Memory, and Cognition, 24,* 336–349.

Martin, M., & Kliegel, M. (2003). The development of complex prospective memory performance in children. *Zeitschrift für Entwicklungspsychologie und Pädagogische Psychologie, 35,* 75–82.

Martin, M., Kliegel, M., & McDaniel, M. A. (2003). The involvement of executive functions in prospective memory performance of adults. *International Journal of Psychology, 38,* 195–206.

Maylor, E. A. (1996). Age-related impairment in an event-based prospective-memory task. *Psychology and Aging, 11,* 74–78.

Maylor, E. A., Darby, R. J., Logie, R. H., Della Sala, S., & Smith, G. (2002). Prospective memory across the lifespan. In P. Graf & N. Ohta (Eds.), *Lifespan development of human memory* (pp. 235–256). Cambridge, MA: MIT Press.

McDaniel, M. A., & Einstein, G. O. (2000). Strategic and automatic processes in prospective memory retrieval: A multiprocess framework. *Applied Cognitive Psychology, 14,* 127–144.

McDaniel, M. A., Glisky, E. L., Rubin, S. R., Guynn, M. J., & Routhieaux, B. C. (1999). Prospective memory: A neuropsychological study. *Neuropsychology, 13,* 103–110.

Meacham, J. A. (1982). A note on remembering to execute planned actions. *Journal of Applied Developmental Psychology, 3,* 121–133.

Meacham, J. A., & Colombo, J. A. (1980). External retrieval cues facilitate prospective remembering in children. *Journal of Educational Research, 73,* 299–301.

Mills, V., Kixmiller, J. S., Gillespie, A., Allard, J., Flynn, E., Bowman, A., et al. (1997). The correspondence between the Rivermead Behavioral Memory Test and ecological prospective memory. *Brain and Cognition, 35,* 322–325.

Okuda, J., Fujii, T., Yamadori, A., Kawashima, R., Tsukiura, T., Fukatsu, R., et al. (1998). Participation of the prefrontal cortices in prospective memory: Evidence from a PET study in humans. *Neuroscience Letters, 253,* 127–130.

Park, D. C., Hertzog, C., Kidder, D. P., Morrell, R. W., & Mayhorn, C. B. (1997). Effect of age on event-based and time-based prospective memory. *Psychology and Aging, 12,* 314–327.

Park, D. C., Lautenschlager, G., Hedden, T., Davidson, N. S., Smith, A. D., & Smith, P. K. (2002). Models of visuospatial and verbal memory across the adult life span. *Psychology and Aging, 17,* 299–320.

Phillips, L. H., MacLeod, M., & Kliegel, M. (2005). Adult aging and cognitive planning. In G. Ward & R. Morris (Eds.), *The cognitive psychology of planning* (pp. 111–134). Hove, UK: Psychology Press.

Rendell, P. G., & Craik, F. I. M. (2000). Virtual week and actual week: Age-related differences in prospective memory. *Applied Cognitive Psychology, 14,* 43–62.

Schaie, K. W. (2005). *Developmental influences on adult intelligence: The Seattle Longitudinal Study.* New York: Cambridge University Press.

Schmidt, I. W., Berg, I. J., & Deelman, B. G. (2001). Prospective memory training in older adults. *Educational Gerontology, 27,* 455–478.

Schneider, W. (2002). Memory development in childhood. In U. Goswami (Ed.), *Blackwell handbook of childhood cognitive development* (pp. 236–256). Oxford, UK: Blackwell.

Schneider, W., & Lockl, K. (2002). The development of metacognitive knowledge in children in children and adolescents. In B. L. Schwartz & T. J. Perfect (Eds.), *Applied metacognition* (pp. 224–257). New York: Cambridge University Press.

Shallice, T. (1982). Specific impairments of planning. *Philosophical Transactions, Royal Society of London. B. Biological Science, 298,* 199–209.

Shallice, T., & Burgess, P. W. (1991). Deficits in strategy application following frontal lobe damage in man. *Brain, 114,* 727–741.

Shum, D., Leung, J. P., Ungvari, G. S., & Tang, W. K. (2001). Schizophrenia and prospective memory: A new direction for clinical practice and research? *Hong Kong Journal of Psychiatry, 11,* 23–26.

Smith, R. E., & Bayen, U. J. (2004). A multinomial model of event-based prospective memory. *Journal of Experimental Psychology: Learning, Memory, and Cognition, 30,* 756–777.

Somerville, S. C., Wellman, H. M., & Cultice, J. C. (1983). Young children's deliberate reminding. *Journal of Genetic Psychology, 143,* 87–96.

Terry, W. S. (1988). Everyday forgetting: Data from a diary study. *Psychological Reports, 62,* 299–303.

Uttl, B., Graf, P., Miller, J., & Tuokko, H. (2001). Pro- and retrospective memory in late adulthood. *Consciousness and Cognition, 10,* 451–472.

Villa, K. K., & Abeles, N. (2000). Broad spectrum intervention and the remediation of prospective memory declines in the able elderly. *Aging and Mental Health, 4,* 21–29.

Wang, L., Kliegel, M., Liu, W., & Yang, Z. (in press). Prospective memory performance in preschoolers: Inhibitory control matters. *European Journal of Developmental Psychology.*

Welsh, M., Pennington, B. F., & Groisser, D. B. (1991). A normative-developmental study of executive function: A window on prefrontal function in children. *Developmental Neuropsychology, 7,* 131–149.

West, R. (1996). An application of prefrontal cortex function theory to cognitive aging. *Psychological Bulletin, 120,* 272–292.

West, R., & Craik, F. I. M. (1999). Age-related decline in prospective memory: The roles of cue accessibility and cue sensitivity. *Psychology and Aging, 14,* 264–272.

Winograd, E. (1988). Some observations on prospective remembering. In M. M. Gruneberg, P. M. Morris, & R. N. Sykes (Eds.), *Practical aspects of memory: Current research and issues* (pp. 348–353). Chichester, UK: Wiley.

Zöllig, J., Schwank, O., Lemke, U., & Kliegel, M. (2005, July). *What do we know about neural and behavioral correlates of prospective memory in children?* Paper presented at the 2nd International Conference on Prospective Memory, Zurich, Switzerland.

10

Commentary
Prospective Memory through the Ages

ELIZABETH A. MAYLOR

Department of Psychology
University of Warwick, United Kingdom

*T*he number of published articles on prospective memory has increased markedly over the past 15 years (see Marsh, Cook, & Hicks, 2006; Figure 1.1). A recent *Web of Science* search revealed that almost 40% of 421 articles that included the term *prospective memory* (PM) were concerned with some aspect of age, whether childhood or adult age (the majority on the latter). My task here is to summarize, comment on, and discuss general themes and unresolved issues arising from the chapters in this volume on development (Kvavilashvili, Kyle, & Messer, chap. 6, this volume), aging (McDaniel, Einstein, & Rendell, chap 7, this volume; Phillips, Henry, & Martin; chap. 8, this volume), and the life span (Kliegel, Mackinlay, & Jäger, chap. 9, this volume). The composition of this section reflects not only the continued interest (and controversy) surrounding PM across adulthood (which was similarly present in the previous volume [Brandimonte, Einstein, & McDaniel, 1996] but also the growing evidence on the early development of PM and the need to take an integrative approach to understanding the processes and mechanisms that drive change in PM across the life span (cf. Bialystok & Craik, 2006; Graf & Ohta, 2002).

THE DEVELOPMENT OF PM

Kvavilashvili et al.'s (chap. 6, this volume) comprehensive review of the development of PM in children begins by noting the paucity of studies in this area (an unusual case of development lagging aging research). They attribute this to the (mistaken, they argue) assumption that developmental work is unlikely to tell us anything new about PM and also to the undoubted challenges in collecting PM data from young children. (To these explanations, one could perhaps add that it might be easier to justify the study of aging PM to funding bodies because of the obvious importance of everyday PM tasks, such as remembering to take medication and pay bills on time, to living independently in old age.) Nevertheless, there clearly has been some success in designing PM paradigms suitable for children to address these methodological issues, many of which have been encountered previously in the aging literature (see Maylor, 1993b, 1996b; Uttl, 2005, for summaries). For example, it seems to me that the failure of the "feeding the dog" scenario described by Kvavilashvili et al. illustrates the need to avoid the PM requirement becoming a vigilance or monitoring task in the sense that it occupies working memory or conscious awareness throughout the retention interval (see Graf & Uttl, 2001, on the distinction between PM "proper" and vigilance/monitoring).

Also in common with the aging literature, it seems that the data from developmental studies of PM are somewhat inconsistent, which Kvavilashvili et al. (this volume) attribute in part to different policies on whether or not ongoing task difficulty should be adjusted to match the demands on younger and older children. However, the emerging picture appears to be of quite well-developed PM in preschoolers, with relatively modest improvement with increasing age thereafter. This contrasts with much stronger developmental trends for retrospective memory, but I would argue that such a comparison raises the question of the reliability of PM measures in children. If reliability is low, this limits the amount of systematic variance available to be associated with age. Therefore, a priority for future research should be a study, along the lines of Salthouse, Berish, and Siedlecki's (2004) investigation of PM across adulthood, in which children of different ages are administered multiple PM and retrospective memory tasks (and other measures, such as executive functioning) to first establish their construct validity and only then to compare their developmental sensitivity.

In their concluding remarks, Kvavilashvili et al. suggest that further insights might be gained from applying current theoretical models of PM to development, in particular, McDaniel and Einstein's (2000) multiprocess framework. This would predict stronger developmental trends for PM tasks requiring more strategic resource-demanding monitoring but weaker developmental trends for PM tasks relying on more automatic processing (for similar arguments with respect to aging, see McDaniel et al., chap. 7, this volume). Preliminary evidence consistent with this framework as applied to development comes from a study that was briefly described in Maylor, Darby, Logie, Della Sala, and Smith (2002). Children aged 6 to 11 years old ($N = 200$) were presented with a series of photographs of their teachers and the children were asked to name each of them (ongoing task). In addition, they were to indicate if the teacher was wearing glasses or if there was a plant in the picture (PM task). Although the glasses were visually much less prominent than the plant, the glasses occurred within the focus of attention for the ongoing task, whereas the plant occurred outside the focus of attention (cf. Hicks, Cook, & Marsh, 2005). Responding to the glasses as the PM cue was therefore assumed to

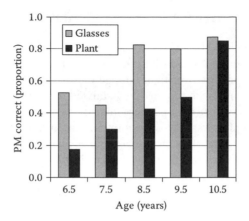

FIGURE 10.1   Proportion of children in each of five age groups (mean ages = 6.5–10.5 years; n = 40 per group) who responded successfully to each of two PM targets (a teacher wearing glasses; a plant in the picture) while naming their teachers from photographs (ongoing task). From Maylor (1996). [Prospective memory performance in 200 children aged 6 to 11 years.] Unpublished data.

be more dependent on automatic processes and less dependent on strategic monitoring processes than responding to the plant.

Almost every child successfully named both the PM target teachers (who were deliberately chosen to be the most familiar to the children). As can be seen in Figure 10.1, there was general improvement in PM performance with increasing age, but this was less striking for the glasses than for the plant, consistent with the predictions from the multiprocess framework. McGann, Defeyter, Reid, and Ellis (2005) reported similar trends in a study of 4- to 7-year-olds in which PM target salience was manipulated by increasing the size of the PM stimulus relative to the non-PM stimuli. Clearly, as Kvavilashvili et al. (chap. 6, this volume) point out, this represents a promising approach for future developmental investigations.

Kvavilashvili et al. suggest that whereas in laboratory-based studies PM performance generally improves with development, in a naturalistic study of children who were asked to remind their caregivers of various everyday tasks, there was no improvement between the ages of 2 and 4 years and PM success rate was high throughout (Somerville, Wellman, & Cultice, 1983). Thus there is an intriguing hint of a developmental PM paradox (although not a complete crossover of developmental effects inside vs. outside the laboratory) that deserves replication and further investigation. However, it would surely be surprising to find younger children performing *better* than older children on PM tasks outside the laboratory. At least in this respect, development is not the mirror-image of aging, for which there is substantial evidence of an age–PM paradox such that young adults outperform older adults on laboratory-based PM tasks, whereas exactly the reverse is the case outside the laboratory (Henry, MacLeod, Phillips, & Crawford, 2004; Rendell & Thomson, 1999). However, a complete explanation for the age–PM paradox remains surprisingly elusive.

THE AGE–PM PARADOX

Phillips et al. (chap. 8, this volume) provide a critical examination of factors that have commonly been held responsible for the age–PM paradox and in particular for the unexpected positive effects of old age on PM performance in naturalistic studies. These data have been too readily dismissed in the past largely because of a lack of experimental control over participants' use of memory aids, ongoing activities, and so on. Note, for example, the comment that "although the study of behavior in context is important, it cannot be a replacement for the systematic study of behavior under laboratory conditions" (Maylor, 1996b, p. 184). However, Phillips et al. argue convincingly that it is still important to understand fully the reasons behind the often superior PM performance of older adults outside the laboratory, and they helpfully outline the missing crucial studies required to test them.

It seems clear to me that older adults are more highly motivated to succeed in naturalistic PM tasks like phoning the experimenter than are young adults, although why is less clear (but note that the majority of young adults in the naturalistic studies of PM included in Henry et al.'s, 2004, meta-analysis were undergraduate students who might have other priorities). For example, Patton and Meit's (1993) older participants "indicated that the task was more important to them than it was to younger subjects, confirming the importance of motivation" (p. 175). Rendell and Thomson's (1999) young adults' poor PM performance was attributable to their failure to keep an electronic organizer with them at all times. Comments from Rendell and Craik's (2000) participants suggested that their older adults took the naturalistic task more seriously than did their young adults. Kvavilashvili and Fisher's (2007) older adults reported "reliably higher levels of (intrinsic) motivation both before and after completion of the task than younger adults" (p. 129).

Age differences in motivation may also interact with other factors discussed by Phillips et al., particularly the use of memory aids. I find it hard to imagine, for example, an undergraduate student turning one item of furniture upside down in every room of the house as a reminder to make a phone call to the experimenter, which was the external cue adopted by one older participant in Maylor's (1990) study. This case (albeit extreme) makes the point that previous categorizations of memory aids as internal, external, or conjunction have overlooked the obvious fact that all cues are not equal. As Phillips et al. suggest, we should be wary of the simplistic view that older adults outperform the young in naturalistic PM tasks because they are more likely to adopt external reminders. Instead, I suggest that we focus on the nature of the cues adopted, the effort involved in setting them up, their potential effectiveness, how they interact with the structure of the person's life, how practiced the person is in using that particular cue, and so on. An additional question is whether a strategy can be imposed or trained, as illustrated by the following instruction to preachers on a Primitive Methodist Plan of 1857: "As forgetfulness is not tolerated, he is desired to mark out his appointments and read them over once a week."

Phillips et al.'s (chap. 8, this volume) interesting discussion of ecological validity (see their Table 8.1) concludes that task setting is most critical in determining whether there are positive or negative age effects on PM, the former being observed "when tasks are set in the day-to-day environment of the participant." It is not clear whether this would include, for example, the population-based study by Huppert, Johnson, and Nickson (2000) in which a random sample of people aged 65 and older were interviewed in their places of residence by a trained experimenter. Performance on a simple PM task administered during the session declined dramatically and linearly with increasing age. However, although the task setting was the everyday environment of the participant, the PM task was still under the control of the experimenter (and the same would apply to the Web-based study to be described later, despite the physical absence of an experimenter in that case); see Phillips et al.'s section on participant control.

The hypothetical scenario posed by Phillips et al. is especially sobering in that it highlights just how little we have learned from decades of both naturalistic and laboratory work on aging and PM about older people's actual performance in everyday PM tasks. These would include not only those habitual PM tasks usually listed in the introductory sections of articles and grant proposals (remembering to take medication, pay the bills, etc.), but also "tasks that crop up unexpectedly during the day" (Rendell & Thomson, 1999, p. 268) such as remembering to set the video to tape a television program, turn off the bath faucet or the electric blanket, prompt a friend who has asked you to remind him or her of something when he or she leaves, phone someone back in an hour when he or she will be available, and so on. As Phillips et al. note, we simply do not know whether aging data from naturalistic- or laboratory-based tasks are more appropriate to everyday PM situations. This seems a disappointing state of affairs but one that could be remedied by following the recommendations for future research outlined in their chapter, including systematic manipulations of relevant factors across both naturalistic and laboratory settings, and also direct observational studies. It would, for instance, be interesting to discover the extent of collaboration and reliance on others in prospective remembering across adulthood (see Schaefer & Laing, 2000).

AGING PM IN THE LABORATORY

The age–PM paradox is, of course, a generalization that ignores the fact highlighted by McDaniel et al. (chap. 7, this volume) that age-related deficits are not always observed in laboratory-based PM tasks. Thus it is now recognized that PM tasks vary in their attentional demands, with age differences greater under more demanding conditions consistent with McDaniel and Einstein's (2000) multiprocess framework (see Henry et al., 2004; Maylor et al., 2002). In their chapter, McDaniel et al. explore in detail a distinction between focal and nonfocal cues in event-based PM tasks, the former eliciting more automatic spontaneous retrieval than the latter because of their "overlap with the information constellation relevant to performing the ongoing task." This is reminiscent of an earlier notion of "task appropriate processing" (Maylor, 1996a, p. 78), which suggested that a key to understanding age differences in PM was in terms of the relationship between the type or level of stimulus processing required to perform the ongoing task and stimulus processing required to perform the PM task (see also Maylor et al., 2002). Although McDaniel et al. argue that these two ideas are not the same, it seems to me that they are conceptually very similar and indeed make identical predictions. Taking their example of making lexical decisions as the ongoing task and indicating a member of the animal category as the PM task, McDaniel et al. define this as task appropriate (because both are semantic tasks) but nonfocal (because deciding if a letter string is a word "does not require processing the semantic features necessary to make a category determination"). Instead, I would define this as task inappropriate because the processing required to decide if a letter string is a word is insufficient for a participant to realize that it is a member of a particular category. Maylor (1996a) similarly defined Mäntylä's (1993) condition in which the ongoing task was word association and the PM cue was any member of a particular category (e.g., liquids) as task inappropriate because a shift was required in the level of processing from the generation of a semantically related word to the categorization of that word as a member of a specific group. A task-appropriate version of McDaniel et al.'s example would be a lexical decision as the ongoing task and indicating the word *cat* as the PM task. Thus, I would claim that all the nonfocal cases in McDaniel et al.'s Table 7.1 are task inappropriate and all the focal cases are task appropriate. In other words, in all the nonfocal cases, some additional (self-initiated) processing, beyond that required by the ongoing task, is necessary for the PM cue to be detected as such.

Terminology aside, the data are reasonably consistent in showing smaller age-related deficits with focal than with nonfocal cues (e.g., Maylor et al., 2002; McDaniel et al., chap. 7, this volume; Rendell, McDaniel, Forbes, & Einstein, 2007; Salthouse et al., 2004). However, the data are less consistent on the question of whether age deficits can be eliminated altogether with focal cues. For example, Salthouse et al. (2004) observed age deficits in their PM tasks with focal cues (namely, "drawing classification" and "concept identification") and several of my own (unpublished) attempts to replicate Einstein and McDaniel's (1990) classic findings of no age deficits with focal cues have failed. Some reasons for these discrepancies are discussed later.

One important possibility identified by McDaniel et al. that has been ignored in past studies is that older adults might be able to achieve an equivalent level of PM performance to that of the young adults but only by sacrificing ongoing task performance. Investigating this obviously requires monitoring ongoing task performance both with and without the PM task to obtain a measure of PM costs (and this should probably be routine in future PM studies). McDaniel et al. present data with focal cues suggesting that the absence of age-related deficits in PM is not accompanied by greater costs to the ongoing task in older adults. These results are striking, but they do raise a couple of concerns. The first is the extent to which performance is at or close to ceiling; note that although focal PM performance was not actually 100%, PM may be subject to a "functional measurement ceiling" (Salthouse et al., 2004, p. 1143) that is effectively lower than 100%. (This ceiling issue also complicates the interpretation of age by condition interactions, where condition might be focal versus nonfocal, salient versus nonsalient, event-based or time-based, etc.).

The second point is that in addition to considering ongoing task performance more closely as advocated by McDaniel et al., we should examine PM performance in greater detail. Traditionally, only accuracy is considered. But evidence that more might be learned from other measures, reaction time in particular, comes from a study by Maylor, Brandimonte, Darby, and Freni (1999). The PM task was embedded within an ongoing letter-matching task. Participants were presented with strings of five letters and were asked to decide whether the second and fourth letters in each string were the same or different (letter-matching task). They were additionally instructed that if one or both of these letters was the letter B, they should press the spacebar before making the usual same or different response (PM task). PM targets occurred twice in each of eight blocks of 65 trials. There were 26 young and 34 older participants with mean ages of 21 and 70 years, respectively, although the data from 4 participants (1 young, 3 older) were excluded from the analysis because they did not perfectly recall every element of the instructions when questioned at the end of the experiment. On the letter-matching task, both age groups were highly accurate (around 97% correct) but young adults were faster than older adults (M reaction times of 839 and 1,267 ms, respectively, an age-related slowing factor of 1.5). For the PM task, young adults were numerically but not significantly more successful than older adults (63% and 57% correct, respectively), consistent with a classification of the PM cue as focal. However, the PM responses of young adults were considerably faster than those of older adults (M reaction times of 1,225 and 2,337 ms, respectively, an age-related slowing factor of 1.9). This particularly marked slowing of older adults' PM responses (also observed by West & Craik, 1999, although using a nonfocal PM cue) could reflect greater difficulty in inhibiting the ongoing task response, slower retrieval of the PM action required, and so forth. Whatever the explanation, the point here is that PM performance in focal tasks may not be entirely indistinguishable between young and older adults and that we may be missing more subtle and potentially interesting age-related deficits in PM by generally focusing on percent correct as the dependent variable.

McDaniel et al.'s (this volume) most intriguing result is the absence of reliable age-related deficits in PM for nonfocal cues (requiring strategic monitoring), which was associated with disproportionate costs to ongoing task performance in older adults. In other words, for whatever reason, their older adults apparently chose to prioritize PM performance at the expense of ongoing task performance. Why older adults in previous studies of nonfocal PM tasks (e.g., Maylor, 1998) apparently chose not to do this is a puzzle (but see discussion later on task instructions) that should be addressed in future research.

It is suggested by McDaniel et al. that their laboratory-based findings can help to reconcile the age–PM paradox. Thus, they argue that age deficits will not occur in naturalistic PM tasks when the cue is focal because performance relies on spontaneous retrieval processes that are preserved in old age. Nor will they necessarily occur in naturalistic PM tasks when the cue is nonfocal because ongoing task performance can be sacrificed or adjusted to take the PM task into account. However, aside from the difficulties in extrapolating from the laboratory to naturalistic settings (see Phillips et al., chap. 8, this volume), such arguments fail to explain the *positive* effects of aging observed in naturalistic PM tasks. Nonetheless, McDaniel et al.'s provocative discussion opens up some interesting new lines of enquiry.

McDaniel et al. (this volume) close by mentioning other factors besides the focal–nonfocal distinction that may influence the extent of age effects in laboratory-based PM tasks, one of which is time of day. Significant effects of time of day were reported by Leirer, Decker Tanke, and Morrow (1994) in a naturalistic study of older adults who were required to simulate taking medication at specified times each day. PM performance was best in the morning, a result they attributed to the morning hours being less busy (see Rendell & Thomson, 1999, for a similar result). If time of day effects were found in laboratory-based PM tasks, they would presumably require a different explanation because ongoing activity would be controlled.

Time of day has received some recent attention in the aging literature (see Yoon, May, & Hasher, 2000, for a review) because whereas most young adults describe themselves as "neutral" or "evening" types, most older adults are "morning" types. Moreover, cognitive performance for young adults tends to be better when tested in the afternoon than in the morning, with precisely the reverse for older adults. For example, May, Hasher, and Stoltzfus (1993) observed substantial age deficits in recognition memory in the late afternoon (optimal for young but not older adults) but no age deficits in the morning (optimal for older but not young adults). Therefore, a potential explanation for the conflicting effects of aging on laboratory-based PM tasks in the literature is that studies have been conducted at different times of the day, with those showing no age deficits conducted in the morning and those showing age deficits conducted in the afternoon. Unfortunately, such information is not usually reported in laboratory-based PM studies.

Preliminary evidence from young adults in the laboratory comes from a study by Maylor (1996d) in which 94 undergraduate students were tested either in the morning or in the afternoon. The ongoing task was either to name famous people from their photographs or to provide their occupations (half assigned to each condition) and the PM task was to indicate those wearing glasses (cf. Maylor, 1996a, 1998). Figure 10.2 shows correct performance on the ongoing and PM tasks (name and occupation data were combined) as a function of time of day. There was no overall effect of time of day but there was a significant interaction with task ($p < .05$), indicating that PM performance was relatively better in the morning and ongoing performance was relatively better in the afternoon. The reason for this is unclear; one possibility is that there are differential and independent effects of time of day on retrieval from semantic memory (ongoing task) and PM; another possibility is that participants adopt different strategies or trade-offs in the allocation of attentional resources between the ongoing and PM tasks in the morning and afternoon. Whatever the explanation, these data suggest that time of day should be considered in future studies (although time of day effects may be more apparent with nonfocal than with focal PM cues), particularly those involving different age groups.

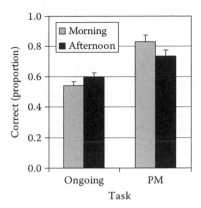

FIGURE 10.2 Mean correct performance from 94 undergraduate students, half of whom were tested in the morning and half in the afternoon, for the ongoing task (providing the names or occupations of famous people from their photographs) and the PM task (circling the trial number of those people wearing glasses; $n = 8$ out of 120). Error bars indicate 1 SEM. From Maylor (1996d).

LIFE-SPAN CHANGES IN COMPLEX PM

In contrast to the rather weak developmental improvements in PM reviewed by Kvavilashvili et al. (chap. 6, this volume) and the absence of age deficits in PM obtained by McDaniel et al. (chap. 7, this volume), Kliegel et al. (chap. 9, this volume) report a wealth of data showing marked inverted-U-shaped changes in performance across the life span. Importantly, their task is a complex planning task with presumably high demands on executive functioning, in which the PM component as I have previously understood it—for example, "the requirement to remember to perform an action at some point in the future ... in the absence of any prompting by the experimenter" (Maylor, 1996b, p. 175)—is only one element (i.e., intention initiation) of the intention formation–retention–initiation–execution process. Kliegel et al.'s paradigm was designed to explore life-span changes in each of these phases in a complex PM task. Impressive data and combined plots from 555 participants over a wide age range (6–84 years) show that growth, stability, and then decline (in some cases accelerating) are evident in all phases but particularly for initiation and execution. Furthermore, an increase in the need for inhibitory control in the execution phase exaggerated age effects across the life span.

At least as implemented in sections 2 and 3 of Kliegel et al., the task's emphasis is on how participants form a plan to follow a set of arbitrary rules, retain the plan, and then later carry it out without breaking the rules (see their footnotes 1, 2, and 4). However, I would argue that the paradigm fails to capture what is perhaps most relevant to PM and that is the formation, retention, and execution of a plan for initiating an intention. Thus, in view of the PM instructions to self-initiate the multitask set on encountering the PM cue (i.e., a request to write date of birth at the top of a questionnaire; see their footnote 3), of most interest is what participants of different ages do to ensure that they will remember, whether their methods are effective, and so forth. In fact, section 4 begins to address this potential criticism by introducing conditions that include specifically instructing participants to consider planning aids that would target the intention initiation component. Nonetheless, it remains of interest to discover the extent to which participants of different ages focus on intention initiation or execution in their spontaneous plans and how these then relate to success or otherwise in each phase.

Another possible reservation concerning Kliegel et al.'s paradigm is that it may not be relevant to performance outside the laboratory (although this criticism also applies to other laboratory PM tasks, of course). For example, Kliegel et al. consistently observed that older adults formed less elaborate plans in comparison with young adults. However, although others have also found age deficits in formulating and executing plans with novel tasks, it seems that if the planning task is more familiar or ecologically valid, age differences disappear (see Phillips et al., chap. 8, this volume). This is not to deny the potential value of Kliegel et al.'s paradigm for addressing questions such as the role of various explanatory mechanisms in each of the phases, but it does suggest some caution in interpreting the data and drawing conclusions from the paradigm.

GENERAL THEMES, UNRESOLVED ISSUES, AND AN INTERNET STUDY

One common theme running through these chapters is the age–complexity effect, which refers to the tendency for age (and developmental) differences in performance to increase with the complexity of the task (see Salthouse, 1991, for discussion). Age–complexity is related to the reduced processing resources view whereby older adults and young children have fewer processing resources or less attentional capacity than young adults; they are therefore particularly disadvantaged in complex tasks that are more demanding and less automatic (Hasher & Zacks, 1979). Although this view enables us to make relative predictions such as life-span changes should be more dramatic for nonfocal than for focal PM cues, it is less helpful in making absolute predictions about whether any particular PM task will show age differences. The argument becomes circular if we find a reliable age difference in PM performance and therefore conclude that retrieval was not automatic. A possible added complication is that sometimes PM tasks that appear more complex result in superior performance. For example, Maylor (1993a) asked participants to name famous faces and to circle the trial number if the person had a beard and cross out the trial number if the person was smoking a pipe. Maylor (1996a) asked participants to name famous faces and to circle the trial number if the person was wearing glasses. PM performance in the first block of trials was much higher with the former more complex instructions than with the simpler instructions (68% vs. 42% correct). It seemed that greater effort was made to encode the complex instructions, which may also have been mentally rehearsed more often subsequently because of their perceived difficulty. A related argument was made by Henry et al. (2004) in categorizing 6-event and 12-event PM conditions as requiring high and low strategic demands, respectively, on the grounds that the greater frequency of PM cues would "presumably maintain activation of the PM task" (p. 29). In short, the age–complexity notion may not necessarily prove to be so helpful in the context of PM.

Another emerging theme is the somewhat inconsistent nature of the PM findings in both the developmental and aging literatures. Of course, some contrasting data patterns have led to interesting proposals like the age–PM paradox that should continue to inspire researchers. However, other inconsistencies raise the general issue of the reliability and validity of PM measures across the life span. In the only large-scale study of several different laboratory event-based PM tasks, Salthouse et al. (2004) found that although their PM tasks showed both convergent and discriminant validity, little of the variance in each task was associated with what they had in common (unlike, e.g., retrospective memory). They therefore concluded with a note of caution to researchers trying to make inferences about the construct of PM based on results from a single task. No such equivalent data exist for naturalistic PM tasks, which represents a gap that urgently needs to be filled.

Inconsistent results also highlight both the logical and methodological problems associated with the investigation of PM. Thus, single binary measures of success or failure on laboratory tasks such as remembering to ask for a red pen at the appropriate moment (designed to simulate everyday "crop-up" tasks mentioned earlier) are noisy, coarse indexes of PM ability. Increasing the number of PM trials introduces other complications; for example, it risks the task becoming one of vigilance (Uttl, 2005); also, performance on the first PM trial may be influenced differently by factors such as aging to performance on subsequent PM trials (Maylor, 1996b).

A novel way of producing a more finely grained index of PM performance from a single PM response was recently described by Graf, Uttl, and Dixon (2002). Participants are shown the PM cue (e.g., a picture of a helicopter) and instructed to stop performing the ongoing task (e.g., categorizing letters presented in the center of the computer screen) when the PM cue occurs in one of the corners of the screen. Each ongoing task trial is accompanied by four pictures of different sizes. The PM cue, when it first appears, is small and if the participant fails to respond, it reappears a few trials later but slightly larger. This procedure continues until the participant responds, the dependent variable being the size of the cue at that point. Using this simple method, Uttl (2006) observed significant age-related deficits in PM with both visual and auditory cues, with older adults requiring larger and louder PM cues, respectively, before responding. It would seem quite straightforward and potentially interesting to extend this paradigm to the study of PM development.

An alternative solution to the problem of noisy, coarse data from single-event PM tasks is to compensate by increasing the numbers of participants in the study. This could be achieved by collecting data via the Internet. With the enormous recent growth in access to the Internet has come a rapidly expanding literature reporting psychological experiments conducted online (see Birnbaum, 2004; Reips, 2002, for reviews). There are many obvious advantages of such a methodology. For example, it can save researchers both time and money as once an experiment is set up, it can be run concurrently on large numbers of unpaid volunteers. These generally represent a wider demographic than the usual undergraduate population and hence the results may be more generalizable. Experimenter bias can be avoided because Internet experiments run automatically. To these can be added a couple of particular advantages with respect to research on aging, namely, participants are not required to travel for testing, and older adults are probably less anxious when tested in their own familiar environment.

Of course, there are also some obvious disadvantages associated with Internet experimentation. These include the possibility of a biased sample as although most people now have access to computers, not everyone will have the appropriate software installed for downloading and running experiments. People might not be honest, for example, in answering questions about demographics (age, education, gender, etc.). More important, they might not always understand the instructions and, unlike laboratory research, there is no opportunity to check and provide further instructions if necessary. Internet studies provide no control over the conditions under which the experiment is conducted; uncontrolled factors include monitor size, hand positions, distractions, noise, time of day, and so on. Also, there is no control over the state of participants who, for example, may be tired, intoxicated, or not wearing their glasses.

However, in view of the large numbers of people who can be tested in Internet studies, researchers can ensure the integrity of their data by taking a conservative approach to the data sets they allow to enter the analysis. In general, this methodology tends to produce effects that account for only a small proportion of the variance but are highly significant. The effects may be more generalizable to real-world situations if they emerge from experiments conducted on diverse samples under poorly controlled conditions. It is therefore argued that the considerable advantages more than outweigh the disadvantages, particularly as evidence suggests that Web-based studies can reliably replicate laboratory findings (see Buchanan & Smith, 1999; Gosling, Vazire, Srivastava, & John, 2004; McGraw, Tew, & Williams, 2000).

Access to the Internet is now widespread in schools; older adults are also increasingly being encouraged to use the Internet, although home access decreases with age (Cutler, Hendricks, & Guyer, 2003; Selwyn, Gorard, Furlong, & Madden, 2003). Thus there is currently enormous potential for conducting lifespan research online. Recent published examples include a study on self-esteem by Robins, Trzesniewski, Gosling, and Potter (2002) with 326,641 individuals aged between 9 and 90 years, and a study of task switching by Reimers and Maylor (2005) with 5,271 participants between 10 and 66 years.

In collaboration with Robert Logie and the British Broadcasting Corporation (BBC), Internet data are currently being collected on a set of memory experiments that include a simple PM task. Toward the beginning of the session, participants view a screen informing them that later in the test, they will see a smiley face and they have to remember to click on the smiley face when it appears. This PM cue is presented in the top right corner of the screen that provides feedback to the participant after the tests have been completed. There is no time limit imposed on viewing either the instruction screen or the feedback screen. Preliminary results from

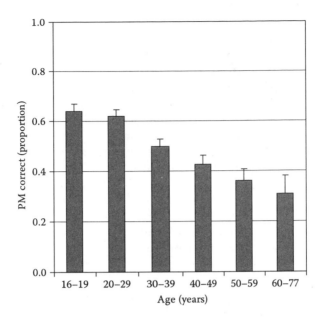

FIGURE 10.3 Mean proportion of participants in each of seven age groups from 16 to 77 years (n = 232, 343, 283, 188, 111, and 42, respectively) who responded correctly to a single PM target event in an Internet study of memory run from the BBC's Science and Nature Web site. Error bars indicate 1 SEM. Preliminary results from U.K. participants in the first 5 days of data collection (Logie & Maylor, 2006).

1,199 U.K. volunteers aged between 16 and 77 years from the first 5 days of data collection are presented in Figure 10.3.[1] The point-biserial correlation between exact age and PM success was weak but highly significant, r_{pb} = –.201, p < .001. Thus, although the task setting was the participants' own familiar environment, there was approximately linear age-related decline in PM performance from young adulthood. Internet methodology may therefore be a promising avenue to pursue in the future, particularly with respect to the investigation of PM in neglected age groups such as adolescents and 20- to 40-year-olds.

Returning to the issue of discrepancies in the literature, a significant source of variance across PM studies may lie in the exact wording of the task instructions, which are not always reported but perhaps should be routinely included in appendices. As noted by Phillips et al. (chap. 8, this volume), age deficits can vary in the laboratory depending on the relative emphasis in the instructions on the ongoing versus PM tasks. Performance may also be influenced by whether the PM task is

---

[1] Participants were in fact randomly assigned by the computer program to one of four conditions in this PM experiment; for present purposes, the data have been combined across the different conditions to produce Figure 10.3.

described explicitly as a test of memory as shown by Gao, Cuttler, and Graf (2005), who administered a neuropsychological test battery to 141 community-living adults. Prior to starting the tests, the experimenter unplugged the phone to prevent disruptions and asked the participant to remind the experimenter to plug the phone back in when testing was completed. Half of the participants were assigned to an "informed" condition in which they were told that the phone task was designed to assess their memory, whereas the other half were in a "naive" condition in which they were not told that the phone task was a memory test. Informed participants were significantly more successful in remembering to remind the experimenter than were naive participants (approximately 59% and 28%, respectively).

The importance of the precise wording of instructions with respect to aging is highlighted by intriguing data from a study of retrospective memory by Rahhal, Hasher, and Colcombe (2001; see also Desrichard & Köpetz, 2005). When the instructions emphasized the memory component of the task (e.g., "You will be tested on your memory of this information in Phase 2"), age deficits were observed. However, when the instructions were phrased more neutrally (e.g., "You will be tested on this information in Phase 2"), there were no age differences. Although task instructions are unlikely to account entirely for discrepancies in the PM literature,[2] they surely deserve serious consideration in the design of future aging (and perhaps developmental) studies.

From a life span perspective, several important issues remain largely unresolved. First, as mentioned in more than one chapter, all our present conclusions are based on cross-sectional data, so there is obviously a need to replicate PM findings longitudinally. Second, there are at least some hints that PM may be more strongly related to retrospective memory and other aspects of cognition in childhood and old age than in adulthood, consistent with the differentiation–dedifferentiation view of intellectual development across the life span (see Li et al., 2004), but clearly further data are required. Third, although there appear to be some parallels between the two ends of the life span in terms of mechanisms and processes underlying the development and aging of PM (changes in executive functioning, inhibitory control, speed of processing, etc.), there may also be some differences (cf. Craik & Bialystok, 2006). For example, it seems unlikely that the significant contribution to PM performance from sensory functioning found in old age (Uttl, 2006) will be replicated in development.

In summary, over recent years there has been considerable progress in research on PM in both development and aging. Studies are now more theory-driven and beginning to benefit from improved methods and insights from wider domains. However, a nagging question relevant to all these chapters is whether any of the

---

[2] For example, compare the PM instructions in a study with no age deficits in which participants were told that the experimenters "had a secondary interest in their ability to remember to do something in the future" (Einstein & McDaniel, 1990, p. 719), and a study with age deficits in which the experimenter told participants "If you see a person wearing glasses, then I want you to put a circle around the number of that slide" (Maylor, 1996a, p. 75).

findings would particularly surprise a developmental or aging retrospective memory researcher. The age–PM paradox perhaps stands out as the most unexpected; it would perhaps further surprise a retrospective memory researcher to learn that there is still no completely satisfactory explanation for it.

ACKNOWLEDGMENTS

Thanks to Richard Darby, Victoria Holman, and Joanne Rodger for help with data collection and to Stian Reimers for useful discussions.

REFERENCES

Bialystok, E., & Craik, F. I. M. (Eds.). (2006). *Lifespan cognition: Mechanisms of change.* New York: Oxford University Press.

Birnbaum, M. H. (2004). Human research and data collection via the Internet. *Annual Review of Psychology, 55,* 803–832.

Brandimonte, M., Einstein, G. O., & McDaniel, M. A. (Eds.). (1996). *Prospective memory: Theory and applications.* Mahwah, NJ: Lawrence Erlbaum Associates, Inc.

Buchanan, T., & Smith, J. L. (1999). Using the Internet for psychological research: Personality testing on the World Wide Web. *British Journal of Psychology, 90,* 125–144.

Craik, F. I. M., & Bialystok, E. (2006). Cognition through the lifespan: Mechanisms of change. *Trends in Cognitive Sciences, 10,* 131–138.

Cutler, S. J., Hendricks, J., & Guyer, A. (2003). Age differences in home computer availability and use. *Journal of Gerontology Series B: Psychological Sciences and Social Sciences, 58,* S271–S280.

Desrichard, O., & Köpetz, C. (2005). A threat in the elder: The impact of task-instructions, self-efficacy and performance expectations on memory performance in the elderly. *European Journal of Social Psychology, 35,* 537–552.

Einstein, G. O., & McDaniel, M. A. (1990). Normal aging and prospective memory. *Journal of Experimental Psychology: Learning, Memory, and Cognition, 16,* 717–726.

Gao, J., Cuttler, C., & Graf, P. (2005, November). *Prospective memory, instructions and personality.* Poster presented at the annual meeting of the Psychonomic Society, Toronto, Canada.

Gosling, S. D., Vazire, S., Srivastava, S., & John, O. P. (2004). Should we trust Web-based studies? A comparative analysis of six preconceptions about Internet questionnaires. *American Psychologist, 59,* 93–104.

Graf, P., & Ohta, N. (Eds.). (2002). *Lifespan development of human memory.* Cambridge, MA: MIT Press.

Graf, P., & Uttl, B. (2001). Prospective memory: A new focus for research. *Consciousness and Cognition, 10,* 437–450.

Graf, P., Uttl, B., & Dixon, R. (2002). Prospective and retrospective memory in adulthood. In P. Graf & N. Ohta (Eds.), *Lifespan development of human memory* (pp. 257–282). Cambridge, MA: MIT Press.

Hasher, L., & Zacks, R. T. (1979). Automatic and effortful processes in memory. *Journal of Experimental Psychology: General, 108,* 356–388.

Henry, J. D., MacLeod, M. S., Phillips, L. H., & Crawford, J. R. (2004). A meta-analytic review of prospective memory and aging. *Psychology and Aging, 19,* 27–39.

Hicks, J. L., Cook, G. I., & Marsh, R. L. (2005). Detecting event-based prospective memory cues occurring within and outside the focus of attention. *American Journal of Psychology, 118,* 1–11.

Huppert, F. A., Johnson, T., & Nickson, J. (2000). High prevalence of prospective memory impairment in the elderly and in early-stage dementia: Findings from a population-based study. *Applied Cognitive Psychology, 14,* S63–S81.

Kvavilashvili, L., & Fisher, L. (2007). Is time-based prospective remembering mediated by self-initiated rehearsals? Role of incidental cues, ongoing activity, age, and motivation. *Journal of Experimental Psychology: General, 136,* 112–132.

Leirer, V. O., Decker Tanke, E., & Morrow, D. G. (1994). Time of day and naturalistic prospective memory. *Experimental Aging Research, 20,* 127–134.

Li, S.-C., Lindenberger, U., Hommel, B., Aschersleben, G., Prinz, W., & Baltes, P. B. (2004). Transformations in the couplings among intellectual abilities and constituent processes across the life span. *Psychological Science, 15,* 155–163.

Logie, R. H., & Maylor, E. A. (2006). [Prospective memory performance from an initial sample of 1,199 adults in an Internet study.] Unpublished data.

Mäntylä, T. (1993). Priming effects in prospective memory. *Memory, 1,* 203–218.

Marsh, R. L., Cook, G. I., & Hicks, J. L. (2006). An analysis of prospective memory. In B. H. Ross (Ed.), *The psychology of learning and motivation* (Vol. 46, pp. 115–153). San Diego, CA: Elsevier Academic.

May, C. P., Hasher, L., & Stoltzfus, E. R. (1993). Optimal time of day and the magnitude of age differences in memory. *Psychological Science, 4,* 326–330.

Maylor, E. A. (1990). Age and prospective memory. *Quarterly Journal of Experimental Psychology, 42A,* 471–493.

Maylor, E. A. (1993a). Aging and forgetting in prospective and retrospective memory tasks. *Psychology and Aging, 8,* 420–428.

Maylor, E. A. (1993b). Minimized prospective memory loss in old age. In J. Cerella, J. Rybash, W. Hoyer, & M. L. Commons (Eds.), *Adult information processing: Limits on loss* (pp. 529–551). San Diego, CA: Academic.

Maylor, E. A. (1996a). Age-related impairment in an event-based prospective memory task. *Psychology and Aging, 11,* 74–78.

Maylor, E. A. (1996b). Does prospective memory decline with age? In M. Brandimonte, G. O. Einstein, & M. A. McDaniel (Eds.), *Prospective memory: Theory and applications* (pp. 173–197). Mahwah, NJ: Lawrence Erlbaum Associates, Inc.

Maylor, E. A. (1996d). [Young adults' performance of ongoing and prospective memory tasks as a function of time of day.] Unpublished data.

Maylor, E. A. (1998). Changes in event-based prospective memory across adulthood. *Aging, Neuropsychology, and Cognition, 5,* 107–128.

Maylor, E. A., Brandimonte, M. A., Darby, R. J., & Freni, G. (1999). *Effects of irrelevant information on prospective remembering.* Unpublished manuscript.

Maylor, E. A., Darby, R. J., Logie, R. H., Della Sala, S., & Smith, G. (2002). Prospective memory across the lifespan. In P. Graf & N. Ohta (Eds.), *Lifespan development of human memory* (pp. 235–256). Cambridge, MA: MIT Press.

McDaniel, M. A., & Einstein, G. O. (2000). Strategic and automatic processes in prospective memory retrieval: A multiprocess framework. *Applied Cognitive Psychology, 14,* S127–S144.

McGann, D., Defeyter, M. A., Reid, C., & Ellis, J. A. (2005, July). *Prospective memory in children: The effects of age and target salience.* Paper presented at the Second International Conference on Prospective Memory, Zurich, Switzerland.

McGraw, K. O., Tew, M. D., & Williams, J. E. (2000). The integrity of Web-delivered experiments: Can you trust the data? *Psychological Science, 11,* 502–506.

Patton, G. W. R., & Meit, M. (1993). Effect of aging on prospective and incidental memory. *Experimental Aging Research, 19,* 165–176.

Rahhal, T. A., Hasher, L., & Colcombe, S. J. (2001). Instructional manipulations and age differences in memory: Now you see them, now you don't. *Psychology and Aging, 16,* 697–706.

Reimers, S., & Maylor, E. A. (2005). Task switching across the life span: Effects of age on general and specific switch costs. *Developmental Psychology, 41,* 661–671.

Reips, U.-D. (2002). Standards for Internet-based experimenting. *Experimental Psychology, 49,* 243–256.

Rendell, P. G., & Craik, F. I. M. (2000). Virtual week and actual week: Age-related differences in prospective memory. *Applied Cognitive Psychology, 14,* S43–S62.

Rendell, P. G., McDaniel, M. A., Forbes, R. D., & Einstein, G. O. (2007). Age-related effects in prospective memory are modulated by ongoing task complexity and relation to target cue. *Aging, Neuropsychology, and Cognition, 14,* 236–256.

Rendell, P. G., & Thomson, D. M. (1999). Aging and prospective memory: Differences between naturalistic and laboratory tasks. *Journal of Gerontology: Psychological Sciences, 54B,* P256–P269.

Robins, R. W., Trzesniewski, K. H., Gosling, S. D., & Potter, J. (2002). Global self-esteem across the life span. *Psychology and Aging, 17,* 423–434.

Salthouse, T. A. (1991). *Theoretical perspectives on cognitive aging.* Hillsdale, NJ: Lawrence Erlbaum Associates, Inc.

Salthouse, T. A., Berish, D. E., & Siedlecki, K. L. (2004). Construct validity and age sensitivity of prospective memory. *Memory & Cognition, 32,* 1133–1148.

Schaefer, E. G., & Laing, M. L. (2000). "Please, remind me...": The role of others in prospective remembering. *Applied Cognitive Psychology, 14,* S99–S114.

Selwyn, N., Gorard, S., Furlong, J., & Madden, L. (2003). Older adults' use of information and communications technology in everyday life. *Ageing and Society, 23,* 561–582.

Somerville, S. C., Wellman, H. M., & Cultice, J. C. (1983). Young children's deliberate reminding. *Journal of Genetic Psychology, 143,* 87–96.

Uttl, B. (2005). Age-related changes in event cued prospective memory proper. In N. Ohta, C. M. MacLeod, & B. Uttl (Eds.), *Dynamic cognitive processes* (pp. 273–303). Tokyo: Springer.

Uttl, B. (2006). Age-related changes in event-cued visual and auditory prospective memory proper. *Aging, Neuropsychology, and Cognition, 13,* 141–172.

West, R., & Craik, F. I. M. (1999). Age-related decline in prospective memory: The roles of cue accessibility and cue sensitivity. *Psychology and Aging, 14,* 264–272.

Yoon, C., May, C. P., & Hasher, L. (2000). Aging, circadian arousal patterns, and cognition. In D. Park & N. Schwarz (Eds.), *Cognitive aging: A primer* (pp. 151–171). Hove, UK: Psychology Press.

11

On the Role of Rostral Prefrontal Cortex (Area 10) in Prospective Memory

PAUL W. BURGESS

Institute of Cognitive Neuroscience & Psychology Department
University College London

IROISE DUMONTHEIL

Institute of Cognitive Neuroscience & Psychology Department
University College London and
Laboratoire de Physiologie de la Perception et de l'Action
Collège de France, Paris

SAM J. GILBERT

Institute of Cognitive Neuroscience & Psychology Department
University College London

JIRO OKUDA

Institute of Cognitive Neuroscience & Psychology Department
University College London and
Tamagawa University Research Institute, Tokyo

MARIEKE L. SCHÖLVINCK

Institute of Cognitive Neuroscience & Psychology Department
University College London

JON S. SIMONS

Brain Mapping Unit
University of Cambridge, Addenbrooke's Hospital, Cambridge, United Kingdom

*T*his book is testament to the wonderful advances that have been achieved in the last few years in the field of prospective memory (PM[1]) research. However this is still a very new area of study. Also relatively new are the methods in cognitive neuroscience that enable us to localize the neural underpinnings of specific behavioral functions. So one might expect, at this early scientific stage, that the evidence that links particular brain regions to PM might be somewhat contradictory. Very surprisingly, however, this is not the case, at least for the frontal lobes. There is a general consensus that the executive functions of the frontal lobes play some part in supporting PM. This comes both from evidence of structural abnormality in the frontal lobes in people with an acquired PM deficit (e.g., Fortin, Godbout, & Braum, 2003) or through studies linking executive processing with PM performance (e.g., Kliegel, Eschen, & Thone-Otto, 2004; Knight, Titov, & Crawford, 2006; Mantyla, 2003; Marsh & Hicks, 1998; McDaniel, Glisy, Rubin, Guynn, & Routhieaux, 1999; Salthouse, Berish, & Siedlecki, 2004; but see Mathias & Mansfield, 2005).

Most recently, there is early evidence that suggests a special role for one subregion of the frontal lobes: area 10. This region is also rather confusingly referred to in the literature as Brodmann's area 10, rostral prefrontal cortex, anterior prefrontal cortex, frontopolar cortex, or the frontal pole. This is a very interesting brain region. It is very large in humans: In volumetric terms, it is probably the largest single architectonic region of the frontal lobes (Christoff et al., 2001), covering approximately 25 to 30 cubic centimeters (Semendeferi, Armstrong, Schleicher, Zilles, & Van Hoesen, 2001; see Figure 11.1). It is also in relative terms much larger in the human brain than in other animals, including the great apes (Semendeferi et al., 2001; but see Holloway, 2002). Additionally, this region is probably the last to achieve myelination, and it has been argued that tardily myelinating areas engage in complex functions highly related to the organism's experience (Fuster, 1997). These are all good reasons to imagine that the rostral prefrontal cortex may support cognitive processing which is especially important to humans. Very recent evidence seems to suggest that this brain region may play a critical part in supporting the processes that enable PM, which is perhaps one of the behavioral functions that most distinguishes humans from other animals (see, e.g., Einstein et al., 2005). This chapter is a review of the currently available evidence, which comes from two main sources. The first is lesion evidence; the second is evidence from functional brain imaging.

---

[1] Delegates at the Second International Conference on Prospective Memory held in Zurich, Switzerland, in July 2005 voted to use the abbreviation PM in the future to refer to prospective memory. It should be noted, however, that this vote was not carried with an overwhelming majority, and elegant and principled arguments were presented in favor of other abbreviations, especially by Peter Graf.

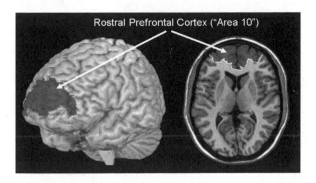

FIGURE 11.1   Approximate location of rostral prefrontal cortex, or Area 10 of the human brain (shaded in dark gray). It is the most anterior part of the brain, located just behind the forehead. The panel on the left shows the whole brain, with the front of the brain facing forward. The panel on the right is a transverse slice through the brain that shows the approximate depth of rostral prefrontal cortex. A simple way of understanding the orientation of this transverse slice is to imagine that the top of someone's head has been cut off, and the picture is what you would see if you were looking down into the skull.

AREA 10 AND PROSPECTIVE MEMORY: HUMAN LESION EVIDENCE

Perhaps the easiest way of making a link between the functions of particular brain regions and prospective memory would be to find a series of people with circumscribed cerebral involvement who have either isolated PM impairments (i.e., show no impairment on any other kind of test), or show isolated impairments at different stages of remembering to carry out a delayed intention. However, to our knowledge this has not yet occurred. Of course, this could be because the appropriate patient has not yet been discovered. However, it is also possible that this is consistent with a view of prospective memory as a function rather than a construct, where *a function* is an observable set of behaviors evinced in pursuit of a particular contextually defined purpose, and *constructs* are hypothetical processing resources used in support of many functions (e.g., memory, attention, etc.; see Burgess, Alderman et al., 2006, for definitions of functions and constructs). On this account, many theoretically independent processing resources (e.g., sustained attention, retrospective memory, inhibition, etc.) work together to enable the behavior called prospective memory. Consistent with this account is the view that these resources are used to enable other forms of behavior as well. If this is correct, then a processing impairment that produces a PM deficit will also be likely to cause observable deficits in other functions. Indeed, it is central to the notion of central processes in the field of executive functions that executive control processes contribute to a range of different behaviors, and low process–behavior correspondence is therefore concomitant (see Burgess, 1997, for further details).

Prima facie, this complicates investigations. However, this situation, if true, actually means that examining the symptoms that coexist with the PM ones, and the situations in which they occur, can give a key insight into the processing components of PM. Indeed, in this way, to study only performance on PM tests would be a mistake. Instead, one ideally needs to understand the totality of the clinical picture of which a PM deficit is one component. This is most likely to give the concordant evidence that is required to characterize the central process. We illustrate this point next by demonstrating that prospective failures in everyday life, even where they occur in the context of unimpaired intellect, retrospective memory, or problem-solving skills, usually do so in the context of a specific problem with behavioral organization, of which PM problems are one symptom.

PROSPECTIVE MEMORY FAILURES AS ONE SYMPTOM OF A WIDER SYNDROME

What would the everyday behavior of a person with a severe acquired PM deficit look like? If every intended action that could not be enacted immediately was not carried out, or was executed out of sequence, or in response only to environmental prompts, then the result would be widespread behavioral disorganization, not just failure on PM tests.

Perhaps the first description of such a person was reported 70 years ago. Penfield and Evans (1935) described the symptoms that Penfield's sister was experiencing after the removal of a right frontal glioma:

> She had planned to get a simple supper for one guest and four members of her family. She looked forward to it with pleasure and had the whole day for preparation. When the appointed hour arrived she was in the kitchen, the food was all there, one or two things were on the stove, but the salad was not ready, the meat had not been started and she was distressed and confused by her long continued effort alone. (p. 131).

This impairment in carrying out daily activities would not have been remarkable were it the case that the patient was suffering from serious disabilities in basic cognitive systems (e.g., classic dense amnesia, visuospatial/perceptual or agnosic problems, disorders of motor control, etc.). However this was not the case with Penfield and Evans's patient, nor with others who were soon reported (e.g., Ackerly & Benton, 1947; Brickner, 1936). These established, at least on the grounds of clinical observation alone, that this kind of behavioral disorganization can be seen in the absence of these kinds of impairments.

However, it was not until 50 years after Penfield and Evans's paper that an attempt was made to isolate the critical cognitive deficit underpinning this disorder. Eslinger and Damasio (1985) described the case of EVR, who had undergone surgical removal of a large bilateral frontal meningioma. At the time of his operation, EVR was a financial officer with a small company and a respected member of his community. He was married and the father of two children; his brothers and sisters considered him a role model and a natural leader. After the operation however, EVR lost his job, went bankrupt, was divorced by his wife, and moved in with his parents. He subsequently married a prostitute and was divorced again within 2 years. Extensive psychological evaluations found no deficit; in fact, he was superior or above average on most tests (e.g., Verbal IQ of 125; Performance IQ of 124; no difficulty on Wisconsin Card Sorting Test [WCST]). He was also able to discuss intelligently matters such as the economy, foreign affairs, financial matters, and moral dilemmas. Despite these normal findings, EVR was often unable to make simple everyday decisions, such as which toothpaste to buy, what restaurant to go to, or what to wear. He would instead make endless comparisons and contrasts, often being completely unable to come to a decision at all. Further, Eslinger and Damasio (1985) reported PM problems: "It was as if he forgot to remember short- and intermediate-term goals" (p. 1737).

Eslinger and Damasio's (1985) paper was particularly important because it was the first convincing demonstration that this level of behavioral disorganization could occur in the context of intact intellect, and intact performance on some tests traditionally thought to be sensitive to deficits in "frontal lobe" executive functions. However, it was not possible to determine from this case alone whether the emotional and psychosocial problems that EVR displayed were necessarily linked to his prospective memory problems, or whether they were just associated deficits resulting from a large frontal lesion. Scientific progress on this front was limited at that time by two interlinked shortcomings: (a) No qualitative assessment had yet been undertaken of these kinds of patients' everyday life problems, and (b) no laboratory task had been developed that a priori reflected these difficulties. Without a qualitative assessment, one could not begin to determine the range of behaviors under examination, or the characteristics of the situations that presented problems for the patients, and without a representative laboratory task there was no simple "model of the world" that could form the basis for scientific investigation of the disorder at an information processing level.

DISORGANIZATION IN EVERYDAY LIFE: FROM OBSERVATION TO EXPERIMENTATION

Shallice and Burgess (1991), however, addressed these issues. They presented three patients who had all suffered frontal lobe damage following traumatic brain injury. All three had no significant impairment on formal tests of perception, language, and intelligence, and two performed well on a variety of traditional tests of executive function. Indeed, one of these cases (AP) was probably the best example of the syndrome so far reported (this case was later called NM by Metzler & Parkin, 2000). AP had sustained an open head injury in a road-traffic accident when he was in his early 20s. The injury caused a virtually complete removal of the rostral prefrontal cortex bilaterally plus damage to surrounding regions. On standard neuropsychological measures of intellectual functioning, memory, perception, and even traditional tests of executive function, AP performed within the superior range.

This is not to say that AP was unimpaired in other regards, however (Metzler & Parkin, 2000; Shallice & Burgess, 1991). The most noticeable of these in everyday life was a marked multitasking and PM problem. This manifested itself as tardiness and disorganization, the severity of which ensured that despite his excellent intellect and social skills, he never managed to make a return to work at the level he had enjoyed premorbidly. Shallice and Burgess (1991) invented two new tests of multitasking to assess these problems. The first of these tests, called the Multiple Errands Test (MET), is a real-life multitasking test carried out in a shopping center. Participants have to complete a number of tasks, principally involving shopping in an unfamiliar shopping center, while following a set of rules (e.g., no shop should be entered other than to buy something). The tasks vary in terms of complexity (e.g., buy a small loaf of bread vs. discover the exchange rate of the Euro yesterday), and there are a number of "hidden" problems in the tasks that have to be appreciated and the possible courses of action evaluated (e.g., one item asks that participants write and send a postcard, yet they are given no pen, and although they cannot use anything not bought on the street to help them, they are also told they need to spend as little money as possible). In this way, the task is quite open-ended or ill-structured (i.e., there are many possible courses of action, and it is up to the individuals to determine for themselves which one they will choose).

The second task that Shallice and Burgess (1991) invented was a more controlled experimental task (the Six Element Test [SET]). This requires participants to swap efficiently among three simple subtasks, each divided into two sections within 15 minutes, while following some arbitrary rules (e.g., You cannot do Part A of a subtask followed immediately by Part B of the same subtask). There are no cues as to when to switch tasks, and although a clock is present, it is covered, so that checking it has to be a deliberate action. Thus this paradigm has a strong component of voluntary time-based task switching, one form of PM.

Despite their excellent general cognitive skills, AP and the other cases reported by Shallice and Burgess (1991) all performed these tasks below the 5% level compared with age- and IQ-matched controls. On the MET, the participants made a range of types of errors, many of which could be interpreted as PM failures. For instance, they would find themselves having to go into the same shop more than once to buy items that could all have been bought at one visit; not completing tasks that they had previously learned that they needed to do; not remembering to come over to the experimenter and tell them what they had bought when leaving a shop (a prelearned task rule); or going outside the boundaries of the shopping center (at the start of the test participants are shown the boundaries and told not to cross them; see Figure 11.2). They also made a range of social behavior errors (e.g., leaving a shop without paying, offering sexual favors in lieu of payment). Shallice and Burgess rather inelegantly termed this kind of behavioral disorganization in the context of preserved intellect and other cognitive functions the "strategy application disorder."

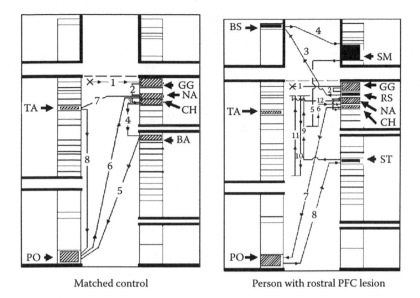

Matched control   Person with rostral PFC lesion

FIGURE 11.2 Performance of a patient with rostral prefrontal cortex damage on the Multiple Errands Test (Shallice & Burgess, 1991), and a typical control matched for age, sex, and estimated premorbid IQ (NART). The patient took twice as long as the control yet failed to complete a number of tasks (the control completed them all). He also went out of bounds (boundary indicated by hatched line at end of street), entered shops more times than was needed, entered shops that were not necessary for the task, and made a number of task and social rule breaks. The patient was, however, able to repeat the task rules correctly both before and after the test.

It was not possible on the basis of Shallice and Burgess's (1991) data, however, to speculate on the anatomical localization of the lesion critical for this pattern of deficit, as the patients had suffered large traumatic lesions. Two years later, however, Goldstein, Bernard, Fenwick, Burgess, and McNeil (1993) described a case that began to suggest a possible locus. This 51-year-old right-handed man (GN) had undergone a left frontal lobectomy 2.5 years earlier following the discovery of a frontal lobe tumor (mixed astrocytoma-oligodendroglioma). A 5-cm resection of the left frontal lobe from the frontal pole was undertaken. From the point of view of traditional neuropsychological tests, this surgery made little difference to his cognitive abilities (e.g., Verbal IQ of 129, Performance IQ of 111; Story Recall Immediate 75–90th percentile, Delayed 50–70th percentile; Rey–Osterreith Delayed Figure Recall 80–90th percentile; Trail-Making 70–75th percentile). However, this did not reflect the change in his everyday competence. The patient had held a senior management position within an international company, but 2 years after surgery he had to take medical retirement because of increasing lethargy. He worked from home as a freelance management consultant, but had difficulty making decisions, culminating in his taking 2 weeks to decide which slides to use for a work presentation but never actually reaching a decision. He also experienced anger control difficulties.

Goldstein et al. (1993) administered Shallice and Burgess's (1991) MET. GN made significantly more errors than controls, being less efficient (e.g., having to return to a shop), breaking task rules (e.g., using a stamp that another customer gave him), misinterpreting tasks (e.g., sticking the stamp on the wrong card), and failing to complete some tasks altogether, reporting that he had known he had to do them but somehow "forgot" them. He also showed some social rule breaks. For instance, he had forgotten to find out the price of tomatoes while in the grocery store earlier, and realizing that he should not go back into the shop unless he was to buy something, he very conspicuously climbed onto the fruit display outside the shop and peered in the shop window.

This case, and others reported in the literature, show a remarkably similar pattern of neuropsychological test performance. Burgess (2000b) summarized the performance of eight well-known cases: None of the cases had any language or visuoperceptual impairment, and all scored within the superior range on tests of current intellectual functions. Four of the seven showed no impairment on any memory test. Furthermore, two showed no impairment on a range of clinical executive function tests known to be sensitive to frontal lobe lesions. Moreover, no executive test had been failed by more than two of the eight cases. Most remarkably, two tasks had been administered to all the patients—the WCST and Verbal Fluency—and had been performed well by every case. This contrasts with the observation that all of the reported cases of strategy application disorder who had been given either the MET or SET had failed at least one of them.

THE RELATION BETWEEN PROSPECTIVE MEMORY AND LONG-TERM MULTITASKING

The kind of multitasking just described critically requires PM. Multitasking is a behavioral-level description that has a precise meaning in cognitive neuroscience. Burgess (2000a, 2000b) describes eight features of a situation that requires multitasking, the first five of which are axiomatic, plus a further three that are usually true of everyday-life multitasking situations:

Many tasks. A number of discrete and different tasks have to be completed.
Interleaving required. Performance on these tasks needs to be dovetailed to be time-effective.
One task at a time. Due to either cognitive or physical constraints, only one task can be performed at any one time.
Delayed intentions. The times for returns to task are not signaled directly by the situation.
No immediate feedback. There is no moment-by-moment performance feedback of the sort that participants in many laboratory experiments will receive. Typically, failures are not signaled when they occur.

Interruptions and unexpected outcomes. Unforeseen interruptions, sometimes of high priority, will occasionally occur, and things will not always
go as planned.

Differing task characteristics. Tasks usually differ in terms of priority, difficulty, and the length of time they will occupy.

Self-determined targets. People decide for themselves what constitutes adequate performance.

In this way, multitasking may be different, at least in some regards, in the information processing demands it makes from multiple-task performance, which is
where someone is performing several tasks simultaneously (or dual-tasking where
there are two tasks; e.g., Baddeley, Della Salla, Gray, Papagno, & Spinnler, 1997).
Prototypical dual- or multiple-task situations are air traffic control, or operating
a computer while talking to someone on a telephone. There is little obvious PM
demand in dual-task situations because the retention interval over which an intention is to be maintained is typically so short. By contrast, many real-life multitasking situations involve the coordination and dovetailing of many activities over
longer time scales (e.g., Alderman, Burgess, Knight, & Henman, 2003). These typically require one to perform one particular task at a time (e.g., writing a scientific
paper) while bearing in mind that other unrelated tasks have to be performed
before completion of this task (e.g., collect the car from the shop at 1 p.m.) and often
having to periodically check the state of something else (e.g., has the expected e-mail
arrived yet?). In other words, multitasking and multiple-task situations share characteristics 1 and 2 above (plus in some situations 5), but only multitasking has
characteristics 3 and 4. These characteristics necessitate the involvement of PM
(e.g., Kvavilashvili & Ellis, 1996) or the carrying out of an intended action—in this
case a task switch—after a delay. Indeed, we would argue that the most common
example of a PM action in everyday life is in the dovetailing of one's daily activities. Without this ability, one's behavior would be very inefficient. For instance, one
would have to always finish one task (e.g., cooking the vegetables for a meal) before
starting another (e.g., cooking other parts of the main meal), and operations that
involve the integration of many subgoals (e.g., visiting a number of different shops
during one shopping trip) would be performed highly inefficiently.

WHAT ARE THE CRITICAL BRAIN REGIONS
THAT SUPPORT THE PROSPECTIVE MEMORY
COMPONENT OF MULTITASKING?

There is now some evidence that this PM component of multitasking can be
localized. The largest human group lesion study to date in this area was published by Burgess, Veitch, Costello, and Shallice (2000), who examined a series
of 60 acute neurological patients (approximately three quarters of whom were
suffering from brain tumors) and 60 age- and IQ-matched healthy controls on a
multitasking test called the Greenwich Test. In this test, participants are presented

with three different simple tasks and told that they have to attempt at least some of each of the tasks in 10 minutes, while following a set of rules. One of these rules relates to all subtests ("In all three tasks, completing a red item will gain you more points than completing an item of any other color") and there are four task-specific rules (e.g., "In the tangled lines test you must not mark the paper other than to write your answers down"). Thus this is a multitasking test where the majority of the variance in performance of the test comes from rule infractions rather than task-switching problems. The Greenwich Test was administered in a form that allowed consideration of the relative contributions of task rule learning and remembering, planning, plan following, and remembering one's actions to overall multitasking performance. Specifically, before participants began the test, their ability to learn the task rules (by both spontaneous and cued recall) was measured; this measure was called learn. They were then asked how they intended to do the test, and a measure of the complexity and appropriateness of their plans was gained (a variable called plan). This enabled us to look at whether their failures could be due to poor planning (see Kliegel, McDaniel, & Einstein, 2000; Kliegel, Phillips, Lwemke, & Kopp, 2005, for a similar approach). The participants then performed the task itself and, by comparing what they did with what they had planned to do, a measure of plan following was made. Multitasking performance (the number of task switches minus the number of rule breaks) was referred to as the test score. After these stages were finished, participants were asked to recollect their own actions by describing in detail what they had done (variable name: recount). Finally, delayed memory for the task rules was examined (remember).

A basic finding was that this sort of procedure is sensitive to a range of cognitive problems: Despite no differences between the controls and patients on measures of premorbid (NART) or current fluid intelligence (Raven's Advanced Progressive Matrices), the patients showed significant impairment on most of the variables (a similar finding is reported by Levine et al., 2000). At a more specific level, however, lesions in different brain regions were associated with impairment at different stages in the multitasking procedure. Lesions to a large region of superior posterior medial cortex including the left posterior cingulate and forceps major gave deficits on all measures except planning. Remembering task contingencies after a delay was also affected by lesions in the region of the anterior cingulate. Critically, however, Burgess et al. (2000) found that patients with left hemisphere rostral prefrontal cortex lesions, when compared with patients with lesions elsewhere, showed a significant multitasking impairment (i.e., the variable score) despite no significant impairment on remembering task rules (remember variable). Indeed, the left rostral prefrontal cases showed no significant impairment on any variable except the one reflecting multitasking performance. In other words, despite being able to learn the task rules, form a plan, remember their actions, and say what they should have done, they nevertheless did not do what they said that they intended to do. This can make a striking impression when one is administering the test: The participant says, for example, that he or she will attempt Tasks X, Y, and Z in that order, and may even say how long he or she intends to spend on each, plus describes how he or she will follow the task rules (e.g., "I will replace the lid on the bead box every time I take a bead out of the bead box."). However, after starting the test just a minute or so later, the participant will actually not carry out any of these intended acts.

This link between rostral prefrontal cortex damage and this PM component of multitasking accorded well with the lesion location of Goldstein et al.'s (1993) previous single case. Moreover, two of the original three patients reported by Shallice and Burgess (1991) also had lesions affecting the rostral parts of the left frontal lobe. However, a specific problem is presented by other findings. Thus one of Shallice and Burgess's (1991) cases had principally a right frontal lesion. Moreover, Levine and colleagues (e.g., Levine, Freedman, Dawson, Black, & Stuss, 1999; Levine et al., 2000; Levine et al., 1998) have repeatedly implicated right hemisphere lesions in poor performance on their multitasking test, the R-SAT. As Levine et al. (2000) pointed out, these apparently conflicting results may be a result of the use of multitasking tests with differing characteristics: The Burgess et al. (2000) study applied a test where the variable taken as an estimate of multitasking ability was based principally on rule following rather than task switching. However, Levine et al.'s task (R-SAT) is more similar to Shallice and Burgess's (1991) original SET, in that the emphasis is on voluntary time-based task switching rather than rule following. So the lesion location differences could occur if task switching and rule following are not equivalent in information processing terms. This is certainly plausible with reference to the known characteristics of event- or time-based PM (see, e.g., Kvavilashvili & Ellis, 1996). Moreover, a recent group study of real-world multitasking in mixed etiology neurological patients (Alderman et al., 2003) demonstrated a double dissociation between rule following and failures to initiate tasks. An alternative possibility, however, is that the difference between the findings of Levine's group and Burgess's group may instead be due to the differing populations studied by them: Levine's finding are based principally on traumatic brain injury, but the Burgess et al. (2000) study used acute circumscribed lesions (principally tumors).

A resolution to this apparent paradox was provided by a recent human group lesion study by Burgess, Veitch, and Costello (reported in Burgess, Gilbert et al., 2006). In this study, a new version of the Burgess et al. (1996) SET of multitasking was given to 69 acute neurological patients with circumscribed focal lesions and 60 healthy adults, using the administration framework of Burgess et al. (2000). The SET differs from the Greenwich Test in that the multitasking score reflects mainly voluntary time-based switching rather than rule following. Compared with other patients, those whose lesions involving the rostral prefrontal regions of the right hemisphere made significantly fewer voluntary task switches, attempted fewer subtasks, and spent far longer on individual subtasks. They did not, however, make a larger number of rule breaks (in contrast to the left rostral patients in the Burgess et al., 2000, study). As with the study of Burgess et al. (2000), these multitasking deficits could not be attributed to deficits in general intellectual functioning, rule knowledge, planning, or retrospective memory.

Considering now the previous single case studies in the context of these group study findings, it is clear that there is a remarkably consistent finding of involvement of Area 10 in patients who have high-level disorganization in everyday life. For instance, in the six cases reviewed by Burgess (2000b) for whom good brain scan data were available, all of them had rostral prefrontal cortex involvement of either the left or right hemisphere (or both). In addition to these cases, we might now also add the recent case of Bird, Castelli, Malik, Frith, and Husain (2004) who had suffered a rare form of stroke affecting the medial aspects of Area 10 bilaterally, and who failed the SET, despite passing some other executive tests (e.g., the WCST). It seems likely that PM problems (and therefore multitasking ones) are just one indicator of the problems these unfortunate people experience.

SUMMARY OF EVIDENCE FROM HUMAN LESION STUDIES

Although it is a widespread belief that human lesion studies show that PM must be supported in part by the frontal lobes (e.g. Cockburn, 1995), there is actually surprisingly little direct evidence (see, e.g., Daum & Mayes, 2000). However, what little evidence there is broadly supports this view. We have argued here that some of the critical components supported by the frontal lobes that contribute to PM also contribute to other behaviors. In this way we expect that patients with even relatively isolated PM deficits will show concomitant deficits (i.e., will fail tests other than PM ones, if the appropriate procedure is given). However, there is now enough evidence to suggest that these concomitant deficits need not be in the domains of language, simple memory (e.g. recognition), perception, or even those abilities indexed by performance on many traditional executive function tests (e.g., Tower of London, WCST). There is also enough evidence to suggest that, more specifically, rostral prefrontal cortex plays a critical part in the ability to carry out what you intended to do after a delay, beyond what can be explained by planning or retrospective memory. So what is the nature of this processing impairment that can leave so many domains of cognition intact but cause PM failures and also other symptoms (e.g., social behavior abnormalities)?

THE ROLE OF ROSTRAL PREFRONTAL CORTEX IN PROSPECTIVE MEMORY: NEUROIMAGING EVIDENCE

Working on the basis that deficits in PM were the core impairment in rostral patients with multitasking deficits, Burgess, Quayle, and Frith (2001) tested the link between rostral prefrontal cortex and PM using positron emission tomography (PET). Regional cerebral blood flow (rCBF) increases in lateral Brodmann's area (BA) 10 were indeed found in PM conditions relative to the ongoing task alone. This finding was in agreement with that of Okuda et al. (1998), who also found increases in the left frontal pole. However, Okuda et al. were unable to determine whether this activation was associated with intention maintenance, target detection, or the requirement for "dividing attention between the planned action and the routine activity" (p. 127). The Burgess et al. (2001) study helped in this respect, by including a condition where participants were told that an intention cue or target might appear, but none actually did. Critically, rCBF increases in lateral BA 10 were also discovered in this condition, where there is only the expectation of an intention cue, and a cue is never witnessed or responded to. Thus lateral BA 10 is more involved with the maintenance of an intention rather than cue recognition or intention execution.

A second PET study confirmed the role of lateral BA 10 in PM conditions, but also showed that medial BA 10 is more active in ongoing conditions than PM ones (Burgess, Scott, & Frith, 2003). Furthermore, medial BA 10 was also more active (compared with PM conditions) in a simple attentional baseline condition where the participant just responded as fast as possible to any change on the display.

The two Burgess et al. PET studies had used a conjunction experimental design in which one investigates hemodynamic changes common to tasks that putatively stress the process of interest (Shallice, 1988) but where the other demands of the tasks are made quite different, by, for example, using spatial material for one and verbal for the other. Accordingly, Burgess et al. (2003) interpreted their results as suggesting that the functions supported by BA 10 in PM are "central" in the respect that they are material nonspecific, and unrelated to precise intention retrieval or cue recognition demands. Instead, Burgess et al. favored an explanation in terms of one of the possibilities raised by Okuda et al. (1998), that the rostral prefrontal cortex rCBF changes were related to the attentional demands made by having to "bear in mind" an intention while performing an ongoing task.

Simons, Schölvinck, Gilbert, Frith, and Burgess (2006) explicitly tested this hypothesis by measuring brain activity (using functional MRI [fMRI] and a conjunction of two different PM tasks: words and shapes) while manipulating the demands on either recognizing the appropriate context to act (cue identification) or remembering the action to be performed (intention retrieval). In the word task, each trial consisted of two nouns presented next to each other in the middle of the screen, one of which was written in uppercase and the other in lowercase letters. For ongoing trials, participants were instructed to indicate using a keypad whether the left or the right word contained more letters. However, if the words belonged to the same semantic category (e.g., *cow* and *horse*), a different key was to be pressed (cue identification PM condition). Furthermore, if the words were written in the same case, participants were required to count up the syllables of both words and indicate using the keypad whether the total was four or less, or higher than four (intention retrieval PM condition).

The stimuli in the shape task consisted of a 4 × 4 grid, in which a colored triangle and a random other shape, such as a pentagon, were presented. For ongoing trials, participants were instructed to indicate whether the shape that was not the triangle was presented to the left or the right of the triangle. However, if the two shapes were, spatially, a chess knight's move away from each other, participants were instructed to press a different key (cue identification PM condition). In the intention retrieval PM condition, if the two shapes were of the same color, participants were required to determine the number of sides of the shape other than the triangle, and indicate whether this number was below or equal to five, or above five (intention retrieval PM condition).

A consistent pattern of hemodynamic changes was found in anterior prefrontal cortex (BA 10) across both types of tasks, and across both PM conditions (compared with the ongoing task): There was activation in lateral BA 10, which was

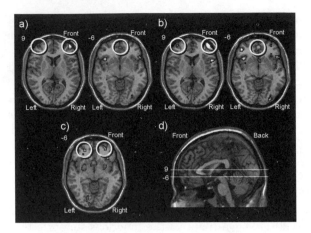

FIGURE 11.3 Data from Simons, Schölvinck, Gilbert, Frith, and Burgess (2006) indicating that cue identification and intention retrieval components of prospective memory have a largely common neural basis in anterior prefrontal cortex (BA 10). Activations of principal interest are circled. Z coordinates are shown in the top left corner of each axial image, and the inferior–superior location of the slices is indicated on the sagittal projection shown in (d). (a) Contrasting the cue identification PM trials with ongoing trials, bilateral BA 10 activation (9 slice), and medial BA 10 deactivation (-6 slice) was observed. A highly similar pattern is shown in (b), the intention retrieval PM versus ongoing contrast. Differences between conditions emerge in (c), the direct intention retrieval PM > cue identification PM contrast, with significantly greater activation in anterior prefrontal cortex bilaterally in the intention retrieval PM condition, and evidence of deactivation in medial anterior BA 10.

accompanied by deactivation in medial BA 10. However, direct comparison of the high intention retrieval demand with the high cue recognition demand PM conditions also revealed greater activation in lateral BA regions bilaterally in the intention retrieval condition. These regions were located somewhat more medially than those that showed activation common to both conditions (see Figure 11.3). Simons et al. (2006) argued that the regions that were activated in both PM conditions may reflect the requirement in PM tasks for the biasing of attention between external events (e.g., identifying the cue amid distracting stimuli) and internal thought processes (i.e., maintaining the intention and remembering the intended actions). However, it also seems from the comparison of the two PM conditions that there are some subregions of BA 10 that are more sensitive to particular PM task characteristics.

Further evidence for the specificity of some regions of BA 10 comes from a recent paper by Okuda et al. (2006). In two PET studies, brain activity associated with time-based versus event-based PM tasks was examined. In the time-based condition of the first study, young healthy volunteers were asked to make a response based on their self-estimation of the passage of time while engaged in an attention-demanding ongoing activity. In the time-based condition of the second study, participants had a clock available. Both studies showed activation differences in rostral prefrontal cortex (principally BA 10) according to whether the task was time- or event-based.

In Study 1, participants performed two prospective memory tasks (time, event) and a baseline task requiring the ongoing activity alone. The ongoing activity was a serial addition task. A digit, randomly selected from one to nine, was presented binaurally every 3 seconds and the participants were required to add up the digits one by one and report the sum immediately after the presentation of each digit. The prospective response was to clench both hands. In the time-based task, the participants were asked to make the prospective response once during the first 30 seconds, twice during the next 30 seconds, once during the third 30 seconds, and once during the last 30 seconds after the task started. In the event-based task, they were asked to make the prospective memory response when a cue stimulus (the number 7) was presented during the ongoing activity. The cue stimulus was presented once during the first 30 seconds, twice during the next 30 seconds, once during the third 30 seconds, and once during the last 30 seconds. Okuda et al. (2006) found in this experiment that an area of left lateral superior rostral prefrontal cortext (BA 9/10; peak coordinates $x = -16$, $y = 48$, $z = 24$) was more active during the time-based PM condition than during either the event-based PM one or the ongoing task alone (see Figure 11.4).

Okuda et al.'s (submitted) second experiment used a conjunction design, looking at the activations common to two different PM tasks: verbal or nonverbal, each presented in three conditions (time PM, event PM, ongoing task only). In the verbal tasks, the ongoing task required the participants, when presented with pairs of words, to make a same–different judgment based on the number of syllables in each word. For the ongoing task of the nonverbal conditions, participants were presented with a pair of rectangles and had to judge if the shapes were identical, regardless of their orientation. In the time PM conditions of each task, a clock was always presented at the center of the screen, which updated every 1 second to indicate current time from the start of the task. Participants were asked to press a button every 1 minute after starting the task, and were told that they could use the information of the clock to help them. In the event PM conditions, participants were asked to press a button whenever they encountered a cue stimulus, which was the word *guitar* in the verbal tasks or exact squares in the nonverbal tasks.

In contrast to the first study, a region of increased rCBF was found in left lateral rostral prefrontal cortex during the event-based PM conditions compared with the time-based conditions (Figure 11.4c). This region was somewhat inferior within BA 10 to that found in Experiment 1 (Figure 11.4a). Across both studies, rCBF in the rostro-medial prefrontal cortical regions increased during the time-based task and the ongoing-alone task as compared with the event-based task. These regions were more rostral, superior, and closer to the midline than the medial BA 10 regions identified in Experiment 1. (The aspect of exactly *where* within BA 10 the activations occurred will become important in the discussion of the functions of BA 10 later.) It is probably too early within our understanding both of the dynamics of PM tasks and of the functional architecture of BA 10 to

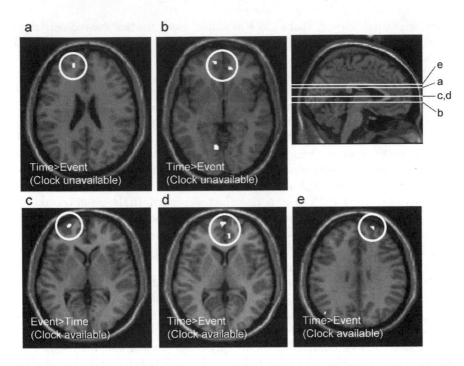

FIGURE 11.4 Areas of activation during time- and event-based prospective memory tasks according to Okuda et al. (2006). Activation foci, encircled with a white ring, were superimposed on horizontal sections of anatomical MRI of the standard brain. (a) and (b) show greater activation during time-based tasks than during event-based tasks, where participants had to estimate timing for time-based prospective response (Study 1). (c) shows greater activation during event-based tasks than during time-based tasks, where a clock was available for time-based prospective response (Study 2). (d) and (e) show greater activation during time-based tasks than during event-based tasks in Study 2. The top right panel shows the height level of each section (white lines) within the brain on a midsagittal section of the standard anatomical MRI.

reach a full explanation of these results. However, they do seem to suggest that brain activity in the rostral prefrontal cortex shows different patterns during the performance of time- and event-based PM tasks. Furthermore, they seem to suggest that subregions of BA 10 are differentially involved in time-based tasks according to whether or not a clock is present as an aid to the passage of time. One possibility to explain this latter phenomenon that relates to the explanation of the Simons et al. (2006) findings earlier is that having a clock available increases the degree to which the participant attends to environmental stimuli rather than maintaining a continually updated, self-generated representation of the passage of time. In other words, it changes the relative amount of stimulus-oriented or stimulus-independent attending.

FROM PROSPECTIVE MEMORY TO THE "GATEWAY HYPOTHESIS" OF BA 10 FUNCTION

In a series of experiments in our lab, we have investigated this possibility that BA 10 is sensitive to differences in the degree to which cognition is stimulus-oriented or stimulus-independent. If BA 10 supports a mechanism that enables us to either maintain thoughts in our head (i.e., stimulus-independent cognition) while doing something else, or switch between the thoughts in our head and attending to events in the environment (stimulus-oriented attending), then one would indeed expect that BA 10 would play a central role in prospective memory. However, it should not be the only ability that this region supports, because one can conceive of situations that require these psychological functions without having the characteristic of maintaining an intention over a delay period. So if we could design a paradigm that stresses this psychological mechanism but is not a PM task, and it activates BA 10 in a neuroimaging experiment, then this account is lent weight.

Accordingly, three functional neuroimaging experiments carried out in our laboratory investigated the evidence that BA 10 is sensitive to differences in the source of the representations that are currently active in one's mind (for overviews see Burgess, Gilbert, Okuda, & Simon, 2006; Burgess, Simons, Dumontheil, & Gilbert, 2005). On this account, some thoughts are stimulus independent, in the sense that they are self-generated (e.g., inventing a novel story) or are not prompted by things currently experienced or witnessed (e.g., mind wandering). However, some thoughts are directly provoked by, or oriented toward, stimuli that one can see (e.g., reading). In this way, the hypothesis was that BA 10 might act as an attentional gateway between inner mental life and the external world as experienced through the senses.

The first experiment to test this hypothesis was presented by Gilbert, Frith, and Burgess (2005). They contrasted, using fMRI, the neural activation that occurs when people are performing tasks using stimuli presented on a display with activation that occurs when they are performing the same tasks "in their heads." Medial BA 10 was found to be activated in the condition where people are using externally displayed stimuli (i.e., stimulus-oriented attending or SO) compared with when they are doing the same task in the absence of relevant stimuli (stimulus-independent cognition or SI). By contrast, lateral BA 10 activation was observed at the points where participants switched between either condition, regardless of the direction of the switch (i.e., SO -> SI; SI -> SO). Thus the existence of a neural mechanism that arbitrates between stimulus-independent and stimulus-oriented thought received support, and a link between this mechanism and rostral prefrontal cortex seemed a promising line of enquiry. A further fMRI study (Gilbert, Simons, Frith, & Burgess, 2006) demonstrated performance-related activation (i.e., increased activation was associated with faster reaction times) in medial BA 10 in simple reaction time conditions that did not require substantial stimulus processing. Thus the characterization of medial rostral prefrontal cortex as most active when an unusual degree of attention to external stimuli is required was supported.

Burgess et al. then considered the possible role of lateral rostral prefrontal cortex. The findings of a patient's problems with multitasking, and previous functional imaging studies of prospective memory (e.g., Burgess et al., 2001; Burgess et al., 2003), suggest a role for this subregion of BA 10 in stimulus-independent cognition. However, there are different forms of both stimulus-oriented and stimulus-independent attending. So Burgess, Dumontheil, Gilbert, and Frith (submitted) examined the main forms of both to determine whether the lateral–medial distinction holds for all forms, and whether there is evidence for further functional specialization within lateral or medial BA 10. Two quite different tasks were given under four conditions in a conjunction design. The conditions varied in the degree to which they made demands on five attentional constructs, two of which were stimulus oriented (vigilance and stimulus attending) and three of which were stimulus independent in nature (mind wandering, use of self generated representations, and maintenance over a delay). Regardless of the task, conditions stressing both of the stimulus-oriented attentional forms activated medial BA 10, and all three that stressed stimulus-independent cognition activated lateral BA 10 (see Figure 11.5). There was

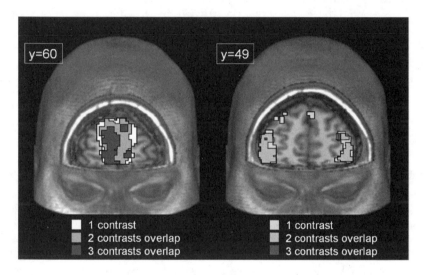

FIGURE 11.5 Results from Burgess, Dumontheil, et al. (submitted). On the left is shown a coronal slice of the brain at $y = 60$. The shades of gray represent the areas of activation, and overlaps between the activations, during three conditions (Conditions 1, 2, and 4) that stressed stimulus-oriented cognition compared with a condition that made a high demand on stimulus-independent thought (Condition 3). So the darkest shaded regions, for instance, indicate that all three stimulus-oriented conditions activated this area: a large region of medial BA 10. On the right is a coronal slice of the brain at $y = 49$, demonstrating a second set of contrasts, and the overlaps between the areas revealed by them. The contrasts compare Conditions 1, 3, and 4, which had a substantial stimulus-independent component, to Condition 2, where attention is just maintained on stimulus-oriented thoughts. Lateral BA 10 regions are revealed by these contrasts, and there is substantial overlap in the location of the activations demonstrated by them.

limited evidence for further functional specialization. Thus the gateway hypothesis did indeed approximate BA 10 findings across a range of conditions and tasks.

FROM THE GATEWAY HYPOTHESIS
BACK TO PROSPECTIVE MEMORY

These results indicate that there may be a general principle for the functional organization of at least some parts of human brain BA 10. This view receives further support from a meta-analysis conducted by Gilbert, Spengler, Simons, Frith, and Burgess (2006). They analyzed the reaction times to paradigms from 104 PET/fMRI studies, yielding 133 independent contrasts. The tasks that had provoked these activations came from a wide range of functions (e.g., memory, mentalizing, perception, and PM). A fascinating general principle emerged. Gilbert, Spengler, Simons, Frith, et al. (2006) found that reaction times to tasks that had provoked lateral BA 10 activations tended to be slower than reaction times in whatever control task had been used. However, reaction times to tasks provoking medial BA 10 activations were, if anything, faster than the control task. The pattern occurred regardless of the type of task under study, and thus seems to be a general principle of BA 10 neuroimaging findings. If lateral BA 10 plays some part in effecting tasks that require the various forms of stimulus-independent cognition as argued here, this pattern would be expected. This is because reaction times to tasks that require attending to stimuli plus some form of stimulus-independent thought (e.g., performing an ongoing task while maintaining an intention, checking for PM cues, etc.) will be longer, typically, than to tasks that only require the stimulus-attending component (e.g., the ongoing task alone). This result also accounts for the consistent findings of rostral prefrontal cortex activation in paradigms where a novel degree of juxtapositione may be expected between stimulus-oriented and stimulus-independent thought, either induced intentionally by the task or because of spontaneous task-irrelevant thoughts (e.g., PM and other multitask and switching paradigms; e.g., Braver & Bongiolatti, 2002; Burgess et al., 2001; Burgess et al., 2003; Dreher, Koechlin, Ali, & Grafman, 2002; Koechlin, Basso, Pietrini, Panzer, & Grafman, 1999; Koechlin, Corrado, Pietrini, & Grafman, 2000; Okuda et al., 1998; Pollmann, 2001, 2004; or memory control processing, e.g., Fletcher & Henson, 2001; Herron, Henson, & Rugg, 2004; see Gilbert, Spengler, Simons, Steele, et al., 2006, for review).

However, although there may be general principles for the organization of BA 10 functions, this does not mean that there is no specialization within these parameters. Thus Gilbert, Spengler, Simons, Steele, et al. (2006) investigated, using the neuroimaging database described earlier, the location of activations within BA 10 according to the type of task being used. They found evidence for specialization of function within BA 10, with mentalizing tasks tending to provoke activations within caudal medial aspects of BA 10, episodic memory tasks (i.e., retrospective memory) being associated with lateral BA 10 activations, and paradigms that required the coordination of two or more activities (including prospective memory) being associated with very rostral activations within BA 10 (see Figure 11.6).

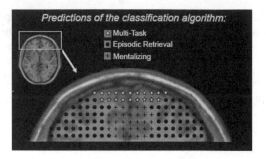

FIGURE 11.6 Results from the classification algorithm developed by Gilbert, Spengler, Simons, Steele, et al. (2006). This figure shows the predicted regions of activation for three types of tasks: those involving episodic retrieval (i.e., retrospective memory), mentalizing (e.g., theory of mind and other metacognitive judgments), and multitasking (any task involving the coordination of more than one task, including prospective memory paradigms). Results are plotted on an axial slice of a normalized T1 weighted image ($z = 0$).

CONCLUSION

There is a gathering consensus among PM researchers that the cognitive resources that underpin the episodic memory aspects of remembering a delayed intention are in some senses separable from those that support the control processing and attentional aspects of performance (e.g., Brandimonte & Passolunghi, 1994; Ellis, Kvavilashvili, & Milne, 1999; Groot, Wilson, Evans, & Watson, 2002; Marsh, Hicks, & Cook, 2005; Maylor, Smith, Della Sala, & Logie, 2002; McDaniel, Guynn, Einstein, & Breneiser, 2004; Park, Hertzog, Kidder, Morrell, & Mayborn, 1997; Sheeran, Webb, & Gollwitzer, 2005; Smith & Bayen, 2006; West, Bowry, & Krompinger, 2006; see also Burgess & Shallice, 1997; chap. 11, this volume; Guynn, chap. 3, this volume; Kliegel, Jäger, Altgassen, & Shum, chap. 13, this volume; Marsh, Hicks, & Cook, chap. 4, this volume; Maylor, chap. 10, this volume; Smith, chap. 2, this volume). On most conceptions, episodic (or retrospective) memory resources are used principally in, for example, maintenance of the intention trace, recognizing the prospective cue, remembering what it was that had to be performed, and so forth. By contrast, the control, executive, or attentional resources are used to effect active rehearsal of the intention; monitoring and maintaining an increased state of preparedness; dividing attention or switching between the ongoing task and intention rumination; determining the allocation of attentional resources to either the ongoing task or to detecting the PM cue; and also strategic and motivational aspects of performance. Indeed, much recent research into the experimental psychology of PM is concentrating on the nature of these attentional resources and the demands made on them by PM tasks (e.g., Cohen, Dixon, Lindsay, & Masson, 2003; Einstein et al., 2005; Hicks, Cook, & Marsh, 2005; McGann, Ellis, & Milne, 2002; Nowinski & Dismukes, 2005; West, Krompinger, & Bowry, 2005; see also Guynn, chap. 3, this volume; Kliegel, Jäger, Altgassen, & Shum, chap. 13, this volume; Marsh, Hicks, & Cook, chap. 4, this volume; McDaniel, Einstein, & Rendell, chap. 7, this volume; Moscovitch, chap. 14, this volume; Phillips, Henry, & Martin, chap. 8, this volume; Smith, chap. 2, this volume). Moreover, it is in support of this resource that many researchers identify the role of frontal lobe structures (e.g. McDaniel et al., 1999).

However, it seems that we can now be a little more precise than referring just to the frontal lobes in general. No doubt processes supported by many structures within the frontal lobes are utilized in the formulation and execution of delayed intentions. However, one subregion of the frontal lobes that seems on present evidence to play a particularly significant role is BA 10, the most anterior aspect of the frontal lobes. Patients with damage to this region show various forms of failing to carry out delayed intentions, and neuroimaging studies of PM paradigms have consistently activated this region. However, patients with damage to this region need not show retrospective memory problems, and neuroimaging studies of episodic memory have tended to associate BA 10 with control or executive aspects of memory. Therefore it seems most plausible at present that the role that the processes that BA 10 supports in PM are bound up with the control or attentional components of PM functions.

As outlined earlier, one hypothesis that we have been pursuing is the role of BA 10 in PM and the requirement that PM tasks make on the active control of stimulus-independent versus stimulus-oriented (or driven) cognition, and especially in the requirement to switch between these attentional modes. This is because actively maintaining an intention while performing some other task necessarily requires stimulus-independent thought (i.e., because you are thinking about something other than what you are currently witnessing), and also stimulus-oriented cognition (i.e., processing stimuli in the performance of the ongoing task), and especially, the dovetailing of the two.

This explanation has the potential to explain many of the findings relating to the performance of different forms of PM tasks. For instance, one might think in these terms when hypothesizing about the processing differences made by (a) time-based PM tasks (when no clock is available) versus event-based PM tasks, and (b) between time-based tasks where a clock is not available and the same task where a clock is available. In the former cases of both examples there is an increased need to maintain a stimulus-independent representation (e.g., a continually updated representation of the passage of time) and therefore considerable switching between this mode of attending and stimulus-oriented attending, as required by the ongoing task. By comparison, in the latter examples one might expect relatively increased attendance to information available in the environment, that is, stimulus-oriented attending.

However, we are at such an early stage of our understanding both of PM and of the functions of BA 10 that this must remain a hypothesis at present. In particular, although our experimental findings have emphasized a medial/lateral BA 10 functional distinction, the results from our meta-analyses suggest that there are additional functional distinctions to be made in BA 10 along a rostral-caudal dimension, and that this may relate somehow to the varying demands that PM tasks make on retrospective memory versus executive control processing. Moreover, we have yet to discover how the processes supported by BA 10 that we suggest are involved in PM may also be used in the furtherance of other behaviors. For instance, (a) our lab has also shown substantial BA 10 activations that are provoked by context memory paradigms, and these seem to show anatomical overlap with some of those activated by both PM and SI/SO attentional switching paradigms (Simons, Gilbert, Owen, Fletcher, & Burgess, 2005; Simons, Owen, Fletcher, & Burgess, 2005), and (b) prospective memory failures do not seem to be the only symptom shown by patients with rostral prefrontal cortex damage. Clearly we still have a great deal to learn. However, progress both in our understanding of the experimental and motivational psychology of PM, and also in the neuroscience of PM, has been so rapid over the last 10 years that there must be considerable hope for our future understanding of this important human behavior, and how the brain supports it. Moreover, it seems increasingly likely that progress in both fields will go hand-in-hand.

REFERENCES

Ackerly, S. S., & Benton, A. L. (1947). Report of a case of bilateral frontal lobe defect. *Research Publications: Association for Research in Nervous and Mental Disease, 27,* 479–504.

Alderman, N., Burgess, P. W., Knight, C., & Henman, C. (2003). Ecological validity of a simplified version of the multiple errands shopping test. *Journal of the International Neuropsychological Society, 9,* 31–44.

Baddeley, A., Della Salla, S., Gray, C., Papagno, C., & Spinnler, H. (1997). Testing central executive functioning with a pencil-and-paper test. In P. Rabbitt (Ed.), *Methodology of frontal and executive function* (pp. 61–80). Hove, UK: Psychology Press.

Bird, C. M., Castelli, F., Malik, O., Frith, U., Husain, M. (2004). The impact of extensive medial frontal lobe damage on theory of mind and cognition. *Brain, 127,* 914–928.

Brickner, R. M. (1936). *The intellectual functions of the frontal lobes: A study based upon observation of a man after partial bilateral frontal lobectomy.* New York: Macmillan.

Burgess, P. W. (1997). Theory and methodology in executive function research. In P. Rabbitt (Ed.), *Methodology of frontal and executive function* (pp. 81–116). Hove, UK: Taylor & Francis.

Burgess, P. W. (2000a). Real-world multitasking from a cognitive neuroscience perspective. In S. Monsell & J. Driver (Eds.), *Control of cognitive processes: Attention and performance XVIII* (pp. 465–472). Cambridge, MA: MIT Press.

Burgess, P. W. (2000b). Strategy application disorder: The role of the frontal lobes in human multitasking. *Psychological Research, 63,* 279–288.

Burgess, P. W., Alderman, N., Emslie, H., Evans, J. J., Wilson, B. A., & Shallice, T. (1996). The simplified six element test. In B. A. Wilson, N. Alderman, P. W. Burgess, H. Emslie & J. J. Evans (Eds.), *Behavioural assessment of the dysexecutive syndrome.* Bury St. Edmunds, UK: Thames Valley Test Company.

Burgess, P. W., Alderman, N., Forbes, C., Costello, A., Coates, L. M.-A., Dawson, D. R., et al. (2006). The case for the development and use of "ecologically valid" measures of executive function in experimental and clinical neuropsychology. *Journal of the International Neuropsychological Society, 12,* 1–16.

Burgess, P.W., Dumontheil, I., Gilbert, S. J. and Frith, C. D. (submitted) Area 10 (rostral PFC) is involved in the attenuation of many forms of stimulus-oriented vs. stimulus-independent attending.

Burgess, P. W., Gilbert, S. J., Okuda, J., & Simons, J. S. (2006). Rostral prefrontal brain regions (area 10): A gateway between inner thought and the external world? In W. Prinz & N. Sebanz (Eds.), *Disorders of volition* (pp. 373–396). Cambridge, MA: MIT Press.

Burgess, P. W., Quayle, A., & Frith, C. D. (2001). Brain regions involved in prospective memory as determined by positron emission tomography. *Neuropsychologia 39*, 545–555.

Burgess, P. W., Scott, S. K., & Frith, C. D. (2003). The role of the rostral frontal cortex (area 10) in prospective memory: A lateral versus medial dissociation. *Neuropsychologia, 41*, 906–918.

Burgess, P. W. and Shallice, T. (1997) The relationship between prospective and retrospective memory: Neuro psychological evidence. In: M.A. Conway (Ed.) *Cognitive Models of Memory* (pp. 247–272). Hove, UK: Taylor and Francis.

Burgess, P. W., Simons, J. S., Dumontheil, I., & Gilbert, S. J. (2005). The gateway hypothesis of rostral PFC function. In J. Duncan, L. Phillips, & P. McLeod (Eds.), *Measuring the mind: Speed, control and age* (pp. 215–246). London: Oxford University Press.

Burgess, P. W., Veitch, E., Costello, A., & Shallice, T. (2000). The cognitive and neuroanatomical correlates of multitasking. *Neuropsychologia, 38*, 848–863.

Brandimonte, M. A., & Passolunghi, M. C. (1994). The effect of cue-familiarity, cue-distinctiveness, and retention interval on prospective remembering. *Quarterly Journal of Experimental Psychology, 47*, 565–587.

Braver, T. S., & Bongiolatti, S. R. (2002). The role of the frontopolar prefrontal cortex in subgoal processing during working memory. *Neuroimage, 15*, 523–536.

Christoff, K., Prabhakaran, V., Dorfman, J., Zhao, Z., Kroger, J. K., Holyoak, K. J., et al. (2001). Rostrolateral prefrontal cortex involvement in relational integration during reasoning. *Neuroimage, 14*, 1136–1149.

Cockburn, J. (1995). Task interruption in prospective memory: A frontal lobe function? *Cortex, 31*, 87–97.

Cohen, A. L., Dixon, R. A., Lindsay, D. S., & Masson, M. E. (2003). The effect of perceptual distinctiveness on the prospective and retrospective components of prospective memory in young and old adults. *Canadian Journal of Experimental Psychology, 57*, 274–289.

Daum, I., & Mayes, A. R. (2000). Memory and executive function impairments after frontal or posterior cortex lesions. *Behavioral Neurology, 12*, 161–173.

Dreher, J. C., Koechlin, E., Ali, S. O., & Grafman, J. (2002). The roles of timing and task order during task switching. *Neuroimage, 17*, 95–109.

Einstein, G. O., McDaniel, M. A., Thomas, R., Mayfield, S., Shank, H., Morrisette, N., et al. (2005). Multiple processes in prospective memory retrieval: Factors determining monitoring versus spontaneous retrieval. *Journal of Experimental Psychology: General, 134*, 327–342.

Ellis, J., Kvavilashvili, L., & Milne, A. (1999). Experimental tests of prospective remembering: The influence of cue-event frequency on performance. *British Journal of Psychology, 90*, 9–23.

Eslinger, P.J., & Damasio, A. R. (1985). Severe disturbance of higher cognition after bilateral frontal lobe ablation: Patient E.V. R. *Neurology, 35*, 1731–1741.

Fletcher, P. C., & Henson, R. N. (2001). Frontal lobes and human memory: Insights from functional neuroimaging, *Brain, 124* (5), 849–881.

Fortin, S., Godbout, L., & Braum, C. M. (2003). Cognitive structure of executive deficits in frontally lesioned head trauma patients performing activities of daily living. *Cortex, 39*, 273–291.

Fuster, J. M. (1997). *The prefrontal cortex: Anatomy, physiology, and neuropsychology of the frontal lobe.* Philadelphia: Lippincott-Raven.

Gilbert, S. J., Frith, C. D., & Burgess, P. W. (2005). Involvement of rostral prefrontal cortex in selection between stimulus-oriented and stimulus-independent thought. *European Journal of Neuroscience, 21*, 1423–1431.

Gilbert, S. J., Simons, J. S., Frith, C. D., & Burgess, P. W. (2006). Performance-related activity in medial rostral prefrontal cortex (Area 10) during low demand tasks. *Journal of Experimental Psychology: Human Perception and Performance, 32,* 45–58.

Gilbert, S. J., Spengler, S., Simons, J. S., Frith, C. D., & Burgess, P. W. (2006). Differential functions of lateral and medial rostral prefrontal cortex (area 10) revealed by brain–behavior associations. *Cerebral Cortex, 16,* 1783–1789.

Gilbert, S. J., Spengler, S., Simons, J. S., Steele, J. D., Lawrie, S. M., Frith, C. D., et al. (2006). Functional specialization within rostral prefrontal cortex (area 10): A meta-analysis. *Journal of Cognitive Neuroscience, 18,* 932–948.

Goldstein, L. H., Bernard, S., Fenwick, P. B. C., Burgess, P. W., & McNeil, J. (1993). Unilateral frontal lobectomy can produce strategy application disorder. *Journal of Neurology, Neurosurgery and Psychiatry, 56,* 274–276.

Groot, Y. C., Wilson, B. A., Evans, J., & Watson, P. (2002). Prospective memory functioning in people with and without brain injury. *Journal of the International Neuropsychological Society, 8,* 645–654.

Herron, J. E., Henson, R. N., & Rugg, M. D. (2004). Probability effects on the neural correlates of retrieval success: An fMRI study. *Neuroimage, 21,* 302–310.

Hicks, J. L., Cook, G. I., & Marsh, R. L. (2005). Detecting event-based prospective memory cues occurring within and outside the focus of attention. *American Journal of Psychology, 118,* 1–11.

Holloway, R. L. (2002). Brief communication: How much larger is the relative volume of area 10 of the prefrontal cortex in humans? *American Journal of Physical Anthropology, 118,* 399–401.

Kliegel, M., Eschen, A., & Thone-Otto, A. I. (2004). Planning and realization of complex intentions in traumatic brain injury and normal aging. *Brain and Cognition, 56,* 43–54.

Kliegel, M., McDaniel, M. A., & Einstein, G. O. (2000). Plan formation, retention, and execution in prospective memory: A new approach and age-related effects. *Memory and Cognition, 28,* 1041–1049.

Kliegel, M., Phillips, L. H., Lwemke, U., & Kopp, U. A. (2005). Planning and realisation of complex intentions in patients with Parkinson's disease. *Journal of Neurology, Neurosurgery and Psychiatry, 76,* 1501–1505.

Knight, R. G., Titov, N., & Crawford, M. (2006). The effects of distraction on prospective remembering following traumatic brain injury assessed in a simulated naturalistic environment. *Journal of the International Neuropsychological Society, 12,* 8–16.

Koechlin, E., Basso, G., Pietrini, P., Panzer, S., & Grafman, J. (1999). The role of the anterior prefrontal cortex in human cognition. *Nature, 399,* 148–151.

Koechlin, E., Corrado, G., Pietrini, P., & Grafman, J. (2000). Dissociating the role of the medial and lateral anterior prefrontal cortex in planning. *Proceedings of the National Academy of Science USA, 97,* 7651–7656.

Kvavilashvili, L., & Ellis, J. (1996). Varieties of intention: Some distinctions and classifications. In M. Brandimonte, G. Einstein, & M. McDaniel (Eds.), *Prospective memory: Theory and applications* (pp. 23–51). Hillsdale, NJ: Lawrence Erlbaum Associates, Inc.

Levine, B., Freedman, M., Dawson, D., Black, S. E., & Stuss, D. T. (1999). Ventral frontal contribution to self-regulation: Convergence of episodic memory and inhibition. *Neurocase, 5,* 263–275.

Levine, B., Robertson, I., Clare, L., Carter, G., Hong, J., Wilson, B. A., et al. (2000). Rehabilitation of executive functioning: An experimental–clinical validation of goal management training. *Journal of the International Neuropsychological Society, 6,* 299–312.

Levine, B., Stuss, D., Milberg, W. P., Alexander, M. P., Schwartz, M., & Macdonald, R. (1998). The effects of focal and diffuse brain damage on strategy application: Evidence from focal lesions, traumatic brain injury and normal aging. *Journal of the International Neuropsychological Society. 4,* 247–264.

Mantyla, T. (2003). Assessing absentmindedness: Prospective memory complaint and impairment in middle-aged adults. *Memory and Cognition, 31,* 15–25.

Marsh, R. L., & Hicks, J. L. (1998). Event-based prospective memory and executive control of working memory. *Journal of Experimental Psychology: Learning, Memory, and Cognition, 24,* 336–349.

Marsh, R. L., Hicks, J. L., & Cook, G. I. (2005). On the relationship between effort towards an ongoing task and cue detection in event-based prospective memory. *Journal of Experimental Psychology: Learning, Memory, and Cognition, 31,* 68–75.

Mathias, J. L., & Mansfield, K. M. (2005). Prospective and declarative memory problems following moderate and severe traumatic brain injury. *Brain Injury, 19,* 271–282.

Maylor, E. A., Smith, G., Della Sala, S., & Logie, R. H. (2002). Prospective and retrospective memory in normal aging and dementia: An experimental study. *Memory and Cognition, 30,* 871–884.

McDaniel, M. A., Glisy, E. L., Rubin, S. R., Guynn, M. J., & Routhieaux, B. B. (1999). Prospective memory: A neuropsychological study. *Neuropsychology, 13,* 103–110.

McDaniel, M. A., Guynn, M. J., Einstein, G. O., & Breneiser, J. (2004). Cue-focused and reflexive-associative processes in prospective memory retrieval. *Journal of Experimental Psychology: Learning, Memory, and Cognition, 30,* 604–614.

McGann, D., Ellis, J. A., & Milne, A. (2002). Conceptual and perceptual processes in prospective remembering: Differential influence of attentional resources. *Memory and Cognition, 30,* 1021–1032.

Metzler, C., & Parkin, A. J. (2000). Reversed negative priming following frontal lobe lesions. *Neuropsychologia, 38,* 363–379.

Nowinski, J. L., & Dismukes, K. R. (2005). Effects of ongoing task context and target typicality on prospective memory performance: The importance of associative cueing. *Memory, 13,* 649–657.

Okuda, J., Fujii, T., Yamadori, A., Kawashima, R., Tsukiura, T., Fukatsu, R., et al. (1998). Participation of the prefrontal cortices in prospective memory: Evidence from a PET study in humans. *Neuroscience Letters, 253,* 127–130.

Okuda, J., Fujii, T., Ohtake, H., Tsukiura, T., Yamadori, A., Frith, C.D. & Burgess, P.W. (2006). Differential involvement of regions of rostral prefrontal cortex (Brodmann area 10) in time- and event-based prospective memory. *International Journal of Psychophysiology,* Nov. 23, [Epub ahead of print.].

Park, D. C., Hertzog, C., Kidder, D. P., Morrell, R. W., & Mayborn, C. B. (1997). Effect of age on event-based and time-based prospective memory. *Psychology and Ageing, 12,* 314–327.

Penfield, W., & Evans, J. (1935). The frontal lobe in man: A clinical study of maximum removals. *Brain, 58,* 115–133.

Pollmann, S. (2001). Switching between dimensions, locations, and responses: The role of the left frontopolar cortex. *Neuroimage, 14,* S118–S124.

Pollmann, S. (2004). Anterior prefrontal cortex contributions to attention control. *Experimental Psychology, 51,* 270–278.

Salthouse, T. A., Berish, D. E., & Siedlecki, K. L. (2004). Construct validity and age sensitivity of prospective memory. *Memory and Cognition, 32,* 1133–1148.

Semendeferi, K., Armstrong, E., Schleicher, A., Zilles, K., & Van Hoesen, G. W. (2001). Prefrontal cortex in humans and apes: A comparative study of area 10. *American Journal of Physical Anthropology, 114,* 224–241.

Shallice, T. (1988). *From neuropsychology to mental structure*. New York: Cambridge University Press.

Shallice, T., & Burgess, P. W. (1991). Deficits in strategy application following frontal lobe damage in man. *Brain, 114*, 727–741.

Sheeran, P., Webb, T. L., & Gollwitzer, P. M. (2005). The interplay between goal intentions and implementation intentions. *Personality and Social Psychology Bulletin, 31*, 87–98.

Simons, J. S., Gilbert, S. J., Owen, A. M., Fletcher, P. C., & Burgess, P. W. (2005). Distinct roles for lateral and medial anterior prefrontal cortex in contextual recollection. *Journal of Neurophysiology, 94*, 813–820.

Simons, J. S., Owen, A. M., Fletcher, P. C., & Burgess, P. W. (2005). Anterior prefrontal cortex and the recollection of contextual information. *Neuropsychologia, 43*, 1774–1783.

Simons, J. S., Schölvinck, M., Gilbert, S. J., Frith, C. D., & Burgess, P. W. (2006). Differential components of prospective memory? Evidence from fMRI. *Neuropsychologia, 44*, 1388–1397.

Smith, R. E., & Bayen, U. J. (2006). The source of adult age differences in event-based prospective memory: A multinomial modelling approach. *Journal of Experimental Psychology: Learning, Memory, and Cognition, 32*, 623–635.

West, R., Bowry, R., & Krompinger, J. (2006). The effects of working memory demands on the neural correlates of prospective memory. *Neuropsychologia, 44*, 197–207.

West, R., Krompinger, J., & Bowry, R. (2005). Disruptions of preparatory attention contribute to failures of prospective memory. *Psychonomic Bulletin, 12*, 502–507.

12

The Cognitive Neuroscience of Prospective Memory

ROBERT WEST

Department of Psychology
Iowa State University

From the chapters included in this volume it is clear that much has been learned over the last decade regarding the fundamental cognitive processes that underlie prospective memory, how the efficiency of these processes develops and then declines over the course of the life span, and what interventions may be undertaken to remediate deficits in the ability to realize delayed intentions. In one form or another some evidence related to each of these themes was considered in the 1996 volume on prospective memory (Brandimonte, Einstein, & McDaniel, 1996). In contrast, a consideration of evidence related to the neurobiological underpinnings of prospective memory in intact individuals was essentially absent in the earlier edition. This chapter is designed to provide an overview of the growing literature related to the neurobiological basis of prospective memory in the hope of illustrating what progress has been made within this area of research and also to inspire other investigators to join those of us who have spent considerable energy over the last several years laying the foundation for studies to be conducted in the coming decade and beyond.

A review of the literature reveals that progress in identifying the neural architecture of prospective memory has been made in studies using two complimentary methodologies. Studies using functional neuroimaging methods (i.e., positron emission tomography [PET] and functional magnetic resonance imaging [fMRI]) have served to identify some of the functional neuroanatomy that is related to the maintenance of intentions during performance of an ongoing activity (Burgess, Quayle, & Frith, 2001; Okuda et al., 1998; Simons, Schölvinck, Gilbert, Frith, & Burgess, 2005) and neural activity that is related to processes that are engaged when a candidate prospective cue is encountered in the environment (De Bruycker, Verhoef, d'Ydewalle, & Orban, 2005). Studies using scalp recorded event-related potentials (ERPs) have allowed investigators to identify the time course of neural activation that is differentially related to the detection of a prospective cue, the retrieval of an intention from memory, and postretrieval processes that serve to coordinate the ongoing and prospective aspects of the task (West, 2005).

The chapter is divided into three sections. The first section is designed to provide a review of the literature related to the neurobiological basis of prospective memory in intact humans. This is in fact a quite manageable task given that the extant literature includes only about 20 primary empirical works. The second section of the chapter is relatively brief and is designed to identify some of the methodological pitfalls that have been considered in the published literature. My intent is that this section may assist future researchers in designing studies that guard against such factors that can lead to ambiguous results. The final section of the chapter provides an integration of findings from studies using ERP and functional neuroimaging methodologies and considers potential avenues for future research. My hope is that this may serve as the sketch of a roadmap for some of the directions that research in this area may follow in the coming years.

ERP AND FUNCTIONAL NEUROIMAGING EVIDENCE

ERPs and Prospective Memory: Basic Findings

Studies using ERPs to examine the neural correlates of prospective memory have primarily focused on identifying modulations of the electrophysiology that are associated with the realization of event-based delayed intentions and determining whether these modulations of the ERPs can be dissociated from aspects of the physiology that are generally related to target processing and memory retrieval. This work has revealed two modulations of the ERPs that are differentially related to the detection of prospective cues (i.e., N300) and postretrieval processes (i.e., prospective positivity). The following section of the chapter provides an overview of the empirical work examining the functional characteristics of these two modulations of the ERPs.

N300 and Cue Detection The N300 represents a negativity over the occipital-parietal region of the scalp that emerges between 300 and 400 ms after stimulus onset (Figure 12.1; West, Herndon, & Crewdson, 2001). In some studies the N300 is rather phasic in nature, lasting from 200 to 400 ms (West & Ross-Munroe, 2002). In other studies the negativity associated with the N300 may last for several hundred milliseconds, persisting until the time of the prospective response (West & Krompinger, 2005). The occipital-parietal manifestation of the N300 is often accompanied by an enhanced positivity over the frontal midline region that begins at about the same time as the N300 and may persist beyond the duration of the N300 (West et al., 2001; West & Krompinger, 2005). The amplitude of the N300 is typically greater for prospective cues that elicit a prospective response (i.e., prospective hits) than for prospective cues that fail to elicit a prospective response

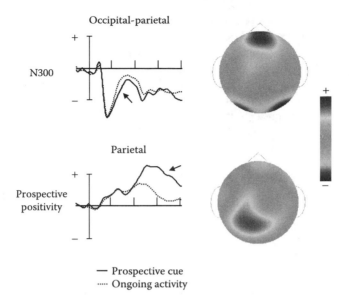

FIGURE 12.1 Grand average ERPs and scalp topography maps as viewed from above demonstrating the time course and topography of the N300 and prospective positivity. Adapted from West and Wymbs (2004) and West & Ross-Munroe (2002).

(i.e., prospective misses; West & Ross-Munroe, 2002; West & Krompinger, 2005, West, in press). These findings led to the suggestion that the N300 is associated with processes that support the detection of prospective cues when they are encountered in the environment (West & Ross-Munroe, 2002). The N300 is associated with the activity of a relatively general process that subserves the detection of prospective cues as it is elicited when prospective cues are embedded in a variety of ongoing activities and when prospective cues are defined by different attributes of the stimuli (West, Bowry, & Krompinger, 2006; West et al., 2001; West & Krompinger, 2005).

The time course and topography of the N300 are relatively similar to that of the N2 and N2pc. These modulations of the ERPs reflect phasic negativities over the occipital-parietal region of the scalp and are associated with target processing or the processing of a physically deviant stimulus. This observation served as the motivation for a line of research designed to determine whether the N300 could be distinguished from modulations of the ERPs that are generally related to target processing. In our first study using ERPs to examine the neural correlates of prospective memory we employed a prospective cue that was perceptually distinct relative to the stimuli presented for the ongoing activity trials (i.e., words presented in uppercase letters relative to words presented in lowercase letters; West et al., 2001, Experiment 1). The fact that the prospective cues were perceptually distinct led us to wonder whether the N300 reflected a general sensitivity to stimulus deviance or was more specifically related to the detection of prospective cues.

To address this issue we performed an experiment that was designed to tease apart the contribution of perceptual salience and prospective memory to generation of the N300 (West et al., 2001, Experiment 2). In this experiment individuals were instructed to perform the ongoing activity during the first half of the task and that the prospective cues were irrelevant; in the second half of the task individuals were instructed to perform the ongoing activity in addition to making a prospective response when the prospective cues were presented. The logic behind this design was that any negativity elicited by the prospective cues during the first half of the task would be associated with stimulus deviance; in contrast, in the second half of the task the negativity would reflect the influence of stimulus deviance and any additional activity that was distinctly related to processing prospective cues. The results of this experiment revealed that the amplitude of the N300 was similar over the left hemisphere in the first and second halves of the task and greater over the right hemisphere in the second half of the task relative to the first half of the task (West et al., 2001). These findings were taken to indicate that the N300 over the right hemisphere reflected neural activity associated with processes that are somewhat distinct to prospective memory.

In a second study examining similarities and differences between the N300 and modulations of the ERPs associated with target processing we sought to compare the N300 and the N2pc. The N2pc represents an enhancement of the occipital-parietal N2 that is associated with target selection in visual search (Luck & Hillyard, 1994) and visual discrimination (Eimer, 1996) tasks where individuals search for a target represented in working or visual memory over the course of the task. A defining characteristic of the N2pc is that it is greater in amplitude over the occipital-parietal region of the scalp that is contralateral to the visual field in which a target is presented. If similar processes underlie the detection of prospective cues and the selection of target stimuli, one could expect the N300 to respond in a manner similar to the N2pc. In contrast, if the N300 reflects processes that are distinct to prospective memory, one could expect to observe a dissociation between the N300 and the N2pc.

To test these predictions we embedded a prospective memory component in a target discrimination task wherein half of the targets and prospective cues appeared in the left visual field and half of the targets and prospective cues appeared in the right visual field (West & Wymbs, 2004). In this study the N2pc was elicited by both target stimuli and prospective cues between 250 and 270 ms after stimulus onset. In contrast, between 340 and 360 ms after stimulus onset the N300 was elicited for prospective cues and there was no significant difference in voltage between target and nontarget trials. Furthermore, the amplitude of the N300 was greater for prospective cues presented to the right hemisphere (in the left visual field) relative to those presented to the left hemisphere (in the right visual field). Together the findings of this study indicate that the N300 and N2pc reflect temporally and functionally distinct modulations of the ERPs. Also, extending the findings of West et al. (2001), these data indicate there is an advantage for prospective cues that are initially processed in the right hemisphere relative to those that are initially processed in the left hemisphere.

Prospective Positivity and Postretrieval Processes   The prospective positivity is typically observed between 400 and 1,200 ms after stimulus onset and is broadly distributed over the central, parietal, and occipital regions of the scalp (Figure 12.1; West et al., 2001). The label for this modulation is designed to distinguish it from other positivities (P3 and parietal old–new effect) that are observed over the parietal region and that are elicited by the recognition of task-relevant stimuli. Like the N300, the prospective positivity is elicited when prospective cues are embedded in a variety of ongoing activities (i.e., semantic judgment, N-back, target discrimination) and defined by a number of attributes of the prospective cues (i.e., letter case, color, letter or word identity; West et al., 2006; West et al., 2001; West & Krompinger, 2005; West & Wymbs, 2004). Also, the prospective positivity is greater in amplitude for prospective hits than for prospective misses, at least when prospective cues are not repeated over the course of task performance (West, in press; West & Krompinger, 2005).

The parietal distribution of the prospective positivity bears some resemblance to the topography of the P3 component that is associated with target categorization (Kok, 2001) and the recognition old–new effect that is associated with the retrieval of a previous episode from memory (Rugg, 1995). Given similarities between the prospective positivity and the P3 and old–new effect, one goal of studies conducted in my laboratory has been to determine whether or not the prospective positivity merely reflects the manifestation of these components in prospective memory tasks or whether it reflects the activity of processes that are uniquely associated with the realization of delayed intentions.

One demonstration of a dissociation between the P3 and the prospective positivity is found in the study by West and Wymbs (2004). In this study a different target stimulus (a letter) was encoded for each trial and individuals then determined whether the target was presented in a test display including two letters presented to the left or right of fixation. In analyzing the data we used partial least squares analysis (PLS; Lobaugh, West, & McIntosh, 2001; McIntosh, Bookstein, Haxby, & Grady, 1996) to identify modulations of the ERPs that distinguished prospective cues and target stimuli in a visual discrimination task. PLS is a multivariate statistical technique that is similar to principle components analysis that allows one to identify latent variables that are differentially sensitive to experimental conditions or elements of the task design. The application of this technique to the data reported by West and Wymbs (2004) revealed one latent variable that expressed the prospective positivity and contrasted prospective hits with target hits and target absent trials. The clustering of target present and target absent trials in this analysis indicates that the prospective positivity cannot merely be conceptualized as a general index of target processing or the P3 component. A second latent variable from this analysis contrasted target trials and prospective cues presented to the left hemisphere with target absent trials and expressed the P3 component. Together these data demonstrate that the P3 component may contribute to the manifestation of the prospective positivity. However, these data also indicate that the prospective positivity does not solely reflect an index of the processes underlying target processing that lead to generation of the P3 (West, Wymbs, Jakubek, & Herndon, 2003).

The data reported in the previous paragraph provide a statistical dissociation of the prospective positivity and the P3 component, leading one to wonder whether it

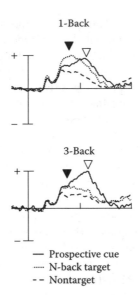

1-Back

3-Back

— Prospective cue
····· N-back target
- - Nontarget

FIGURE 12.2 Grand average ERPs for prospective cue, N-back target, and nontarget trials at electrode Pz demonstrating the effect of N-back load on the P3, but not the prospective positivity. The filled arrows mark the P3 and the unfilled arrows mark the prospective positivity. Adapted from West et al. (2006).

might also be possible to empirically dissociate these two modulations of the ERPs. Such a dissociation has been observed in a study when a prospective memory task was embedded in an N-back working memory task. In this study the amplitude of the P3 elicited by N-back target stimuli was dramatically attenuated in 2-back or 3-back conditions relative to the 1-back condition (West & Bowry, 2005; West et al., 2006), replicating previous research with this paradigm (Gevins et al., 1996). In contrast, the amplitude of the prospective positivity was insensitive to N-back load in two samples of younger adults (Figure 12.2). These data clearly demonstrate that the prospective positivity and P3 component are sensitive to different experimental manipulations, providing additional evidence that the prospective positivity arises from the activity of processes that are somewhat specific to prospective memory.

Other work has sought to determine whether the prospective positivity might reflect a manifestation of the recognition old–new effect in prospective memory. These studies were motivated by theories of prospective memory wherein similar processes are thought to underlie the recollection of prior episodes in the service of explicit episodic memory and prospective memory (Guynn, McDaniel, & Einstein, 2001). One methodological issue that had to be addressed in this line of research was related to differences in the way that assessments of prospective memory and explicit episodic memory are typically constructed. For instance, encoding in prospective memory is presumably always intentional, whereas encoding in episodic memory tasks can be intentional or incidental. Also, in prospective memory tasks a small number of items are typically encoded, whereas in episodic memory tasks a moderate to large number of items may be encoded. In an effort to address these methodological issues we designed a paradigm where for each of a series of blocks of trials, individuals encoded one prospective cue and one recognition (Experiment 1) or cued-recall (Experiment 2) target under intentional encoding conditions (West & Krompinger, 2005). Individuals then encountered the prospective cue during the ongoing task and made a forced choice recognition or cued-recall judgment at the end of each block of trials following a signal to prepare for the recognition or cued-recall test.

The ERP data from these experiments revealed two interesting findings. In Experiment 1, where a recognition test was used, recognition hits and prospective hits both elicited a positivity over the parietal region, reflecting the old–new effect and a slow wave over the right frontal region; in Experiment 2, where a cued-recall test was used, cued-recall hits and prospective hits both elicited a slow wave that was broadly distributed over the central-parietal region of the scalp. The time course and topography of these modulations were highly consistent with what has been observed in previous studies of recognition (Rugg, 1995) and cued-recall (Allan & Rugg, 1998) and converge with the idea that similar processes underlie the retrieval of a prior episode in prospective memory and explicit episodic memory tasks (Guynn et al., 2001). In addition, a second pattern was observed that distinguished prospective hits from recognition hits and cued-recall hits that reflected a sustained positivity over the parietal region of the scalp. The findings of this study led to the suggestion that the prospective positivity reflects two distinct types of processes, some that are common to prospective memory and explicit episodic memory and are associated with the retrieval of a prior episode from memory, and others that may be unique to prospective memory and associated with postretrieval processes that foster realization of the intention once it is retrieved from memory (West & Krompinger, 2005).

ERPs and Prospective Memory: Implications for Cognitive Models

The work described in the previous section was primarily designed to identify and characterize the ERP correlates of processes underlying the realization of delayed intentions in event-based prospective memory tasks. A second, and perhaps more important, goal of studies using ERPs from the perspective of cognitive neuroscience is to consider how evidence from studies using neuromonitoring methodologies may serve to inform theories of the cognitive processes underlying prospective memory. In this section of the chapter the results of two studies that were conducted in the pursuit of this goal are described to portray the potential utility of ERP methods in understanding the cognitive processes underlying prospective memory.

The first study was designed to examine the locus of the effect of variation in the availability of working memory resources on the processes underlying prospective memory. This study was motivated by evidence from a number of studies demonstrating that increasing the working memory and attentional demands of the ongoing activity can, in some cases, lead to a decrement in prospective memory

(Marsh & Hicks, 1998). Based on current theories of prospective memory, this effect might be expected to arise from at least two different sources. Within the preparatory attentional processes and memory processes (PAM) theory, increasing the working memory demands of the ongoing activity would be thought to draw capacity away from processes that support the detection of prospective cues (R. E. Smith, 2003; R. E. Smith & Bayen, 2004). In contrast, within the noticing and discrepancy plus search theory of prospective memory, increasing the working memory demands of the task might be expected to have little effect on processes underlying the detection of prospective cues and to disrupt processes that support directed search (Einstein & McDaniel, 1996; McDaniel, Guynn, Einstein, & Breneiser, 2004) or strategic processing (Guynn et al., 2001; West & Krompinger, 2005).

To examine these two hypotheses we conducted an experiment where individuals were to respond to nonfocal prospective cues (McDaniel & Einstein, 2000) while performing an N-back working memory task under loads of 1-back or 3-back. The data from this study revealed several interesting findings within the context of the noticing plus search and PAM theories. The amplitude of the N300 was attenuated in the 3-back condition relative to the 1-back condition, and the prospective positivity was insensitive to variation in the working memory demands of the ongoing activity (West et al., 2006). These results seem to support predictions derived from the PAM theory. However, a more detailed analysis of the data reveals a somewhat different story. For this analysis we utilized PLS analysis (Lobaugh et al., 2001; McIntosh et al., 1996). The PLS analysis of this data set revealed two latent variables that expressed the neural correlates of prospective memory. The first latent variable was insensitive to N-back load and expressed the N300 over the occipital-parietal and midline frontal regions and the prospective positivity over the parietal region. The pattern of data revealed in this latent variable is consistent with what would be expected based on the noticing plus search theory of prospective memory. Specifically, the N300 that is associated with the detection of prospective cues was tightly coupled to the prospective positivity that is associated with postretrieval processes, and this effect was not sensitive to the working memory demands of the ongoing activity. The second latent variable from this analysis was sensitive to N-back load. This latent variable expressed a phasic modulation of the N300 over the right occipital-parietal region and a sustained modulation over the midline frontal region, and did not express the prospective positivity. The effect of N-back load on the N300 over the right occipital-parietal region is consistent with other evidence indicating that the right hemisphere supports an attentional mechanism that facilitates the detection of prospective cues (West et al., 2001; West & Wymbs, 2004).

The findings of this study support three conclusions related to the cognitive processes underlying prospective memory. First, both capacity-demanding and capacity-independent processes expressed in the N300 may underlie the detection of prospective cues. This conclusion seems inconsistent with PAM theory and lends support to the multiprocess view of prospective memory (McDaniel & Einstein, 2000). Second, processes underlying the detection of prospective cues reflected in the N300 are tightly coupled to postretrieval processes reflected in the prospective positivity. This proposal follows from the noticing plus search theory of prospective memory wherein the detection of a prospective cue leads to the recruitment of processes supporting directed search to establish the significance of the prospective cue (Einstein & McDaniel, 1996). Furthermore, these data may indicate that directed search is more strongly aligned with postretrieval processes than with memory retrieval per se. Finally, increasing the working memory demands of the ongoing activity has a somewhat localized effect on the processes underlying prospective memory. Specifically, increasing demand appears to influence the allocation of processes underlying the detection of prospective cues that may be mediated by the right hemisphere (West & Wymbs, 2004) and more sustained processes that give rise to neural activity over the midline frontal region that could be associated with disengagement from the ongoing activity or coordination of the ongoing and prospective aspects of the task following the detection of prospective cues (Cockburn, 1995).

In a second study we sought to examine the effects of strategic monitoring (Guynn, 2003) on the ERP correlates of prospective memory. Current theories of the processes underlying prospective memory differ substantially with regard to the degree that the realization of delayed intentions requires strategic monitoring for a prospective cue. Within the strategic monitoring (Guynn, 2003) and PAM (R. E. Smith & Bayen, 2004) theories, individuals are believed to engage in strategic processes that support the detection or recognition of prospective cues. In contrast, within the automatic associative activation theory (Guynn et al., 2001) the retrieval of an intention from memory is thought to occur when a focally attended prospective cue interacts with a memory trace representing the cue–intention association. The result of this interaction is the obligatory delivery of the intention to conscious awareness that is presumably followed by realization of the intention.

To examine the influence of strategic monitoring on the N300 and prospective positivity we designed a paradigm where for each block of trials individuals encoded a single word as a prospective cue and were then engaged in a continuous recognition memory test for the ongoing activity (West, in press). In this task the stimuli for the ongoing activity were presented in gray letters for the first 10 trials of each block, in green letters for the next 10 trials of each block, and in gray letters for the last 10 trials of each block. Individuals were instructed to make a prospective response to prospective cues that appeared in green letters (i.e., prospective attend condition) and to ignore prospective cues that were presented in gray letters (i.e., prospective ignore condition). Given this instruction we hoped that individuals would monitor for prospective cues during the middle third of the blocks when words were presented in green letters and not during the first and last thirds of the blocks when words were presented in gray letters. The response time data for ongoing activity trials confirmed the presence of monitoring, revealing a roughly 60-ms increase in response time from the first to the second thirds of the trials.

The ERP data for this study also revealed a clear effect of monitoring that provides support for processes described in both the strategic monitoring (Guynn, 2003) and the automatic associative activation (Guynn et al., 2001) theories of prospective memory. The occipital-parietal and midline frontal components of the N300 distinguished prospective hits in the prospective attend condition from prospective cues in the prospective ignore condition, new items, and prospective

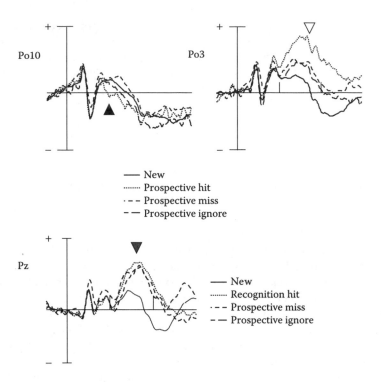

FIGURE 12.3 Grand average ERPs demonstrating the effect of monitoring on the N300, prospective positivity, and old–new effect elicited by prospective cues. The upper panel demonstrates for the N300 (black arrow) and prospective positivity (white arrow) for prospective cues when the cues were either relevant or irrelevant to task performance. The lower panel demonstrates the old–new effect (gray arrow) elicited by recognition hits, prospective cues in the prospective ignore condition, and prospective misses in the prospective attend condition.

misses in the prospective attend condition (Figure 12.3). This finding indicates that the N300 and accompanying frontal activity were only observed when individuals were expected to be engaged in monitoring and the intention was actually realized. The amplitude of the prospective positivity decreased from prospective hits in the prospective attend condition to prospective cues in the prospective ignore condition, was similar for prospective misses in the prospective attend condition and prospective cues in the prospective ignore condition, and then decreased for the ERPs elicited by new items. This pattern of data is somewhat ambiguous with regard to the monitoring and automatic activation theories in that it may indicate that memory retrieval and postretrieval processes were elicited for missed prospective cues and in the prospective ignore condition. A comparison of the ERPs elicited by prospective cues and those elicited by recognition hits in the ongoing activity, however, serves to resolves this ambiguity. This comparison reveals that the amplitude of the old–new effect that is associated with recognition was similar for recognized old items, prospective cues in the prospective ignore condition, and prospective misses in the prospective attend condition (Figure 12.3). Given this finding, it seems reasonable to suggest that the intention was retrieved from memory in the prospective ignore condition and for prospective misses in the prospective attend condition but went unrealized either due to task instructions or the failure to engage strategic processes reflected in the N300 and prospective positivity.

The findings of this study support a number of tentative conclusions. First, it appears that active monitoring may not be required for a delayed intention to be retrieved from memory because the old–new effect was elicited by prospective cues regardless of the intention to make a prospective response to these stimuli. This finding supports a fundamental assumption of the automatic associative activation theory of prospective memory (Guynn et al., 2003). Second, the engagement of monitoring processes may be essential for the recruitment of processes that support the detection of prospective cues that in turn lead to the activation of processes that support disengagement from the ongoing activity and postretrieval processes. Finally, these data may indicate that processes supporting the retrieval of an intention from memory and the coordination of the ongoing and prospective components of the task once the cue is detected operate in parallel to facilitate the realization of delayed intentions (West, in press).

ERPs, Prospective Memory, and Development

In addition to being used to characterize the basic processes underlying the realization of delayed intentions, ERPs have also been used to examine the developmental trajectory of prospective memory. Most of this work has focused on the effects of aging in later adulthood on the neural correlates of prospective memory (West & Covell, 2001; West, Herndon, & Covell, 2003), although some progress has been made in examining the development of prospective memory from adolescence to early adulthood (Zöllig, 2005).

The effects of aging on the N300 and prospective positivity have been examined in three studies conducted in my laboratory using nonfocal prospective cues (West & Bowry, 2005; West & Covell, 2001; West, Herndon, & Covell, 2003). In each of these studies the amplitude of the N300 was attenuated in older adults relative to younger adults, and the effect of aging on the prospective positivity was somewhat mixed. The effect of aging on the N300 appears to result from a decline in the ability of older adults to recruit attentional processes that facilitate the detection of prospective cues. This proposal is supported by two findings. First, West, Herndon, and Covell (2003) observed that the amplitude of the N300 was similar for younger and older adults over the left hemisphere but was attenuated in older adults relative to younger adults over the right hemisphere, where effects of attention on the N300 have been observed in previous studies (West et al., 2006; West & Wymbs, 2004). Second, the effect of N-back load on the N300 over the right hemisphere that is observed in younger adults was not expressed in older adults (West & Bowry, 2005). Additionally, other data reported by West and Bowry indicate that older adults may recruit somewhat different neural generators to support the detection of prospective cues and that this system may be relatively insensitive to the effect of variation in the working memory demands of the ongoing activity.

As mentioned previously, the effects of aging on the prospective positivity revealed in previous research have been somewhat mixed. West and Covell (2001) observed a clear decrease in the amplitude of the prospective positivity in older adults relative to younger adults. In contrast, West, Herndon, and Covell (2003) reported that the amplitude of the prospective positivity was similar in younger and older adults when the ERPs elicited by prospective hits were compared to those elicited by ongoing activity trials. Two factors appear to have contributed to differences in the findings of these studies. A confounding of the P3 component and the prospective positivity appears to reflect one source of variation between the findings of these two studies (West, Wymbs, et al., 2003). A second, and perhaps more interesting, source of variation is revealed in the study by West and Bowry (2005). In this study, the prospective positivity was expressed by two latent variables, one that was more strongly expressed in younger adults than in older adults and one that was more strongly expressed in the older adults than in the younger adults. Inspection of the electrode saliences for these latent variables revealed a similar topography over the parietal region of the scalp for each latent variable and differences in topography over the frontal regions of the scalp. These data may indicate that younger and older adults recruit somewhat different neural generators that overlap for the parietal region to support postretrieval processes (West & Bowry, 2005).

Functional Neuroanatomy of Prospective Memory

Studies using PET and fMRI have focused on patterns of neural recruitment related to tonic or sustained processes that may support prospective memory in addition to neural activity that is more specifically related to the processing of prospective cues when they are encountered in the environment. Given evidence from a number of studies, it seems clear that the realization of delayed intentions is supported by a broadly distributed neural network that includes structures within the rostral prefrontal cortex (PFC), the parietal cortex, and the hippocampal complex (Burgess et al., 2001; Burgess, Scott, & Frith, 2003; Okuda et al., 2001; Okuda et al., 1998). Also, consistent with the ERP data described in the pervious section, there is growing evidence that the functional neuroanatomy underlying prospective memory can be distinguished from that associated with vigilance, dual-task performance, and working memory (De Bruycker et al., 2005; Reynolds, West, & Braver, 2003).

The rostral PFC is one of the most commonly activated regions in studies examining the functional neuroanatomy of prospective memory. In an early study Burgess et al. (2001) sought to determine whether this region was related to processes that support one's ability to hold an intention in mind or to realize the intention when a prospective cue was encountered. To this end individuals performed one of four tasks under three different conditions: a baseline condition where the ongoing activities were performed in isolation, a prospective expectation condition where prospective cues were anticipated but never occurred, and a prospective

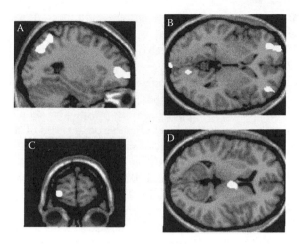

FIGURE 12.4 Functional activation differentiating (execution + expectation) – ongoing alone (A–C) and execution – expectation (D) conditions. A and B portray activation within lateral rostral PFC, C portrays activation in right lateral PFC, and D portrays thalamic activation. Adapted from Burgess et al. (2001).

execution condition where cues were presented. The comparison of the execution plus expection conditions with the baseline condition revealed bilateral activation in the lateral rostral PFC in addition to the right parietal and precuneus regions (Figure 12.4). The recruitment of these structures in both the execution and expectation conditions was interpreted as reflecting a network that supports the maintenance of intentions during the course of the ongoing activity (Burgess et al., 2001). The comparison of the execution condition to the expectation condition revealed activation that was limited to the right thalamus, which was interpreted as reflecting neural recruitment specifically associated with the realization of delayed intentions (Burgess et al., 2001; Okuda et al., 2001).

A more recent study by this group was designed to further characterize the contribution of the rostral PFC and its associated network to the realization of delayed intentions (Simons et al., 2005). In this study there were two prospective memory conditions. The cue identification condition was designed to place greater demands on the detection or identification of the prospective cue than the retrieval or execution of the intention. In contrast, the intention retrieval condition was designed to place greater demands on the retrieval or execution of the intention than on the detection or identification of the prospective cue. The behavioral data from this study revealed that the accuracy of prospective memory was lower in the cue identification condition than the intention retrieval condition, and response time for prospective responses was longer in the intention retrieval condition than in the cue identification condition. The imaging data replicated previous findings, revealing greater activation in the rostral PFC for both prospective memory conditions relative to when the ongoing activity was performed alone. Furthermore, greater activation was observed in the rostral PFC for the intention retrieval condition than the cue identification condition, indicating that activity in this region was more strongly aligned with the complexity of the intention than with the ease with which the prospective cue could be detected or recognized (Simons et al., 2005).

In a study conducted in collaboration with Reynolds and Braver at Washington University we were interested in whether a common network involving the rostral PFC might be involved in supporting both prospective memory and working memory. This study was motivated by evidence from a series of studies indicating that rostral PFC is activated in a variety of tasks when individuals are required to either maintain or frequently switch between multiple goals (Braver & Bongiolatti, 2002; Braver, Reynolds, & Donaldson, 2003). For instance, Braver et al. (2003) observed sustained activity in right rostral PFC when individuals were required to switch between two task sets relative to when either of the tasks was performed throughout the block of trials.

The design of the study was similar to that reported in West et al. (2006), wherein a prospective component was embedded in an N-back working memory task that included N-back loads of one or three items (Reynolds et al., 2003). An increase in working memory load from the 1-back to the 3-back condition resulted in the recruitment of right dorsolateral PFC and bilateral parietal cortex in addition to left rostral PFC. In contrast, the addition of a prospective memory load to the 1-back task led to the recruitment of a similar area of rostral PFC relative to when the 1-back condition was performed in isolation or during a vigilance control condition, but did not lead to the recruitment of right dorsolateral PFC. These findings are interesting in two regards. First, these data reveal that rostral PFC may be generally recruited when individuals are required to balance multiple goals across a variety of tasks (O'Reilly, Noelle, Braver, & Cohen, 2002). Second, they indicate that there is only partial overlap between the neural networks that are recruited in the service of working memory and prospective memory, providing additional evidence that somewhat distinct processes underlie prospective memory and working memory (West et al., 2006).

In addition to success in identifying the functional anatomy of sustained processes underlying the realization of delayed intentions, fMRI has also been used to examine trial-specific processes related to cue processing that are elicited when a stimulus is encountered. For instance, De Bruycker et al. (2005) reported data that appear to reveal the neural correlates of processes related to checking for a prospective cue (Guynn, 2003) in addition to the detection and realization of delayed intentions. In this study individuals performed four task conditions while undergoing fMRI scanning. For the ongoing activity condition individuals were simply required to make a binary judgment related to stimuli that were presented. For the prospective memory condition individuals performed the ongoing activity and also made prospective responses. In contrast, for the vigilance condition individuals were only required to respond to the prospective cues. Finally, in the dual-task condition individuals were required to make both the ongoing and prospective judgments for each trial.

Examination of the event-related fMRI data from this study revealed a number of interesting findings. A comparison of activity elicited by ongoing activity stimuli revealed greater activity in the medial and lateral extrastriate cortex in the prospective memory condition relative to the ongoing activity alone condition. The data from this study also revealed neural activity that differentiated the processing of prospective cues from the processing of identical stimuli in the vigilance and dual-task conditions, and included regions within occipital, parietal, and dorso-lateral PFC. In addition, activation of rostral PFC was not observed in any of the task contrasts, consistent with the idea that activation of rostral PFC reflects tonic or sustained processing rather than item-specific processing (Burgess et al., 2001; Reynolds et al., 2003).

One surprising finding to emerge from the functional neuroimaging literature related to prospective memory is a dissociation between the roles of the lateral and medial rostral PFC. As we have seen in the studies described to this point, lateral rostral PFC is consistently activated when a prospective memory component is added to the task. In contrast, medial rostral PFC is often deactivated in the prospective memory condition relative to the baseline condition (Burgess et al., 2003). Complementing this finding, other work has revealed a double dissociation between these two regions with lateral rostral PFC being more strongly activated in a prospective memory condition relative to a baseline condition, and medial ros-tral PFC being more strongly activated when individuals were required to reflect on intentional causality relative to when they were required to reflect on physi-cal causality (den Ouden, Frith, Frith, & Blakemore, 2005). Together these and other findings have led to the "gateway hypothesis" of the rostral PFC wherein interactions between the lateral and medial rostral PFC can been seen to direct the flow of information between the internal and external worlds of the individual (Burgess, Simons, Dumontheil, & Gilbert, 2005). This account is clearly consistent with the data of Reynolds et al. (2003), wherein monitoring the environment for prospective cues and updating the representation of a memory set in the N-back task led to similar levels of recruitment within the lateral rostral PFC. Interest-ingly, the interaction between prospective memory load and N-back load observed by Reynolds et al. may indicate that the gating function of the rostral PFC can be disrupted when multiple competing goals simultaneously vye for access to the information processing system.

LESSONS LEARNED: ISSUES RELATED TO EXPERIMENTAL DESIGN IN ERP AND FUNCTIONAL IMAGING STUDIES

As is evident from the research reviewed in this chapter, significant progress has been made in identifying the functional neuroanatomical and electrophysiological correlates of the processes underlying prospective memory. Furthermore, given the number of talks and posters that were presented at the Second International Conference on Prospective Memory in the summer of 2005 and the lively discus-sion surrounding these presentations, it seems clear that an increasing number of investigators are being attracted to this area of research. Given this, there seems to be some providence in devoting at least a section of the chapter to describing some of the methodological advances that have been made in studies of the neural basis of prospective memory. This should not be taken as an effort to constrain the range of paradigms that various investigators may wish to employ to address questions related to the neural correlates of prospective memory, but rather as a guide that may help others avoid some of the pitfalls that have emerged from previous work in the area.

Three salient issues have emerged from our studies using ERPs to examine the neural correlates of prospective memory. The first of these is related to the relative frequency with which one can present prospective cues. The conceptual issue is focused on this question: At what point does a task move from being a prospective memory task to being a dual or working memory task, wherein individuals adopt the strategy of continuously rehearsing the prospective cues? In our research we have utilized several strategies that we hope discourage active rehearsal. First, we hold the frequency of prospective cues to between 5% and 10% of the total trials (West et al., 2001; West & Krompinger, 2005) and try to maintain a minimum of five trials between prospective cues in tasks where multiple cues can appear within a single block (West et al., 2006; West & Ross-Munroe, 2002). Second, in studies where a single prospective cue is presented within each block of trials, care is taken to present the cues in the last 50% to 60% of the trials for the blocks with the expectation that the prospective cue should fade from conscious awareness by the time that it is encountered. Finally, we have typically employed ongoing activities that require either fairly deep processing of the stimuli (e.g., semantic categorization; West et al., 2001; West & Krompinger, 2005) or possess an inherent working memory load (West et al., 2006; West & Wymbs, 2004) in the hope of discouraging rehearsal.

The second issue is that care should be taken to avoid selecting prospective cues that could be expected to strongly elicit modulations of the ERPs that are not specific to prospective memory. As an example of this, in some of our early work we used prospective cues that were perceptually distinct from the ongoing activity trials (West et al., 2001) that led to a confounding of the prospective positivity and the P3 component (West, Wymbs, et al., 2003). The potential problem of component overlap is highlighted by a comparison of the effects of aging on the amplitude of the prospective positivity in two studies. West and Covell (2001) used a distinct prospective cue that could be expected to elicit a P3—which is known to be highly sensitive to the effects of aging (Friedman, Kazmerski, & Fabiani, 1997)—and observed a strong effect of aging on the amplitude of parietal activity. In contrast, West, Herndon, and Covell (2003) used a prospective cue that was less likely to elicit a large P3 and observed minimal or no age-related differences in the amplitude of parietal activity. These findings clearly demonstrate that the outcome of a given study and the potential theoretical implications of the data can be strongly dependent on the nature of the prospective cues that are utilized.

A third issue rests in how often one should repeat the same prospective memory cue during the task. The relevance of this issue is demonstrated by an examination of the effect of the accuracy of prospective responding on the amplitude of prospective positivity. In West and Ross-Munroe (2002), we observed that the amplitude of the prospective positivity was similar for prospective hits and prospective misses when four prospective cues were each presented 12 times over the course of the task. In contrast, more recent work using unique prospective cues for each block of trials has demonstrated that the amplitude of the prospective positivity is greater for prospective hits than for prospective misses and that there may be little difference in the amplitude of the ERPs for prospective misses and ongoing activity trials (West, in press; West & Krompinger, 2005). Given these findings, it seems that one would like to use a unique stimulus for each presentation of a prospective cue when possible.

As is the case for studies using ERPs to examine the neural correlates of prospective memory, work using functional neuroimaging methods has revealed several design features that may serve to optimize data collection and interpretation. The first of these is the use of multiple ongoing activities in concert with a common prospective memory component (Burgess et al., 2001; Burgess et al., 2003). This allows one to minimize the degree that material-specific aspects of an ongoing activity influence the neural response and to focus on neural activity that is common to prospective memory across different ongoing activities. A second is the use of what could be considered multiple baseline conditions. Examples of this are found in the work of De Bruycker et al. (2005) and Reynolds et al. (2003), described earlier in the chapter. In both of these studies the investigators were able to demonstrate that both tonic and item-specific activities associated with the maintenance and realization of delayed intentions were distinct from that related to vigilance, dual-task performance, or working memory using identical stimulus materials across conditions. Finally, it may be important in incorporate what Burgess et al. (2001) identified as expectation and execution conditions in the task design. The results of De Bruycker et al. (2005) demonstrate that this element of the design may not only reveal patterns of activation that are sustained over time, as was the case in the study by Burgess et al. (2001), but may also reveal item-specific processes such as checking (Guynn, 2003) that are carried out on ongoing activity stimuli when individuals expect to encounter a prospective cue.

INTEGRATION AND FUTURE DIRECTIONS

To this point in the chapter findings from studies using ERP and neuroimaging methods to examine the neurobiology of prospective memory have been considered rather independently. Given the relative infancy of the literature in these two areas, this seems somewhat justified, yet there are a number of promising points of convergence that are worth highlighting. One point of convergence is the apparent role of extrastriate cortex in processing prospective cues. De Bruycker et al. (2005) observed greater activation associated with processing stimuli that were prospective cues than when the same stimuli were processed as targets within the context of a vigilance or dual-task paradigm (De Bruycker et al., 2005). Consistent with this finding, the N300 is maximal in amplitude over the occipital-parietal region of the scalp (West, 2005) and is limited to instances where prospective cues are directly relevant to task performance. Although the neural generators of the N300 have not been modeled in previous studies, similarities in the topography of this modulation and modulations of the N2 component that are commonly localized to the extrastriate cortex lead to the reasonable suggestion that the N300 may reflect activity in extrastriate cortex.

A second point of convergence is the observation that hippocampal or medial temporal structures are consistently activated during prospective remembering (Okuda et al., 1998; Okuda et al., 2002; Reynolds et al., 2003) and that a parietal old–new effect is elicited by prospective cues (West & Krompinger, 2005). The contribution of the medial temporal lobe to the generation of the old–new effect has been revealed in a study demonstrating that the amplitude of this component is significantly attenuated during the performance of a recognition memory task in patients with damage to the medial temporal lobe (M. E. Smith & Halgren, 1989). These findings provide support for the idea that a hippocampally dependent retrieval process underlies prospective memory and explicit episodic memory (Guynn et al., 2001).

A third point of convergence rests in the effects of comparable experimental manipulations on modulations of the ERPs and activation of functional neuroanatomy during prospective remembering. For instance, Simons et al. (2005) observed that increasing the complexity of the intention led to greater activation within the right hemisphere for Brodmann's area 6. Consistent with this finding, evidence from a study using ERPs revealed a sustained modulation extending from the right frontal to right parietal regions that increased in amplitude with the complexity of the prospective cue–intention associations (West, Wymbs, et al., 2003). A final point of convergence reflects activity associated with processes that serve to monitor the environment for the occurrence of a prospective cue such as checking (Guynn, 2003). Supporting the existence of such a process, DeBruycker et al. (2005) reported that there was greater activity in extrastriate cortex for ongoing activity stimuli in a prospective memory condition relative to a no prospective memory condition. In agreement with this finding, we have observed sustained activity over the occipital-parietal region of the scalp that is greater for target stimuli in a prospective memory condition than for target stimuli in a no prospective memory condition (West & Bowry, 2005; West et al., 2006). The evidence reviewed in these paragraphs offers a glimpse of what seems to be a promising start in building a cognitive neuroscience of prospective memory by revealing points of contact between processes described in various cognitive theories of prospective memory and patterns of neural recruitment observed in studies using ERP and functional neuroimaging methodologies.

In this chapter I have tried to provide a relatively comprehensive review of the literature related to the neurobiological foundations of prospective memory focusing on evidence from studies using ERP and functional neuroimaging methodologies. In the closing section of the chapter it seems warranted to look forward and consider what future directions research in this area might pursue. It is self-evident that further basic research related to fundamental aspects of the neurophysiological basis of prospective memory is required in the coming years to gain a clearer understanding of the neural processes underlying the realization of delayed intentions. Additionally, incorporating the paradigms and measures that have emerged from this research may provide insight into the locus of individual and group differences in the efficiency of prospective memory. For instance, the inclusion of ERP or functional neuroimaging methods in studies examining deficits of prospective memory arising from various forms of neuropathology could serve to identify the locus of the impairment.

As an example, evidence from a growing number of studies indicates that traumatic brain injury (TBI) is commonly associated with impairments of prospective memory (Kliegel, Eschen, & Thone-Otto, 2004; Schmitter-Edgecombe & Wright, 2004; Shum, Valentine, & Cutmore, 1999). Given the known contribution of the rostral PFC to prospective memory and the sensitivity of this region to the effects of TBI, one might expect deficits of prospective memory following TBI to be associated with underrecruitment within the rostral PFC. If this were the case, it could also lead to the prediction that such patients should also experience difficulties in settings where switching between tasks is required (Braver et al., 2003). Such evidence could reveal a common causal mechanism for behavioral deficits that at the surface may seem unrelated.

A related target area could be the integration of neurophysiological and pharmacological studies. Recent evidence indicates that nicotine can have both positive and negative effects on the efficiency of prospective memory, depending on the attentional demands of the ongoing activity (Rusted, 2005; Rusted, Trawley, Heath, Kettle, & Walker, in press). Integrated studies could provide investigators a means of identifying the specific processes underlying the realization of intentions that are modulated by the administration of nicotine or other pharmacological challenges that have been identified in basic research examining the neurobiological basis of prospective memory. Finally, it seems possible that ERP and functional neuroimaging methodologies may hold some promise in understanding the effects of intervention programs designed to ameliorate disruptions of prospective memory. For instance, these methodologies might provide insight into whether restored function arises from the repair of existing neural networks or from plasticity within the information processing system that allows for a compensatory network to be recruited in the service of prospective memory.

REFERENCES

Allan, K., & Rugg, M. D. (1998). Neural correlates of cued recall with and without retrieval of source memory. *Neuroreport, 9*, 3463–3466.

Brandimonte, M., Einstein, G. O., & McDaniel, M. A. (1996). *Prospective memory: Theory and applications*. Mahwah, NJ: Lawrence Erlbaum Associates, Inc.

Braver, T. S., & Bongiolatti, S. R. (2002). The role of frontopolar cortex in subgoal processing during working memory. *Neuroimage, 15*, 523–536.

Braver, T. S., Reynolds, J. R., & Donaldson, D. I. (2003). Neural mechanisms of transient and sustained cognitive control during task switching. *Neuron, 39*, 713–726.

Burgess, P. W., Quayle, A., & Frith, C. D. (2001). Brain regions involved in prospective memory as determined by positron emission tomography. *Neuropsychologia, 39*, 545–555.

Burgess, P. W., Simons, J. S., Dumontheil, I., & Gilbert, S. J. (2005). The gateway hypothesis of rostral prefrontal cortex (area 10) function. In J. Duncan, L. Phillips, & P. McLeod (Eds.), *Measuring the mind: Speed, control, and age* (pp. 217–248). Oxford, UK: Oxford University Press.

Burgess, P. W., Scott, S. K., & Frith, C. D. (2003). The role of the rostral frontal cortex (area 10) in prospective memory: A lateral versus medial dissociation. *Neuropsychologia, 41,* 906–918.

Cockburn, J. (1995). Task interruption in prospective memory: A frontal lobe function. *Cortex, 31,* 87–97.

De Bruycker, W., Verhoef, B., d'Ydewalle, G., & Orban, G. A. (2005, July). *Brain regions associated with retention and retrieval in event-based prospective memory.* Paper presented at the Second International Conference on Prospective Memory, Zurich, Switzerland.

den Ouden, H. E. M., Frith, U., Frith, C., & Blakemore, S.-J. (2005). Thinking about intentions. *Neuroimage, 28,* 787–796.

Eimer, M. (1996). The N2pc component as an indicator of attentional selectivity. *Electroencephalography and Clinical Neurophysiology, 99,* 225–234.

Einstein, G. O., & McDaniel, M. A. (1996). Retrieval processes in prospective memory: Theoretical approaches and some new empirical findings. In M. Brandimonte, G. O. Einstein, & M. A. McDaniel (Eds.), *Prospective memory: Theory and applications* (pp. 115–142). Mahwah, NJ: Lawrence Erlbaum Associates, Inc.

Friedman, D., Kazmerski, V., & Fabiani, M. (1997). An overview of age-related changes in the scalp distribution of P3b. *Electroencephalography and Clinical Neurophysiology, 104,* 498–513.

Gevins, A., Smith, M. E., Le, J., Leong, H., Bennett, J., Martin, N., et al. (1996). High resolution evoked potential imaging of the cortical dynamics of human working memory. *Electroencephalography and Clinical Neurophysiology, 98,* 327–348.

Guynn, M. J. (2003). A two-process model of strategic monitoring in event-based prospective memory: Activation/retrieval mode and checking. *International Journal of Psychology, 38,* 245–256.

Guynn, M. J., McDaniel, M. A., & Einstein, G. O. (2001). Remembering to perform intentions: A different type of memory? In H. D. Zimmer, R. L. Cohen, M. J. Guynn, J. Engelkamp, R. Kormi-Nouri, & M. A. Foley (Eds.), *Memory for action: A distinct form of episodic memory?* (pp. 25–48). Oxford, UK: Oxford University Press.

Kliegel, M., Eschen, A., & Thone-Otto, A. I. (2004). Planning and realization of complex intentions in traumatic brain injury and normal aging. *Brain and Cognition, 56,* 43–54.

Kok, A. (2001). On the utility of P3 amplitude as a measure of processing capacity. *Psychophysiology, 38,* 557–577.

Lobaugh, N. J., West, R., & McIntosh, A. R. (2001). Spatiotemporal analysis of experimental differences in event-related potential data with partial least squares. *Psychophysiology, 38,* 517–530.

Luck, S. J., & Hillyard, S. A. (1994). Electrophysiological correlates of feature analysis during visual search. *Psychophysiology, 31,* 291–308.

Marsh, R. L., & Hicks, J. L. (1998). Event-based prospective memory and executive control of working memory. *Journal of Experimental Psychology: Learning, Memory, and Cognition, 24,* 336–349.

McDaniel, M. A., & Einstein, G. O. (2000). Strategic and automatic processes in prospective memory retrieval: A multiprocess framework. *Applied Cognitive Psychology, 14,* S127–S144.

McDaniel, M. A., Guynn, M. J., Einstein, G. O., & Breneiser, J. (2004). Cue-focused and reflexive-associative processes in prospective memory retrieval. *Journal of Experimental Psychology: Learning, Memory, and Cognition, 30,* 605–614.

McIntosh, A. R., Bookstein, F. L., Haxby, J. V., & Grady, C. L. (1996). Spatial pattern analysis of functional images using partial least squares. *Neuroimage, 3,* 143–157.

Okuda, J., Fujii, T., Ohtake, H., Tsukiura, T., Umetsu, A., Suzuki, M., et al. (2001). Brain mechanisms underlying human prospective memory. In A. Yamadori, R. Kawashima, T. Fujii, & K. Suzuki (Eds.), *Frontiers in human memory* (pp. 79–96). Sendai, Japan: Tohoku University Press.

Okuda, J., Fujii, T., Yamadori, A., Kawashima, R., Tsukiura, T., Fukatsu, R., et al. (1998). Participation of the prefrontal cortices in prospective memory: Evidence from a PET study in humans. *Neuroscience Letters, 253,* 127–130.

O'Reilly, R. C., Noelle, D. C., Braver, T. S., & Cohen, J. D. (2002). Prefrontal cortex and dynamic categorization tasks: Representational organization and neuromodulatory control. *Cerebral Cortex, 12,* 246–257.

Reynolds, J., West, R., & Braver, T. (2003). Differentiation of prospective memory and working memory using a mixed state and event-related fMRI design. *Journal of Cognitive Neuroscience, p.* 147(Suppl.).

Rugg, M. D. (1995). ERP studies of memory. In M. D. Rugg & M. G. H. Coles (Eds.), *Electrophysiology of mind: Event-related brain potentials and cognition* (pp. 132–170). Oxford, UK: Oxford University Press.

Rusted, J. (2005, July). *Examining the pharmacology of prospective memory: Implications for psychological models.* Paper presented at the Second International Conference on Prospective Memory, Zurich, Switzerland.

Rusted, J. M., Trawley, S., Heath, J., Kettle, G., & Walker, H. (2005). Nicotine improves memory for delayed intentions. *Psychopharmacology, 182,* 355–365.

Schmitter-Edgecombe, M., & Wright, M. J. (2004). Event-based prospective memory following severe closed-head injury. *Neuropsychology, 18,* 353–361.

Shum, D., Valentine, M., & Cutmore, T. (1999). Performance of individuals with severe long-term traumatic brain injury on time-, event-, and activity-based prospective memory tasks. *Journal of Clinical and Experimental Neuropsychology, 21,* 49–58.

Simons, J. S., Schölvinck, M. L., Gilbert, S. J., Frith, C. D., & Burgess, P. W. (2005). *Differential components of prospective memory: Evidence from behavioral and fMRI studies.* Manuscript submitted for publication.

Smith, M. E., & Halgren, E. (1989). Dissociation of recognition memory components following temporal lobe lesions. *Journal of Experimental Psychology: Learning, Memory, and Cognition, 15,* 50–60.

Smith, R. E. (2003). The cost of remembering to remember in event-based prospective memory: Investigating the capacity demands of delayed intention performance. *Journal of Experimental Psychology: Learning, Memory, and Cognition, 29,* 347–361.

Smith, R. E., & Bayen, U. J. (2004). A multinomial model of event-based prospective memory. *Journal of Experimental Psychology: Learning, Memory, and Cognition, 30,* 756–777.

West, R. (2005a). *The influence of strategic monitoring on the neural correlates of prospective memory.* Memory and Cognition.

West, R. (2005b). The neural basis of age-related decline in prospective memory. In R. Cabeza, L. Nyberg, & D. Park (Eds.), *Cognitive neuroscience of aging* (pp. 246–264). New York: Oxford University Press.

West, R., & Bowry, R. (2005). Effects of aging and working memory demands on prospective memory. *Psychophysiology, 42,* 698–812.

West, R., Bowry, R., & Krompinger, J. (2006). The effects of working memory demands on the neural correlates of prospective memory. *Neuropsychologia, 44,* 197–207.

West, R., & Covell, E. (2001). Effects of aging on event-related neural activity related to prospective remembering. *Neuroreport, 12,* 2855–2858.

West, R., Herndon, R. W., & Covell, E. (2003). Neural correlates of age-related declines in the formation and realization of delayed intentions. *Psychology and Aging, 18,* 461–473.

West, R., Herndon, R. W., & Crewdson, S. J. (2001). Neural activity associated with the realization of a delayed intention. *Cognitive Brain Research, 12,* 1–10.

West, R., & Krompinger, J. (2005). Neural correlates of prospective and episodic memory. *Neuropsychologia, 43,* 418–433.

West, R., & Ross-Munroe, K. (2002). Neural correlates of the formation and realization of delayed intentions. *Cognitive, Affective, & Behavioral Neuroscience, 2,* 162–173.

West, R., & Wymbs, N. (2004). Is detecting prospective cues the same as selecting targets? An ERP study. *Cognitive, Affective, & Behavioral Neuroscience, 1,* 354–363.

West, R., Wymbs, N., Jakubek, K., & Herndon, R. W. (2003). Effects of intention load and background context on prospective remembering: An event-related brain potential study. *Psychophysiology, 40,* 260–276.

Zöllig, J. (2005, July). *What do we know about the neural and behavioral correlates of prospective memory in children?* Paper presented at the Second International Conference on Prospective Memory, Zurich, Switzerland.

13

Clinical Neuropsychology of Prospective Memory

MATTHIAS KLIEGEL

Department of Psychology
University of Zurich, Switzerland

THEODOR JÄGER

Department of Psychology
Saarland University, Saarbrücken, Germany

MAREIKE ALTGASSEN

Department of Psychology
University of Zurich, Switzerland

DAVID SHUM

School of Psychology
Griffith University, Brisbane, Australia

THE NEED FOR A CLINICAL NEUROPSYCHOLOGY OF PROSPECTIVE MEMORY

Prospective memory refers to the cognitive ability of remembering to carry out intended actions and is an essential precursor of independent living, as the necessity to prospectively remember is highly prevalent in the organization of one's daily routine and in the challenge of accomplishing occupational and social demands. The variety of prospective memory situations has been categorized into *event-based* tasks, where the appropriate moment for executing an intended action is triggered by an external event (e.g., to deliver a message to a friend on seeing him); *time-based* tasks, where the intended action has to be executed at a specific point in time or after a particular elapsed time (e.g., to visit the dentist at 10 a.m.); and *activity-based* tasks, where it is necessary to perform an intended action after the completion of another activity (e.g., to take medication after the meal; Einstein & McDaniel, 1990; Kvavilashvili & Ellis, 1996).

Given the high prevalence of day-to-day prospective memory situations, it is evident that the lives of individuals with severely diminished prospective memory abilities may be compromised by a substantial loss of independence. For instance, persistent failures in prospective remembering may impede professional activities (e.g., incessantly forgetting about errands one is supposed to do at work), endanger the maintenance of intimate social relationships (e.g., chronically forgetting to keep promises to close friends), or even impose serious risks on physical well-being (e.g., failing to regularly take medication). In sum, the negative outcomes of prospective memory deficits may be highly embarrassing, frustrating, or even life-threatening, and can impose a substantial burden on the individuals' significant others or care-givers. Importantly, one source or amplifier of such difficulties with carrying out intended actions are disorders such as physical illness, injuries, or psychopathological disorders. However, although it has been relatively well investigated whether various clinical populations exhibit deficits in cognitive domains such as attention, speed of processing, retrospective memory, or executive functioning, it was not until the beginning of the new millennium that research on the clinical aspects of prospective memory increased considerably. This new interest in the clinical neuropsychology of prospective memory was also reflected in the amount of posters tapping various clinical populations presented at the Second International Conference on Prospective Memory held in Zurich in July 2005. Thus, the purpose of this chapter is to provide a first overview of the currently available literature on prospective memory in clinical populations. Besides describing possible impairments and areas of spared performance, we also discuss initial evidence on the potential mechanisms underlying these findings. Finally, another aim of this chapter is to provide some suggestions for future research on the clinical neuropsychology of prospective memory.

COGNITIVE AND NEURAL SUBSTRATES OF PROSPECTIVE MEMORY

It is important to note that the term *prospective memory* refers to an interaction of various cognitive processes during several consecutive phases. Specifically, the prospective memory process can be subdivided into the phases of (a) *intention formation,* the point at which an intention to perform a future activity is formed and encoded; (b) *intention retention,* the period during which the intention is retained in memory while performing other ongoing activities; (c) *intention initiation,* the moment at which the execution of the intention should be initiated; and (d) *intention execution,* the actual execution of the intended action(s) according to the previously formed plan (Kliegel, Mackinlay, & Jäger, chap. 9, this volume; Kliegel, Martin, McDaniel, & Einstein, 2002; cf. also Ellis, 1996, who proposed a fifth phase that is concerned with monitoring the output of an executed intention). Distinct cognitive processes have been identified as playing the predominant roles during the completion of a particular phase (e.g., Kliegel et al., chap. 9, this volume, 2002). Because the processes underlying these phases will be important determinants as to when and why one might expect specific effects of distinct neuropsychological conditions on prospective remembering, we briefly review those cognitive and neural underpinnings of prospective memory (for more details see Burgess et al., chap. 11, this volume; Kliegel et al., chap. 9, this volume; West, chap. 12, this volume).

During intention formation, *planning skills* are assumed to be the most influential cognitive function, especially when an intention is somewhat complex. Furthermore, an *efficient encoding* of the intention is needed during this first phase of prospective remembering. Intention retention seems to primarily require storing the content of the intention in *retrospective memory*. Finally, intention initiation and execution seem to rely on processes such as *monitoring, cognitive flexibility*, or *inhibition*. Obviously, the cognitive abilities *retrospective remembering* and *executive functioning* are thought to play the major roles during the prospective memory process. Although distinct executive functions are suggested to be intimately involved during intention formation, intention initiation, and intention execution, they seem to play only a negligible role during intention retention (however, executive control may be required during intention retention to some degree to periodically rehearse or check for uncompleted intentions; Carlesimo, Casadio, & Caltagirone, 2004; Kliegel et al., chap. 9, this volume). Hence, the process of becoming aware of the appropriate moment that an intended action has to be initiated and executed (the so-called prospective component of prospective memory tasks; Einstein & McDaniel, 1996) may strongly rely on executive functions. By contrast, the process of retrieving the content of the intention and the specific actions that have to be carried out (the so-called retrospective component of a prospective memory task) is mediated by retrospective memory abilities.

Based on this analysis of cognitive processes involved in prospective memory tasks, a putative neuroanatomical basis of prospective memory has been postulated (e.g., Burgess, Veitch, de Lacy Costello, & Shallice, 2000; Cohen & O'Reilly, 1996; McDaniel, Glisky, Rubin, Guynn, & Routhieaux, 1999; Vogels, Dekker, Brouwer, & de Jong, 2002). On the one hand, it is assumed that the *prefrontal cortex* mostly mediates those processes involved in prospective remembering that are thought to be executive, such as the planning of an intention or the executive control mechanisms required to successfully initiate and execute an intention. In the light of the intimate link between executive functions and the prefrontal cortex (e.g., Miller, 2000; Miller & Cohen, 2001), a strong involvement of this large brain region in specific phases of the prospective memory process has been suggested (see also the evidence from functional neuroimaging; Burgess, Quayle, & Frith, 2001; Burgess, Scott, & Frith, 2003; Okuda et al., 1998; Simons et al., 2006; Yamadori et al., 1997). On the other hand, the memory system of the *medial temporal lobes* is assumed to be essential for the retrospective component of prospective memory tasks to retrieve the content of an intention (e.g., Guynn, McDaniel, & Einstein, 2001). In summary, it has been postulated that specific subprocesses of prospective memory strongly rely on the prefrontal cortex, the medial temporal lobes, and on interactions between these structures (Cohen & O'Reilly, 1996). It has been this conceptual context that has stimulated the rationale of several research groups to start looking at the impact of neuropsychological conditions on the efficiency of prospective remembering, and we use these assumptions on the nature of prospective remembering to guide the following discussion of relevant empirical findings in this area.

MAJOR FINDINGS ON PROSPECTIVE MEMORY IN VARIOUS CLINICAL POPULATIONS

In this main section of the chapter, we provide a comprehensive (although not always detailed) review of the available studies on prospective memory in a variety of clinical aetiologies (see Table 13.1). As will become apparent to the reader, there clearly is a need to carry out further studies on each of these populations and to extend the investigation to populations of other aetiologies (Knight, 1998). With regard to each investigated population, we briefly specify the theoretical or empirical grounds that have led to the expectation of prospective memory difficulties among the respective patients and summarize the studies' main findings.

Prospective Memory in Patients with Head Injuries

Overview   The clinical neuropsychology of prospective memory has been most extensively studied in patient populations suffering from brain damage. The relevance of this population is reflected in patients' reports that failures to execute intended actions are their most significant area of memory deficits (Hannon, Adams, Harrington, Fries-Dias, & Gibson, 1995; Shum, Valentine, & Cutmore, 1999). In the light of the putative cognitive and neural correlates of prospective memory, substantial difficulties of particular neurological patients in mastering prospective memory tasks were expected. For instance, traumatic brain injury (TBI) often involves damage to the prefrontal cortex. Given the conceptual background described earlier, it was assumed that prefrontal cortex damage may have particular deleterious effects on the prospective component. On the other hand, damage to the medial temporal lobes resulting in amnesia possibly disrupts prospective memory as well, as the retrospective component may be impaired by such brain lesions, which might result in forgetting the intention content during the delay, but might also result in failing to retrieve the intention at the appropriate point in time (see Guynn et al., 2001).

Relevant Findings   Some investigators found that patients with circumscribed lesions to the prefrontal cortex (i.e., lesions to frontopolar Brodmann's area 10) exhibit substantial difficulties in performing real-life multitask situations that involve prospective remembering, such as planning and preparing a meal (Burgess, 2000; Burgess et al., 2000; Fortin, Godbout, & Braun, 2002, 2003; Shallice &

TABLE 13.1   Overview

Patient Group	Authors	Main Findings
Patients with head injuries		
Lesions to the frontal lobes	Burgess (2000), Burgess et al. (2000), Cockburn (1995), Daum & Mayes (2000), Fortin et al. (2002), Fortin et al. (2003), Palmer & McDonald (2000), Shallice & Burgess (1991)	Difficulties with real-life multitask situations Poor prospective remembering
Traumatic brain injury	Carlesimo et al. (2004), Hannon et al. (1995), Henry et al. (in press), Kinch & McDonald (2001), Kinsella et al. (1996), Kliegel et al. (2004), Knight et al. (2005), Knight et al. (2006), Mateer et al. (1987), Mathias & Mansfield (2005), Maujean et al. (2003), McCauley & Levin (2004), Roche et al. (2002), Schmitter-Edgecombe & Wright (2004), Shum et al. (2002), Shum et al. (1999), Ward et al. (2004)	Impairment in time-, event-, and activity-based intentions Prospective memory failures in daily life
Brain injuries of various other etiologies	Brooks et al. (2004), Cockburn (1996), Groot et al. (2002), Kopp & Thöne-Otto (2003), Palmer & McDonald (2000)	Impairments in time-, event-, and activity-based prospective remembering
Patients with dementia		
Dementia	Huppert & Beardsall (1993), Huppert et al. (2000), Jones et al. (2006), Kazui et al. (2005), Maylor et al. (2002), Smith et al. (2000)	Impairments in time- and event-based prospective remembering Prospective memory failures in daily life
Patients with Parkinson's disease		
Parkinson's disease	Katai et al. (2003), Kliegel, Phillips, et al. (2005)	No impairment in time-based tasks, but in event-based tasks Impaired ability to plan the execution of an intention
Patients with other neuropathological diseases		
Multiple sclerosis	Bravin et al. (2000), West et al. (2005)	Impaired prospective remembering in time-, event-, and activity-based tasks
HIV	Carey et al. (2006)	Impaired prospective remembering in time- and event-based tasks
Herpes simplex encephalitis	Sgaramella et al. (2000)	Impairment in time-based tasks

(Continued)

TABLE 13.1   Overview (Continued)

Patients with substance abuse

Alcohol	Brunfaut et al. (2000), Heffernan et al. (2004), Heffernan et al. (2002), Ling et al. (2003)	Impairments in event-based prospective remembering Prospective memory failures in daily life
MDMA	Heffernan, Jarvis, et al. (2001), Heffernan, Ling, & Scholey (2001), J. Rodgers et al. (2001), Zakzanis et al. (2003)	Prospective memory failures in daily life and in time- and event-based laboratory tasks
Cannabis	J. Rodgers et al. (2001)	Impaired prospective remembering in daily life

Patients with schizophrenia

Schizophrenia	Elvevåg et al. (2003), Kondel (2002), Kumar et al. (2005), Meissner et al. (2001), Shum et al. (2004)	Deficits in performing time-, event-, or activity-based intentions

Patients with affective disorders

Depression	Rude et al. (1999)	Impairment in a time-based task

Patients with developmental disorders

ADHD	Clark et al. (2000), Kerns & Price (2001), Kliegel et al. (2006) Siklos & Kerns (2004)	Impairments in multitasks, time-based tasks
Autism	Mackinlay et al. (2006)	Impairment in a multitask

Burgess, 1991). Interestingly, these patients showed severe difficulties in everyday life despite exhibiting intact levels of executive functioning or retrospective memory when tested using neuropsychological batteries. Hence, common activities of daily living but not necessarily neuropsychological tests seem to be especially challenging for these patients. In consequence, these findings underline the potential utility of ecologically valid clinical assessments of prospective memory abilities to accurately assess the neuropsychological profile and everyday functioning of patients (cf. the approaches by Brooks, Rose, Potter, Jayawardena, & Morling, 2004; Knight, Harnett, & Titov, 2005; Knight, Titov, & Crawford, 2006; Titov & Knight, 2000).

By applying laboratory-based prospective memory tasks to TBI patients and normal controls, several studies have strongly suggested that TBI results in a diminished ability to carry out time-, event-, or activity-based intentions (Carlesimo et al., 2004; Hannon et al., 1995; Henry et al., in press; Kinch & McDonald, 2001; Kinsella et al., 1996; Kliegel, Eschen, & Thöne-Otto, 2004; Knight et al., 2005; Knight et al., 2006; Mathias & Mansfield, 2005; Maujean, Shum, & McQueen, 2003; McCauley & Levin, 2004; Schmitter-Edgecombe & Wright, 2004; Shum, Fleming, & Neulinger, 2002; Shum et al., 1999; for a partial quantitative review see Henry et al., in press). Patients' poor prospective memory performance mainly seems to result from momentary lapses of intention rather than from a complete forgetting of the intention, as Schmitter-Edgecombe and Wright's (2004) data showed that the TBI patients demonstrated a significant tendency to recover from a miss on the following event trial, indicating that the prospective memory success or failure of the TBI participants fluctuated over the course of task performance rather than being an all-or-none phenomenon.

The magnitude of the deficit has been found to depend on the severity of the brain injury (McCauley & Levin, 2004), the difficulty of the particular prospective memory task (Maujean et al., 2003; but see Henry et al., in press), or the levels of distraction involved in the ongoing activity (Knight et al., 2006). Furthermore, difficulties of TBI patients may be especially pronounced in time-based tasks as these tasks generally rely on a higher degree of self-initiated, controlled cognitive processes relative to event- or activity-based tasks (e.g., Groot, Wilson, Evans, & Watson, 2002; Mathias & Mansfield, 2005). Disruptions in estimating the time (Shum et al., 1999) or in externally monitoring the passage of time (Carlesimo et al., 2004) may be partly responsible for the deficit in time-based tasks. Importantly, the deficits of TBI patients seem to emerge despite substantial efforts to succeed in the prospective memory tasks as reflected in costs on ongoing task performance (McCauley & Levin, 2004; cf. Schmitter-Edgecombe & Wright, 2004).

Similarly, brain injuries of various other etiologies are associated with impairments in prospective remembering (Brooks et al., 2004; Cockburn, 1996; Groot et al., 2002; Kopp & Thöne-Otto, 2003; Palmer & McDonald, 2000). The findings of some studies are consistent with the hypothesis that damage to the prefrontal cortex invariably results in poor prospective remembering (Burgess, 2000; Cockburn, 1995; Fortin et al., 2002, 2003). For instance, Cockburn (1995) reported a patient with bilateral frontal lobe infarcts who showed an inability to interrupt ongoing activities to carry out an intended action at the appropriate moment. However, the proposal that prospective memory deficits are especially sensitive to prefrontal cortex lesions remains controversial. Daum and Mayes (2000) recruited nonamnesic patients with either frontal or posterior cortex lesions. Both of these patient groups were found to be similarly impaired in event-based prospective memory compared to normal controls. Hence, frontal and posterior cortex lesions did not result in differential prospective memory deficits (cf. Palmer & McDonald, 2000), suggesting that prospective memory tasks do not only tap prefrontal functions. However, given that prospective memory may rely on widely distributed neural networks, posterior lesions are likely to result in prospective memory impairments as well. Hence, future studies should identify the particular locus of patients' prospective memory deficits to examine the possibility that different forms of brain damage may have differential effects on the cognitive processes involved in prospective remembering.

Providing further support for the aforementioned findings, questionnaire and interview studies have revealed that patients with TBI (Hannon et al., 1995; Mateer, Sohlberg, & Crinean, 1987) or parents of children with TBI (Ward, Shum, Dick, McKinlay, & Baker-Tweney, 2004) report a high incidence of day-to-day prospective memory problems associated with the brain injury. However, it was found that TBI patients may largely underestimate their prospective memory deficits and thus show a reduced self-awareness of their impairments (see Brooks et al., 2004;

Knight et al., 2005; Roche, Fleming, & Shum, 2002). Clearly, these findings point to the need for more tools enabling objective assessments of prospective memory performance in clinical practice.

With regard to the mechanisms underlying the prospective memory difficulties of patients with brain injury, some studies suggest that the deficits are mainly due to the prospective rather than the retrospective component of prospective memory, as patients are often fully aware of the content of the intention when asked for it (Cockburn, 1995; Daum & Mayes, 2000; Henry et al., in press; Kopp & Thöne-Otto, 2003; Maujean et al., 2003; Shum et al., 1999). However, contrasting findings come from a study that specifically aimed at disentangling deficits of TBI patients in the prospective and retrospective component, where patients were found to be impaired in both components relative to normal controls (Carlesimo et al., 2004; see Brooks et al., 2004, for similar findings). Hence, in some patients, deficits in retrospective memory are at least partially responsible for their poor prospective remembering. For example, amnesics or other patients with retrospective memory deficits may encounter situations in which they realize that something has to be done, but do not remember what specifically it was (cf. Carlesimo et al., 2004). The finding that both the prospective and retrospective components may be disrupted in some patients with brain injury is also in line with the proposal that their prospective memory deficits may result from a general reduction in processing capacity or cognitive resources (Maujean et al., 2003).

Another line of evidence closely links the prospective memory deficits of patients with brain injury to their concomitant executive dysfunctions (Daum & Mayes, 2000; Kliegel et al., 2004; Kopp & Thöne-Otto, 2003; Mathias & Mansfield, 2005; Maujean et al., 2003). Importantly, there is evidence that prospective memory is more sensitive to executive dysfunction than to retrospective storage deficits. Specifically, impairments in executive functioning, but not impairments in retrospective memory, were found to result in diminished abilities to perform prospective memory tasks (e.g., Kopp & Thöne-Otto, 2003; cf. Kliegel et al., 2004). This pattern of findings is thus consistent with the suggestion that prospective memory may more strongly rely on prefrontally mediated (executive control) processes than on temporally mediated (retrospective memory) processes (Brunfaut, Vanoverberghe, & d'Ydewalle, 2000; McDaniel et al., 1999). However, it is important to note that, in general, patients with severe amnesia are unable to perform prospective memory tasks (Kopp & Thöne-Otto, 2003). To conclude, a certain level of retrospective memory functioning is a prerequisite for prospective memory, as the content of an intention has to be recalled to perform it. This ability is obviously disrupted in patients with severe retrospective memory deficits. It seems, however, that prospective memory is already lowered through relatively mild disruptions of executive functioning. This has led to the proposal that prospective memory performance is especially sensitive to executive dysfunctions compared to retrospective memory deficits. However, it is notable that a considerable number of studies have found deficits of patients in prospective memory tasks that were not accompanied by concomitant deficits in executive functioning (Burgess, 2000; Burgess et al., 2000; Bisiacchi, 1996; Fortin et al., 2002, 2003; Palmer & McDonald, 2000; Schmitter-Edgecombe & Wright, 2004; Shallice & Burgess, 1991).

Prospective Memory in Alzheimer's Disease

Overview   Cognitive impairments that occur due to Alzheimer's disease or other forms of dementia have been well described in terms of retrospective memory deficits or executive dysfunction, with the predominant difficulties in retrospective memory, at least in earlier stages of the disease (Collie & Maruff, 2000; Duke & Kaszniak, 2000). The neuropathology of Alzheimer's disease is characterized by a widespread neuronal cell loss, together with an inflammatory response to the deposition of amyloid plaques and neurofibrillary tangles. It is known that both frontal and temporal brain regions are damaged through these mechanisms, even in preclinical forms of the disease (Jones, Livner, & Bäckman, 2006). On the basis of these neurocognitive disruptions, substantial deficits in performing prospective memory tasks were expected among patients with Alzheimer's disease (Knight, 1998). Until recently there has not been much research investigating this hypothesis (Maylor, 1995). Currently, there is a handful of studies that indeed revealed that a severe prospective memory deficit is highly prevalent in Alzheimer's disease, even in preclinical or mild forms of the disease. Most of these studies have targeted dementia of Alzheimer's type, and there is a lack of studies investigating other forms of dementia (e.g., cortical dementia such as vascular or frontotemporal dementia, or subcortical dementia such as Huntington's disease, etc.).

Relevant Findings   An initial study applied the prospective memory subtests of the Rivermead Behavioral Memory Test (RBMT; Wilson, Cockburn, & Baddeley, 1985) as well as retrospective memory tests to patients with minimal dementia, moderate dementia (mostly patients with Alzheimer's disease), and normal controls (Huppert & Beardsall, 1993). This study revealed that in retrospective memory, the patients with minimal dementia scored intermediate relative to the other two groups. In contrast, in the prospective memory tasks, patients with minimal dementia showed a similar performance as moderately demented patients, with both patient groups scoring substantially worse than controls (see Kazui et al., 2005, for a similar finding, and see Driscoll, McDaniel, & Guynn, 2005, for initial converging evidence in participants whose apolipoprotein E (APOE) status indicates that they are at risk for Alzheimer's disease). Based on this outcome, Huppert and Beardsall (1993) concluded that prospective memory might be more susceptible to the adverse effects of early stages of dementia compared to retrospective memory (see Kixmiller, 2002; Knight, 1998, for similar arguments; see also Craik, 1986; Jones et al., 2006; but see Maylor, 1995).

Subsequent studies provided further evidence that dementia is associated with prospective memory impairments. In a questionnaire study, Smith, Della Sala, Logie, and Maylor (2000) found that Alzheimer's disease results in chronic prospective memory failures in everyday life. These failures were even reported to have a greater negative impact on caregivers' lives in comparison to patients' retrospective memory failures. Three further studies applying laboratory-based tasks supported the notion that prospective memory decline is a characteristic of dementia. Specifically, in a large-scale population-based study, participants with very mild dementia were almost unable to perform a prospective memory task with respect to both the prospective and the retrospective components (Huppert, Johnson, & Nickson, 2000). In another study, patients with Alzheimer's disease were substantially impaired in time- and event-based prospective memory relative to healthy controls (Maylor, Smith, Della Sala, & Logie, 2002). Here, it seemed to be primarily the prospective component that was disrupted by Alzheimer's disease. Finally, extending the studies on clinical forms of Alzheimer's disease, Jones et al. (2006) provided evidence that prospective memory impairments are already evident in preclinical forms of Alzheimer's disease. Here, the prospective and the retrospective components were similarly impaired. Importantly, Jones et al.'s study indicated that prospective memory performance has an independent contribution to the prediction of Alzheimer's disease over and above that of retrospective memory performance. In summary, there is initial evidence of highly prevalent prospective memory failures in dementia, even in preclinical or mild forms of the disease. Clearly, the low number of empirical studies argues for cautious interpretation of the findings and highlights the need for further research in this area.

Prospective Memory in Parkinson's Disease

Overview   Patients suffering from Parkinson's disease have been found to develop severe cognitive deficits predominantly in terms of executive dysfunction. Parkinson's disease also results in retrospective memory problems, but these deficits are generally milder than in dementia (Zgaljardic, Borod, Foldi, & Mattis, 2003). The primary site of pathology among patients with Parkinson's disease lies in the midbrain, where a loss of dopamine-producing neurons is observed. Until recently, it remained unclear whether the disease disrupts prospective memory as well, although such a deficit was expected in the light of the neuropsychological profile of patients with Parkinson's disease (Knight, 1998).

Relevant Findings   So far only two studies have addressed prospective memory abilities in Parkinson's disease. Katai, Maruyama, Hashimoto, and Ikeda (2003) administered a time-based and an event-based task and found that the patients were significantly impaired only in the latter task relative to healthy controls (note that this finding was somewhat surprising given that time-based tasks are typically found to be more sensitive to cognitive decline than event-based tasks; see, e.g., Einstein, McDaniel, Richardson, Guynn, & Cunfer, 1995). Importantly, the deficit of the patients in the event-based task seemed to be due to failures in the prospective component rather than to failures in retrospectively remembering the content of the intention. Patients' diminished event-based prospective memory performance was attributed to a disruption of executive control processes necessary for the task, whereas patients' spared performance in the time-based task may result from preserved time-estimation abilities through the administration of dopamine agonists. Alternatively, different neural networks may be involved in time- versus event-based tasks, and thus these neural networks may have been differentially disrupted by the disease.

Kliegel, Phillips, Lemke, and Kopp (2005) applied a complex prospective memory paradigm that disentangles the four phases of prospective memory (see earlier; chapter 9) to examine the locus of the particular deficits associated with Parkinson's disease. Relative to healthy controls, the patients were found to be impaired in the intention formation phase in terms of developing less complex plans. Regarding intention initiation, patients also showed a trend toward diminished performance. By contrast, no group differences were found in retrospective memory for the self-generated plans and in the actual execution of the intention. It was thus concluded that Parkinson's disease might be associated with a relatively specific deficit in the ability to execute intended activities, namely with a poor ability to adequately plan the execution of an intention. Moreover, for these patients prospective memory deficits do not seem to result from failures in retrospective memory for the content of an intention but rather from a disruption of the prospective component. With regard to potential mechanisms underlying these deficits, Kliegel, Phillips, et al. revealed that the Parkinson's patients' impairment in prospective memory planning could be linked to working memory deficits.

Prospective Memory in Other Neuropathological Diseases (Multiple Sclerosis, HIV, and Herpes Simplex Encephalitis)

Relevant Findings   The first experimental investigation of prospective memory in patients with multiple sclerosis was carried out by Bravin, Kinsella, Ong, and Vowels (2000). Given that this disease has been found to result in deficits in retrospective memory and executive functioning, which could partly be due to dysfunctions of prefrontal and medial temporal lobe interactions, substantial deficits of the patients in prospective remembering were expected. Consistently, across two time-based tasks patients performed significantly worse than healthy controls. Importantly, although the patients appeared to be slightly impaired in the prospective component, their deficit was more pronounced in the recall of the specific actions that had to be carried out. This indicates that multiple sclerosis may particularly impair the retrospective component of prospective memory tasks. Further studies are necessary to investigate the exact nature of prospective memory deficits associated with multiple sclerosis.

In an interesting case report, West, McNerney, and Krauss (2005) described a patient suffering from multiple sclerosis who appeared to have a focal and selective deficit in prospective memory in conjunction with fully intact general intelligence, executive functioning, and retrospective memory. Hence, this single-case study suggests that there may be neurocognitive processes that are somewhat unique to prospective remembering and may even be selectively disrupted.

Carey et al. (2006) provided the first study on prospective memory in patients with HIV infection. HIV infection is known to result in neuropathology, particularly in a disruption of prefrontal-striatal neural circuits. Moreover, patients with HIV infection display cognitive impairments in processing speed, working memory, retrospective memory, and executive functioning. Across several prospective memory tasks, Carey et al. were able to confirm their hypothesis that patients with HIV are disrupted in their prospective memory abilities relative to healthy controls.

Finally, Sgaramella, Borgo, Fenzo, Garofano, and Toso (2000) first investigated prospective memory performance in patients with herpes simplex encephalitis. Given that these patients are reported to exhibit impairments in retrospective memory and executive functioning, substantial deficits of the patients in prospective remembering were expected. Consistently, patients appeared to be severely impaired in executing time- and event-based prospective memory tasks; however, no control group was included in the design.

Prospective Memory in Substance Abuse

Overview   Over the past decades, there has been an increasing use of recreational drugs in many countries. Cognitive deficits due to the abuse of drugs such as alcohol, MDMA (ecstasy), or cannabis have been well described in various domains (Parrott, 2001; Pope, 2002; B. Rodgers et al., 2005). A considerable number of studies have begun to address whether drug abusers have impaired prospective memory abilities. The hypothesis was tested that prospective memory is disrupted due to the abuse of drugs that have been found to produce deficits in retrospective memory or particularly in executive functioning. There is increasing evidence that long-term abuse of psychoactive drugs such as alcohol, MDMA, or cannabis, and even drugs with relatively weak psychostimulant effects such as nicotine (Heffernan et al., 2005; but cf. Rusted, Trawley, Heath, Kettle, & Walker, 2005) has detrimental effects on everyday prospective memory functioning.

Relevant Findings

Alcohol   One line of research has been concerned with the potential deleterious effects of chronic alcohol abuse on prospective remembering. Persistent abuse of alcohol results in cortical and subcortical damage, neurotransmitter impairments, brain shrinkage, inhibition of prefrontal cortex functioning, and reduction of the number of cholinergic neurons in the basal forebrain resulting in reduced hippocampal function (Heffernan, Moss, & Ling, 2002; Ling et al., 2003). These brain anomalies have been found to be associated with impaired retrospective memory, working memory, and executive functioning (Heffernan, Ling, & Bartholomew, 2004; Heffernan et al., 2002). On the basis of this neuropsychological profile, an adverse effect of alcohol abuse on prospective memory was expected.

An initial study investigated prospective memory in amnesic Korsakoff patients and nonamnesic chronic alcoholics by administering an event-based prospective memory task (Brunfaut et al., 2000). Because Korsakoff patients are known to suffer from severe retrospective memory deficits, it was expected that they would be strongly impaired in the retrospective component. Moreover, given the pronounced cerebral atrophy in the prefrontal cortex of Korsakoff patients, they were also expected to be disrupted in the prospective component. Indeed, across two experiments the Korsakoff patients showed significantly impaired prospective memory performance relative to the nonamnesic alcoholics. However, it remained unclear whether the deficit of the Korsakoff patients was mainly due to disruptions of the prospective or the retrospective component of the task.

Some further studies using questionnaires (Heffernan et al., 2004; Heffernan et al., 2002) or Web-based designs (Ling et al., 2003) have consistently revealed that chronic alcohol consumers report a higher incidence of day-to-day prospective memory problems relative to normal controls, although the cognitive deficits seem to be generalized and not specific to prospective memory (Ling et al., 2003). Moreover, chronic alcohol users may not show adequate self-awareness or management of their prospective memory deficits, as they do not use the support of external memory aids to a higher degree than controls (Heffernan et al., 2002). Importantly, the prospective memory deficits of chronic alcohol users are reported to be accompanied by impairments in everyday executive functioning (Heffernan et al., 2004), which provides further evidence for the suggestion that efficient executive functioning is an important precursor for prospective memory. Future work will have to further investigate the putative deficit of alcoholics in carrying out intended actions by applying objective tests of prospective memory performance.

Recreational Drugs   Another line of research has investigated disruptions in prospective remembering due to MDMA. The persistent use of this drug leads to psychopathological symptoms (e.g., irritability or depression) and results in cognitive dysfunctions such as mental confusion or decrements in retrospective memory, working memory, and executive functioning. These adverse effects are supposed to result from the neurotoxic effects of MDMA on prefrontal and medial temporal brain regions (Heffernan, Ling, & Scholey, 2001; Zakzanis & Young, 2001). Studies using questionnaires assessing day-to-day prospective memory abilities (Heffernan, Jarvis, Rodgers, Scholey, & Ling, 2001; Heffernan, Ling, & Scholey, 2001; J. Rodgers et al., 2001) consistently revealed that regular MDMA users seem to experience substantially more problems in a variety of everyday prospective memory tasks than normal controls. Importantly, the adverse effects of the drug do not seem to result from the concomitant use of other substances such as alcohol, tobacco, marijuana, or cocaine (Heffernan, Ling, & Scholey, 2001) or from the possibility that MDMA users may generally perceive their cognitive functioning as more flawed (Heffernan, Jarvis, et al., 2001). Moreover, MDMA users do not seem to compensate for their prospective memory difficulties by the use of external memory aids (Heffernan, Ling, & Scholey, 2001), which seems to indicate that they may not dispose of adequate self-awareness or management of their deficits (which would in turn challenge the validity of self-report data in these groups). Importantly, concomitant impairments in executive functions were found to accompany the prospective memory deficits of MDMA users (Heffernan, Jarvis, et al., 2001).

In a Web-based survey, J. Rodgers et al. (2001) focused on the relative contributions of MDMA and cannabis on self-rated memory performance. The abuse of both cannabis and MDMA seems to result in impaired prospective memory, but the two drugs were associated with differential adverse effects. Specifically, cannabis was associated with disruptions of short-term and internally cued prospective memory, whereas MDMA was related to problems in long-term prospective memory tasks. Hence, the possibility exists that different kinds of drugs differentially affect prospective memory performance, presumably due to differences in the drug effects' neural underpinnings.

In the only study applying laboratory-based prospective memory tasks to MDMA users, there was further indication that the use of this drug may lead to substantially impaired prospective memory skills, whereas there was no similar deficit in retrospective memory tasks (Zakzanis, Young, & Campbell, 2003). Hence, this study underlines the suggestion that prospective memory tests may have a higher sensitivity for detecting cognitive deficits relative to tests tapping retrospective memory (Palmer & McDonald, 2000).

Prospective Memory in Schizophrenia

Overview   Schizophrenia is a psychopathological disorder that is associated with neuropsychological dysfunctions in the areas of attention, retrospective memory, working memory, and executive functioning (Aleman, Hijman, de Haan, & Kahn, 1999; Egeland et al., 2003; Hoff & Kremen, 2003; Kremen, Seidman, Faraone, & Tsuang, 2001; Meissner, Hacker, & Heilemann, 2001), possibly due to subtle damage of the medial temporal lobes and prefrontal cortex. On the basis of these impairments, it was expected that schizophrenia patients would also exhibit substantial problems in performing prospective memory tasks (Shum, Leung, Ungvari, & Tang, 2001).

Relevant Findings   A handful of studies have consistently revealed that schizophrenia is associated with deficits in performing time-, event-, or activity-based intentions (Elvevåg, Maylor, & Gilbert, 2003; Kumar, Nizamie, & Jahan, 2005; Meissner et al., 2001; Shum, Ungvari, Tang, & Leung, 2004), with a somewhat pronounced difficulty in time-based tasks that may be due to the patients' poor time monitoring (Shum et al., 2004). Importantly, the deficits do not seem to result from disruptions of the retrospective component (Kumar et al., 2005; Shum et al., 2004), but they seem to be partly mediated by executive dysfunction as indicated by correlations of participants' performance in executive tests and prospective memory tests (Shum et al., 2004).

Elvevåg et al. (2003) pointed out that prospective memory tasks are sensitive for problems in internal source monitoring, as they require evaluating whether an intended action still has to be performed or whether it has already been carried out. This requirement is especially relevant for habitual tasks where an intended action is often repeated (e.g., taking medicine every morning). As confusions about the source of actions or thoughts and reality monitoring errors are characteristic symptoms of schizophrenia, Elvevåg et al. hypothesized that schizophrenic patients have pronounced difficulties in judging whether an intended action waits to be carried out or whether it has already been performed. Indeed, it was found that relative to normal controls, the patients reported significantly more often having carried out the intended action in a habitual prospective memory task where in fact they had not. It would be interesting to further address the question of whether this kind of prospective memory error is specific to schizophrenia or also occurs in other etiologies.

Prospective Memory in Affective Disorders

Overview   There is nearly a complete lack of studies investigating prospective memory in affective disorders such as major depression or bipolar disorder, although some studies have addressed this issue in nonclinical samples (see Kliegel, Jäger, et al., 2005; see Kliegel & Jäger, 2006, for a review). As impairments in retrospective memory (Austin, Mitchell, & Goodwin, 2001; Burt, Zembar & Niederehe, 1995; Rogers et al., 2004) and executive functions (Channon, 1996; Elliott et al., 1997; Robertson & Taylor, 1985) have been found in major depression and bipolar disorder (Quraishi & Frangou, 2002), one can expect prospective memory deficits in patients suffering from affective disorders.

Relevant Findings   So far, only one study has addressed prospective remembering in major depression (Rude, Hertel, Jarrold, Covich, & Hedlund, 1999). In this study, patients demonstrated substantial deficits in their ability to carry out a time-based prospective memory task relative to normal controls. This is consistent with the proposal that depression-related impairments may be especially pronounced in tasks that require a high degree of self-initiated, controlled cognitive processes such as time-based prospective memory tasks (Kliegel & Jäger, 2006). Importantly, the findings of Rude et al. (1999) also point to the methodological issue of controlling for the effects of comorbid depression on prospective memory performance when examining other clinical populations.

Prospective Memory in Developmental Disorders

Overview   There is currently little research on prospective memory in childhood and adolescence, and even fewer studies have investigated whether the development of prospective memory skills is negatively affected by psychopathologies such as autism or Attention Deficit Hyperactivity Disorder (ADHD). In individuals with autism (Ozonoff & Jensen, 1999; Ozonoff & McEvoy, 1994; Prior & Hoffmann, 1990; Rumsey & Hamburger, 1988) and in those with ADHD (Willcutt, Doyle, Nigg, Faraone, & Pennington, 2005) executive dysfunctions are well documented. Hence, given the assumed involvement of executive functions in prospective memory, it was expected that children with autism or ADHD would be impaired in carrying out intended actions.

Relevant Findings

ADHD   Two studies on multitasking found that children diagnosed with ADHD have difficulties in the coordination of several to-be-performed tasks where the switching from one task to another may require some form of prospective remembering (Clark, Prior, & Kinsella, 2000; Siklos & Kerns, 2004). Additionally, one of these studies indicated that the deficits seem to be specific for ADHD and are not attributable to oppositional defiant/conduct disorder (Clark et al., 2000).

Kerns and Price (2001) administered a time-based prospective memory task in the form of a computer game to children with ADHD. Moreover, an event-based task was applied in which children were required to perform specific actions during the course of the experiment. Kerns and Price found that relative to a sample of normal controls, children with ADHD performed significantly worse in the time-based but not in the event-based task. This differential pattern of findings was explained by the assumption that time-based tasks generally rely more heavily on executive control processes than event-based tasks, and thus only the former was sensitive for disruptions due to ADHD.

Kliegel, Ropeter, and Mackinlay (in press) applied a complex prospective memory paradigm to children with ADHD (cf. Kliegel et al., chap. 9, this volume). By this means, Kliegel et al. aimed at identifying the locus of the prospective memory deficit associated with ADHD. It was hypothesized that the impairments are pronounced in those phases of prospective remembering where a high degree of executive control is required. Consequently, Kliegel et al. found that compared to a group of normal controls, the children with ADHD showed particular deficits in the intention formation phase as indicated by impulsive intention planning. Importantly, this planning deficit had further negative implications for the retention and implementation of the delayed intentions.

Autism   Only one study has so far investigated processes related to prospective memory in autistic patients. Similar to the findings on ADHD, Mackinlay, Charman, and Karmiloff-Smith (2006) reported impaired prospective memory performance in children with high-functioning autism or Asperger's syndrome as compared with typically developing controls. In a novel test of multitasking (Battersea Multitask Paradigm) the clinical group showed difficulties with planning, task switching, and inhibition of rule-breaking behavior. Consequently, the authors concluded that children with autism display deficits in the prospective organization of activities.

MAJOR ISSUES AND DIRECTIONS FOR FUTURE RESEARCH: TOWARD A CLINICAL NEUROPSYCHOLOGY OF PROSPECTIVE MEMORY

Since the publication of the last edition of this volume in 1996, quite a number of studies have been conducted to examine the effects of different clinical conditions on prospective memory. As can be seen in Table 13.1, only 7 of the 61 studies reviewed in this chapter were published in 1996 or before. In this section, we attempt to integrate the findings of the studies reviewed already and postulate the potential explanations or mechanisms for prospective memory impairment. In addition, we discuss issues that are relevant and important for advancing a clinical neuropsychology of prospective memory and provide suggestions for future research.

Apart from studying individual cases with localized damage to the prefrontal cortex and individuals with TBI, the studies reviewed have examined the effects of a wide range of clinical conditions on prospective memory. These conditions include other brain diseases (e.g., Alzheimer's disease, Parkinson's disease, multiple sclerosis), psychiatric disorders (e.g., schizophrenia, depression), substance abuse (e.g., alcohol, cannabis, MDMA), viral infections (e.g., HIV and Herpes Simplex Encephalitis), and developmental disorders (e.g., ADHD, autism). The patient groups were chosen in these studies mainly because they were reported to have prospective memory problems or because their pathology is related to brain areas that are supposed to be related to prospective memory. Most of these studies compared the performance of clinical groups and matched controls on one or more types of prospective memory (e.g., time-, event-, or activity-based) using tasks developed in the experimental literature. Typically, the results of these studies indicate that these patients tend to be impaired on one or more types of prospective memory (refer to Table 13.1).

These significant results confirm the reports and observations by patients, significant others, and health professionals that prospective memory impairment is a common symptom in many clinical conditions. The impairment is most likely related to the prospective component of the tasks (see Carlesimo et al., 2004, for exceptions). However, this finding might be limited by the fact that in many laboratory tasks applied the retrospective component is usually minimized following Ellis and Kvavilashvili's (2000) suggestion and that often postexperimental interviews were conducted to ensure that only participants who remembered the retrospective component were included in data analysis. These results underscore the importance of a valid assessment of this construct in clinical practice. Whereas retrospective memory is routinely assessed in many clinical settings, the assessment of prospective memory is neither common nor widespread. The introduction of clinical assessment of prospective memory may provide important additional insights into the neuropsychological profiles of patients (Carey et al., 2006) and the impact of prospective memory failures on patients' everyday lives (Mathias & Mansfield, 2005). In terms of research, it is imperative to conduct more prospective memory studies on other clinical groups that are commonly reported to have memory problems. Examples of these groups include patients with epilepsy and stroke, older individuals with mild cognitive impairment, and children with acquired brain injury.

Among the patient groups that were found to be impaired on time-, event-, or activity-based prospective memory, damage to the prefrontal area of the brain is common. The results of the studies reviewed, therefore, provide evidence to support the involvement of prefrontal processes and functions in prospective remembering. This is not surprising given the discussion earlier in this chapter. However, it should be pointed out that most of the patient groups included in the studies reviewed have damage (either localized or diffused) to other parts of the brain as well. For example, the medial temporal area and the hippocampus are areas commonly damaged in patients with TBI and patients who abuse alcohol. Therefore, one cannot rule out the involvement of other parts of the brain in prospective remembering. In fact, this is highly likely given that prospective memory is a complex construct that has multiple stages and components and requires more than one skill. To clearly and directly evaluate the unique contribution of the prefrontal lobe to prospective remembering, studies of patients with localized prefrontal lesions need to be conducted. This type of study, however, is difficult to conduct because it can take a long time to recruit patients. Moreover, as pointed out by Burgess and Shallice (1997), it is practically impossible to demonstrate a double dissociation between prospective and retrospective memory using patients with localized frontal and temporal damage because the latter group of patients is likely to show impairment on both retrospective and prospective memory. Another way to investigate the unique contribution of the prefrontal cortex in prospective memory is to monitor and compare the brain activity of patients and controls while they are performing different types of prospective memory tasks.

Among some of the studies reviewed, however, researchers have included experimental manipulations to evaluate the contribution of specific prefrontal functions to prospective memory. For example, Shum et al. (2004) hypothesized that patients with schizophrenia would be significantly more impaired in time-based rather than event-based tasks. The results confirmed this hypothesis. According to Shum et al., patients with damage to the prefrontal cortex have difficulty initiating actions. As such, they would have more difficulty in retrieving and carrying out an intended action in the experimental condition where external cues did not appear to prompt the intended action. However, it should be noted that this finding is not always reliable. For example, Shum et al. (1999) did not find patients with TBI to be significantly more impaired on time-based than event-based tasks. It is difficult to interpret this inconsistent finding because in the literature different researchers have used different ongoing and prospective memory tasks in their studies. Therefore, even though two studies claim to use a time-based PM task on the same clinical population, their results may not be the same and directly comparable. This lack of convergence of evidence is likely due to a lack of agreement on the procedure for assessing the same construct. One suggestion for future research, therefore, is for researchers to come to some agreement about the format and difficulty level of tasks used to assess different types of prospective memory. One promising approach that has recently been introduced to further classify event-based prospective memory tasks is the differentiation of focal and nonfocal event-based tasks (see McDaniel, Einstein, & Rendell, chap. 7, this volume). Resting on ideas developed in the context of the multiprocess framework (McDaniel & Einstein, 2000), this distinction proposes that in tasks that require focal processing the ongoing task encourages processing of the prospective cue. Importantly, in those tasks, more automatic retrieval processes will be involved. In contrast, in nonfocal tasks, more effortful, executive (monitoring) processes are assumed to be involved. In consequence, one could predict that (only) nonfocal event-based tasks may be affected by prefrontal impairments (see McDaniel et al., chap. 7, this volume, for consistent evidence in older adults).

Although it is important to know that individuals with different clinical conditions are impaired on different types of prospective memory, it is also important to ascertain the reason underlying the impaired performance. Among the studies reviewed, few studies were designed for this latter purpose. One exception is Kliegel, Phillips, et al.'s (2005) study that utilized a complex prospective memory paradigm in patients with Parkinson's disease and was able to show that these patients are impaired in the formation and initiation but not execution of intention.

Theoretically, a more detailed analysis of the reasons for failure in terms of either stages of prospective memory or other cognitive processes such as retrospective memory and executive functioning could help to build a more analytical theory and model of this construct. Practically, a better identification of the locus of prospective memory impairment could lead to better differential diagnoses among clinical groups. Furthermore, this could enable clinicians to design better or more effective rehabilitation techniques that specifically target the problem of a particular clinical group. For example, patients who have problems in forming and planning intentions can be provided more time and taught techniques during the intention-formation-encoding phase and patients who have problems in executing intentions can be taught to build more routine habits in their everyday life. One suggestion for future research, therefore, is to apply these more analytical tasks of prospective memory to different clinical groups to isolate or identify the locus of impairment.

One of the main findings in reviewing the recent studies is that patients or individuals with damage to the brain (particularly to the prefrontal cortex) are impaired on different types of prospective memory. However, it is interesting to note that none of the studies reviewed have examined or established the relationship between these impairments and outcomes (e.g., functional, vocational, and psychological). This is surprising given that the construct of prospective memory has its root in the applied tradition of memory research and that this construct is considered by clinicians and significant others of patients to be relevant and important for everyday functioning. One suggestion for future research, therefore, is to design studies that allow researchers to examine and clarify the relationships between prospective memory and outcome measures in different clinical groups. Another suggestion is to compare the relative importance of prospective memory measures with other demographics, neurological measures, and cognitive measures (e.g., IQ, retrospective memory, executive functions) in predicting outcomes. The results of these studies have the potential to validate the importance and utility of the construct of prospective memory in the clinical context.

As mentioned before, most of the tasks used to assess prospective memory in the reviewed studies were adapted from the experimental literature. Although these tasks were found to be sensitive in detecting prospective memory impairment in a number of clinical groups, they might not be suitable for use in clinical practice. This is because they usually require a substantial amount of time to administer and undertake, and clinicians might not be able to fit it in the existing assessment schedule and battery. In addition, some of these tasks require computer hardware and software that might not be easily available to clinicians in a hospital or rehabilitation setting. Finally, given that the psychometric properties of these tasks are seldom reported and that normative data for these tasks are usually lacking, these tasks do not meet the professional standards as psychological tests.

In response to this need, two psychometric tests of prospective memory have been developed. They are the Cambridge Prospective Memory Test (CAMPROMPT; Wilson et al., 2005) and the Memory for Intentions Screening Test (MIST; Raskin, 2004). The CAMPROMPT is an individually administered test designed for individuals 16 years and older and it takes 25 minutes to administer. It comprises three time-based and three event-based prospective memory tasks.

Norms of the test include a group of 212 controls and a group of 72 individuals with brain injury (mainly TBI). The MIST is also an individually administered test designed for adults and it takes about; 30 minutes to administer. There are eight prospective memory tasks in the test, half of them are time-based and half of them are event-based. The MIST is yet to be published, but norms have been collected for younger, middle-aged, and older adults. Although both of these tests look promising, they have mainly been applied to individuals with TBI. Therefore, more research is needed to demonstrate their utility in other clinical populations. Moreover, given that theories and models of prospective memory are still being developed in the experimental and clinical literature, it is expected that these tests may need to be modified or updated in the future.

In conclusion, as a construct that has recently gained considerable attention in the literature, prospective memory is considered to have implications for everyday, independent living. Individuals who are impaired on various types of prospective memory, therefore, may experience substantial difficulties personally, socially, and vocationally. In this chapter, we reviewed studies that had investigated prospective memory performance in a number of clinical populations. Most of these studies were conducted after the publication of the first edition of this volume and their results indicate that prospective memory impairments are very common in the patient populations reviewed. Although there is evidence to suggest that the impairments reported might be related to damage to the prefrontal area of the brain, more research is needed to confirm the unique contribution of this area to prospective remembering. To advance a clinical neuropsychology of prospective memory, it is also important to (a) utilize more analytical methodologies or tasks that allow researchers to identify or isolate the stage(s) or component(s) of prospective memory that are affected in the different conditions; (b) examine and establish the relationships between measures of prospective memory and outcome; and (c) develop and validate psychometric tests of prospective memory for use in clinical practice.

REFERENCES

Aleman, A., Hijman, R., de Haan, E. H. F., & Kahn, R. S. (1999). Memory impairment in schizophrenia: A meta-analysis. *American Journal of Psychiatry, 156*, 1358–1366.

Austin, M.-P., Mitchell, P., & Goodwin, G. M. (2001). Cognitive deficits in depression. *British Journal of Psychiatry, 178*, 200–206.

Bisiacchi, P. S. (1996). The neuropsychological approach in the study of prospective memory. In M. Brandimonte, G. O. Einstein, & M. A. McDaniel (Eds.), *Prospective memory: Theory and applications* (pp. 297–318). Mahwah, NJ: Lawrence Erlbaum Associates, Inc.

Bravin, J. H., Kinsella, G. J., Ong, B., & Vowels, L. (2000). A study of performance of delayed intentions in multiple sclerosis. *Journal of Clinical and Experimental Neuropsychology, 22*, 418–429.

Brooks, B. M., Rose, F. D., Potter, J., Jayawardena, S., & Morling, A. (2004). Assessing stroke patients' prospective memory using virtual reality. *Brain Injury, 18*, 391–401.

Brunfaut, E., Vanoverberghe, V., & d'Ydewalle, G. (2000). Prospective remembering of Korsakoffs and alcoholics as a function of the prospective-memory and on-going tasks. *Neuropsychologia, 38*, 975–984.

Burgess, P. W. (2000). Strategy application disorder: The role of the frontal lobes in human multitasking. *Psychological Research, 63,* 279–288.

Burgess, P. W., Quayle, A., & Frith, C. D. (2001). Brain regions involved in prospective memory as determined by positron emission tomography. *Neuropsychologia, 39,* 545–555.

Burgess, P. W., Scott, S. K., & Frith, C. D. (2003). The role of the rostral frontal cortex (area 10) in prospective memory: A lateral versus medial dissociation. *Neuropsychologia, 41,* 906–918.

Burgess, P. W., & Shallice, T. (1997). The relationship between prospective and retrospective memory: Neuropsychological evidence. In M. A. Conway (Ed.), *Cognitive models of memory* (pp. 247–272). Cambridge, MA: MIT Press.

Burgess, P. W., Veitch, E., de Lacy Costello, A., & Shallice, T. (2000). The cognitive and neuroanatomical correlates of multitasking. *Neuropsychologia, 38,* 848–863.

Burt, D. B., Zembar, M. J., & Niederehe, G. (1995). Depression and memory impairment: A meta-analysis of the association, its pattern, and specificity. *Psychological Bulletin, 117,* 285–305.

Camp, C. J., Foss, J. W., Stevens, A. B., & O'Hanlon, A. M. (1996). Improving prospective memory task performance in persons with Alzheimer's disease. In M. Brandimonte, G. O. Einstein, & M. A. McDaniel (Eds.), *Prospective memory: Theory and applications* (pp. 351–367). Hillsdale, NJ: Lawrence Erlbaum Associates, Inc.

Carey, C. L., Woods, S. P., Rippeth, J. D., Heaton, R. K., Grant, I., & the HNRC Group (in press). Prospective memory in HIV-1 infection. *Journal of Clinical and Experimental Neuropsychology.*

Carlesimo, G. A., Casadio, P., & Caltagirone, C. (2004). Prospective and retrospective components in the memory for actions to be performed in patients with severe closed-head injury. *Journal of the International Neuropsychological Society, 10,* 679–688.

Channon, S. (1996). Executive dysfunction in depression: The Wisconsin Card Sorting Test. *Journal of Affective Disorders, 39,* 107–114.

Clark, C., Prior, M., & Kinsella, G. J. (2000). Do executive function deficits differentiate between adolescents with ADHD and oppositional defiant/conduct disorder? A neuropsychological study using the six elements test and Hayling sentence completion test. *Journal of Abnormal Child Psychology, 28,* 403–414.

Cockburn, J. (1995). Task interruption in prospective memory: A frontal lobe function? *Cortex, 31,* 87–97.

Cockburn, J. (1996). Failure of prospective memory after acquired brain damage: Preliminary investigation and suggestions for future directions. *Journal of Clinical and Experimental Neuropsychology, 18,* 304–309.

Cohen, J. D., & O'Reilly, R. C. (1996). A preliminary theory of the interactions between prefrontal cortex and hippocampus that contribute to planning and prospective memory. In M. Brandimonte, G. O. Einstein, & M. A. McDaniel (Eds.), *Prospective memory: Theory and applications* (pp. 267–296). Mahwah, NJ: Lawrence Erlbaum Associates, Inc.

Collie, A., & Maruff, P. (2000). The neuropsychology of preclinical Alzheimer's disease and mild cognitive impairment. *Neuroscience and Biobehavioral Reviews, 24,* 365–374.

Craik, F. I. M. (1986). A functional account of age differences in memory. In F. Klix & H. Hagendorf (Eds.), *Human memory and cognitive capabilities: Mechanisms and performances* (pp. 409–422). Amsterdam: Elsevier.

Daum, I., & Mayes, A. R. (2000). Memory and executive function impairments after frontal or posterior cortex lesions. *Behavioural Neurology, 12,* 161–173.

Driscoll, I., McDaniel, M. A., & Guynn, M. J. (2005). Apolipoprotein E and prospective memory in normally aging adults. *Neuropsychology, 19,* 28–34.

Duke, L. M., & Kaszniak, A. W. (2000). Executive control functions in degenerative dementias: A comparative review. *Neuropsychology Review, 10,* 75–99.

Egeland, J., Sundet, K., Rund, B. R., Asbjornsen, A., Hugdahl, K., Landro, N. I., et al. (2003). Sensitivity and specificity of memory dysfunction in schizophrenia: A comparison with major depression. *Journal of Clinical and Experimental Neuropsychology, 25,* 79–93.

Einstein, G. O., & McDaniel, M. A. (1990). Normal aging and prospective memory. *Journal of Experimental Psychology: Learning, Memory, and Cognition, 16,* 717–726.

Einstein, G. O., & McDaniel, M. A. (1996). Retrieval processes in prospective memory: Theoretical approaches and some new findings. In M. Brandimonte, G. O. Einstein, & M. A. McDaniel (Eds.), *Prospective memory: Theory and applications* (pp. 115–142). Mahwah, NJ: Lawrence Erlbaum Associates, Inc.

Einstein, G. O., McDaniel, M. A., Richardson, S. L., Guynn, M. J., & Cunfer, A. R. (1995). Aging and prospective memory: Examining the influences of self-initiated retrieval processes. *Journal of Experimental Psychology: Learning, Memory, and Cognition, 21,* 996–1007.

Elliott, R., Baker, S. C., Rogers, R. D., O'Leary, D. A., Paykel, E. S., Frith, C. D., et al. (1997). Prefrontal dysfunction in depressed patients performing a complex planning task: A study using positron emission tomography. *Psychological Medicine, 27,* 931–942.

Ellis, J. (1996). Prospective memory or the realization of delayed intentions: A conceptual framework for research. In M. Brandimonte, G. O. Einstein, & M. A. McDaniel (Eds.), *Prospective memory: Theory and applications* (pp. 1–22). Mahwah, NJ: Lawrence Erlbaum Associates, Inc.

Ellis, J., & Kvavilashvili, L. (2000). Prospective memory in 2000: Past, present and future directions. *Applied Cognitive Psychology, 14,* S1–S9.

Elvevåg, B., Maylor, E. A., & Gilbert, A. L. (2003). Habitual prospective memory in schizophrenia. *BMC Psychiatry, 3,* 1–7.

Fortin, S., Godbout, L., & Braun, C. M. J. (2002). Strategic sequence planning and prospective memory impairments in frontally leisoned head trauma patients performing activities of daily living. *Brain and Cognition, 48,* 361–365.

Fortin, S., Godbout, L., & Braun, C. M. J. (2003). Cognitive structure of executive deficits in frontally lesioned head trauma patients performing activities of daily living. *Cortex, 39,* 273–291.

Groot, Y. C. T., Wilson, B. A., Evans, J., & Watson, P. (2002). Prospective memory functioning in people with and without brain injury. *Journal of the International Neuropsychological Society, 8,* 645–654.

Guynn, M. J., McDaniel, M. A., & Einstein, G. O. (2001). Remembering to perform actions: A different type of memory? In H. D. Zimmer, R. L. Cohen, M. J. Guynn, J. Engelkamp, R. Kormi-Nouri, & M. A. Foley (Eds.), *Memory for action: A distinct form of episodic memory?* (pp. 25–48). New York: Oxford University Press.

Hannon, R., Adams, P., Harrington, S., Fries-Dias, C., & Gibson, M. T. (1995). Effects of brain injury and age on prospective memory self-rating and performance. *Rehabilitation Psychology, 40,* 289–297.

Heffernan, T. M., Jarvis, H., Rodgers, J., Scholey, A. B., & Ling, J. (2001). Prospective memory, everyday cognitive failure and central executive function in recreational users of ecstasy. *Human Psychopharmacoloy, 16,* 607–612.

Heffernan, T. M., Ling, J., & Bartholomew, J. (2004). Self-rated prospective memory and central executive deficits in excessive alcohol users. *Irish Journal of Psychological Medicine, 21,* 122–124.

Heffernan T. M., Ling, J., Parrott, A. C., Buchanan, T., Scholey, A. B., & Rodgers, J. (2005). Self-rated everyday and prospective memory abilities of cigarette smokers and nonsmokers: A www study. *Drug & Alcohol Dependence, 78,* 235–241.

Heffernan, T. M., Ling, J., & Scholey, A. B. (2001). Subjective ratings of prospective memory deficits in MDMA ("ecstasy") users. *Human Psychopharmacology, 16,* 339–344.

Heffernan, T. M., Moss, M., & Ling, J. (2002). Subjective ratings of prospective memory deficits in chronic heavy alcohol users. *Alcohol and Alcoholism, 37,* 269–271.

Henry, J. D., Phillips, L. H., Crawford, J. R., Kliegel, M., Theodorou, G., & Summers, F. (in press). Traumatic brain injury and prospective memory: Influence of task complexity. *Journal of Clinical and Experimental Neuropsychology.*

Hoff, A. L., & Kremen, W. S. (2003). Neuropsychology in schizophrenia: An update. *Current Opinion in Psychiatry, 16,* 149–156.

Huppert, F. A., & Beardsall, L. (1993). Prospective memory impairment as an early indicator of dementia. *Journal of Clinical and Experimental Neuropsychology, 15,* 805–821.

Huppert, F. A., Johnson, T., & Nickson, J. (2000). High prevalence of prospective memory impairment in the elderly and in early-stage dementia: Findings from a population-based study. *Applied Cognitive Psychology, 14,* 63–81.

Jones, S., Livner, A., & Bäckman, L. (2006). Patterns of prospective and retrospective memory impairment in preclinical Alzheimer's disease. *Neuropsychology, 2,* 144–152.

Katai, S., Maruyama, T., Hashimoto, T., & Ikeda, S. (2003). Event based and time based prospective memory in Parkinson's disease. *Journal of Neurology, Neurosurgery, and Psychiatry, 74,* 704–709.

Kazui, H., Matsuda, A., Hirono, N., Mori, E., Miyoshi, N., Ogino, A., et al. (2005). Everyday memory impairment of patients with mild cognitive impairment. *Dementia and Geriatric Cognitive Disorders, 19,* 331–337.

Kerns, K. A., & Price, K. J. (2001). An investigation of prospective memory in children with ADHD. *Child Neuropsychology, 7,* 162–171.

Kinch, J., & McDonald, S. (2001). Traumatic brain injury and prospective memory: An examination of the influences of executive function and retrospective memory. *Brain Impairment, 2,* 119–130.

Kinsella, G., Murtagh, D., Landry, A., Homfray, K., Hammind, M., O'Beirne, L., et al. (1996). Everyday memory following traumatic brain injury. *Brain Injury, 10,* 499–507.

Kixmiller, J. S. (2002). Evaluation of prospective memory training for individuals with mild Alzheimer's disease. *Brain and Cognition, 49,* 237–241.

Kliegel, M., Eschen, A., & Thöne-Otto, A. I. T. (2004). Planning and realization of complex intentions in traumatic brain injury and normal aging. *Brain and Cognition, 56,* 43–54.

Kliegel, M., & Jäger, T. (2006). The influence of negative emotions on prospective memory: A review and new data. *International Journal of Computational Cognition, 4,* 1–17.

Kliegel, M., Jäger, T., Phillips, L. H., Federspiel, E., Imfeld, A., Keller, M., et al. (2005). Effects of sad mood on time-based prospective memory. *Cognition and Emotion, 19,* 1199–1213.

Kliegel, M., Martin, M., McDaniel, M. A., & Einstein, G. O. (2002). Complex prospective memory and executive control of working memory: A process model. *Psychologische Beiträge, 44,* 303–318.

Kliegel, M., Phillips, L. H., Lemke, U., & Kopp, U. A. (2005). Planning and realisation of complex intentions in patients with Parkinson's disease. *Journal of Neurology, Neurosurgery, and Psychiatry, 76,* 1501–1505.

Kliegel, M., Ropeter, A., & Mackinlay, R. J. (in press). Complex prospective memory in children with ADHD. *Child Neuropsychology.*

Knight, R. G. (1998). Prospective memory in aging and neurodegenerative disease. In A. Troster (Ed.), *Memory in neurodegenerative disease: Biological, cognitive, and clinical perspectives* (pp. 172–183). New York: Cambridge University Press.

Knight, R. G., Harnett, M., & Titov, N. (2005). The effects of traumatic brain injury on the predicted and actual performance of a test of prospective remembering. *Brain Injury, 19,* 27–38.

Knight, R. G., Titov, N., & Crawford, M. (2006). The effects of distraction on prospective remembering following traumatic brain injury assessed in a simulated naturalistic environment. *Journal of the International Neuropsychological Society, 12,* 8–16.

Kondel, T. K. (2002). Prospective memory and executive function in schizophrenia. *Brain and Cognition, 48,* 405–410.

Kopp, U. A., & Thöne-Otto, A. I. T. (2003). Disentangling executive functions and memory processes in event-based prospective remembering after brain damage: A neuropsychological study. *International Journal of Psychology, 38,* 229–235.

Kremen, W. S., Seidman, L. J., Faraone, S. V., & Tsuang, M. T. (2001). Intelligence quotient and neuropsychological profiles in patients with schizophrenia and in normal volunteers. *Biological Psychiatry, 50,* 453–462.

Kumar, D., Nizamie, S. H., & Jahan, M. (2005). Event-based prospective memory in schizophrenia. *Journal of Clinical and Experimental Neuropsychology, 27,* 867–872.

Kvavilashvili, L., & Ellis, J. (1996). Varieties of intention: Some distinctions and classifications. In M. Brandimonte, G. O. Einstein, & M. A. McDaniel (Eds.), *Prospective memory: Theory and applications* (pp. 23–52). Mahwah, NJ: Lawrence Erlbaum Associates, Inc.

Ling, J., Heffernan, T. M., Buchanan, T., Rodgers, J., Scholey, A. B., & Parrott, A. C. (2003). Effects of alcohol on subjective ratings of prospective and everyday memory deficits. *Alcoholism: Clinical and Experimental Research, 27,* 970–974.

Mackinlay, R., Charman, T., & Karmiloff-Smith, A. (in press). High functioning children with autism spectrum disorder: A novel test of multitasking. *Brain & Cognition.*

Mateer, C. A., Sohlberg, M. M., & Crinean, J. (1987). Focus on clinical research: Perceptions of memory function in individuals with closed-head injury. *Journal of Head Trauma Rehabilitation, 2,* 74–84.

Mathias, J. L., & Mansfield, K. M. (2005). Prospective and declarative memory problems following moderate and severe traumatic brain injury. *Brain Injury, 19,* 271–282.

Maujean, A., Shum, D., & McQueen, R. (2003). Effect of cognitive demand on prospective memory in individuals with traumatic brain injury. *Brain Impairment, 4,* 135–145.

Maylor, E. A. (1993). Aging and forgetting in prospective and retrospective memory tasks. *Psychology and Aging, 8,* 420–428.

Maylor, E. A. (1995). Prospective memory in normal ageing and dementia. *Neurocase, 1,* 285–289.

Maylor, E. A. (1996). Age-related impairment in an event-based prospective-memory task. *Psychology and Aging, 11,* 74–78.

Maylor, E. A., Smith, G., Della Sala, S., & Logie, R. H. (2002). Prospective and retrospective memory in normal aging and dementia: An experimental study. *Memory & Cognition, 30,* 871–884.

McCauley, S. R., & Levin, H. S. (2004). Prospective memory in pediatric traumatic brain injury: A preliminary study. *Developmental Neuropsychology, 25,* 5–20.

McDaniel, M. A., & Einstein, G. O. (2000). Strategic and automatic processes in prospective memory retrieval: A multiprocess framework. *Applied Cognitive Psychology, 14,* S127–S144.

McDaniel, M. A., Glisky, E. L., Rubin, S. R., Guynn, M. J., & Routhieaux, B. C. (1999). Prospective memory: A neuropsychological study. *Neuropsychology, 13,* 103–110.

Meissner, F., Hacker, W., & Heilemann, H. (2001). Gedächtnisleistungen und Instruktionseffekte bei Schizophrenie: Eine vergleichende Untersuchung an chronische

Schizophrenen und Gesunden [Memory performance and instructional effects in schizophrenia: A comparison between schizophrenics and Sane persons]. *Psychiatrische Praxis, 28,* 180–188.

Miller, E. K. (2000). The prefrontal cortex and cognitive control. *Nature Reviews Neuroscience, 1,* 59–65.

Miller, E. K., & Cohen, J. D. (2001). An integrative theory of prefrontal cortex function. *Annual Review of Neuroscience, 24,* 167–202.

Okuda, J., Fujii, T., Yamadori, A., Kawashimi, R., Tsukiura, T., Fakatsu, R., et al. (1998). Participation of the prefrontal cortices in prospective memory: Evidence from a PET study in humans. *Neuroscience Letters, 253,* 127–130.

Ozonoff, S., & Jensen, J. (1999). Brief report: Specific executive dysfunction profiles in three neurodevelopmental disorders. *Journal of Autism and Developmental Disorder, 29,* 171–177.

Ozonoff, S., & McEvoy, R. E. (1994). A longitudinal study of executive function and theory of mind development in autism. *Development and Psychopathology, 6,* 415–431.

Palmer, H. M., & McDonald, S. (2000). The role of frontal and temporal lobe processes in prospective remembering. *Brain and Cognition, 44,* 103–107.

Parrott, A. C. (2001). Human psychopharmacology of ecstasy (MDMA): A review of 15 years of empirical research. *Human Psychopharmacology, 16,* 557–577.

Pope, H. C., Jr. (2002). *Cannabis, cognition, and residual confounding. Journal of the American Medical Association, 287,* 1172–1174.

Prior, M. R., & Hoffmann, W. (1990). Brief report: Neuropsychological testing of autistic children through an exploration with frontal lobe tests. *Journal of Autism and Developmental Disorder, 20,* 581–590.

Quraishi, S., & Frangou, S. (2002). Neuropsychology of bipolar disorder: A review. *Journal of Affective Disorders, 72,* 209–226.

Raskin, S. (2004). Memory for intentions screening test (abstract). *Journal of the International Neuropsychological Society, 10*(Suppl. 1), 110.

Robertson, G., & Taylor, P. J. (1985). Some cognitive correlates of affective disorders. *Psychological Medicine, 15,* 297–309.

Roche, N. L., Fleming, J. M., & Shum, D. (2002). Self-awareness of prospective memory failure in adults with traumatic brain injury. *Brain Injury, 16,* 931–945.

Rodgers, B., Windsor, T. D., Anstey, K. J., Dear, K. B. G., Jorm, A. F., & Christensen, H. (2005). Non-linear relationships between cognitive function and alcohol consumption in young, middle-aged and older adults: The PATH Through Life Project. *Addiction, 100,* 1280–1290.

Rodgers, J., Buchanan, T., Scholey, A. B., Heffernan, T. M., Ling, J., & Parrott, A. (2001). Differential effects of ecstasy and cannabis on self-reports of memory ability: A Web-based study. *Human Psychopharmacology, 16,* 619–625.

Rogers, M. A., Kasai, K., Koji, M., Fukuda, R., Iwanami, A., Nakagome, K., et al. (2004). Executive and prefrontal dysfunction in unipolar depression: A review of neuropsychological and imaging evidence. *Neuroscience Research, 50,* 1–11.

Rude, S. S., Hertel, P. T., Jarrold, W., Covich, J., & Hedlund, S. (1999). Depression-related impairments in prospective memory. *Cognition and Emotion, 13,* 267–276.

Rumsey, J. M., & Hamburger, S. D. (1988). Neuropsychological findings in high-functioning men with infantile-autism, residual state. *Journal of Clinical and Experimental Neuropsychology, 10,* 201–221.

Rusted, J. M., Trawley, S., Heath, J., Kettle, G., & Walker, H. (2005). Nicotine improves memory for delayed intentions. *Psychopharmacology, 182,* 355–365.

Schmitter-Edgecombe, M., & Wright, M. J. (2004). Event-based prospective memory following severe closed-head injury. *Neuropsychology, 18,* 353–361.

Sgaramella, T. M., Borgo, F., Fenzo, F., Garofano, P., & Toso, V. (2000). Memory for/and execution of future intentions: Evidence from patients with herpes simplex encephalitis. *Brain and Cognition, 43,* 388–392.

Shallice, T., & Burgess, P. W. (1991). Deficits in strategy application following frontal lobe damage in man. *Brain, 114,* 727–741.

Shum, D., Fleming, J., & Neulinger, K. (2002). Prospective memory and traumatic brain injury: A review. *Brain Impairment, 3,* 1–16.

Shum, D., Leung, J. P., Ungvari, G. S., & Tang, W. K. (2001). Schizophrenia and prospective memory: A new direction for clinical practice and research? *Hong Kong Journal of Psychiatry, 11,* 23–26.

Shum, D., Ungvari, G. S., Tang, W.-K., & Leung, J. P. (2004). Performance of schizophrenia patients on time-, event-, and activity-based prospective memory tasks. *Schizophrenia Bulletin, 30,* 693–701.

Shum, D., Valentine, M., & Cutmore, T. (1999). Performance of individuals with severe long-term traumatic brain injury on time-, event-, and activity-based prospective memory tasks. *Journal of Clinical and Experimental Neuropsychology, 21,* 49–58.

Siklos, S., & Kerns, K. A. (2004). Assessing multitasking in children with ADHD using a modified Six Elements Test. *Archives of Clinical Neuropsychology, 19,* 347–361.

Simons, J. S., Schölvinck, M. L., Gilbert, S. J., Frith, C. D., & Burgess, P. W. (in press). Differential components of prospective memory? Evidence from fMRI. *Neuropsychologia.*

Smith, G., Della Sala, S., Logie, R. H., & Maylor, E. A. (2000). Prospective and retrospective memory in normal ageing and dementia: A questionnaire study. *Memory, 8,* 311–321.

Titov, N., & Knight, R. G. (2000). A procedure for testing prospective remembering in persons with neurological impairments. *Brain Injury, 14,* 877–886.

Vogels, W. A., Dekker, M. R., Brouwer, W. H., & de Jong, R. (2002). Age-related changes in event-related prospective memory performance: A comparison of four prospective memory tasks. *Brain and Cognition, 49,* 341–362.

Ward, H., Shum, D., Dick, B., McKinlay, L., & Baker-Tweney, S. (2004). Interview study of the effects of paediatric traumatic brain injury on memory. *Brain Injury, 18,* 471–495.

West, R., McNerney, W., & Krauss, I. (2005, July). *Exploring the locus of a focal prospective memory deficit: A case study.* Poster presented at the Second International Conference on Prospective Memory, Zurich, Switzerland.

Willcutt, E. G., Doyle, A. E., Nigg, J. T., Faraone, S. V., & Pennington, B. F. (2005). Validity of the executive function theory of attention-deficit/hyperactivity disorder: A meta-analytic review. *Biological Psychiatry, 57,* 1336–1346.

Wilson, B. A., Cockburn, J., & Baddeley, A. D. (1985). *The Rivermead Behavioral Memory Test.* Titchfield, UK: Thames Valley Test.

Wilson, B. A., Emslie, H., Foley, J., Shiel, A., Watson, P., Hawkins, K., et al. (2005). *Cambridge Prospective Memory Test (CAMPROMPT): Manual.* Oxford, UK: Harcourt Assessment.

Yamadori, A., Okuda, J., Fujii, T., Kawashima, R., Kinomura, S., Ito, M., et al. (1997). Neural correlates of prospective memory: A positron emission tomography study. *Brain and Cognition, 35,* 366–369.

Zakzanis, K. K., & Young, D. A. (2001). Memory impairment in abstinent MDMA ("ecstasy") users: A longitudinal investigation. *Neurology, 56,* 966–969.

Zakzanis, K. K., Young, D. A., & Campbell, Z. (2003). Prospective memory impairment in abstinent MDMA ("ecstasy") users. *Cognitive Neuropsychiatry, 8,* 141–153.

Zgaljardic, D. J., Borod, J. C., Foldi, N. S., & Mattis, P. (2003). A review of the cognitive and behavioral sequelae of Parkinson's disease: Relationship to frontostriatal circuitry. *Cognitive and Behavioral Neurology, 16,* 193–210.

14

Commentary: A Perspective on Prospective Memory

MORRIS MOSCOVITCH

Department of Psychology
University of Toronto

I imagine I was invited to discuss the papers because of my very early contribution to this area, which consisted of a single paragraph describing a real-life experiment on memory and aging (Moscovitch, 1982). In that study, Nina Minde[21] found that older adults were as good or better than younger adults at keeping phone appointments. This age advantage on naturalistic tasks as compared to an age deficiency on laboratory-based tasks is now known as the *age prospective memory paradox* and has been studied extensively since then (see Phillips, Henry, & Martin, chap. 8, this volume). I return to it at the end of this commentary. I also noted that some people have incorporated some ideas from my neuropsychologically based, component process model (Moscovitch, 1992, 1994; Moscovitch & Winocur, 1992) into their theories of prospective memory (see especially the work of McDaniel & Einstein summarized in this). Although I have a nodding familiarity with some of the current literature on the topic, my comments are not those of an expert, but of an interested observer. From that point of view, I found the following chapters in this book by Kliegel, Jäger, Altgassen, and Shum (chap. 13, this volume), West (chap. 12, this volume), and Burgess et al. (chap. 11, this volume) to be not only enjoyable, but enlightening.

Three major themes are apparent in reading the chapters. The first, which the authors perhaps take for granted and so do not state explicitly, is that research on prospective memory is about the only major enterprise in memory research in which the problem is not memory itself, but the uses to which memory is put. This is an extremely neglected area of research, with the vast majority of papers on memory dealing only with memory itself, as if memory evolved for its own sake rather than for the service of action or goal-directed behavior. This tendency to separate cognition from action is not peculiar to research on memory but can be found in other domains, such as perception, even though there is much evidence to indicate that doing so provides an incomplete, and probably erroneous, view of how cognition works (Goodale &Wolf, 2006). The essays on prospective memory do not go so far as to speculate how, or if, our views of retrospective memory would be altered by thinking of the uses to which it is put, although such considerations have contributed to evolving views of perception (Goodale & Milner, 1992; Goodale & Milner, 2004). Nonetheless, research on prospective memory moves things in the right direction (see especially Zimmer et al., 2006).

The second major theme is front and center in all the chapters: What are the components of prospective memory? Each of the chapters addresses this issue in a number of ways. What they all acknowledge is that prospective memory is a complex *function*, to use Burgess et al.'s nomenclature, that requires the identification of various *constructs* that contribute to the execution of that function. As I understand it, Burgess et al.'s use of the term *construct,* insofar as it applies to things such as memory, refers to what I call *components.* I hope Burgess et al. will forgive me for adopting my own terminology, with which I am more comfortable. Thus, research on prospective memory requires the identification of various components that make it up. What was surprising to me, however, was how much weight the concept of prospective memory had been made to bear, and how many components are now considered part of the function or concept of prospective memory. Prospective memory not only embodies the requirement to carry out some particular task in the future, but also to keep in mind a number of such tasks and the rules for executing them, to select among the best alternatives, to devise and keep in mind an order (plan) in which to carry them out, and to monitor the outcome to see if the tasks we executed according to plan. The multiple elements tasks that began with Shallice and Burgess's (1991) attempt to capture in a "laboratory" (I put this in quotation marks because some of the tasks actually were required to be executed on the street) the difficulties that some of their patients had in leading productive lives despite adequate perception, memory, and intelligence have now been incorporated into the general framework of prospective memory by many researchers in the field (see Burgess et al., chap. 11, this volume; Kliegel et al., chap. 13, this volume; Levine et al., 1998). Although everyone acknowledges that in real life knowing how to plan one's activities requires all these components, I think it is a mistake to include them in a scientific investigation of prospective memory, if one wants to get to the bottom of what is unique to it, as compared, say, to decision making under uncertainty, or to solving open-ended problems, or to planning in general.

How prospective memory interacts with those functions and the cognitive processes that mediate them is an interesting question in its own right, but it presupposes that we first know something about prospective memory independently of these other aspects. It may even be the case that prospective memory shares components with each of these other functions, but that is something to be proven, not something to be assumed at the beginning. My reading of the chapters suggests that all the authors would agree with many of these observations, although they sometimes blur the distinctions I am making. In rereading the chapters, a good exercise would be to isolate what one believes is peculiar to prospective memory and leave aside the other aspects of the tasks to get at what is special about prospective memory.

The third major theme is linked closely to the second, namely, to identify the neural substrates or correlates that are associated with the various components of prospective memory. This enterprise needed to await the development of some good theories of prospective memory before it became worthwhile. Such theories are now available, and the cognitive neuroscience of prospective memory not only complements these theories by helping to specify the neural mechanisms that support the different components that comprise prospective memory, but also can be used to determine the cognitive components themselves or corroborate that they are crucial. In short, evidence from neuropsychology and cognitive neuroscience can inform psychological theory. Thus, for example, by first demonstrating that rostral prefrontal cortex (area 10) is implicated in prospective memory tasks, and then by showing that it also is implicated on other tasks that involve stimulus-independent cognition, Burgess and his collaborators (chap. 11, this volume) bolster their case that stimulus-independent cognition is a crucial component of prospective memory.

THEME 1: THE USES TO WHICH MEMORY IS PUT

A major distinction in research on prospective memory is between it and retrospective memory. In almost all the studies, one wants to be reassured that the content of the memory that forms the basis for future action and the rules for its execution are retained (retrospective memory) if one is to examine the ability to retrieve them when required or desired (the prospective aspect). Although such a procedure is necessary, too often one reaches the conclusion that retrospective memory is relatively spared (or even completely intact) relative to impaired prospective memory, or at the very least, that performance on tests of retrospective memory cannot account fully for performance on tests of prospective memory. This conclusion is true only insofar as one's view of spared retrospective is restricted to the content of the memory and the rules for its execution. Research on retrospective memory, however, has shown that it encompasses much more than that. Although I profess my ignorance of much of the recent literature on prospective memory, I was struck by the articles that I read that there was little attempt to see if deficits in prospective memory also are related to deficits in more complex tests of retrospective memory such as recollection as compared to familiarity, temporal ordering, source memory, and self-ordered pointing. The list is not exhaustive, but I mention these in particular because they seem to have components in common with those that are needed to perform well on tests of prospective memory, such as stimulus-independent thought, ordering responses, responding based on what has been remembered before, and so on. To my mind, the important distinction, therefore, is not between retrospective and prospective memory, but between the components needed for prospective memory and those that are not needed on some, but not all, tests of retrospective memory.

A second problem that has not been addressed in any of the readings is whether memory that has not been encoded for its prospective use actually contributes to performance. In proposing the component process model (Moscovitch, 1992, 1994; Moscovitch & Winocur, 1992), I drew the distinction between modular and central systems in memory. I noted that the hippocampus and related structures in the medial temporal lobes can be considered as memory modules that obligatorily encode any information that is fully attended (in consciousness) and also obligatorily and relatively automatically retrieve the encoded information when supplied with appropriate cues. This relatively automatic and "stupid" process is supplemented by strategic processes, mediated by the prefrontal cortex, that, at encoding, draw attention to information depending on the context and plan available at the time (intentions). At retrieval, these strategic processes are implicated in setting up a retrieval mode, which involves a search plan, and postretrieval monitoring, verification, and placing items in the proper temporal order so as to put the recovered memory to its proper use. Although models of prospective memory make use of the associative, automatic, and strategic components at retrieval, most of the research on encoding has focused only on the strategic aspects, the encoded intention to perform an act at a particular time. One reason for including a modular component at encoding, however, was that in real life we rarely know at any given time to what use the memory will be put, so we encode everything to which we attend fully. To what extent is this information, which was not part of intentional encoding on the prospective memory task, brought to bear on later prospective memory? For example, suppose that you encoded, without intending to act on it, that your friend likes to read novels by a particular author. When visiting this friend, what is the likelihood that you will think of bringing a novel as a present? Is this ability related at all to prospective memory abilities? It would seem to me that it is according to some models but not according to others, depending on how the prospective task is designed and implemented. Such unintended uses of memory on prospective tasks are very common; whether they typically are a crucial part of prospective memory or merely contribute to it, in the way that problem-solving ability does, remains to be seen.

THEMES 2 AND 3: COMPONENTS OF PROSPECTIVE MEMORY AND THEIR NEURAL CORRELATES AND SUBSTRATES

If there was any doubt that successful performance on tests of prospective memory depends on the contribution of many components, Kliegel et al. (chap. 13, this volume) should put those doubts to rest. All patient groups reported in their chapter showed impaired prospective memory despite having different disorders of different etiologies that affect different brain areas. There are many ways to fail a prospective memory task, and these findings support Kliegel et al.'s contention that tests of prospective memory should be part of a standard neuropsychological assessment, especially considering that problems with prospective memory and related functions are among the chief complaints of patients and their caretakers.

The issue with which the clinical neuropsychologist is faced, no less than the cognitive psychologist or neuroscientist, is specifying the source of the problem; that is, identifying the component(s) whose damage leads to the deficit. Kliegel and his colleagues, like Burgess, Levine, and others, have made a good start with their complex tasks, but my concern is that the tasks are too complex to administer in any routine way in the clinic. Moreover, in trying to imagine taking Kliegel et al.'s complex task myself, I felt disheartened. It felt as if I was being subjected to one of those awful days at work or at home where I would have to devise a plan to handle a variety of demands, run from one errand to another, and do it all under some time pressure while keeping some arcane rules and goals in mind. Indeed, the requirement to train participants extensively so that they can know the parameters of the task and what is expected of them indicates how difficult it is to do all this. My inclination, and I imagine anyone else's except for perhaps some people with brain damage, is to write a checklist that also contains the plan of action and then proceed to check items off as they are completed. If the goal is to create tests that can be used routinely in the clinic, I think one would have to sacrifice thoroughness for a rough and ready test of prospective memory, such as those developed by Wilson and her collaborators (Wilson, Cockburn, & Baddeley, 1985; Wilson et al., 2005) and then use additional tests to home in on the particular deficits that are primarily responsible for the impairment.

I found it appealing, and I must say satisfying, in reading the chapters, especially West's (chap. 12, this volume), to learn that the component process model with an associative, hippocampal component, and a strategic, frontal component, which I proposed for dealing with memory in general (see earlier), also is being applied, with little modification, to studies of prospective memory. In evaluating various theories, West notes that "within the automatic associative activation theory (a variant of McDaniel and Einstein's earlier detection and discrepancy theory [Guynn, 2003; Guynn, McDaniel, & Einstein, 2001]) the retrieval of an intention from memory is thought to occur when a focally attended prospective cue interacts with a memory trace representing the cue–intention association. The result of this interaction is the obligatory delivery of the intention to conscious awareness that is presumably followed by realization of the intention."

Although the general framework is consistent with the component process model, research on prospective memory has gone beyond it by identifying the strategic components at both a psychological and a neurological level more precisely than Winocur and I ever could in 1992 (but see Moscovitch & Winocur, 2002, for an update). Some general principles, however, apply, and I want to emphasize these, although I believe the authors noted them clearly. Each single component that supports performance on tests of prospective memory is not unique to it, but likely will be found on other tests that bear little resemblance to prospective memory on the surface. What distinguishes prospective memory from other functions is the constellation of components that comprise it. Thus, as West noted, the component needed to disengage from ongoing tasks to deal with the cues that call for the execution of delayed intentions may be the same as the one that is implicated in other tests that call for disengagement, such as task switching (see Braver, Reynolds, & Donaldson, 2003) or attention (Posner & Peterson, 1990), and would draw on similar neural structures in the prefrontal cortex. Likewise, as Burgess et al. (chap. 11, this volume) speculated, if stimulus-independent cognition and switching attention from internal to external events are crucial components of prospective memory, then these same components should be evident on tasks that make comparable demands but have no prospective component, and should activate comparable brain regions. Indeed, this seems to be the case, as when matching objects based on derived commonalities that are not directly observable in the stimulus itself (see Christoff, Ream, Geddes, & Gabrieli, 2003), and the same region of prefrontal cortex, rostral area 10, is activated in both instances (see also the studies by Gilbert, Frith, & Burgess, 2005; Gilbert, Simons, Frith, & Burgess, 2006, mentioned in the Burgess et al. chapter). This observation is consistent with the general idea that the prefrontal cortex is organized along a caudal-rostral dimension, with increasing abstractness or internalization as one moves rostrally toward the frontal poles (Christoff et al., 2003; Petrides, 2005).

A final case in point concerns following rules or a plan of action, which is crucial if delayed intentions are to guide behavior. Rule breaking or ignoring (or perhaps a kind of obliviousness to them) seems to be a hallmark of people with deficits in prospective memory (see Burgess et al., chap. 11, this volume). This behavior is reminiscent of a finding noted by B. Milner (1965) and Corkin (1965) in observing patients with frontal lesions as they were learning a visually guided or tactile maze, respectively. I quote this passage at length because it is almost indistinguishable from the description of Shallice and Burgess's patients who have impaired prospective memory though the maze test is one of simple learning.

The object of the task was to learn the correct path in a maze made up of an 8 × 8 grid of equally spaced boltheads by going from one to another:

> With a metal-pointed stylus in his preferred hand, he proceeds, one step at a time, from bolthead to bolthead, with the loud click of an electrical error-counter informing him whenever he leaves the correct path. The rules are few: he must go back to the preceding bolthead whenever the counter clicks; he must not retrace portions of the correct path; and he *must* not move diagonally across the board. . . . [one] patient, however, repeatedly failed to go back to the preceding bolthead when the error counter clicked, although he knew that he was supposed to do so. Thenceforth all such instances of "rule-breaking" were systematically recorded. Some patients with frontal-lobe lesions persisted in back-tracking towards the starting-point (cf. Case A. N.); others omitted some of the steps on the route, or made diagonal moves in an attempt to approach the goal more directly. Many disregarded the clicking of the counter and the subsequent warning cries of the experimenter. . . . Some frontal-lobe patients would go back only one step after making an error (thus complying with the rules), but then, after a brief pause, would repeat their previous incorrect response. This kind of behaviour was rarely exhibited by the other subjects ... subjects with intact frontal lobes rarely, if ever, failed to carry out the test instructions, and the ability of the patients with bilateral hippocampal lesions to follow instruction is particularly noteworthy, in view of their difficulty in learning the correct path. (B. Milner, 1965, pp. 330–331.)

Significantly, although damage to either frontal lobe was associated with rule breaking, right-sided damage was particularly detrimental, as one might have expected given the recent literature on prospective memory (see Burgess et al., chap. 11, this volume). Moreover, the lesion included the frontal pole (rostral prefrontal cortex) in the most severe cases, although a deficit was observed in a patient with damage confined to the superior aspect of the prefrontal cortex. Of course, one could argue that the maze task was a prospective memory task of sorts, with the participant having to remember what to do at each bolthead, but that would be stretching the notion of prospective memory too far for it to be useful.

Given the variety of components that contribute to prospective memory, I was relieved to discover that it is possible to distinguish them from those implicated in some tests of free recall, cued recall and recognition, working memory, vigilance, and divided attention in elegant experiments either conducted by the authors of these chapters or reported by them (see especially West, chap. 12, this volume). What seems to make prospective memory different from all these is the requirement to act on delayed intentions. A crucial region is the rostral prefrontal cortex, or area 10, with the lateral aspect acting in conjunction with the medial aspect, to maintain intentions and shift attention from internal thoughts or intentions to external stimuli, as Burgess et al.'s (chap. 11, this volume) gateway theory posits.

As attractive as the theory is, it needs to be combined, in my opinion, with the detection and discrepancy and search model if it is to be viable. That area 10 may be in a state of heightened activation in anticipation of a prospective cue is not in doubt (see Burgess et al.). That it can stay in this state of heightened activation for months or years, considering that one can have intentions to act in the distant future, is very unlikely, especially if we consider that we hold many different intentions simultaneously. Some mechanism is required to store the intentions offline and revive them in response to internal or external cues as needed, and deliver the output to area 10 to begin the process of implementing them. Along with area 10, therefore, the medial temporal lobe and other regions of prefrontal and posterior cortex (not to mention subcortical structures, whose contribution has hardly been examined) play a crucial role. Although such a neuropsychological model of prospective memory may exist in the literature, I am not aware of one that takes all these aspects into account.

A study on Prospective Memory for Telephone Appointments Let me end by returning to the only study I conducted on prospective memory. To remind you, Nina Minde, the moving force behind this study, and I found that older adults were no worse, and sometimes even better, than younger adults in keeping phone appointments. The data have never been published, but they appear in Table 14.1 through Table 14.5, for the different conditions we tried. In the first experiment, participants had to remember to make phone calls to an answering service 5 days a week for 2 weeks. As a reminder, each person was given a piece of paper with the telephone number and the times of his or her calls. Participants had to call within 3 minutes of the appointed time. As can be seen from Table 14.1, older adults missed far fewer appointments than younger adults.

TABLE 14.1   Total Number of Appointments Missed by Younger and Older Adults in Experiment 1

	Forgot (11 Minutes or More)	Forgot (4–10 Minutes)	Excuse	Early (4 Minutes or Before)
Older ($n = 10$)	8	3	2	5
Young ($n = 10$)	16	9	3	12

Note. Participants were required to call once a day for 5 days a week for 2 weeks.

To control for the possibility that older adults relied on external cues whereas younger adults relied on internal ones, and that requiring so many phone calls puts an undue strain on younger adults' schedules, we did the following in Experiment 2: Participants were asked to keep only two telephone appointments, scheduled 4 to 6 days apart, one in the morning and one in the afternoon. *Each person was given a card with the telephone number on it but was specifically instructed not to make any written reminder of the appointments.* The number was to be kept hidden and only retrieved at the time that it was needed. Again, older adults outperformed younger ones (See Table 14.2). In Experiment 3, we added even more to prospective memory demands. Participants were asked to keep two appointments 4 to 6 days apart, one in the morning and the other in the afternoon, using a different phone number for each. The times in this experiment, and the others, were chosen in consultation with the participant. We were encouraged by the finding that now there was little difference between the performances of older and younger adults (Table 14.3), but dismayed that even on such a difficult task, older adults' performance was not worse.

TABLE 14.2   Total Number of Appointments Missed by Younger and Older Adults in Experiment 2

	Early Excuse	Late Excuse	Forgetting
Older ($n = 10$)	1	2	3
Young ($n = 10$)	2	2	4

Note. Participants were required to call only twice, 4 to 6 days apart.

TABLE 14.3   Total Number of Appointments Missed by Younger and Older Adults in Experiment 3

	Early Excuse	Late Excuse	Forgetting
Older ($n = 15$)	3	2	12
Young ($n = 15$)	4	3	14

Note. Participants were required to call only twice, 4 to 6 days apart, each time to a different phone number.

To bring older adults to their knees, we repeated Experiment 3, but now had them keep three appointments at three different numbers over a 2-week period, and as in Study 2, each person was specifically instructed not to make any written reminder of the appointments. If anything, this variation had the opposite effect (see Table 14.4) in that older adults outperformed the young.

TABLE 14.4   Total Number of Appointments Missed by Younger and Older Adults in Experiment 4

	Forgot(11 Minutes or More)	Forgot (4–10 Minutes)	Excuse	Early (4 Minutes or Before)
Older (n = 8)	1	1	2	2
Young (n = 10)	8	2	2	5

Note. Participants were required to call three times over a 2-week period, each time to a different phone number.

Discouraged from lowering the older adults' performance, we resorted to trying to improve the performance of younger adults. Conjecturing that perhaps younger adults did not take their task seriously or were otherwise unmotivated, we offered a monetary incentive of their own choosing, up to $20, which was quite a bit for an undergraduate in 1980. Also, to make it easy on them, they could choose to call at whatever time they wished, and if they were on time, they would receive their reward. This monetary incentive seemed merely to widen the gap in favor of the older adults (see Table 14.5). It was the older adults who rose to the occasion, whereas the young adults became worse; only one of the young adults kept the appointment on time. Although many of the older adults declined the incentive at the end of the study, it presumably spurred them to greater heights perhaps because they interpreted the incentive as indicating how serious we were about their keeping the appointment.

TABLE 14.5   Total Number of Appointments Missed by Younger and Older Adults in Experiment 4

	Early Excuse	Late Excuse	Forgetting
Older (n = 11)	1	1	1
Young (n = 11)	—	3	7

Note. Participants were required to call only once, and received a monetary reward if they called on time.

We did not have a ready interpretation of these findings, and we certainly did not conduct the study to test theories of prospective memory, which I am not sure even existed as a technical term at the time. Our point in conducting the study was to see whether older adults would be as debilitated in real life (naturalistic setting) as their performance on laboratory tests of episodic memory would lead us to expect. To our surprise, they were not. We speculated that good organizational skills and a sense of responsibility or conscientiousness, combined with an awareness of memory's unreliability from a lifetime of experience, can more than make up for a loss of memory power with age.

In reviewing these chapters, I learned that this conundrum, as to why older adults who consistently perform poorly on many laboratory tests of prospective memory can perform so well on many comparable tests of prospective memory in real life, now has an official designation: *age prospective memory paradox*. Phillips et al. (chap. 8, this volume) thoroughly review the evidence associated with this paradox and consider a number of explanations of it, some similar to our own. From reading their review, it is clear that no single factor or hypothesis will account for all, or even most, of the data, although a combination of them may account for many of the findings.

Let me add a neuropsychological hypothesis to many of their functional ones. The emerging consensus is that area 10 in rostral prefrontal cortex plays a pivotal role in prospective memory, although other regions certainly contribute. Considering that this area is one of the last to develop, and that development proceeds well into adolescence, it is possible that this region is not fully functional in young adult undergraduates, and may be in no better (and possibly worse) shape than in our well-educated and accomplished older volunteers. Certainly, the data on aging to which West (chap. 12, this volume) and Phillips et al. (chap. 8, this volume) allude do not speak against it. This neurodevelopmental hypothesis complements some of the hypotheses offered by Phillips et al. and suggests a possible neural underpinning for some of them. If recruitment of area 10 is crucial for performance on self-initiated tests of prospective memory, then older adults should perform well, relative to younger adults, on those tests that are especially reliant on this structure. Of course, in conducting experiments based on this hypothesis, care must be taken to control for other components that may contribute to performance.

In this light, it is interesting to consider the role of ecological validity in determining age differences in performance (Phillips et al., chap. 8, this volume). Combined with the neuropsychological hypothesis, it suggests that there is an interaction between the component process that is engaged in a task and the information or action on which it operates. Doing something familiar allows that component, which may be functional in older adults, to be expressed. If the task is less familiar or well practiced, that component may not be expressed or it may be expressed less reliably. (This interaction between task and components is valid whether the component is fully functional or somewhat deteriorated.) For example, in a study conducted by Baddeley (1986) on short-term memory for digits, older adults show little deficit if they merely have to repeat the digits but show a noticeable deficit if they have to dial the digits. Likewise, in a set of studies on memory for objects in infants, Kates and I Kates, 1995; Kates and Moscovitch found that memory was much better if the infants indicated their knowledge by moving their eyes than by reaching. Applying this rationale to neuroimaging studies, it would be interesting to see whether activation of area 10 was modulated by the familiarity of the task in older adults, and possibly younger adults, too.

CONCLUSION

If research on the cognitive neuroscience of memory has revealed that memory can be fractionated into different types, each mediated by different structures and governed by different principles, then research on prospective memory has gone that much further. More than research on any other aspect of memory, it places memory in the context of action and planning. Much has yet to be learned about the different components that are peculiar to prospective memory itself and those that it shares with other functions. Research on prospective memory, however, is at the vanguard of opening the study of memory to the broader cognitive and social contexts in which it exists. This, I hope, will be a direction in which the study of memory will be heading.

REFERENCES

Baddeley, A. D. (1986). Working Memory. Oxford University Press.

Braver, T. S., Reynolds, J. R., & Donaldson, D. I. (2003). Neural mechanisms of transient and sustained cognitive control during task switching. *Neuron, 39,* 713–726.

Christoff, K., Ream, J. M., Geddes, L. P. T., & Gabrieli, J. D. E. (2003). Evaluating self-generated information: Anterior prefrontal contributions to human cognition. *Behavioral Neuroscience, 11,* 1161–1168.

Corkin, S. (1965). Tactually-guided maze learning in man: Effects of unilateral cortical excisions and bilateral hippocampal lesions. *Neuropsychologia, 3,* 339–351.

Gilbert, S. J., Frith, C. D., & Burgess, P. W. (2005). Involvement of rostral prefrontal cortex in selection between stimulus-oriented and stimulus-independent thought. *European Journal of Neuroscience, 21,* 1423–1431.

Gilbert, S. J., Simons, J. S., Frith, C. D., & Burgess, P. W. (2006). Performance-related activity in medial rostral prefrontal cortex (area 10) during low demand tasks. *Journal of Experimental Psychology: Human Perception and Performance, 32,* 45–58.

Goodale, M. A., & Milner, A. D. (1992). Separate visual pathways for perception and action. *Trends in Neuroscience, 15,* 20–25.

Goodale, M. A., & Wolf, M. E. (2006). Vision for action. In *Essays in honor of Zenon Pylyshyn.*

Guynn, M. J. (2003). A two-process model of strategic monitoring in event-based prospective memory: Activation/retrieval mode and checking. *International Journal of Psychology, 38,* 245–256.

Guynn, M. J., McDaniel, M. A., & Einstein, G. O. (2001). Remembering to perform intentions: A different type of memory? In H. D. Zimmer, R. L. Cohen, M. J. Guynn, J. Engelkamp, R. Kormi-Nouri, & M. A. Foley (Eds.), *Memory for action: A distinct form of episodic memory?* (pp. 25–48). Oxford, UK: Oxford University Press.

Levine, B., Stuss, D., Milberg, W. P., Alexander, M. P., Schwartz, M., & Macdonald, R. (1998). The effects of focal and diffuse brain damage on strategy application: Evidence from focal lesions, traumatic brain injury and normal aging. *Journal of the International Neuropsychological Society, 4,* 247–264.

Milner, B. (1965). Visually-guided maze learning in man: Effects of bilateral hippocampal, bilateral frontal, and unilateral cerebral lesions. *Neuropsychologia, 3,* 317–338.

Moscovitch, M. (1982). A neuropsychological approach to perception and memory in normal and pathological aging. In F. I. M. Craik & S. Trehub (Eds.), *Aging and cognitive processes.* New York: Plenum.

Moscovitch, M. (1992). Memory and working with memory: A component process model based on modules and central systems. *Journal of Cognitive Neuroscience, 4,* 257–267.

Moscovitch, M. (1994). Cognitive resources and dual-task interference effects at retrieval in normal people: The role of the frontal lobes and medial temporal cortex. *Neuropsychology, 8,* 524–534.

Moscovitch, M., & Winocur, G. (1992). The neuropsychology of memory and aging. In F. I. M. Craik & T. A. Salthouse (Eds.), *The handbook of aging and cognition* (pp. 315–372). Hillsdale, NJ: Lawrence Erlbaum Associates, Inc.

Moscovitch, M., & Winocur, G. (2002). The frontal cortex and working with memory. In D. T. Stuss & R. T. Knight (Eds.), *The frontal lobes.* Oxford, UK: Oxford University Press.

Petrides, M. (2005). Lateral prefrontal cortex: Architectonic and functional organization. *Philisophical Transactions of the Royal Society of London, B Biological Sciences, 360,* 781–795.

Posner, M. I., & Peterson, S. E. (1990). The attention system of the human brain. *Annual Review of Psychology, 13,* 25–42.

Shallice, T., & Burgess, P. W. (1991). Deficits in strategy application following frontal lobe damage in man. *Brain, 114,* 727–741.

Wilson, B. A., Cockburn, J., & Baddeley, A. D. (1985). *The Rivermead Behavioral Memory Test.* Titchfield, UK: Thames Valley Test.

Wilson, B. A., Emslie, H., Foley, J., Shiel, A., Watson, P., Hawkins, K., et al. (2005). *Cambridge Prospective Memory Test (CAMPROMPT): Manual.* Oxford, UK: Harcourt Assessment.

Zimmer, H. D., Cohen, R. L., Guynn, M. J., Engelkamp, J., Kormi-Nouri, R., & Foley, M. A. (Eds.). (2001). *Memory for action: A distinct form of episodic memory?* Oxford, UK: Oxford University Press.

15

Assessment and Treatment of Prospective Memory Disorders in Clinical Practice

ANGELIKA I. T. THÖNE-OTTO

Outpatient Clinic of Cognitive Neurology
University of Leipzig

KATRIN WALTHER

Outpatient Clinic of Cognitive Neurology
University of Leipzig

As the preceding chapters in this book have shown, there has been increased understanding of the processes involved in prospective remembering within recent years. In line with this development, there has been increasing interest in a better understanding and treatment of prospective memory disorders in clinical settings, given that many day-to-day activities of patients involve the ability to remember performing an intention in the future (e.g., remembering to take medication or remembering to go to physiotherapy at the appropriate time) and that this ability is critical for social integration and independent living (Kinsella, Murtagh, & Landry, 1996).

Nevertheless, until now there have been hardly any well-standardized measures or intervention methods for prospective memory disorders. The assessment techniques reviewed in this chapter include clinical tests and questionnaires. Experimental procedures are described in several of the other chapters. Most of the clinical procedures, however, lack a firm theoretical basis, adequate norms, and strong psychometric properties. To reliably assess patients' prospective memory abilities, therefore, the measures have to be combined with careful observation in everyday life.

The second part of this chapter reviews therapy strategies and techniques available to improve performance on prospective memory tasks in patients with brain injuries. The organization of this part relies on the distinction between functional training, which basically deals with drill and practice of the impaired memory function, and compensating therapy, in which patients learn strategies to cope with their memory deficits (Thöne-Otto & Markowitsch, 2004). Within those strategies, on the one hand there are more internal strategies, which patients use to improve encoding or retrieval (e.g., visual imagery or verbal elaboration), and on the other hand there are so-called external memory aids, which can be further subdivided into nonelectronic (e.g., diaries and notebooks) and electronic memory aids (e.g., Palm organizers or the memory function of mobile phones).

ASSESSMENT OF PROSPECTIVE MEMORY

Psychological Tests

Few psychological tests have been developed to directly measure prospective memory. In traditional test batteries such as the Wechsler Memory Scale–III (Wechsler, 1997) there are no subtests designed for measuring the fulfillment of future intentions. Until 2005, the only clinical test that tested prospective memory was the Rivermead Behavioral Memory Test (RBMT; Wilson, Cockburn, & Baddeley, 1985). The two items for measurement of prospective memory were (a) remembering where a belonging is hidden and asking for it to be returned at the end of the test, and (b) asking for the next appointment time when an alarm sounds.

The RBMT does not provide standardized scores for individual items from which to compute a prospective memory index, but only offers a score of the overall memory impairment. Nevertheless, some studies have used the specific prospective memory item scores. Because the purposes of these studies are quite heterogeneous, they are summarized in Table 15.1.

Wilson and colleagues have been working on a new test that specifically measures prospective memory. An early version, which was mentioned in a publication by Kime, Lamb, and Wilson (1996) and modified by Groot, Wilson, Evans, and Watson (2002), consisted of four time-based and four event-based prospective memory tasks and took about 40 minutes to administer. They found that clinical examinees performed significantly worse than controls, time-based tasks were more difficult than event-based tasks for both patients and control groups, and note-taking significantly benefited prospective memory performance. After extensive pilot studies, the authors decided that some changes needed to be made. In particular, they had to ensure that the time intervals between being asked to do the task and responding appropriately at the right moment had to be balanced across cuing conditions (i.e., time and event). In addition, the new version of the test provides a set pattern of responses to examinees' actions or lack of actions; for example, it specifies how the tester should react if the examinee carries out the wrong task at the wrong time or does not react to a predefined stimulus. Finally, the authors improved the scoring system, which now takes into account both the timing of the action and the action itself. The new version of this test was published in 2005 as the Cambridge Test of Prospective Memory (CAMPROMT; Wilson et al., 2005) and is "the first standardised test to have been designed to assess prospective memory within an ecologically plausible context" (p. 1).

TABLE 15.1   Studies Applying RBMT Prospective Memory Items

Authors	Sample	Purpose of the Study	Method	Main Results
Mills et al. (1997)	6 neurologically impaired outpatients	Examine the correspondence between the Rivermead Behavioral Memory Test and ecological prospective memory	Patients were asked to complete everyday tasks in the morning without any verbal or visual cues. After lunch break, staff gave patients a verbal cue, reminding them that their daily responsibilities needed to be completed before the beginning of afternoon activities.	Correlations between responsibilities completed and the prospective memory tasks on the RBMT were low and nonsignificant, whereas a high correlation was found between responsibilities completed and the retrospective RBMT tasks ($r = .83$, $p < .05$).
Keil (2005)	Assisted-living community residents	Neuropsychological assessment in the prediction of everyday functional abilities of older adults	Relationships among a comprehensive range of neuropsychological tests, including the Repeatable Battery for the Assessment of Neuropsychological Status (RBANS; Randolph, 1998), everyday functional skills measured using the Direct Assessment of Functional Status (DAFS; Loewenstein et al, 1989), measures of prospective memory from the RBMT, and self- and caregiver reports of functional memory skills were evaluated.	Superior predictions of performance on the DAFS was made when combining both global (RBANS) and specific tests (RBMT) in regression on DAFS.
Kazui et al. (2005)	24 patients with mild cognitive impairment	Examination of everyday memory impairment in patients with mild cognitive impairment	RBMT scores of patients with mild cognitive impairment were compared to those of normal controls and patients with Alzheimer's disease.	Overall everyday memory was impaired in patients with mild cognitive impairment, but the severity was milder than that in Alzheimer's patients. Patients with mild cognitive impairment showed deficits of everyday memory tasks requiring delayed recall, whereas prospective memory tasks were not useful for detecting the patients with mild cognitive impairment.
Zakzanis, Young, & Campbell (2003)	15 abstinent MDMA (ecstasy) users	Exploring the nature and pattern of memory impairment found in abstinent MDMA users	Abstinent MDMA users and normal controls were compared on RBMT, a stem-completion task, and the Vocabulary Subtest of the Wechsler Adult Intelligence Scale–III.	MDMA users were impaired on the time-based appointment and event-based message subtest of the RBMT. The results also indicate that the ability to recall a future appointment may be related to the frequency of MDMA use and the absolute length of time MDMA was used.

The Cambridge Prospective Memory Test

The CAMPROMT consists of two parallel versions, each consisting of three event-based and three time-based prospective memory tasks that have to be completed over a period of 25 minutes. Most of that time is filled with distractor paper-and-pencil tasks such as a general knowledge quiz and a word-finder puzzle. Examinees are allowed to use any strategy as an aid to remembering the tasks (e.g., writing a reminder on the paper provided). The time-based tasks are as follows:

Remind the tester to ring the garage (reception). The task has to be carried out at a specified time (e.g., 10 minutes past five), which is 5 minutes after a 20-minute distracter task interval. The cue comes from a clock sitting on the table.

Remind the tester not to forget his or her keys (mug). Here the time interval is 13 minutes and the response should be made "when there are 7 minutes left," which is indicated by a timer on the table.

Switch to another task (pen) "in 7 minutes time," or when the timer shows there are 8 minutes left.

The event-based tasks are cued by a verbal prompt from the tester, by the beeper going off followed by a prompt from the tester, or by a specific quiz question. The tasks are as follows:

Remind the tester of five hidden objects, when a beeper goes off.

Switch to another task when there is a quiz question about *East Enders* (a long-running British television show).

Give the tester a message envelope when the tester says there are 5 minutes left.

The test was standardized with 237 healthy participants, from 16 to 92 years old ($M = 42.4$, $SD = 17.1$) and a mean estimated IQ of 105.5 ($SD = 15.5$, range = 69–131). In addition, there are data from 72 patients with a variety of neurological disorders, for whom other neuropsychological tests such as the RBMT, the MAP Search from the Test of Everyday Attention (TEA; Robertson, Ward, Ridgeway, & Nimmo-Smith, 1994), and the modified six-elements test from the Behavioural Assessment of the Dysexecutive Syndrome (BADS; Wilson, Alderman, Burgess, Emslie, & Evans, 1996) were collected. There are significant correlations between the RBMT and the CAMPROMT total scores ($r = .38$) and the event-based total score ($r = .47$) but not the time-based total score ($r = .22$). These findings, according to the authors, confirm the validity of the CAMPROMT and show that by including the additional time-based tasks, the CAMPROMT is a more comprehensive test of prospective memory. According to the manual, there are also reasonable reliability scores; test–retest reliability was .64 (Kendall's Jau-b) in those control participants who were tested again 7 to 10 days after first testing. The detailed analysis of the participants' behavior revealed very little change in note-taking between the two testing occasions and although, as expected, there was a significant practice effect ($z = 3.26$, $p = .001$, Wilcoxon), this was for only 11 of the 20 participants and was small in magnitude.

Thus the CAMPROMT may prove to be a useful clinical instrument to get a valid and reliable measure of prospective memory performance.

There are some other test procedures with everyday life characteristics, however, that so far have not been standardized. In this chapter we only chose those procedures that have some kind of everyday life characteristic. Experimental procedures to examine prospective memory are described in other chapters of this book. One such test for the assessment of prospective memory is the Memory for Intentions Screening Test (MIST; Shum, Fleming, & Neulinger, 2002). This test takes about half an hour to administer and has two parallel forms with eight prospective memory tasks in each. Half the tasks require verbal responses, such as "Tell me that it is time to take a break," and half require an action, such as "Sign your name on your paper." In addition, four tasks are time-based (e.g., "In 15 minutes...") and four are event-based or cue-based (e.g., "When I hand you a red pen..."). These types of tasks are not evenly distributed on the types of reactions, thus there are three time-based tasks that require a verbal response and only one that requires an action. The instrument itself has not been published, but it was described in a review by Shum et al. (2002).

Finally, there is a procedure developed by Titov, Knight, and colleagues, who simulated with video technology everyday situations to evaluate prospective memory performance under standardized conditions (Knight, Harnett, & Titov, 2005; Titov & Knight, 2000). A video sequence of about 18 minutes presents a situation in which the participant goes to either a department store or the city center. While watching this sequence, 10 or 20 different prospective tasks have to be accomplished (e.g., buying a CD, booking a flight, etc.). According to Titov and Knight (2000), the video test led to the same results as real department store attendance, so that these authors regard this technique as a suitable procedure for the estimation of prospective memory performance in everyday life. The video method is restricted to event-based tasks only, and time-based tasks remain unconsidered. In everyday life, however, people would use external aids (e.g., a shopping list) in the face of such a high number of prospective tasks; thus, the test seems to have quite a high retrospective memory load, and therefore seems to resemble a list-learning task. Thus, it is not surprising that the authors found high correlations with performance on a list-learning test.

Questionnaires

Questionnaires are the most frequently assigned method for the evaluation of prospective memory, although there are only few questionnaires that concentrate only on prospective memory. Instead, some items concerning prospective remembering were embedded into general questionnaires concerning memory in everyday life (for an overview, see Shum et al., 2002). In the following, only those procedures are described that permit a more comprehensive evaluation. All the questionnaires reported indicate the frequency of forgetting on a Likert scale.

Prospective and Retrospective Memory Questionnaire (PRMQ; Smith, Della Sala, Logie, & Maylor, 2000)
For the evaluation of memory in the everyday life of patients with Alzheimer's disease, Smith et al. (2000) provided the

PRMQ. This instrument consists of eight items concerning prospective memory and eight items concerning retrospective memory. In addition, length of storage interval (short vs. long interval) as well as the recall context (time-based vs. event-based) were varied. Crawford, Smith, Maylor, Della Sala, and Logie (2003) accomplished a comprehensive standardization study, which also allows statements about important differences between prospective and retrospective memory.

Prospective Memory Questionnaire (PMQ; Hannon, Adams, Harrington, & Fries-Dias, 1995)

The PMQ is a questionnaire specifically tailored to the assessment of prospective memory. The PMQ consists of 52 questions that may be assigned to four subscales: frequency of forgetting short-term habitual intentions, long-term episodic intentions, internal cued intentions, and strategy use. This questionnaire assesses strategy use, which most others do not.

Comprehensive Assessment of Prospective Memory (CAPM; Waugh, 1999)

The CAPM not only asks for the frequency of forgetting, it also asks for information concerning the severity of memory errors, as well as reasons for memory failure. Thirty-nine items ask for prospective memory failures in different everyday situations. Roche, Fleming, and Shum (2002) tested the questionnaire with 33 patients with brain injuries, as well as 29 healthy control participants. The groups did not differ in self-assessment, but there were significant differences in the relatives' ratings. Whereas patients with brain injuries usually overestimated their performance and underestimated everyday failures, the opposite response behavior was observed in healthy participants, who overestimated the frequency of their errors. The authors concluded that self-ratings are less reliable in individuals with brain injuries, but that relatives' ratings may offer a more reliable and valid assessment of patients' performance. Walther and Thöne-Otto (2005) used a German translation of the CAPM in a clinical study of 26 patients with brain injuries. The CAPM rating of relatives' was correlated with patients' performance on two experimental tasks of prospective remembering (calling an answering machine at designated times, and mailing a letter) and self-reported dysexecutive problems (BADS-DEX), but not with other neuropsychological test parameters (reactions times, word-list learning, digit span, Behavioural Assessment of the Dysexecutive Syndrome [BADS]). This result was in line with other studies, which failed to find correlations between psychometric parameters and everyday prospective memory performance (Fortin, Godbout, & Braun, 2003; Shallice & Burgess, 1991). This may be due to the fact that a complex interaction among several cognitive functions is necessary to provide successful prospective remembering in everyday life. Correlations between individual test scores may not be able to represent these interrelations, whereas a self- or relative's estimation measured by a questionnaire may be able to.

One problem with questionnaires is that they are not able to differentiate whether forgetting few intentions is actually due to good prospective memory or rather, based on good compensatory strategies. Thus, if patients use their memory books reliably, they may not forget appointments in everyday life, although they do not remember them without the book. In addition, there are some problems that apply to the use of questionnaires with patients with brain injuries in general.

These patients may have difficulties estimating the frequencies of their memory deficits accurately because they forget about having forgotten things or their awareness of deficits may be impaired. In addition, in patients with perceptual deficits or neglect, errors may occur because they fail to see some of the answer choices.

On the other hand, self-rating questionnaires give a good idea of the patient's perception of his or her everyday problems and not necessarily a realistic view of his or her prospective memory performance. The employment of ratings by relatives may supplement the picture generated by self-assessment.

TREATMENT OF PROSPECTIVE MEMORY IMPAIRMENT IN CLINICAL PRACTICE

Functional Training of Prospective Memory Components

Is it possible to improve a patient's ability to self-initiate a delayed intention at the appropriate time (time-based) or when the appropriate event occurs (event-based)? If so, what kinds of patients are able to improve their performance on prospective memory tasks on the basis of what kind of training?

Sohlberg, White, Evans, and Mateer (1992) and Raskin and Sohlberg (1996) each evaluated single cases in which they trained patients to improve prospective memory. Raskin and Sohlberg asked the patient to clap his hands whenever the experimenter got up (event-based) or to blink his eyes every 3 minutes (time-based). The time delay was increased when the patient was able to complete the task successfully. In 37 training sessions, they were able to increase the time interval up to 12 minutes. They were even able to show transfer to everyday tasks, but it took much longer. Both patients made phone calls, which they were asked to make at a predefined time. Although self-initiation seemed to improve, patients did not perform the tasks at the precise time at which they were supposed to perform them. Interestingly enough, the authors reported that training only improved performance on prospective but not on retrospective memory tasks.

Whereas Sohlberg et al. (1992), as well as Raskin and Sohlberg (1996), concentrated on the prospective component of the tasks during training, Camp, Foss, Stevens, and O'Hanlon (1996) tried to improve memory performance by exercising and repeating the retrospective component. Thirty patients with mild Alzheimer's dementia were asked to repeat what they were supposed to do when coming to the next therapy session (ask for a coupon). One week later, 73% of the patients completed the prospective task correctly. Unfortunately, no baseline or control-group data were reported, so it is impossible to evaluate training effects.

Shum et al. (2002) discussed several reasons for the success of repetitive training on prospective remembering:

- An intense activation of control processes as well as a deeper level of processing.
- Learning specific skills (e.g., monitoring time- and task-relevant information).
- Procedural or implicit learning.

Regarding the different phases of prospective remembering, repetitive training tries to influence encoding or the self-initiated retrieval.

All in all, repetitive training of prospective memory might have some positive effect on everyday functioning. Data, however, are too scarce to determine which kind of training may be effective for this purpose, and which patients may profit from this kind of training.

Compensatory Strategies

When normal participants try to remember to fulfil some kind of delayed intention of importance to them, most often they say they would use some kind of compensatory strategy: external aids (timers, writing on their hands, placing something in view, asking someone to remind them, making notes, etc.), internal aids (rehearsal, imagery, and stating aloud the reheasal of the intention to be remembered) or conjunction aids (planning or rearranging the day, and tying intention to events; Penningroth, 2005). Participants use external aids more than internal or conjunction aids and judge external aids more effective.

Similarly, compensational strategies (especially external memory aids) are of high importance in compensating for problems of prospective memory in patients with brain injuries.

There are hardly any studies concerning internal strategies and prospective memory in patients. Only Kaschel et al. (2002) trained patients to use visual imagery, and prospective memory performance was one of the outcome measures they used. Patients were asked to imagine themselves fulfilling the intention at the appropriate time or situation. Training took 20 sessions and patients in the imagery training group showed higher rates of keeping appointments than patients in a control group.

According to the model of Ellis (1996) and Kvavilashvili and Ellis (1996), internal strategies improve encoding of the delayed intention. Repeated imagination of the retrieval situation may increase detection of retrieval cues once the situation occurs. This is more likely for event-based situations, because there are external cues to be detected, whereas such cues are missing in time-based tasks. Here it would be necessary to combine the critical time with the imagination of the activity in which participants plan to be involved. Thus, if I plan to make a phone call at 3 p.m., I should try to imagine what I will be doing at that time, and I should imagine how, while I am doing my work, I will look at the phone and remember to make the phone call. Thus, imagination may help to transfer a time-based task into an event-based one. This, however, presumably will only be possible in patients with rather mild impairments.

External memory aids are used by patients more often than internal strategies, and they are also examined more often by researchers. Herrmann, Brubaker, Yoder, Sheets, and Tio (1999) distinguished between passive and active memory aids. Passive aids store only the content of the intention, and thus basically compensate for the retrospective memory component. Typically, passive aids include calendars, to-do lists, notes, or pill boxes. They are helpful only if the person remembers to look at the aid at the proper time.

Active aids, instead, trigger retrieval at the appropriate time. There are systems that only remind the individual of his or her intention to do something, without telling what to do (e.g., alarms, a knot in the handkerchief), as well as systems that combine an active alarm with the information about what to do (electronic calendars, electronic timers, another person). Alarms are well suited only if they are very specific, such as the alarm in the car, which reminds you to switch off the lights after stopping the engine, or the alarm that tells you to get up in the morning. If you set your alarm during the day, however, to remind you of any kind of intention, retrospective retrieval must be working reasonably well to allow you to complete the relevant task. In our clinical work we have been observing more and more patients (especially younger ones) using the alarm function on their mobile phones to remind themselves of intentions.

Relying on someone else is a very common strategy. The vast majority of managers rely entirely on their secretaries to remind them of anything they have to do. If patients, however, rely on their relatives, this may highly restrict their own and their relatives' independence and may result in conflicts or burnout within the patient's family. In a study by Thöne-Otto and Walther (2001), strategy use seemed to be correlated with independence in everyday life, defined by a number of criteria (e.g., managing one's household oneself, organizing one's financial businesses, or being in paid employment). Thus, the more independent participants used a number of external as well as internal strategies, whereas those who were less independent used the same number of external and internal strategies but also relied heavily on their relatives in terms of memory.

Nonelectronic External Memory Aids   As mentioned earlier, there are quite a few nonelectronic memory aids that can be used in memory therapy. Empirical evaluations, however, have only been undertaken for memory books. Sohlberg and Mateer (1989) developed a training program to teach a memory-impaired patient the use of a memory book. The program is based on learning theories and consists of three phases. In the initial acquisition phase, patients are taught what they can do with the memory book. Patients are introduced to the different functions of the memory book (e.g., orientation, calendar, telephone numbers, and addresses) and learn how to use it. The second phase concentrates on application. By means of role play, patients learn when and where the book is to be used and situations in which its use is suitable. The final adaptation phase strengthens transfer into everyday life, as well as applications to new situations. The authors defined effectiveness criteria, which specified which goals had to be met to move on to the next level of training. Before moving to the next level, knowledge had to be demonstrated over a longer period. For the severely impaired patient reported by Sohlberg and Mateer (1989), training took 6 months.

Schmitter-Edgecombe, Fahy, Whelan, and Long (1995) used a similar procedure and compared training of memory book use with a more social therapy. In a group-therapeutic setting, four patients were trained in the application of a calendar, and its use was supplemented by a regular alert from a wristwatch. In a control condition, four other patients received a social therapy in which problem-solving strategies concerning more general changes in their cognitive and psychosocial situation were discussed. The number of errors in everyday life was reduced only in the memory book group. On a follow-up 6 months later, however, there were no longer differences between the two groups.

Squires, Hunkin, and Parkin (1997) showed that the method of errorless learning was effective to teach patients memory book use. A combination of memory book training with metamemory strategies based on self-instruction also proved to be helpful (Ownsworth & Mcfarland, 1999).

Table 15.2 provides a summary of memory aids available in everyday life.

Electronic Memory Aids   Based on the massive increase in electronic memory aids on the commercial market, opportunities for patients have increased, as well. During the 1990s there were still very few publications on electronic memory aids in patients, but since the beginning of the 21st century a continuous increase has been observed.

Kapur, Glisky, and Wilson (2002) pointed out the following circumstances in which electronic memory aids may be especially useful.

TABLE 15.2   Nonelectronic Memory Aids: Overview

Memory Aid	Advantages	Disadvantages	Comments
Calendar	Available in different sizes Highly accepted as memory aid in normal adults	No alarm when the critical time arrives (it does not help when self-initiated retrieval is the problem)	If a calendar is used as a diary for daily notes, it needs to have a reasonable page size (at least one page per day). Many families use one calendar for all family members placed, for example, in the kitchen. In that case patients need an additional one to carry around.
Notes	Very frequently used Sticky notes are easy to post in view	Easy to lose Danger of mixing them up	Not very suitable for patients due to high risk of loss.
Notebook	Better than sheets of paper because it does not get lost as easily	If not embedded into an agenda, the date needs to be written on the pages	
Pin-board	Everything in view at the same time	Old information needs to be removed regularly; if too much accumulates, patient cannot find relevant information	
Timer	Good reminder for short intervals Suitable for patients who forget to return to tasks after an interruption	Timer only reminds the patient that he or she needs to do something; it does not tell what	

- There are different tasks to be fulfilled between the forming of an intention and the execution interval.
- There is a long interval between formation of the intention and execution (days or months).
- High time accuracy is necessary for the execution of the intention, and internal strategies might fail (e.g., remembering to take the cake out of the oven at a certain time).
- Several alarms are necessary during a day (e.g., taking medication at different times of the day).

Because there is such a vast number of devices, similar kinds of aids described in the literature are summarized here as follows:

- PC-based aids.
- Alarms.
- Commercial organizers with visual displays.
- Commercial organizers with speech output.
- Paging systems.
- Interactive systems.

Table 15.3 gives an overview of available systems.

PC-Based Aids   Cole, Dehdashti, Petti, and Angert (1994), Cole (1999), and Flannery, Butterbaugh, Rice, and Rice (1997) reported the use of personal computers or laptop computers. Cole (1999) used individually designed user interfaces to support his patients. Flannery et al. (1997) reported a reduction in reminders necessary by nursing staff from 78% during baseline to 5% with the help of his notebook in a 17-year-old spina bifida patient with hydrocephalus. The notebook was mainly used to remind him of everyday routine activities. The patient's reactions were stored in the systems; thus, the patient as well as significant others could use this history to make sure he had fulfilled his intentions. Given that desktop computers, and even notebook computers, are not very convenient to use unless they are always on, these devices are restricted to the patients' home environment.

Alarms   Several single-case studies report use of wristwatches with alarms (Fowler, Hart, & Sheehan, 1972; Kime et al., 1996; Kurlychek, 1983; Naugle, Naugle, Prevey, & Delaney, 1988).

While some alarms were set at regular intervals (e.g., 1 hour), others had to be set again after each alarm. The alarm reported by Naugle et al. (1988) was able to store up to 50 different times and was also able to give a text reminder of up to five letters on the display (e.g., the hint to look into the memory book).

In the studies, alarms were usually used to support memory book use. Most of the patients were not able to use a memory book independently in spite of a phase of intensive memory book training. The patient reported by Naugle et al. (1988) took another 3 months to learn the association between the alarm and the use of the memory book. He either ignored the alarm or switched it off in advance.

TABLE 15.3 Electronic Memory Aids: Overview

Memory Aid	References	General Features	Advantages	Disadvantages
PC-based aids				
PC	Cole et al. (1994) Cole (1999)	Calendar systems with alarm	Software adapted to patient with brain injury; reactions of the alarm are collected in log files and examined by caregivers	Too heavy and bulky to carry with you; computer has to be permanently on, needs permanent power supply
Notebook	Flannery et al. (1997)			
Alarms				
	Fowler et al. (1972) Kime et al. (1996) Kurlychek (1983) Naugle et al. (1988)	Programmable alarms without the storage of messages or text	Easily available, inexpensive to purchase, worn all the time	Storage of messages not possible or very limited; need an additional memory book
Organizer (PDA)				
PSION organizer Sharp organizer PSION organizer PSION organizer PALM III	Giles & Shore (1989) Mohr et al. (1997) Kim et al. (2000) Kim et al. (1999) Kapur (1995) Kissel et al. (2002)	Programmable alarms with messages displayed on a screen	Easily available, relatively inexpensive to purchase and maintain; commonly used by individuals with no brain injury	Data entry too difficult for most patients with brain injury; use can be limited by other impairments (e.g., vision, fine motor control)
Palm, mobile phone	Thöne-Otto & Walther (2003)			
Voice organizer				
IQ voice organizer Voice organizer Sony IC recorder	van den Broek et al. (2000) Oriani et al. (2003) Yasuda et al. (2002)	Voice messages are stored with a programmable alarm	Easily available, inexpensive to purchase and maintain; suitable for patients with visual impairments, sometimes used by individuals with no brain injury	Data entry too difficult for some patients with brain injury; other individuals can hear the messages, which might be embarrassing in public

Paging systems

System	References	Description	Advantages	Limitations
NeuroPage Mobile phone Postie© Yahoo	Evans et al. (1998) Hersh & Treadgold (1994) Wilson et al. (1999, 2001) Wilson et al. (1997) Wilson et al. (2003) Wade & Troy (2001) Kirsch et al. (2004) O'Connell et al. (2003)	Messages are entered into a schedule on PC and then transmitted at the appropriate time to a pager	Device very easy to use	Transmission of messages at the right time is not always guaranteed, expensive to transmit messages, no overview of all daily tasks available to user

Interactive systems

System	References	Description	Advantages	Limitations
Cognitive Orthosis (COGORTH)	Kirsch et al. (1987) Kirsch et al. (1992)	Computer systems that guide patients step by step through complex tasks	System detects errors in execution and corrects them with the prompts that follow	Limited to two complex tasks (baking and cleaning)
Planning and Execution Assistant and Training (PEAT)	Levinson (1997)		Checks schedule to prevent overlapping events, schedule can be adapted during execution of the task according to priorities	Expensive to purchase, new appointments only with connection to PC, no published behavioral data
Autominder	McCarthy & Pollack (2002) Pollack et al. (2003) Pollack et al. (2002)		Sensors monitor individuals' behavior and remind only when needed	No published behavioral data, limited to in-house use, person is followed all the time by a robot
ISAAC	Gorman et al. (2003)		Step-by-step guidance can be requested by the patient only when needed	New appointments only entered at the rehabilitation center
Memojog Mobile Extensible Memory and Orientation System (MEMOS)	Szymkowiak et al. (2004) Thöne-Otto & Walther (2005) Walther & Thöne-Otto (2005)		Easy to use, caregiver can monitor patient's behavior and is informed by missing confirmation of critical prompt, patient can enter appointments	Sometimes problems making connections between device and server, expensive to run

Nevertheless, all four patients reported in the literature were able to improve their performance on memory book use, and support of significant others could be reduced.

Although the studies reported in the literature describe the alarms as successful in the long run, training is very time consuming because the retrospective memory load is very high; that is, patients have to remember what they are supposed to do when the alarm goes off. Today, mobile phone alarms may easily be combined with more elaborate information concerning the task to be done. Therefore, it may now be much easier for patients to learn the association. Interestingly enough, no further studies have been published on the topic of alarms alone. This is probably because more sophisticated devices are now available.

Commercially Available Organizers with Visual Displays   The organizers mentioned here have been developed since the late 1990s and can be purchased as personal digital assistants (PDA) or Palmtops. They are hand-held computers that can easily be carried around.

All the devices have a display large enough to save some information concerning the task to be executed. The message is shown on the screen in combination with an audible alarm. Usually repeated appointments (daily or monthly) may be easily entered.

Again, most reports evaluating the efficacy of PDA use are case histories. Giles and Shore (1989) reported on a young patient with subarachnoidal hemorrhage who was supported in the execution of household tasks by a PSION organizer. She was able to increase task performance from 0% without any memory aids to 60% with a memory book and to 90% with the PDA.

Mohr, Kraeber, and Jochum (1997) were able to increase performance of a severely impaired patient with hypoxic brain injury. With the help of a Sharp organizer he was able to go independently to his occupational therapies in 70% of the cases, whereas his performance was at 10% without the memory aid.

Similarly, the patient reported by Kim, Burke, Dowds, and George (1999) was able to go to his therapy sessions independently with the help of the organizer. In a follow-up study, Kim, Burke, Dowds, Boone, and Park (2000) examined use of the organizer in 12 patients, and asked them, between 2 months and 4 years after therapy, whether they were still using the aid. Seven of the 12 patients were still using the device, and 9 of the 12 patients stated that they found it helpful. Among the remaining 3 patients, there was 1 who had never learned to use it, and the other 2 did not find any situations in their everyday activities of which they wanted to be reminded.

Kapur (1995) reported the use of electronic memory aids in five patients. Four of those improved their performance with the help of the device. The patient who was not improving had a more severe memory deficit, but he also showed reduced initiative and little insight into his impairment.

Kissel, Simonis-Gaillard, and Borbring (2002) reported that two patients, whose amnesia was due to chronic alcoholism, were also able to improve their independent attendance at occupational therapy with the help of an electronic memory aid. Within 8 weeks of training they were able to learn how to react to the device's alarm. Their performance with the device was as good as with the help of some other person during baseline. Aside from the reduced workload for staff members, the device led to improved self-esteem in the patient.

All the studies reported so far show an increase in patients' completion of tasks with the help of the electronic devices. In none of the studies, however, did patients seem to have learned how to enter appointments themselves. Training and evaluation of device usage was restricted to the reaction to an alarm. Data apparently had been entered by nursing staff or the experimenters.

In a study reported by Thöne-Otto and Walther (2003), a Palm organizer and the memory function of a mobile phone were compared as to their effectiveness for a group of 12 memory-impaired patients. Patients were trained to enter appointments into the devices. Training was accomplished in a staged manner: All patients learned the basic functions of the data input, however some more complex functions (e.g., postponing tasks with the Palm) were learned only by some patients. All patients were trained in the use of both devices; order was counterbalanced. Only patients with mild memory disturbances were able to learn the operation of the Palm organizer. The operation of the mobile phones seemed to be learned more easily. Once the appointments were entered correctly into the memory aids, this led to increased task completion in experimental tasks dictated by the experimenter, just like in individual tasks (those the patient chose individually). The study, however, showed that only mildly impaired patients were able to learn the independent use of commercially available electronic memory aids.

Commercially Available Organizers with Speech Output   Organizers with speech output are comparable to dictaphones. Verbal messages are entered into the device and are played back to the patient when the alarm goes off. Depending on the device, (a) patients can enter the verbal message and speak the instructions for when the message should be played (IQ Voice Organizer; van den Broek, Downes, Johnson, Dayus, & Hilton, 2000), (b) timing information has to be entered separately from the verbal message (Voice Organizer reported by Oriani et al., 2003), or (c) all relevant information has to be entered by the experimenter (Sony IC Recorder; Yasuda et al., 2002). All devices described in the literature seem to improve patients' performance on prospective memory tasks compared to baseline conditions. In a posttreatment phase, after withdrawal of the memory aid, most patients' performance dropped to baseline; thus, the memory aids will have to be used for a long time because there are no indications that regular routines may be established with the help of the memory devices.

Paging Systems   The most famous and well-evaluated paging system is the NeuroPage, developed by Hersh and Treadgold (1994) and evaluated by Wilson and colleagues (Wilson, Emslie, Quirk, & Evans, 1999, 2001; Wilson, Evans, Emslie, & Malinek, 1997; Wilson, Scott, Evans, & Emslie, 2003) and Evans, Emslie, and Wilson (1998).

A central computer stores and administers dates of different patients. Therapists or service personnel enter appointments for the patients into the system. The dates are transmitted by modem to a telephone company and from there are sent to the paging system at the appropriate time. The pager has a large display and few buttons. If a message is conveyed, an alarm goes off acoustically or with vibration and indicates the task as a text message. Message receipt has to be confirmed by the patient by calling an answering machine. If there is no confirmation, the message is dispatched again. All messages are stored on the equipment and can be sent again if necessary. Wilson and colleagues proved the efficacy of the system in several single cases (Evans et al., 1998; Wilson et al., 1999), as well as in a large group of 143 patients (Wilson et al., 2001). In this study, a group of unselected patients with disorders of memory, executive functioning, and attention used NeuroPage in a crossover design with a waiting list control group. Patients' performance improved from 48% during baseline to 75% with NeuroPage. Of the patients, 84% showed a significant improvement. Whereas in the studies mentioned earlier, posttreatment performance was similar to baseline, Wilson et al. (2001) reported better performance after treatment, compared to the pretreatment baseline. They presumed that use of NeuroPage may be able to establish some kind of routine in some patients, whereas other patients are not able to build up a routine. Meanwhile, NeuroPage has been accepted by a national health company in Great Britain and can be obtained by a majority of patients.

Other authors have evaluated similar devices. Wade and Troy (2001) used electronic phone calls that reached the patient via mobile phone. Kirsch, Shenton, and Rowan (2004) used a freeware program (Postie©) that is able to send e-mails at predefined times. Again messages were sent to a pager. Finally, O'Connell, Mateer, and Kerns (2003) used the Yahoo-Calendar System to enter information that was sent to a pager via a telephone company. They were even able to teach the patient how to enter information into the calendar system; thus, this system increased independence significantly. For the other systems, authors were able to demonstrate their efficacy in improving patients' performance.

One important disadvantage of the paging systems is that usually appointments are sent at the critical time. Due to problems with radio transmission, however, messages may reach their recipient with delay or be truncated. Because the system works basically on a one-way basis, patients have no opportunity to postpone an intention, if the situation is not suitable for execution, once they have received their reminder.

Thus, although there are quite a few studies to date that demonstrate the efficacy of electronic reminding systems, technical problems may require interactive systems for better support of patients' needs.

Interactive Systems   The electronic memory aids presented so far mainly compensate for problems in storage of the intention content and support retrieval at the appropriate time. Execution of delayed intentions, however, requires more. Once an intention has been retrieved, the individual has to decide whether task execution is possible. If not, the intention has to be postponed and retrieved again later. If execution is possible in complex tasks, it may well be that execution is interrupted before the task can be completely finished. In this case, sometimes patients need help to find their way back to their tasks. Interactive systems, which may be paced by patients' reactions, are able to support prospective memory in a more sophisticated way.

The following systems are described in the literature:

- *Cognitive Orthosis* (COGORTH; Kirsch, Levine, Fallon-Krueger, & Jaros 1987; Kirsch, Levine, Lajiness-O'Neill, & Schnyder, 1992). COGORTH is a computerized interactive system that supports patients in everyday tasks such as baking a cake or cleaning a room in public nursing homes. Instructions are presented step by step on the screen of a mobile computer. Every step has to be confirmed by pressing a button; only then will the next step be presented. The system is able to interrupt a task if another task of higher priority needs to be started. One patient improved her competence at baking a cake, and two of four patients improved their ability to clean their rooms with the help of the system. The authors mentioned a lack of motivation as a reason why the other patients did not improve performance. One problem of the system may be that only predefined and analyzed tasks may be supported. Thus, its application is not very flexible.
- *Planning and Execution Assistant and Training* (PEAT; Levinson, 1997). The PEAT system represents a superordinate monitoring unit, which supervises processes of planning and execution. Different alternatives are taken into account and the most suitable process is selected. For step-by-step guidance, scripts of routine activities (e.g., morning routine, shopping) are available, which are divided into individual steps. The scripts can be provided by the responsible person or—as far as possible—by the patient himself or herself. They are entered into a daily schedule. The system reacts independently and flexibly to situations deviating from the plan. This presupposes, however, that all alternatives are sufficiently considered during the description of the scripts. The system sounds highly sophisticated; no evaluative data, however, are available so far.
- *Autominder* (McCarthy & Pollack, 2002; Pollack et al., 2003; Pollack et al., 2002). Autominder was developed for elderly patients with mild to moderate memory disorders. A robot-like piece of equipment with a screen accompanies the client in the dwelling and reminds him or her of tasks to be executed. The system called Autominder has been integrated into this robot. Autominder consists of three components. In the Plan Manager (PM) a caretaker can create the daily plan based on predefined plan fragments. Several links are to be made between the tasks, which specify under which circumstances and in which time window tasks are to be implemented (e.g., latest time for taking medication 1 hour after noon). Afterward, the PM simulates the daily plan and eliminates or changes incorrect plans. The Client Manager (CM) supervises the client's behavior using different sensors stationed in the dwelling. On the basis of the plan designed in the PM, the CM offers feedback about whether or not the ongoing action is in line with the plan or if adjustments or changes are necessary. The last component, the Personalized Cognitive Orthotic (PCO), decides whether and when the client is supposed to receive a reminder message. Thus the PCO coordinates tasks on the basis of the user's preferences. So it may remind the patient to go to the bathroom right before

a television show starts. If, on the basis of the feedback system, the PCO concludes that an intention has already been executed without a reminder, then no further reminder will be given. Autominder was evaluated in the laboratory, but no application in everyday life or with elderly people has been reported. It sounds intriguing to have a system that is able to supervise a patient's reactions and to adapt necessary reminders to the patient's actions. On the other hand, the elderly patients may not desire permanent supervision of their actions, and the permanent presence of the robot may be an intrusion into privacy.

- *ISAAC* (Gorman, Dayle, Hood, & Rumrell, 2003). ISAAC allows patients to choose whether they only need an oral reminder of a task, or if they need a checklist to guide them through an action. The checklist is displayed on a computer screen, and patients may confirm every step by touching the screen. The chance to choose between more elaborate support and only a brief reminder seems to support patients' independence. Two patients reported in the study were able to get along without the system after 11 to 12 months. One of the patients was even able to go back to work with the help of the system.

- *Memojog* (Szymkowiak et al., 2004). Memojog is a memory aid system developed at Applied Computing at the Dundee University of Scotland in collaboration with the Oliver Zangwill Centre in Ely. Memojog is a remote and interactive communication system that functions as a prompting device for memory-impaired people. Similar to MEMOS (discussed next), Memojog works with a PDA equipped with a mobile phone, which gives text-based action prompts to memory-impaired clients. Via the PDA or an Internet-accessible PC, a Web site is accessed from which the reminders can be entered into a central database. If necessary, patients may phone an administrator who would enter data for them into the system. At the appropriate time, action prompts are wirelessly transmitted from an Internet database to the PDA, where the patient confirms task execution. Initial evaluation showed that patients were able to manage the interface. One problem, however, was "lack of coverage of the system." Thus, due to connection problems, patients were unable to connect to the relevant Web site, which, according to the authors, "upset clients and their caretakers as they are attempting to use something they are unfamiliar with" (Szymkowiak et al., 2004, p. 21). Thus, they are unsure whether they are doing something wrong or if the system simply does not work properly at that time. The authors call those connectivity problems the "biggest challenge" because this was something that was not under their control. All in all, they described the system as promising and especially emphasized the important role of the relatives "by keeping the clients motivated" (p. 23), as they felt the benefit of using the memory aid.

- *Mobile Extensible Memory and Orientation System* (MEMOS; Thöne-Otto & Walther, 2005; Walther & Thöne-Otto, 2005). MEMOS is a memory aid system tailored to the special needs of patients with brain injuries. A commercially available handheld computer with an integrated mobile phone is used as a personal memory assistant (PMA). Instead of the Windows interface, however, a specially designed MEMOS interface appears on the display. The PMA reminds patients of future intentions at the appropriate time. Online connection to a base station allows interactive guidance through activities. At the service center, the client's appointments are entered into the system by caregivers or service personnel via a Web-based interface and sent to the PMA via mobile phone networks. Because most of the appointments are sent to the PMA at night, problems with radio transmission will not disturb data transfer. At the designated time an alarm goes off at the PMA and reminds the patient of his or her tasks. Tasks may be divided into individual steps to guide patients through complex situations. Task execution has to be confirmed by the patient, which allows monitoring via wireless connection. Tasks such as taking relevant medication can be classified as critical. If execution of critical tasks is not confirmed, the caregiver is informed by an alarm. If necessary, he or she can call the patient via the integrated mobile phone and remind him or her again of the relevant task. The phone, in addition, allows the patient to call the service center to leave information concerning new appointments on a voice box and to call for help in case of emergency.

Thöne-Otto and Walther (2005) compared the use of MEMOS with a commercially available Palm organizer in 13 patients with head injuries. The Palm organizer reminded participants of their intentions with an alarm, but did not require task confirmation and did not guide patients through their tasks.

All patients used both devices in a counterbalanced order. Performance on experimental tasks was assessed during baseline, either Palm or PMA usage, and posttreatment. Patients fulfilled significantly more experimental tasks with both the Palm and the PMA compared to baseline. In addition, performance with the PMA was better than with the Palm. In a semistructured interview, patients were asked about their satisfaction with the systems. Comparing Palm and PMA, more patients stated that the PMA was helpful in the execution of daily prospective memory tasks and more patients said they would like to continue using the PMA.

Walther and Thöne-Otto (2005) evaluated the long-term use of the MEMOS system in three single cases. By analyzing the task histories (i.e., protocols of patients' task confirmations), the authors reported that once the system had been successfully implemented, two of the three patients seemed to get used to its regular support and showed a high level of acceptance over time. The number and type of tasks entered were highly stable over time. This indicates high acceptance as well as the necessity of long-term use. In patients with severe memory problems and apathy, such as the third case in the study, MEMOS alone was not able to compensate for the deficits. Here, additional support provided by relatives was necessary. Nevertheless, in this case MEMOS was able to reduce the burden on the spouse, at least to some extent.

Major Issues and Future Directions

In this chapter, we aimed to review the literature on the clinical assessment and therapy of prospective memory in patients with brain injuries. What are, from a clinical point of view, the relevant questions for the future?

Integrating experimental and clinical measures to predict prospective memory performance in everyday life. Despite the fact that research in the field of prospective memory has increased enormously within recent years, there are still hardly any reliable and valid clinical assessment tools. In 2005, the CAMPROMT was published as the first clinical test devoted to the assessment of prospective memory (Wilson et al., 2005). In addition, there are some questionnaires available that ask for relatives' observations and patients' self-ratings in a standardized manner. Thus, they may help to enhance the clinical impression. Of course, experimental procedures are more well defined and analytical and allow assessment under better controlled conditions; nevertheless, they often lack ecological validity. Thus integration of experimental procedures and clinical measures is needed.

Providing electronic memory aids tailored to the patients' needs. In terms of rehabilitation, there is quite reliable evidence by now that with the use of any kind of electronic memory aid that compensates for impaired self-initiated retrieval in the relevant situation, patients' performance on those tasks may be improved. The problem, however, may be that most patients are not able to learn the operation of commercially available devices, such as the alarm function of a mobile phone or any kind of Palm organizer. This, however, may be of less relevance in a couple of years, when there are more and more individuals who have been using electronic devices before brain injury. In any case, there is potential for the future development of electronic memory aids, with more and more sophisticated technology being put on the market.

Integrating the use of electronic memory aids into a holistic neuropsychological therapy. Aside from technology, however, the most relevant aspect seems to be whether or not patients are aware of their deficits, and therefore willing to use any kind of compensation. In any case, training of memory aid use needs to be integrated into a more general neuropsychological therapy. Before administering any kind of therapy, the therapist needs to analyze what the patient must do in his or her everyday life, his or her skills and abilities, and possible social support systems. Therapy has to reflect the fact that acceptance of any device is highly related to the acceptance of impairment and handicap. In addition, external memory aids may be combined with other compensational strategies, such as changes in work behaviors, management of work breaks, and so on. Finally, relatives' needs have to be kept in mind; thus, they may have to learn to allow more independence or a memory system has to be chosen that guarantees relevant safety for the patient. These considerations show that the application of suitable memory aids for the treatment of patients with prospective memory impairment always have to be embedded in a neuropsychological therapy individually tailored to the patient's needs.

REFERENCES

Cole, E. (1999). Cognitive prosthetics: An overview to a method of treatment. *Neurorehabilitation, 12,* 39–51.

Cole, E., Dehdashti, P., Petti, L., & Angert, M. (1994). Design and outcomes of computer-based cognitive prosthetics for brain injury: A field study of three subjects. *Neurorehabilitation, 4,* 174–186.

Crawford, J. R., Smith, G., Maylor, E. A., Della Sala, S., & Logie, R. H. (2003). The Prospective and Retrospective Memory Questionnaire (PRMQ): Normative data and latent structure in a large non-clinical sample. *Memory, 11,* 261–275.

Ellis, J. (1996). Prospective memory or the realization of delayed intentions: A conceptual framework for research. In M. Brandimonte, G. O. Einstein, & M. A. McDaniel (Eds.), *Prospective memory: Theory and applications* (pp. 1–22). Mahwah, NJ: Lawrence Erlbaum Associates, Inc.

Evans, J. J., Emslie, H., & Wilson, B. A. (1998). External cueing systems in the rehabilitation of executive impairments of action. *Journal of the International Neuropsychological Society, 4,* 399–408.

Flannery, M. A., Butterbaugh, G. J., Rice, D. A., & Rice, J. C. (1997). Reminding technology for prospective memory disability: A case study. *Pediatric Rehabilitation, 1,* 239–244.

Fortin, S., Godbout, L., & Braun, C. M. (2003). Cognitive structure of executive deficits in frontally lesioned head trauma patients performing activities of daily living. *Cortex, 39,* 273–291.

Fowler, R. S., Hart, J., & Sheehan, M. (1972). A prosthetic memory: An application of the prosthetic environment concept. *Rehabilitation Counseling Bulletin, 16,* 80–85.

Giles, G. M., & Shore, M. (1989). The effectiveness of an electronic memory aid for a memory-impaired adult of normal intelligence. *American Journal of Occupational Therapy, 43,* 409–411.

Gorman, P., Dayle, R., Hood, C. A., & Rumrell, L. (2003). Effectiveness of the ISAAC cognitive prosthetic system for improving rehabilitation outcomes with neurofunctional impairment. *Neurorehabilitation, 18,* 57–67.

Groot, Y. C., Wilson, B. A., Evans, J., & Watson, P. (2002). Prospective memory functioning in people with and without brain injury. *Journal of the International Neuropsychological Society, 8,* 645–654.

Hannon, R., Adams, P., Harrington, S., & Fries-Dias, C. (1995). Effects of brain injury and age on prospective memory self-rating and performance. *Rehabilitation Psychology, 40,* 289–298.

Herrmann, D., Brubaker, B., Yoder, C., Sheets, V., & Tio, A. (1999). Devices that remind. In F. T. Durso, R. S. Nickerson, R. W. Schvaneveldt, S. T. Dumais, D. S. Lindsay, & M. T. H. Chi (Eds.), *Handbook of applied cognition* (pp. 377–407). New York: Wiley.

Hersh, N. A., & Treadgold, L. G. (1994). NeuroPage: The rehabilitation of memory dysfunction by prosthetic memory and cueing. *Neurorehabilitation, 4,* 187–197.

Kapur, N. (1995). Memory aids in the rehabilitation of memory disordered patients. In A. D. Baddeley, B. A. Wilson, & F. N. Watts (Eds.), *Handbook of memory disorders* (pp. 533–556). Chichester, UK: Wiley.

Kapur, N., Glisky, E. L., & Wilson, B. A. (2002). External memory aids and computers in memory rehabilitation. In A. D. Baddeley, M. D. Kopelman, & B. A. Wilson (Eds.), *The handbook of memory disorders* (2nd ed., pp. 757–783). Chichester, UK: Wiley.

Kaschel, R., Della Sala, S., Cantagallo, A., Fahlboeck, A., Laaksonen, R., & Kazen, M. (2002). Imagery mnemonics for the rehabilitation of memory: A randomised group controlled trial. *Neuropsychological Rehabilitation, 12,* 127–153.

Kazui, H., Matsuda, A., Hirono, N., Mori, E., Miyoshi, N., Ogino, A., et al. (2005). Everyday memory impairment of patients with mild cognitive impairment. *Dementia and Geriatric Cognitive Disorders, 19,* 331–337.

Keil, M. M. (2005). Brief neuropsychological assessment in the prediction of everyday functional abilities of older adults. *Dissertation Abstracts International B: The Sciences and Engineering, 66*(4-B), 2309.

Kim, H. J., Burke, D. T., Dowds, M. M., Jr., Boone, K. A., & Park, G. J. (2000). Electronic memory aids for outpatient brain injury: Follow-up findings. *Brain Injury, 14,* 187–196.

Kim, H. J., Burke, D. T., Dowds, M. M., & George, J. (1999). Utility of a microcomputer as an external memory aid for a memory-impaired head injury patient during in-patient rehabilitation. *Brain Injury, 13,* 147–150.

Kime, S. K., Lamb, D. G., & Wilson, B. A. (1996). Use of a comprehensive programme of external cueing to enhance procedural memory in a patient with dense amnesia. *Brain Injury, 10,* 17–25.

Kinsella, G., Murtagh, D., & Landry, A. (1996). Everyday memory following traumatic brain injury. *Brain Injury, 10,* 499–507.

Kirsch, N. L., Levine, S. P., Fallon-Krueger, M., & Jaros, L. A. (1987). Focus on clinical research: The microcomputer as an "orthotic" device for patients with cognitive deficits. *Journal of Head Trauma Rehabilitation, 2*(4), 77–86.

Kirsch, N. L., Levine, S. P., Lajiness-O'Neill, R., & Schnyder, M. (1992). Computer-assisted interactive task guidance: Facilitating the performance of a simulated vocational task. *Journal of Head Trauma Rehabilitation, 7*(3), 13–25.

Kirsch, N. L., Shenton, M., & Rowan, J. (2004). A generic, "in-house," alphanumeric paging system for prospective activity impairments after traumatic brain injury. *Brain Injury, 18,* 725–734.

Kissel, A., Simonis-Gaillard, U., & Borbring, K. (2002). Elektronische Gedächtnishilfen bei amnestischen Alkoholikern [Electronic memory aids in amnestic alcoholics]. *Praxis Klinische Verhaltensmedizin und Rehabilitation, 60,* 306–308.

Knight, R. G., Harnett, M., & Titov, N. (2005). The effects of traumatic brain injury on the predicted and actual performance of a test of prospective remembering. *Brain Injury, 19,* 19–27.

Kurlychek, R. T. (1983). Use of a digital alarm chronograph as a memory aid in early dementia. *Clinical Gerontologist, 1*(3), 93–94.

Kvavilashvili, L., & Ellis, J. (1996). Varieties of intention: Some distinctions and classifications. In M. Brandimonte, G. O. Einstein, & M. A. McDaniel (Eds.), *Prospective memory: Theory and applications* (pp. 23–51). Mahwah, NJ: Lawrence Erlbaum Associates, Inc.

Levinson, R. (1997). The planning and execution assistant and trainer (PEAT). *Journal of Head Trauma Rehabilitation, 12*(2), 85–91.

Mills, V., Kixmiller, J. S., Gillespie, A., Allard, J., Flynn, E., Bowman, A., et al. (1997). The correspondence between the Rivermead Behavioral Memory Test and ecological prospective memory. *Brain and Cognition, 35,* 322–325.

Mohr, G., Kraeber, A., & Jochum, I. (1997). *Die Effekte externer Speichermedien auf die Orientierung amnestischer Patienten: eine Einzelfallstudie* [The effects of external memory aids on the orientation of amnesic paients: A single case study]. Unpublished manuscript, University of Saarland, Saarbrucken, Germany.

Naugle, R. I., Naugle, C. G., Prevey, M., & Delaney, R. C. (1988). New digital watch as a compensatory device for memory dysfunction. *Cognitive Rehabilitation, 4,* 22–23.

O'Connell, M. E., Mateer, C. A., & Kerns, K. A. (2003). Prosthetic systems for addressing problems with initiation: Guidelines for selection, training, and measuring efficacy. *Neurorehabilitation, 18,* 9–20.

Oriani, M., Moniz-Cook, E., Binetti, G., Zanieri, G., Frisoni, G. B., Geroldi, C., et al. (2003). An electronic memory aid to support prospective memory in patients in the early stages of Alzheimer's disease: A pilot study. *Aging and Mental Health, 7,* 22–27.

Ownsworth, T. L., & Mcfarland, K. (1999). Memory remediation in long-term acquired brain injury: Two approaches in diary training. *Brain Injury, 13,* 605–626.

Penningroth, S. (2005, July). *Strategy differences for remembering important and less important real-life intentions.* Paper presented at the Second International Conference on Prospective Memory, Zurich, Switzerland.

Pollack, M. E., Brown, L., Colbry, D., McCarthy, C. E., Orosz, C., Peintner, B., et al. (2003). Autominder: An intelligent cognitive orthotic system for people with memory impairments. *Robotics and Autonomous Systems, 44,* 273–282.

Pollack, M. E., McCarthy, C. E., Tsamardinos, I., Ramakrishnan, S., Brown, L., Carrion, S., et al. (2002, March). *Autominder: A planning, monitoring, and reminding assistive agent.* Paper presented at the 7th International Conference on Intelligent Autonomous Systems (IAS). Retrieved February 2, 2005, from http://citeseer.ist.psu.edu/561745.html

Raskin, S. A., & Sohlberg, M. M. (1996). The efficacy of prospective memory training in two adults with brain injury. *Journal of Head Trauma Rehabilitation, 11*(3), 32–51.

Robertson, I. H., Ward, T., Ridgeway, V., & Nimmo-Smith, T. (1994). *Test of Everyday Attention (TEA).* Harcourt Assessment.

Roche, N. L., Fleming, J. M., & Shum, D. H. (2002). Self-awareness of prospective memory failure in adults with traumatic brain injury. *Brain Injury, 16,* 931–945.

Schmitter-Edgecombe, M., Fahy, J. F., Whelan, J. P., & Long, C. J. (1995). Memory remediation after severe closed head injury: Notebook training versus supportive therapy. *Journal of Consulting and Clinical Psychology, 63,* 484–489.

Shallice, T., & Burgess, P. W. (1991). Deficits in strategy application following frontal lobe damage in man. *Brain, 114,* 727–741.

Shum, D., Fleming, J., & Neulinger, K. (2002). Prospective memory and traumatic brain injury: A review. *Brain Impairment, 3,* 1–16.

Smith, G., Della Sala, S., Logie, R. H., & Maylor, E. A. (2000). Prospective and retrospective memory in normal ageing and dementia: A questionnaire study. *Memory, 8,* 311–321.

Sohlberg, M. M., & Mateer, C. A. (1989). Training use of compensatory memory books: A three stage behavioral approach. *Journal of Clinical and Experimental Neuropsychology, 11,* 871–891.

Sohlberg, M. M., White, O., Evans, E., & Mateer, C. (1992). An investigation of the effects of prospective memory training. *Brain Injury, 6,* 139–154.

Squires, E. J., Hunkin, N. M., & Parkin, A. J. (1997). Take note: Using errorless learning to promote memory notebook training. In A. J. Parkin (Ed.), *Case studies in the neuropsychology of memory* (pp. 191–203). Hove, UK: Psychology Press.

Szymkowiak, A., Morrison, K., Shah, P., Gregor, P., Evans, J. J., Newell, A. F., et al. (2004, March). *Memojog: An interactive memory aid with remote communication.* Paper presented at the Workshop on Universal Access and Assistive Technology (CWUAAT), Cambridge, UK. Retrieved February 1, 2005, from www.computing.dundee.ac.uk/projects/memojog/publications.html

Thöne-Otto, A. I. T., & Markowitsch, H.-J. (2004). Gedächtnisstörungen nach Hirnschädigung [Memory deficits following brain injury]. In H. Flor, S. Gauggel, S. Lautenbacher, H. Niemann, & A. Thöne-Otto (Eds.), *Fortschritte der Neuropsychologie.* Göttingen, Germany: Hogrefe.

Thöne-Otto, A. I. T., & Walther, K. (2001). Neuropsychologische Störungen als Prädiktoren von Selbstständigkeit im Alltag [Neuropsychological impairments as predictors of independence in everyday life]. *Zeitschrift für Neuropsychologie, 12,* 102–103.

Thöne-Otto, A. I. T., & Walther, K. (2003). How to design an electronic memory aid for brain-injured patients: Considerations on the basis of a model of prospective memory. *International Journal of Psychology, 38,* 236–244.

Thöne-Otto, A. I. T., & Walther, K. (2005, July). *Evaluation of MEMOS, an interactive memory aid system for brain injured patients: Personal memory assistant vs. Palm organizer.* Poster presented at the Second International Conference on Prospective Memory, Zurich, Switzerland. Retrieved August 23, 2005, from http://www.h5197.serverkompetenz.net/1312/wcms/conference/content/docs/Abstracts.pdf

Titov, N., & Knight, R. G. (2000). A procedure for testing prospective remembering in persons with neurological impairments. *Brain Injury, 14,* 877–886.

van den Broek, M. D., Downes, J., Johnson, Z., Dayus, B., & Hilton, N. (2000). Evaluation of an electronic memory aid in the neuropsychological rehabilitation of prospective memory deficits. *Brain Injury, 14,* 455–462.

Wade, T. K., & Troy, J. C. (2001). Mobile phones as a new memory aid: A preliminary investigation using case studies. *Brain Injury, 15,* 305–320.

Walther, K., & Thöne-Otto, A. I. T. (2005, July). *Long-term usage of the interactive memory aid system MEMOS.* Poster presented at the Second International Conference on Prospective Memory, Zurich, Switzerland. Retrieved August 23, 2005, from http://www.h5197.serverkompetenz.net/1312/wcms/conference/content/docs/Abstracts.pdf

Thöne-Otto, A. I. T & Walther, K. (2005). Neuropsychologische Diagnostik prospektive & Erinnerungsleistungen in Alltag. *Zeitschrift für Neuropsychologie, 16* (SA), F.

Waugh, N. (1999). *Self-report of the young, middle-aged, young-old and old-old individuals on prospective memory functioning.* Unpublished honours thesis, School of Applied Psychology, Griffith University, Brisbane, Australia.

Wechsler, D. (1997). *Wechsler Memory Scale* (3rd ed.). London: Psychological Corporation.

Wilson, B. A., Alderman, N., Burgess, P. W., Emslie, H. C., & Evans, J. J. (1996). *The Behavioural Assessment of the Dysexecutive Syndrome (BADS).* Bury St. Edmunds, UK: Thames Valley Test.

Wilson, B. A., Cockburn, J., & Baddeley, A. (1985). *Rivermead Behavioral Memory Test (RBMT).* Bury St. Edmunds, UK: Thames Valley Test.

Wilson, B. A., Emslie, H., Foley, J., Shiel, A., Watson, P., Hawkins, K., et al. (2005). *Cambridge Prospective Memory Test (CAMPROMT).* London: Harcourt Assessment.

Wilson, B. A., Emslie, H., Quirk, K., & Evans, J. (1999). George: Learning to live independently with NeuroPage. *Rehabilitation Psychology, 44,* 284–296.

Wilson, B. A., Emslie, H. C., Quirk, K., & Evans, J. J. (2001). Reducing everyday memory and planning problems by means of a paging system: A randomized control crossover study. *Journal of Neurology, Neurosurgery, and Psychiatry, 70,* 477–482.

Wilson, B. A., Evans, J. J., Emslie, H., & Malinek, V. (1997). Evaluation of NeuroPage: A new memory aid. *Journal of Neurology, Neurosurgery, and Psychiatry, 63,* 113–115.

Wilson, B. A., Scott, H., Evans, J., & Emslie, H. (2003). Preliminary report of a NeuroPage service within a health care system. *Neurorehabilitation, 18,* 3–8.

Yasuda, K., Misu, T., Beckman, B., Watanabe, O., Ozawa, Y., & Nakamura, T. (2002). Use of an IC recorder as a voice output memory aid for patients with prospective memory impairment. *Neuropsychological Rehabilitation, 12,* 155–166.

Zakzanis, K. K., Young, D. A., & Campbell, Z. (2003). Prospective memory impairment in abstinent MDMA ("ecstasy") users. *Cognitive Neuropsychiatry, 8,* 141–153.

16

The Social Side of Prospective Memory

MARIA A. BRANDIMONTE

Laboratory of Experimental Psychology
Suor Orsola Benincasa University, Naples, Italy, and
University of Trieste, Italy

DONATELLA FERRANTE

Department of Psychology
Suor Orsola Benincasa University, Naples, Italy, and
University of Trieste, Italy

Prospective remembering is distinctive by virtue of its basis in interpersonal relations... The social-mind perspective might yield some gain in understanding *intentionality and prospective remembering.*

—Meacham (p. 355, 1988)

Since the publication of the first book fully devoted to prospective memory (Brandimonte, Einstein, & McDaniel, 1996), an increasing number of researchers have considered prospective remembering as one aspect of cognitive functioning that is central to developing our understanding of how intentions are translated into action and under which conditions they fail. In fact, the past decade has seen a veritable explosion of research on prospective memory with the field enriched by studies relying on different approaches by behavioral and brain scientists employing a variety of methods to investigate normal and abnormal prospective memory phenomena in adults, children, and the elderly. Yet, very little has been said on the social aspects of prospective memory. Only recently, prospective memory researchers (Ellis & McGann, 2003) argued that the degree to which specific cognitive skills are required for successful prospective memory depends not only on the characteristics of an intention but also on the circumstances under which it should be realized. In other words, investigating this important aspect of human activity in terms of a cognitive analysis only neglects the fundamental social component of the activity.

The purpose of this chapter is to draw the reader's attention to some issues that may be relevant to the development of the still neglected social side of prospective memory research, namely, the role of social interaction and that of the social value of the to-be-performed action in activating and inhibiting prospective remembering. Both these topics are prototypical issues in the field of social cognition, which attempts to understand and explain how individuals' behavior is influenced by the actual, imagined, or implied presence of others (Allport, 1985). In this view, the study of social interaction and of the social value of goals as potential determinants of prospective memory performance can be conceptualized as the study of remembering to do actions, respectively, with others and for others (M. Kliegel, personal communication, November 23, 2005).

SOCIAL INTERACTION, MOTIVATION, AND MEMORY

The simplest type of social interaction is the real or imagined pure presence of others. The way in which the presence of others affects individuals' performance has been a topic of interest in social psychology since its very beginning (Allport, 1924; Triplett, 1898). Many studies have been conducted (for a meta-analytic review see Bond & Titus, 1983) that showed that the presence of a coactor increases the speed of performance of well-learned, simple tasks and improves performance accuracy (*social facilitation*), but decreases the speed of performance of poorly learned complex tasks and impairs performance accuracy (*social inhibition*). Several explanations have been proposed for social facilitation and inhibition (SFI) effects. In the 1980s, the predominant explanation was that proposed by Zajonc (1965). According to Zajonc, by increasing the individual's level of generalized drive and arousal, the presence of others enhances the tendency to provide the so-called dominant response (i.e., the response that appears first in the person's repertoire of responses to a specific situation or stimulus in the environment), which is typically the correct answer in simple tasks, and it is often the wrong answer in complex tasks. Subsequent studies showed that the very presence of others is not sufficient, per se, to warrant a state of activation; that, rather, is prompted by such motivational mechanisms as evaluation apprehension (Cottrell, 1968, 1972) and expectations on one's own performance (Sanna, 1992).

On the other hand, when the social context makes the individual's response difficult to identify, as with collective tasks in which individuals' efforts are combined to form a single product, a reduction in the individual's motivation will take place, thereby producing a decrease in performance. Although intuition might lead us to think that working with others should maximize an individual's performance, research on social psychology has revealed that individuals frequently exert less effort on collective tasks than on individual tasks.

The most general phenomenon that is characterized by a decrement of the individual output is *social loafing*. The term was introduced by Latané, Williams, and Harkins (1979) and refers to the loss of motivation that occurs when individuals work together for the same aim (Steiner, 1972). Research revealed that social loafing does not depend on a coordination loss. Individuals working alone but believing that others are simultaneously working on the same task and that the outputs of all members would be combined exert less effort than those who know they are working individually (Latané et al., 1979).

A dramatic decrease in individual performance was also reported in several studies aimed at investigating the effects of collaboration on memory performance (Andersson & Rönnberg, 1997; Basden, Basden, Bryner, & Thomas, 1997; Clark & Stephenson, 1989; Meudell, Hitch, & Kirby, 1992; Weldon & Bellinger, 1997). In general, results showed that group interaction may strongly impair retrieval performance, hence reducing the amount of joint information available to the group. In particular, it was shown that although collaboration was better than individual recall, collaboration did not optimize individual performance. Collaborative recall exceeded mean individual recall, but collaborative groups recalled less than nominal groups.[1] Weldon and Bellinger (1997) referred to this poorer recall of collaborative groups as *collaborative inhibition.*

Different kinds of mechanisms have been proposed to explain collaborative inhibition. One explanation focuses on such motivational factors as evaluation apprehension, personal accountability, and diffusion of responsibility. A second explanation suggests a cognitive mechanism for collaborative inhibition: It would depend on retrieval interference. Namely, group interaction may strongly disrupt a given individual's retrieval strategy, providing inconsistent cues. Current evidence seems to provide more support for the cognitive explanation of collaborative inhibition (Basden et al., 1997). However, it is widely acknowledged (Andersson & Rönnberg, 1997; Basden et al., 1997; Weldon & Bellinger, 1997) that the experimental procedure typically adopted (i.e., turn taking), as well as task demands, may have minimized the role of motivational factors.

The role of social and motivational factors in influencing memory encoding and retrieval has long been known (e.g., Bartlett, 1932). People's memories are typically affected by schemas that reflect the body of knowledge that is transmitted by the members of their own culture. In turn, social interactions are highly dependent on individual memory: Being a forgetful person may cause our personal relationships with other people to deteriorate. Given this interplay between memory and social processes, any account of memory, at some point in its development, should consider the impact of social variables on memory processes and performance. Prospective memory is no exception.

SOCIAL INTERACTION, MOTIVATION, AND PROSPECTIVE MEMORY

Our interaction with other people influences (and is influenced by) our memory capability not only when we recall information that was acquired in the past (retrospective memory), but also when we perform actions based on previously formed

---

[1] Nominal groups are control groups formed by pooled individual performances (total nonredundant outputs) of an equal number of participants tested individually.

intentions (prospective memory). In both cases, memory failures in social contexts are deeply embarrassing, as they affect the credibility that other people give us.

Prospective memory failures are particularly relevant in people's social lives. As Winograd (1988) noted in his seminal paper "Some Observations on Prospective Remembering," there is a moral aspect that accompanies prospective memory failures: If retrospective memory fails, the person's memory is seen as unreliable, but if prospective memory fails, the person is seen as unreliable (Munsat, 1966). The responsibility given to the person whose prospective memory performance is unsatisfactory is therefore clearly social in nature. In the same years, Meacham (1988) argued that to understand prospective remembering, research should consider the quality of interpersonal relations within which the rememberer is enmeshed. Indeed, according to Meacham, if the intention remains a private fact, it can be conveniently forgotten or even denied. On the other hand, from a social-mind perspective, intentions are stable and long-lasting, thereby playing a causal role in behavior (Meacham, 1988, pp. 355–356) by modulating the strength of motivation and volition.

Like needs and goals, intentions are motivational states. Theories of both cognitive and social psychology suggest that such motivational states are characterized by enhanced accessibility of motivation-related concepts and representations (Anderson, 1983; Bruner, 1957; Förster, Lieberman, & Higgins, 2005). For example, in Anderson's (1983) adaptive control of thought (ACT*) model, goals are considered as sources of activation capable of sustaining activation even without rehearsal. In this perspective, enhanced accessibility of intention-relevant concepts derives from goals' strengths and values (i.e., from motivation-based mechanisms) rather than from rehearsal and strategic monitoring (i.e., from attention-based mechanisms). Of course, this is not to say that cognitive, attention-based mechanisms are not at work, only that they are not the original source of activation, which is instead motivational.

Motivation theories of volition converge on the idea that enhanced accessibility of goal-related concepts may contribute to effective goal pursuit (e.g., Goshke & Kuhl, 1993). For example, Gollwitzer (e.g., Gollwitzer, 1996; see also Cohen & Gollwitzer, chap. 17, this volume), in his *implementation intention* theory,[2] suggested that activation of intention-relevant representations prepares the individual to efficiently, and often automatically, detect goal-relevant cues in the environment (see also Bargh, 1997; Custers & Aarts, 2005; Gollwitzer & Bargh, 2005). In this perspective, automatic or unconscious motivations respond immediately and effortlessly to environmental conditions that promote or support the goal in question, hence keeping a person on task, even when the conscious mind is focused elsewhere. As Gollwitzer and Bargh (2005) suggested, "the efficient nature of unconscious motivation makes it an especially effective means of goal pursuit in complex and busy *social environments* in which conscious attention is divided and in short supply" (p. 624). For example, Gollwitzer, Bayer, and McCullock (2005) recently identified a factor able to reduce the impact of social loafing. In their study,

---

[2] Implementation intentions refer to an act of willing that furnishes the goal intention with an if–then plan that specifies the when, where, and how the person will realize the goal.

which was aimed at testing the effect of plans on social loafing, they showed that forming implementation intentions is sufficient to eliminate the tendency to loaf in a cognitive task (i.e., generating ideas).

Strength of motivation, strength of a person's intention or goal, and quality of implementation are all variables that may be modulated by social factors. Indeed, classic motivational theories hold that people are more prone to commit for those goals the attainment of which is perceived as both highly desirable and feasible. Typically, it is the social group to which the person belongs that establishes which goals are or are not desirable, feasible, or socially important (e.g., Atkinson, 1957; Lewin, 1951). As we discuss later in the chapter, prospective remembering seems particularly sensitive to the social value (i.e., social importance) of the action to be performed (Brandimonte, Ferrante, Bianco, & Villani, 2007a; Cicogna & Nigro, 1998; Kvavilashvili, 1987; Meacham & Kushner, 1980).

IMPORTANCE OF INTENTIONS

In 1988 Winograd wrote, "important future events ... cast a long shadow forward in time ... Normal activities are altered in concrete ways ... and are subordinated to or colored by the special activity. (We don't need external reminders for these important occasions)" (p. 352). Since then, theorizing on prospective memory has often included some reference to the influence of task importance on the realization of intentions (e.g., Cockburn, 1996; Kvavilashvili & Ellis, 1996; McDaniel & Einstein, 2000). However, so far, only a handful of studies have addressed this issue empirically, from different perspectives, producing quite different results (Andrzejewski, Moore, Corvette, & Herrmann, 1991; Brandimonte et al., 2007a; Cicogna & Nigro, 1998; Einstein, M'Daniel, Thomas, Mayfield, Shank, Morrisette & Breneiser, 2005; Ellis, 1988; Goshke & Kuhl, 1996; Kliegel, Martin, McDaniel, & Einstein, 2001, 2004; Kvavilashvili, 1987; Meacham & Kushner, 1980; Meacham & Singer, 1977; Somerville, Wellman, & Cultice, 1983).

One of the first demonstrations that task importance may have beneficial effects on prospective memory performance was that by Meacham and Singer (1977). The study was conducted in a natural setting where participants were asked to mail postcards to the experimenter over a period of 8 weeks. Half the participants were told that from all the postcards received on time, four would be drawn to win a maximum of $5. The results showed that under high-incentive conditions, participants performed significantly better. Since then, the beneficial effect of perceived task importance on prospective remembering has been documented in several studies ranging from questionnaire or diary studies (e.g., al., 1991; Ellis, 1988) to experimental studies (Brandimonte et al., 2007a; Cicogna & Nigro, 1998; Einstein et al., 2005; Kliegel et al., 2001, 2004; Kvavilashvili, 1987; Somerville et al., 1983). However, other studies reported no effects of importance on goal recall (Goshke & Kuhl, 1996) or prospective memory performance (Brandimonte et al., 2007a, 2007b; Kliegel et al., 2001, 2004).

Given the practical relevance for everyday life of importance effects in prospective memory, researchers have recently devoted their attention to the analyses of the factors that modulate importance effects. For example, Kliegel and colleagues (2001, 2004) recently proposed a theoretical explanation for the differential effects of importance reported in the literature. Namely, these authors suggest that task importance improves prospective memory performance if the prospective memory task requires the strategic allocation of attentional monitoring resources but not if the prospective memory task can be accomplished by relying on relatively automatic processes. Consistent with this view, Kliegel and colleagues found that importance instructions improved performance in a time-based prospective memory task and in an event-based task that required strategic monitoring to be successfully performed (Kliegel et al., 2004), but not in an event-based task that relied on relatively automatic processes (Kliegel et al., 2001, 2004). Most recently, Einstein and colleagues (2005) extended Kliegel et al.'s results by showing that importance instructions led to greater monitoring for the prospective memory targets, as measured by costs on the ongoing task, but improved prospective memory performance only with tasks that required monitoring (so-called nonfocal tasks).

In Kliegel et al.'s (2001, 2004) research, as well as in Einstein et al.'s (2005) studies, importance was manipulated with no regard to the degree of personal involvement in the task. Instructions were "neutral" as to the participant's degree of personal involvement and participants were simply told that either the prospective memory task or the ongoing task was "more important." In fact, the typical distinction in most studies that manipulated importance has been the important–unimportant (high–low importance) dichotomy, independently of the direction of benefit (i.e., whether the performed action would benefit the person himself/herself or another person). Sometimes, even though social importance was introduced in the study, it was not considered as such (Kvavilashvili, 1987). Two notable exceptions are the studies by Meacham and Kushner (1980) and Cicogna and Nigro (1998). Meacham and Kushner (1980) reported that social tasks such as meeting someone or keeping an appointment were more likely to be remembered and performed than tasks of a less social nature. Cicogna and Nigro (1998) explicitly referred to the social importance of the action to be performed. Participants were asked to fill out a questionnaire for 15 minutes. Immediately after giving the instructions, the experimenter said that he had to go away and took the receiver of the telephone off the hook. On leaving the room, the experimenter asked the participant to put the receiver back after 5 minutes. Importance was manipulated by either informing the participant that the experimenter was waiting for an important call and asking him or her to answer in case the telephone rang 5 minutes later (high importance), or generically saying that the experimenter was waiting for a call from a colleague (low importance). Results showed that significantly more participants performed the time-based task when the action was socially relevant. However, in that study, social importance was investigated within a time-based, attention-demanding prospective memory task. Therefore, one cannot disentangle motivational from attention-based influences.

By identifying some of the conditions under which task importance does or does not influence memory for intentions, the previously mentioned studies advanced our understanding of the cognitive mechanisms underlying the realization of intentions. However, in these studies manipulating importance always implied a correspondent variation in the amount of active monitoring. Thus, the question remains open as to whether, in the realization of an intention, importance-related, motivational factors such as a goal's value can have effects that are not mediated by strategic monitoring (see Gollwitzer, 1996; Gollwitzer & Bargh, 2005).

In an attempt to investigate the potentially important role of motivation in the activation of the intention, we have recently manipulated the direction of benefit (for the participant or for the experimenter) of the to-be-performed action within an activity-based (see Kvavilashvili & Ellis, 1996) prospective memory paradigm (Brandimonte et al., 2007a, 2007b). In addition, to study the role of social interaction in prospective remembering, we manipulated the presence of another person and the familiarity between the persons participating in the experimental session. Two hundred undergraduates recruited from the University of Naples participated in the study. There were 12 conditions obtained by crossing three independent variables (presence of another person, social importance, personal importance) in a $3 \times 2 \times 2$ between-participants design. The variable of presence of another person included three levels (alone, friend, stranger), and the other two factors varied on two levels (presence vs. absence of benefit).

In the alone condition, the participant was informed that he or she would perform a verb verification task (identifying regular and irregular verbs within three prose texts; ongoing task) and that at the end of each text he or she should remember to sign a form (maximum of three times). The importance of the to-be-performed action was manipulated by attaching to the action a different value in terms of the benefit that it would produce. Namely, no mention to any a priori evaluation of the degree of importance by the experimenter was made. Rather, each participant would perform the prospective memory task in accordance with his or her own evaluation of the goal's value. To this aim, participants in the alone condition received one of the following instructions, according to the experimental conditions: (a) If you remember to sign the form, you'll receive one course credit (personal importance); (b) If you do not remember to sign the form, important information will be missed and the experiment will be invalid (social importance); or (c) If you remember to sign the form, important information will be collected and you'll get one course credit (social and personal importance).

Importantly, the form was always out of the participant's sight. In addition, before starting with the task, each participant was required to recall instructions, to ensure that he or she had understood what, when, and how to do the tasks. Similarly, at the end of the experimental session, each participant was interviewed again about the tasks he or she was supposed to do. In so doing, we ensured that any failure to perform the prospective memory task was not due to forgetting the content of the to-be-performed action (the what and when retrospective components).

For the conditions in which another person was present during the test, the procedure involved testing couples of participants. Each couple was composed of a participant and a confederate. The latter was selected to be either a participant's friend or a stranger. On arrival, the two persons were required to choose who would be the participant. Afterward, the participant was informed that he or she would perform a verb verification task (identifying regular and irregular verbs within three prose texts; ongoing task) and that, in case he or she was uncertain about some responses, he or she could ask the confederate for help. However, the participant could do that no more than three times overall (this variation was introduced to justify the presence of another person during the test). For the prospective memory task, each participant was also told that at the end of each text, he or she should remember to remind the confederate to sign a form for the experimenter to keep track of the number of persons participating in the study. As for the alone conditions, the importance of the to-be-performed action was manipulated by attaching to the action a different value in terms of the benefit that it would produce. Thus, participants received one of the following instructions, according to the experimental conditions: (a) If you remember to remind the confederate to sign the form, you'll receive one course credit (personal importance); (b) If you do not remember to remind the confederate to sign the form, important information will be missed and the experiment will be invalid (social importance); or (c) If you remember to remind the confederate to sign the form, the experimenter will get important information and you'll get one course credit (social and personal importance).

A no importance condition served as the control. The no importance conditions resulted from crossing presence or absence of personal and social importance variables (i.e., absence of social importance and absence of personal importance). As for the alone conditions, pre- and postexperimental interviews were administered.

It is important to notice that although the ongoing task was very demanding (identifying Italian regular vs. irregular verbs), the prospective memory task was chosen to be very simple and relatively automatic. We assumed that doing one thing before or after another (activity-based intentions; see Kvavilashvili & Ellis, 1996) may be the simplest situation among prospective memory paradigms because it does not require either the interruption of an ongoing activity or monitoring for the target event. Interrupting the current activity to perform the prospective memory action may place some demands on current attentional resources (although that is not always the case; see Brandimonte, Ferrante, Feresin, & Delbello, 2001; Einstein et al., 2005). Retrieval of an activity-based intention, on the other hand, may fully rely on a kind of association that is very similar to an if–then plan (implementation intentions). In fact, when requested to recall instructions, before the experimental session, all participants recalled their goals in the form of when–then plans. As for implementation intentions (Gollwitzer et al., 2005), a strong mental link was created between the critical situation (finishing each verb verification task) and the goal-directed response (turning to the confederate—who was always out of sight—and reminding him or her to sign the form or, in the alone condition, turning behind and signing the form), such that the system may respond in a relatively automatic way to the event in the environment (see Einstein et al., 2005; McDaniel & Einstein, 2000). In our paradigm, finishing the verb verification task was the event that represented the critical situation in the environment. Such a paradigm may allow for vast opportunities to investigate motivation-based importance, as the prospective memory task clearly does not depend on strategic, active monitoring. Plausibly, one does not need to monitor the environment to detect the end of the task.

Extrapolating from these theories, we reasoned that if goals, desires, and if–then plans are sources of activation capable of sustaining activation even without monitoring (i.e., in a relatively automatic fashion; Anderson, 1983; Gollwitzer, 1999; Gollwitzer & Bargh, 2005), then any effects of importance under activity-based prospective memory conditions should reflect precognitive, motivation-based mechanisms rather than attention-based mechanisms. Namely, we hypothesized that manipulating the goals' value should affect the strength of motivation and, as a consequence, the activation of the intention.

Results revealed that social importance, but not personal importance, had the effect of facilitating retrieval of intentions, and this effect was limited to the prospective memory task. In fact, no effects of the importance manipulation were found on the ongoing task performance, hence supporting the assumption that the prospective memory task we chose was a relatively automatic task. To the opposite, participants were significantly better at performing the prospective memory task when they formed the socially relevant intention of avoiding damages to the experimenter (i.e., missing data for the experiment) than when they could obtain a benefit for themselves. No difference was found between the personal importance condition and the control, noimportance conditions.

Postexperimental interviews revealed that failures to perform the action were not due to noncompliance or forgetting of the content of the action. First, the activity-based intention was so simple that there is no reason to believe that one could decide not to do the action once he or she has retrieved it. Second, all participants recalled correctly what to do and when to do it.

The most interesting result, however, was a dramatic difference in the alone conditions between the social importance condition and the condition with the two joint benefits (social plus personal). Namely, whereas the expectancy of a personal benefit had no effect on prospective memory performance in the conditions with another person present during the test (i.e., either friend or stranger), in the alone condition the expectancy of a personal benefit while performing a socially relevant task significantly reduced prospective memory performance, as compared to the social importance condition. In other words, when people are alone while doing a socially relevant task, providing explicit incentives (personal benefit) reduces task performance. At first sight, this result might seem very surprising. After all, one of the broadest principles of behaviorism is concerned with how incentives increase the frequency of our behavior. In addition, as already mentioned, research on the effects of incentives on prospective memory has documented better performance in the high-incentive conditions (Meacham & Singer, 1977; Somerville et al., 1983). However, a large literature in social psychology documented how, under certain conditions, explicit incentives can lead to decreased motivation and unchanged or reduced task performance (see, e.g., Deci, 1975; Deci & Ryan, 1985). In addition, most recent theorizing in the economic literature (Bénabou & Tirole, 2005; Wichardt, 2005) has provided an important contribution to the comprehension of prosocial behavior and individual altruism.

PROSOCIAL PROSPECTIVE MEMORY:
A BROADER PERSPECTIVE

The concept of social importance is strictly related to that of altruism. Many studies confirm that a significant fraction of people engage in altruistic or prosocial behaviors. People commonly perform actions that benefit others and are costly to themselves, like volunteering, helping strangers, giving to charitable organizations, donating blood, and sometimes sacrificing their lives for strangers (Bénabou & Tirole, 2006).

Altruism cannot be easily defined. Typically, social scientists prefer the concept of *behavioral altruism*, which refers to the costly act of conferring benefits (economic, psychological, etc.) to other individuals (Fehr & Fischbacher, 2003). It is not clear what governs this kind of behavior. However, the social value of cooperative behavior in economic and political contexts is without doubt (see Wichardt, 2005). Behavioral altruism, as does any exchange, involves social interaction. It is widely acknowledged that utility in terms of individual life satisfaction or happiness is—at least in part—derived through favorable social interpersonal or intergroup comparisons. In other words, ego utility is derived through status (see Frank, 1985; Frey & Stutzer, 2002; Layard, 2005). Prominent theories of altruism provide a purely selfish motivation for human altruism (Wichardt, 2005), which is based on personal status seeking. Indeed, prosocial behavior seems typically driven by concerns for social reputation or self-respect (Bénabou & Tirole, 2006). We try to analyze the results observed under joint benefit (personal and social) conditions in the light of these theories.

Economic models of altruism provide clear and convincing explanations for the mechanisms underlying prosocial behavior (e.g., Wichardt, 2005), as well as for the negative (or lack of) effects of personal incentives. The assumption of these models is that an individual's well-being (i.e., utility) derives not only from the possession of a certain good, or, more generally, from the individual's wealth, but also—and predominantly—from the individual's status within some reference group (e.g., his or her family, acquaintances, or colleagues; Bénabou & Tirole, 2005). Recent studies indicate that a higher socioeconomic status positively influences subjective life expectancy (Mirowsky & Ross, 2000) and mental health (Miech & Shanahan, 2000). Thus, it seems reasonable to assume a causal relationship between individual status and individual well-being. Prosocial behavior and behavioral altruism, in this perspective, derive from a purely selfish motivation of improving an individual's status within a group through self-reputation or self-respect. The mirror image of such a perspective is that providing rewards (to do something) or punishments (not to do something) results in a detrimental effect of not affecting, or even reducing, task performance. For instance, paying blood donors can reduce supply, whereas imposing penalties can undermine an individual's motivation to obey the law. The psychological mechanism underlying such effects is linked to the strength of the so-called social signaling motives (Bénabou & Tirole, 2006). People care about the opinions others have of them (i.e., they care about their own self-image), and this concern contributes to prosocial behavior in a substantial way. Altruistic behaviors function as signals for the social group. If extrinsic incentives are introduced, they may have the detrimental effect of crowding out intrinsic motivation, hence reducing prosocial behavior (Frey & Jegen, 2001). In other words, rewards act like an increase in the noise-to-signal ratio. However, this is not to say that incentives systematically crowd out spontaneous prosocial behavior. Rather, the assumption of this economic model is that agents' pro-social or anti-social behavior reflects an endogenous and unobservable mix of three motivations: intrinsic, extrinsic, and reputational (Bénabou & Tirole, 2006). This mix varies across individuals and situations and can be altered by such variables as the introduction of rewards or punishments, the publicity or disclosure of the giving behavior, and the nature and amount of reward. The latter variable is particularly relevant to our results, as we found that a small positive reward (personal incentive) did not significantly affect prosocial behavior in any direction when another person was present during the test. However, in the alone condition, introducing a personal—although small—benefit crowded out prosocial prospective memory. This is in line with those models that hold that explicit incentives can lead to decreased motivation and unchanged or reduced task performance (see, e.g., Deci, 1975; Deci & Ryan, 1985). The results also showed that such social factors as the presence of another person during the socially relevant activity interact with the presence of the personal benefit in a way that attenuates any crowding out effects.

An important and intriguing question arising from these findings is what kind of incentive makes intrinsic motivation decrease to crowd out prosocial behavior. Is there a breakpoint in the prospective memory curve from no incentives to high incentives, as economic models of prosocial behavior seem to predict (Gneezy & Rustichini, 2000)? To answer this question, we are currently collecting data from a second study (Brandimonte et al., 2007b) in which the amount of personal reward is manipulated to obtain no incentive, high (money) and low (one course credit) incentive conditions crossed with the presence or absence of social importance. If current models of altruism are correct, we expect to replicate and extend our previous results and to observe high, unchanged, or reduced prosocial behavior according to the amount and nature of the rewards.

In any case, the results from our first study clearly indicate that (a) importance effects can emerge even with relatively automatic prospective memory tasks; (b) these effects are mediated by precognitive, motivation-based mechanisms; and (c) retrieval of an intention is influenced by such social factors as the direction of benefit and the presence of other people. In fact, as mentioned earlier, another social factor that influenced prospective memory performance was the presence of a stranger during the task. Indeed, memory for intentions is systematically better when a stranger is present during the task rather than a friend, providing further support for the notion of evaluation apprehension as a determinant of social facilitation.

THE ROLE OF OTHERS IN PROSPECTIVE REMEMBERING

Very few studies explored the role of others in prospective remembering. Kobayashi and Maruno (1994) compared two groups of participants. In one group, all participants shared the date on which they had to mail a questionnaire, whereas in the other group, mailing dates varied across participants. Contrary to the authors' prediction, the percentage of returned questionnaires was significantly lower for the group with a common mailing date. To explain these data, Kobayashi and Maruno (1994) proposed that the worse performance of participants who shared the mailing date was caused by the implicit expectation of a reminder from others. Most recently, Schaefer and Laing (2000) reexamined the effects of reminding expectations on prospective remembering. Participants were asked to perform six prospective memory tasks and were informed that at the time for performance they were to remind another participant (confederate) about the tasks, receive a reminder about the tasks from the confederate, or both. In a control condition participants heard nothing about reminders. Results showed that those participants who expected to provide a reminder performed more tasks than controls, although this difference just failed to reach significance. On the other hand, those who expected a reminder performed fewer tasks than those who did not expect any reminder. However, a closer analysis reveals that reminding expectations impaired prospective memory performance only in that they affected the retrospective memory component of the task (i.e., retention of the content). Thus, these results do not speak clearly either to the question of whether taking the responsibility to remind someone else to do something increases prospective memory or to the question of whether expecting a reminder from other people actually impairs prospective memory. The reason is that, as the authors themselves acknowledged (Schaefer & Laing, 2000, p. S109), the prospective memory task was a demanding multiple task (six different actions) and reminding instructions were worded in such a way that they may have unduly stressed the remembering of the content of the action, rather than the action itself. In addition, in the conditions in which the participant had to remind another person to perform multiple prospective memory tasks, the reminding action was a further prospective memory task, thereby introducing a confounding into the study. Thus, although interesting, the question of the role that other people may have in activating or inhibiting prospective remembering has not received a clear answer yet, for not only are there too a few studies on this topic, but the question itself, in our opinion, needs to be more focused and requires more theoretical elaboration.

For instance, the results from the study by Kobayashi and Maruno (1994) could be easily explained by the social impact theory (Latané, 1981; Latané & Nida, 1980). In a group subjected to social forces, the impact of those forces on each person in the group is diminished in inverse proportion to the strength (e.g., status, power), immediacy, and number of persons in the group. The division of impact is predicted to follow an inverse power function, with a negative exponent having an absolute value less than 1, thereby resulting in a marginally decreasing impact as the group size increases. In this perspective, the experimenter serves as a single source of social impact, whereas the group of participants serves as multiple targets of social impact. The influence of instructions—the main source of the effect—is therefore diluted among participants, hence weakening the effects.

Recently Johansson, Andersson, and Rönnberg (2000) reported a decrement of individual output in situations characterized by collaborative prospective memory. In their experiment, Johansson et al. measured the productivity (i.e., the level of performance) of couples of individuals in retrospective and prospective memory tasks. They compared the performances of old married couples, old non-friend couples, and nominal groups of two old individuals working on their own. The hypothesis was that only the old nonfriend couples should exhibit a negative effect of collaboration, whereas the productivity of the old married couples should approach the productivity of the control group. The idea that guided this hypothesis was that old married couples might use a shared language to reduce the amount of distraction on each other's retrieval processes and to cue one another more efficiently. This hypothesis was only partially supported by the results: The collaboration between the members of the couples inhibited optimal performances, but did so for both the old married couples and the nonfriends couples. However, a closer inspection of the results revealed that the married couples, who claimed to use a joint memory in a questionnaire filled in at home 1 week before, performed as well as the control pairs in both the prospective and retrospective tasks. Therefore, using a *transactive memory* seems to be sufficient to prevent collaborative inhibition. According to Johansson et al., the reduction of collaborative inhibition for the couples who claimed to use transactive memory supports a cognitive explanation of this phenomenon in terms of reduced-cue effectiveness. However, it seems plausible that longtime married couples who developed transactive memory also developed a special ability to share the responsibility of the different tasks. This could have eliminated the main determinant of social loafing, that is, *unidentified responsibility*.

To investigate whether and, if so, under which conditions prospective memory performance can be influenced by social loafing, we conducted an exploratory study in which we manipulated individual versus shared responsibility of performing a prospective memory task (Ferrante, Brandimonte, & Pelizzon, 2007). In particular, we were interested in exploring the impact of social loafing during the different phases of a prospective memory task. In this study, we used a very simple disjunctive task (Steiner, 1972) as a prospective memory task, which implied that any of the members of a group could perform the planned action. Importantly, the task did not require direct interaction between the participants during the experimental session, or special skills for its execution. Namely, the participants were requested to remember to switch off the light when leaving the laboratory, on completion of the task. To ensure that a simple everyday task such as switching off the light could be used as a reliable prospective memory task when included in a paradigm like the one used in this study, we conducted a pilot study with an ongoing task only condition. Indeed, participants could have switched off the light simply because they do so as a habit many times a day when they leave a room in everyday life. The ongoing task only condition served as a control for this possible confounding. The ongoing activity included a verb discrimination task and a questionnaire. Results from this pilot study showed that only 24% of participants switched off the light spontaneously on leaving the laboratory when they were alone. In the proper experiment, participants were assigned to four experimental conditions that varied according to the level of shared responsibility: without sharing, shared responsibility at encoding, shared responsibility at retrieval, and full sharing. In all four conditions, after instructions on the ongoing activity, the participant was informed that the experimenter would leave the room to look for the next participants and that he or she should remember to switch off the light on leaving the lab. Because the top of the door was made of glass, this action (turning off the light) would let the experimenter know that nobody was in the lab and that she could go in with the new participant. In the three conditions with shared responsibility, a collaborator of the experimenter (a confederate) participated in the task. In the full sharing condition, the confederate was in the lab when the participant arrived and received the instructions together with the participant. The confederate finished the task at the same time as the participant and then left the lab just before the participant, hence leaving the participant with the responsibility of performing the prospective action in isolation. In the shared responsibility at encoding condition, the initial phase of the task was the same as that in the full sharing condition. The difference was that, at some point during the task, the confederate pretended to have finished the task and left the room, leaving the participant alone until the time at which the prospective memory action was to be executed. In the shared responsibility at retrieval condition, after instructions on the ongoing task but before the prospective memory instructions, the experimenter informed the participant that in a few minutes another participant would arrive who had already received instructions about the task. Then, the experimenter gave the participant instructions on the prospective memory task. Afterward, the experimenter left the room and soon the confederate arrived and remained in the room until the end of the task. In the without sharing condition, the participant worked alone. Results showed that the presence of another person who shared the responsibility of doing an action determined a decrease in prospective memory performance according to the level of sharing. In particular, whereas in the without sharing condition, 96% of participants turned off the light before leaving the laboratory, in the condition with shared encoding, the percentage of participants who executed the prospective task dropped to 68%, in the condition of shared responsibility at retrieval it was 56%, and it dropped to 40% in the condition of full sharing, hence supporting a social loafing hypothesis.

One obvious concern may refer to the possibility that the decrease in prospective memory performance from the without sharing to the full sharing conditions are due to noncompliance. However, our data speak against such an interpretation. In fact, only in the full sharing condition could the participant decide not to perform the action and leave the responsibility to perform it to the confederate. In the other conditions, either the confederate left the room at some point during the task (shared responsibility at encoding) or the participant did not know what kind of instructions the confederate had received (shared responsibility at retrieval). Thus the observed decrement in the full sharing condition could be mostly due to a prospective memory failure deriving from the interference produced by the social interaction. Most interestingly, in the shared responsibility at encoding condition the participant is left alone and, in fact, he or she remains the only one who can do the prospective task. This reminds us of a typical social loafing situation, in which the sharing of responsibility for doing a very simple task lowers the level of motivation, thereby making it less likely that the trace of the to-be-performed task will be activated.

MAJOR ISSUES AND FUTURE DIRECTIONS

Prospective memory is a multifaceted phenomenon that can involve a wide variety of processes. The specific nature of the task will determine which type of processes, cognitive and noncognitive, are emphasized or attenuated, hence allowing for vast opportunities to alter and study different processing attributes of this fundamental function of everyday life (Dobbs & Reeves, 1996). In this chapter, we discussed some issues that may be relevant to our understanding of when and how prospective memory performance is affected by such noncognitive factors as the social relevance of the to-be-performed action and the nature and quality of social interaction. We argued that in the realization of an intention, importance-related motivational factors such as goals' value might have effects that are not mediated by strategic monitoring (see Gollwitzer, 1996). Rather, motivation-driven intentions seem to be characterized by enhanced accessibility of motivation-related representations capable of sustaining activation even without monitoring. We showed that an important class of motivation-driven intentions refers to prosocial intentionality: Avoiding damages to another person is a better activator of people's prospective memory performance than obtaining a material reward. However, prosocial prospective memory may function just as predicted by psychological and economic models of behavioral altruism, with memory for the intention activated on the basis of purely selfish motivation of self-image and reputation maintenance. We also showed that another social factor that seems to activate prospective remembering is the presence of an unknown person.

On the other hand, in this chapter we have also documented effects of inhibition of prospective memory due to diffusion of responsibility (social loafing). Of course, many questions are still open as to the relationship between social loafing and prospective memory. As an initial step, research could address the key question of which factors, among those that are known to produce social loafing, may have a role in prospective memory failures. Some of the findings discussed in this chapter are certainly new and counterintuitive. For example, the result that giving the responsibility of performing a specific, simple action to two persons increases the probability that the participants forget to do the task is a new finding that requires further investigation. It remains to be established whether this result holds when group performance, rather than individuals' performance, is considered. Analogously, the social relevance of intentions (importance or social value of the goal) and the motivational mechanisms associated with them are variables that need to be explored because they seem to affect prospective memory just as cognitive factors do. Future research, for example, might investigate such motivational qualities of prosocial prospective memory as sustained goal activation, persistence, and resumption of intentions (Atkinson & Birch, 1970; Gollwitzer & Bargh, 2005; Goshke & Kuhl, 1993, 1996; Lewin, 1951) as related to social versus personal benefits or to the presence of others.

A related area of research that might shed light on the questions addressed in this chapter refers to the investigation of social importance effects with focal prospective memory target events (Einstein et al., 2005). A target event becomes a focal one when it is part of the information extracted by the person in the service of her or his ongoing activity. For example, encountering and pausing to converse with the friend to whom one intended to give a message makes the cue focal by virtue of the overlap between the ongoing activity and the prospective memory action. In accordance with the multiprocess framework (Einstein et al., 2005; McDaniel & Einstein, 2000), recent results indicate that participants rely on spontaneous retrieval processes with a focal target event, as evidenced by the lack of significant costs (both in the accuracy and speed of performing the ongoing task) associated with performing a prospective memory task.

An interesting twist toward the study of the relationship between social motivation and memory for intentions would be to explore the effects of social versus personal importance with focally cued prospective memory tasks. According to our model, a lack of costs in the ongoing task should be associated with an improvement of prospective memory accuracy under social importance conditions and, possibly, with an impairment of prospective memory accuracy under joint social and personal importance conditions.

To sum up, in this chapter we have sketched a few new ideas for capturing some of the social aspects of prospective memory. We believe that if we want to progress in our understanding of prospective memory functioning, it is time to consider questions and theories that extend well beyond the study of an individual's prospective memory taken in isolation. We hope that the ideas that emerged from this analysis may represent an initial step toward the comprehension of this fundamental side of memory for intentions.

ACKNOWLEDGMENT

The writing of this chapter was supported by a grant from the Italian Ministry of Education, University, and Research (PRIN 2004) to Maria A. Brandimonte and Donatella Ferrante.

REFERENCES

Allport, F. H. (1924). *Social psychology*. Boston: Houghton Mifflin.

Allport, A. (1985). The historical background of social psychology. In G. Lindzey & E. Aronson (Eds.). *Handbook of social psychology* (Vol. 1, 3rd ed., pp. 1–46). New York: Random House.

Anderson, J. R. (1983). *The architecture of cognition*. Cambridge, MA: Harvard University Press.

Andersson, J., & Rönnberg, J. (1997). Cued memory and collaboration: Effects of friendship retrieval and type of retrieval cue. *European Journal of Cognitive Psychology, 9*, 273–287.

Andrzejewski, S. J., Moore, C. M., Corvette, M., & Herrmann, D. (1991). Prospective memory skill. *Bulletin of the Psychonomic Society, 29*, 304–306.

Atkinson, J. W. (1957). Motivational determinants of risk taking behavior. *Psychological Review, 64*, 359–372.

Atkinson, J. W., & Birch, D. (1970) A dynamic theory of action. New York: Wiley.

Bargh, J. (1997), The automaticity of every day life, in R.S. WYER-J.R. MAHWAH (a cura di), The automaticity of Everyday Life: Advances in Social Cognition, vol. X, Erlabaum, NJ, pp. 1–61.

Baron, R. S. (1986). Distraction-conflict theory: Progress and problems. In L. Berkovitz (Ed.), *Advances in experimental social psychology* (pp.1–40). New York: Academic.

Bartlett, F. C. (1932). *Remembering: A study in experimental and social psychology.* Cambridge, UK: Cambridge University Press.

Basden, B. H., Basden, D. R., Bryner, S., & Thomas, R. L. (1997). A comparison of group and individual remembering: Does collaboration disrupt retrieval strategies? *Journal of Experimental Psychology: Learning, Memory, and Cognition, 23,* 1176–1189.

Bénabou, R., & Tirole, J. (2006). Incentives and prosocial behavior. *American Economic Review, 26* (5), 1652–1658.

Bond, C. F., & Titus, L. J. (1983). Social facilitation: A meta-analysis of 241 studies. *Psychological Bulletin, 94,* 265–292.

Brandimonte, M. A., Einstein, G. O., & McDaniel, M. A. (1996). *Prospective memory: Theory and applications.* Mahwah, NJ: Lawrence Erlbaum Associates, Inc.

Brandimonte, M. A., Ferrante, D., Bianco, C., & Villani, M. G. (2007a). *Pro-social prospective memory.*

Brandimonte, M. A., Ferrante, D., Bianco, C., & Villani, M. G. (2007b). Remembering to do things for others: When incentives hurt. (submitted)

Brandimonte, M. A., Ferrante, D., Feresin, C., & Delbello, R. (2001). Dissociating prospective memory from vigilance processes. *Psicologica, 22,* 97–113.

Bruner, J. S. (1957). Going beyond the information given. In H. E. Gruber, K. H. Hammond, & R. Jessor (Eds.), *Contemporary approaches to cognition* (pp. 41–69). Cambridge, MA: Harvard University Press.

Cicogna, P. C., & Nigro, G. (1998). Influence of importance of intention on prospective memory performance. *Perceptual and Motor Skills, 87,* 1387–1392.

Clark, N. K., & Stephenson, G. M. (1989). Group remembering. In P. B. Paulus (Ed.), *Psychology of group influence* (2nd ed., pp. 357–391). Hillsdale, NJ: Lawrence Erlbaum Associates, Inc.

Cockburn, J. (1996). Assessment and treatment of prospective memory deficits. In M. A. Brandimonte, G. O. Einstein, & M. McDaniel (Eds.), *Prospective memory: Theory and applications* (pp. 199–225). Mahwah, NJ: Lawrence Erlbaum Associates, Inc.

Cottrell, N. B. (1968). Performance in the presence of other human beings: Mere presence audience and affiliation effects. In E. C. Simmel, R. A. Soppe, & G. A. Milton (Eds.), *Social facilitation and imitative behavior* (pp. 245–250). Boston: Allyn & Bacon.

Cottrell, N. B. (1972). Social facilitation. In C. G. Milton (Ed.), *Experimental social psychology* (pp. 185–236). New York: Holt, Rinehart & Winston.

Custers, R., & Aarts, H. (2005). Positive affect as implicit motivator: on the nonconscious operation of behavioral goals. *Journal of Personality and Social Psychology, 89,* 129–142.

Deci, E. (1975). *Intrinsic motivation.* New York: Plenum.

Deci, E., & Ryan, R. (1985). *Intrinsic motivation and self-determination in human behavior.* New York: Plenum.

Dobbs, J., & Reeves, H. (1996). Prospective memory: More than memory. In M. A. Brandimonte, G. O. Einstein, & M. A. McDaniel (Eds.), *Prospective memory: Theory and applications* (pp. 199–225). Mahwah, NJ: Lawrence Erlbaum Associates, Inc.

Einstein, G. O., McDaniel, M. A., Thomas, R. A., Mayfield, S., Shank, H., Morrisette, N., et al. (2005). Multiple processes in prospective memory retrieval: Factors determining monitoring versus spontaneous retrieval. *Journal of Experimental Psychology: General.*

Ellis, J. A. (1988). Memory for future intentions: Investigating pulses and steps. In M. M.Gruneberg, P. E. Morris, & R. N. Sykes (Eds.), *Pratical aspects of memory: Current research and issues* (Vol.1 , pp. 371–376). Chichester, UK: Wiley.

Ellis, J., & McGann, D. (2003, September). *Prospective remembering: A socially relevant activity.* Paper presented at the ESCoP Symposium on Prospective Memory, Granada.

Fehr, E., & Fischbacher, U. (2003). The nature of human altruism. *Nature, 425,* 785–791.

Ferrante, D., Brandimonte, M. A., (olreft). Pelizzon, L. & Marcotto, F. (2007). *Social loafing effects on memory for intentions.*

Förster, J., Lieberman, N., & Higgins, E. T. (2005). Accessibility from active and fulfilled goals. *Journal of Experimental Social Psychology, 41,* 220–239.

Frank, R. (1985). *Choosing the right pond.* Oxford, UK: Oxford University Press.

Frey, B. S., & Jegen, R. (2001). Motivation crowding theory: A survey of empirical evidence. *Journal of Economic Surveys, 15,* 589–611.

Frey, B. S., & Stutzer, A. (2002). What can economists learn from happiness research? *Journal of Economic Literature, 15,* 402–435.

Gneezy, U., & Rustichini, A. (2000). Pay enough or don't pay at all. *Quarterly Journal of Economics, 115,* 791–810.

Gollwitzer, P. M. (1996). The volitional benefits of planning. In P. M. Gollwitzer & J. A. Bargh (Eds.), *The psychology of action: Linking cognition and motivation to behavior* (pp. 287–312). New York: Guilford.

Gollwitzer, P. M. (1999). Implementation intentions: Strong effects of simple plans. *American Psychologist, 54,* 493–503.

Gollwitzer, P. M., & Bargh, J. A. (2005). Automaticity in goal pursuit. In A. J. Elliot & C. S. Dweck (Eds.), *Handbook of competence and motivation.* New York: Guilford.

Gollwitzer, P. M., Bayer, U. C., & McCulloch, K. C. (2005). The control of the unwanted. In R. Hassin, J. Uleman, & J. A. Bargh (Eds.), *The new unconscious* (pp. 485–515). Oxford, UK: Oxford University Press.

Gollwitzer, P.M., Bayer, U., McCullouch, K. (2005). The control of the unwanted. In R. Hassin, J. Uleman, & J.A. Bargh (Eds.), *The new unconscious* (pp. 485–515). Oxford: Oxford University Press.

Goschke, T., & Kuhl, J. (1993). Representation of intention: Persisting activation in memory. *Journal of Experimental Psychology: Learning, Memory, and Cognition, 19,* 1211–1226.

Goschke, T., & Kuhl, J. (1996). Remembering what to do: Explicit and implicit memory for intentions. In M. A. Brandimonte, G. O. Einstein, & M. A. McDaniel (Eds.), *Prospective memory: Theory and applications* (pp. 53–91). Mahwah, NJ: Lawrence Erlbaum Associates, Inc.

Johansson, O., Andersson, J., & Rönnberg, J. (2000). Do elderly couples have a better prospective memory than other elderly people when they collaborate? *Applied Cognitive Psychology, 14,* 121–133.

Kliegel, M. K., Martin, M., McDaniel, M. A., & Einstein, G. O. (2001). Varying the importance of a prospective memory task: Differential effects across time- and event-based prospective memory. *Memory, 9,* 1–11.

Kliegel, M. K., Martin, M., McDaniel, M. A., & Einstein, G. O. (2004). Importance effects on performance in event-based prospective memory tasks. *Memory, 12,* 553–561.

Kobayashi, K., & Maruno, S. (1994). The role of other persons in prospective memory: Dependence on other persons inhibits remembering and execution of a task. *Japanese Journal of Psychology, 64,* 482–487.

Kvavilashvili, L. (1987). Remembering intention as a distinct form of memory. *British Journal of Psychology, 78,* 507–518.

Kvavilashvili, L., & Ellis, J. (1996). Varieties of intention: Some distinctions and classifications. In M. A. Brandimonte, G. O. Einstein, & M. A. McDaniel (Eds.), *Prospective memory: Theory and applications* (pp. 23–51). Mahwah, NJ: Lawrence Erlbaum Associates, Inc.

Latané, B. (1981). The psychology of social impact. *American Psychologist, 36,* 343–356.

Latané, B., & Nida, S. (1980). Social impact theory and group influence: A social engineering perspective. In P. Paulus (Ed.), *Psychology of group influence*, pp. 3–36. Hillsdale, NJ: Lawrence Erlbaum Associates, Inc.

Latané, B., Williams, K., & Harkins, S. (1979). Many hands make light the work: The causes and the consequences of social loafing. *Journal of Personality and Social Psychology, 37*, 822–833.

Layard, R. (2005). *Happiness: Lessons from a new science*. New York: Penguin.

Lewin, K. (1951). Intention, will, and need. In D. Rapaport (Ed.), *Organization of and pathology of thought*. New York: Columbia University Press.

McDaniel, M. A., & Einstein, G. O. (2000). Strategic and automatic processes in prospective memory retrieval: A multiprocess framework. *Applied Cognitive Psychology, 14*, S127–S144.

Meacham, J. A. (1988). Interpersonal relations and prospective remembering. In M. M. Gruneberg, P. E. Morris, & R. N. Sykes (Eds.), *Practical aspects of memory: Current research and issues* (Vol. 1, pp. 354–359). Chichester, UK: Wiley.

Meacham, J. A., & Kushner, S. (1980). Anxiety, prospective remembering, and performance of planned actions. *Journal of General Psychology, 103*, 203–209.

Meacham, J. A., & Singer, J. (1977). Incentive effects in prospective remembering. *The Journal of Psychology, 97*, 191–197.

Meudell, P. R., Hitch, G. J., & Kirby, P. (1992). Are two heads better than one? Experimental investigations of the social facilitation of memory. *Applied Cognitive Psychology, 6*, 525–543.

Miech, R., & Shanahan, M. (2000). Socioeconomic status and depression over the life course. *Journal of Health and Social Behavior, 41*, 162–176.

Mirowsky, J., & Ross, C. (2000). Socioeconomic status and subjective life expectancy. *Social Psychology Quarterly, 63*, 133–151.

Munsat, S. (1966). *The concept of memory*. New York: Random House.

Sanna, L. J. (1992). Self-efficacy theory: Implications for social remembering. In M. M. Gruneberg, P. E. Morris, & R. N. Sykes (Eds.), *Practical aspects of memory: Current research and issues* (Vol. 1, pp. 348–353). Chichester, UK: Wiley.

Schaefer, E. G., & Laing, M. L. (2000). "Please, remind me…": The role of others in prospective remembering. *Applied Journal of Cognitive Psychology, 14*, S99–S114.

Somerville, S. C., Wellmann, H. M., & Cultice, J. C. (1983). Young children's deliberate reminding. *Journal of Genetic Psychology, 143*, 87–96.

Steiner, I. D. (1972). *Group processes and productivity*. New York: Academic.

Triplett, N. D. (1898). The dynamogenic factor in pacemaking and competition. *American Journal of Psychology, 9*, 507–533.

Weldon, M. S., & Bellinger, K. D. (1997). Collective memory: Collaborative and individual processes in remembering. *Journal of Experimental Psychology: Learning, Memory, and Cognition, 23*, 1160–1175.

Wichardt, P. C. (2005). *A status based motivation for behavioural altruism* (Working paper). University of Bonn, Bonn, Germany.

Winograd, E. (1988). Some observations on prospective remembering. In M. M. Gruneberg, P. E. Morris, & R. N. Sykes (Eds.), *Practical aspects of memory: Current research and issues* (Vol. 2, pp. 348–353). Chichester, UK: Wiley.

Zajonc, R. B. (1965). Social facilitation. *Science, 149*, 269–274.

17

The Cost of Remembering to Remember

Cognitive Load and Implementation Intentions Influence Ongoing Task Performance

ANNA-LISA COHEN

Department of Psychology
New York University

PETER M. GOLLWITZER

Department of Psychology
New York University and University of Konstanz

I magine the following scenario: You need to remember to execute an important intention, such as turning off your cell phone before an important meeting. In the past, you may have been embarrassed by the failure to complete such an intention, thereby disturbing an entire room of colleagues, not to mention the invited speaker. Therefore, you are especially determined to successfully complete this goal. However, at the same time, you may need to keep your phone activated until the last possible minute because of an impending vital phone call from a family member. How do you successfully fulfill these conflicting objectives? Cognitively speaking, are there differential attentional requirements (more or less resources) depending on the quality or complexity of the intention? Are there strategies one can employ to ensure a higher likelihood of fulfilling an intention while reducing the resources required to execute it? In this chapter, we describe research that attempts to answer such questions.

Reasons for prospective memory failure are often attributed to the person becoming absorbed in some other ongoing thoughts or activity such that the opportunity for execution of the intention passes. For example, the need to turn off the cell phone may be temporarily forgotten if the individual becomes engrossed in a conversation with the department chair prior to the meeting. This example underscores the key feature of prospective memory: the idea that prospective memory is inherently effortful because an intention must be retrieved when one is in the midst of some other competing activity (Maylor, 1996). For example, successful realization of the intention requires that the person disengage and interrupt the ongoing flow of thought and activity for it to be properly executed. Therefore, prospective memory is thought to require a higher degree of self-initiated processing (Craik, 1986). The more engrossing the ongoing task, the more prospective memory may suffer due to increased competition (d'Ydewalle, 1995). Thus, prospective memory involves striking a balance between executing an intention and maintaining ongoing task activities.

Based on some recent research on a phenomenon known as the *intention superiority effect*, intentions are thought to have some built-in qualities that make it more likely that they will be completed. For example, a number of researchers (e.g., Cohen, Dixon, & Lindsay, 2005; Freeman & Ellis, 2003; Goschke & Kuhl, 1993; Marsh, Hicks, & Bink, 1998; Marsh, Hicks, & Bryan, 1999) have shown that information related to intentions was highly accessible compared to information that was not future oriented. For example, results revealed that undergraduate participants showed better access to material that was intended for some future activity compared to material that was not future oriented. This phenomenon was termed the intention superiority effect (Goschke & Kuhl, 1993). In the typical paradigm, participants are asked to memorize written descriptions of two activities. Next, participants in an "execute" condition are informed that they will have to execute one of these activities (e.g., setting a table) later, whereas those in an "observe" condition only observe the experimenter carrying out the task. Then participants from both conditions receive a recognition memory test or lexical decision task that includes words from both scripts. Experimenters assume that the time it takes to match a probe item with its match in long-term memory is inversely related to the accessibility of that representation (Anderson, 1983).

Results from a number of studies showed faster reaction times for the items related to the to-be-executed task (e.g., Goschke & Kuhl, 1993; Marsh et al., 1998; Marsh et al. 1999). These results were thought to demonstrate that material related to intentions may experience some type of increased accessibility or superiority relative to information that is not future oriented. These findings lead to a question: If representations of intentions have increased activation or can be accessed more easily, do they compete or interfere with other ongoing activities? That is, does holding an intention in mind consume attentional resources?

THE COST OF HOLDING AN INTENTION IN MIND

Increasingly, there is growing interest in examining this issue of whether ongoing task performance is affected by the presence of an embedded intention. More simply, the question is whether there are costs to holding an intention in mind.

Some researchers (e.g., Smith, 2003, chap. 2, this volume; Smith & Bayen, 2004) argue that prospective memory is capacity dependent because at some level one is always monitoring the environment for a cue. Others (e.g., Einstein & McDaniel, 1996; Einstein et al., 2005; Guynn, McDaniel, & Einstein, 2001) argue that prospective memory can be automatic in the sense that the intention sometimes seems to pop into mind with little or no effort. The logic is as follows: When the intention is encoded, a representation is established that involves the target event and the response that is to be performed. Automatic retrieval of the response is assumed to occur once the target is identified because the representation has either a reduced threshold or a heightened level of activation. Therefore, conscious processes were involved at the time that the intention was formed but were not needed before the occurrence of the target event.

In contrast to this idea of automatic retrieval, Smith (2003) examined the issue of costs to ongoing task performance and showed that reaction time performance on an ongoing task was significantly increased by the presence of an embedded intention. More interestingly, these increased reaction times occurred even on neutral trials when no prospective memory target was present. Smith (2003) interpreted her findings as support for the preparatory attentional and memory processes (PAM) theory, which suggests that capacity-demanding attentional resources are needed for successful prospective memory performance (see also Smith & Bayen, 2004). In Smith's (2003) paradigm, both groups learned a list of six prospective memory target words. One group (embedded condition) was told to make a certain response when any of these words appeared during the lexical decision task, whereas the other group (delayed condition) was told that they should make their response at the end of the experiment, after the lexical decision task was finished. Thus, in one condition, the prospective memory task was embedded within a lexical decision task, and in the second condition the participants performed only the lexical decision task. In the embedded case, participants were instructed to try to remember to press the F1 key when they saw any of the six target words during the lexical decision task. In the delayed case, participants were told that they did not have to remember to press the key until after the lexical decision task had been completed. The two groups learned the same prospective memory target words and received the same prospective memory instructions, except for the delay.

According to PAM theory, preparatory attentional processes are engaged before the occurrence of the target event, and it is these processes that draw on limited resources. Therefore, Smith (2003) hypothesized that reallocation of resources would be necessary in an embedded prospective memory group, but that a delayed prospective memory group would not have to engage in the preparatory processing during the lexical decision task. She predicted that lexical decision reaction times to nontarget control words would be longer in the prospective memory embedded case than in the prospective memory delayed situation.

Not only did participants have longer reaction times on prospective memory trials, but latencies were longer on the nonprospective memory trials as well. The author interpreted these findings as evidence for PAM theory as they showed that capacity-consuming resources are needed to discriminate between target and nontarget events, as well as to recollect the intention even on trials where there is no target present. Smith (2003) made the fairly strong claim that the results are inconsistent with a view of prospective memory that proposes that intentions can be retrieved automatically (e.g., Einstein & McDaniel, 1996; Guynn et al., 2001) and are more consistent with the suggestion that successful event-based prospective memory tasks require attentional resources. (See Einstein et al. [2005], for an alternative view providing empirical support for spontaneous retrieval in a prospective memory task.)

Marsh, Hicks, Cook, Hansen, and Pallos (2003) conducted a study in which they examined slowing to the ongoing task more specifically by exploring whether it is due to several subcomponents of prospective memory. For example, they reasoned that cue detection may be achieved through four processes, including (a) recognition of a cue that was previously associated with an intention, (b) verification of whether that cue meets the requirements that were specified during encoding, (c) retrieval of the correct action, and (d) coordination of executing the action and maintaining ongoing task performance. In four experiments, they manipulated performance to examine whether slowing occurs due to verification processes (Experiments 1 and 2), or whether it was due to retrieval processes of the response action (Experiments 3 and 4). These experiments were undertaken to explore which cognitive processes of prospective memory are resource demanding and therefore cause slowing to ongoing task performance. Results showed that both of these processes contributed to ongoing task slowing. For example, Experiment 2 demonstrated that cues that were unrelated to each other showed more task interference than cues that were related to each other (e.g., animal words). This result was seen as evidence that the process of verifying the cue does require processing resources that interfere with prospective memory performance. Furthermore, target–response pairings that were highly associated (e.g., photo–album) showed much less interference than cue–target pairings that were not associated (e.g., dog–album). This indicated that processes devoted to retrieval of the response do interfere with ongoing task performance. In general, results showed that attention allocated to ongoing task performance resulted in more resources being available for cue detection.

NEW EXPERIMENTS

In a line of experiments that we recently carried out (e.g., Cohen, Jaudas, & Gollwitzer, in preparation), we attempted to replicate results by Smith (2003).[1] In contrast to Smith's paradigm, our paradigm required participants to make their lexical decision on each trial first, before they made their prospective memory response (if appropriate). This change to the protocol (also used by Marsh, Hicks, Cook, Hansen, & Pallos 2003) ensured that any observed cost was not due to participants withholding their lexical decision response because they were trying to decide whether it was a prospective memory target. Therefore, increased costs would have to be due to a process other than item checking. For example, observed

---

[1] We would like to thank Rebekah Smith for her generosity in sharing her materials with us and for her helpful comments when we were deciding on the experimental design.

costs may be a result of the need to periodically bring the intended action to mind, thereby maintaining the association between the prospective memory target and the intended action, similar to suggestions made by Guynn (2003). Alternatively, increased costs could be due to increased working memory load. For example, the need to hold an intention in mind, depending on the complexity of it, may result in increased memory load. This latter possibility was specifically examined in Experiment 3 of the current line of experiments.

In Experiment 1, participants were randomly assigned to either a control condition or an intention condition. Participants performed a first block of a lexical decision task that consisted of 126 word trials and 126 nonword trials (252 in total). After the first block of trials, participants received instructions for the prospective memory task. They were asked to take 2 minutes to memorize six target words (e.g., *blue, girls, decided, member, maybe, husband*). Participants in the control condition were told that they would have to recall the six words at the end of the experiment. Those in the intention condition were told that they would have to make an additional response to these words if they encountered them in the second half of the lexical decision task (see Figure 17.1 for a schematic of the experimental design). Participants were told to press the F1 key on the computer keypad (after first making their lexical decision) if they saw any one of these words during the experiment. We emphasized the lexical decision task and told them that they should be sure to respond as quickly and accurately as possible in the word–nonword decisions. However, we told them to also keep in mind that they must perform an additional response to the six target items.

Our results replicated those of Smith (2003). In Block 1, response latencies did not differ between conditions; therefore, we computed difference scores in which

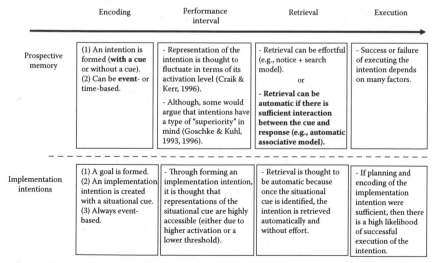

	Encoding	Performance interval	Retrieval	Execution
Prospective memory	(1) An intention is formed (**with a cue** or without a cue). (2) Can be **event**- or time-based.	- Representation of the intention is thought to fluctuate in terms of its activation level (Craik & Kerr, 1996). - Although, some would argue that intentions have a type of "superiority" in mind (Goschke & Kuhl, 1993, 1996).	- Retrieval can be effortful (e.g., notice + search model). or - **Retrieval can be automatic if there is sufficient interaction between the cue and response (e.g., automatic associative model).**	- Success or failure of executing the intention depends on many factors.
Implementation intentions	(1) A goal is formed. (2) An implementation intention is created with a situational cue. (3) Always event-based.	- Through forming an implementation intention, it is thought that representations of the situational cue are highly accessible (either due to higher activation or a lower threshold).	- Retrieval is thought to be automatic because once the situational cue is identified, the intention is retrieved automatically and without effort.	- If planning and encoding of the implementation intention were sufficient, then there is a high likelihood of successful execution of the intention.

Note: Bold font indicates aspects of prospective memory that are similar to those of implementation intention processes.

FIGURE 17.1   Schematic of the experimental design in Experiment 1.

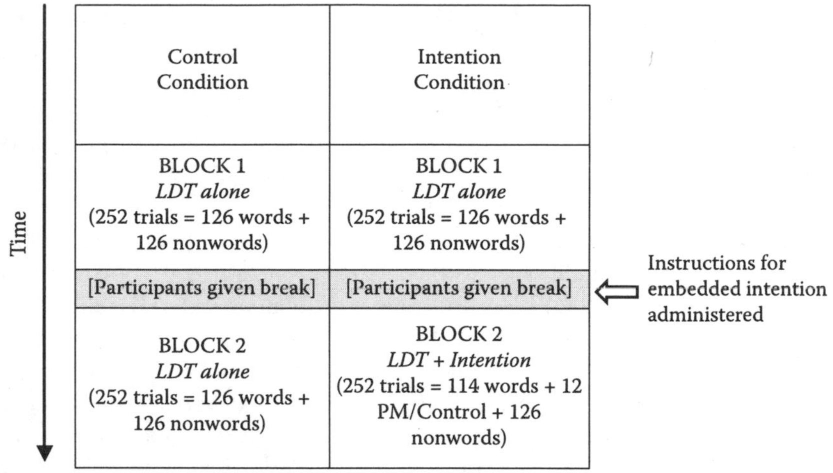

Control Condition	Intention Condition
BLOCK 1 *LDT alone* (252 trials = 126 words + 126 nonwords)	BLOCK 1 *LDT alone* (252 trials = 126 words + 126 nonwords)
[Participants given break]	[Participants given break]
BLOCK 2 *LDT alone* (252 trials = 126 words + 126 nonwords)	BLOCK 2 *LDT + Intention* (252 trials = 114 words + 12 PM/Control + 126 nonwords)

Time

Instructions for
embedded intention
administered

FIGURE 17.2 Reaction time latencies on ongoing lexical decision task trials in Experiment 1 as a function of condition. Bars represent standard error.

we subtracted Block 1 latencies from Block 2. Results showed that participants in the control condition exhibited a large practice effect, but that those in the intention condition did not benefit from practice due to the embedded intention (see Figure 17.2). It is worth mentioning that the latencies in our analyses of ongoing task costs in all our experiments did not include prospective memory trials. In fact, to reduce the likelihood that any "switch costs" would inflate our measure of ongoing task costs, we did not include the first three trials following a prospective response.

In our next experiment, we were interested in investigating whether the costs associated with executing the intention could be due to the coordination of two manual key presses. Some researchers might argue that participants were required to hold in mind two sets of instructions, both of which involved a manual key press. The fact that these two responses involved similar output channels (manual) could have created a type of response confusion, or conflict, leading to increased response times. That is, participants in the intention condition had to coordinate the act of pressing a computer key (yes or no) in response to the lexical decision task, while they also had to press another key (F1) for the prospective memory task. It is plausible that coordinating two manual responses led to the observed costs in the previous experiment. Therefore, the method was exactly the same in this experiment as in the previous experiment, except that participants were required to say "word" aloud when they saw one of the six target prospective memory cues instead of pressing the F1 key. Furthermore, we were interested in examining whether changing the retrospective memory component of the prospective memory intention to a verbal response would decrease observed costs.

Results for Experiment 2 were similar to those of the previous experiment in that participants in the control condition exhibited a large practice effect from Block 1 to Block 2 but participants in the intention condition did not benefit from practice

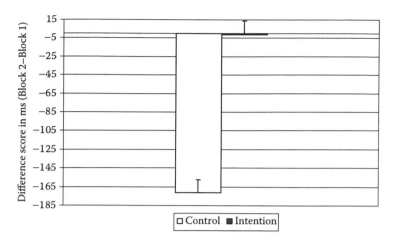

FIGURE 17.3 Reaction time latencies on ongoing lexical decision task trials in Experiment 2 as a function of condition. Bars represent standard error.

(see Figure 17.3). Our results are in line with those found by Marsh, Hicks, Cook, Hansen & Pallos (2003), who also showed that there is cue interference when participants perform a vocal prospective memory response. Prospective memory performance was considerably lower in Experiment 2 (53%) compared to Experiment 1 (82%). It may be that making a vocal response to a prospective memory cue was more difficult and led to more forgetting than making a manual key press response. Possibly the manual prospective memory response served as a type of reminder in the first experiment, whereas this was not the case in Experiment 2 with the verbal mode of responding.[2] However, we are reluctant to make any strong claims about this discrepancy based on a cross-experiment comparison. It may be interesting to deliberately manipulate response modality in subsequent experiments to examine how prospective memory and ongoing task performance are affected.

In the previous two experiments, participants were required to memorize six target words. It is possible that holding six targets in mind taxed working memory, causing excessive cognitive load, and that it was this aspect of the task that led to increased costs. Therefore, ongoing task costs may not be due to item checking but rather to periodic retrieval of the target + action association with ongoing task latencies increasing with the numbers of targets held in mind. Marsh, Hicks, Cook, Hansen & Pallos (2003)varied cue set size because they were interested in the effect that this manipulation could have on verification processes. The logic was that a larger cue set size would take longer to verify and this load on verification processing would increase ongoing task costs. The authors asked participants to memorize either four or eight target cues. Indeed, results showed that costs were increased for those in the eight versus four cue set size condition. Furthermore, a more recent study by Einstein et al. (2005) supported the multiprocess view by demonstrating that

---

[2] We thank Mark McDaniel for suggesting this interpretation.

participants rely on different processes for different task demands. That is, results of Experiment 3 of their line of studies showed significantly more ongoing task costs with six-target events compared to a condition involving one target.

We conducted a study to examine more specifically when cue set size begins to interfere with ongoing task performance. It may be that there is a point at which working memory load becomes taxed and ongoing task performance begins to suffer. That is, we wanted to explore at what exact point working memory load begins to interfere with ongoing task performance. In our study, we varied cognitive load across seven conditions in which participants received no intention (control condition) or one, two, three, four, five, and six target cue words. Each target occurred 12 times; therefore, those in the two-word condition had each target appear six times and those in the three-word condition had each target appear four times each, and so on. Therefore, the only aspect of the design that varied was the number of targets that participants had to hold in mind. Surprisingly, there were no significant differences for prospective memory performance as a function of condition (proportion correct ranged between .70 and .80). Thus, prospective memory was not significantly affected by our manipulation of working memory load. However, there were significant differences for ongoing task costs. Similar to findings by Einstein et al. (2005), our results showed that there were no costs to ongoing task performance in the one-word condition and only marginal costs in the two-word condition. Significant costs emerged in the three-word condition and increased in magnitude to the six-word condition (see Figure 17.4). Our results suggest that working memory load may influence the way that attention is allocated over the course of the task as a function of cognitive load. In a recent paper by Unsworth and Engle (2006), the authors suggested that primary memory is thought to have an upper bound of approximately four items. They provided evidence that when

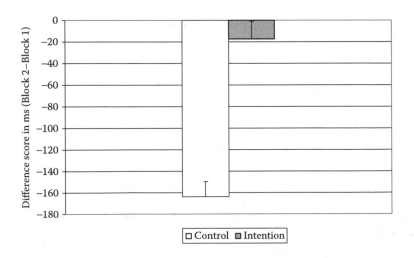

FIGURE 17.4 Reaction time latencies on ongoing lexical decision task trials in Experiment 3 as a function of condition. Bars represent standard error.

more than four items are present, items within primary memory are probabilistically displaced and must be recalled from secondary memory. Therefore, items are displaced from primary memory and must be retrieved from secondary memory, which may require additional resources leading to increased ongoing task costs.

These results provide support for the multiprocess framework (Einstein et al., 2005), which suggests that prospective memory may be mediated by spontaneous processing such that there are little or no costs to ongoing task performance under conditions of low working memory load. To further examine our findings, we conducted a regression model analysis in which we modeled ongoing task performance (difference scores) as a function of condition. In Fit 1, we entered a model to test the linear function, which was significant ($p < .05$) with a slope of 27. Thus, the slope could be interpreted to mean that difference score latencies decreased by 27 ms (signifying costs to ongoing task performance) with each unit increase of condition. Inspection of Figure 17.5 shows that the linear fit is generalizing across performance in the one-word condition. In a sense, the significant linear function implies that there is an increase in cognitive load from the control condition to the one-word condition when that is obviously not the case. Therefore, in Fit 2, we entered a model that takes into account performance in the one-word condition. The trend approached significance ($p = .09$) and the slope was 24. Although this second model was only marginally significant, it is suggestive that performance in the one-word condition is best explained by a model with a J-type function.

Results from this regression analysis are important in helping to quantify the increased costs to ongoing task performance as a function of each unit increase in cognitive load. Our results show that there was little or no cost when participants had to hold one target in mind. Smith (2003) stated that successful event-based

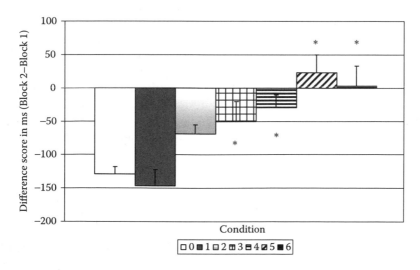

FIGURE 17.5 Regression model of ongoing task performance (difference scores) in Experiment 3 as a function of condition. Fit 1 was significant and Fit 2 showed a trend toward significance.

prospective memory responding always requires attentional resources. However, our results suggest that participants are able to juggle multiple demands (ongoing task + prospective memory task) when cognitive load is minimal, providing support for the multiprocess view (McDaniel & Einstein, 2000).

SELF-REGULATORY STRATEGIES AND PROSPECTIVE MEMORY

In the previous section, we described the tension between holding an intention in mind and the potential effect it can have on other ongoing activity. An interesting question to examine is whether these costs are amenable to self-regulatory strategies. More specifically, can one influence prospective memory and ongoing task performance by adopting a particular mind state or strategy? Marsh, Hicks, and Cook (2005) proposed that cue detection may be negatively affected when the intention and ongoing task are similar in nature (both semantic or both orthographic) because they compete for the same resources. The experimenters also used an effort manipulation wherein participants were instructed to allocate low, medium, or high effort toward the ongoing task. Results showed that there was a general interference effect when participants had to execute an intention versus a condition with no intention. Furthermore, increased effort toward semantic analysis of a letter string reduced the detection of semantic cues but not orthographic cues, and high effort in analyzing orthography of words resulted in reduced detection of orthographic cues. Marsh et al. (2005) made a distinction between overall general costs to ongoing task performance because of an embedded intention and the changing allocation of attention over the course of the task. Thus, the authors concluded that the relationship between ongoing task performance and cue detection is more complicated in that slower ongoing task performance may indicate sloppy inattentive processing in which cues may go unattended. By contrast, faster ongoing task latencies may reflect increased attention to the ongoing task; if the cue detection is competing for the same resources, it will be negatively affected (Marsh et al., 2005). Therefore, consequences of an adopted strategy depend on the degree to which a participant allocates attention to either the prospective memory task and the ongoing task and the degree to which he or she focuses on particular aspects of that task (e.g., semantic or orthographic).

Implementation Intentions

In Experiment 4 of our line of experiments, we had two related objectives: (a) to examine whether using a self-regulatory strategy known to enhance controlled processing would benefit prospective memory accuracy, and, more interestingly, (b) to examine whether enhancing prospective memory performance through the use of a self-regulatory strategy would come at a cost to ongoing task performance. Similar to questions posed in Marsh et al. (2005), we were interested in the relationship between cue detection and ongoing task performance. If we enhance performance on one component (prospective memory), does it necessarily come at a cost to the other component (ongoing task)? Therefore, in Experiment 4, we employed a self-regulatory strategy that is thought to enhance prospective memory performance known as implementation intentions.

Implementation intentions have been attracting increasing interest in the realm of prospective memory even though this strategy has been studied in the social cognitive domain for well over a decade (e.g., Gollwitzer, 1993). In prospective memory, researchers tend to stress the memory aspect of this executing intention. For example, failures to execute an intention are explained in terms of some type of cognitive failure. In social cognition, by contrast, the memory aspect is less the focus. Rather, failure to realize one's goal or intention is explained in terms of implemental problems (e.g., one is absorbed by competing goal pursuits, wrapped up in ruminations, gripped by intense emotional experiences, or simply unmotivated). Intentions are defined more broadly with the terms goal and intention being used interchangeably. An *intention* is defined as a mental representation that has been formed in relation to a desire to accomplish a task or direct behavior to achieve some desired state in the world (Kruglanski, 1996). The concept of intention is central in human goal striving (e.g., Bandura, 1991; Gollwitzer & Moskowitz, 1996; Locke & Latham, 1990; Wicklund & Gollwitzer, 1982).

In traditional theories on goal striving, the intention to achieve a certain goal was seen as an immediate determinant (or at least predictor) of goal-directed action. Thus, it was expected that the strength of an intention (i.e., how much one wants to realize it) would determine whether it is implemented or not (Ajzen, 1991; Godin & Kok, 1996; Sheeran, 2002).

However, research shows that intention–behavior relations are modest due to the fact that people, despite having formed strong intentions, often fail to act on them (Orbell & Sheeran, 1998). Evidence has shown that forming strong intentions does not guarantee goal attainment, as there are a host of subsequent implemental problems that need to be solved successfully (Gollwitzer, 1996). For instance, after having set a goal, people may procrastinate in acting on their intentions and thus fail to initiate goal-directed behavior. Furthermore, in everyday life, people often strive to attain multiple or even competing goals, many of which require repeated efforts (e.g., buying a new car) rather than the execution of simple short-term projects. Also, to meet their goals, people have to seize viable opportunities to act, a task that becomes particularly difficult when attention is allocated elsewhere or when these opportunities are not obvious at first sight or only present themselves briefly. Therefore, in the realm of social cognitive research, a failure to execute a goal or intention is examined not solely in terms of failure of memory, but also in terms of a host of other implemental problems that are considered as potential impediments to intention realization.

Previous theories of goal pursuit emphasized conscious choice and it was thought that behavior was guided on a moment-to-moment basis (e.g., Bandura, 1986). More recently, research has shown that mental representations of goals can become activated without an act of conscious will such that behavior is guided by these goals within the current situational context (Bargh & Gollwitzer, 1994). *Automatic action initiation* is the notion that established routines linked to a relevant context are released when the necessary conditions exist, without the need for controlled or conscious intent (Bargh, 1989). Bargh, Gollwitzer, Lee-Chai, Barndollar, and Troetschel (2001) showed that representations of goal-directed activity do not need to be put into motion by an act of conscious choice. In their study, Bargh and colleagues demonstrated that nonconsciously activated goals effectively guided action, enabling participants to adapt to ongoing situational demands.

Furthermore, Gollwitzer (1993, 1999) suggested that forming a certain type of intention called an implementation intention is a powerful self-regulatory strategy that alleviates the need for conscious control by delegating control to prespecified environmental cues. More specifically, implementation intentions link anticipated opportunities with goal-directed responses and thus commit a person to respond to a certain critical situation in a stipulated manner. Implementation intentions take the format "If situation X is encountered, then I will perform behavior Y!" They are to be distinguished from the more simple structure of a goal intention, which has the form "I intend to reach Z," whereby Z may relate to a certain outcome or behavior to which the individual feels committed.

An everyday example would be the following. You need to remember to tell a colleague an important message but are in the midst of a busy day of meetings and finishing a grant application. In this example, the goal intention is "I intend to give my colleague a message." Forming an implementation intention that links this goal with a specific situational cue might be "As soon as I finish my grant application, I will call my colleague." Therefore, you establish a specific cue (finishing the application) that is linked with a desired response (remembering to call your colleague). Implementation intentions are formed in the service of more general goal intentions and specify the when, where, and how a goal-directed response will be executed. Forming implementation intentions involves the selection of a critical future situation, and it is assumed that implementation intentions lead to a heightened accessibility of the situational cue (Gollwitzer, 1999). This in turn facilitates the detection of the situational cue in the environment and alleviates the need for effortful conscious control.

There is strong evidence for this perceptual readiness effect (Aarts, Dijksterhuis, & Midden, 1999; Gollwitzer & Schaal, 1998; Webb & Sheeran, 2003). For example, Aarts et al. (1999) investigated cognitive and behavioral effects of planning (i.e., forming implementation intentions) on goal pursuit during the performance of mundane behaviors. Participants received a goal to collect a coupon in the cafeteria among a variety of other task-related behaviors. Half of the participants enriched their goal with implementation intentions, whereas the other half did not. Results showed that participants who formed implementation intentions were more effective in goal pursuit than the control group. More important, results from a lexical decision task that included target words associated with the goal showed faster latencies to words associated with the attainment of the goal. Based on the assumption that the formation of implementation intentions creates a strong link between situations and behavior in memory, these findings point to the fact that planning increased the probability of goal achievement through a heightened accessibility of the mental representations of situational features related to the goal-directed behavior.

One published study examined whether using implementation intentions enhanced the prospective memory performance of older adults relative to a group of younger adults. Chasteen, Park, and Schwarz (2001) showed that forming implementation intentions significantly enhanced older adults' prospective memory performance. The authors concluded that implementation intentions benefited older adults' prospective memory functioning by allowing them to take advantage of the fact that this technique recruits automatic rather than effortful controlled memory processes. Their results showed that creating an implementation intention allowed behavior to become reflexive, thus eliminating the need for conscious control once the prospective memory cue target was encountered. The authors concluded that encoding an implementation set stored action schemas into a state of readiness and, when the appropriate trigger conditions were satisfied, the intention could be executed without mediation of a conscious recollection of the intention. This research demonstrated that implementation intentions facilitated the attainment of goal intentions in a situation where it was easy to forget to act on them. It is important to note that instructions in the Chasteen et al. (2001) study involved an imagery component. For example, participants were instructed to picture themselves writing the day of the week as a way to help them remember to execute this intention. Implementation intentions do not typically involve an explicit imagery component. There are three crucial issues in forming implementation intentions: selecting a critical situation, selecting a suitable goal-directed response, and strongly linking the two cognitions with the relational construct of if–then. Use of imagery techniques to achieve these three tasks is optional, and it may be a good technique for some people (those high in imagery), and for some "if" and "then" components that are easy to imagine.

As mentioned previously, we devised an experiment examining whether forming an implementation intention would improve prospective memory performance and, more interestingly, whether this improvement would be at the cost of ongoing task performance. In this paradigm, we compared three conditions: a control condition (no intention), an intention only condition, and an intention + implementation intention condition. The method was largely based on that of Experiment 2 from Marsh, Hicks, Cook, Hansen & Pallos (2003). In that study, participants memorized unrelated (e.g., dog–album) and related (e.g., photo–album) word pairs. Participants were told that they should respond with the second member of the word pair if they saw the first member of the word pair in a lexical decision task. Therefore, if they encountered *dog*, they should respond by saying "album" out loud. Results showed that target–response pairings that were highly associated (e.g., photo–album) showed less interference to ongoing task performance than cue–target pairings that were not associated (e.g., dog–album).

Based on these findings, we speculated that implementation intentions that form a link or an association between two previously unassociated components may function similarly to the inherent semantic association between two related words. That is, we predicted that a condition in which an unassociated word pair was furnished with an implementation (thereby creating a link between the two components) might lead to a reduction in interference compared to an unassociated word pair condition with no implementation intention.

In our paradigm, participants in all three conditions (control, intention only, intention + implementation intention) performed a lexical decision task. Halfway through the experiment, participants were asked to memorize three unassociated word pairs. Participants in the two intention conditions were instructed to say the second member of the word pair if they saw the first member during the lexical decision task. Participants in the implementation intention condition also formed an implementation intention for one of the word pairs. They were asked to write down the following phrase three times: "If I see the word *window* at any point in the task, then I will say *wrapper* as fast as possible!" So in a sense, the implementation intentions created an association between each member of the word pair similar to the inherent association that exists between semantically associated word pairs. Therefore, we predicted that those in the intention + implementation intention condition would show improved prospective memory performance in terms of accuracy and less interference in ongoing task performance in terms of less costs than those in the intention only condition.

Our predictions were confirmed. There was a significant improvement in prospective memory accuracy for those in the intention + implementation intention condition compared to the intention only condition; however, performance was near ceiling for both conditions. Most interestingly, there was a significant main effect for ongoing task costs, with ongoing task costs reduced for those in the implementation intention condition. Specifically, post-hoc analyses revealed that there was a significant difference between ongoing task costs in the control condition and the intention only condition, but no difference between control and intention + implementation intention conditions. Furthermore, ongoing task costs were significantly higher for those in the intention only condition compared to the intention + implementation intention condition. This study showed that improvement in prospective memory performance does not necessarily come at a cost to ongoing task performance (see Figure 17.6). As Marsh et al. (2005) concluded, the relationship

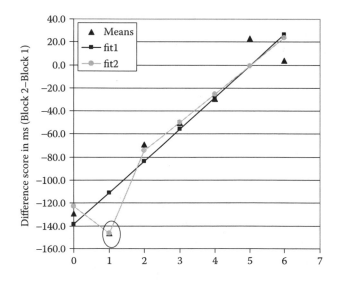

FIGURE 17.6 Reaction time latencies on ongoing lexical decision task trials in Experiment 4 as a function of condition. Bars represent standard error.

between prospective memory performance and ongoing task costs is complicated. The authors stated that slower ongoing task performance may indicate sloppy inattentive processing in which cues may go unattended. Along the lines of this statement, our findings suggest that participants in the intention only condition detected fewer cues than those in the intention + implementation intention condition, but this was not because they had faster performance in the ongoing task.

COMPARING AND CONTRASTING PROSPECTIVE MEMORY AND IMPLEMENTATION INTENTIONS

As mentioned earlier, there is increasing interest in the self-regulatory strategy of implementation intentions, perhaps due to its striking structural similarities to prospective memory. If we decompose each phenomenon into its component parts, there are some undeniable commonalities. For example, McDaniel and Einstein (1992) proposed that successful prospective memory is supported by two related component processes. The prospective component (prospective memory) is defined as the realization that some prospective action is to be performed when an appropriate cue is encountered. The retrospective component is defined as the ability to recall an intention when the prospective cue is detected. Thus, we must remember at an appropriate moment that we must do something (prospective memory component), and we have to recall what is to be done (retrospective memory component). For example, if an individual has to remember to give a friend a message, successful prospective memory requires that the appearance of the friend trigger the memory that a message has to be given (prospective component). Successful prospective memory also requires that the individual remember the content of the message (retrospective component).

Implementation intentions can be decomposed into components similar to those specified in the McDaniel and Einstein (1992) distinction. For example, when participants form an implementation intention, they say, "If situation X arises, then I will perform response Y." Therefore, the first portion of the implementation intention, "If situation X arises," is focused on specifying a situational cue that will eventually be linked with the goal-directed behavior. It focuses on the "I will have to do something when I encounter X." Therefore, this first half of the implementation intention may serve to establish the noticing process or prospective memory component of prospective memory. The second part of the implementation intention, "I will perform response Y," may serve to establish or strengthen memory for the content of the intention. This enables the individual to remember what that "something" actually is; therefore, it strengthens the search process or retrospective memory component of prospective memory. By forming an implementation intention, participants establish a link between both components. It may be this association that leads to a benefit in performance.

Ellis and Freeman (chap. 1, this volume) compare and contrast prospective memory and implementation intentions and pose important questions concerning the point at which the similarities between these two phenomena begin and end. They acknowledge that the role of commitment to one's goal or intention plays an important role in implementation intentions research but fails to be measured or acknowledged in prospective memory research. Furthermore, Ellis and Freeman suggest that implementation intention researchers fail to acknowledge sufficiently the wide variation in intention characteristics (e.g., nature of the cue, nature of the ongoing task) and in the ways that implementation intentions are encoded (e.g., written or read aloud and imagined). In the domain of prospective memory, Ellis and Freeman suggest that researchers may have become too focused on experimental paradigms and fail to acknowledge the importance of the commitment of the individual to the intention, how the intention is formed, and whether the intention is social or not social. Ellis and Freeman also question the proposed automaticity of implementation intentions. We return to this issue of automaticity in the next section, as it is important.

If we compare prospective memory and implementation intentions from the point of encoding to execution (see Figure 17.7 for a conceptual model), we can see that implementation intentions may be a special case of prospective memory tasks. In prospective memory tasks, intentions can be thought of as *cue specific* or *cue unspecific*. An example of a cue-specific intention would be "I need to give a colleague a message when I see him or her during the colloquium," with the cue being the colleague. In contrast, an example of an intention that is cue unspecific would be "I need to remember to write a recommendation letter for my student." In implementation intention research, a goal intention takes the form, "I intend to write a recommendation letter." This type of intention is thought to be unreliable in

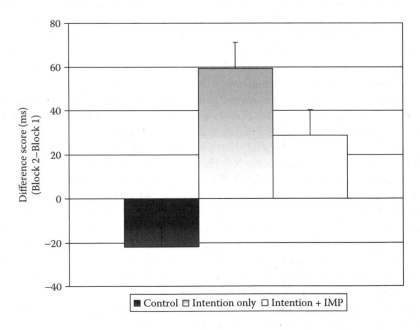

FIGURE 17.7 Conceptual model highlighting similarities and differences between prospective memory and implementation intentions.

the sense that one may not realize the goal, as there are a host of implemental problems (procrastination, distraction) that need to be solved successfully (Gollwitzer, 1996). However, when intentions take the form of an implementation intention ("If or when I finish my meeting, then I will write the recommendation letter"), a link is specified in the form of an if–then plan between a specific cue and desired response. It is in this form that there is higher likelihood that the intention will be successfully carried out. If we compare the cue-specific and cue-unspecific intentions, one can detect structural similarities between the goal intention, and the implementation intention. For example, one can see that the cue-specific intention is structurally similar to an implementation intention and the cue-unspecific intention is structurally similar to a goal intention. Therefore, it is with a cue-unspecific intention that using implementation intentions should benefit overall prospective memory performance. In cases where the cue is clearly specified, the intention already has the form of an implementation intention and benefits would not be expected. Therefore, implementation intentions can be thought of as a subpart of prospective memory in the sense that it is a strategy that helps to translate an ill-defined intention into a more clearly specified intention, which, in turn, has a higher likelihood of being successfully carried out.

As Chasteen et al. (2001) noted, implementation intentions only lead to a benefit with tasks that require a certain degree of self-initiation. In their background pattern task, implementation intentions did not lead to a significant improvement, whereas in the day-of-the-week task (which required a higher level of self-initiation), forming implementation intentions did lead to an improvement. In their background pattern task, the cue was highly integrated with the primary ongoing task. Therefore, little benefit was observed. Implementation intentions are if–then statements that are formed on top of "I will behave in such-and-such way in such-and-such situation" statements. In the statement "Please press the F1 key if you see the word *flower*," there is no selective specification of the if, or selective specification of the then. Therefore, explicit formation of an if–then link may not be achieved.

AUTOMATICITY

According to the multiprocess view (McDaniel & Einstein, 2000), successful prospective remembering can be mediated by strategic monitoring processes and in other cases by more automatic reflexive processes. This latter aspect of the multiprocess model builds on the earlier automatic associative module model (McDaniel, Robinson-Riegler, & Einstein, 1998). In this model, a cue must automatically interact with a memory trace for a prospective memory intention to be retrieved. When there is sufficient interaction between a prospective cue and an associated memory trace, this results in the memory trace for the intended action being delivered automatically to consciousness. Thus, successful prospective remembering is determined by the strength of association between the cue and the associated memory trace. If the cue does not automatically interact with a memory trace, that memory trace is not retrieved unless another memory module (prefrontal component) initiates a strategic memory search. Thus, the planning and encoding stage of prospective memory is critical for successful performance because an association between a cue and intention must be made to ensure successful prospective remembering (Kliegel, McDaniel, & Einstein, 2000).

Aspects of the automatic associative module model of prospective memory have implications for theory building in implementation intentions. Earlier in the chapter, we stated that forming an implementation intention causes the mental representation of the situational cue to become highly accessible, and that it is this heightened accessibility that makes it easier to detect the critical situation in the surrounding environment and readily attend to it even when one is busy with other ongoing activity. Moreover, this heightened accessibility should facilitate the recall of the critical situation because a strong link had been formed between the two components (situation cue + response). Implementation intentions are a strategy that can transform an intention that may require effort and attention into an intention that can be realized by more automatic processing. Thus, implementation intentions may increase the likelihood that there will be a strong association between the cue and associated memory trace, resulting in the memory trace for the intended action being delivered automatically to consciousness, as outlined by the automatic associative module model.

As stated earlier, it is important to be clear when we use the term *automaticity* in the context of implementation intentions. We use the word *automatic* in terms of Bargh's (1994) definition. Bargh argued that "mental processes at the level of complexity studied by social psychologists are not exclusively automatic or exclusively controlled but are in fact combinations of the features of each" (p. 3). Bargh suggested that there are three ways in which an individual may be unaware of a mental process: (a) A person may be unaware of the stimuli itself (e.g., subliminal perception), (b) a person may be unaware of the way in which he or she categorizes a stimulus event (e.g., stereotyping), and (c) a person may be unaware of the way in which his or her judgments or subjective feeling states are determined or influenced. For example, one may find a perceptual categorization task very fluid and easy to complete and may misattribute this feeling of ease to an incorrect cause because it is most available as an explanation. Therefore, forming an implementation intention results in a sensitivity to environmental cues that elicit a response or behavior that was previously paired with that cue, reducing the need for continued conscious control.

We understand this type of automatic action control as *strategic automaticity* or *instant habits* (Gollwitzer, 1999), as it originates from a single act of will rather than being produced by repeated and consistent selection of a certain course of action in the same situation (i.e., principles of routinization; Anderson, 1987; Fitts & Posner, 1967; Newell & Rosenbloom, 1981). Bargh and Chartrand (1999) suggested that mental representations that are designed to perform a certain function will perform that function once activated (regardless of the origin of that activation). The authors suggest that the representation does not "care" about the source of its activation because the mental representation is similar to a button being pushed. They stated, "In whatever way the start button is pushed, the mechanism subsequently behaves in the same way" (p. 476). Thus, similar to descriptions of the automatic associative model (McDaniel et al., 1998), if there is sufficient association between a situational cue and a desired behavior or response, the behavior will unfold automatically once the cue is successfully identified.

MECHANISM OF IMPLEMENTATION INTENTIONS

Automatic action initiation is the notion that established routines linked to a relevant context are released when the necessary conditions exist without the need for controlled or conscious intent (Bargh, 1989). Forming implementation intentions involves the establishment of a critical situation, and it is assumed that implementation intentions lead to a heightened accessibility of the situational cue, which in turn facilitates the detection of the situational cue in the environment. Sohn and Anderson (2001) proposed an ACT–R (adaptive control of thought–rational) model to explain task-switching costs. Their model assumes that information processing involves a sequence of production rule firings, and each of these production rules involves "retrieving some declarative information, called chunks, to transform the current goal state" (Sohn & Anderson, 2001, p. 764). They also suggested that the speed of retrieval of information depends on the level of activation of these rules. In a similar vein, implementation intentions are thought to lead to successful goal attainment based on the heightened activation level of a situational cue, which in turn eases retrieval of the associated response. Therefore, it may be that implementation intentions facilitate retrieval of intentions because the necessary "chunk" of declarative information for performing the intention is highly activated through the formation of an implementation intention.

Some confusion arises with standard prospective memory tasks, which often use instructions that resemble the wording of an implementation intention (e.g., "Press the F1 key when you see an animal word"). However, implementation intentions involve a purposeful and deliberate act in which a strong if–then link is created in a situation where the intention has not been so deliberately specified. It is possible that an individual may respond to prospective memory instructions by spontaneously forming a strong if–then link and creating conditions similar to those in implementation intentions, thereby enhancing their prospective memory performance.

MAJOR ISSUES AND FUTURE DIRECTIONS

In this chapter, we had two primary objectives. First, we examined the delicate balance between prospective memory and ongoing task performance. Second, we examined how a self-regulatory strategy known in the social cognitive domain has relevance in the realm of prospective memory. Regarding the former objective (examining the balance between prospective memory and ongoing task costs), it may be useful to consider the task-switching literature. Surprisingly, these two domains have not been thoroughly compared to date.

It is important to address the extent to which task switching and prospective memory are distinct or share common features, on the construct level and on the operational level. Often prospective memory failures are blamed on the fact that a

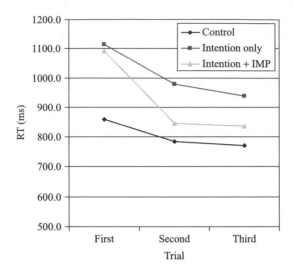

FIGURE 17.8 Reaction time latencies (switch costs) on the first three trials following a prospective memory target as a function of condition.

person becomes so engrossed in an ongoing task that he or she fails to remember to execute an intention. In other words, failures in prospective memory may be due to an inability to switch attention from ongoing task activity to execution of an intention. In our Experiment 4, we examined lexical decision task latencies on the first three trials following a prospective memory response. The resulting pattern of responding was similar to costs observed in a task-switching scenario (see Figure 17.8). That is, after making the response to the prospective memory target, there were increased costs for the first three trials before performance leveled off. This seems to suggest that there is some recovery time before participants are able to get back into the mindset of the ongoing task. Therefore, these costs may reflect a "reconfiguring of task set" similar to that described by Rogers and Monsell (1995) in the task-switching literature. Although not statistically significant, inspection of Figure 17.8 shows that those in the intention + IMP condition recovered more quickly from switch costs compared to those in the intention only condition in the second trial following a prospective memory target. An interesting future study would be to examine whether forming implementation intentions can reduce switch costs. Future research would benefit by comparing and contrasting processes shared in prospective memory and task-switching paradigms.

Another primary objective of this chapter was to examine the influence of a self-regulatory strategy on ongoing task costs. Results from Experiment 4 showed that forming an implementation intention may facilitate the switch of attention from an ongoing activity to remembering to execute an intention. Most interestingly, results showed that improvement in prospective memory performance was not necessarily at a cost to ongoing task performance.

Some researchers may have assumed that implementation intentions are a form of a motivational manipulation in the sense intentions furnished with an implementation intention may be perceived by the participant as more important compared to the ongoing task requirements. However, the lack of increased ongoing task costs in the implementation intention condition compared to the intention only condition did not support this interpretation. Implementation intentions create a strong link between an anticipated situational cue and a desired response, and this link may facilitate the switch of attention from an ongoing activity to retrieving an intention. There are two reasons why implementation intentions are thought to benefit performance. First, encoding an implementation intention leads to a heightened accessibility of the situational cue (either by increased activation or a reduced threshold), therefore helping to facilitate the detection of that cue in the environment. In a sense, they create a state of perceptual readiness. Second, implementation intentions establish a situation–behavior or response link, and in turn, established routines linked to a relevant context release the critical goal-directed behavior once the situational cue is encountered. By forming implementation intentions, people can strategically switch from conscious and effortful control of their goal-directed behaviors to behavior being automatically elicited by selected situational cues. According to automotive theory (Bargh, 1999), the heightened accessibility of goal-relevant information results in the processing of these stimuli preconsciously, which in turn leads to the direct activation of a behavior without conscious intent (Bargh, 1999). As Bargh and Chartrand (1999) suggested, mental representations that are goal directed to perform a certain function will perform that function once activated without the need for conscious control. Using this framework, it is possible that information related to an intention is processed more efficiently when that information is furnished with an implementation intention.

This examination also revealed the importance of cognitive load in determining the degree of ongoing task costs. Our results showed that there were no costs to ongoing task performance in the one-word condition and only marginal costs in the two-word condition, with significant costs emerging in the three-word condition. Similar to ideas expressed by Unsworth and Engle (2006), we suggest that there are few ongoing task costs in the one-word and two-word conditions because targets can be maintained in primary memory. Primary memory is thought to maintain four or fewer separate representations active for ongoing processing. When the number of targets exceeds this limit, they must be retrieved from secondary memory, yielding significant ongoing task processing costs (Unsworth & Engle, 2006). Furthermore, there can be instances in which primary memory is only able to hold less than its maximal limit, such as when trying to maintain information in the presence of an ongoing goal representation (i.e., lexical decision task).

To summarize, our results suggest that working memory load may influence the way that attention is allocated over the course of the task. Increased ongoing task costs may reflect the need to retrieve targets from secondary memory when the number of targets exceeds the capacity of primary memory. Results from our Experiment 4 suggest that self-regulatory strategies known as implementation intentions may help to reduce this cognitive burden by freeing up resources for ongoing task processing.

REFERENCES

Aarts, H., Dijksterhuis, A., & Midden, C. (1999). To plan or not to plan? Goal achievement or interrupting the performance of mundane behaviors. *European Journal of Social Psychology, 29,* 971–979.

Ajzen, I. (1991). The theory of planned behavior. *Organizational Behavior and Human Decision Processes, 50,* 179–211.

Anderson, J. R. (1983). A spreading activation theory of memory. *Journal of Verbal Learning & Verbal Behavior, 22,* 261–295.

Anderson, J. R. (1987). Skill acquisition: Compilation of weak-method problem solutions. *Psychological Review, 94,* 192–210.

Bandura, A. (1986). *Social foundations of thought and action: A social cognitive theory.* Englewood Cliffs, NJ: Prentice Hall.

Bandura, A. (1991). Self-regulation of motivation through anticipatory and self-reactive mechanisms. In R. A. Dienstbier (Ed.), *Nebraska symposium on motivation: Perspectives on motivation* (Vol. 38, pp. 69–164). Lincoln: University of Nebraska Press.

Bargh, J. A. (1989). Conditional automaticity: Varieties of automatic influence in social perception and cognition. In J. S. Uleman & J. A. Bargh (Eds.), *Unintended thought* (pp. 3–51). London: Guilford.

Bargh, J. A. (1994). The four horsemen of automaticity: Awareness, intention, efficiency, and control in social cognition. In R. S. Wyer, Jr. & T. K. Srull (Eds.), *Handbook of social cognition: Vol. 1. Basic processes* (2nd ed., pp. 1–40). Hillsdale, NJ: Lawrence Erlbaum Associates, Inc.

Bargh, J. A., & Chartrand, T. L. (1999). The unbearable automaticity of being. *American Psychologist, 54,* 462–479.

Bargh, J. A., & Gollwitzer, P. M. (1994). Environmental control of goal-directed action: Automatic and strategic contingencies between situations and behavior. In W. D. Spaulding (Ed.), *Integrative views of motivation, cognition, and emotion: Nebraska symposium on motivation* (pp. 71–124). Lincoln: University of Nebraska Press.

Bargh, J. A., Gollwitzer, P. M., Lee-Chai, A., Barndollar, K., & Troetschel, R. (2001). The automated will: Nonconscious activation and pursuit of behavioral goals. *Journal of Personality and Social Psychology, 81,* 1014–1027.

Chasteen, A. L., Park, D. C., & Schwarz, N. (2001). Implementation intentions and facilitation of prospective memory. *Psychological Science, 12,* 457–461.

Cohen, A.-L., Dixon, R. A., & Lindsay, D. S. (2005). The intention interference effect and aging: Similar magnitude of effects for young and old adults. *Applied Cognitive Psychology, 19,* 1177–1197.

Cohen, A-L., Jaudas, A., & Gollwitzer, P. M. (Under review). *Working Memory Load and the Cost of Remembering to Remember.*

Craik, F. I. M. (1986). A functional account of age differences in memory. In F. Klix & H. Hagendorf (Eds.), *Human memory and cognitive capabilities: Mechanisms and performances* (pp. 409–422). Amsterdam: Elsevier.

d'Ydewalle, G. (1995). Age-related interference of intervening activities in a prospective memory task. *Psychologica Belgica, 35,* 189–203.

Einstein, G. O., & McDaniel, M. A. (1996). Retrieval processes in prospective memory: Theoretical approaches and some new empirical findings. In M. Brandimonte, G. O. Einstein, & M. A. McDaniel (Eds.), *Prospective memory: Theory and applications* (pp. 115–141). Mahwah, NJ: Lawrence Erlbaum Associates, Inc.

Einstein, G. O., McDaniel, M. A., Thomas, R., Mayfield, S., Shank, H., Morrisette, N., et al. (2005). Multiple processes in prospective memory retrieval: Factors determining monitoring versus spontaneous retrieval. *Journal of Experimental Psychology: General, 134,* 327–342.

Fitts, P. M., & Posner, M. I. (1967). *Human performance.* Monterey, CA: Brooks-Cole.

Freeman, J. E., & Ellis, J. A. (2003). Aging and the accessibility of performed and to-be-performed actions. *Aging, Neuropsychology, & Cognition, 10,* 298–309.

Godin, G., & Kok, G. (1996). The theory of planned behavior: A review of its applications in health-related behaviors. *American Journal of Health Promotion, 11,* 87–98.

Gollwitzer, P. M. (1993). Goal achievement: The role of intentions. *European Review of Social Psychology, 4,* 141–185.

Gollwitzer, P. M. (1996). The volitional benefits of planning. In P. M. Gollwitzer & J. A. Bargh (Eds.), *The psychology of action: Linking cognition and motivation to behavior* (pp. 287–312). New York: Guilford.

Gollwitzer, P. M. (1999). Implementation intensions: Strong effects of simple plans. *American Psychologist, 54,* 493–503.

Gollwitzer, P. M., & Moskowitz, G. B. (1996). Goal effects on action and cognition. In E. T. Higgins & A. W. Kruglanski (Eds.), *Social psychology: Handbook of basic principles* (pp. 361–399). New York: Guilford.

Gollwitzer, P. M., & Schaal, B. (1998). Metacognition in action: The importance of implementation intentions. *Personality and Social Psychology Review, 2,* 124–136.

Goschke, T., & Kuhl, J. (1993). The representation of intentions: Persisting activation in memory. *Journal of Experimental Psychology: Learning, Memory, and Cognition, 19,* 1211–1226.

Guynn, M. J., McDaniel, M. A., & Einstein, G. O. (2001). Remembering to perform actions: A different type of memory? In H. Zimmer & R. Cohen (Eds.), *Memory for action: A distinct form of episodic memory?* (pp. 25–48). New York: Oxford University Press.

Guynn, M. J. (2003). A two-process model of strategic monitoring in event-based prospective memory: Activation/retrieval mode and checking. *International Journal of Psychology, 38,* 245–256.

Kliegel, M., McDaniel, M. A., & Einstein, G. O. (2000). Plan formation, retention, and execution in prospective memory: A new approach and age-related effects. *Memory & Cognition, 28,* 1041–1049.

Kruglanski, A. W. (1996). Goals as knowledge structures. In P. M. Gollwitzer & J. A. Bargh (Eds.), *The psychology of action: Linking cognition and motivation to behavior* (pp. 599–618). New York: Guilford.

Locke, E. A., & Latham, G. P. (1990). *A theory of goal setting and task performance.* Englewood Cliffs, NJ: Prentice-Hall.

Marsh, R. L., Hicks, J. L., & Bink, M. L. (1998). Activation of completed, uncompleted, and partially completed intentions. *Journal of Experimental Psychology: Learning, Memory, and Cognition, 24,* 350–361.

Marsh, R. L., Hicks, J. L., & Bryan, E. S. (1999). The activation of unrelated and canceled intentions. *Memory and Cognition, 27,* 320–327.

Marsh, R. L., Hicks, J. L., & Cook, G. I. (2005). On the relationship between effort toward an ongoing task and cue detection in event-based prospective memory. *Journal of Experimental Psychology: Learning, Memory, and Cognition, 31,* 68–75.

Marsh, R. L., Hicks, J. L., Cook, G. I., Hansen, J. S., & Pallos, A. L. (2003). Interference to ongoing activities covaries with the characteristics of an event-based intention. *Journal of Experimental Psychology: Learning, Memory, and Cognition, 29,* 861–870.

Maylor, E. A. (1996). Does prospective memory decline with age? In M. Brandimonte, G. O. Einstein, & M. A. McDaniel (Eds.), *Prospective memory: Theory and applications* (pp. 173–197). Mahwah, NJ: Lawrence Erlbaum Associates, Inc.

McDaniel, M. A., & Einstein, G. O. (1992). Aging and prospective memory: Basic findings and practical applications. *Advances in Learning and Behavioral Disabilities, 7,* 87–105.

McDaniel, M. A., & Einstein, G. O. (2000). Strategic and automatic processes in prospective memory retrieval: A multiprocess framework. *Applied Cognitive Psychology, 14,* S127–S144.

McDaniel, M. A., Robinson-Riegler, B., & Einstein, G. O. (1998). Prospective remembering: Perceptually driven or conceptually driven processes? *Memory & Cognition, 26,* 121–134.

Newell, A., & Rosenbloom, P. S. (1981). Mechanisms of skill acquisition and the law of practice. In J. R. Anderson (Ed.), *Cognitive skills and their acquisition* (pp. 1–55). Hillsdale, NJ: Lawrence Erlbaum Associates, Inc.

Orbell, S., & Sheeran, P. (1998). "Inclined abstainers": A problem for predicting health-related behavior. *British Journal of Social Psychology, 37,* 151–165.

Rogers, R. D., & Monsell, S. (1995). Costs of a predictable switch between simple cognitive tasks. *Journal of Experimental Psychology: General, 124,* 207–231.

Sheeran, P. (2002). Intention–behavior relations: A conceptual and empirical review. *European Review of Social Psychology, 12,* 1–30.

Smith, R. E. (2003). The cost of remembering to remember in event-based prospective memory: Investigating the capacity demands of delayed intention performance. *Journal of Experimental Psychology: Learning, Memory, and Cognition, 29,* 347–361.

Smith, R. E., & Bayen, U. (2004). A multinomial model of event-based prospective memory. *Journal of Experimental Psychology: Learning, Memory, and Cognition, 30,* 756–777.

Sohn, M.-H., & Anderson, J. R. (2001). Task preparation and task repetition: Two-component model of task switching. *Journal of Experimental Psychology: General, 130,* 764–778.

Unsworth, N., & Engle, R. W. (2006). A temporal-contextual retrieval account of complex span: An analysis of errors. *Journal of Memory and Language, 54,* 346–362.

Webb, T. L., & Sheeran, P. (2003). Can implementation intentions help to overcome ego depletion? *Journal of Experimental Social Psychology, 39,* 279–286.

Wicklund, R. A., & Gollwitzer, P. M. (1982). *Symbolic self-completion.* Hillsdale, NJ: Lawrence Erlbaum Associates, Inc.

18

Prospective Memory and Health Behaviors
Context Trumps Cognition

ELIZABETH A. H. WILSON and DENISE PARK

The Beckman Institute
University of Illinois

Prospective memory is an extraordinarily important behavior in maintaining the fabric of one's everyday life. To maintain social and professional function, an individual needs to keep appointments and remember plans for social events. Prospective memory is also viewed as an important component of maintaining one's health. Not only must an individual remember to keep medical appointments, there is also a substantial prospective component to the performance of common health behaviors, including remembering to take medications; performance of monitoring tasks (e.g., monitoring blood glucose in diabetics); and compliance with other medical regimens that may involve diet, exercise, or other behavioral modifications. In this chapter, we ask how important prospective memory is in complying with medical instructions. We make the case that there are different components of medical adherence, and that the prospective memory component is particularly reactive to contextual factors rather than to cognitive factors. Because of the important role of context in governing the prospective component of medical adherence, the individuals most vulnerable to prospective failures in adhering to medications are, quite surprisingly, younger rather than older adults. To make this case, we first provide an overview of the different components of medical adherence behaviors.

COMPONENTS OF MEDICAL ADHERENCE

The basic components we consider in understanding adherence to a medical regimen are (a) the physical effects associated with adherence, (b) patient beliefs associated with the regimen, (c) cognitive aspects of the regimen, and (d) contextual factors associated with the regimen. We also note that the bulk of the literature on medical adherence is associated with adherence to taking pills, and much of the discussion focuses on this literature, although we also consider glucose monitoring and appointment keeping when relevant literature is available.

Physical Effects of an Adherence Behavior

It is often the case that there are side effects associated with adherence behaviors. Taking a particular pill may make an individual sleepy, achy, nauseous, or irritable, to name a few possible side effects. We take the position (Park & Kidder, 1996), in agreement with that proposed by Leventhal, Leventhal, and Schaefer (1992), that it is the individual's mental construction of side effects or physical effects that is important in understanding the impact of such symptoms on medical adherence, rather than the symptoms per se. If, for example, an individual feels mildly nauseous a few hours after taking a particular medication, but attributes this feeling to a "nervous stomach" rather than to the medication, the individual will be likely to continue the medication. Similarly, if an individual has chronic back pain every morning when he or she gets out of bed, he or she could attribute the pain to the medication taken each night at bedtime, even though the real cause is an old mattress. Nevertheless, if the individual believes that it is the medication causing the pain, he or she might be likely to stop taking it. Thus, we believe that people's beliefs about the effects of a medication play a more important role in determining their adherence to it than do the actual effects. Often, people will have accurate beliefs about a medication (e.g., people correctly believe that an anti-inflammatory medication is making them have stomach pain) and will then cease taking it. Even in this case, however, it is the belief, rather than the side effect, per se, that drives the decreased adherence.

Beliefs About Medications and Medical Activities

There is a lengthy literature on the role that health beliefs play in medical adherence (Becker, 1989; Leventhal & Cameron, 1987; Rosenstock, 1990). Even more sophisticated than a simple beliefs model is the self-regulatory model of medical adherence (Leventhal & Cameron, 1987), which emphasizes the role of patient values, beliefs, and constructions of illness as the predictors of how an individual regulates medication-taking behavior. The patient is viewed as an intelligent problem solver who will utilize and adjust medication dosages based on experience. For the purposes of this chapter, which is focused on the role of prospective memory in medical adherence, we limit our discussion to individuals who have an illness representation that is consistent with medical adherence; that is, they believe that the medicine they are to take will be helpful to them, and they want to take it. Once an individual has an illness representation consistent with adherence (and also has access to the medication, as financial limitations sometimes play a role in nonadherence), cognitive factors become important in determining adherence behaviors.

Cognitive Aspects of Medical Adherence

Once an individual has formed an illness representation that is consistent with the desire to adhere to a prescribed medical regimen (e.g., take pills twice a day and monitor glucose three times a day), there are four major cognitive factors that play an important role in adherence (Park, 1992). These factors include (a) comprehending the different instructions associated with each medication or task, (b) integrating that information across the different items into a plan for each day, (c) remembering the plan, and (d) remembering to execute the plan. The comprehension and integration of the plan relies primarily on working memory, remembering the plan relies on retrospective memory (Einstein, Holland, McDaniel, & Guynn, 1992); and executing the plan relies on prospective memory.

It is our contention in this chapter that the cognitive components of adherence differ in their importance and relative contribution to adherence in adults of different ages. We present evidence that suggests that much of the problem in medical adherence in older adults involves the first three components of cognition (comprehension, working memory, and retrospective memory) and that prospective memory for taking medications is actually quite good in older adults. We also present evidence suggesting that prospective memory is a pressing problem for young and middle-aged adults in adhering to a medication regimen, and that this difficulty in prospective memory is related to age differences in the contexts in which medical adherence occurs.

Contextual Factors Associated with Medical Adherence

Context is a factor that has typically not played a large role in understanding prospective memory function. This is surprising because it is generally considered a socially acceptable excuse to indicate that one missed an appointment because one was "very busy" and that this busyness led to a prospective memory failure. For example, if your girlfriend failed to meet you at the coffee shop for a planned hour-long chat, you would probably find it acceptable if she told you that she forgot because she was extremely busy and had a grant deadline, multiple house guests, and a sick child, but you would find it less acceptable if she told you that she was home knitting a sweater and just did not remember until it was too late. We have suspected that how busy and how routine people's lives are might play a role in medical adherence, with the idea that the more busy an individual is, the less likely that he or she is to adhere. To assess this, we developed the Martin and Park Environmental Demands Questionnaire (Martin & Park, 2003), which provides an index of how busy and how routine people's lives are. The questions associated with the scale are presented in Table 18.1. The scales have a high degree of reliability for both old and young, and their validity was demonstrated when we noted that high scores on the scale were related to nonadherence to a pill regimen in a life-span sample.

Overall, we believe that the context in which the adherence occurs and the nature of an individual's lifestyle are factors that have been greatly underestimated in understanding the role of prospective memory in adherence. We came to this notion based on the consistent but puzzling finding that individuals with

TABLE 18.1   Items from the Martin and Park Environmental Demands (MPED) Questionnaire

Busyness Items

How busy are you during an average day?

How often do you have too many things to do each day to actually get them all done?

How often do you find yourself rushing from place to place trying to get to appointments or to get things done?

How often are you so busy that you miss scheduled breaks or rest periods?

How often are you so busy that you miss your regular meal times?

How often do you rush out of the house in the mornings to get to where you need to be?

How often do you have so many things to do that you go to bed later than your regular bedtime?

Routine Items

How often do your days follow a basic routine?

How often do you get out of bed in the morning and go to bed at about the same time?

How often do you eat all of your meals at the same time each day and night?

How often do you engage in activities at home at a specific time (i.e., read the paper after work, watch a particular television show, children, hobbies, etc.)?

---

high cognitive vulnerability (older adults) were actually more adherent than those with stronger cognitive systems. In the remainder of this chapter, we focus on two issues. First, we review our findings that indicate that age is an important factor in understanding susceptibility to medication adherence errors and that older adults have more trouble with comprehension and retrospective memory for a regimen, whereas young adults are particularly susceptible to prospective memory failure. Second, we discuss cognitive interventions designed to improve adherence, with a focus on contrasting interventions that operate on the retrospective versus prospective components of medical adherence.

UNDERSTANDING THE ROLE OF AGE AND COGNITION IN MEDICAL ADHERENCE

Cognitive Vulnerability Increases with Age

There is convincing evidence that as people age, there are declines in speed of information processing, working memory, and long-term memory (Park et al., 2002; Park et al., 1996). At the same time that basic cognitive processes decrease with age, there is also evidence that world knowledge remains intact (Park et al., 2002; Park et al., 1996). Thus, although cognitive processes operate less efficiently, knowledge—the product of experience—is preserved. Figure 18.1 displays this relationship. With respect to prospective memory, there is evidence that when participants are provided with a cue for prospective memory (event-based memory), age differences are small or nonexistent (Einstein, McDaniel, Richardson, Guynn, & Cunfer, 1995; Park, Hertzog, Kidder, Morrell, & Mayhorn, 1997). However, when an individual must remember to perform an action in the absence of a cue at

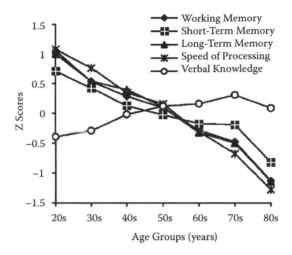

FIGURE 18.1   A composite view of life-span performance on measures of processing (working memory, short-term memory, long-term memory, and speed of processing) and verbal knowledge. Composite scores for each construct represent the z score of the average of all measures for that construct. (Adapted from Park et al., 2002. Copyright © 2002 by the American Psychological Association. Adapted by permission.)

a specific time (time-based prospective memory), age differences are quite large, with older adults performing more poorly than younger adults (Einstein et al., 1995; Park et al., 1997). When this pattern of findings is extrapolated to the real-world behavior of medical adherence, it suggests that older adults should have difficulty with most aspects of medical adherence (comprehension, working memory, long-term memory, and time-based prospective memory), with the only exception being event-based medical adherence events, where young and old should be equal. In contrast, young adults should outperform older adults on all aspects of medical adherence except for event-based tasks. A summary of findings with respect to these different components of medical adherence appears next.

Comprehension and Memory for Medical Information

In an initial study, Morrell, Park, and Poon (1989) studied comprehension and memory for a fictitious medical regimen in old and young adults. They reported that older adults showed poorer memory than young adults for the adherence instructions associated with the medications. The deficits persisted even when the older adults were able to have these written instructions available to them while they planned their medication schedules, as well as when the older adults had unlimited time to encode the information. These data are suggestive of comprehension, working memory, and long-term (retrospective) memory difficulties in planning and remembering a medical regimen. The working memory difficulties were manifested by older adults' difficulty in integrating an accurate adherence schedule across the multiple medications, even when the medications were available to them. The increased deficits observed when older adults were required to remember, rather than merely comprehend, the regimen points to retrospective memory problems as well.

In an effort to relieve the working memory and retrospective memory burden associated with prescription labels, Morrell, Park, and Poon (1990) hypothesized that pictorial labels may improve older adults' knowledge about prescriptions when compared to labels that only include text because older adults maintain stable memory for pictures (Park, Puglisi, & Smith, 1986; Park, Royal, Dudley, & Morrell, 1988). Surprisingly, the presence of the pictures on some of the labels increased younger adults' performance on tasks related to the information these labels contained, but this pictorial label type did not help older adults, and in fact for this group the picture labels were associated with lower levels of performance than were the text-based labels.

The advantage of word-based mediums to communicate information also extends to other domains; older adults are also better at remembering instructions about time of day when they are shown the relevant information in words as opposed to by pictures of clocks (Morrow, Leirer, & Andrassy, 1996). Because presentation of medical information via pictures is a relatively novel way to communicate such information, Morrell et al. (1990) suggested that encoding information shown in this modality may require higher levels of effortful processing, and they ideated that any novel methods used should be introduced slowly to increase familiarity before they are implemented as tools used to increase understanding of medical material. Within the domain of text, presentation style can also affect ease of comprehension and remembrance. For example, presenting information in list format as opposed to paragraph format can increase comprehension and memory for medical information by older adults (Morrow, Leirer, & Altieri, 1995; Morrow, Leirer, Andrassy, Hier, & Menard, 1998). Overall, these data suggest that older adults have comprehension difficulties as well as working memory and long-term (retrospective) memory difficulties.

The Retrospective Component of Prospective Memory

Although prospective memory primarily involves remembering to perform a future action, prospective memory has a significant retrospective component— that is, a component that requires that individuals remember past information and actions. In the discussion in the preceding section, we presented data suggesting that older adults have difficulty remembering medical information and that this difficulty has the potential to impact medical adherence. Other data have focused on individuals' ability to remember what prospective actions they have performed in the past. A key aspect of adherence is performing the action at the right time and the right number of times. All of us have had the experience of wondering whether we have performed an action (like taking a medication) or merely thought about performing the action. If someone concludes that he or she performed the action when he or she did not, an error of omission will occur (i.e., a medication event will be skipped), even though the prospective component of the event (remembering to take the medication) occurs at the proper time. Similarly, if someone concludes that he or she did not perform the action when he or she did, an error of commission will occur, and an individual will take an extra dose of the medication based on his or her faulty retrospective memory. Older adults have much more difficulty with this reality monitoring aspect of memory, and this again is a retrospective component that is more problematic for older adults.

Related to difficulties with reality monitoring, research on false memory has demonstrated that imagining the occurrence of an event that did not happen inflates participants' later confidence that the event did happen. This effect, known as imagination inflation (e.g., Einstein, McDaniel, Smith, & Shaw, 1998; Garry, Manning, Loftus, & Sherman, 1996; Goff & Roediger, 1998), has been shown to be especially pronounced in older adults (Lyle, Bloise, & Johnson, 2006). Imagination inflation is a retrospective memory phenomenon and may be another mechanism accounting for medical adherence errors in older adults.

The Prospective Aspect of Prospective Memory

Another aspect of prospective memory relates to the ability to remember to execute the prospective task. Sometimes an individual may encounter an external cue that successfully catches his or her attention to remind him or her to perform a prospective action, but the cue occurs at a time or in a context where it is inconvenient or impossible to act on the individual's intention (e.g., one's medication bottle is at home while one is at the grocery store). To address this issue, Einstein et al. (1998) gave people an overt experimental task and within this task also presented cues that needed to be acted on only after the participants had waited 30 seconds from the onset of the cue's appearance. Some participants were also asked to complete a distracter task simulating the busyness of multitasking in daily life. Einstein et al. found that older adults had a harder time responding accurately to the cues than did younger adults, and at the beginning of the experiment these differences were exaggerated when older adults were also responsible for completing the distracter task. Similarly, in an experiment by Einstein, McDaniel, Mazzi, Cochran, and Baker (2000), when older adults had to wait to act on a cue, they performed at much lower levels than younger adults, despite equivalent performance when they could respond to cues immediately. These problems were not likely due to the increased cognitive load on working memory that resulted from the distracter tasks because the presence of such extraneous tasks did not affect performance. In fact, older adults were still at a deficit when they did not have to do anything but wait between cue and appropriate response time (McDaniel, Einstein, Stout, & Morgan, 2003). In the real world, the problems that older adults have when they cannot immediately act on external cues is a relevant factor because often people remember to take their medicines at times when they cannot immediately act on these intentions due to inconvenient timing or other life responsibilities, such as answering the phone or driving to work. Again, this is a problem where older adults accurately remember to perform the event but due to distractions are unable to maintain the event in working memory at a level that is sufficiently effective that they remember to take their medications later.

Prospective Memory in the Real World: The Case of Medical Adherence and Aging

All of the literature reviewed thus far presents a convincing picture of the deficits that older adults evidence in many different components of cognitive function involved in medical adherence. Remembering to take medications and perform medical actions such as glucose monitoring are among the most important memory behaviors an individual must perform, particularly because the consequences of failing to do so can result in illness, hospitalization, and even death. There is a wealth of literature suggesting that older adults have significant problems with medical adherence due to some of the cognitive deficits outlined in the preceding sections, along with a great deal of information about how to remedy adherence problems. In an effort to document precisely how problematic medication adherence is in older adults, we conducted an initial study where we examined adherence rates in adults aged 60 and older using microelectronic devices (Park, Morrell, Frieske, & Kincaid, 1992). We sampled adults with a range of different illnesses, all of whom were taking at least four different medications. We followed the adults for 2 weeks and found that individuals who were 60 to 76 years old had an adherence rate of 94%, whereas adults 77 years old and older made more adherence errors and had an adherence rate of 85%. We were very surprised by the excellent adherence rates in the young-old adults, as we had expected nonadherence to be as high as 40%.

Because the sample in this study (Park et al., 1992) was heterogeneous, we thought that perhaps we should examine adherence as a function of specific diseases, and we opted to conduct a new study on a life-span sample of adults with hypertension. We selected hypertension because it is a silent disorder with no obvious consequences associated with nonadherence, as well as no cues, such as pain or other discomfort, to remind an individual to adhere. We studied 48 adults, 36 to 87 years old, for a 4-week period. We found that adults 65 to 74 years old had by far the lowest number of adherence errors (a total of less than 4%), whereas the highest number of errors was made by middle-aged adults (ages 55–64), with a rate of 18%, and by the oldest adults (those 75 years old and older), with a rate of 21% (Morrell, Park, Kidder, & Martin, 1997). These data, like the Park et al. (1992) data, suggested that young-old adults were the most adherent group for following medication instructions. This result was particularly puzzling because we also had cognitive data on these participants, and the 65- to 74-year-olds with such excellent adherence showed significant age-related decline in measures of cognition.

In an effort to better understand the mechanisms contributing to adherence and nonadherence, we conducted another study, this time on a large life-span sample of rheumatoid arthritis patients, 34 to 84 years old, who were followed for 4 weeks. Adherence was measured by providing participants with microchips embedded in their medication bottles so that the date and time that the bottles were opened was inconspicuously recorded. In addition to measuring nonadherence, we collected measures of belief systems about the illness and medications to develop stable measures of illness representation, a complete neurocognitive battery, and measures of anxiety and depression as well as measures of routine and busyness (Park et al., 1997). The results from this study indicated again that (a) older participants showed decreased speed of processing, working memory, and long-term memory compared to younger participants; (b) middle-aged adults (those from 34 to 54) made the most adherence errors; (c) the oldest adults had the best rate of adherence; and (d) structural equation modeling indicated that the best predictor of nonadherence was busyness rather than cognition. So again, in this study, we reported that old adults, despite their cognitive frailties, were the most adherent, contrary to the many suggestions in the literature that were largely based on speculation rather than empirical data. By including a large array of individual differences measures and controlling for both age and cognitive function, we were able to determine that measures of busyness and routine were the most important factors in determining adherence. Middle-aged adults scored much higher on the Martin and Park Environmental Demands Questionnaire (Martin & Park, 2003), and this measure of contextual press (shown in Table 18.1) proved to be more important than cognitive function in determining adherence behavior.

Overall, our research has shown that age is indeed a risk factor for nonadherence, but it is younger rather than older adults who are more at risk for making medication errors. The data (Park et al., 1997) show that older adults evidenced significant cognitive decline relative to younger adults but still had sufficient cognitive resources to take medication with a high degree of accuracy, agreeing with data reported by Morrell et al. (1997). The data suggest that with respect to medical regimens, context may take precedence over cognition. Additionally, the individuals most at risk of nonadherence are busy, middle-aged adults who are experiencing sufficient contextual press that they regularly experience prospective memory failures and do not remember to take their medications. In contrast, older adults who lead highly routine, less busy lives may repeatedly encounter the same cues each time they take a medication, such as taking a morning pill with the orange juice that they have every morning (Park, Gutchess, Meade, & Stine-Morrow, in press; Park & Meade, 2007). In this example, the orange juice quickly becomes an event-based cue for a time-based prospective behavior. Eventually, the act of picking up the glass of orange juice each morning will lead to the individual picking up his or her medication with little or no thought, as the behavior becomes automatized (Park, 2000). The fact that older adults showed vastly more routine and less busy lives in the Park et al. (1999) adherence study, and that this decreased busyness led directly to increased adherence, argues for the notion that older adults are more likely to automatize medication adherence behaviors by transforming time-based medical events into more easily remembered and automatized event-based behaviors.

One interesting question is whether it is how busy one is or how routine one's life is that affects adherence. The Martin and Park Environmental Demands Questionnaire (Martin & Park, 2003), utilizing the questions that appear in Table 18.1, determined that busyness and routine are independent factors. Using multiple regression analysis, they determined that busyness was more important in determining adherence behaviors than routine. So, for example, a very busy physician who sees many patients per day may lead an intensely busy, yet routine life and would be at greater risk of nonadherence than a physician who saw few patients, but on a sporadic schedule.

It is important to note that participants in the studies described thus far were using medications that they had taken for some time, and they were highly familiar with their regimen. We hypothesize that older adults may be at the most risk for nonadherence when they are prescribed new medications or medical procedures with which they are highly unfamiliar. In these cases, they would have to comprehend and remember a considerable amount of information utilizing retrospective memory, and at the same time learn a new prospective behavior. Future research, contrasting familiar routines with more novel routines in older adults, would be welcome. Another important aspect contributing to adherence behavior in older adults may be the fact that they are taking medications that are more critical to maintain their function (e.g., heart medications) than young adults (e.g., allergy medications). Additionally, older people generally have far more cues suggesting their physical vulnerability than younger adults, which may make medication-taking behavior more important and contribute to an overall level of higher adherence in this age group. Congruent with this notion, Kliegel, Martin, McDaniel, and Einstein (2004) reported a higher completion rate for prospective memory manipulated to appear important, and Horne and Weinman (1999) reported that individuals who believed a medication to be important were more likely to be adherent to it.

IMPROVING THE PROSPECTIVE MEMORY COMPONENT OF MEDICAL ADHERENCE

In this final section, we consider what techniques can be used to improve the prospective component of medical adherence behaviors. There is evidence that environmental aids can be helpful for improving prospective memory when used effectively. Einstein and McDaniel (1990) showed that when participants used external devices such as paper clips or posted paper notes with reminders of when critical tasks should be completed, these cues increased participants' performances on prospective memory tasks relative to the performance of participants who also had these items present but who were not allowed to use them as aids. Outside the laboratory, external aids such as medication organizers, charts and checklists, electronic monitors, and external reminders can serve these functions to help people remember when and how to take medications.

In the real world, medication organizers are currently commonly used devices aimed at increasing medication adherence. However, we caution that these devices will only be helpful for maintaining medication adherence if they are used correctly. Medication organizers with dividers for the days of the week can help enforce appropriate scheduling of doses and assist patients in knowing if they have taken their medication as needed, but these devices will only work effectively if loaded correctly. Additionally, different kinds of medication dividers are more effective than others: Park, Morrell, Frieske, Blackburn, and Birchmore (1991) found that medication organizers that included divisions for different times of day in addition to the days of the week were associated with lower levels of loading errors by participants than 7-day organizers that did not include time-of-day information. Park et al. (1991) suggested that these weekly organizers without time divisions are less effective not only because they are linked to higher error rates in loading, but also because they inherently carry less information about the schedule of when medicines should be taken, leaving room for even more errors at time of dosage.

Although weekly medication loaders that include time divisions are better than their non-time-divided counterparts, these loaders also may not be ideal for achieving high levels of adherence. Once medication is loaded into an organizer, all extraneous information about that medicine that is present on the bottle label, such as special instructions and information about how the medication should be taken, will be lost. Without this information present, patients will not have salient reminders of any special precautions, such as drug, alcohol, or food interactions, available to them when it is time for them to actually take their medications, which can be especially problematic for people taking complex mixtures of multiple medications at once, as is the case for many older adults. Even with these drawbacks, well-made medication organizers can assist patients in developing effective routines for taking their medicines, so these aids should not be discounted when developing adherence strategies.

Charts and checklists can also offer benefits for increasing and maintaining medication adherence, especially when used in addition to well-organized medication loaders. Park et al. (1992) showed that when old-old adults (aged 71 and older) were given a chart for their refrigerator that relieved comprehension load by providing explicit instructions on how to take all medications hour by hour and used a 7-day medication organizer with time divisions, these adults were more adherent than others without the use of these aids. Interestingly, young-old adults (aged 60–70) did not benefit from the charts and organizers, but the authors suggested that because this group already showed very high levels of adherence even without the external aids, these devices may not have been as necessary for this highly compliant group as they would be for groups farther from maximal performance. Interestingly, old-old participants did not benefit from the use of only one of the two memory aids and only showed increased levels of adherence when given both the chart and the organizer. Park et al. suggested that these results imply that prospective memory assistance may be driving these effects because both aids together not only lower the cognitive demands of understanding medication regimens, but also effectively double the external aid to prospective memory.

Other external aides of note-involving technology include electronic monitors and telephone reminders. Electronic monitors and diaries that allow patients to record the time at which they take their medication can also increase medication adherence, and older adults show high levels of adherence when using devices such as these (Morrell et al., 1997; Park et al., 1992). However, in the Park et al. and Morrell et al. studies the monitors, along with serving as external cues, may also have served motivational purposes by reminding participants of their involvement in the experiment. Other studies have shown benefits of automated reminding services. Telephone reminders with voice-mail instructions have been shown to increase levels of adherence for influenza vaccinations (Leirer, Morrow, Pariante, & Doksum, 1989) as well as for following medication schedules (Leirer, Morrow, Tanke, & Pariante, 1991). With Internet and cell phone use increasing rapidly, these modes of communication may provide current and future prescription users with interactive reminders, such as e-mails and text messages, that can travel with them conveniently and unobtrusively throughout the day. Even people who are currently unexposed to these technologies can benefit from such aids. With relatively straightforward training, older adults can effectively learn to use personal digital assistants (PDAs) to keep track of schedules (Sterns, 2005), and these devices can also help remind people to take their medication.

Enhancing Medical Adherence with Implementation Intentions

While external aids may provide effective environmental cues to assist people in remembering to adhere to their medication schedules, a relatively simple and potentially cost-effective way to increase adherence is through the use of implementation intentions. Gollwitzer (1999) described an implementation intention as the action of predictively imagining in what behaviors you will engage when you encounter certain critical situations to achieve desired goals. Implementation intentions are distinct from goal intentions because while the latter idea describes intent, implementation intentions also detail the plans necessary to achieve those goals if certain contexts are encountered. By planning out responses to specific contexts, implementation intentions can help people consider what types of situations may be relevant to their ability to achieve their goals. Implementation intentions can also help them recognize when these critical situations are occurring and spur them into the desired actions that will increase the likelihood of goal attainment.

Just as external aids can help link time-based tasks to event-based cues, implementation intentions can help people be medically adherent by linking through imagination intended actions with available situations, thus changing the time-based task of remembering to take medicine into a task of event-based prospective memory (Park, 2000). Because strong implementation intentions involve vividly imagining reacting to specific situations, the act of picturing these situations and their optimal responses can leave these contexts and their associated behaviors strongly activated. Later, when these situations are encountered in the real world, they will be easily recognized as critical times to act, and the activated intention will assist in making the desired behavior more automatic when these critical situations are encountered (Gollwitzer, 1999). Implementation intentions have the same underlying mechanisms as habits: They both link situational cues with behavioral responses (Aarts & Dijksterhuis, 2000a; Sheeran, Webb, & Gollwitzer, 2005). Because habit formation can help make behaviors more automatic (Aarts & Dijksterhuis, 2000a, 2000b; Wood, Quinn, & Kashy, 2002), it reasonably follows that implementation intentions may be promising tools for increasing the automaticity of accurately taking medications in appropriate situations.

Implementation intentions have affected behavior in laboratory settings. In a lexical decision task, words describing situations that were detailed in implementation intentions were recognized more quickly than neutral words, and greater levels of accessibility of intention words were positively associated with achievement of the intended goals (Aarts, Dijksterhuis, & Midden, 1999). Chasteen, Park, and Schwarz (2001) also showed that implementation intentions can increase desired behaviors in experimental situations. In Chasteen et al.'s experiment, older adults completed a working memory task and were also asked to complete two prospective memory tasks: responding with a certain key press whenever a specific series of numbers was presented on screen during the cover task (which occurred randomly within 2-minute intervals), and writing the current day of the week on worksheets that were completed during a later portion of the experiment. Before engaging in the working memory task, participants formed implementation intentions about either the number sequence and its subsequent desired key press or the worksheets and the desired act of writing the current weekday. Creating an implementation intention about pressing a key in response to a number sequence did not better participants' performance on this task (possibly because the numerical cue alone served as a salient cue to respond, and participants performed well on this task even without forming implementation intentions), but participants did benefit significantly from forming intentions about writing the day of the week. Notably, the older adults who imagined writing the current day on each worksheet before the working memory task actually completed this behavior more than twice as often as the older adults who did not utilize the implementation strategy!

Commitment to achieving goals can influence the effectiveness of implementation intentions, but even when commitment level is controlled, the formation of implementation intentions can improve performance on tasks that lead toward goal achievement. Implementation intentions do have stronger effects when commitment toward achieving the goal is relatively strong. Regarding health behaviors, people who had stronger intentions to achieve the goal of completing breast exams were more likely to benefit from the use of implementation intentions than were people with relatively weak intentions (Orbell, Hodgkins, & Sheeran, 1997). Implementation intentions are especially effective when people believe that the goal that they are trying to attain is relatively difficult to achieve. Gollwitzer and Brändstatter (1997) found that when people attempt to achieve goals that they believe to be difficult, they are three times more likely to be successful when they have formed implementation intentions. Similarly, Sheeran et al. (2005) showed that having ambitious goal intentions increased the effectiveness of implementation intentions in students with independent study goals.

Although increased goal commitment is associated with increased effectiveness of implementation intentions, implementation intentions do not work simply because they cause greater goal commitment. In a study of opiate addicts in withdrawal who were experiencing the conscious distraction of cravings, when these participants were given the goal of completing a new curriculum vita by the end of the day, 12 out of the 20 participants who had formed implementation intentions were able to do so, but none of the 21 participants who did not form these intentions were able to complete the task. These discrepancies in performance occurred despite the fact that both groups reported high levels of commitment to achieving their goal (Brandstätter, Lengfelder, & Gollwitzer, 2001).

A recent study by Sheeran et al. (2005) highlights circumstances in which implementation intentions are activated and are useful at improving performance. Sheeran et al. found that implementation intentions are especially effective when they are relevant to desired outcomes of tasks and unconsciously primed into action. In their study, Sheeran et al. gave all participants a cover puzzle task. Some of the participants had the conscious goal of completing the task as quickly as possible, and some participants also formed a relevant implementation intention relating to speed, whereas others formed an irrelevant implementation intention that was unlinked to the goal of the cover task. Before completing the cover task (but after forming the relevant or irrelevant implementation intentions) participants completed a word search with either words priming for speed or neutral words. On the actual task that followed the word search, people who had formed the implementation intentions regarding speed performed faster than those who had formed the irrelevant intentions, and priming was only effective if relevant implementation intentions had been formed. These results show that implementation intentions, even when activated outside of consciousness, can automatically lead to changes in behavior. Because older adults are spared from significant declines in performance related to automatic processes, the use of implementation intentions to automatically link appropriate situations with desired actions can be of particular use to these populations.

Implementation Intentions in the Real World

Implementation intentions are also effective at producing desired outcomes outside of the laboratory. Health behaviors are more likely to be completed when people have formed implementation intentions about them, and this effect has been shown experimentally by studies concerning breast examinations even when participants have equivalent goal strengths (Orbell et al., 1997) and attendance of screenings for cervical cancer when motivation to attend is equivalent (Sheeran & Orbell, 2000). Maintaining regular exercise regimens, an important goal that many people find quite difficult to achieve, can also be made easier through the use of implementation intentions. In one study, when people were told the risks of heart disease and the preventative benefits of exercise, the formation of implementation intentions was the strongest predictor for increased amounts of exercise (Milne, Orbell, & Sheeran, 2002). Similarly, people who wrote down when and where they intended to watch and follow an exercise video were more likely to actually engage in these behaviors over 3 subsequent days (Walsh, Soares, DaFonseca & Banta, 2005). Implementation intentions are also strong predictors of regular exercise among college students (Rise, Thompson, & Verplanken, 2003). Implementation intentions have even proven to be effective strategies for increasing rates of health behaviors that are unpleasant or easy to forget, such as regular intake of vitamins (Sheeran & Orbell, 1999). Implementation intentions have also helped people eat better: Imagining specifically what is eaten at each meal helps people engage in generally healthier eating practices (Verplanken & Faes, 1999), and people who form implementation intentions are more likely to lower their daily intake of fats than are equally motivated people who do not form these plans (Armitage, 2004).

As discussed in the previous paragraphs, once they are formed, implementation intentions can help make desired behaviors automatic at appropriate times, and because older adults are able to maintain relatively high levels of automatic processing as compared to effortful processing and show few declines on event-based prospective tasks, this population can especially benefit from the advantage gleaned from the formation of these intentions. Implementation intentions can also help other populations that often experience difficulties in achieving goals. As discussed earlier, opiate addicts can benefit from such strategies, and schizophrenics who completed a key press exercise showed speed benefits only after completing implementation intentions (Brandstätter et al., 2001). Similarly, patients with frontal lobe lesions who had difficulties in deliberating about goals also benefited from the formation of implementation intentions (Lengfelder & Gollwitzer, 2001). Because implementation intentions can work even for populations that experience cognitive impairments, they can be very useful in helping older adults and people suffering from illnesses that cause cognitive deficits to maintain high levels of medication adherence.

Despite the fact that being adherent to medication regimens is a common and important task that requires effective prospective memory, little research has yet been completed regarding medication adherence and implementation intentions, but the following studies highlight the benefits of this strategy for helping people remember to medicate appropriately. In one example, Sheeran and Orbell (1999) examined vitamin use and implementation intentions. Sheeran and Orbell gave undergraduates bottles of vitamin C and measured how many pills participants who formed detailed implementation intentions actually took over the course of 3 weeks when compared to controls who did not use this intention strategy that involved imagining when and where the implementers would take the vitamins. After 3 weeks, implementers had forgotten to take their pills significantly fewer times than controls.

Benefits of adherence for older adults are also evident in experiments that examine real-world use. Liu and Park (2004) measured adherence for testing blood glucose levels and found that the formation of implementation intentions led to greater compliance with recommendations regarding this behavior. The use of glucose monitors provides an unobtrusive way to measure adherence to the task by recording the date and time of all readings, which can help experimenters avoid problems associated with self-reporting (Mazze et al., 1984). Although diligent monitoring can help diabetics maintain stable blood glucose levels, many people do not engage in this activity as often as their doctors suggest (Harris, Cowie, & Howie, 1993; Karter, Ferrara, Darbinian, Ackerson, & Selby, 2000). This issue is especially relevant to our elderly population because the majority of people with Type 2 diabetes are older adults (U.S. Food and Drug Administration, 2002), and older adults often experience difficulties with the task of measuring blood glucose levels (Rogers, Mykityshyn, Campbell, & Fisk, 2001).

To simulate newly diagnosed diabetics who would not yet be familiar with the associated routine of self-care, Liu and Park (2004) recruited older adults who were free of diabetes and did not already know how to use a blood glucose monitor. After participants were trained to use the equipment and were assessed individually to ensure that all could use the monitors correctly, they were instructed to test their blood glucose levels without the use of external aids (e.g., alarms) four times a day, as a typical diabetic would be expected to do (American Diabetes Association, 2001). Additionally, during the instruction phase, some participants repeated aloud what they intended to do, whereas some participants deliberated on the pros and cons of regularly testing themselves. In contrast to these two approaches, a third group of participants formed implementation intentions including a specific plan of action and vividly imagined exactly when and where they would be, along with what they would be doing, at each time they intended to measure their blood glucose levels. All three groups of participants spent the same amount of time (3 minutes) on this phase of the experiment, ensuring that any differences in monitoring practices would not be due to varying amounts of rumination about the goal behavior.

Three weeks after the instruction session adherence rates were measured, and as expected, older adults who had formed implementation intentions were more likely to have remembered to test themselves within 10- and 20-minute time windows surrounding the desired times of monitoring than both members of the deliberation group and participants who had merely stated their goals aloud. Participants who had formed implementation intentions were also more likely to test themselves at least once a day (an objective of many Type 2 diabetics) than were deliberators or controls. Perhaps most strikingly, over the course of the 3 weeks of the study, the group that engaged in forming implementation intentions completed 50% more tests than did participants from the other two instruction groups. There were no significant differences between the deliberation group and the goal intention group, and all groups evidenced equivalent levels of motivation as well as comparable levels of cognitive function, suggesting that the formation of implementation intentions was the main force driving the relatively high levels of adherence to the desired testing schedule.

Collectively, implementation intentions can be useful tools for increasing desired behaviors, but certain styles of implementation intention formation may be more effective than others. One example that showcases such differences in effectiveness involves intentions that relate to shunning temptations, and implementation intentions that focus on ignoring temptations can often work better than those that emphasize increasing efforts on current tasks. Gollwitzer and Schaal (1998) discussed an experiment where participants completed a relatively mundane cover task involving math problems while attempting to avert their attention from a series of exciting television commercials that involved fun activities and attractive people. To keep their attention on the arithmetic problems, participants were either instructed to ignore the commercials or work harder at the math problems, and the participants formed implementation intentions relating to their specific instructions. The group that formed intentions that included ignoring the distracters was more successful than the group that tried to increase their efforts on the cover task, suggesting that the former type of implementation intention is more effective than the latter. Additionally, Gollwitzer and Oettingen (2007) suggested that tailoring implementation intentions to suit patients can also help increase their effectiveness. In one example supporting this idea, Murgraff,

White, and Phillips (1996) showed that when alcoholics are forming implementation intentions, when they are given options of possible ways to respond when being offered a drink, they report less drinking after 2 weeks than participants who did not form these intentions. Similarly, formatting patients' implementation intentions to complement their own lifestyles and schedules may increase the efficacy of these intentions by utilizing cues that are both often experienced by and salient to these patients.

SUMMARY

Medical adherence behaviors are among the most important memory tasks that people perform on a regular basis. Despite declines in many aspects of cognition, older adults do a better job than younger adults at adhering to a medical regimen in the real world. It increasingly appears that how busy and chaotic an individual's life is will better predict medical adherence than will cognitive function, leading to the conclusion that context trumps cognition with respect to this behavior. Older adults who would appear to be at high risk of nonadherence due to cognitive frailty are actually at relatively low risk because the highly routine, less busy lives led by older adults result in reliable environmental cues that effectively maintain adherence behaviors. The use of techniques that rely on imagining a medical adherence behavior in the context of cues one will encounter when performing the behavior is a highly effective procedure for enhancing and maintaining adherence, particularly in older adults. Understanding the interplay between context and cognition in predicting adherence to medical regimens has been studied in only a limited way and is an important avenue for understanding and advancing adherence behaviors.

REFERENCES

Aarts, H., & Dijksterhuis, A. (2000a). Habits as knowledge structures: Automaticity in goal-directed behavior. *Journal of Personality and Social Psychology, 78,* 53–63.

Aarts, H., & Dijksterhuis, A. (2000b). On the automatic activation of goal-directed behavior: The case of travel habit. *Journal of Environmental Psychology, 20,* 75–82.

Aarts, H., Dijksterhuis, A., & Midden, C. (1999). To plan or not to plan? Goal achievement or interrupting the performance of mundane behaviors. *European Journal of Social Psychology, 29,* 971–979.

American Diabetes Association. (2001). Standards of medical care for patients with diabetes mellitus [Position statement]. *Diabetes Care, 24*(Suppl. 1), S33–S43.

Armitage, C. J. (2004). Evidence that implementation intentions reduce dietary fat intake: A randomized trial. *Health Psychology, 23,* 319–323.

Becker, L. A. (1989). Family systems and compliance with medical regimens. In C. N. Ramsey, Jr. (Ed.), *Family systems in medicine* (pp. 416–431) New York: Guilford.

Brandstätter, V., Lengfelder, A., & Gollwitzer, P. M. (2001). Implementation intentions and efficient action initiation. *Journal of Personality and Social Psychology, 81,* 946–960.

Chasteen, A. L., Park, D. C., & Schwarz, N. (2001). Implementation intentions and facilitiation of prospective memory. *Psychological Sciences, 6,* 457–461.

Einstein, G. O., Holland, L. J., McDaniel, M. A., & Guynn, M. J. (1992). Age-related deficits in prospective memory: The influence of task complexity. *Psychology and Aging, 7,* 471–478.

Einstein, G. O., & McDaniel, M. A. (1990). Normal aging and prospective memory. *Journal of Experimental Psychology: Learning, Memory, and Cognition, 16,* 717–726.

Einstein, G. O., McDaniel, M. A., Mazzi, M., Cochran, B., & Baker, M. (2000). Prospective memory and aging: Forgetting intentions over short delays. *Psychology and Aging, 15,* 671–683.

Einstein, G. O., McDaniel, M. A., Richardson, S. L., Guynn, M. J., & Cunfer, A. R. (1995). Aging and prospective memory: Examining the influences of self-initiated retrieval processes. *Journal of Experimental Psychology: Learning, Memory, and Cognition, 21,* 996–1007.

Einstein, G. O., McDaniel, M. A., Smith, R. E., & Shaw, P. (1998). Habitual prospective memory and aging: Remembering intentions and forgetting actions. *Psychological Science, 9,* 284–288.

Garry, M., Manning, C. G., Loftus, E. F. & Sherman, S. J. (1996). Imagination inflation: Imagining a childhood event inflates confidence that it occurred. *Psychonomic Bulletin & Review, 3,* 208–214.

Goff, L. M., & Roediger, H. R. (1998). Imagination inflation for action events: Repeated imaginings lead to illusory recollections. *Memory and Cognition, 26,* 20–33.

Gollwitzer, P. M. (1999). Implementation intentions: Strong effects of simple plans. *American Psychologist, 54,* 493–503.

Gollwitzer, P. M., & Brandstätter, V. (1997). Implementation intentions and effective goal pursuit. *Journal of Personality and Social Psychology, 73,* 186–199.

Gollwitzer, P. M., & Oettingen, G. (2007). In medical adherence: The role of goal setting and goal striving. In D. Park & L. Liu (Eds.), *Social and cognitive perspectives on medical adherence* (pp. 23–47). Washington, DC: American Psychological Association.

Gollwitzer, P. M., & Schaal, B. (1998). Metacognition in action: The importance of implementation intentions. *Personality and Social Psychology Review, 2,* 124–136.

Harris, M. I., Cowie, C. C., & Howie, L. J. (1993). Self-monitoring of blood glucose by adults with diabetes in the United States population. *Diabetes Care, 16,* 1116–1123.

Horne, R., & Weinman, J. (1999). Patients' beliefs about prescribed medicines and their role in adherence to treatment in chronic physical illness. *Journal of Psychosomatic Research, 47,* 555–567.

Karter, A. J., Ferrara, A., Darbinian, J. A., Ackerson, L. M., & Selby, J. V. (2000). Self-monitoring blood glucose. *Diabetes Care, 23,* 477–483.

Kliegel, M., Martin, M., McDaniel, M. A., & Einstein, G. O. (2004). Importance effects on performance in event-based prospective memory tasks. *Memory, 12,* 553–561.

Leirer, V. O., Morrow, D. G., Pariante, G. M., & Doksum, T. (1989) Increasing influenza vaccination adherence through voice mail. *Journal of the American Geriatric Society, 37,* 1147–1150.

Leirer, V. O., Morrow, D. G., Tanke, E. D., & Pariante, G. M. (1991). Elders' nonadherence: Its assessment and medication reminding by voicemail. *The Gerontologist, 31,* 514–520.

Lengfelder, A., & Gollwitzer, P. M. (2001). Reflective and reflexive action control in patients with frontal brain lesions. *Neuropsychology, 15,* 80–100.

Leventhal, H., & Cameron, L. (1987). Behavioral theories and the problem of compliance. *Patient Education and Counseling, 10,* 117–138.

Leventhal, H., Leventhal, E. A., & Schaefer, P. M. (1992). Vigilant coping and health behavior. In M. G. Ory, R. P. Abeles, & P. D. Lipman (Eds.), *Aging, health, and behavior* (pp. 109–140). Newbury Park, CA: Sage.

Liu, L. L., & Park, D. C. (2004). Aging and medical adherence: The use of automatic processes to achieve effortful things. *Psychology and Aging, 19,* 318–325.

Lyle, K. B., Bloise, S. M., & Johnson, M. K. (2006). Age-related binding deficits and the contents of false memories. *Psychology and Aging, 21,* 86–95.

Martin, M., & Park, D. C. (2003). The Martin and Park Environmental Demands (MPED) Questionnaire: Psychometric properties of a brief instrument to measure self-reported environmental demands. *Aging: Clinical and Experimental Research, 15,* 77–82.

Mazze, R. S., Shamoon, H., Pasmantier, R., Lucido, D., Murphy, J., Hartmann, K., et al. (1984). Reliability of blood glucose monitoring by patients with diabetes mellitus. *American Journal of Medicine, 77,* 211–217.

McDaniel, M. A., Einstein, G. O., Stout, A. C., & Morgan, Z. (2003). Aging and maintaining intentions over delays: Do it or lost it. *Psychology and Aging, 18,* 823–835.

Milne, S., Orbell, S., & Sheeran, P. (2002). Combining motivational and volitional interventions to promote exercise participation: Protection motivation theory and implementation intentions. *British Journal of Health Psychology, 7,* 163–184.

Morrell, R. W., Park, D. C., Kidder, D. P., & Martin, M. (1997). Adherence to antihypertensive medications across the life span. *The Gerontologist, 37,* 609–619.

Morrell, R. W., Park, D. C., & Poon, L. W. (1989). Quality of instructions on prescription drug labels: Effects on memory and comprehension in young and old adults. *The Gerontologist, 29,* 345–353.

Morrell, R., Park, D. C., & Poon, L. W. (1990). Effects of labeling techniques on memory and comprehension of prescription information in young and. *Journal of Gerontology: Psychological Sciences, 45,* 166–172.

Morrow, D. G., Leirer, V. O., & Altieri, P. (1995). List formats improve medication instructions for older adults. *Educational Gerontology, 21,* 151–166.

Morrow, D. G., Leirer, V. O., & Andrassy, J. M. (1996). Using icons to convey medication schedule information. *Applied Ergonomics, 27,* 267–275.

Morrow, D. G., Leirer, V. O., Andrassy, J. M., Hier, C. M., & Menard, W. E. (1998). The influence of list format and category headers on age differences in understanding medication instructions. *Experimental Aging Research, 24,* 231–256.

Murgraff, V., White, D., & Phillips, K. (1996). Moderating binge drinking: It is possible to change behavior if you plan it in advance. *Alcohol & Alcoholism, 31,* 577–582.

Orbell, S., Hodgkins, S., & Sheeran, P. (1997). Implementation intentions and the theory of planned behavior. *Personality and Social Psychology Bulletin, 23,* 945–954.

Park, D. C. (1992). Applied cognitive aging research. In F. I. M. Craik & T. A. Salthouse (Eds.), *Handbook of cognition and aging* (pp. 449–493). Mahwah, NJ: Lawrence Erlbaum Associates, Inc.

Park, D. C. (2000). The basic mechanism accounting for age-related decline in cognitive function. In D. C. Park & N. Schwarz (Eds.), *Cognitive aging: A primer* (pp. 3–21). Philadelphia: Psychology Press.

Park, D. C., Gutchess, A., Meade, M. L., & Stine-Morrow, E. (in press). Improving cognitive function in older adults: Nontraditional approaches. *Journal of Gerontology: Psychological Sciences.*

Park, D. C., Hertzog, C., Kidder, D. P., Morrell, R. W., & Mayhorn, C. B. (1997). Effect of age on event-based and time-based prospective memory. *Psychology and Aging, 12,* 314–327.

Park, D. C., Hertzog, C., Leventhal, H., Morrell, R. W., Leventhal, E., Birchmore, D., et al. (1999). Medication adherence in rheumatoid arthritis patients: Older is wiser. *Journal of American Geriatrics Society, 47,* 172–183.

Park, D. C., & Kidder, D. (1996). Prospective memory and medication adherence. In M. Brandimonte, G. Einstein, & M. McDaniel (Eds.), *Prospective memory: Theory and application,* (pp. 369–390). Mahwah, NJ: Lawrence Erlbaum Associates, Inc.

Park, D. C., Lautenschlager, G., Hedden, T., Davidson, N., Smith, A. D., & Smith, P. (2002). Models of visuospatial and verbal memory across the adult life span. *Psychology and Aging, 17,* 299–320.

Park, D. C., & Meade, M. L. (2007). A broad view of medical adherence: The importance of cognitive, social, and contextual factors. In L. L. Liu & D. C. Park (Eds.), *Social and cognitive perspectives on medical adherence.* Washington, DC: APA.

Park, D. C., Morrell, R. W., Frieske, D., Blackburn, B., & Birchmore, D. (1991). Cognitive factors and the use of over-the-counter medication organizers by arthritis patients. *Human Factors, 33,* 57–67.

Park, D. C., Morrell, R. W., Frieske, D., & Kincaid, D. (1992). Medication adherence behaviors in older adults: Effects of external cognitive supports. *Psychology and Aging, 7,* 252–256.

Park, D. C., Puglisi, J. T., & Smith, A. D. (1986). Memory for pictures: Does an age-related decline exist? *Psychology and Aging, 1,* 11–17.

Park, D. C., Royal, D., Dudley, W., & Morrell, R. (1988). Forgetting of pictures over a long retention interval in old & young adults. *Psychology and Aging, 3,* 94–95.

Park, D. C., Smith, A. D., Lautenschlager, G., Earles, J., Frieske, D., Zwahr, M., et al. (1996). Mediators of long-term memory performance across the life span. *Psychology and Aging, 11,* 621–637.

Rise, J., Thompson, M., & Verplanken, B. (2003). Measuring implementation intentions in the context of the theory of planned behavior. *Scandinavian Journal of Psychology, 44,* 87–95.

Rogers, W. A., Mykityshyn, A. L., Campbell, R. H., & Fisk, A. D. (2001). User-centered analysis of a "simple" medical device. *Ergonomics in Design, 9,* 6–14.

Rosenstock, I. M. (1990). The health belief model: Explaining health behavior through expectancies. In K. Glanz, F. M. Lewis, & B. K. Reiner (Eds.), *Health behavior and health education* (pp. 39–62). San Fransisco: Jossey-Bass.

Sheeran, P., & Orbell, S. (1999). Implementation intentions and repeated behavior: Augmenting the predictive validity of the theory of planned behaviour. *European Journal of Social Psychology, 29,* 349–369.

Sheeran, P., & Orbell, S. (2000). Using implementation intentions to increase attendance for cervical cancer screening. *Health Psychology, 19,* 283–289.

Sheeran, P., Webb, T. L., & Gollwitzer, P. M. (2005). The interplay between goal intentions and implementation intentions. *Personality and Social Psychology Bulletin, 31,* 87–98.

Sterns, A. A. (2005). Curriculum design and program to train older adults to use personal digital assistants. *The Gerontologist, 45,* 828–834.

U.S. Food and Drug Administration. (2002, January–February). Diabetes: A growing public health concern. *FDA Consumer Magazine, 36*(1). Retrieved March 9, 2006, from http://www.fda.gov/fdac/features/2002/102_diabetes.html

Verplanken, B., & Faes, S. (1999). Good intentions, bad habits, and effects of forming implementation intentions on healthy eating. *European Journal of Social Psychology, 29,* 591–604.

Walsh, J. J., Soares Da Fonseca, R., & Banta, A. (2005). Watching and participating in exercise videos: A test of the theory of planned behaviour, conscientiousness, and the role of implementation intentions. *Psychology and Health, 20,* 729–741.

Wood, W., Quinn, J. M., & Kashy, D. (2002). Habits in everyday life: Thought, emotion, and action. *Journal of Personality and Social Psychology, 83,* 1281–1297.

19

Prospective Memory in Aviation and Everyday Settings

R. KEY DISMUKES

NASA *Ames Research Center*
Moffett, California

O
n the morning of August 31, 1988, Flight 1141, a Boeing 727, was moving slowly in a long taxi queue for departure from Dallas-Fort Worth, Texas. Because of the delay, the crew shut down the number three engine to conserve fuel. When the flight was fourth in line for takeoff, the crew restarted the engine and began running the checklists used to confirm that the airplane's systems were properly set. While they were running the checklists the air traffic controller unexpectedly told them to move up past the other airplanes to the runway, and 30 seconds later the controller cleared Flight 1141 to take off. The crew rushed to complete preparations for takeoff. When the flight engineer, who was reading the checklists aloud, called out the item for verifying that wing flaps and leading edge slats were set to the takeoff position, the first officer quickly responded "Fifteen, fifteen, green light," indicating that the inboard flaps and outboard flaps were correctly set to 15 degrees and that the green light indicating the slats were deployed was illuminated.

In fact, however, the crew had forgotten to set the flaps and slats to the takeoff position, which is essential for large airplanes to generate enough lift to climb at takeoff speeds. Unfortunately the configuration warning system, which should have alerted the crew when the throttles were advanced that the airplane was not properly configured for takeoff, failed to activate because of a mechanical failure. The airplane accelerated normally and began to climb from the runway, but then stalled, crashing a few thousand feet beyond the end of the runway. The airplane was destroyed by the impact and resulting fire; 12 passengers and 2 crew members were killed, and many others were seriously injured.

Accident investigators attribute most airline accidents primarily to crew error (Boeing, 2005). Between 1987 and 2001, 27 major airline accidents occurred in the United States in which crew error was found to be a causal or contributing factor. In five of these accidents, inadvertent omission of a normal procedural step by pilots played a central role (National Transportation Safety Board [NTSB], 1988, 1989, 1995, 1997, 2001). Two accidents, including Flight 1141, involved failing to set flaps and slats to takeoff position. The other three involved failing to set hydraulic boost pumps to the high position before landing, causing the landing gear to not extend on command; failing to turn on the pitot heat,[1] causing erroneous airspeed indications on takeoff; and failing to arm the spoilers before landing, which combined with other errors and a wet runway to prevent the airplane from stopping before the end of the runway.

Perhaps I should reassure readers at this point that airliners are not raining from the sky. About 1 flight in 1.14 million departures worldwide results in an accident with fatalities or hull loss, and the accident rate for developed countries is around 1 in 5 million departures (Boeing, 2005). However, maintaining the aviation system at such a high level of reliability requires constant effort as the skies become more crowded and new challenges emerge. Because more than half of airline accidents are attributed to crew error (Boeing, 2005), it is crucial to identify the types of errors pilots make, to analyze the causes of those errors, and to avoid simplistic assumptions about the reliability of human performance (Dismukes, Berman, & Loukopoulos, 2005; Dekker, 2002).

Many factors beyond the scope of this discussion played a role in each of the five accidents already mentioned, but at the heart of each was failure by highly experienced pilots to remember to perform a fairly simple procedural step that they had executed successfully on thousands of previous occasions. Also noteworthy is that in each case the memory lapse by one pilot was not detected by the other pilot in the cockpit and was not discovered when the crew ran the associated checklist.

In this chapter I review several studies that enabled my research group to characterize the nature of prospective memory task demands in flight operations, and then compare these findings to those of a diary study of everyday prospective memory tasks, which share some features with many flight tasks. From these studies it is clear that real-world prospective memory tasks have aspects that have not yet been well explored in laboratory studies, and it seems likely that these aspects contribute to much of the variance in performance. Field studies and diary studies are by their nature rather phenomenological, and cannot resolve questions about underlying cognitive processes. Thus my discussion of cognitive issues involved in these real-world tasks is of necessity quite speculative, but this speculation points to new research issues with both practical and theoretical implications. Finally, I discuss a laboratory study we conducted as a first attempt at studying some of those implications empirically.

---

[1] Pitot tubes provide atmospheric pressure readings for altimeters. These tubes are mounted on the outside of the aircraft and are heated to prevent freezing, which would cause erroneous readings.

AVIATION STUDIES

Airline operations lend themselves to study of skilled human performance of complex tasks because detailed written procedures, in the form of flight operations manuals (FOMs), guide almost every aspect of flight from before starting the engines to shutting them down after landing. The procedures are designed to ensure that crew actions are correct, safe, and efficient, and to provide standardization so that crew members who have never flown together (which is often the case in large airlines) can readily coordinate their actions. Also facilitating research is that a fair degree of consensus exists among aviation experts about what constitutes appropriate or inappropriate action in specific situations.

We have recently completed three studies that enable us to describe the kinds of prospective memory tasks that commonly occur in flight operations, to identify the forms of errors that occur, and to speculate about the causes of those errors. The first was an ethnographic study in which we collected information about normal flight operations on Boeing 737 aircraft (Dismukes, Loukopoulos, & Barshi, 2003; Loukopoulos, Dismukes, & Barshi, 2003). One author observed 60 normal flights by 36 crews from two major airlines by sitting in the cockpit jumpseat and taking notes. (In the Boeing 737 the jumpseat is between and behind the two pilots' seats.) The other two authors participated as pilots in one airline's flight simulation training for first officers. We also analyzed FOMs and participated in classroom training to characterize how pilots were ideally expected to execute procedures. We searched the Aviation Safety Reporting System's (ASRS) extensive database of voluntary reports from pilots to find examples of prospective memory errors and other errors associated with concurrent task demands.

In a second study we analyzed the NTSB reports of the 19 major U.S. airline accidents between 1991 and 2001 in which crew error played a central role, and attempted to determine the task, cognitive, and organizational factors contributing to those errors. (This study and the ethnographic study address many crew performance issues beyond prospective memory that are not discussed in this chapter.)

The third study sampled 20% of all ASRS reports from airline pilots over a 12-month period to obtain descriptions of any type of memory error (Nowinski, Holbrook, & Dismukes, 2003). A startling finding of this study was that, of the 75 reports with sufficient information to clearly identify a memory failure, 74 involved prospective memory rather than retrospective memory. This is not necessarily evidence that prospective memory errors are more common than retrospective errors—the frequency of reporting of different types of errors to ASRS reflects factors beyond the frequency of occurrence. Pilots are motivated to submit ASRS reports in part because submission provides immunity from prosecution for the reporter's errors, so pilots are more likely to submit reports about the kinds of errors that might get them in trouble. However, this finding does suggest that prospective memory errors are more consequential, more frequent, or more memorable than retrospective memory errors.

On reflection, it would not be surprising if experts are more vulnerable to prospective memory errors than to retrospective memory errors. The high level of experience and proficiency of airline pilots greatly reduces their vulnerability to retrospective memory errors, but may provide less protection against prospective memory errors, and may even increase vulnerability in certain situations, discussed later in this chapter. Operational procedures provide safeguards, such as checklists, to support performing intended actions, but these safeguards are themselves vulnerable to inadvertent errors of omission. In several airline accidents, crews that were distracted, interrupted, or overloaded forgot to begin or to resume a checklist.

By combining the findings from these three studies we began to get a picture of prospective memory demands in the cockpit. We have categorized these demands into five general situations that differ in terms of the associated cognitive demands. The situations are illustrated with examples in the following discussion.

Episodic Tasks

These tasks correspond to the type of prospective memory task most commonly studied in laboratory paradigms. In these situations the pilot must remember to perform at a later time some task that is not habitually performed. For example, an air traffic controller might instruct a crew to report passing through 10,000 feet (altitude) while the airplane is descending through 15,000 feet, a task that would require the crew to hold the instruction in memory for perhaps 5 minutes as the airplane descends. The way pilots typically perform this type of task seems to combine aspects of both event-based and time-based prospective memory. Although the condition for executing the intended action is ostensibly framed in terms of an event—passing through 10,000 feet—to know that the airplane has reached this altitude requires the crew to monitor an altimeter as it winds down during descent, similar to monitoring a clock. During descent pilots are occupied with diverse flight tasks that divert their attention from the altimeter, so awareness of time probably plays a role in the altitude task. With experience, some pilots may develop scanning routines in which they perform several steps of an ongoing task and then switch attention to the altimeter, in which case the ongoing task steps may serve as event-based cues for monitoring. Also, all of the ongoing tasks are part of the overarching goal of managing the flight path, and this context may provide associative cuing that help the pilots remember to check the altimeter (see Cook, Marsh, & Hicks, 2005; Nowinski & Dismukes, 2005, for context effects).

The window of opportunity for executing a deferred intention and the nature of the cues signaling that opportunity in real-world situations are far more variegated than in most prospective memory laboratory paradigms. (See Ellis's [1996] discussion of retrieval context.) In the laboratory the prospective memory target cue uniquely defines the opportunity to respond and is usually presented in a discrete trial, in most cases lasting only a few seconds. In contrast, consider an aviation situation in which the crew decides to defer setting the flaps to takeoff position until they reach the end of the taxi rather than at the usual time (for reasons explained later). The window of opportunity here is defined not by a single perceptual cue but by a constellation of cues that must be interpreted as a set to recognize that the time has come to set the flaps. When the crew reaches the end of the taxi they begin performing the last preparations for takeoff and may not consciously frame their situation as "we are at the end of the taxi." Also, the crew's ongoing tasks at this point may or may not direct attention to happenstance cues associated with the intention, for example, the flap handle.

Habitual Tasks

Crews perform many tasks in the course of a flight, and many tasks involve multiple steps. Most of the tasks and many of the intermediate steps of the tasks are specified by written procedures and are normally performed in the same sequence. Thus, for experienced pilots, execution presumably becomes largely automatic and does not require a deliberate search of memory to know what to do next. Pilots do not need to form an episodic intention to perform each task and each action step—rather, the intention is implicit in the action schema for the task, stored as procedural memory. It would be uncommon for a pilot to arrive at work thinking "I will lower the landing gear today when I turn onto final approach" (and it would be rather alarming if a pilot found this necessary).

This raises the question of whether performing habitual tasks should be considered a form of prospective memory—certainly habitual tasks differ substantially from episodic tasks in the way intentions are encoded. We come down on the side of including habitual tasks as a special form of prospective memory for largely practical reasons. When individuals forget to perform a habitual task, they generally report having intended to perform the task, and consider not having done so a failure of memory. Regardless of how we label these memory failures, it is important to study them: It is noteworthy that all five of the memory failures resulting in accidents described earlier involved habitual tasks.

Remembering to perform habitual tasks seems quite reliable normally—individuals in aviation and in everyday life perform enormous numbers of habitual activities with few complaints—but performance is undermined if normally present cues are for some reason removed. Apparently, execution of habitual tasks depends heavily on cuing (Meacham & Leiman, 1982), an aspect shared with event-based episodic tasks. For example, at a given airline, the procedure may be for the captain to call for flaps to be set for takeoff immediately following completion of the after engine start checklist and before starting to taxi. Setting the flaps occurs as part of a habitual sequence of actions, and the captain is normally prompted to remember to call for the flaps by the strong association in memory with completing the preceding checklist. Further, the context of the perceptual environment of the ramp area outside the cockpit is associated with setting the flaps, and recent research reveals that context can support retrieval of intentions (although this has not been studied with habitual tasks; Cook et al., 2005; Nowinski & Dismukes, 2005).

What happens, however, if the crew must defer setting the flaps until after taxi to prevent freezing slush on the taxiway from being thrown up on the flaps? The cues that normally trigger crews to set the flaps are no longer present—this action is now out of sequence, temporally separated from completion of the after engine start checklist and removed from the normal environmental context provided by being at the ramp. By deferring the task of setting the flaps, the crew has essentially changed a habitual task to an episodic task. They may not realize that this increases their vulnerability to forgetting and may not elaborate encoding of the intention or identify or create specific cues as reminders.

An even more insidious vulnerability of habitual tasks occurs when external circumstances remove a cue that normally triggers execution of a task. For example, a highly experienced airline captain reported landing his private airplane gear-up. The captain's own analysis was that he had developed the habit of lowering the landing gear as he entered the downwind leg of the landing pattern when the runway passed under the wing (in visual rather than instrument conditions). On this occasion he made a rare visual straight-in approach to the airport and thus the runway never passed under the wing, removing the cue that normally prompted him to lower the gear. This suggests that the captain relied on automatic retrieval of the action, rather than consciously monitoring for the opportunity to lower the gear. We suspect that pilots rely heavily on automatic retrieval of habitual actions because otherwise the volume of action steps required to operate an airplane during busy periods would be overwhelming.

Although the distinction between episodic and habitual tasks goes back to the early days of prospective memory research (Ellis, 1996; Meacham & Leiman, 1982), few empirical studies have addressed habitual tasks, and those few have not examined tasks as deeply engrained and situation dependent as those of experts performing highly practiced tasks (Einstein, McDaniel, Smith, & Shaw, 1998). It would be useful to know more about the factors determining retrieval of individual steps by experts performing habitual concurrent tasks. Is retrieval driven by a single cue or interaction of multiple cues? How do cues interact with the expert's action schema and goal structures? How do automatic and conscious processing interact? Performance on event-based prospective memory tasks in the laboratory has been shown to improve when the importance of the prospective tasks is emphasized, presumably because participants shift their strategy for allocation of attention (see, e.g., Kliegel, Martin, & McDaniel, 2004). Given the extensive role of habitual procedures in the work of experts in many domains, it would be worthwhile to explore the role of importance in habitual prospective memory tasks. For example, even though pilots are quite cognizant that omitting certain procedural steps could have fatal consequences, the successful execution of those steps many thousands of times over years of experience may remove the sense of threat. Combined with sometimes heavy task loading, this may undercut pilots' incentive to carefully monitor the execution of procedures that can be performed in a largely automatic fashion (Dismukes et al., 2007).

Atypical Actions Substituted for Habitual Actions

Circumstances sometimes require crews to modify a well-established procedural sequence. If the modified procedure resembles the normal procedure, differing only in a single step, the crew is vulnerable to unintentionally reverting to the normal procedure unless they carefully monitor execution when the step is to be substituted. For example, departing from a particular runway at a certain airport, crews might almost always be given a standard instrument departure (SID) procedure that requires them to turn left to 300 degrees on reaching 2,000 feet.

Through long experience the sequence of actions to execute this procedure would become habitual. If on one occasion a crew is directed before takeoff to modify the SID to turn to 330 degrees instead of 300, the crew would need to form an episodic intention to continue their turn to 330. Crews are quite busy with multiple attention-demanding tasks during early departure; when the crew levels the airplane at 2,000 feet and sets the cockpit automation to start a left turn they are vulnerable to setting 300 degrees out of habit instead of 330, without noticing the error. Reason (1990) discussed memory errors of this sort as *habit intrusions*. The idea is that cues that normally trigger the habitual action are so strongly associated that the habitual action is often retrieved and executed automatically instead of the intended action if the individual does not consciously supervise the process.

Kvavilashvili and Ellis (1996) argued that habit intrusion errors of this sort are not truly prospective memory errors, which they would restrict to situations in which no intention is retrieved at all. (In habit intrusion the habitual action is retrieved and executed inappropriately.) Regardless of nomenclature, it seems important for prospective memory researchers to investigate errors in execution of habitual tasks. Highly practiced tasks make up much of the work of experts, and it seems that errors of omission in these practiced tasks occur mainly when normal cues are removed (as when habitual tasks are deferred) or when an atypical action step is substituted for a habitual step. The latter may suffer from a double vulnerability. Not only must the pilot remember a new, episodic task; the intended action must also compete for retrieval with the habitual action, which is strongly associated in memory with cues present in the environment or generated by preceding actions.

Interrupted Tasks

Interruptions of cockpit procedures are quite frequent, especially when crews are at the gate preparing the airplane for departure (Dismukes, Young, & Sumwalt, 1998; Latorella, 1999; Loukopoulos et al., 2003). Flight attendants, gate agents, mechanics, and jumpseat riders require the pilots' attention as the pilots perform a fairly long sequence of procedural steps before starting the engines. Interruptions are so abrupt, salient, and common that pilots may do little if anything to encode an explicit intention to resume the interrupted task. After the interruption is over, a common error is to go on to the next task, forgetting to complete the interrupted task. In many cases the perceptual cues available in the cockpit do not provide a salient indication of the status of the interrupted task, and the perceptually rich environment of the cockpit is associated with many tasks that remain to be done at this point. If the pilot thinks to ask, "What was I doing when I was interrupted?" he or she may remember the interrupted task, but sometimes this question is not asked, and the pilot simply responds to the next task demand.

We speculate that source memory confusion may play a role here (Johnson, Hashtroudi, & Lindsay, 1993). Having performed cockpit preparation tasks thousands of times previously (and perhaps on earlier flights the same day), a specific instance of performing the interrupted task may not be very distinctive in memory from the many times it *has* been completed. Further, the memory of having started the interrupted task may lead to the belief that it has been accomplished, and this may help trigger the initiation of the next task in the sequence.

Interleaving Tasks and Monitoring

While performing ongoing tasks pilots are often required to monitor the status of other tasks. Some tasks, such as the requirement to report passing through an altitude, previously discussed, involve monitoring for an event that is known *will* occur. In other situations, pilots must monitor for events that occur infrequently, if at all. For example, when flying in visual meteorological conditions, pilots must scan outside the cockpit windows for other airplanes that might be on a conflicting path. This may seem a topic of more interest to attention researchers than memory researchers, but in fact pilots report becoming preoccupied with ongoing tasks and forgetting to monitor the status of other tasks for dangerously long periods (Dismukes et al., 1998). The problem is probably greatest when high workload preempts limited resources: Bargh and Chartrand (1999) argued that conscious control of behavior (which monitoring presumably requires at least to some extent) is a very limited resource. However, lapses in monitoring also occur in low and moderate workload situations in which enough time exists to switch attention back and forth between the ongoing task and monitoring and to perform both tasks adequately.

In a flight simulation study, pilots' scanning outside the cockpit increased substantially when potentially conflicting airplanes started appearing, but returned to near baseline levels minutes after the last airplane appeared (Colvin, Dodhia, & Dismukes, 2005). We speculate that it is difficult to maintain the monitoring task goal in working memory when the result of each inspection of the monitored scene reveals that no event has occurred. In this sense the monitoring aspect of the pilots' dual tasks somewhat resembles vigilance tasks (Parasuraman, 1986). Apparently humans are wired to allocate attention heavily toward sources of high information content, and thus have difficulty maintaining monitoring for low-probability events, even when those events may have high consequences (see Wickens, Goh, Helleberg, Horrey, & Talleur, 2003, for a model of attention allocation among tasks). However, this sort of monitoring differs from traditionally studied vigilance tasks in that the pilot must interrupt an ongoing task and shift attention to the thing being monitored. When the pilot goes too long without shifting attention, the monitoring task may slip from working memory, and then must somehow be retrieved, just as in other types of prospective memory situations. This conclusion is supported by a study in which Einstein et al. (2005) found that the level of monitoring declined over the course of the experiment. (The level of monitoring was inferred from the cost to response time of an ongoing task.)

Much of prospective memory laboratory research has focused on stimulus-driven responding, and only a few studies have addressed monitoring as a prospective memory task. Park, Hertzog, Kidder, Morrell, and Mayhorn (1997) required participants to remember to make a response at either 1-minute or 2-minute intervals while performing an ongoing working memory task. Participants were allowed to check elapsed time during the intervals. Monitoring performance was worse with 2-minute intervals, suggesting difficulty maintaining the monitoring task in working memory.

The six-element task developed by Shallice and Burgess (1991) and adapted for prospective memory studies by Kliegel and colleagues (Kliegel, McDaniel, & Einstein, 2000) shares some features with cockpit monitoring tasks. The six-element task requires participants to remember to switch tasks on their own as a function of how far they have progressed on the current task, rather than remembering to switch when a prearranged cue is perceived or at a predetermined interval. Similarly, many cockpit monitoring tasks also require pilots to remember to switch attention periodically from an ongoing task, without the benefit of any specific cue. In both the six-element task and cockpit tasks, the individual's perception of passage of time presumably plays a role, although the mechanisms of this are not understood (see Cicogna, Nigro, Occhionero, & Esposito, 2005, for theoretical speculation about mechanisms of time-based prospective memory).

Many interesting research questions about performance of monitoring tasks of this sort invite study. When the goal of monitoring slips from working memory it eventually reappears—its reappearance triggered by the passage of time, happenstance cues, the context of the cockpit environment, performance of steps of the ongoing task, or something else altogether. What is the relation of the goal and action structures of the ongoing task and the monitoring task? What role does task importance play when monitoring for low-probability, high-consequence events? Do individual differences and situational factors such as fatigue and stress affect monitoring performance? Could pilots and other individuals learn techniques to reduce vulnerability to lapses in monitoring?

EVERYDAY PROSPECTIVE MEMORY

Our ethnographic study revealed the structure of prospective memory situations in the cockpit, but too few errors were observed for analysis. Review of accident and incident reports provided plentiful examples of errors, but did not provide access to the pilots involved. We recently completed a diary study of everyday prospective memory to explore the structure of these real-world tasks, to compare them to aviation prospective memory tasks, and to take advantage of individuals' abilities to report the nature of their intentions (Holbrook, Dismukes, & Nowinski, 2005). Eight participants, all with at least some graduate-level training in psychology and familiarity with prospective memory concepts, were used on the assumption that these individuals would be better able to recognize and describe prospective memory situations than untrained individuals. We recognize that our participants' reports are undoubtedly colored by their theoretical perspectives.

Participants were asked to record at least one prospective memory task in which they succeeded or failed each day for a week. Each participant received a digital voice recorder and worksheets with questions to elicit a detailed description of the intention, prior experience performing this type of intention, how the intention was encoded, length of retention interval, whether the intention came to mind during the retention interval, and the window of opportunity for executing the intention. Voice recorders were used to make brief notes at the time the intention was retrieved; these notes helped participants fill out the worksheets at the end of the day.

Sixty-nine worksheets were collected, describing 29 successes and 40 failures to perform an intended action during the intended period. The types of intentions reported fell into four categories: event-based episodic (e.g., buy toothpaste while at a drugstore), time-based episodic (e.g., take car to garage before 5 p.m.), habitual (close top of bottle of contact lens solution), and multiple component. The last category consists of intentions with multiple intended actions grouped under a superordinate goal, such as going to a store to buy several items. Failing to pick up one item of several might be viewed as a failure of the retrospective component of prospective memory in some situations, but in other situations it seemed clearly a problem with the prospective component. For example, one participant reported going to a store to buy an item, then thinking of additional items while at the store and buying those items, but forgetting to buy the item originally intended. Perhaps picking up the unplanned items induced a sense of having completed the intention and triggered the action schema of going to the cash register.

No habit intrusion errors were reported in this sample, although these were reported in the larger sample of another study of everyday tasks not discussed here. No failures of interleaving tasks or monitoring were reported, which may indicate that this type of task is less common in everyday affairs than in aviation or that monitoring failures are less likely to be noticed.

It is not likely that the relative proportion of successes and failures or the numbers of each type of prospective memory task reported in this study represent actual exposure. For example, success at habitual tasks, such as brushing one's teeth, are so common as to seem trivial, and were almost certainly underreported. Thus our analysis focuses on interrelations among variables described next.

Participants were asked to indicate which of four statements best described their encoding of each intention. Table 19.1 shows that most intentions were encoded in ways that did not fully specify the window of opportunity for executing the intention and did not identify specific cues that might be encountered to trigger retrieval of the intention. Intentions for which more specific information was encoded were more likely to be remembered ($r = .34$). (All correlations reported

TABLE 19.1   Extent of Encoding

Level of Encoding	No.	%
You did not think very much about the intention, just assumed you would remember to perform it.	16	23
You made a "mental note" to perform your intention, but didn't think specifically about how, where, or when you would perform it.	24	35
You thought about how or where you would perform your intention, but did not identify exactly when you would perform it.	23	16
You developed a specific plan for how, where, and when you would perform your intention.	35	24

TABLE 19.2   Retention Interval

Retention Interval	No.	%
Less than 1 hour	15	22
1 to 12 hours	28	41
12 to 24 hours	7	10
More than 24 hours	19	28

here were statistically significant.) Also, intentions that were rated as more important were encoded more completely $(r = .32)$ and were remembered better $(r = .26)$.
Participants were more likely to create a cue to help them remember intentions
they considered important $(r = .24)$.

The retention interval ranged from 30 seconds to 3 weeks (Table 19.2). The
length of most retention intervals makes it seem unlikely that individuals could
continuously and actively monitor for the opportunity to execute the intention.
No participant reported monitoring for cues in his or her narrative descriptions,
which is consistent with reports from other diary studies (e.g., Kvavilashvili,
2005; Marsh, Hicks, & Landau, 1998; Sellen, Louie, Harris, & Wilkins, 1997).
This does not rule out the possibility of some sort of unconscious monitoring
or, alternately, of individuals being in a state of heightened retrieval sensitivity
(Mäntylä, 1993).

Participants were asked to report spontaneous retrievals during the retention
interval. Spontaneous retrievals were reported for 59% of successfully executed
intentions and 33% of failures $(r = .26)$, and multiple spontaneous retrievals were
reported for 48% of successes and 18% of failures.

The window of opportunity for successfully executing intentions (retrospectively defined by participants when filling out the worksheets) ranged from 1 minute to 3 weeks (Table 19.3). Thus most of these everyday tasks provided a broad
window of opportunity to execute the intention. In 51% of successful retrievals
during the execution window, individuals reported that retrieval occurred when
they noticed a happenstance cue, that is, a cue the individual had not identified
when forming the intention. In some sense even the "failures" in our sample represented some level of success, because participants eventually retrieved the intention after the execution window had passed. Forty-eight percent of late retrievals

TABLE 19.3   Window of
Opportunity for Execution

Execution Window	No.	%
Less than 1 hour	23	33
1 to 12 hours	31	45
12 to 24 hours	3	4
More than 24 hours	12	17

were reported to have been associated with noticing a happenstance cue. Thus, happening to encounter unplanned cues may account for a major portion of the variance in performance of these everyday prospective memory tasks. Happenstance cues are more likely to be encountered, of course, when the window of opportunity for execution is broad.

In comparison, how effective were planned cues (those identified during encoding)? Participants reported encoding specific cues in 22 instances. The planned cues were actually encountered in only 14 of these 22 instances, and retrieval was successful in 8 of these 14 cases. Thus planned cues played a smaller role than happenstance cues in successful performance in this study.

Summing across this diary study (not all of which is reported here), I posit that several factors account for much of the outcome of executing intentions in everyday situations. The following factors are internal to the individual:

Intention is not explicitly specified at all—intention is *implicit*, as in habitual tasks and some interrupted tasks.

Intention is poorly specified—few details are encoded about opportunities for execution.

Cue is ineffective—individuals habituate to cues continuously present, cues are not sufficiently associated with the intention, cues have many other associations.

These factors are environmental:

Ongoing task demands direct attention away from cues.
Planned cues do not occur or are not encountered.
Happenstance cues are encountered.
Breadth of window of opportunity for execution.

Our subjective impression is that these factors also account for much of the variance in prospective memory performance in aviation settings, but we have not studied this directly. It is noteworthy that the experimental literature on prospective memory has not yet addressed many of these factors in any depth, perhaps in part because it is difficult to manipulate these factors in a controlled way in most existing laboratory paradigms. For example, a large number of experimental studies have explored the crucial role of cuing in event-based prospective memory (e.g., Brandimonte & Passolunghi, 1994; Ellis & Milne, 1996; McDaniel & Einstein, 1993; Meacham & Colombo, 1980; Richards & Krauter, 1999; Vortac, Edwards, Fuller, & Manning, 1993), but both our diary study and a recent diary study by Kvavilashvili (2005) suggest we should pay more attention to happenstance cues not encoded with the intention. Also, experimental studies have typically not explored how individuals encode intentions and what they encode in real-world situations. (However, Kliegel et al. [2000], did use the six-element task to look at participants' planning and adherence to their plans.) Our studies suggest self-initiated encoding varies considerably, partly as a function of the situation, and the implementation planning literature (Chasteen, Park, & Schwarz, 2001; Gollwitzer, 1999) reveals that prospective memory performance can be enhanced by more elaborate or more specific encoding. (This conclusion is supported by the interruption study described next.)

The factors identified in our studies have practical implications, such as pointing to ways to protect against prospective memory failures. One can also see interesting theoretical issues lurking within these sources of variance. For example, is self-encoding more effective than experimenter instructions (when content is comparable), analogous to the generation effect for retrospective memory (Slamencka & Graf, 1978)? By what mechanisms do spontaneous retrievals during the retention interval affect performance (Kvavilashvili, 2005)? Are individuals more sensitive to noticing happenstance cues when retaining an intention to which those cues are related (see Mäntylä, 1993)? Do stored intentions alter how individuals allocate attention, consciously or nonconsciously, while performing ongoing tasks? Are the goal structures for ongoing tasks and prospective memory tasks independent or do they interact, and if so how?

AN EXPERIMENTAL STUDY OF INTERRUPTIONS

Our group is attempting to develop experimental paradigms that would allow exploration of the factors identified in our studies of prospective memory in aviation and everyday settings. We have developed a paradigm that allows us to study how some of these factors play in interrupted tasks. Interruptions are a major source of errors of omission in cockpit operations (Dismukes et al., 1998) and in aviation maintenance (Hobbs & Williamson, 2003), and interruptions may contribute to errors of omission in other domains, such as medicine (Gawande, Studdert, Orav, Brennan, & Zinner, 2003), although this has not been studied explicitly in other domains. Several experimental studies have found that interruptions contribute to delays, impaired retrospective memory, and errors of commission after the interrupted task resumes (Edwards & Gronlund, 1998; Speier, Valachich, & Vessey, 1999; Trafton, Altmann, Brock, & Mintz, 2003), but interruptions have not been studied as a form of prospective memory task until recently.

Dodhia and Dismukes (2005) hypothesized that individuals forget to resume interrupted tasks for three reasons. First, the salient intrusion of interruptions often diverts attention quickly, undercutting encoding of an explicit intention to resume the interrupted task. If no explicit intention is encoded, then remembering to resume will depend on noticing happenstance cues that remind the individual of the status of the interrupted task and of the original motivation to undertake that task. In this case one might say that an *implicit* intention to resume exists. Even if the individual does explicitly think at the moment of interruption of the need to resume the interrupted task, encoding is likely to be abbreviated, conditions for resuming may be poorly specified, and cues indicating the opportunity to resume may not be encoded. This situation may somewhat resemble that presented by a paradigm reported by Einstein, McDaniel, Williford, Pagan, and Dismukes (2003) in which participants retrieved a deferred intention but had to defer executing the intention for a short period in which they continued an ongoing task. Even a 15-second delay in execution of the retrieved intention reduced performance substantially. The need to execute the retrieved intention after a short delay is essentially a new prospective task. Perhaps participants underestimated the difficulty of retaining the retrieved intention for such a period and did little to encode or rehearse this new prospective task after the initial intention was retrieved.

A second reason individuals may forget to resume interrupted tasks is that, after the end of an interruption, individuals are often presented with new task demands and opportunities that capture their attention, giving them little time to interpret the end of the interruption or to process cues that might remind them of the implicit or explicit intention to resume the interrupted task. A third reason is that cues indicating the window of opportunity for resuming the interrupted task at the end of the interruption may not closely match the form in which the intention to resume (implicit or explicit) was encoded. The end of an interruption is not a simple perceptual cue, but a state of affairs that requires interpreting diverse perceptual cues to recognize. Although the individual may process these diverse cues as part of the ongoing task, he or she may not frame the situation as "this is the end of an interruption," unless consciously monitoring for this event. Rather, the individual may frame the situation only as the transition from one task to another, or may not even consciously frame the situation at all, simply responding to the flow of demands posed by a series of tasks. This third hypothesis goes beyond the issue of how individual cues are processed and suggests that how individuals frame the ongoing task might have an effect on retrieval, a sort of metacognitive influence. This idea is partially related to the concept of transfer-appropriate processing and to the finding that changes in conceptual context (McGann, Ellis, & Milne, 2002) or semantic context (McDaniel, Robinson-Riegler, & Einstein, 1998) between encoding and testing impair the retrieval of intentions.

We designed an experimental paradigm to investigate these three hypotheses. Participants were required to answer a series of questions resembling the Scholastic Aptitude Test, arranged in blocks of different types of questions (e.g., analogies, vocabulary, math). They were instructed that when blocks were occasionally interrupted by the sudden onset of a different block of questions they should remember to return to the interrupted block, after completing the interrupting block and before continuing to the next block in the series. Five of the 20 blocks were interrupted. In the baseline condition these occasional interruptions were abrupt: The screen with the question participants were currently working on was suddenly replaced before the question could be answered with a screen with a different type of question, and the background color of the screen changed.

After the last question of the interrupting block was answered, a screen appeared for 2.5 seconds with the message "Loading next section" (this screen also appeared between all blocks that were not interrupted), and then the next block of questions appeared without any reference to the incomplete block that was interrupted. Without receiving any explicit prompt, participants had to remember to return to the interrupted block at this time by pressing a key. Participants in the baseline condition frequently forgot to resume the interrupted task (discussed later) and instead continued with the next block in the series after the interruption. These failures to return to the interrupted block were due to memory failures, rather than to misunderstanding the task requirements, as shown by participants' correct description of task requirements when debriefed after the experiment and by the distribution of errors among the five prospective memory trials for individual participants.

The first experiment included three manipulations, conducted across participants. To address the first hypothesis, that the sudden intrusion of an interruption discourages adequate encoding of an intention to resume the interrupted task, we used an encoding reminder condition in which the interruption began with a 4-second text message: "Please remember to return to the block that was just interrupted." This manipulation increased the proportion of resumptions from the baseline condition of .48 to .65, which was highly significant statistically (as were the results of all other manipulations discussed here). It was not clear whether the encoding reminder manipulation improved performance because of the explicit reminder or because of the 4-second delay before participants had to start performing the interrupting task. Therefore we included an encoding pause manipulation in which participants saw only a blank screen for 4 seconds at the beginning of the interruption. This manipulation also improved performance to .65. We interpret this result as indicating that a short pause before starting to perform an interrupting task allows individuals time to recognize the implications of being interrupted and to encode information that helps them remember to resume the interrupted task. Providing an explicit reminder to resume the interrupted task apparently does not provide any additional advantage over the pause.

This experiment also included a manipulation to address the second hypothesis, that individuals sometimes forget to resume an interrupted task because interruptions are often quickly followed by other task demands that attract attention and prevent the individual from fully processing and interpreting environmental conditions and retrieving the intention to resume the interrupted task. One might imagine that the "Loading next section" message that appeared for 2.5 seconds after the end of interrupting blocks (and between all other blocks) would give participants enough time to reflect on whether they should do anything else before starting the block after the interruption. However, we suspected that this short pause, coupled with the message that the next section was about to start, might orient participants toward mentally preparing to start the next section and might make them less likely to think about the implications of a new block of questions being loaded (implicitly signaling that the interrupted task should be resumed rather than starting the next block). To address this we created a retrieval pause condition in which the delay between all completed blocks, including the delay after interruptions, was increased to between 8 and 12 seconds. (No delay occurred in the onset of the interruption, as in the baseline condition.) During the delay between blocks a countdown clock displayed the remaining time to the next block so it would be obvious to participants that they had plenty of time before new task demands would begin. This manipulation increased performance to .88, supporting the idea that individuals fail to resume interrupted tasks in part because their attention is sometimes quickly diverted to new task demands arising after an interruption's end.

A second experiment, conducted within participants, addressed the third hypothesis, that individuals are vulnerable to forgetting to resume interrupted tasks because the diverse cues indicating the end of an interruption do not provide a simple match to the encoded intention and must be integrated for the individual to interpret their significance. As before, participants were interrupted on five blocks; two of these blocks were interrupted in the manner of the baseline condition, but for three of the blocks the "Loading next section" screen that appeared after the interruption also included the message "End of interruption." This message increased performance from the baseline condition of .52 to .88, supporting our hypothesis.

Although more studies will be required to fully elucidate the cognitive mechanisms underlying these effects, this interruption study demonstrates that hitherto unexplored sources of variance in real-world prospective memory studies can be studied in controlled laboratory paradigms. The sources of variance we hypothesize for interruptions may also apply in other prospective memory situations. For example, in many real-world situations individuals may fail to elaborate an intention or the conditions for execution—someone might have a fleeting thought at night to call a colleague the next day but not encode conditions for execution in detail. One interpretation of the improvement in performance associated with forming implementation plans (Gollwitzer, 1999) is that planning provides better matching between the encoded intention and cues that may occur during the window of opportunity for execution (Chasteen et al., 2001).

Also, in many real-world situations the window of opportunity requires interpretation of diverse cues to frame the situation as the window of opportunity. In the preceding example, you might frame the window for calling the colleague as "when in my office tomorrow." If asked the next day, you would certainly report being aware of being in your office, but until asked you might not consciously frame your situation that way. Of course individual perceptual cues within the office are associated with the concept of office and thus should provide some associative cuing, at least indirectly. Indeed, the office provides many cues, so in one sense the opportunities for reflexive retrieval are large. However, the point here is the lack of direct correspondence between how the intention was encoded—as an abstraction not depending on any single perceptual cue—and how the individual frames the ongoing situation in the office. Most likely the individual's stream of consciousness will revolve around the tasks being performed rather than an explicit frame of "Now I am in my office." We can only speculate how this might affect prospective memory processes, as most laboratory studies have used simple perceptual cues—mainly words and pictures—as targets to signal the opportunity to execute deferred intentions. Some experimental studies have used more complex situations to define the window of opportunity, for example, asking participants to remind the experimenter to look up some data after the end of the experiment, but the effects of using more complex situations, and the underlying cognitive processes, have not been explored systematically (see discussion in Kvavilashvili, 1992).

The difference between using single perceptual cues and more complex situations as conditions for retrieving intentions may be somewhat analogous to the difference between using single targets and conjoint targets in visual search (Triesman & Gelade, 1980). When searching for a target that differs from distracters only in a single dimension, the target appears to "pop out" automatically, but when the target is defined by conjunction among two or more variables, individuals must search serially and effortfully. By analogy, individuals may be able to retrieve intentions automatically and fairly reliably if the opportunity for retrieval is defined by a simple perceptual cue and if the ongoing task directs their attention to this cue. But if the opportunity for retrieval is defined by conjoint occurrence of several cues, relying on automatic retrieval may be much less reliable. (West & Craik [1999], used a conjoint prospective memory target in which both words of a pair had to be either green or uppercase, but this study was directed to other issues.)

CONCLUSION

Field studies of prospective memory in everyday settings and in the tasks of expert professionals reveal dimensions and sources of variance not fully explored by existing laboratory paradigms. These field studies are by their nature rather phenomenological and cannot resolve questions about underlying cognitive processes, but they do suggest fruitful avenues for experimental research. They also raise theoretical issues that might not be identified in experimental studies that eliminate some of the real-world sources of variance. Finally, field studies are a necessary precursor to developing practical measures to improve prospective memory performance, pointing to sources of variance that may affect prospective memory performance substantially in various real-world situations and that might be manipulated usefully. Also, one must understand the structure of tasks and goals in specific real-world situations to assess whether potential countermeasures are likely to be practical.

Only well-controlled experimental paradigms can resolve issues hinted at by field studies and elucidate the underlying cognitive mechanisms. Prospective memory research has progressed to the point that it is now useful to develop new paradigms to explore the more complex aspects of prospective memory. For example, Kvavilashvili's (1998) word substitution paradigm provides a way to study habit intrusion errors, the six-element task (Kliegel et al., 2000) can be used to explore retrieval of intentions in the absence of explicit cues, and our paradigm can be used to study interruptions.

Many other topics in prospective memory would benefit from new paradigms. Expertise plays a large role in many real-world prospective memory situations and thus warrants experimental study. In contrast to most laboratory paradigms, the world is rich in perceptual stimuli related to individuals' diverse intentions, and individuals often maintain multiple goals, waiting for appropriate opportunities to pursue them. Retrieval of intentions may depend on happenstance cues as much or more as on encoded cues. Opportunities for executing goals are often defined by the conjunction of multiple conditions, rather than by simple perceptual stimuli. Priming experiments (e.g., Mäntylä, 1993) and context experiments (Cook et al., 2005; Nowinski & Dismukes, 2005) suggest that multiple cues may interact to trigger retrieval in ways that have not yet been fully explored. It might also be useful to study what factors belatedly prompt the retrieval of intentions that were not executed when intended—this might point to ways to help individuals detect and recover from prospective memory errors before the opportunity is lost completely. Opportunities for research abound!

ACKNOWLEDGMENTS

Portions of this work were supported by NASA's Aviation Safety Program and Aviation System Program. Many of the ideas in this chapter arose from stimulating conversations with my colleagues Rahul Dodhia, Jon Holbrook, Kim Jobe, Loukia Loukopoulos, Jessica Nowinski, and Xidong Xu.

REFERENCES

Bargh, J., & Chartrand, T. L. (1999). The unbearable automaticity of being. *American Psychologist, 54*, 462–479.

Boeing. (2005). *Statistical summary of commercial jet airplane accidents: Worldwide operations 1959–2004. Aviation safety.* Seattle, WA: Author.

Brandimonte, M., & Passolunghi, M. C. (1994). Effect of cue familiarity, cue distinctiveness, and retention interval on prospective memory. *Quarterly Journal of Experimental Psychology, 47A*, 565–587.

Chasteen, A. L., Park, D. C., & Schwarz, N. (2001). Implementation intentions and facilitation of prospective memory. *Psychological Science, 12*, 457–461.

Cicogna, P. C., Nigro, G., Occhionero, M., & Esposito, M. J. (2005). Time-based prospective remembering: Interference and facilitation in a dual task. *European Journal of Cognitive Psychology, 17*, 221–240.

Colvin, K., Dodhia, R., & Dismukes, R. K. (2005). Is pilots' visual scanning adequate to avoid mid-air collisions? In *Proceedings of the 13th International Symposium on Aviation Psychology* (pp. 104–109). Oklahoma City, OK: Wright State University.

Cook, G. I., Marsh, R. L., & Hicks, J. L. (2005). Associating a time-based prospective memory task with an expected context can improve or impair intention completion. *Applied Cognitive Psychology, 19*, 345–360.

Dekker, S. (2002). *The field guide to human error investigations.* Hampshire, UK: Ashgate.

Dismukes, R. K., Loukopoulos, L. D., & Barshi, I. (November, 2003). *Concurrent task demands and pilot error in airport surface operations.* Paper presented at the joint meeting of the 56th Annual International Air Safety Seminar IASS, IFA 33rd International Conference, and IATA, Washington, DC.

Dismukes, R. K., Young, G. E., & Sumwalt, R. L. (1998). Cockpit interruptions and distractions: Effective management requires a careful balancing act. *ASRS Directline, 10*, 4–9.

Dodhia, R. M., & Dismukes, R. K. (2005, January). *A task interrupted becomes a prospective memory task.* Paper presented at the biennial meeting of the Society for Applied Research in Memory and Cognition, Wellington, New Zealand.

Edwards, M. B., & Gronlund, S. D. (1998). Task interruption and its effects on memory. *Memory, 6*, 665–687.

Einstein, G. O., McDaniel, M. A., Smith, R. E., & Shaw, P. (1998). Habitual prospective memory and aging: Remembering intentions and forgetting actions. *Psychological Science, 9*, 284–288.

Einstein, G. O., McDaniel, M. A., Thomas, R., Mayfield, S., Shank, H., Morrisette, N., et al. (2005). Multiple processes in prospective memory retrieval: Factors determining monitoring versus spontaneous retrieval. *Journal of Experimental Psychology: General, 134*, 327–342.

Einstein, G. O., McDaniel, M. A., Williford, C. L., Pagan, J. L., & Dismukes, R. K. (2003). Forgetting of intentions in demanding situations is rapid. *Journal of Experimental Psychology: Applied, 9*, 147–162.

Ellis, J. A. (1996). Prospective memory or the realization of delayed intentions: A conceptual framework for research. In M. Brandimonte, G. O. Einstein, & M. A. McDaniel (Eds.), *Prospective memory: Theory and applications* (pp. 1–22). Mahwah, NJ: Lawrence Erlbaum Associates, Inc.

Ellis, J. A., & Milne, A. (1996). Retrieval cue specificity and the realization of delayed intentions. *Quarterly Journal of Experimental Psychology, 49A*, 862–887.

Gawande, A. A., Studdert, D. M., Orav, E. J., Brennan, T. A., & Zinner, J. J. (2003). Risk factors for retained instruments and sponges after surgery. *The New England Journal of Medicine, 348*, 229–235.

Gollwitzer, P. M. (1999). Implementation intentions: Strong effects of simple plans. *American Psychologist, 54*, 493–503.

Hobbs, A., & Williamson, A. (2003). Associations between errors and contributing factors in aircraft maintenance. *Human Factors, 45*, 186–201.

Holbrook, J. B., Dismukes, R. K., & Nowinski, J. L. (2005, January). *Identifying sources of variance in everyday prospective memory performance.* Presented at the biennial meeting of the Society for Applied Research in Memory and Cognition, Wellington, New Zealand.

Johnson, M. K., Hashtroudi, S., & Lindsay, D. S. (1993). Source monitoring. *Psychological Bulletin, 114*, 3–28.

Kliegel, M., Martin, M., & McDaniel, M. A. (2004). Importance effects on performance in event-based prospective memory tasks. *Memory, 12*, 553–561.

Kliegel, M., McDaniel, M. A., & Einstein, G. O. (2000). Plan formation, retention, and execution in prospective memory: A new approach and age-related effects. *Memory and Cognition, 28*, 1041–1049.

Kvavilashvili, L. (1992). Remembering intentions: A critical review of existing experimental paradigms. *Applied Cognitive Psychology, 6*, 507–524.

Kvavilashvili, L. (1998). Remembering intentions: Testing a new method of investigation. *Applied Cognitive Psychology, 12*, 533–554.

Kvavilashvili, L. (2005, July). *Automatic or controlled? Rehearsal and retrieval processes in everyday time- and event-based prospective memory tasks.* Paper presented at the 2nd International Conference on Prospective Memory, Zurich, Switzerland.

Kvavilashvili, L., & Ellis, J. A. (1996). Varieties of intention: Some distinctions and classifications. In M. Brandimonte, G. O. Einstein, & M. A. McDaniel (Eds.), *Prospective memory: Theory and applications* (pp. 1–22). Mahwah, NJ: Lawrence Erlbaum Associates, Inc.

Latorella, K. (1999). *Investigating interruptions: Implications for flightdeck performance* (NASA Tech. Memo. No. 209707). Hampton, VA: Langley Ames Research Center.

Loukopoulos, L. D., Dismukes, R. K., & Barshi, I. (2003). Concurrent task demands in the cockpit: Challenges and vulnerabilities in routine flight operations. In R. S. Jensen (Ed.), *Proceedings of the 12th International Symposium on Aviation Psychology* (pp. 737–742). Dayton, OH: Wright State University.

Mäntylä, T. (1993). Priming effects in prospective memory. *Memory, 1*, 203–218.

Marsh, R. L., Hicks, J. L., & Landau, J. D. (1998). An investigation of everyday prospective memory. *Memory & Cognition, 26*, 633–643.

McDaniel, M. A., & Einstein, G. O. (1993). The importance of cue familiarity and cue distinctiveness in prospective memory. *Memory, 1*, 23–41.

McDaniel, M. A., Robinson-Riegler, R., & Einstein, G. O. (1998). Prospective remembering: Perceptually driven or conceptually driven processes? *Memory & Cognition, 26*, 121–134.

McGann, D., Ellis, J. A., & Milne, A. (2002). Conceptual and perceptual processes in prospective remembering: Differential influence of attentional resources. *Memory and Cognition, 30*, 1021–1032.

Meacham, J. A., & Colombo, J. A. (1980). External retrieval cues facilitate prospective remembering in children. *Journal of Educational Research, 73*, 299–301.

Meacham, J. A., & Leiman, B. (1982). Remembering to perform future actions. In R. C. Atckinson, J. Freedman, G. Lindzey, & R. F. Thompson (Eds.), *Memory observed: Remembering in natural contexts*, pp. 327–336. San Francisco: Freeman.

National Transportation Safety Board. (1988). *Aircraft accident report: Northwest Airlines, McDonnell Douglas DC-9-82, N312RC, Detroit Metropolitan Wayne Country Airport, Romulus, Michigan, August 16, 1987* (NTSB/AAR-88/05). Washington, DC: Author.

National Transportation Safety Board. (1989). *Aircraft accident report: Delta Air Lines, Boeing 727-232, N473DA, Dallas-Fort Worth International Airport, Texas, August 31, 1988* (NTSB/AAR-89/04). Washington, DC: Author.

National Transportation Safety Board. (1995). *Aircraft accident report: Runway overrun following rejected takeoff. Continental Airlines flight 795, McDonnell-Douglas MD-82, N18835, LaGuardia Airport, Flushing, New York, March 2, 1994* (NTSB/AAR-95/01). Washington, DC: Author.

National Transportation Safety Board. (1997). *Aircraft accident report: Wheels-up landing, Continental Airlines Flight 193, Douglas DC-9, N10556, Houston, Texas, February 19, 1996* (NTSB/AAR-97/01). Washington, DC: Author.

National Transportation Safety Board. (2001). *Aircraft accident report: Runway overrun during landing, American Airlines flight 1420, McDonnell Douglas MD-82, N215AA, Little Rock, Arkansas, June 1, 1999* (NTSB/AAR-01/02). Washington, DC: Author.

Nowinski, J. L., & Dismukes, R. K. (2005). Effects of ongoing task context and target typicality on prospective memory performance: The importance of associative cuing. *Memory, 13*, 649–657.

Nowinski, J. L., Holbrook, J. B., & Dismukes, R. K. (2003). Human memory and cockpit operations: An ASRS study. In R .S. Jensen (Ed.), *Proceedings of the 12th International Symposium on Aviation Psychology* (pp. 888–893). Dayton, OH: Wright State University.

Parasuraman, R. (1986). Vigilance, monitoring, and search. In K. R. Boff, L. Kaufman, & J. P. Thomas (Eds.), *Handbook of perception and human performance: Vol. II: Cognitive processes and performance* (pp. 43.1–43.39). New York: Wiley.

Park, D. C., Hertzog, C., Kidder, D. P., Morrell, R. W., & Mayhorn, C. B. (1997). Effect of age on event-based and time-based prospective memory. *Psychology and Aging, 12*, 314–327.

Reason, J. (1990). *Human error.* New York: Cambridge University Press.

Richards, A. M., & Krauter, E. E. (1999). Cue competition in prospective memory. *Psychological Reports, 85*, 1011–1024.

Sellen, A. J., Louie, G., Harris, J. E., & Wilkins, A. J. (1997). What brings intentions to mind? An in situ study of prospective memory. *Memory, 5*, 483–507.

Shallice, T., & Burgess, P. W. (1991). Deficits in strategy application following frontal lobe damage in man. *Brain, 114*, 727–741.

Slamencka, N. J., & Graf, P. (1978). The generation effect: Delineation of a phenomenon. *Journal of Experimental Psychology: Human Learning and Memory, 4*, 592–604.

Speier, C., Valachich, J. S., & Vessey, I. (1999). The influence of task interruption on individual decision making: An information overload perspective. *Decision Sciences, 30*, 337–360.

Trafton, J. G., Altmann, E. M., Brock, D. P., & Mintz, F. E. (2003). Preparing to resume an interrupted task: Effects of prospective goal encoding and retrospective rehearsal. *International Journal of Human-Computer Studies, 58*, 583–603.

Triesman, A., & Gelade, G. (1980). A feature-integration theory of attention. *Cognitive Psychology, 12*, 97–136.

Vortac, O. U., Edwards, M. B., Fuller, D. K., & Manning, C. A. (1993). Automation and cognition in air traffic control: An empirical investigation. *Applied Cognitive Psychology, 7*, 631–651.

West, R., & Craik, F. I. M. (1999). Age-related decline in prospective memory: The roles of cue accessibility and cue sensitivity. *Psychology and Aging, 14*, 264–272.

Wickens, C. D., Goh, J., Helleberg, J., Horrey, W. J., & Talleur, D. A. (2003). Attentional models of multitask pilot performance using advanced display technology. *Human Factors, 45*, 360–380.

20

Commentary
Goals and the Intentions Meant to Fulfill Them

PETER M. GOLLWITZER

Department of Psychology
New York University and University of Konstanz

ANNA-LISA COHEN

Department of Psychology
New York University

As described in the first paragraph by Dismukes (chap. 19, this volume), a forgotten intention had drastic and tragic consequences for Flight 1141. Without a doubt, all of the crew members, engineers, pilots, and air traffic controllers shared a common goal: to make sure that the plane flew safely, ensuring the health and welfare of all passengers. However, one intention in a series of intentions meant to fulfill that goal, namely to prepare the plane for takeoff, was forgotten.

Typically in the prospective memory literature, the term *goal* is used very seldom and it is memory for *intention* that is the focus of scholarly inquiry. However, it may be useful to consider the relative obscurity of the term *goal* in the prospective memory literature as it may reflect that we are missing one piece of the puzzle. Baldwin (1897; as cited in Olson, Astington & Zelazo, 1999) defined intentional action in terms of goal-directed behavior. He described it as "the emergence of desire, deliberation, and effort: the conscious representation of a goal, the active consideration of alternative means and ends, and the feeling accompanying the selection and execution of a plan (p. 2, Olson et al., 1999). The term *goal* is used to refer to the idea that a mental representation of a desired future state is formed and in turn directs behavior to find a way to achieve that state. It may be that the airline employees in the Dismukes example had no problem maintaining their *goal* in mind, but their failure to implement their various intentions in an effort to achieve the goal led to trouble. Substantial failures of prospective memory may thus occur not merely due to cognitive failure, but also due to implemental problems.

In fact, Wilson and Park (chap. 18, this volume) propose that aspects of prospective memory related to medication adherence are very sensitive to contextual (as opposed to cognitive) factors. They present the counterintuitive result that younger adults are more at risk than older adults for making medication adherence errors. Wilson and Park found that those who were most at risk for nonadherence were middle-aged adults with busy schedules. In comparison, older adults who had more routine and less busy lives made fewer errors. If younger adults are making a greater proportion of adherence errors compared to the more cognitively vulnerable population of older adults, then we must examine what noncognitive factors are to blame. Indeed, further analysis revealed that it was the level of busyness specifically that seemed most predictive of medication adherence errors.

As Brandimonte and Ferrante (chap 16, this volume) note in their chapter, very little has been published on the social aspects of prospective memory. Most theories within the prospective memory literature tend to be solely cognitive in nature. Based on comparing the prospective memory performance of younger and older adults, Wilson and Park suggest that situational contexts are more determinative of medication adherence performance than cognitive factors. Following Brandimonte and Ferrante, one wonders, therefore, whether the older adults' positive performance in medical adherence may also be produced by a comparatively stronger social motivation (along with different levels of business as suggested by Wilson & Park). Older adults may have a stronger desire than younger adults to avoid a potential situation in which their memory is seen as unreliable. The stakes may be higher regarding perceived memory functioning for older rather than young adults in terms of both social interaction and social values.

THE IMPORTANCE OF CUES

The findings from Dismukes (chap. 19, this volume) indicate that interference in the form of distractions may be most to blame for prospective memory failures in aviation. Similarly, within the social cognitive realm, evidence shows that forming strong intentions does not guarantee goal attainment, as there are a number of subsequent implemental problems (distraction, competing goals) that need to be solved successfully (Cohen & Gollwitzer, chap. 17, this volume; Gollwitzer, 1993). If the environmental context poses obstacles for prospective memory, then, in a sense, one must find a way to control its potentially distracting effects. If we can use the environment to facilitate remembering, then prospective memory will likely be more successful. One way to manipulate our environment to facilitate prospective memory is to establish cues that trigger associated intentions. In that way, we can relieve ourselves of the laborious task of maintaining an intention in mind. Instead, we rely on a prespecified cue that triggers the intention when the cue is encountered.

Dismukes (chap. 19, this volume) asked research participants to choose one of four statements that best described their encoding of intentions. Most participants reported that they did not identify a specific cue to help them trigger an intention. This finding demonstrates that participants were not spontaneously forming cue + intention links. Rather, they seemed to rely on more internal strategies for remembering the intention. By electing not to choose an environmental cue or aid to trigger an intention, participants may have unknowingly made themselves more vulnerable to the environmental context. In their automatic associative module model, McDaniel et al. (1998) proposed that whenever there is sufficient interaction between a prospective cue and an associated memory trace, the memory trace for the intended action is delivered automatically to consciousness. If we accept that proposition, prospective remembering is dependent on the strength of the association between the cue and the associated memory trace. This suggests that the planning and encoding stage of prospective memory is critical for successful performance. Along these lines, Gollwitzer (1993, 1999) suggested that one is more likely to achieve a goal when he or she forms a certain type of intention called an *implementation intention*. As described in Cohen and Gollwitzer (chap. 17, this volume), an implementation intention is the formation of a plan that specifies how one will respond to a prespecified cue or situation. For example, if I need to remember to turn off the oven after dinner, then I may form an implementation intention that links the desired response with a specific context. If, as Dismukes found, participants are not likely to form cue + intention pairings spontaneously, it may be necessary to have them deliberately form implementation intentions so that they can use the environment to their advantage.

In a clinical population, there is commonly an even greater need to establish strategies that help patients overcome prospective memory deficits. As many scholarly articles on the topic of prospective memory are quick to state, prospective memory is critical to daily functioning (e.g., the need to remember to take medication, turn off a stove). Therefore, patients with brain injuries can suffer severe liabilities in their ability to live independently when their prospective memory functioning is impaired. However, as Thöne-Otto and Walther (chap. 15, this volume) note in their very thorough review of the literature on clinical assessment and therapy of prospective memory in patients with brain injury, compensatory memory aids often involve external reminders rather than internal strategies. Due to the expense and technological challenges associated with electronic memory aids, there may be a need for more research investigating internal prospective memory strategies.

One study examined the effects of a self-regulatory strategy in a population with brain injuries. Specifically, Lengfelder and Gollwitzer (2001) studied the effects of implementation intentions with frontal lobe patients. Typically, patients with frontal lobe injury display difficulty with tasks that require high levels of conscious control. In contrast, tasks that require more automatic behaviors are not impaired (e.g., Shallice, 1982). Lengfelder and Gollwitzer asked a sample of frontal lobe patients to perform a go/no-go task, as well as a secondary tracking task of varying difficulty. Their results showed that even at a high level of difficulty on the tracking task, implementation intentions improved performance on the go/no-go task. Moreover, the effect of implementation intentions was stronger in frontal lobe patients than in a control group of university students. This study showed that using implementation intentions helped participants recruit automatic rather than effortful controlled memory processes, which enhanced their performance.

HOW TO ENHANCE THE POWER OF IMPLEMENTATION INTENTIONS?

The State of the Superordinate Goal

Sheeran, Webb, and Gollwitzer (2005, Study 2) found that implementation intention effects are sensitive to the (even subliminal) activation of the superordinate goal. In other words, implementation intentions only affect behavior when the superordinate goal is activated. As a consequence, people who use implementation intentions to avoid forgetting to act on their goals should seek out situational contexts that implicitly or explicitly activate the respective goal. However, implementation intention effects are not only found to be sensitive to goal activation, they also respect the strength of and commitment to the superordinate goal (e.g., Sheeran et al., 2005, Study 1). The more hours college students wanted to engage in independent study, the greater the beneficial effects of respective implementation intentions specifying when, where, and how to study. If implementation intentions fail to benefit goal attainment given that the goal is weak, people have to ensure that goal strength and goal commitment are high. Otherwise they cannot rely on the beneficial effects of forming implementation intentions. It becomes important therefore that people keep up high motivation throughout goal striving. Strong motivation is dependent not only on high perceived desirability, but also on high perceived feasibility of the wanted future event. Accordingly, people have to retain high self-efficacy beliefs throughout the process of goal striving if they want to profit from their if–then plans.

Single Plans or Multiple Plans

Given the beneficial effects of if–then planning on acting on one's goals, one wonders how many individual if–then plans people should form for any given goal. If the goal at hand can be served in many different situations and various ways (e.g., the goal to do more physical exercise), it seems wise to specify multiple plans that make use of the many suitable opportunities and instrumental goal-directed responses available. Still, there is the question of whether it is better to solely focus on one particular situation and making several plans that link this very situation to various different instrumental goal-directed behaviors, or to focus on just one particular goal-directed behavior and making plans that link it to the various available suitable situations. Or should people go ahead and first list various highly suitable situations and then link each of them to a unique, most fitting, goal-directed behavior? Alternatively, people might first list various instrumental goal-directed behaviors and then select the most appropriate situations for each of these behaviors.

Answers to these questions need to consider the moderators of implementation intention effects as well as the mechanisms on which they are based. Next to high goal strength and goal commitment, a further important moderator is a person's commitment to the formed plan (Gollwitzer & Sheeran, 2006). Only if a person strongly commits to a formed if–then plan are we to expect beneficial effects on goal attainment. Intuitively it seems easier to commit to plans that specify either one critical situation only (that is then linked to a multitude of goal-directed behaviors) or just one critical goal-directed behavior (that is then linked to a multitude of suitable situations) than to a multitude of if–then links between critical situations and behaviors. However, it is up to empirical research to find decisive answers to this question.

If one considers the mechanisms on which implementation intentions are based, one has to distinguish between the mechanisms that relate to the if part (i.e., identification processes) versus the mechanisms that relate to the then part of implementation intentions (i.e., response initiation processes). The postulated heightened activation of the cues specified in the if part of implementation intentions implies that if–then planning that focuses on one specific cue only and is then linked to multiple goal-directed behaviors is to be preferred over the forming of plans each using a different situational cue (principle of cue competition). The postulated automated initiation of the response specified in the then part of implementation intentions suggests that the formation of plans that link just one goal-directed behavior to a select situational cue should facilitate automation of action initiation and should thus be preferred in comparison to making if–then plans that link various different goal-directed behaviors to one and the same situational cue (principle of response competition).

Individual Differences

The role of individual differences can also be discussed from various different perspectives. First, there is the straightforward applied question of which people should not bother to make plans, as implementation intentions will fail to have beneficial effects for them. This question should be answered by taking into consideration that implementation intention effects know certain moderators but are based on very simple psychological mechanisms. With respect to moderation, we know that high goal strength and goal commitment are a prerequisite (see earlier), and thus, to give an example, one cannot expect people with strong power and low affiliation motives to benefit from implementation intention formation when trying to meet goals geared at socializing with others. Moreover, as a person's commitment to an if–then plan formed also moderates goal attainment effects (see Gollwitzer & Sheeran, 2006), certain groups of people may not benefit from forming implementation intentions because they find it aversive to plan out goal striving in advance and thus do not commit to if–then plans (e.g., for individuals high on socially prescribed perfectionism, if–then planning was found to arouse negative affect; Powers, Koestner, & Topciu, 2005).

When one considers the psychological mechanisms on which implementation intention effects are based, it is hard to conceive of a group of individuals who cannot take advantage of these simple mechanisms (i.e., facilitated cue identification and automated action initiation). As long as people succeed in specifying suitable cues (i.e., cues that actually arise) in the if part of their implementation intentions, and then link them to instrumental goal-directed responses in the then part that can actually be preformed in the presence of these cues, if–then plans should achieve their beneficial effects. Some groups of individuals may need help with this task (e.g., highly depressed individuals), but once if–then plans with appropriate if and then parts are in place they should succeed in facilitating goal attainment. Indeed, even individuals with chronic problems in action control (e.g., frontal lobe patients, Lengfelder & Gollwitzer, 2001; schizophrenics and heroin addicts under withdrawal, Brandstätter, Lengfelder, & Gollwitzer, 2001; children with attention deficit hyperactivity disorder, Gawrilow & Gollwitzer, in press) showed an increased rate of goal attainment when if–then plans were assigned to them by the experimenter.

Still, there is the issue of whether there are certain individuals who are particularly skilled in forming if–then plans. We have recently started to analyze this question by developing a computer task that allows determining how good a person is in creating strong mental links between anticipated critical cues and goal-directed responses (Grant, Gollwitzer, & Oettingen, 2006). If one conceives of personality in terms of "intra-individually stable, if … then … , situation-behaviour relations" (Mischel & Shoda, 1995, p. 248), the question of skilful if–then plan formation also refers to the types of situations and responses that are linked. Let us assume that a person has the goal to reduce aggression in relating to others, and he or she also knows about his or her respective situation-behavior profile (i.e., he or she knows what kind of social situations elicit aggressive responses in him or her and how staying calm and collected is possible in other social situations). Given this goal and knowledge, the person can now tailor his or her implementation intentions to those critical, anger-eliciting situations specifying responses that allow him or her to stay calm. Thus, it seems likely that people differ not only in terms of the strength of the if–then links they are able to create but also in terms of coming up with if parts and then parts that take into account their unique chronic situation-behavior profiles, specifying implementation intentions exactly where and how they are needed.

CONCLUSION

This commentary began by highlighting the fact that most prospective memory laboratory studies do not specify a goal; rather, the majority of studies require participants to encode an arbitrary intention that is removed from daily experience (e.g., "Press the F1 key anytime you see an animal word"). In the absence of a clearly specified goal, it may be that factors determining success or failure in such a task are altogether different from those that influence prospective memory functioning in everyday life. In the social cognitive domain, intentions are formed in the hopes of fulfilling a goal. For example, a person may have the goal of attaining a higher grade-point average (GPA). The student may form an intention to spend four nights a week at the library in the hopes of raising his or her GPA. Thus, intentions are formed in the service of clearly specified goals. Most laboratory prospective memory studies involve instructions that are fairly arbitrary with no clearly specified goal. Future research would benefit by creating goals and intentions that are more in line with an individual's true interests. For example, the goal could be maximizing "points" in an online video game. The intention that would help to attain that goal would be to strike a computer key every time a certain prespecified stimulus appears.

Failures to carry out an intention can result in consequences ranging from burning one's toast to a fatal airplane crash. Relegating our study of prospective memory to controlled laboratory settings has helped us establish some core features of this relatively new area of memory research. However, if we are to continue making theoretical advances, it is vital that we begin to study prospective memory in more varied settings and with more diverse methods. Several chapters in this part present examinations of prospective memory in more diverse settings and they help to underscore the need for continued work in this direction.

REFERENCES

Brandstätter, V., Lengfelder, A., & Gollwitzer, P. M. (2001). Implementation intentions and efficient action initiation. *Journal of Personality and Social Psychology, 81,* 946–960.

Gawrilow, C., & Gollwitzer, P. M. (in press). Implementation intentions facilitate response inhibitions in children with ADHD. *Cognitive Therapy and Research.*

Gollwitzer, P. M. (1993). Goal achievement: The role of intentions. *European Review of Social Psychology, 4,* 141–185.

Gollwitzer, P. M. (1999). Implementation intentions: Strong effects of simple plans. *American Psychologist, 54,* 493–503.

Gollwitzer, P. M., & Sheeran, P. (2006). Implementation intentions and goal achievement: A meta-analysis of effects and processes. *Advances in Experimental Social Psychology, 38,* 69–119.

Grant, H., Gollwitzer, P. M., & Oetingen, G. (2006). Individual differences in the self-regulation of goal striving by forming implementation intentions. Manuscript submitted for publication.

Lengfelder, A., & Gollwitzer, P. M. (2001). Reflective and reflexive action control in patients with frontal brain lesions. *Neuropsychology, 15,* 80–100.

McDaniel, M. A., Robinson-Riegler, B., & Einstein, G. O. (1998). Prospective remembering: Perceptually driven or conceptually driven processes? *Memory & Congnition, 26,* 121–134.

Mischel, W., & Shoda, Y. (1995). A cognitive-affective system theory of personality: Reconceptualizing situations, dispositions, dynamics, and invariance in personality structure. *Psychological Review, 102,* 246–268.

Olson, D. R., Astington, J. W., & Zelazo, P. D. (1999). Introduction: Actions, intentions, and attributions. In P. D. Zelazo, J. W. Astington & D. R. Olson (Eds.), *Developing theories of intention* (pp. 1–13). Mahwah, NJ: Erlbaum.

Powers, T. A., Koestner, R., & Topciu, R. A. (2005). Implementation intentions, perfectionism, and goal progress: Perhaps the road to hell *is* paved with good intentions. *Personality and Social Psychology Bulletin, 31,* 902–912.

Sheeran, P., Webb, T. L., & Gollwitzer, P. M. (2005). The interplay between goal intentions and implementation intentions. *Personality and Social Psychology Bulletin, 31,* 87–98.

Shallice, T. (1982). Specific impairments of planning. *Philosophical Transactions of the Royal Society London, B 298,* 199–209.

Index